KT-462-874

FROM OLD ENGLISH TO STANDARD ENGLISH

Studies in English Language series

A Course Book in English Grammar, 2nd Edition –
Dennis Freeborn
From Old English to Standard English, 2nd Edition –
Dennis Freeborn
Style: Text Analysis and Linguistic Criticism – Dennis Freeborn
Varieties of English, 2nd Edition – Dennis Freeborn with
Peter French and David Langford
Analysing Talk – David Langford
English Language Project Work – Christine McDonald

FROM OLD ENGLISH TO STANDARD ENGLISH

A COURSE BOOK IN LANGUAGE VARIATION ACROSS TIME

Second Edition

Dennis Freeborn

palgrave

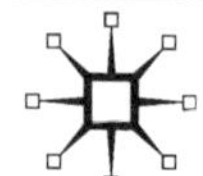

© Dennis Freeborn 1992, 1998

All rights reserved. No reproduction, copy or transmission of this publication may be made without written permission.

No paragraph of this publication may be reproduced, copied or transmitted save with written permission or in accordance with the provisions of the Copyright, Designs and Patents Act 1988, or under the terms of any licence permitting limited copying issued by the Copyright Licensing Agency, 90 Tottenham Court Road, London W1T 4LP.

Any person who does any unauthorised act in relation to this publication may be liable to criminal prosecution and civil claims for damages.

The author has asserted his right to be identified as the author of this work in accordance with the Copyright, Designs and Patents Act 1988.

Published by
PALGRAVE
Houndmills, Basingstoke, Hampshire RG21 6XS and
175 Fifth Avenue, New York, N.Y. 10010
Companies and representatives throughout the world

PALGRAVE is the new global academic imprint of
St. Martin's Press LLC Scholarly and Reference Division and
Palgrave Publishers Ltd (formerly Macmillan Press Ltd).

ISBN 0–333–69154–7 hardcover
ISBN 0–333–69155–5 paperback

This book is printed on paper suitable for recycling and made from fully managed and sustained forest sources.

A catalogue record for this book is available
from the British Library

14 13 12 11 10 9 8 7
11 10 09 08 07 06 05 04 03

Printed and bound in Great Britain by
Antony Rowe Ltd, Chippenham, Wiltshire

Contents

Preface to the second edition

The text of the first edition has been completely revised and enlarged to include nearly two hundred historical texts, of which more than half are reproduced in facsimile. The facsimiles are primary sources of our knowledge of the language, illustrating the development of handwriting, printing, punctuation and spelling in a way which is not possible using modern printed versions of old texts.

The practice of modernising the spelling of modern printed texts of earlier English like, for example, the 15th-century *Paston Letters* and Shakespeare's late 16th- and early 17th-century plays has obscured important and interesting changes that have taken place. Literary texts are generally printed with modern spelling and punctuation, and though editions of Old and Middle English retain much of the original spelling, they usually add present-day punctuation.

The texts

The core of the book is the series of texts exemplifying the changes in the language from Old English to the establishment of Standard English. The texts have been selected for a number of reasons. The Old English texts are almost all from the *Anglo-Saxon Chronicle*, and so provide something of the historical context of the language a thousand years ago. Some texts have aspects of language itself as their subject. As we have no authentic records of the spoken language before the invention of sound recording, letters and diaries of the past are included, because they are likely to provide some evidence of informal uses of English. Some literary texts have been chosen, but the series does not constitute a history of English literature.

Readership

The first edition was intended for students of English Language at Advanced Level, but since publication in 1992 the book has been used in university departments of English, both in Britain and in over thirty overseas countries. As a result, the enlarged text aims to provide more material and commentary which is suitable for study in higher education. For example, Chapter 6 demonstrates how a relatively short extract from an early Middle English text can be analysed to demonstrate the evidence for changes from Old English in spelling, pronunciation, vocabulary and grammar that had occurred.

Activities

The Activities are designed to encourage students to find out for themselves – to answer the question 'how do you know?' and to consider possible reasons for what they observe. They are able to study data at first hand and to consider hypotheses, rather than to accept the answers to problems of interpretation that others have given. The process of analysing the texts in itself demonstrates how our knowledge of earlier English has been arrived at. The surviving corpus of Old and Middle English texts is all the evidence we have about the language as it was. There are no grammar books, descriptions of pronunciation, spelling books or dictionaries of English before the 16th century. The tasks in the Activities are no more than suggestions, and teachers will omit, modify and add to them as they think useful.

Many of the simpler, basic activities in the first edition have, however, been omitted, and teachers will readily devise them if they are needed.

Levels of study

It is helpful to consider three levels of study which may be followed according to students' needs, or to the amount of time available for study.

- At the first, observational level, features of the language can be simply noted and listed as interesting or different.
- At the second, descriptive level, such features are identified more specifically, using appropriate descriptive terms from a model of language.
- At the third, explanatory level, they are placed in their relation to general processes of language change, and in their social, political and historical context.

Language change

The English language, like all living languages, is in a continuous state of variation across time. The language of one generation of speakers will differ slightly from another, and at any one time there are 'advanced' and 'conservative' forms, whether they belong to regional, educational or class dialects. Change takes place at every level of language:

- **Lexical level** – new words are needed in the vocabulary to refer to new things or concepts, while other words are dropped when they no longer have any use in society.

- **Semantic level** – the meaning of words changes – *buxom* once meant *obedient*, *spill* meant *kill*, and *knight* meant *boy*.
- **Syntactic level** – a word-for-word translation of some Old English is unlikely to read like grammatical contemporary English, because word order and grammatical structure have changed as well as vocabulary.
- **Phonological level** – pronunciation in particular is always being modified and varies widely from one regional or social group to another.

The process of change has, however, considerably slowed since the 18th century, because the spelling system and grammatical structure have been standardised and are therefore highly resistant to further change.

Standard English

Standard English has a unique and special status. Its prestige is such that for many people it is synonymous with 'the English language'. This book sets out to show what the origins of present-day Standard English were in the past. It is concerned principally with the forms of the language itself, and makes reference to the historical, social and political background to the establishment of Standard English in outline only.

Commentaries

Analytic commentaries are provided for some of the texts in the book. Each commentary is a case-study based upon the text itself, which provides some of the evidence for change in the language. Other texts are provided without commentary.

Supplementary Materials

Two supplementary books in typescript (photocopiable) and a cassette tape are available from the author for teachers, lecturers and advanced students.

- ***Text Commentary Book***
  The *Text Commentary Book* contains additional descriptive textual analyses which are indicated in *From Old English to Standard English* after the relevant texts and the sign 🕮. There is also one further chapter:
  Chaucer's rhymes as evidence of changes in pronunciation.

- ***Word Book***
  The *Word Book* contains a complete word-list in alphabetical order for each Old and Middle English text. The lists for the Old English texts give the base form of inflected words and a translation, so that students can refer to an Old English dictionary or grammar more easily. Those for the Middle English texts include the derivation of each word. The *Word Book* also contains selected

lists of words in present-day English which are derived from Old English, Old French, Old Norse or Celtic. These supplement the lists of loan-words which are included at the end of many of the chapters.

- ***Cassette tape***
  The cassette tape contains readings of the following texts:

1	Texts 4 & 5b	*Peterborough Chronicle*	Old English
2	Text 14	*Cædmon's hymn*	West Saxon & Northumbrian Old English
3	Text 33	*Peterborough Chronicle*, 1140	Early Middle English
4	Text 35	*Ormulum*, late 12th C	Early East Midlands Middle English
5	Text 53	*Ayenbyte of Inwit*, 1340	Kentish Middle English
6	Text 59	Barbour's *Bruce*, c. 1375	Scots Middle English
7	Text 62	*York Pentecost Play*, c. 1470	Northern Middle English
8	Text 66	*Sir Gawayn and þe Grene Knyȝt*	West Midland Middle English
9	Text 68	*Piers Plowman*, c. 1370	West Midland Middle English
10	Text 82	*Friar's Tale*, late 14th C	East Midland/London Middle English
11	Text 85	*Boke of Margery Kempe*, c. 1420	East Midland Early Modern English
12	Text 89	*Paston Letters*, c. 1480	East Midland Early Modern English
13	Text 109	John Hart's *An Orthographie*, 1569	London Early Modern English
14	Text 120	Sir Thomas Browne's *Of the Badger*, 1646	Early Modern English
15	Text 146	Rhymes in John Dryden's *Aeneis*, 1697	Early Modern English

Versions of 'Peter's denial' – St Matthew's Gospel, 26: 69–75

16	Text 174	Late West Saxon Old English
17	Text 175	14th C South Midlands Middle English
18	Text 176	Early 16th C Scots Middle English
19	Text 177	Early Modern English late 16th C
20	Text 178	Early Modern English early 17th C
21	Text 179	20th C Scots
22	Text 180	20th C Modern English
23	Text 181	20th C Bislama (Vanuatu Pidgin English)

A phonetic transcription follows each recorded text in this book.

The supplementary books and cassette tape can be obtained directly from the author:

- by post: PO Box 82, Easingwold, York YO61 3YY
- by e-mail: dennis.freeborn@btinternet.com

or visit his website

- www.btinternet.com/~dennis.freeborn/

Dennis Freeborn
1997

Acknowledgements

The author and publishers wish to thank the following for permission to use copyright material:

Guardian News Services Ltd, for the extract from *The Guardian*, 24 August 1989;
Newspaper Publishing plc, for the letters to *The Independent* by Daniel Massey, 14 November 1987, and Carol Clark, 25 November 1987.

Every effort has been made to trace all the copyright holders, but if any have been inadvertently overlooked the publishers will be pleased to make the necessary arrangement at the first opportunity.

Symbols

Languages

OE	Old English
ME	Middle English
EMnE	Early Modern English
MnE	Modern English
Fr	French
OF	Old French
ONF	Old Northern French
AN	Anglo-Norman
AF	Anglo-French
ON	Old Norse
MS	manuscript
fr	from

Grammar

m	masculine (gender)
f	feminine
n	neuter
nom	nominative (case)
acc	accusative
gen	genitive
dat	dative
sg	singular (number)
pl	plural
S	subject (in clause structure)
P	predicator
C	complement
O	object
A	adverbial
Ø	stands for a deleted element in grammatical analysis

Writing and printing

Symbols used for OE letters in transcriptions of facsimiles:

ſ	long ⟨s⟩
ꞅ	insular ⟨s⟩
ı	letter ⟨i⟩ in manuscript (no dot)
þ/Þ	letter thorn (lower case and capital)
ð/Đ	letter eth (lower case and capital)
ȝ/Ȝ	letter yogh (lower case and capital)
ƿ/Ƿ	letter wynn (lower case and capital)
ꝥ	abbreviation for *þæt*

Letters in caret brackets identify written letters of the alphabet, e.g. ⟨e⟩.

Letters in square brackets identify spoken sounds, using the symbols of the International Phonetic Alphabet (IPA), e.g. [ə], [ʃ], [iː]. The IPA symbols can be found in *Gimson's Pronunciation of English*, 5th edn, revised by Alan Cruttenden (London: Edward Arnold, 1994), p. 32, and *Varieties of English*, 2nd edn, Dennis Freeborn, with Peter French and David Langford (Basingstoke: Macmillan, 1993), Chapter 4, pp. 67–8.

Texts and facsimiles

Chapter 8

Chapter 9

Chapter 10

Chapter 11

Chapter 12

Chapter 13

Chapter 14

Chapter 15

Chapter 16

1. Introduction

1.1 English today

Four hundred years ago, at the turn of the 16th and 17th centuries, English was spoken almost exclusively by the English in England, and by some speakers in Wales, Ireland and Scotland, and this had been so for hundreds of years since the language was first brought to Britain in the 5th century.

English today is a worldwide international language. It is spoken as a mother tongue by about 400 million people in the British Isles, Canada, the United States of America, Australia and New Zealand. It is a second language for many others in, for example, India and Pakistan and in some African states, where it is used as an official language in government and education.

New Englishes

Many different national and regional varieties of English have therefore developed, and will continue to do so. They have been called 'new Englishes', with their own characteristics of vocabulary, grammar and pronunciation, in the different states of Africa, India and Pakistan, Singapore and the Philippines for example.

Standard English

In Britain there are many regional and social dialects, but there is one variety which is not confined to any geographical region. It originally developed as a common system of writing, but it is also the dialect of what is called 'educated speech':

> Educated English naturally tends to be given the additional prestige of government agencies, the professions, the political parties, the press, the law court and the pulpit – any institution which must attempt to address itself to a public beyond the smallest dialectal community. It is codified in dictionaries, grammars, and guides to usage, and it is taught in the school system at all levels. It is almost exclusively the language of printed matter. Because educated English is thus accorded implicit social and political sanction, it comes to be referred to as STANDARD ENGLISH...
> (R. Quirk *et al.*, *A Comprehensive Grammar of the English Language* (Longman, 1985) p. 18)

The object of this book is to provide an outline of how the English language, and Standard English in particular, has developed into its present form. It says little about the changes since the late 18th century, because the standard language which had been established in written English by that time has not changed significantly, apart from losses and gains in vocabulary. Its usage and styles have of course continued to change, but the underlying system has not. The book also says nothing about the development of American English during the last four hundred years.

The texts and facsimiles which illustrate the development of English in England make up a series of potential 'case studies', available to students and readers according to their interest. Some record historical events in the language of the time at which they happened; others contain earlier descriptions of and comments on language use. They provide an opportunity for studying a little of the development of the early conventions of handwriting, printing, punctuation and spelling which are not reproduced in modern printed versions of old texts. The practice of modernising the spelling of texts of earlier English has obscured important changes, interesting to students of English language, that have in fact taken place.

The texts and facsimiles can be used in a variety of ways, according to the needs of students and readers. The straighforward observation of differences may be followed by more detailed description and explanation in depth.

1.2 Studying variety across time in language

To study languages and dialects we focus our attention on:

(i)	Meaning:	the **semantic** level.
(ii)	Vocabulary (lexis):	the **lexical** level – loss of old words, gain of new words.
(iii)	Word-structure:	the **morphological** level – prefixes, suffixes and internal changes
(iv)	Grammar:	the **syntactic** level – word order in sentences and phrases.

1.3 How has the English language changed?

If we look at versions of the same text at successive historical periods, we can quickly observe some of the changes in the language. The Bible is a most useful source, because translations have been continuously made from Old English, a thousand years ago, to the present day.

Activity I.I

Describe some of the differences you can observe in the following texts, which are the beginning of the parable of the Prodigal Son from St Luke's Gospel, chapter 15 (the verses of the chapter are numbered). Look at vocabulary, spelling, word structure and word order, and try to identify Old English words that are still part of present-day English, though sometimes considerably changed in their spelling. Notice which Old English words appear to have been lost.

Text 1 – Late West Saxon Old English *c.* 1050

Œ 11 He cwæð. soðlice sum man hæfde twegen suna. 12 þa cwæð se gingra to hys
fæder. fæder syle me mynne dæl mynre æhte. þe me to gebyreð. þa dælde he hym
hys æhta. 13 þa æfter feawa dagum ealle hys þyng gegaderode se gingra sunu 7
ferde wræclice on feorlen ryce. 7 þær forspylde hys æhta lybbende on hys gælsan.

The OE vocabulary of Text 1 is listed in the *Word Book*

WW 11 He quoth (*spoke*). soothly (*truly*) some (*a certain*) man had two sons.
12 then quoth the younger to his father. father sell (*give*) me my deal (*part*) of-
my property. that me to belongs. then dealed (*gave*) he him his property. 13 then
after few days all his things gathered the younger son & fared abroad in far-off
country. & there spilled (*wasted*) his property living in his luxury.

Text 2 – Late 14th-century Middle English, South Midlands

ME 11 And he seide, A man hadde twei sones; 12 and the ȝonger of hem seide to the
fadir, Fadir, ȝyue me the porcioun of catel, that fallith to me. And he departide to
hem the catel. 13 And not aftir many daies, whanne alle thingis weren gederid
togider, the ȝonger sone wente forth in pilgrymage in to a fer cuntre; and there he
wastide hise goodis in lyuynge lecherously.

Text 3 – Early Modern English 1582

EMne 11 And he said, A certaine man had tvvo sonnes: 12 and the yonger of them
said to his father, Father, giue me the portion of substance that belongeth to me.
And he deuided vnto them the substance. 13 And not many daies after the
yonger sonne gathering al his things together vvent from home into a farre
countrie: and there he vvasted his substance, liuing riotously.

An analysis is in the *Text Commentary Book*.

I.4 How can we learn about Old English and later changes in the language?

The evidence for changes in the language lies in the surviving manuscripts of older English going back to the 8th century, and in printed books since the end of the

15th century. A lot of older English texts have been reprinted in modern editions, and so can be readily studied.

All our knowledge of pronunciation, however, has to be inferred from written evidence. So we can never reproduce for certain the actual pronunciation of English before the invention of sound recording in the late 19th century, but we try to make a reasonable guess by putting together different kinds of evidence.

1.5 Changes of meaning – the semantic level

Some people believe that words have 'real meanings', and object to evidence of change in current usage. Favourite words for teachers today are, for instance, *aggravate* and *disinterested*, which have taken on the meanings of *annoy* and *uninterested* in addition to those of *make worse* and *impartial*. It is argued that the new meanings are wrong, and an appeal is made to the **derivation** or **etymology** of a word – that is, what its original meaning was in the language it came from. Here is an example from the 'Letters to the Editor' columns of a newspaper. The first writer is arguing that Latin should be taught in schools; the second is one of the replies that were printed later:

Activity 1.2

Discuss the argument and the response. The dictionary definitions (from the *OED*) of the words mentioned in the letters are printed below.

1st letter:

It is demonstrably more easy to explain the function of a word when you know what it means. The very word 'education' provides me with a wonderful example. In Latin *e* from *ex* meaning 'out' and ducare 'to lead' – literally, therefore to lead out. To lead out of ignorance into the light of knowledge.

(*The Independent*, 14 November 1987)

2nd letter

Knowing the derivation of the word education is of as much help to us in deciding how children should be educated as knowing the derivation of, say, 'hysteria' would be in choosing a treatment for that condition. May I suggest that your etymologically minded correspondents look up 'treacle' in a good dictionary? They will then know what to do if ever bitten by a snake.

(*The Independent*, 25 November 1987)

Latin *educare – to lead out*
education

1. The process of nourishing or rearing a child or young person, an animal. (*obsolete*)
2. The process of bringing up (young persons); the manner in which a person has been brought up; with reference to social station, kind of manners and habits acquired, calling or employment prepared for, etc. (*obsolete*)

3. The systematic instruction, schooling or training given to the young in preparation for the work of life; by extension, similar instruction or training obtained in adult age. Also, the whole course of scholastic instruction which a person has received.
4. [*From sense 3, influenced by sense 2 and sometimes by the quasi-etymological notion 'drawing out'.*] Culture or development of powers, formation of character, as contrasted with the imparting of mere knowledge or skill.

hysteria – modern (1801) medical Latin, formed as abstract noun to hysteric – a functional disturbance of the nervous system.

hysteric from Latin *hysteric-us*, from Greek *ὑστερικ-ός belonging to the womb, suffering in the womb, hysterical*, from *ὑστέρα womb.*

treacle
Middle English *triacle*, from Old French *triacle – antidote against a venomous bite*. The sense development in English has proceeded further than in other languages.

1. A medicinal compound, originally a kind of salve, composed of many ingredients (*obsolete*)

    I almoost haue caught a Cardynacle
    By corpus bones but I haue triacle...
    (1386, Chaucer's *Pardoner's Prologue*)

2. The uncrystallized syrup produced in the process of refining sugar.

To understand that words change their meaning over time is to understand that words like *aggravate* and *disinterested* can have two current meanings. Many words have changed so much that their original meaning seems quite remote, and it is interesting to use a dictionary to trace the sequence of meanings, and to see how one leads to another. For example, the earliest written record of the word *buxom* in the OED is dated 1175, and spelt *buhsum*.

Beo **buhsum** toward gode
Be obedient to God

It is recorded in a modern dictionary of Anglo-Saxon as *bocsum*, meaning *flexible, obedient*, and its first syllable *boc-/buh-* came from the OE word *bugan*, meaning to *bow down* or *bend* – that is, *bocsum/buhsum* means 'bow-some', 'pliable'. Its present-day meaning is defined in the *Concise Oxford Dictionary* as 'plump and comely'. How did *buxom* change its meaning from *obedient* to *plump and comely*, and what then is its 'true meaning'? Here is the sequence:

I easily bowed or bent

1 **morally**

a **obedient**
*Be **obedient** to God*
This meaning survives into the 19th century:
To be **buxom** and obedient to the laws and customs of the republic
(George Borrow, 1843)

b **submissive, humble, meek**
þat lauedi til hir lauerd lute
Wit **buxum** reuerence and dute (*c.* 1300, *Cursor Mundi*)
The lady bowed to her lord
*With **humble** and fearful reverence*

c **gracious, indulgent, favourable; obliging, amiable, courteous, affable, kindly**
Meek and **buxom** looke thou be
And with her dwell
(*c.* 1460, Mystery Play, *The Annunciation*, Angel to Joseph)

d **easily moved, prone, ready, willing**
And many a beggere for benes **buxum** was to swynke
(1377, Langland, *Piers Plowman*)
And many a beggar was ***willing*** *to toil for (a meal of) beans*

2 **physically**

flexible, pliant, unresisting
Then gan he scourge the **buxome** aire so sore
That to his force to yielden it was faine
(1596, Spenser, *The Faerie Queene*)

II **blithe, jolly, well-favoured**

3 **bright, lively, gay**
A Souldier firme and sound of heart, and of **buxome** valour
(1599, Shakespeare, *Henry V*)

4 **Full of health, vigour and good temper; well-favoured, plump and comely, 'jolly', comfortable-looking (in person). (Chiefly of women)**
She was a **buxom** dame about thirty
(1823, Scott, *Peveril of the Peak*)

These meanings overlapped for centuries in the course of the development of the present-day meaning of the word, which is confined to references to women as 'comfortable-looking in person'. It cannot be said that the 'real meaning' today is 'obedient', though it was for Samuel Johnson. He wrote in his *The Plan of a Dictionary* (1747),

> And *buxom*, which means only *obedient*, is now made, in familiar phrases, to stand for *wanton*, because in an antient form of marriage, before the reformation, the bride promised complaisance and obedience in these terms, 'I will be bonair and *buxom* in bed and at board.'
>
> (*bonair* derived from OF *bonnaire* – gentle, courteous, affable, shortened from *debonnaire*.)

The meaning *wanton* for *buxom* is mentioned in the *Oxford English Dictionary* as 'apparently only contextual' and is not recorded as one of the word's meanings.

Here are some more examples of words whose present-day meaning has evolved from a quite different original:

Word	*Original meaning, now obsolete*
bachelor	a young knight, not old enough, or having too few vassals, to display his own banner, and who therefore followed the banner of another; a novice in arms.
beam	a tree
career	the ground on which a race is run, a racecourse
cloud	a mass of rock; a hill
danger	power of a lord or master, jurisdiction, dominion; power to dispose of, or to hurt or harm

dizzy	foolish, stupid
eerie	fearful, timid
fowl	any feathered vertebrate animal; = bird
gentle	well-born, belonging to a family of position; originally used synonymously with *noble*
girl	a child or young person of either sex, a youth or maiden
harlot	a vagabond, beggar, rogue, rascal, villain, low fellow, knave
horrid	bristling, shaggy, rough
knave	a male child, a boy
knight	a boy, youth, lad (Only in OE)
lady	one who kneads bread
loft	air, sky, upper region
meat	food in general; anything used as nourishment for men or animals; usually, solid food, in contradistinction to *drink*
mess	portion of food
naughty	having or possessing naught; poor, needy
nice	foolish, stupid, senseless
organ	a musical instrument
parliament	a speech; a talk, colloquy, conversation, conference, consultation
pen (writing)	a feather of a bird, a plume
quell	to kill, slay, put to death, destroy
read	to have an idea; to think or suppose *that*, etc.
rid	to clear (a way or space), *esp.* to clear (land) of trees, undergrowth, etc.
sad	satisfied; sated, weary or tired (of something)
sell	to give, to hand over something
silly	deserving of pity, compassion, or sympathy
spill	to put to death; to slay or kill
starve	to die; to die a lingering death, as from hunger, cold, grief, or slow disease
team	the bringing forth of children; childbearing
town	an enclosure; a field, garden, yard, court
want (vb)	to be lacking or missing; not to exist
worm	a serpent, snake, dragon

Activity I.3

See if you can pair off the following words with their original meanings listed alphabetically below.
(The correct pairings are printed at the end of the chapter.)

Words	*Meanings*
coin	animal, beast
deer	cloud
dreary	cunning, crafty, wily, artful, astute
giddy	gory, bloody, cruel
honest	held in honour; respectable
nerve	mad, insane, foolish, stupid
pretty	reason as a faculty of the mind
sincere	sinew or tendon
skill	true, correct, exact
sky	wedge, corner, angle

Activity 1.4

(i) Choose some of the words in the preceding lists and trace their successive meanings in a dictionary.

(ii) The words in the following list have all changed their meaning in time. Choose some words from the list and use a dictionary to trace the successive changes of meaning.

can (vb)	flour	meal (to eat)	Pope	shut	toil
castle	harvest	medley	prestige	sleuth	toy
chore (n)	holiday	mole (spot)	pudding	slogan	try
control	kind (n)	mood	rather	smite	very
deal (n)	left(-hand)	moss	saucer	soft	walk
delicate	lewd	must (vb)	sergeant	solve	weird
faint	lord	pastor	shall	spoon	whine
false	lose	pester	share (n)	stomach	win
fear	may (vb)	pharmacy	shroud	stool	womb

The original meanings are listed in the *Text Commentary Book*.

Answer to Activity 1.3 – Correct pairing of words and meanings

Word	*Original meaning*	*Source*	*Earliest recorded date*
coin	wedge, corner, angle	F *coin* wedge, corner	1350
deer	animal, beast	OE deor	*c.* 950
dreary	gory, bloody, cruel,	OE dreorig	8th C (*Beowulf*)
giddy	mad, insane, foolish, stupid	OE gidig	*c.* 1000
honest	held in honour; respectable	OF honeste	1325
nerve	sinew or tendon	L nervus	1538
pretty	cunning, crafty, wily, artful, astute	OE prættig	*c.* 1000
sincere	true, correct, exact	L sincerus	1536
skill	reason as a faculty of the mind	ON skil	1200
sky	cloud	ON sky	1220

The date is that of the earliest occurrence of the word recorded in the *OED*.
OF = Old French; ON = Old Norse; F = French; L = Latin

2. The English language is brought to Britain

2.1 Roman Britain

In the middle of the 5th century Britain had been a province of the Roman Empire for over 400 years, and was governed from Rome. The official language of government was **Latin**. It would have been spoken not only by the Roman civil officials, military officers and settlers, but also by those Britons who served under the Romans, or who needed to deal with them. The term **Romano-British** is used to describe those 'Romanised' Britons and their way of life.

The native language was **British**, one of a family of **Celtic** languages. Its modern descendants are **Welsh**, and **Breton** in Brittany (Britons migrated across the Channel in the 6th century to escape the Anglo-Saxon invasions). There were also speakers of **Cornish** up to the 18th century. Irish and Scots **Gaelic** today come from a closely related **Celtic** dialect. None of these languages resembles English, which comes from the family of **West Germanic** languages.

The Saxons had been raiding the east coast of Roman Britain for plunder since the early 3rd century, and a Roman military commander had been appointed to organise the defence of the coastline. He was called, in Latin, *Comes litoris Saxonici*, the 'Count of the Saxon Shore'. But Roman power and authority declined throughout the 4th century, and we know that a large-scale Saxon raid took place in AD 390.

2.2 *The Anglo-Saxon Chronicle*

Here are two short texts that were originally written down in the 9th century in what we now, from our point of view, call **Old English** (OE), but which was simply *Englisc* at the time. They are from *The Anglo-Saxon Chronicle*, which has survived in several manuscripts. Extracts and facsimiles from it in this book are taken from the versions known as the *The Peterborough Chronicle* and *The Parker Chronicle*. The differences between them provide useful evidence for changes in the language that were taking place a thousand or more years ago.

The two texts will give you a first impression of Old English. Text 4 is the beginning of the description of the island of Britain from the *Peterborough Chronicle*. Text 5 tells how the Britons had been conquered by the Romans in AD 47. The word-for-word translations (WW) are followed by paraphrases in Modern English (MnE).

The transcriptions use many of the OE letter shapes, which you should try to work out for yourself at present. The OE alphabet is described in more detail in chapter 3.

Text 4 – The opening of the *Peterborough Chronicle* (facsimile)

rıttene ıʒland ıſ ehta hund mıla lanʒ.
7 ƿpa hund brad. 7 her ſınd on þıs
ıʒlande fıf ʒeþeode. enʒlıſc. 7 brıt
tıſc. 7 pılſc. 7 ſcyttıſc. 7 pyhtıſc. 7
boc leden. Ereſt peron buʒend þıſeſ
landeſ brıtteſ.

ŒE

B
rıttene ıʒland ıſ ehta hund mıla lanʒ.
7 tpa hund brad. 7 her ſınd on þıs
ıʒlande fıf ʒeþeode. enʒlıſc. 7 brıt
tıſc. 7 pılſc. 7 ſcyttıſc. 7 pyhtıſc. 7
boc leden. Ereſt peron buʒend þıſeſ
landeſ brıtteſ.

(See section 3.1.2.1 for a description of the letter shapes.)

WW

of-Britain island is eight hundred miles long.
& two hundred broad. & here are in this
island five languages. english. & british.& welsh. & scottish. & pictish. &
book latin. First were inhabitants of-this
land britons.

MnE

The island of Britain is eight hundred miles long and two hundred broad. There are five languages, English, Brito-Welsh, Scottish, Pictish and Latin. The first inhabitants of this land were the Britons.

The scribe copied *fif ʒeþeode – five languages* and then divided the list into six. He had mistaken what should have been one language – *Brito-Welsh* – for two. The Old English words *brittisc* and *wilsc* referred to the same people.

📖 The vocabulary of Text 4 is listed in the *Word Book*.

Text 5a – *Parker Chronicle* for AD 47 (facsimile)

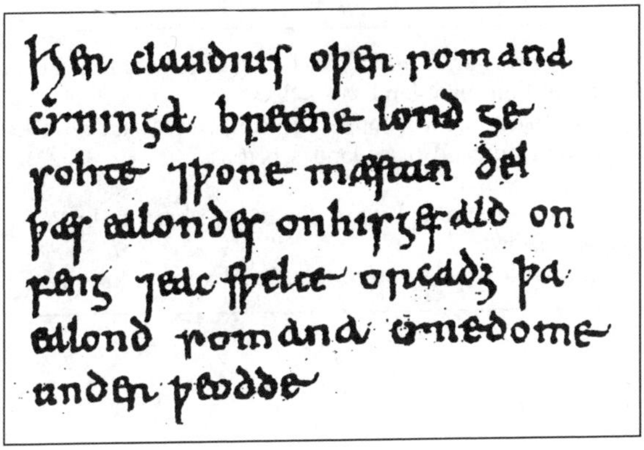

Œ

Her Claudıuꞅ oþer romana
cynınʒa bretene lond ʒe
ꞅohte 7 þone mæꞅtan del
þæꞅ ealondeꞅ on hıꞅ ʒeƿald on
fenʒ 7 eac ꞅƿelce orcadʒ þa
ealond romana cynedome
under þeodde

WW

Here Claudius second of-romans
kings of-britain land
attacked & the most part
of-the island into his power
seized & also orkney the
island to-romans empire
subjected

ME

In this year Claudius, the second Roman emperor, invaded Britain and conquered most of the land. He also subjected the Isle of Orkney to the rule of the Roman Empire.

The *Peterborough Chronicle* account differs in its detail:

Text 5b – *Peterborough Chronicle* for AD 47

Œ

Her Claudius romana cininʒ ʒeƿat mid here on brytene.
7 ıʒland ʒeeode. 7 ealle ƿyhtas. 7 ƿalas underþeodde romana rice.

WW Here Claudius romans' king went with army in britain.
& island over-ran. & all picts. & welsh made-subject-to romans' empire.

MnE In this year the Roman emperor Claudius invaded Britain with his army and overran the island. All the Picts and Welsh were also made subject to the Roman empire.

The vocabulary of Texts 5a & 5b is listed in the *Word Book*.

Texts 4 and 5b are recorded on the cassette tape.

brɪtːənə iːjlənd is ɛhta hʊnd miːla laŋg ənd twaː hʊnd braːd
ənd heːr sɪnd ɔn ðɪs iːjlənd viːf jəðeːədə
ɛŋglɪʃ ənd brɪtɪʃ ənd wɪlʃ ənd ʃʏtɪːʃ ənd pʏçtɪʃ ənd boːk leːdən
ɛːrəst wɛːrən buːʏənd ðɪsəs ləndəs brɪtːəs

heːr klaʊdɪʊs roːmaːnə kɪnɪŋg jəwaːt mɪd hɛrə ɔn brɪtənə
ənd iːjlənd jəeːɔdə
ənd æəlːə pʏhtas ənd walas ʊndərðeːədːə roːmaːnə riːtʃə

2.3 How the English language came to Britain

By AD 443, the Roman legions had been withdrawn from Britain to defend Rome itself, so when the Romano-British leader Vortigern invited the Angles Hengest and Horsa to help defend the country, they found Britain undefended, and open not only for raiding and plunder, but for invasion and settlement.

2.3.1 *The coming of the Angles, Saxons and Jutes*

This was not a peaceful process. Bede describes what happened in his *History of the English Church and People*, which was written in Latin in the 8th century (see section 3.2.3):

> It was not long before such hordes of these alien peoples crowded into the island that the natives who had invited them began to live in terror. . . . They began by demanding a greater supply of provisions; then, seeking to provoke a quarrel, threatened that unless larger supplies were forthcoming, they would terminate the treaty and ravage the whole island. . . . These heathen conquerors devastated the surrounding cities and countryside, extended the conflagration from the eastern to the western shores without opposition, and established a stranglehold over nearly all the doomed island. A few wretched survivors captured in the hills were butchered wholesale, and others, desperate with hunger, came out and surrendered to the enemy for food, although they were doomed to lifelong slavery even if they escaped instant massacre. Some fled overseas in their misery; others, clinging to their homeland, eked out a wretched and fearful existence among the mountains, forests, and crags, ever on the alert for danger.
>
> (Translation from the Latin by Leo Sherley-Price, Penguin, 1955)

Activity 2.1

In the following accounts of the coming of the Angles (Texts 6, 7 and 8), abbreviated words in the manuscript have been filled out in the transcriptions, but the punctuation is the original. Here are some suggestions for study:

(i) Compare the word-for-word translations with the Old English facsimiles.

- (a) List some OE words which are still used in MnE (some will be different in spelling), and
- (b) List some OE words which have not survived into MnE.
- (c) List those letters of the alphabet which are not used in MnE or which have changed a lot in shape
- (d) Comment on the punctuation.

(ii) Read the MnE version, and consider some of the reasons why the word-for-word translation does not read like present-day English.

Text 6a – *Peterborough Chronicle* for AD 443 (facsimile)

OE

Her ſen
don brytƿalaſ oferſ^{æ}to
rome. 7 heom fultumeſ
bædon ƿıð peohtaſ. ac hı
þær nefdon nænne. forþan
ðe hı feordodan ƿıð ætlan
huna cınınʒe. 7 þa ſendon
hı to anʒlū. 7 anʒel cyn/
neſ æðelınʒaſ ðeſ ılcan
bædon.

WW

Here sent
britons over sea to
rome. & them troops
asked against picts. but they
there had not none. because
they fought against attila
huns king. & then sent
they to angles & angle peo/
ples princes the same
asked.

MnE In this year the Britons sent overseas to Rome and asked the Romans for forces against the Picts, but they had none there because they were at war with Attila, king of the Huns. Then the Britons sent to the Angles and made the same request to the princes of the Angles.

Text 6b – *Parker Chronicle* for AD 443 (facsimile)

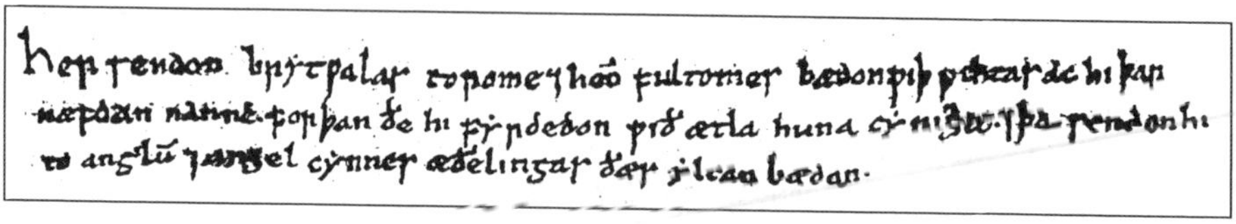

OE her ꞅendon brẏtalaꞅ to rome 7 heō fultomeꞅ bædon ƿıþ pıhtaꞅ ac hı þar næfdan nanne. forþan ðe hı fẏrdedon ƿıþ ætla huna cẏnıngæ. 7 þa ꞅendon hı to anglū 7 angel cẏnneꞅ æðelıngaꞅ ðæꞅ ẏlcan bædan.

📖 The vocabulary of Texts 6a and 6b is listed in the *Word Book*.

Text 7 – *Peterborough Chronicle* for AD 449 (facsimile)

Her martıa/	Here martia-
nuſ 7 ualentın' onfenȝon	nus & valentinus took
rıce 7 rıxadon.vıı. pıntra.	kingdom & reigned 7 winters.
7 on þeora daȝum ȝelaðode	& in their days invited
pyrtȝeorn anȝel cın hıder.	vortigern angle people hither.
7 hı þa coman on þrım ceo/	& they then came in three ships
lum hıder to brytene. on	hither to britain. at
þam ſtede heoppıne[s] fleot.	the place heopwinesfleet.
Se cynınȝ pyrtȝeorn ȝef	The king vortigern gave
heom land on ſuðan eaſ /	them land in south east
tan ðıſſum lande. pıððan	of-this land. provided
þe hı ſceoldon feohton pıð	that they should fight against
pyhtaſ. Heo pa fuhton	picts. They then fought
pıð pyhtaſ. 7 heofdon ſı/	against picts. & had vic-
ȝe ſpa hper ſpa heo co/	tory wherever they came.
mon. Hy ða ſendon to	They then sent to
anȝle heton ſendon mara	anglen ordered send more
fultum. 7 heton heom ſec/	help. & ordered them say
ȝan brytpalana nahtſcı/	britons' coward-
pe. 7 þeſ landeſ cyſta.	ice. & the land's goodness.
Hy ða ſona ſendon hıder	They then at-once sent hither
mare peored þam oðrum	greater force to others
to fultume. Ða comon	as help. Then came
þa men of þrım meȝðum	these men from three nations
ȝermanıe. Of ald ſeaxum.	germany. From old saxons.
of anȝlum. of ıotum. Of	from angles. from jutes. From
ıotum comon cantpara. 7 pıht/	jutes came kent-people. & wight-
para. ꝥ ıſ ſeo meȝð þe nu	people. that is the race which now
eardaþ on pıht. 7 þæt cyn on	dwells in wight. & the race among
peſt ſexum þe man nu ȝıt	west saxons that one now still
hæt ıutna cyn. Of eald	calls jutes' race. From old
ſeaxum coman eaſt ſeaxa.	saxons came east saxons
7 ſuð ſexa 7 peſt ſexa. Of	& south saxons & west saxons. From
anȝle comon ſe a ſyððan	anglen came it ever since
ſtod peſtıȝ betpıx ıutum	stood waste between jutes
7 ſeaxum. eaſt anȝla. mıd/	and saxons. east angles. mid-
del anȝla. mearca. 7 ealla	dle angles. mercians & all
norþhymbra. Heora he/	northumbrians. Their lead-
retoȝan pæron tpeȝen	ers were two
ȝebroðra. henȝeſt. 7	brothers. hengest. &
horſa.	horsa.

MnE In this year Marcian [*Eastern Roman Emperor*] and Valentinian [*Western Roman Emperor*] came to power and reigned seven years. In their days Vortigern invited the Angles here and they then came hither to Britain in three ships, at a place called Ebbsfleet [*in Kent*]. King Vortigern gave them land in the south-east of this country, on condition that they fought against the Picts. They fought the Picts and were victorious wherever they fought. Then they sent to Anglen, and ordered the Angles to send more help, and reported the cowardice of the Britons and the fertility of the land. So the Angles at once sent a larger force to help the others. These men came from three Germanic nations – the **Old Saxons**, the **Angles** and the **Jutes**. From the Jutes came the people of **Kent** and the **Isle of Wight** – that is, the people who now live in the Isle of Wight, and the race among the West Saxons who are still called Jutes. From the **Old Saxons** came the men of **Essex**, **Sussex** and **Wessex**. From **Anglen**, which has stood waste ever since, between the Jutes and Saxons, came the men of **East Anglia**, **Middle Anglia**, **Mercia** and the whole of **Northumbria**. Their leaders were two brothers, Hengest and Horsa.

📖 The vocabulary of Text 7 is listed in the *Word Book*.

Text 8 – *Peterborough Chronicle* for AD 455 (facsimile)

OE

Her hen
ʒeſt 7 horꞅa fuhton pıð
pyrtʒerne þā cınınʒe
on þære ꞅtope þe ıꞅ cpe/
den æʒeleꞅþrep. 7 hıꞅ bro/
þor horꞅan man ofꞅloh.
7 æfter þonn fenʒ to
rıce henʒeꞅt. 7 æꞅc hıꞅ
ꞅunu.

WW

Here hen-
gest & horsa fought against
vortigern the king
in the place that is call-
ed aylesford. & his bro-
ther horsa one slew.
& after that came to
kingdom hengest. & æsc his
son.

MnE In this year Hengest and Horsa fought against king Vortigern at a place called Aylesford, and Hengest's brother Horsa was killed. Then Hengest became king and was succeeded by his son Æsc.

📖 The vocabulary of Text 8 is listed in the *Word Book*.

2.3.2 'Englaland' established

The complete conquest of *Englaland* – 'the land of the Angles' – took another two centuries. There are tales of a Romano-British king called Arthur who led successful resistance in the 470s, winning battles that are recorded in Welsh heroic legends. He would have been a Romano-British noble, and was probably a commander of cavalry. Twelve victories against the Saxons are recorded, and much of the country remained under British rule for some time. But Arthur's

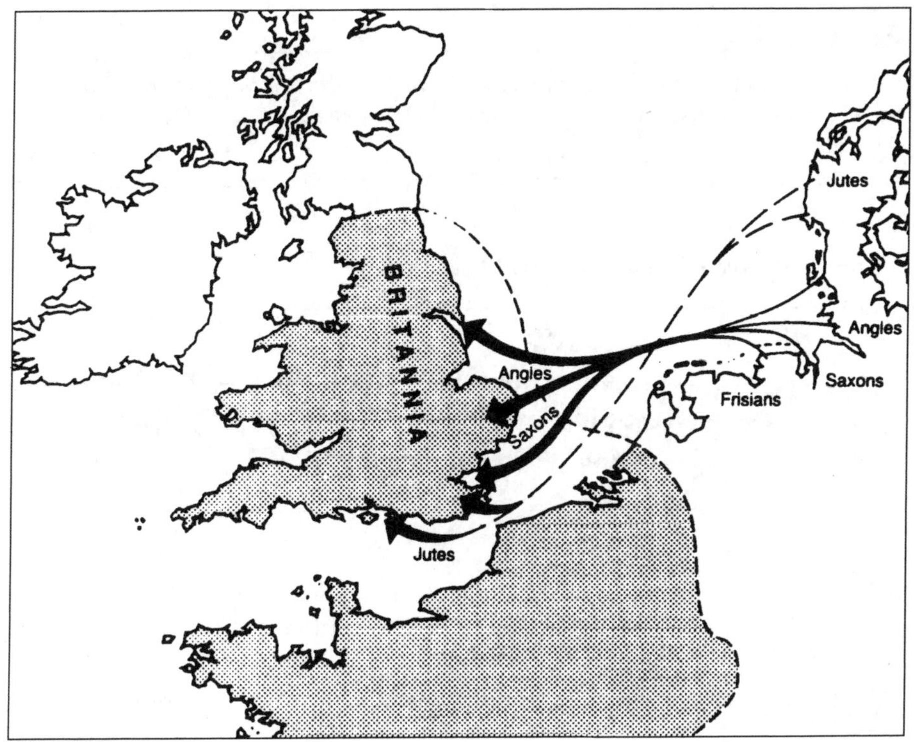

Map 1 The invasions of the Angles, Saxons and Jutes

name does not appear in *The Anglo-Saxon Chronicle*, and his historical existence is still disputed, though the chronicle does tell of other battles that took place, as in the following example.

Text 9a – *Peterborough Chronicle* for AD 519 (facsimile)

OE

Her. certıc 7 kynrıc onfenȝon
ƿeꞅt ꞅeaxna rıce. 7 þı ılcan ȝeare hı gefuhton ƿıð
bryttaꞅ. ðer man nu nemnað certıceꞅ ford. 7 ꞅıððan
rıxadon ƿeꞅt ꞅeaxna cynebarn of þam dæȝe.

WW

Here certic & cynric took
west saxons' kingdom . & the same year they fought against
britons. where one now names certic's ford. & afterwards
ruled west saxons' princes from that day.

Activity 2.2

Compare the *Peterborough Chronicle* text above with the following version from the *Parker Chronicle*. What differences are there? Can you suggest any reason for these differences?

Text 9b – *Parker Chronicle* for AD 519 (facsimile)

OE

ƿeſt ſexena
Her cerdic 7 cynric , rice onfenȝun. 7 þy ilcan ȝeare hie fuhton
ƿiþ brettaſ. þær mon nu nemneþ cerdiceſ ford. 7 ſiþþan ricſa-
dan ƿeſt ſexana cynebearn of þam dæȝe.

WW

Here cerdic & cynric west saxons' kingdom seized. & the same year they fought
against britons. where one now names cerdic's ford. 7 after ruled
west saxons' princes from that day.

The vocabulary of Texts 9a and 9b is listed in the *Word Book*.

Similar entries about fighting against the Britons are recorded throughout the 6th century and into the 7th and 8th centuries, by which time they would have been driven as a fighting force from England.

In the *Chronicle* they are called both *Wealas*, or *Walas – foreigners*, and *Bretwalas*. *Walas* is the origin of the modern words *Wales*, *Welsh* and *Cornwall* (*Cornwalas*). The singular noun *wealh* was also used to mean *slave* or *serf*, which is an indication of the status of the Britons under Anglo-Saxon rule. For example, the entry for AD 755 in *The Parker Chronicle* tells of Cynewulf, King of Wessex:

> 7 se Cyneƿulf oft miclum ȝefeohtum feaht wiþ bretƿalum.
>
> *& that Cynewulf often great battles fought against brito-welsh.*

and mentions in passing how a Welsh hostage became caught up in a local fight against Cyneheard, a prince of Wessex,

> hie simle feohtende ƿæran oþ hie alle læȝon butan anum bryttiscum ȝisle.
> 7 he spiþe ȝeƿundad ƿæs.
>
> *they continuously fighting were until they all lay (dead) except one british hostage.*
> *& he badly wounded was.*

Here are two typical 7th-century short entries in *The Peterborough* and *Parker Chronicles*. The annal for AD 614 is evidence of continued British resistance.

Text 10a – *Peterborough Chronicle* for AD 611 (facsimile)

OE Her kyneʒılſ fenʒ to rıce. on ƿeaſt ſeaxum. 7 heol^{d} .xxxı. ƿıntra.

WW Here cynegils took to kingdom. among west saxons. & held 31 winters.

MnE AD 611. In this year Cynegils succeeded to the West Saxon kingdom and reigned for 31 years.

Text 11a – *Peterborough Chronicle* for AD 614 (facsimile)

OE Her kyneʒılſ 7 cƿıchelm ʒefuhton on beandune. 7 ofſloʒon .ıı. þuſend ƿalana. 7 lxv.

WW Here cynegils & cwichelm fought at beandune & slew 2 thousand welsh. & 65.

MnE 614. In this year Cynegils and Cwichelm fought at Beandune and slew two thousand and sixty-five Welsh.

Texts 10b and 11b – *Parker Chronicle* for AD 611 & 614 (facsimile)

OE Her cyneʒılſ fenʒ to rıce on ƿeſſeaxum. 7 heold .xxxı. ƿıntra.

þuſend ƿala. 7 lxv

Her cyneʒılſ 7 cuıchelm ʒefuhton on bean dune. 7 ofſloʒon .ii.

The vocabulary of Texts 10a and 10b, 11a and 11b is listed in the *Word Book*.

2.3.3 Celtic words in English today

There is no surviving evidence of the British or Celtic language as it was used in the 5th century, and few Old Celtic words are to be found in MnE, such as *ass*, *bannock*, *brock* (i.e. *badger*), *crag*, *tor*. There is a larger number of Celtic place names of rivers and settlements; the best known include *Avon*, *Carlisle*, *Cornwall*, *Devon*, *Dover*, *Esk*, *Exe*, *London*, *Thames*, *Usk* and *Wye*.

OE *cumb*, like modern Welsh *cwm*, meaning *small valley*, *hollow* is of Celtic origin. It occurs in many place names, like *Batcombe*, *Eastcomb*, *Salcombe* and *Winchcombe*. A number of place-names begin with *Cum-*, like *Cumwhitton*, *Cumdivock*, *Cumlongan*, *Cumloden*.

The reasons for this lack of Old Celtic vocabulary in English must lie in the absence of integration between the British and the Anglo-Saxon invaders. As Bede records, the British were in time either driven westwards into Wales and Cornwall or they remained a subject people of serfs. The dominant language would therefore be English.

tor	probably a Celtic name; cf. Gaelic *torr* – a rocky peak	847
brat	Irish *brat* – cloth, cloak	950
dun (a)	OE *dun*, perhaps from Celtic: cf. Irish and Gaelic *donn* – brown	953
ass	there were two OE words for ass – *esol* and *assa*. OE *assa* was probably from the Celtic (cf. Old Northumbrian *asal*, *assal*, *assald*)	1000
bannock	Gaelic *bannach*	1000
brock	Gaelic *broc* – badger	1000

Celtic loan-words from Scots Gaelic, Irish Gaelic and Welsh are listed in later chapters.

3. Old English (I)

We call the language Old English (OE) during the Anglo-Saxon period and up to about 1100–1150, after the Norman Conquest. Our knowledge about it depends upon the survival of a number of manuscripts from which the grammar and vocabulary of the language have been reconstructed by scholars, working from the 16th century onwards (for a 16th-century example see section 3.1.6), but especially in the 19th and 20th centuries. They have provided us with the dictionaries and grammars of OE and the editions of OE texts to which we can refer.

3.1 Written Old English

3.1.1 *Runes*

The writing system for the earliest English was based on the use of signs called **runes**, which were devised for carving in wood or stone by the Germanic peoples of Northern Europe. The best surviving examples are to be seen in the Scandinavian countries – Sweden, Norway and Denmark – and in the islands of Shetland and Orkney. Few examples of rune-stones have survived in Britain, but the best known is a large 18-foot high cross now in the church at Ruthwell, Dumfriesshire in Scotland. On four sides of the Ruthwell Cross are some runic inscriptions in the Northumbrian dialect, which are part of an OE poem called *The Dream of the Rood* (*rood* comes from the OE word *rod* meaning *cross*), in which the Cross relates the events of the Crucifixion. The Ruthwell Cross probably dates from the 8th century.

3.1.1.1 *Runes, writing & reading*

Here is one version of the runic alphabet:

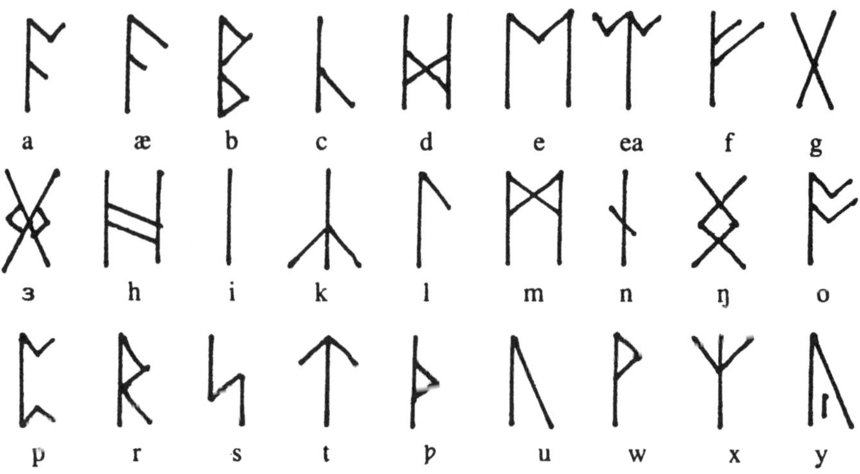

Activity 3.1

Use the chart of the runic alphabet to transcribe the following words from the Ruthwell Cross fragment. They appear at the top of the south-west face of the Cross (see the drawing on p. 23):

ᛣᚱᛁᛋᛏ ᚹᚫᛋ ᚩᚾ ᚱᚩᛞᛁ ᚻᚹᛖᚦᚱᚫ

ᚦᛖᚱ ᚠᚢᛋᚫ ᚠᛠᚱᚱᚪᚾ ᛤᚹᚩᛗᚢ

ᚫᚦᚦᛁᛚᚫ ᛏᛁᛚ ᚪᚾᚢᛗ

The diagram below shows the way in which part of the inscription is carved on the south-west side of the Ruthwell Cross.

OE KRIST WÆS ON RODI HWEÞRÆ
ÞER FUSÆ FEARRAN KWOMU
ÆÞÞILÆ TIL ANUM

WW CHRIST WAS ON CROSS WHETHER (= yet)
THERE EAGER FROM-AFAR CAME
NOBLE-(MEN) TO ONE-ALONE

MnE Christ was on the cross yet eager noblemen came there
from afar to him alone

This part of the inscription in the Northumbrian dialect of OE corresponds to the following lines from the poem *The Dream of the Rood* in the West Saxon dialect:

OE crist wæs on rode
hwæþere þær fuse feorran cwoman
to þæm æþelinge

WW Christ was on cross
yet there eager-(men) from-afar came
to the prince

In the Northumbrian version, the word *æþþilæ* is an adjective, nominative case, masculine plural, and so 'noble-men'. In the West Saxon poem, *æþelinge* is a noun, dative case, masculine singular following the preposition *to*.

The 'noble men' in the extract are Joseph and Nicodemus; cf. the account in St John's Gospel, chapter 19: 38–9: 'After that, Pilate was approached by Joseph of Arimathea, ... who asked to be allowed to remove the body of Jesus. ... He was joined by Nicodemus ....'

3.1.2 *OE handwriting*

3.1.2.1 *Insular book-hand*

Writing in which each letter is formed separately and not joined to the others is called **book-hand** and can be seen in many of its varieties in the facsimiles. The book-hand that developed in England is known as **insular**, because it was the style used by Anglo-Saxon scribes in the island of Britain, in contrast with continental styles. It continued after the Norman Conquest of 1066 until about 1200. (For example, see the letter shapes of ⟨f⟩, ⟨r⟩and ⟨ʒ⟩ in the *Ormulum* of *c*. 1200 in Text 36 in chapter 5.)

Letter shapes

Some of the letters of the alphabet in the facsimile texts in chapter 2 are not at first easily recognisable. In Text 4 reproduced above, for example, notice letters ⟨ı⟩ and ⟨t⟩ in *Brittene*, ⟨ʒ⟩ in *iʒland*, ⟨a⟩ in *ehta*, ⟨d⟩ in *hund* and ⟨f⟩ in *fif*.

There are three forms of ⟨s⟩, 'insular s' ⟨ꞅ⟩ in *sind*, 'long s' ⟨ſ⟩ in *is*, and the familiar 'round s' in *þis*.

Handwriting is studied in **paleography**, which provides part of the evidence for the dating and placing of manuscripts in Old English through Middle English to Early Modern English. A few informal references to handwriting styles are made in later chapters from time to time (see Texts 34, 36, 38, 43, 52, 55, 86), but the topic is not studied in detail.

The Roman alphabet used to write Old English

Written English as we know it had to wait for the establishment of the Church and the building of monasteries in the 7th century in which the monks wrote manuscripts in Latin, the language of the Church. Therefore the Roman alphabet was used to match letters to the nearest equivalent sound in English. But no Roman letter was available for some OE sounds, so other non-Roman letters were adopted. Three of them are always used in modern printed OE texts:

- ⟨æ⟩ – a vowel pronounced [æ] and called *ash* – derived from Latin. It is today popularly known as 'short a', as in MnE *cat*.
- ⟨þ⟩ – a consonant pronounced [θ] or [ð]; the letter is called *thorn* from its runic name (see section 3.1.1 on runes) now replaced by ⟨th⟩.
- ⟨ð⟩ – a consonant also pronounced [θ] or [ð]; the letter is called *eth* – derived from Irish writing and now replaced by ⟨th⟩.

(Letters ⟨þ⟩ and ⟨ð⟩ tended to be interchangeable, and did not separately represent the voiced or voiceless consonant.)

Some of the other non-Roman letters that you will have seen in the facsimiles are:

- ⟨ƿ⟩ – pronounced [w] and called *wynn* from its runic name. This letter is not usually used in printing OE today, and the familiar letter ⟨w⟩ is substituted. Letter ⟨w⟩ was not part of the OE alphabet. The consonant sound [w] was represented in the earliest OE writing by ⟨u⟩ or ⟨uu⟩ ('double-u'), and was then replaced by ⟨ƿ⟩ wynn.
- ⟨ʒ⟩ – The Roman letter ⟨g⟩ was written ⟨ʒ⟩ (called *yogh*) and pronounced [g], [j] or [ɣ]~[x], depending on the sounds that preceded or followed it.

- ⟨⁊⟩ – This sign was used as shorthand for *and*, like the ampersand ⟨&⟩ today.

The OE alphabet therefore consisted of:

Vowel letters:	a æ e i o u y
Consonant letters:	b c d f ʒ h l m n p r s/ſ/ꞅ t þ/ð ƿ> x
	k q z *were rarely used*
	g, j *and* v *were not yet in use*

Present-day printed OE texts almost always use ⟨g⟩ for ⟨ʒ⟩, ⟨w⟩ for ⟨ƿ⟩ and only one form of ⟨s⟩.

Here is a brief summary of some of the developments which can be checked against the facsimiles in later chapters 7–18 which discuss Middle and Early Modern English, including examples of early printing from the late 15th century onwards.

3.1.2.2 *Later changes in letter shapes*

- ⟨ƿ⟩ (wynn) was replaced by ⟨w⟩ or ⟨uu⟩ by *c.* 1300.
- ⟨ð⟩ (eth) had disappeared by about the same time.
- ⟨þ⟩ (thorn) survived much longer, into the 15th century, but often in modified forms, some like the former ⟨ƿ⟩ without its upright stroke ('ascender'), and others like ⟨y⟩. In that case, letter ⟨y⟩ was often dotted, ⟨ẏ⟩, for the vowel ⟨i⟩.
- ⟨g⟩ – the closed continental or 'carolingian' letter was introduced for the consonant ⟨g⟩.
- ⟨ʒ⟩ (yogh) came to be used for a number of different sounds, e.g. for [x], as in *riʒt* [rɪxt] (*right*), for [j] as in *ʒou* (*you*), or for [w] as in *laʒe* (*law*).
- ⟨r⟩ – the insular form was replaced by two forms, one like figure ⟨2⟩ (e.g. Text 37, Laʒamon's *Brut*), and a 'continental' form (e.g. Text 38 *The Owl & the Nightingale*).
- ⟨s⟩ – the insular form ⟨ꞅ⟩ was dropped, but 'long s' ⟨ſ⟩ continued to be used into the 18th-century in writing and printing, as well as the surviving 'round s'.
- ⟨t⟩ – the familiar present-day form with a vertical stroke above the cross-bar, begins to appear in the 13th century.
- ⟨a⟩ – becomes closed to ⟨ɑ⟩ in the 13th century.
- ⟨i⟩ was originally not dotted, ⟨ı⟩. It could be easily confused next to 'minim letters' ⟨m⟩, ⟨n⟩ and ⟨u⟩, so there were two alternative changes, either (1) ⟨y⟩ was used for the vowel, or (2) a slanting line like an accent was adopted as a diacritic mark, ⟨í⟩, which was taken over by early printers in the late 15th century and reduced to the dot, ⟨i⟩ (see, for example, Caxton's printing in Texts 93 and 94 in chapter 14).
- ⟨æ⟩ had been replaced by ⟨a⟩ by the end of the 13th century.

3.1.2.3 Abbreviations

You will have noticed some abbreviations in the facsimiles in chapter 2. They were continued from the writing of Latin manuscripts. The commonest are:

- A line, or 'macron', over a letter shows the omission of ⟨m⟩ or ⟨n⟩, e.g. *oþrū* for *oþrum*.
- The omission of ⟨er⟩, ⟨re⟩ or ⟨ur⟩ is shown by a loop above the line.
- þ^{t} = *þat*; þ^{r}to = *þerto*; þ^{r} = *þer*; p̱ = *per*.

There are others which can be seen in the facsimiles in later chapters.

3.1.3 Long and short vowels and consonants in OE

3.1.3.1 Vowels

OE vowel letters represented both **long** and **short** OE vowels, that is, pairs of vowels with similar **quality** contrasted in **quantity**, or length (though linguists are not in fact agreed as to whether long and short vowels in OE differed only in quantity, and not in quality also).

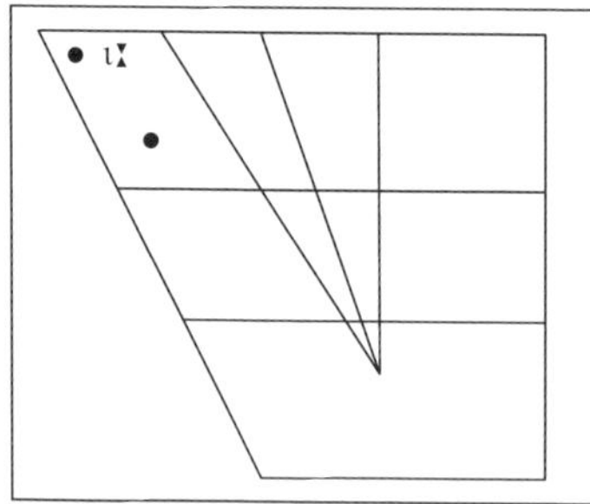

Vowel chart 1
MnE long [iː] and short [ɪ]

There are long and short vowels in present-day English pronunciation, but their length is usually determined by their 'phonetic environment' – the sounds that precede or follow. For example, the [ɑ] in *cart* is shorter than the [ɑː] in *card* because the voiceless [t] of *cart* causes the vowel to be cut off, whereas the voiced [d] of *card* does not. But there are no pairs of words in which only the length (quantity) of the vowel changes meaning. Even between vowels that are very similar, like the [i] of *peat* and the [ɪ] of *pit*, there is always a difference of quality, as the diagrammed Vowel chart 1 illustrates:

📖 The *Text Commentary Book* has a more detailed description.

There are two kinds of evidence that the length of the same vowel sounds in OE was **phonemic**, that is, that length of vowel alone in a word produced a difference of meaning:

- There are some **minimal pairs** of words, spelt identically, but with different meanings, for example,

Long vowel		*Short vowel*	
OE	*MnE*	*OE*	*MnE*
ham	home	ham	ham
is	ice	is	is
rod	rood	rod	rod

The possibility that they were in fact homonyms, spelt and pronounced identically, like MnE *bear* (*animal*) and *bear* (*carry*), is disproved by the second piece of evidence:

- The pronunciation of the vowels in MnE *home*, *ice* and *rood* has clearly changed considerably, from [ɑː] [iː] and [oː] in OE, to [əʊ] [aɪ] and [uː] today, so there must have been significant differences in the pronunciation of the OE vowels for some to have changed and not others. (The changing or 'shifting' of long vowels took place gradually over the period from the 14th to the 17th centuries, and has been called the **Great Vowel Shift** by linguists. It is described in section 15.5.)

The number of OE pure or single vowels (as opposed to glides or diphthongs) was fourteen, twice the number of vowel-letters used in the OE alphabet, for each letter was used to represent both a long and a short vowel. Their position in Vowel chart 2 will help you to remember their relationship.

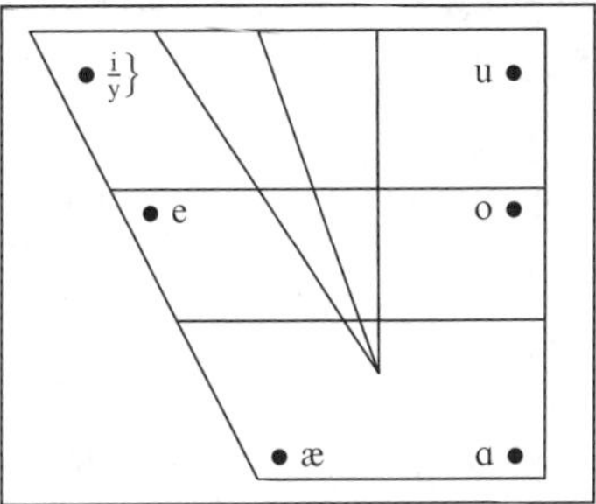

Vowel chart 2
OE single vowels

The contrast between the systems of single vowels in OE and MnE can be seen in Vowel chart 3 which shows the twelve MnE RP vowels.

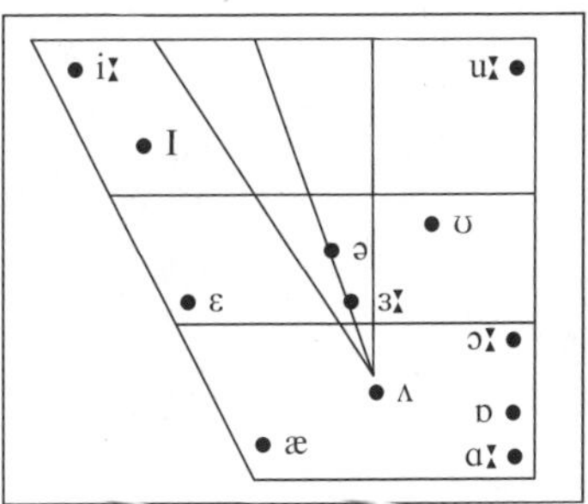

Vowel chart 3
MnE single vowels (RP)

Below are a few OE words containing examples of short and long vowels. The MnE **reflexes** (that is, words that have developed from an earlier stage of the language) have either different long vowels or diphthongs. (There are other changes you can see, but these are not a result of the long-short contrast – sound changes are rather more complex than this simplified account.)

OE		***Mn***		***EOE***		***MnE***	
and	[a]	*and*	[a]	fīf	[iː]	*five*	[aɪ]
tā	[ɑː]	*toe*	[əʊ]	pytt	[y]	*pit*	[ɪ]
bæc	[æ]	*back*	[æ]	fȳr	[yː]	*fire*	[aɪə]
strǣt	[æː]	*street*	[iː]	oxa	[ɔ]	*ox*	[ɒ]
sunne	[ʊ]	*sun*	[ʊ] or RP [ʌ]	gōs	[oː]	*goose*	[uː]
cū	[uː]	*cow*	[aʊ]	west	[ɛ]	*west*	[ɛ]
ribb	[ɪ]	*rib*	[ɪ]	gēs	[eː]	*geese*	[iː]

In printing OE texts today, long vowels are conventionally marked with a macron, e.g. ā ǣ ē ī ō ū ȳ but in this book long vowels are only marked when the information about length is relevant.

3.1.3.2 *Consonants*

OE had both short and long consonants. The pronunciation of **continuants**, that is, consonants that can be held on, like the fricatives [f], [h], [s], can obviously be made longer or shorter. But **plosive (stop)** consonants like [p] and [t], were also doubled in spelling to indicate a pronunciation similar to that of, for example, the MnE ⟨-pp-⟩ combination in a compound word like *hop-pole,* or ⟨-tt-⟩ in *part-time*, or the sequence ⟨-gg-⟩ in the phrase *big game*. There are only a few minimal pairs to prove the contrast, for example:

hopian	[hɔpiən]	to hope
hoppian	[hopːiən]	to hop
cwelan	[kwɛlən]	to die
cwellan	[kwɛlːən]	to kill

but the present and past tenses of certain verbs also formed minimal pairs with single and double consonants. They had the same long vowel in OE, but they have different vowels in their MnE reflexes, and are no longer minimal pairs. For example,

	Present tense	*Past tense*
OE	blēde	blēdde
MnE	bleed	bled
OE	fēde	fēdde
MnE	feed	fed
OE	mēte	mētte
MnE	meet	met

In all three OE verbs, the vowels of both present and past tenses are long [eː]. Both the vowels have since changed, but OE [eː] has shifted to [iː] in the present tense, and has shortened to [ɛ] in the past tense in MnE. The only difference between the two words in OE is in the length of the [d] or [t] consonant, therefore this must in some way have caused the later divergence of the vowels. It is further evidence that there were long and short consonants in OE.

3.1.3.3 *OE letters and sounds*

Here is a list of the letters of the OE alphabet, with a brief indication of their probable pronunciation. A few letters in OE, ⟨c⟩ ⟨ʒ⟩, ⟨f⟩, ⟨þ⟩, ⟨ð⟩, represented more than one sound, but pronunciation and spelling were much closer then than in MnE.

OE letter	OE word	OE sound (IPA)	Modern word with similar sound
Vowels			
⟨i⟩	brinʒan (*bring*)	[ɪ]	*bring*
	rīdan (*ride*)	[iː]	*machine*
⟨y⟩	hyll (*hill*)	[ʏ]	German *schütten*
	hȳf (*hive*)	[y]	German *grün*
⟨e⟩	elm (*elm*)	[e]	*elm*
	fēdan (*feed*)	[eː]	German *gegen*
⟨æ⟩	æsc (*ash*)	[æ]	*ash*
	clǣne (*clean*)	[æː]	
⟨a⟩	sacc (*sack*)	[a]	American English *pot*
	ʒāt (*goat*)	[ɑː]	*cart*
⟨o⟩	fox (*fox*)	[ɔ]	*fox*
	ʒōs (*goose*)	[oː]	German *wohnen*
⟨u⟩	ful (*full*)	[ʊ]	*full*
	fūl (*foul*)	[uː]	*fool*
⟨ea⟩	earnian (*earn*)	[ɛə]	(no equivalent)
	ēast (*east*)	[ɛːə]	
⟨eo⟩	eorþ (*earth*)	[eə]	
	prēost (*priest*)	[eːə]	
Consonants			
⟨p⟩	pullian (*pull*)	[p]	*pull*
⟨b⟩	brid (*bird*)	[b]	*bird*
⟨t⟩	tæʒl (*tail*)	[t]	*tail*
⟨d⟩	doʒʒa (*dog*)	[d]	*dog*
⟨c⟩	col (*coal*)	[k]	*coal*, *king*
or	cirice (*church*)	[tʃ]	*church*
⟨ʒ⟩*	ʒift (*gift*)	[g]	*gift*
or	ʒeonʒ (*young*)	[j]	*young*
or	boʒ (*bough*)	[ɣ]	–
⟨cʒ⟩	hecʒ (*hedge*)	[dʒ]	*hedge*
⟨x⟩	æx (*axe*)	[ks]	*axe*
⟨f⟩	fot (*foot*)	[f]	*foot*
	lufu (*love*)	[v]	*love*
⟨þ⟩ ⟨ð⟩	þæc *or* ðæc (*thatch*)	[θ]	*thatch*
	feþer *or* feðer (*feather*)	[ð]	*feather*
⟨s⟩ ⟨ſ⟩ ⟨ꞅ⟩	sendan (*send*)	[s]	*send*
or	ceosan (*choose*)	[z]	*choose*
⟨sc⟩	sceap (*sheep*)	[ʃ]	*sheep*
⟨h⟩	sihþ (*sight*)	[ç]	German *nichts*
or	boht (*bought*)	[x]	German *nacht*
⟨l⟩	leþer (*leather*)	[l]	*leather*
⟨m⟩	mona (*moon*)	[m]	*moon*
⟨n⟩	niht (*night*)	[n]	*night*
⟨r⟩	rarian (*roar*)	[r]	*roar*
⟨ƿ⟩*	ƿæter (*water*)	[w]	*water*

* Letters ⟨g⟩ and ⟨w⟩ are normally used for ⟨ʒ⟩ and ⟨ƿ⟩ in modern printed editions of OE texts.

📖 There is a more detailed introduction to the pronunciation and spelling of OE in the *Text Commentary Book*.

3.1.4 *The conversion to Christianity*

In the 7th century much of the north of England was converted to Christianity by monks from Ireland, while Augustine had been sent by the Pope in AD 595 to preach Christianity to the English, and had begun in the south, in Kent. Here are the *Chronicle* annals that record the events:

N.B. from this point there will usually be two transcriptions of OE facsimiles, the first matching the original manuscript as far as possible, and the second filling out abbreviations and using the letters as in present-day printed OE – ⟨ð⟩, ⟨þ⟩ and⟨æ⟩. You will be able to infer the functions of the different abbreviations by comparing the two transcriptions.

Text 12a – *Peterborough Chronicle* for AD 595 (facsimile)

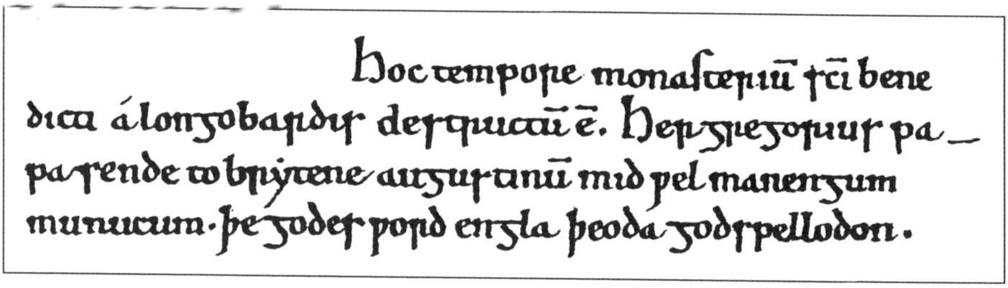
hoc tempore monaſterıū ſcī bene
dıctı á lonʒobardıſ deſtructū ē. her ʒreʒorıuſ pa_
pa ſende to brẏtene auʒuſtınū mıd pel manenʒum
munucum. þe ʒodeſ pord enʒla þeoda ʒodſpellodon.

(*Note that the first sentence is in Latin.*)

ŒE1

hoc tempore monaſterıū ſcī bene
dıctı á lonʒobardıſ deſtructū ē. her ʒreʒorıuſ pa_
pa ſende to brẏtene auʒuſtınū mıd pel manenʒum
munucum. þe ʒodeſ pord enʒla þeoda ʒodſpellodon.

ŒE2

Hoc tempore monasterium sancti benedicti
a longobardis destructum est. Her gregorius papa
sende to brytene augustinum mid wel manegum
munucum. þe godes word engla þeoda godspellodon.

WW

At-this time monastery of-saint benedict
by longobards destroyed was. Here gregory pope
sent to britain Augustine with very many
monks. who god's word to-english nation preached.

MnE

At this time the monastery of St Benedict was destroyed by the Lombards. In this year Pope Gregory sent Augustine to Britain with very many monks, who preached God's word to the English nation.

Text 12b – *Parker Chronicle* version (facsimile)

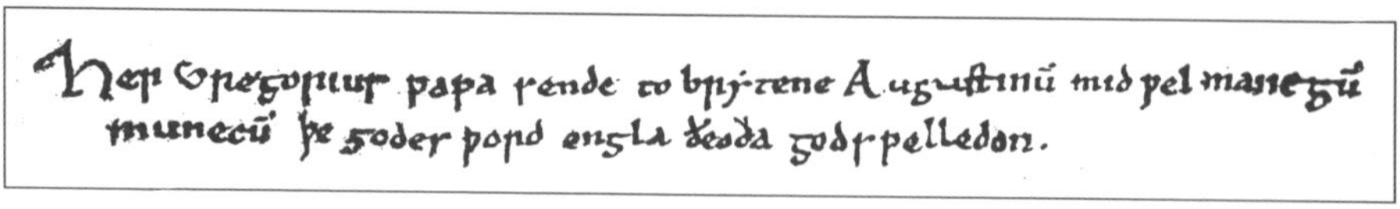
Her Gregoriuſ papa ſende to bryÿtene Auguſtinū mid pel manegū
munecū þe ʒodeſ pord engla ðeoda ʒodſpelledon.

ŒE1 hɛr Greʒorıuꞅ papa ꞅende to brẏtene Auʒuſtınū mıd ƿel maneʒū munecū þe ʒodeꞅ ƿord enʒla ðeoda ʒodꞅpelledon.

ŒE2 Her Gregorius papa sende to brytene Augustinum mid wel manegum munecum þe godes word engla ðeoda godspelledon.

The vocabulary of Texts 12a and 12b is listed in the *Word Book*.

Text 13a – *Peterborough Chronicle* for AD 601 (facsimile)

ŒE1

hɛr ꞅende ʒreʒorıuꞅ papa auʒu__
ꞅtıne arcebıꞅcope pallıum on brẏtene. 7 ƿel maneʒa
ʒodcunde lareƿaꞅ hım to fultume. 7 paulın'bıꞅcop ʒe
hƿırfede eadƿıne nor[ð]hẏmbra cınınʒ to fulluhte.

ŒE2

Her sende gregorius papa aug-
ustine arcebiscope pallium on brytene. 7 wel manega
godcunde larewas him to fultume. 7 paulinus biscop ge-
hwirfede eadwine norðhymbra cining to fulluhte.

WW

Here sent gregory pope augustine
archbishop pallium in britain & very-many
religious teachers him for help &paulinus bishop
converted edwin northumbrians' king to baptism.

MnE In this year Pope Gregory sent the pallium* to archbishop Augustine in Britain, and very many religious teachers to help him; and bishop Paulinus converted Edwin King of Northumbria and baptised him.

* The pallium was a vestment given by the Pope to mark the appointment of an archbishop.

Text 13b – *Parker Chronicle* version (facsimile)

ŒE1

hɛr ꞅende ʒreʒorıuꞅ pap̄ auʒuſtıno. ærce bıꞅcepe pallıum ın
bretene 7 ƿelmonıʒe ʒodcunde lareoƿaꞅ hım to fultome.
7 paulıns bıꞅc ʒ̄hƿerfde edƿıne norþhymbra cynınʒ to fulƿıhte.

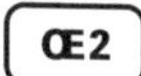

Her sende gregorius papa augustino. ærce biscepe pallium in
bretene 7 welmonige godcunde lareowas him to fultome.
7 paulinus biscop gehwerfde edwine norþhymbra cyning to fulwihte.

The vocabulary of Texts 13a and 13b is listed in the *Word Book*.

The monks had adapted the Roman alphabet from Latin to write English, which means that the spelling of OE gives us a good idea of its pronunciation. We know the sounds of Latin represented by the Roman alphabet, because there has been a continuous tradition of speaking Latin to the present day. This also provides the evidence for the different OE dialects, because different spellings for the same words are likely to indicate differences of pronunciation or word-form.

3.1.5 *Evidence of dialectal variation*

Here are two versions of the earliest known poem in English. It is to be found in the OE translation of Bede's *History of the English Church and People*, which was written in Latin and finished in AD 731. Bede's *History* was translated into English in the late 9th century as part of a great revival of learning under King Ælfred (see section 3.3.1 below). The poem, a hymn to God the Creator, is all that survives of the work of the poet Cædmon, who lived in the 7th century. (For a discussion of OE verse, see chapter 4.)

Text 14 – Cædmon's hymn

West Saxon dialect
Nu we sculan herian heofonrices weard
Metodes mihte and his modgþeonc
weorc wuldorfæder; swa he wundra gehwæs
ece dryhten, ord onstealde.
He ærest gesceop eorðan bearnum
heofon to hrofe, halig scyppend;
ða middangeard, moncynnes weard,
ece dryhten, æfter teode
firum foldan, frea ælmihtig.

Northumbrian dialect
Nu scylun hergan hefænricæs uard
Metudæs mæcti end his modgidanc
uerc uuldurfadur, sue he uundra gihuæs
eci dryctin, or astelidæ.
He ærist scop ælda barnum
heben til hrofe, haleg scepen;
tha middungeard moncynnes uard,
eci dryctin, æfter tiadæ
firum foldu, frea allmectig.

WW

Now we must praise heaven-kingdom's Guardian
Creator's might and his mind-thought
work Glory-father's; as he of-wonders each
everlasting Lord, beginning established.
He first shaped of-earth for-children
heaven as roof, holy Creator;
then middle-earth, mankind's Guardian,
everlasting Lord, after determined
for-men earth, Ruler almighty.

West Saxon dialect

nuː weː ʃulən hɛrɪən heəvənrɪːtʃəs wɛərd
metɔdəs mɪçt ənd hɪs moːdjəðɔŋk
wɛərk wʊldərvædər
zwɑː heː wʊndra jəhwæs
eːtʃə drʏçtən ɔrd ɔnstɛəldə
heː ærəst jəʃɛoːp ɛərðən bɛərnʊm
heəvən toː hroːvə, hɑːlɪj ʃʏpːənd
ðɑː mɪdːənjɛərd, mɔnkʏnːəs wɛərd,
eːtʃə drʏçtən, æftər teːədə
viːrəm vɔldən, vreːə ælmɪçtɪj

Northumbrian dialect

nuː ʃʏlən hɛrgən hɛvænriːtʃæs wɑrd
mɛtʊdæs mæktɪ ɛnd hɪs moːdjɪdɑnk
wɛrk wʊldʊrfɑdʊr,
sweː heː wʊndrɑ jɪhwæs
eːtʃɪ drʏktɪn, oːr ɑːstɛlɪdæ
heː æːrɪst ʃoːp ældɑ bɑrnʊm
hɛbən tɪl hrɔːvə, hɑːlɛj ʃəpən
θɑː mɪdːʊnjɛərd mɔnkʏnːəs wɑrd,
eːtʃɪ drʏktɪn, æftər tiːadæ
fiːtʊm fɔldʊ, frɛːa ɑlːmɛçtij

The vocabulary of Text 14 is listed in the *Word Book*.

Text 14 is recorded on the cassette tape.

3.1.6 *A Testimonie of Antiquitie*

A small book called *A Testimonie of Antiquitie* was printed in London in 1567. Its purpose was to provide evidence, in a contemporary religious controversy, about the Church sacraments. It reproduced, with a translation, a sermon 'in the Saxon tongue' by Ælfric (*c.* 955–*c.* 1010), Abbot of Eynsham near Oxford and a famous English preacher and grammarian.

The book is of interest to students of language, because the translation provides an example of 16th century Early Modern English (EMnE) both in style, spelling and printing, while the Old English sermon is reproduced in a type face which copies OE manuscript letter forms. Here is the beginning of Ælfric's sermon in *A Testimonie of Antiquitie*, with its 16th-century translation, and the list of 'The Saxon Caracters or letters, that be moste straunge' printed at the end of the book.

Text 15 – from *A Testimonie of Antiquitie, A* (1567) (facsimile)

The epiſtle beginneth thus in the Saxon tonge.

Ælꝼɲıc abb. ʒɲeꞇ Sıʒeꝼeɲþ ꝼɲeondlıce; Me ıſ ʒeſæd ꝥ ðu ſædeſꞇ beo me ꝥ ıc oþeɲ tæhꞇe on Enʒlıſcen ʒeƿɲıꞇen. oþeɲ eoƿeɲ ancoɲ æꞇ ham mıd eoƿ tæhþ. ꝼoɲþan ðe he ſƿuꞇelıce ſæʒþ ꝥ hıꞇ ſıe aleꝼd. ꝥ mæſſe pɲeoſꞇaſ ƿel moꞇan ƿıꝼıʒen. and mın ʒeƿɲıꞇen ƿıþcƿeþeþ ðẏſen.

That is, Elfricke abbot doth ſend frendlye ſalutation to Sigeferth. It is tolde me that I teach otherwyſe in my Engliſh writynges, thẽ doth thy anker teach, which is at home wyth thee. For he ſayth playnly that it is a lawfull thing for a prieſt to marye, and my wrytynges doth ſpeake agaynſt thys. &c.

¶ *The Saxon Caracters or letters, that be moſte ſtraunge, be here knowen by other common Caracters ſet ouer them.*

d. th. th. f. g. i. r. ſ. t. w.
¶ ð. ð. þ. ꝼ. ʒ. ı. ɲ. ſ. ꞇ. ƿ.
y. z. and. that.
ẏ. ʒ. ⁊. ꝥ.

¶ Æ. Æ. Th. Th. E. H. M.
¶ Æ. Æ. Ð. Þ. Є. Ƕ. M.
S. W. And.
S. Ƿ. ⁊.

¶ *One pricke ſignifieth an vnperfect point, this figure ; (which is lyke the Greeke interrogatiue) a full pointe, which in ſome other olde Saxon bookes, is expreſſed wyth three prickes, ſet in triangle wyſe thus* ∴

Transcription of the OE

OE1

Ælfrıc abb. ʒret Sıʒeferþ
freondlıce; Me ıs ʒerædþ
ðu rædest beo me ꝥ ıc oþer
tæhte on Enʒlıscen ʒeprı-
ten . oþer eoper ancor æt
ham mıd eop tæhþ . forþan
ðe he sputelıce sæʒþ ꝥ hıt
sıe alefd. ꝥ mæsse preostas
pel motan pıfıʒen . and mın
ʒeprıten pıþcpeþeþ ð > ẏsen.

OE2

Ælfric abbod gret Sigeferþ
freondlice; Me is geræd þæt
ðu rædest beo me þæt ic oþer
tæhte on Engliscen gewri-
ten . oþer eower ancor æt
ham mid eow tæhþ . forþan
ðe he swutelice sægþ þæt hit
sie alefd. þæt mæsse preostas
wel motan wifigen . and min
gewriten wiþcweþeþ ðẏsen.

WW

Ælfric abbot greets Sigeferth
friendlily; to-me is said that
thou saidest about me that I other*
taught in English wri-
tings than your anchorite† at

home with you teaches. because
he clearly says that it
is permitted. that mass priests
well may wive. and my
writings against-speak this.

* oþer . . . oþer = otherwise . . . than = differently from.

† An anchorite is a religious hermit (see section 7.3).

3.2 Dialects and political boundaries

The English were not a politically unified nation until the 10th century, and as they originally came from different parts of western Europe (see Text 7, section 2.3.1 and Map 1), they spoke different dialects of West Germanic. They settled in different parts of Britain, but they were able to communicate with each other. Dialects are varieties of a language which differ in pronunciation, vocabulary or grammar, but not enough to prevent understanding.

The country during the 7th and 8th centuries is sometimes called the **Heptarchy** – that is, the country of seven kingdoms: Northumbria, Mercia, East Anglia, Essex, Kent, Sussex and Wessex.

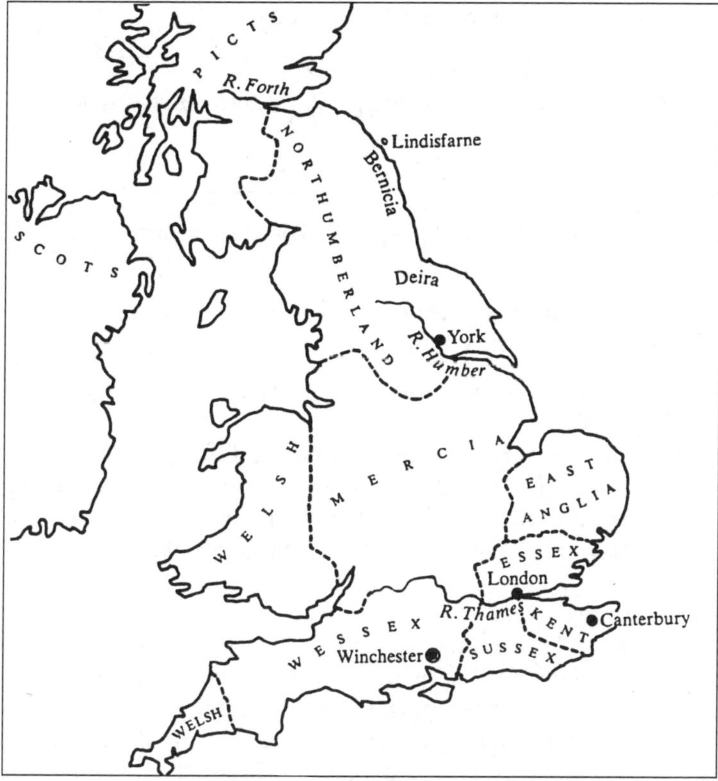

Map 2 The Heptarchy

Wars were frequent, in which one or other of the kingdoms might dominate the others. For example, Wessex *v* Mercia in AD 628:

Text 16a – *Peterborough Chronicle* for AD 628 (facsimile)

OE1 her kẏneʒılꞅ 7 cpıchelm ʒe fuhton
pıð pendan æt cırnceaꞅtre. 7 ʒeþınʒodon þa.

OE2 Her kynegils 7 cwichelm gefuhton
wið pendan æt ċirnceastre. 7 geþingodon þa.

WW Here cynegils & cuichelm fought with penda at cirencester. & settled then.

MnE In this year Cynegils (King of Wessex) and Cwichelm fought against Penda (King of Mercia) at Cirencester, and then they agreed terms.

Text 16b – *Parker Chronicle* for AD 628 (facsimile)

OE1 her cyneʒılꞅ 7 cuıchelm ʒefuhtun pıþ pendan æt cırenceaꞅtre. 7 ʒe
þınʒodan þa.

OE2 Her cynegils 7 cuichelm gefuhtun wiþ pendan æt cirenceastre. 7 ge
þingodan þa.

The vocabulary of Texts 16a and 16b is listed in the *Word Book*.

This does not mean, however, that there were seven different dialects. The evidence from OE manuscripts suggests that there were three or four: **Northumbrian** and **Mercian**, which together are called **Anglian**, from the West Germanic dialect of the Angles; **Kentish** and **West Saxon**, developing from the dialects of the Jutes and Saxons.

All living languages are in a continuous state of change and development, and OE was no exception between the 5th and 12th centuries. So any mention of the forms of OE words, or features of pronunciation, illustrates one dialect of the language at one stage of its development in a generalised way. It is usual to use the late West Saxon dialect of the 10th–11th centuries to describe OE, because West Saxon was by then widely used as a standard form for the written language, and most surviving manuscripts are written in West Saxon.

Map 3 Dialects of Old English

3.3 Danish and Norwegian Vikings

3.3.1 *Invasion, warfare and settlement*

The Peterborough Chronicle records an event in AD 787 which proved to be an ominous portent of things to come:

Text 17a – *Peterborough Chronicle* for AD 787 (facsimile)

Her nam breohtric cining
offan dohter eadburge · 7 on his dagum comon
ærest · iii · scipu norðmanna of hereðalande · 7 þa se ge
refa þær to rad · 7 he wolde drifan to ðes cininges tune
þy he nyste hwæt hi wæron · 7 hine man ofsloh þa · Ðæt
wæron þa erestan scipu deniscra manna þe angelcyn
nes land gesohton ·

ŒE1

her nam breohtrıc cınınʒ
offan dohter eadburʒe.7 on hıſ daʒum comon
ærerſt .ııı. ſcıpu norðmanna of hereða lande. 7 þa ſe ʒe
refa þær to rad. 7 he ƿolde drıfan to ðeſ cınıʒeſ tune
þẏ he nẏſte hƿæt hı ƿæron. 7 hıne man of ſloh þa. Ðat
ƿæron þa ereſtan ſcıpu denıſcra manna þe anʒel cẏn
neſ land ʒeſohton.

ŒE2

Her nam breohtric cining offan dohter eadburge.7
on his dagum comon ærest .iii. scipu norðmanna of hereða
lande. 7 þa se gerefa þær to rad. 7 he wolde drifan to
ðes ciniges tune þy he nyste hwæt hi wæron. 7 hine
man ofsloh þa. Ðæt wæron þa erestan scipu deniscra manna þe
angel cynnes land gesohton.

WW

Here took breohtric king offa's daughter eadburh. &
in his days came first 3 ships of-northmen from hortha
land. & then the reeve there to rode. & he wished drive to
the king's manor because he knew-not what they were. & him
one slew there. that were the first ships danish men's that
Angle-people's land sought.

Text 17b – *Parker Chronicle* for AD 787 (facsimile)

ŒE1

her nom____beorhtrıc cẏnınʒ offan dohtor eadburʒe.
7 on hıſ daʒum cuomon ærerſt . ııı. ſcıpu 7 þa ſe ʒerefa þærto
rad 7 hıe ƿolde drıfan to þæſ cẏnınʒeſ tune þẏ he nẏſte hƿæt
hıe ƿæron 7 hıene mon ofſloʒ þæt ƿæron þa æreſtan ſcıpu
denıſcra monna þe anʒel cẏnneſ lond ʒeſohton:

ŒE2

her nom beorhtric cẏning offan dohtor eadburge.
7 on his dagum cuomon ærest . iii. scipu 7 þa se gerefa þærto
rad 7 hie wolde drifan to þæs cyninges tune þy he nẏste hwæt
hie wæron 7 hiene mon ofslog þæt wæron þa ærestan scipu
deniscra monna þe angel cynnes lond gesohton:

The vocabulary of Texts 17a and 17b is listed in the *Word Book*.

By the end of the 8th century the Angles, Saxons and Jutes had finally occupied and settled almost the whole of England. *The Anglo-Saxon Chronicle* continued to record battles for supremacy between the kings of the seven Anglo-Saxon kingdoms, as for example in the annal dated AD 827:

In this year there was an eclipse of the moon on Christmas morning. And the same year Egbert conquered Mercia, and all that was south of the Humber, and he was the eighth king to be 'Ruler of Britain': the first to rule so great a kingdom was Ælle, king of Sussex; the second was Ceawlin, king of Wessex; the third was Æthelbert, king of Kent; the fourth was Rædwald, king of East Anglia; the fifth was Edwin, king of Northumbria; the sixth was Oswald who reigned after him; the seventh was Oswy, Oswald's brother; the eighth was Egbert, king of Wessex.

But by AD 827, the three ships which the king's reeve had ridden to meet in AD 787 had already been followed by greater numbers of Norsemen, who began to make annual attacks for plunder on the coasts and up the rivers of England and northern France. The *Peterborough Chronicle*'s annal for AD 793 records the first Norwegian Viking attack on the monasteries of Lindisfarne and Jarrow on the north-east coast:

Text 18a – *Peterborough Chronicle* for AD 793 (facsimile)

7 lıtel æfter þam þæꞅ ıl –
can ʒeareꞅ on ·vı· ıd' ıanr̄ earmlıce heðenra manna
herʒunʒ adılıʒode ʒodeꞅ cẏrıcan · ın lındıꞅfarena ee
þurh reaflac · 7 man ꞅleht ·

ŒE1

7 lıtel æfter þam þæꞅ ıl__
can ʒeareꞅ on .vı. ıd' ıanr̄ earmlıce heðenra manna
herʒunʒ adılıʒode ʒodeꞅ cẏrıcan. ın lındıꞅfarena ee
þurh reaflac. 7 man ꞅleht.

ŒE2

7 litel æfter þam þæs ilcan
geares on .vi. ides ianuarium earmlice heðenra manna
hergung adiligode godes cyrican. in lindisfarena ee
þurh reaflac. 7 mansleht.

WW

& little after that the same
year on 6 ides january miserably of-heathen men
raid destroyed god's church. on lindisfarne isle
by robbery. & murder.

MnE

793. and a little after that in the same year on 8th January God's church on the island of Lindisfarne was miserably plundered and destroyed by the heathen, with great slaughter.

Text 18b – *Parker Chronicle* for AD 793

ðes ylcan geares earmlice hæðenra hergung adyligodan godes cyrican in lindisfarena ee. þurh reaflac 7 manslyht.

The vocabulary of Texts 18a and 18b is listed in the *Word Book*.

Norsemen from Norway were soon to raid the north-west coast of England, the north of Ireland, the western islands and coast of Scotland, and the Isle of Man.

Danes began to attack the east coast of England in AD 835. By the middle of the 9th century, large Danish armies regularly ravaged the land and began to occupy and settle permanently in parts of the country.

Here is a typical entry in the *Anglo-Saxon Chronicle* describing the ravages of the Danish armies during king Ælfred's reign:

Text 19a – *Peterborough Chronicle* for AD 878 (facsimile)

OE1

her hıene beꞅtæl ꞅe here on
mıdne pınter ofer tpelftan nıht to cıppanhamme.
7 ʒerıdan peꞅt ꞅeaxna land 7 ʒeꞅetton. 7 mẏcel þæꞅ
folceꞅ ofer ꞅæ adræfdon. 7 þæꞅ oðreꞅ þone mæꞅtan
dæl hı ʒerıdon butan þam cẏnʒe ælfrede lıtle perede
un ẏðelıce æfter pudum for. 7 on morfeꞅtenum...
...7 þæꞅ ON

eaꞅtron ƿrohte ælfred cẏnınʒ lẏtle ƿerede ʒeƿeorc
æt æþelınʒa ıʒe. 7 of þam ʒeƿeorce ƿæꞅ ƿınnende ƿıð
þone here. 7 ꞅumer ꞅetena ꞅe del þe þær nehꞅt ƿæꞅ.
þa on ðere ꞅeofeðan ƿucan ofer eaꞅtron he ʒerad
to ecʒbrıhteꞅ ꞅtane be eaꞅton ꞅealƿudu. 7 hım comon þær
onʒean ꞅumorꞅæte ealle. 7 ƿıllꞅæte. 7 hamtun ꞅcẏr ꞅe
dæl þe hıre beheonan ꞅæ ƿæꞅ. 7 hıꞅ ʒefæʒene ƿæron.
7 he for ẏmb ane nıht of þam ƿıcum to æʒlea. 7 þæꞅ
ẏmb ane nıht to eðan dune. 7 þær ʒefeaht ƿıð ealne he -
re 7 hıene ʒeflẏmde. 7 hım æfter rad oð þet ʒeƿeorc. 7
þær ꞅæt .xıııı. nıht. 7 þa ꞅealde ꞅe here hım ʒıꞅlaꞅ. and
mẏcele aðaꞅ. þet hı of hıꞅ rıce ƿoldon. 7 hım eac ʒehe -
ton þet heora cẏnʒ fulƿıhte onfon ƿolde.

ŒE2

Her hiene bestæl se here on
midne winter ofer twelftan niht to cippanhamme.
7 geridan west seaxna land 7 gesetton. 7 mycel þæs
folces ofer sæ adræfdon. 7 þæs oðres þone mæstan
dæl hi geridon butan þam cynge ælfrede (7 he) litle werede
unyðelice æfter wudum for. 7 on morfestenum
7 þæs on
eastron wrohte ælfred cyning lytle werede geweorc
æt æþelinga ige. 7 of þam geweorce wæs winnende wið
þone here. 7 sumer setena se del þe þær nehst wæs.
þa on ðere seofeðan wucan ofer eastron he gerad
to ecgbrihtes stane be easton sealwudu. 7 him comon þær
ongean sumorsæte ealle. 7 willsæte. 7 hamtun scyr se
dæl þe hire beheonan sæ wæs. 7 his gefægene wæron.
7 he for ymb ane niht of þam wicum to æglea. 7 þæs
ymb ane niht to eðan dune. 7 þær gefeaht wið ealne here 7 hiene geflymde. 7 him æfter rad oð þet geweorc. 7
þær sæt .xiiii. niht. 7 þa sealde se here him gislas. and
mycele aðas. þet hi of his rice woldon. 7 him eac geheton þet heora cyng fulwihte onfon wolde.

WW

Here it[self] stole-away the host in
mid winter after twelfth night to chippenham.
& overran west saxons' land & occupied. & much of-the
folk over sea drove. & of-the other the most
part they subdued except the king Ælfred (& he) with-small band
with-difficulty through woods went & in moor-fastnesses.
& after at
easter built alfred king with-little company fortress
at Athelney & from that fortress was fighting against
the host*. & of-somerset the part that there nearest was.
then in the seventh week after easter he rode
to egbertstone by east of-selwood & to-him came there
back of-somerset-men all. & wiltshire & hampshire
the part that of-it on-this-side-of sea was. & of-him glad they-were.
& he went after one night from those camps to iley. & later
after one night to edington. & there fought against all the
host & it put-to-flight. & it after rode up-to the fortress. &
there sat 14 nights. & then gave the host him hostages and
great oaths. that they from his kingdom wished. & him also
promised that their king baptism receive would.

* The host = the invading Danish army.

Text 19b – *Parker Chronicle* version

Œ

.dccclxxviii. Her hiene bestæl se here on midne winter ofer tuelftan niht to cippanhamme. 7 geridon wesseaxna lond 7 gesæton. 7 micel þæs folces ofer sæ adræfdon. 7 þæs oþres þone mæstan dæl hie geridon buton þam cyninge Ælfrede 7 he lytle werede unieþelice æfter wudum for. 7 on morfæstenum. 7 þæs on eastron worhte Ælfred cyning lytle werede geweorc æt eþelinga eigge. 7 of þam geweorce was winnende wiþ þone here. 7 sumursætna se dæl se þær niehst wæs. þa on þære seofoðan wiecan ofer eastron he gerad to ecgbryhtes stane be eastan seal wyda. 7 him to com þær ongen sumorsæte alle. 7 wilsætan. 7 hamtun scir se dæl se hiere behinon sæ wæs. 7 his geægene wærun. 7 he for ymb ane niht of þam wicum to iglea. 7 þæs ymb ane to eþan dune. 7 þær gefeaht wiþ alne þone here 7 hiene gefliemde. 7 him æfter rad oþ þæt geweorc. 7 þær sæt .xiiii. niht. 7 þa salde se here him fore gislas. 7 micle aþas. þæt hie of his rice uuoldon. 7 him eac geheton þæt hiera kyning fulwihte onfon wolde.

The vocabulary of Texts 19a and 19b is listed in the *Word Book*.

Activity 3.2

Examine the differences between the pairs of words in the two *Chronicle* versions listed below, and discuss the possible reasons for them.

(This topic is discussed in section 4.3.4.)

Peterborough	*Parker*	*Peterborough*	*Parker*	*Peterborough*	*Parker*
æglea	iglea	geflymde	gefliemde	ongean	ongen
Ælfred	Ælfrede	geridan, geridon	geridon	scyr	scir
æþelinga	eþelinga	gesetton	gesæton	sealde	salde
æþelinga ige	eþelinga eigge	geweorc	geweorce	seofeðan	seofoðan
beheonan	behinn	hamtun scyr	hamtun scir	sumorsæte	sumursætna
butan	buton	heora	hiera	ðere	þære
comon	com	nire	niere	þet	þæt
cyng, cynge, cyning	cyninge	ige	eigge	wæron	wærun
dæl, del	dæl	land	lond	west seaxna	wesseaxna lond
ealle, ealne	alle, alne	litle, lytle	lytle	willsæte	wilsætan
easton	eastan	mycel, mycele	micel, micle	wrohte	worhte
ecgbrihtes stane	ecgbryhtes stane	morfestenum	morfæstenum	yðolice	unieþelice

3.3.1.1 *The Danelaw*

After years of continuous war, Ælfred king of Wessex finally defeated the Danes and negotiated treaties with them. By the time of Ælfred's death in AD 899, at the end of the 9th century, only Wessex remained independent. The rest of England, north and east of the old Roman road called Watling Street (from London to Chester), was shared between the English and the Danes, and became known as the **Danelaw**.

The dots on Map 4 mark the sites of towns and villages with whole or part Norse names. The larger dots show names ending in the Norse *-by*, e.g. *Whitby*, *Grimsby*, and smaller dots names with both OE and ON elements, e.g. *Grimston* (*Grim* is a Norse name, and *-tun* the OE for 'settlement'). The large number of ON place names is one of the clearest pieces of evidence for the settlement of Danish or Norwegian Vikings in the Danelaw. (There is a further reference to OE and ON place names in section 3.4.3.)

It was left to Ælfred's son Edward and his three grandsons who succeeded to the kingship of Wessex in turn, Æthelstan, Edmund and Eadred, to create through

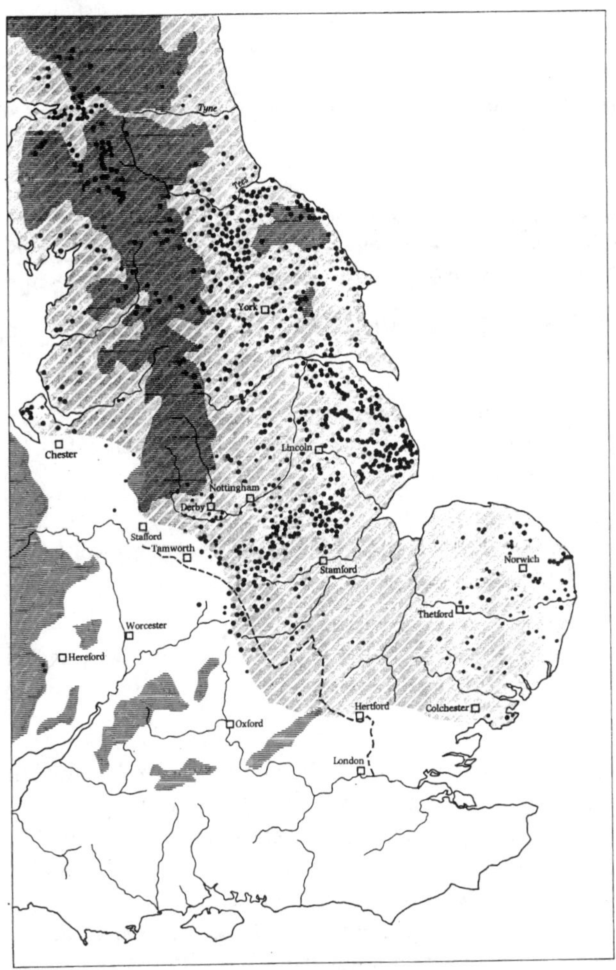

Map 4 The Danelaw

warfare a unified England under Wessex (see, for example, the accounts of Æthelstan's victory at the battle of Brunanburh (AD 937) in sections 3.4.4 and 4.1). But Scandinavian attacks continued throughout the first half of the 10th century, and were recorded in the *Chronicle*.

3.3.2 *King Ælfred and the revival of learning*

Ælfred the Great (AD 848–899) was not only a great military leader, but also a scholar, anxious to restore the tradition of letters which had decayed during the long years of warfare after the destruction of many monasteries. Among other translations, he wrote an English version of the Latin *Cura Pastoralis* of Pope Gregory (AD 540–604) to provide spiritual education for the clergy. A copy was sent to every bishop. Here is the beginning of the copy sent to bishop Wærferth at Worcester:

Text 20 – First lines of King Ælfred's Preface to the West Saxon version of Gregory's *Pastoral Care* (facsimile)

OE ✠ÐEOS BOC SCEAL TO ƿIOGORA CEASTRE
ÆLFred kynıng hateð ʒretan pærferð bıscep hıs pordum luf
lıce 7 freondlıce...

WW ✠THIS BOOK SHALL TO WORCESTER
ALFred king calls (to) greet Wærferð bishop (with) his words lov
ingly & friendlily

MnE THIS BOOK IS TO GO TO WORCESTER
King Ælfred sends greetings to Bishop Wærferth with his loving and friendly words

The vocabulary of Text 20 is listed in the *Word Book*.

The following facsimile is part of Ælfred's Preface to the translation, in which he describes his resolve to remedy the clergy's ignorance of Latin – 'they had little benefit from those books since they were not written in their own language'. King Ælfred has referred to former days of prosperity and learning in England, when men came from abroad in search of knowledge and instruction. But this had now changed, and when he became king there were very few priests who could translate a letter from Latin into English. He deplores this loss of wisdom.

Text 21 – From King Ælfred's Preface to the West Saxon version of Gregory's *Pastoral Care* (facsimile)

Œ1

ʒeðenc hpelcé pıtu uſ ða be comon for ðíſſe porulde . ðaða
pe hıt nohpæðer ne ſelfe ne lufodon . ne eac oðrum monnū ne lefdon;
ðone naman ænne pe lufodon ðætte pe crıſtne pæren : 7 ſpıðe feapa
ða ðeapaſ ; ða ıc ða ðıſ eall ʒemunde: ða ʒemunde ıc eac hú ıc ʒe ſeah
ær ðæm ðe hıt eall for herʒod pære . 7 for bærned . hu ða cırıcean ʒıond
eall anʒel cynn ſtodon maðma 7 boca ʒefylde . Ond eac mıcel menıʒeo ʒo
deſ ðıopa 7 ða ſpıðe lytle fıorme ðara boca pıſton . forðæm ðe hıe
hıora nanpuht ón-ʒıotan ne meahton . forðæm ðe hy næron ón hıo
ra aʒen ʒeðıode aprıtene . Spelce hıe cpæden . ure yldran ða ðe ðaſ
ſtopa ær hıoldon . hıe lufodon pıſdom 7 ðurh ðone hıe beʒeaton pelan
[*7 úr læfdon*]

Œ2 & WW

Geðenc hwelc witu us ða becomon for ðisse worulde, ða ða
Think what punishments upon us then came in this world when

we hit nohwðer ne selfe ne lufodon ne eac oðrum monnum ne lefdon;
we it neither ourselves loved nor also to other men allowed;

ðone naman ænne we lufodon ðæt we Cristne wæren, & swiðe feawa
the name only we loved that we Christian were & very few

ða ðeawas. Ða ic ða ðis eall gemunde, ða gemunde
the virtues When I then this all remembered then remembered

ic eac hu ic geseah,
I also how I had seen,

ærðæmðe hit eall forhergod wære & forbæned, hu ða ciricean giond
before it all ravaged was & burnt, how the churches throughout

eall Angelcynn stodon maðma & boca gefylde.
all England stood with treasures & books filled

Ond eac micel menigeo Godes
And also great multitudes of God's

ðiowa	& ða	swiðe	lytle	fiorme	ðara	boca	wiston,	forðæmðe	hie
servants	*& these*	*very*	*little*	*benefit*	*from those*	*books*	*knew*	*because*	*they*

hiora	nan wuht	ongiotan	ne meahton,	forðæmðe	hie	næron	on	hiora
of them	*nothing*	*understand*	*were able*	*since*	*they*	*were not*	*in*	*their*

agen	geðiode	awritene.	Swelce	hie	cwæden:	ure	ieldran	ða ðe	ðas
own	*language*	*written*	*Such*	*they*	*said*	*Our*	*forefathers*	*who*	*these*

stowa	ær	hiolden,	hie	lufodon	wisdom	&	ðurh	one
places	*formerly*	*held*	*they*	*loved*	*knowledge*	*&*	*through*	*it*

hie	begeaton	welan
they	*acquired*	*wealth*

[&	us	læfdon.]
[*and*	*to us*	*left (it)*]

MnE Think what punishments then came upon us in this world when we neither loved it ourselves nor allowed it to other men – we loved only to be called Christians, and very few loved the virtues. When I remembered all this, then I also remembered how, before it was all ravaged and burnt, I had seen how the churches throughout all England stood filled with treasures and books, and there was also a great multitude of God's servants – they had very little benefit from those books, because they could not understand anything of them, since they were not written in their own language. As if they had said, 'Our forefathers who formerly held these places loved knowledge, and through it they acquired wealth and left it to us.

Ælfred's late 9th-century West Saxon shows some differences from the later 'classical' West Saxon of the 11th century which became a common written standard. One example is the spelling of *giond*, *þiowa*, *fiorme*, *hiora*, *ongiotan*, *geðiode*, *hioldon*, with the *-io-* diphthong. If you look up these words in a dictionary of OE, you will find then under *geond*, *þeow*, *feorm*, *heora*, *ongietan*, *geðeode*, *heoldon*, which must mark a change in the vowel.

📖 The vocabulary of Text 21 is listed in the *Word Book*.

3.4 Effects of Viking settlement on the English language

The settlement of the Norsemen and the occupation of the Danelaw had important effects on the English language.

3.4.1 *Old Norse vocabulary*

Old Norse is the name now given to the group of Scandinavian languages and dialects spoken by the Norsemen – Danish and Norwegian Vikings. It was **cognate** with Old English; that is, they both came from the same earlier Germanic language. It seems likely that the two languages were similar enough in vocabulary for OE speakers to understand common ON words, and vice versa, so that the English and Norsemen could communicate. An Icelandic saga says of the 11th century, 'there was at that time the same tongue in England as in Norway and Denmark'. But speakers would simplify their own language when talking to the other, and OE dialects spoken in the Danelaw in time became modified in ways which were different from the Wessex, West Midland and Kentish dialects. Present-day Northern and East Anglian dialects shown ON features, particularly in vocabulary.

Many of OE words therefore have a similar cognate ON word, and often we cannot be sure whether a MnE reflex has come from OE, or ON, or from both. In a dictionary, the ON cognate of an OE word is given where it is known. If a word is marked '*fr ON*', it means that the OE word was adopted from ON, and is proof of the close contact between the two languages. Here are some examples:

1. Examples of MnE words that are reflexes of both OE and ON

adder	OE næddre ON naðra	lamb	OE lamb ON lamb
bake	OE bacan ON baka	mother	OE mōdor ON mōðir
church	OE cir(i)ce/cyrce ON kirkja	nut	OE hnutu ON hnot
daughter	OE dohtor ON dōttir	oven	OE ofen ON ofn
earth	OE eorþe ON jorð	plum	OE plūma ON ploma
father	OE fæder ON faðir	quick	OE cwicu ON kvikr
green	OE grēne ON groenn	road	OE rād ON reid
hear	OE hȳran/hīeran ON heyra	small	OE smæl ON smalr
iron	OE īren/īsern ON īsarn	thing	OE þing ON ðing
knife/knives	OE cnīf/cnifas ON knifr	wash	OE wæscan ON vaska

From this evidence, it seems likely that an OE or ON speaker would have recognised these words spoken in the other's language.

2. OE words beginning with ⟨sc⟩

The OE digraph ⟨sc⟩ was originally pronounced [sk], but in time the two consonants merged into the consonant [ʃ]. (The spelling ⟨sh⟩, a French convention, was not adopted until after the Norman Conquest.) This sound change did not happen in ON, however, so in the following sample of words, it is the OE pronunciation that MnE reflexes have kept.

OE	***ON***	***MnE***
sceaft	skapt	*shaft*
scell	skell	*shell*
scearp	skarpr	*sharp*
sceran	skera	*shear* (vb)
scinan	skina	*shine*
scield	skjoldr	*shield*
scufan	skufa	*shove*
sceotan	skjota	*shoot*
fisc	fiskr	*fish*
wyscan	œskja	*wish*

OE *scyrte* was cognate with ON *skyrta* and both meant *shirt*, but their MnE reflexes, *shirt* and *skirt*, have taken on different meanings.

OE	*ON*	*MnE*
–	skata	*skate* (fish)
–	skeppa	*skep/skip*
–	skil	*skill*
scinn	skinn	*skin*
–	skifa	*skive*
–	skufr	*skua* (sea-bird)
sceo	sky	*sky*

So one important result of Danish and Norwegian settlement in the Danelaw was its effect on the English language. English and Norse speakers lived in communities which were close enough for contact to take place, sometimes within the same settlement, or in a family after intermarriage. A large number of proper names of Scandinavian origin can be found in late OE and early ME documents. In time, the communities merged. Norse was no longer spoken, but the English dialects spoken in different parts of the Danelaw had been modified – in pronunciation, in vocabulary, and to some extent in grammar. The earliest evidence, however, does not appear in writing until much later, during the Middle English period, because most late OE was written in the standard West Saxon dialect. The long-term effects are still with us in the present-day dialects and accents of East Anglia, the Midlands, northern England and southern Scotland.

Unlike the English, the Danes and Norwegians had not at this time developed a system of writing other than runes, and no evidence of the dialects of the Norse language spoken in the Danelaw has come down to us. Norse must have been spoken throughout, but was gradually assimilated with English.

Some evidence of this assimilation can be seen in the porch of a small church in Kirkdale, North Yorkshire, called St Gregory's Minster. A sundial dating from about 1055 has been preserved, which has the following inscription carved in stone:

Text 22 – Inscription, St Gregory's Minster, Kirkdale, North Yorkshire (facsimile)

+ ORM GAMAL SVNA BOHTESCS GREGORIVS MIN STER ÐONNE HI T ƿES ÆL TOBRO	ÞIS DAGES SOL MERCIA PRS	CAN 7 TO FALAN 7 HE HT LET MACAN NEƿAN FROM GRVNDEXPE7SCSGREGORI VS IN EADƿARDDAGVM CNG 7INTOSTI DAGVM EORL +

7 HAƿARÐ ME ƿROHTE 7 BRAND

The man who carved the stone made the letters and spaces too big to begin with, and had to cram in those in the second part of the inscription, which might have read:

ORM GAMALSUNA BOHTE SCS GREGORIVS MINSTER ÐONNE HIT WES ÆL TOBROCAN 7 TO FALAN 7 HE HIT LET MACAN NEWAN FROM GRUNDE XPE 7 SCS GREGORIVS IN EADWARD DAGUM CNG 7 IN TOSTI DAGUM EORL 7 HAWARÐ ME WROHTE 7 BRAND PRS

SCS = *SANCTUS* = *saint*; XPE = *CHRISTE*; CNG = *CYNING* = *king*; PRS = *PREOSTAS* = *priests*.

Translation

ORM GAMALSON BOUGHT ST GREGORY'S MINSTER WHEN IT WAS ALL BROKEN & FALLEN DOWN & HE CAUSED IT TO BE MADE ANEW FROM THE GROUND TO CHRIST AND ST GREGORY IN KING EDWARD'S DAYS & IN EARL TOSTI'S DAYS & HAWARTH & BRAND PRIESTS MADE ME

The inscription at the top of the sundial reads:

ÞIS IS DAGES SOL MERCA   This is day's sun marker

Tosti, or Tostig, was Earl of Northumberland and brother to Harold Godwinson, who became King of England in 1066, on King Edward's death (see also Texts 24 and 25 in section 3.5). Orm and Gamal are Norse names, but the language is Old English.

📖 The vocabulary of Text 22 is listed in the *Word Book*.

3.4.2 *OE and Scandinavian surnames*

The name *Orm Gamalson* looks familiar to us as the usual way of referring to people by their forename and surname, e.g. *David Williamson*. This name no longer literally means *David, son of William*, and there is nothing strange today about the name *Marion Johnson*, which is unlikely to mean *Marion, son of John*.

But *Orm Gamalsuna* (*Orm Gamalson*) did mean *Orm, son of Gamal*, and this way of creating personal names, by adding *suna*/*-son* as a patronymic suffix (name derived from the father) was in fact a Scandinavian custom, which was in time adopted throughout the country.

The Anglo-Saxon patronymic suffix was *-ing*, as in *Ælfred Æþelwulfing* – *Ælfred, son of Athelwulf* – and was used to name families or peoples as descendants from a common ancestor.

3.4.3 *OE and Scandinavian place names*

These names were also incorporated into place names, as in *Walsingham*, *Billingham*, *Kidlington*, though the *-ing* suffix tended to be used in a more general way as well, and must not be always be taken literally to mean *son of* or *the family of*. Some place names consist of the patronymic alone, for example *Woking*, *Tooting*, *Malling*. The suffixes which indicate place names in OE included *-hyrst* (*copse, wood*), *-ham* (*dwelling, fold*), *-wic* (*village*), *-tun* (*settlement*) and *-stede* (*place*), as in present-day *Wadhurst, Newnham, Norwich, Berwick, Heslington* and *Maplestead.* The detailed study of place-names provides much of the historical evidence for the settlement of Danes and Norwegians in England.

Activity 3.3

Use an atlas and atlas gazetteer of England to identify towns and villages with place-names ending in the Scandinavian suffixes:

(i) -by (town, farm);
(ii) -thorp(e) (village);
(iii) -thwaite (piece of land);
(iv) -toft (piece of land).

If you find a sufficient number, and mark them on a blank map, you should find good evidence of the extent of the Danelaw. You could check the occurrence of these place-names against the map of the Danelaw on p. 43.

3.4.4 *The Battle of Brunanburh (I)*

In the *Peterborough Chronicle* for AD 937 there is the briefest of entries about a battle against Norsemen from Ireland who were defeated by Æthelstan King of Wessex (the site of the battle is not known):

Text 23 – *Peterborough Chronicle* for AD 937 (facsimile)

> A n̄. dcccc xxxvii. her æðelſtan cẏnınȝ lædde fẏr-
> de to brunan bẏrıȝ.

OE M.dcccc XXXVII. her æðelſtan cẏnınȝ lædde fyrde to brunanbẏrıȝ.

WW 937. Here athelstan king led troops to brunanburh.

📖 The vocabulary of Text 23 is listed in the *Word Book*.

A period of twenty-five years of peace after AD 955 was once again broken when more attacks by Norsemen began in the 980s. Some came from Normandy across the Channel, where Norsemen (the Normans) had also settled, as well as from Denmark and Norway. In 1017, the Danish King Cnut (Canute) became 'King of All England', and the line of Danish kings was not ended until 1042, when the English Edward the Confessor became king.

3.5 The Norman Conquest

In 1066, Duke William of Normandy defeated King Harold at Hastings and became King William I of England. This event had the most profound effects on the country and on the language, and when we read English texts from the 12th century onwards, we notice changes at each level of language – spelling and vocabulary, word form and grammar.

Here are two further extracts from *The Anglo-Saxon Chronicle*, one very short and the other much longer, describing the events of 1066. If you study the longer text from *The Peterborough Chronicle*, you will understand a little of how historians have to interpret original sources when writing history. The annal is written in the simple narrative style of the *Chronicle*, with each event prefaced by *and*. Reference to individuals as *he* or *him* is sometimes rather confusing. This outline of the events told in the Chronicle may help:

King Edward the Confessor died on 28 December 1065, and was buried on 6 January 1066. He was succeeded by King Harold, but Duke William of Normandy also claimed the English throne, and prepared a force to attack southern England. But before this, King Harold, with Earls Edwin and Morcar, had to fend off attacks on the north of England by the Norwegian Harald Hardrada. Harold defeated the Norwegian at Stamford Bridge near York. Tostig, the Earl of Northumberland, was King Harold's brother, but he had defected to the Norwegian Harald. King Harold made a forced march southwards immediately after the battle at Stamford Bridge, but his army was defeated by William at the Battle of Hastings. Duke William was crowned William I soon after.

Text 24 – Part of the *Parker Chronicle* for 1066 (facsimile)

ŒE1

. pucena. 7 ænne dæʒ. 7 her
mlxvı. Her forðferde eaduuard kınʒ. 7 harold eorl fenʒ to ðam rıce. 7 heold hıt. xl.
cō pıllelm 7 ʒe wann ænʒla land.

ŒE2

mlxvi. Her forðferde eaduuard king 7 harold eorl feng to ðam rice. 7 heold hit .xl. wucena. 7 ænne dæg 7 her com Willelm 7 gewann ænglaland.

WW

1066. Here died Edward king. & Harold earl seized the kingdom. & held it 40 of-weeks. & one day. & here came William & conquered England.

The vocabulary of Text 24 is listed in the *Word Book*.

Text 25 – Part of *The Peterborough Chronicle* for 1066 (facsimile)

On þissū ʒeare man halʒode þet
mynster æt ƿestmynstre on cilda mæsse dæʒ. ⁊ se cynʒ
eadƿard forðferde on tƿelfta mæsse æfen. ⁊ hine mann
be byrʒede on tƿelftan mæsse dæʒ. innan þære niƿa
halʒodre circean on ƿestmynstre. ⁊ harold eorl fenʒ
to englalandes cyne rice. sƿa sƿa se cynʒ hit him ʒe uðe.
⁊ eac men hine þær to ʒecuron. ⁊ ƿæs ʒebletsod to cyn
ʒe on tƿelftan mæsse dæʒ. ⁊ þy ilcan ʒeare þe he cynʒ
ƿæs. he for ut mid sciphere to ʒeanes ƿillme. ⁊ þa hƿi
le cō tostiʒ eorl into humbran mid .lx. scipū. Ead
ƿine eorl cō land fyrde. ⁊ draf hine ut. ⁊ þa butsecarlas
hine forsocan. ⁊ he for to scotlande mid .xii. snaccū. ⁊ hi
ne ʒe mette harold se norrena cynʒ mid .ccc. scipū. ⁊
tostiʒ hī to beah. ⁊ hi bæʒen foran in to humbran oð þet
hi coman to eoferƿic. ⁊ heō ƿið feaht morkere eorl. ⁊
eadƿine eorl. ⁊ se norrena cynʒ ahte siʒes ʒeƿeald. ⁊ man
cydde harode cynʒ hu hit ƿæs þær ʒedon ⁊ ʒeƿorden.
⁊ he cō mid mycclū here englis cra manna. ⁊ ʒe mette hine
æt stænʒ fordes brycʒe. ⁊ hine ofsloh. ⁊ þone eorl tostiʒ.
⁊ eallne þone here ahtlice ofer cō. ⁊ þa hƿile cō ƿillm eorl
upp æt hestinʒan on scē michaeles mæsse dæʒ. ⁊ harold
cō norðan ⁊ hī ƿið feaht ear þan þe his here come eall. ⁊
þær he feoll. ⁊ his tƿæʒen ʒe broðra ʒyrð ⁊ leofƿine. and
ƿillelm þis land ʒe eode. ⁊ cō to ƿestmynstre. ⁊ ealdred
arceb hine to cynʒe ʒe halʒode. ⁊ menn ʒuldon him ʒyld.
⁊ ʒislas sealdon. ⁊ syððan heora land bohtan.

ŒE

On þissum geare man halgode þet
mynster æt westmynstre on cilda mæsse dæg. ⁊ se cyng
edward forðferde on twelfta mæsse æfen. ⁊ hine mann
bebyrgede on twelftan mæsse dæg. innan þære niwa
halgodre circean on westmynstre. ⁊ harold eorl feng
to englalandes cynerice. swa swa se cyng hit him geuðe.
⁊ eac men hine þærto gecuron. ⁊ wæs gebletsod to cynge on twelftan mæsse dæg. ⁊ þy ilcan geare þe he cyng
wæs. he for ut mid sciphere togeanes Willelme. ⁊ þa hwile com tostig eorl into humbran mid .lx. scipum. Eadwine eorl com landfyrde. ⁊ draf hine ut. ⁊ þa butsecarlas
hine forsocan. ⁊ he for to scotlande mid xii snaccum. ⁊ hine gemette harold se norrena cyng mid .ccc. scipū ⁊
tostig him to beah. ⁊ hi bægen foran into humbran oð þet
hi coman to eoferwic. ⁊ heom wið feaht morkere eorl. ⁊
eadwine eorl. ⁊ se norrena cyng alne siges geweald. ⁊ man
cydde haro⟨l⟩de cyng hu hit wæs þær gedon ⁊ geworden.
⁊ he com mid mycclum here engliscra manna. ⁊ gemette hine
æt stængfordes brycge. ⁊ hine ofsloh. ⁊ þone eorl tostig.
7 eallne þone here ahtlice ofercom. ⁊ þa hwile com willelm eorl
upp æt hestingan on sancte michaeles mæsse dæg. ⁊ harold
com norþhan ⁊ him wið feahte ear þan þe his here come eall. ⁊
þær he feoll. ⁊ his twægen gebroðra Gyrð ⁊ leofwine. and
Willelm þis land ge eode. ⁊ com to westmynstre. ⁊ ealdred
arcebiscop hine to cynge gehalgode. ⁊ menn guldon him gyld.
⁊ gislas sealdon. ⁊ syððan heora land bohtan.

Abbreviations have been filled out.

WW

In this year one consecrated the
minster at westminster on children's mass day*. & the king
edward died on twelfth mass eve†. & him one
buried on twelfth mass day‡. in the new
consecrated church at westminster. & harold earl succeeded
to england's kingdom. as the king it to-him granted.
& as men him thereto chose. & was blessed as king§
on twelfth mass day. & the same year that he king
was. he went out with ship-force against William. & meanwhile
came tostig earl into humber with 60 ships. Ed-
win earl came (with) land- army. & drove him out. & the shipmen
him forsook. & he went to scotland with 12 vessels. & him
met harold the norwegian king with 300 ships. and
tostig him to submitted. & they both went into humber until
they came to york. & them against fought morcar earl.
& edwin earl. & the norwegian king all victory gained. & one
told harold king how it was there done & happened.
& he came with great army of-english men, & met him
at stamford bridge. & slew. & the earl tostig.
& all the host manfully overcame & meanwhile came william earl
up at hastings on st michael's mass day¶. & harold
came from-north & him against fought before his army came all.
& there he fell. & his two brothers Gurth & leofwine. and

William this land conquered. & came to westminster. & Ealdred archbishop him to king consecrated. & men paid him tribute. & hostages gave. & then their lands bought-back.

* children's mass day = Holy Innocent's Day, 28 December.

† twelfth mass eve = the Eve of Epiphany, 5 January.

‡ twelfth mass day = 'Twelfth Night', Epiphany, 6 January.

§ blessed as king = consecrated as king.

¶ st michael's mass day = St Michael's Day, 29 September.

📖 The vocabulary of Text 25 is listed in the *Word Book*.

4. Old English (II)

4.1 The language of Old English poetry

The entry recording the battle of Brunanburh in *The Parker Chronicle* is a graphic poetical account of the battle, in complete contrast to the single terse sentence in the *Peterborough Chronicle* (section 3.4.4). Here are three short extracts from the poem.

4.1.1 *The Battle of Brunanburh (2)*

Text 26 – from the *Parker Chronicle* for AD 937 (facsimile)

dcccc.xxxvıı Her æþelſtan cynınȝ. eorla dryhten. beorna
beahȝıfa. 7 hıƿ broþor eac. eadmund æþelınȝ. ealdor lanȝne tır.
ȝeƿloȝon æt ƿæcce. ſpeorda ecȝum. ymbe brūnanburh.

þær læȝ ƿecȝ mænıȝ. ȝarū aȝeted. ȝuma norþerna.
ofer ƿcıld ƿcoten. ſpılce ſcıttıƿc eac. perıȝ pıȝeƿ ƿæd. peƿƿeaxe forð.
ondlonȝne dæȝ. eorod cıƿtum. on laſt leȝdun. laþum þeodum. heopan
here fleman. hından þearle. mecum mylen ƿcearpan.

ne pearð pæl mare. on þıſ
eıȝlande. æfer ȝıeta. folceƿ ȝefylled. beforan þıƿƿū. ſpeordeƿ
ecȝum. þæƿ þe uƿ ƿecȝað bec. ealde uðpıtan. ſıþþan eaſtan hıder.
enȝle 7 ƿeaxe. up becoman. ofer brad brımu. brytene ƿohtan.
plance pıȝ ſmıðaƿ. peealleƿ ofercoman. eorlaƿ ar hpate. eard
beȝeataN

WW 937. Here Athelstan king. of-earls lord. of-men
ring-giver. & his brother also. Edmund prince. life long honour.
won in battle. of-swords with-edges. by Brunanburh.

there lay man many-a. by-spears killed. man Northern.
over shield shot. also Scots too. weary of-battle sated. West Saxons forth
throughout day. troops in-companies. on trail pursued. loathed people. hacked
from-army fugitives. from-behind harshly. with-swords millstone sharp.

not happened slaughter more. in this
island. ever yet. of-folk felled. before this. of-sword
with-edges. as to-us say books. ancient scholars. since from-east hither.
Angles & Saxons. up came. over broad seas. Britain sought.
proud war smiths. Welshmen overcame. earls for-honour eager. country
conquered

📖 The vocabulary of Text 26 is listed in the *Word Book*.

There was no rhyme or regular syllabic metre in OE verse, which was a 'heightened' form of ordinary speech, with a strong 'falling' rhythm because of the tendency to stress the first syllable of most words. Each line is divided into two half-lines, linked by the **alliteration** of words between the half-lines of each line – that is, they began with same consonant or any vowel. The words carrying stress were lexical words – nouns, adjectives, verbs or adverbs – not function words like pronouns or prepositions:

Her [æ]þelstan cyninȝ. [eo]rla dryhten.
[b]eorna [b]eahȝifa. and his [b]roþor eac.
[ea]dmund [æ]þelinȝ. [ea]ldor lanȝne tir.
ȝe[s]loȝon æt [s]æcce. [s]peorda ecȝum.
ymbe brunanburh.

You can see from the facsimile that verse was set out like prose in OE manuscripts, not in separate lines in the way we are used to. Lines and half-lines were often clearly marked with a dot like our full stop, as in Text 26. Modern printing of OE verse shows the alliterative structure of the lines more clearly, with half-lines marked by a wider space, and with standard sentence punctuation added:

Her æþelstan cyninȝ,   eorla dryhten,
beorna beahȝifa   and his broþor eac,
eadmund æþelinȝ,   ealdor lanȝne tir.
ȝesloȝon æt sæcce   sweorda ecȝum
ymbe brunanburh.

4.1.2 *Beowulf*

Here is another example of OE verse from *Beowulf*, the most famous OE poem. It was probably written in the 8th century (though there is no external evidence and scholars of OE disagree). It is known from a single surviving manuscript that dates from the 10th century. You will see from the facsimile that the manuscript has been damaged. It was scorched in a fire in 1731 and has deteriorated since then, so that many words on the edges are missing or only partly legible.

The historical period of the poem's story is the 6th century, and the hero Beowulf is not Anglo-Saxon, but a Geat from southern Sweden. The tale is legendary, and the following extract from early on in the poem tells how the monster Grendel was harassing Hrothgar, the Danish king of the Scyldings, in his hall, Heorot.

Text 27 – A page from the manuscript of *Beowulf* (facsimile)

Transliteration of MS

(*The lines in italics precede and follow the text of the MS page.*)

þanon untydraſ ealle onpocon
eotenaſ 7ylfe 7orcneaſ ſpylce ʒıʒ-
antaſ, þa pıð ʒode punnon lanʒe þraʒe
he hım ðæſ lean forʒeald.
ʒepat ða neoſıan ſyþðan nıht becom
hean huſeſ hu hıt hrınʒ dene æfter
beor þeʒe ʒe-bun hæfdon. Ꝼand þaðær
ınne æþelınʒa ʒe-drıht ſpefan æfter

ſymble ſorʒe ne cuðon ponſceaft pera
pıht un hælo ʒrım 7ʒrædıʒ, ʒéaro ſona
pæſ reoc 7reþe 7on ræſte ʒenam þrıtıʒ
þeʒna þanon eft ʒepat huðe hremıʒ
to ham faran mıd þære pæl fylle pıca
neoſan. ðapæſ onuhtan mıd ær dæʒe
ʒrendleſ ʒuð cræft ʒumum undẏrne
þa pæſ æfter pıſte pop up ahafen mıcel
morʒen ſpeʒ mære þeoden æþelınʒ ærʒod
un blıðe ſæt þolode ðryð ſpyð þeʒn ſorʒe
dreah ſyð þan hıe þæſ laðan laſt ſcea
pedon perʒan ʒaſteſ pæſ þ́ ʒe pın to
ſtranʒ lað 7lonʒ ſum næſ hıt lenʒra
[*fyrſt ac ymb ane nıht eft ʒefremede*
morð beala mare 7no mearn fore
fæhðe 7fyrene . . .

Modern printed version & translation

[*þanon untydras   ealle onwocon,*
eotenas ond ylfe ond orcneas,
*swylce gig*antas,]   þa wið Gode wunnon
lange þrage;   he him ðæs lean forgeald.
Gewat ða neosian,   syþðan niht becom,
hean huses,   hu hit Hring-Dene
æfter beorþege   gebun hæfdon.
Fand þa ðær inne   æþelinga gedriht
swefan æfter symble;   sorge ne cuðon,
wonsceaft wera.   Wiht unhælo,
grim ond grædig,   gearo sona wæs,
reoc ond reþe,   ond on ræste genam
þritig þegna.   Þanon eft gewat
huðe hremig   to ham faran,
mid þære wælfylle   wica neosan.
Ða wæs on uhtan   mid ærdæge
Grendles guðcræft   gumum undyrne;
þa wæs æfter wiste   wop up ahafen,
micel morgensweg.   Mære þeoden,
æþeling ærgod,   unbliðe sæt;
þolode ðryðswyð,   þegnsorge dreah,
syðþan hie þæs laðan   last sceawedon
wergan gastes.   Wæs þæt gewin to strang,
lað ond longsum.   Næs hit lengra *fyrst,*
[*ac ymb ane niht   eft gefremede*
morðbeala mare   ond no mearn fore,
fæhðe ond fyrene;]

Thence evil broods   all were born:
ogres and elves and goblins
likewise (the) giants who against God strove
(for a) long time   he them their reward paid.
(He) went then (to) seek,   after night came,
(the) lofty house,   how (in) it (the) Ring-Danes,
after beer-drinking,   dwelt had.
(He) found then therein   of-noblemen (a) company,
asleep after (the) banquet; sorrow (they) knew not,

(the) misery of-men. (The) creature damned,
grim and greedy, ready immediately was,
savage and cruel, and at rest seized
thirty thanes. Thence then (he) turned,
(in) plunder exulting, to home go,
with that slaughter (his) dwelling to seek
Then was in (the) half-light before dawn
Grendel's war-strength to-men revealed;
then was after (the) feast weeping, up raised
(a) great morning-cry. (The) great prince,
(a) leader good before others, joyless sat;
suffered (the) mighty one, thane-grief suffered
when they (the) loathsome tracks looked at
of-(the)-accursed devil. Was the contest too fierce,
hateful and long-lasting. Nor-was it longer time,
but within one night again (he) committed
murder more, and no remorse felt,
vengeance and wickedness;

📖 The vocabulary of Text 27 is listed in the *Word Book*.

OE poetic diction

The 'compact' nature of OE verse is partly due to there being fewer function words when compared with MnE (see, for example, the number of determiners and pronouns in brackets marked in the translation above which are grammatically necessary in MnE). This focuses attention on the meaning-bearing lexical words – nouns, verbs, adjectives and adverbs. This effect is also achieved by the number of compound nouns used in OE prose and poetry. The compounds in Text 27 are contrasted with their MnE equivalents, which are usually less compact:

Compound	*Literal translation*	*MnE equivalent*
beorþege	beer + accepting	beer-drinking
wælfylle	the slain + plenty	large numbers of the slain
ærdæge	before + day	before dawn
guðcræft	war + skill	skill in warfare
morgensweg	morning + sound	sound made in the morning
ærgod	before + good	good before others
ðryðswyð	power + strong	very powerful
þegnsorge	thane + sorrow	sorrow for the loss of thanes

4.2 OE prose

Here are two facsimiles of texts for study, one literary, the other 'utility'.

Text 28 – OE *Gospels* (Matthew 28: 8–19) (facsimile)

Ða ferdon hıʒ hrædlıce fram þære býrʒene mıd eʒe 7mıd mýclum ʒefean. 7urnon 7cyð__ don hyt hýſ leornınʒcnıhton7 efne þa com ſe hælýnd onʒean hıʒ 7cpæð. hale pe ſeʒé; **h**ıʒ ʒenealæhton 7ʒe namon hýſ fet. 7to hım ʒe eað__ meddon; **Ð**a cpæð ſe hælýnd to heõ; **Ne ondr**æ de ʒe eop. farað 7cýþað mınum ʒebroþrum ƥhıʒ faron on ʒalıleam þær hıʒ ʒeſeoþ me; **þ**a þa hıʒ ferdon þa comon ſume. þa peardaſ on þa ceaſtre 7 cýðdon þæra ſacerda ealdrum ealle þa ðınʒ þe ðær ʒepordene pærum; **ð**a ʒe ſamnudon þa ealdraſ hıʒ 7porhtun ʒe mot. 7 ſealdon þam ðeʒenum mıcýl feoh.7cpædon; **S**ecʒeað ƥhyýſ leornınʒcnıhtaſ comon nıhteſ 7 forſtælan hýne ða pe slepun; **7** ʒyf se dema þıss ʒe axað. pe lærað hyne 7ʒedoð eop sorh lease; **Ð**a onfenʒon hıʒ þæs feos. 7dýdon eall ſpa hıʒ ʒelærede pæron: 7þıſ purd pæſ ʒe pıd mærſod mıd ıudeum oð þıſne andpeardan dæʒ;

Ða ferdon þa endlufun leomınʒcnıhtaſ on þone munt. þær ſe hælýnd heom dıhte. 7hýne þær ʒeſapun. 7hıʒ to hım ʒe eaðmeddun; **Þ**ıtod__ lıce ſume hıʒ tpeonedon; **Ð**a ʒenealæhte ſe hælýnd 7 ſpræc to heom þaſ þınʒ 7þuſſ cpæð; **Mé** ıſ ʒe ſeald ælc anpeald on heofonan 7 on eorðan. farað pıtodlıce 7lærað ealle þeoda…

4.2.1 *Translations of the Bible*

Transcription into conventional printing of OE, with word-for-word translation

Ða ferdon hig hrædlice fram þære byrgene mid ege and mid myclum
then went they hurriedly from the tomb with fear and with much
gefean, and urnon and
joy and ran and

cyðdon hyt hys leomingcnihton. And efne þa com se hælynd
told it to-his disciples. And behold then came the Lord
ongean hig and
against them and

cwæð, ‘Hale wese ge.’ Hig genealæhton and genamon hys fet and to him
said, ‘Well be you.’ They approached and took his feet and (to) him
geeaðmeddon. Ða cwæð
worshipped. Then said

se hælynd to heom, ‘Ne ondræde ge eow. Farað and cyþað minum
the Lord to them, ‘(Do) not fear (ye) (you). Go and tell my
gebroþrum þæt hig faron
brethren that they go

on galileam. þær hig geseoþ me.'
into Galilee. There they will see me.'

þa þa hig ferdon þa comon sume þa weardas on þa ceastre and
When they went then came some of the watchmen into the city and
cyðdon þæra sacerda
said to the of-priests

ealdrum ealle þa ðing þe ðær gewordene wærum. Đa gesamnudon þa
elders all the things that there happened were. Then gathered the
ealdras hig and worhtun
elders them and held

gemot, and sealdon þam ðegenum micyl feoh, and cwædon, 'Secgeað þæt
meeting and gave to-the soldiers much money, and said, 'Say that
hys leorningcnihtas comon
his disciples came

nihtes and forstælan hyne ða we slepun. And gyf se dema þiss geaxað,
by night and stole him when we slept. And if the judge this asks,
we lærað hyne and
we will advise him and

gedoð eow sorhlease.' Đa onfengon hig þæs feos, and dydon eall swa
make you secure.' Then took they the money, and did all as
hig gelærede wæron, and
they instructed were, and

þis wurd wæs gewidmærsod mid iudeum oð þisne andweardan dæg.
this story was spread abroad among (the) Jews to this present day.

Đa ferdon þa endlufun leorningcnihtas on þone munt þær se hælynd
Then went the eleven disciples to the mountain where the Lord
heom dihte.
them (had) appointed.

And hyne þær gesawun. and hig to him geeaðmeddun. Witodlice sume
And him there saw and they (to) him worshipped. Truly some
hig tweonedon. Đa
them doubted. Then

genealæhte se hælynd and spærc to heom þas þing and þuss cwæð,
came near the Lord and spoke to them these things and thus said,
'Me is geseald ælc anweald
'(To) me is granted all power

on heofonan and on eorðan. Farað witodlice and lærað ealle þeoda…
in heaven and on earth. Go therefore and teach all nations…

The vocabulary of Text 28 is listed in the *Word Book*.

4.2.2 *Wulfstan*

Wulfstan was Archbishop of York from 1003 to 1023, having been Bishop of London in AD 996 and then Bishop of Worcester. He was a distinguished writer of sermons in an alliterative, rhythmic style of prose, but the next facsimile is an example of his 'canonical' writing in a very plain prose style. The *Canons of Edgar* is a book of canon law (church law) for parish priests, a book of reference, written early in Wulfstan's career during the reign of king Edgar (AD 959–975). Later, Wulstan drafted codes of law for king Æthelred (AD 979–1016) and king Cnut (Canute) (AD 1016–1035).

Text 29 – Wulfstan's *Canons of Edgar* (facsimile)

·7 rıht ıſ þ́ ælc
preoſt týlıȝe ȝeorne · þ́ he ȝóde 7huru rıhte
bec hæbbe · 7riht ıſ . þ́ ænıȝ mæſſepreoſt
ana ne mæſſıȝe · þæt he hæbbe þone þe hĩ

acpeðe · 7 riht ıſ ꝥ ǽnıȝ unfæſténde man
huſleſ ne abýrıȝe · bútan hıt for oferſeoc
nýſſe ſý · 7 rıht ıſ ꝥ ǽnıȝ preoſt aneſ dæȝeſ

tpıȝa
oftor ne mæſſıȝe þonne þrıpa mæſtra
ðınȝa · 7 rıht ıſ ꝥ preoſt a ȝeara huſel hæbbe
þam þe þearf ſy · 7 þæt ȝeorne on clænnýſſe
healde . 7 parnıȝe þæt hıt ńe forealdıȝe · ȝyf
ðonne hıt forhealdan ſy · ꝥ hıſ man brucan
ne mæȝe · þonne forbærne hıt man on clænū
fýre · 7 ða axan under peofode ȝebrínȝe ·
7 bete pıð ȝod ȝeorne ſe ðe hıt forȝýme ·

Printed with conventional OE spelling and present-day punctuation:

And riht is þæt ælc
and right is that each

preost tylige georne þæt he gode and huru rihte
priest strives eagerly that he good and at least right

bec hæbbe. And riht is þæt ænig mæssepreost
books has. And right is that any mass-priest

ana ne mæssige; þæt he hæbbe þone þe him
alone does not say Mass; that he has him who for him

acweðe. *And riht is þæt ænig unfstende man
speaks. And right is that any not fasting man

husles ne abyrige, butan hit for oferseoc
without housel not tastes, except it for extreme sick-

nysse sy. And riht is þæt ænig preost anes dæges
ness be. And right is that any priest in one day

oftor ne mæssige þonne riwa mæstra
more often does not say Mass than three most

ðinga. And riht is þæt preost a geara husel hæbbe
times. And right is that priests always ready housel have

þam þe þearf sy, and þæt georne on clænnysse
for them that in want be, and that desirous in purity

healde, and warnige þæt hit ne forealdige. Gyf
keep, and beware that it does not decay. If

ðonne hit forhealdan sy, þæt his man brucan
then it withheld be, that it someone eat

ne mæge, þonne forbærne hit man on clænum
not may, then burn up it someone in clean

fyre, and ða axan under weofode gebringe,
fire, and the ashes under altar bring

and bete wið God georne sc ðe hit forgyme.
and atone with God well he that it neglects.

* And riht is þæt ænig unfæstende man husles ne abyrige . . . = *no one who has not fasted beforehand may receive holy communion.*

📖 The vocabulary of Text 29 is listed in the *Word Book*.

4.3 OE grammar

We have to speak in sentences to convey meanings. **Words** are grouped into **phrases**, and phrases into **clauses**, and in written English one or more clauses make up a **sentence**. There are two principal ways in which words are related to form phrases and clauses and give meanings. One is using an agreed **word order**. The other is changing the form of words, either by adding **inflections** (prefixes or suffixes), or altering part of a word.

In OE, the order of words in a clause was more variable than that of MnE, and there were many more inflections on nouns, adjectives and verbs.

4.3.1 *Word order*

Today, the normal unmarked order of the constituents in a declarative clause (one making a statement) is SP(C/O)(A), that is, the Subject comes first, followed by the Predicator (or Verb), then the Complements or Objects, and last the Adverbials, if any. This was the common pattern already in OE. Examples in this section and the next are from the OE versions of the Garden of Eden (Adam and Eve) or the Flood (Noah) stories in the book *Genesis* from the Old Testament.

S	P	A
seo næddre	cwæþ	to þam wife
the serpent	*said*	*to the woman*

S	P	O
hi	gehyrdon	his stemne
they	*heard*	*his voice*

S	P	O	&	S	P
seo næddre	bepæhte	me	and	ic	ætt
the serpent	*deceived*	*me*	*and*	*I*	*ate*

But there were also different orders of words. For example, after a linking adverb the verb came before the subject:

A	P	S	A	A
þa	cwæþ	seo næddre	eft	to þam wife
then	*said*	*the serpent*	*after*	*to the woman*

A	P	S	cj	S	P	C
þa	geseah	þæt wif	þæt	þæt treow	wæs	god to etenne
then	*saw*	*the woman*	*that*	*the tree*	*was*	*good to eat*

or the verb might sometimes come last in a subordinate clause:

S	P	A	cj	S	C	P
hi	oncneowon	þa	þæt	hi	nacode	wæron
they	*knew*	*then*	*that*	*they*	*naked*	*were*

OE word order also differed from MnE in asking questions and forming the negative,

A	P	S	O	cj	S	neg	P
Hwi	forbead	God	eow	þæt	ge	ne	æton?
Why	*forbade*	*God*	*you*	*that*	*you*	*not*	*eat?*

(= *Why did God forbid you to eat?*)

Many other examples can be found in the OE texts in Chapters 1–4 by reading the word-for-word translations.

Activity 4.1

Identify the clause elements and the order of the subjects and predicators in the following clauses (phrases are bracketed in the first set):

From Text 17a

(Her) (nam) (breohtric cining) (offan dohter eadburge)
7 (on his dagum) (comon) (ærest) (.iii. scipu norðmanna) (of hereða lande)
7 (þa) (se gerefa) (þær to) (rad)
7 (he) (wolde drifan) (to ðes ciniges tune)
ðy (he) (nyste)
(hwæt) (hi) (wæron)
7 (hine) (man) (ofsloh) (þa)
(þæt) (wæron) (þa erestan scipu deniscra manna)
(þe)(angel cynnes land) (gesohton)

From Text 19a

Her hiene bestæl se here on midne winter ofer twelftan niht to cippanhamme
7 Ø geridan west seaxna land
7 Ø gesetton
7 mycel þæs folces ofer sæ adræfdon
7 þæs oþres þone mæstan dæl hi geridon butan þam cynge ælfrede
7 he litle werede yðelice æfter wudum for 7 on morfestenum

4.3.2 *Number, case and gender – inflections on nouns and adjectives*

4.3.2.1 *Number*

There are only a few inflections in MnE today which mark the grammatical functions of nouns. We show the **number** of a noun, that is, whether it is **singular** (sg) or **plural** (pl), by adding [s] [z] or [ɪz] in speech, ⟨s⟩ or ⟨es⟩ in writing,

cat / cats	dog / dogs	church / churches
[kæt/kæts]	[dɒg/dɒgz]	[tʃɜtʃ/tʃɜtʃɪz]

and there are a few irregular plurals which have survived from OE, like *men*, *geese* and *mice* which show plural number by a change of vowel, and *oxen*, whose *-en* plural was very common in OE as *-an*.

4.3.2.2 Case

In MnE today only the personal pronouns (except *you* and *it*) are inflected to show whether they are the subject or object in a clause.

Mn			*OE*		
S	*P*	*O*	*S*	*P*	*O*
I	saw	it	**ic**	seah	**hit**
you (sg)	saw	her	**þu**	sawe	**hi**
he	saw	me	**he**	seah	**me**
she	saw	him	**heo**	seah	**hine**
we	saw	you (pl)	**we**	sawon	**eow**
you (pl)	saw	us	**ge**	sawon	**us**
they	saw	them	**hi**	sawon	**hi**

Adjectives are not inflected to agree with nouns in MnE, nor is the definite article *the*, but they were in OE. The feature of the grammar which marks these functions is called **case**.

subject ⇒ nominative case (nom)
direct object ⇒ accusative case (acc)
indirect object ⇒ dative case (dat)

In a **prepositional phrase** (PrepP) in OE, the noun was in either the accusative or dative case, according to the preposition.

The only other MnE inflection on nouns is the ⟨'s⟩ or ⟨s'⟩ in writing to show possession – called the possessive or **genitive** case (gen). This is the only grammatical case in MnE which survives from OE in nouns. In OE the genitive noun usually preceded the noun head of the phrase:

god**es** cyrican (*Text 18*)	God's church
sweord**a** ecgum (*Text 26*)	(by the) swords' edges
sweord**es** ecgum (*Text 26*)	by the) sword's edges

Place names often begin as genitive + noun constructions:

certic**es** ford (*Text 9a*)	Cerdic's ford (*not identified*)
æþeling**a** ige (*Text 19a*)	Etheling's isle = Athelney
heopwin**es** fleot (*Text 7*)	Ypwine's fleet (*river*) = Ebbsfleet

Phrases of measurement also contained a genitive, as in:

.iii. scipu norðmanna (*Text 17a*)	3 ships of-Norsemen
.xl. wucena (*Text 24*)	40 of-weeks
.xxxi. wintra (*Text 10a*)	31 of-winters = 31 years

4.3.2.3 Gender

In MnE, we have to select the correct pronoun *he*, *she* or *it* according to the sex, or lack of sex, of the referent – *he* is **masculine** (m), *she* is **feminine** (f), *it* is **neuter** (n). This is called **natural gender.** In OE, nouns for things which today are all neuter, and nouns for a male or female person might be masculine, feminine or neuter. For example, *sunne* (*sun*) was feminine, *mona* (*moon*) was masculine, *wif* (*woman*) and *cild* (*child*) were neuter in gender. This is called **grammatical gender**.

So nouns and adjectives in OE, including the equivalent of MnE *the*, were marked by a complex system of inflections for number, case and gender. Here are a few examples; notice that sometimes the inflection is zero (Ø), like the MnE plural of *sheep*, or past tense of *cut*. The inflections are shown after a hyphen:

seo næddr-**e** cwæþ *the serpent said*	sg	nom	f
God-Ø cwæþ to **þære** næddr-**an** *God said to the serpent*	sg	dat	f
þæt wif-Ø andwyrde *the woman answered*	sg	nom	n
God-Ø cwæþ to **þam** wif-**e** *God said to the woman*	sg	dat	n
se hræfn-Ø fleah þa ut *the raven flew then out*	sg	nom	m
he asende ut **þone** hræfn-Ø *he sent out the raven*	sg	acc	m
hi gehyrdon **his** stemn-**e** *they heard his voice*	sg	acc	f
he genam hi in to **þam** arc-**e** *he took her into the ark*	sg	dat	m
heora beg-**ra** eag-**an** wurdon geopenede *their both eyes became opened*	pl	nom	n
ofer **þære** eorþ-**an** bradnysse *over the earth's broadness* (= surface)	sg	gen	f
þa wæter-**u** adruwodon *the waters dried up*	pl	nom	n
he abad oþre seofan dag-**as** *he waited (an)other seven days*	pl	acc	m

Proper nouns also were inflected: *ælfred cyning* (Text 19a) is subject and so nominative case; in the PrepP *butan þam cyng-e ælfred-e* (*except king Ælfred*) (Text 19a), all three words in the NP are in the dative case, following *butan*.

4.3.3 *Verbs*

In MnE there are different ways of forming the **past tense** and **past participle** of verbs.

4.3.3.1 *MnE regular verbs – OE weak verbs*

The majority are regular, and we add /t/, /d/ or /ɪd/ in speech and ⟨ed⟩ (usually) in writing to the verb to form both the past tense and past participle,

MnE			***OE***		
kiss	kissed	kissed	cyssan	cyste	cyssed
fill	filled	filled	fyllan	fylde	fylled
knit	knitted	knitted	cnyttan	cnytte	cnytted

MnE regular verbs derive from a set of OE verbs whose past tense was marked with [t] or [d] in a **dental suffix**, and are called **weak verbs**.

4.3.3.2 *MnE irregular verbs – OE strong verbs*

There is another set of common verbs in MnE whose past tense and past participle are marked by a change of vowel, while the participle has either an ⟨en⟩ suffix (not ⟨ed⟩) or none. These are called **irregular verbs**. Here are a few examples, to which you could add many more:

MnE			***OE***		
ride	rode	ridden	ridan	rad	riden
choose	chose	chosen	ceosan	ceas	coren
drink	drank	drunk	drincan	dranc	druncen
come	came	come	cuman	com	cumen
speak	spoke	spoken	sprecan	sprac	sprecen
see	saw	seen	seon	seah	sewen
fall	fell	fallen	feallan	feoll	feallen

The irregular verbs in MnE derive from a much larger set of verbs in OE, marked by changes of vowel, which linguists have called **strong verbs**. (This is an outline only – the verb systems in both OE and MnE are more varied than shown here.)

4.3.3.3 *Inflections for person and tense*

OE verbs were also marked by different suffixes to agree with their subject – either 1st, 2nd or 3rd **person**, and singular or plural **number**. In MnE, the only present tense inflection is ⟨s⟩, to agree with the 3rd person singular subject:

I/you/we/they drive   he/she/it drive-**s**

In OE, this verb would have a variety of suffixes:

ic drif-**e** þu drif-**st** he/heo/hit drif-**þ** we/ge/hi drif-**aþ**

In MnE, there are no additional suffixes to mark agreement in the past tense:

I/he/she/it/we/you/they drove

In OE the past tense had some suffixes to mark agreement:

ic draf þu drif-**e** he/heo/hit draf we/ge/hi drif-**on**

📖 These examples illustrate only some of the forms of inflection in OE verbs. There is a fuller discussion in the *Text Commentary Book*.

4.3.4 *Evidence of changes in OE pronunciation and grammar*

4.3.4.1 *Loss of inflections in MnE*

One of the important differences between OE and MnE is that MnE has lost most of the inflections of OE. We can observe the beginnings of this loss of word suffixes from evidence in the manuscripts. If you compare the spellings of the same words in the *Anglo-Saxon Chronicle* texts in chapters 2 and 3, you will sometimes find differences in the vowel letters of unstressed syllables, suffixes that marked case in nouns, and tense in verbs (see Activity 3.2 in chapter 3). Here are some examples, with the the two text words followed by the form with the 'correct' OE suffix:

	Peterborough Chronicle	***Parker Chronicle***	***Regular West Saxon OE form***
Text 6	nefdon	næfdan	næfdon = ne hæfdon
	feordodan	fyrdedon	feordodon *or* fyrdedon
	cininge	cyningæ	cyninge
	bædon	bædan	bædon
Text 9	onfengon	onfengun	onfengon
	nemnaþ	nemneþ	nemnaþ
	rixadon	ricsadan	ricsodon
Text 16	gefuhton	gefuhtun	gefuhton
	geþingodon	geþingodan	geþingodon
Text 19	geridan	geridon	geridon
	butan	buton	butan
	sealwudu	sealwyda	sealwudu
	beheonan	behinon	beheonan
	wæron	wærun	wæron

If such spelling irregularities become frequent, we can assume that the vowel sound of these suffixes was no longer a clear [o] [ɑ] or [u], but had reduced to the vowel [ə]. This mid-central vowel is the commonest in present-day English, because we use it in most unstressed syllables, but we have never had a separate letter of the alphabet for it. The scribes of OE therefore began to use vowel letters in these unstressed syllables at random. Eventually letter ⟨e⟩ came to be generally used.

Other spelling differences are evidence of other changes in progress. *þan* (Text 9b) for *þam* (Text 9a) perhaps suggests the beginning of the loss of distinction between [m] and [n] when word-final in unstressed syllables, so that, for example, inflected forms of *tunge* (*tongue*) like *tungan* and *tungum* are both in time reduced firstly to *tungen* and then to *tunge*.

The spelling *cynge* (Text 19a) shows the loss of the second, unstressed syllable of *cyninge* (Text 19b) in the word's development to *king*. *Worhte* (Text 19b) for *wrohte* (Text 19a), in which the consonant [r] and vowel [o] are reversed, illustrates a process called **metathesis** which was not uncommon in the development of OE to ME – other examples are *irnan/rinnan* (*run*), *birnan/brinnan* (*burn*), *berstan/brestan* (*burst*), *þerscan/þrescan* (*thresh*).

So, although in late OE times the West Saxon dialect had become a standard for writing, and therefore did not reflect differences of pronunciation between the dialects, scribes 'mis-spelt' because other changes in pronunciation were taking place.

4.4 Latin loan-words in OE

A great deal of 'Latinate' vocabulary came into English from the 16th century onwards, during the Renaissance, or revival of learning, when both Latin and Greek were generally considered to be languages superior to English. These words are often long and learned, and contrast with shorter Anglo-Saxon words in their use in formal speech and writing. But Old English contained words of Latin origin also, some of which belong to the **core vocabulary** of MnE and are in no way learned or obscure.

4.4.1 *Latin words borrowed before the settlement in England*

Some words borrowed from Latin were in the language brought over with the Angles and Saxons in the 5th century. Old English was a Germanic language, but the Germanic people were in continuous contact with the Latin-speaking Romans. There are no written records from this period, so the evidence for the early adoption of Latin words lies in an analysis of known sound changes.

Here is a selection of words which are reflexes of OE words borrowed from Latin before the Anglo-Saxon settlement in Britain. Many such words have not survived, e.g. *cylle* from Latin *culleus* (*leather bottle*), *mese* from *mensa* (*table*), *sigel* from *sigillum* (*brooch*).

Activity 4.2

Divide the words into sets according to their meanings (e.g. domestic, household articles, etc.). Consider what these sets of borrowed words might suggest about the relationship between the Germanic tribes and the Romans.

Latin	*OE*	*MnE*	*Latin*	*OE*	*MnE*
balteus	belt	*belt*	mulus	mul	*mule*
benna	binn	*bin*	patina	panne	*pan*
episcopus	biscop	*bishop*	pisa	pise	*pease* ⇒ *pea*
butyrum	butere	*butter*	piper	pipor	*pepper*
cattus	catt	*cat*	pulvinus	pylc	*pillow*
calx	cealc	*chalk*	pinna	pinn	*pin*
caseus	cese	*cheese*	pipa	pipe	*pipe* (musical)
cuprum	copor	*copper*	puteus	pytt	*pit*
cuppa	cuppe	*cup*	pix/picem	pic	*pitch* (tar)
discus	disc	*dish*	prunum	plume	*plum*
furca	forca	*fork*	papaver	popig	*poppy*
uncia	ynce	*inch*	pondo	pund	*pound* (weight)
catillus	cetel	*kettle*	bursa	purs	*purse*
culina	cylene	*kiln*	Saturni (dies)	Sæternes (dæg)	*Satur*(day)
cucina	cycene	*kitchen*	secula	sicol	*sickle*
linea	line	*line*	strata	stært	*street*
milea	mil	*mile*	tegula	tigele	*tile*
molinum	mylen	*mill*	telonium	toll	*toll* (tax)
moneta	mynet	*mint* (money)	vallum	wall	*wall*
mango	mangian/	*-monger*	vicus	wic	-*wick* (= town)
	mangere		vinum	win	*wine*
mortarium	mortere	*mortar* (vessel)			

None of these words is polysyllabic or learned, and their Latin origin cannot be guessed from their form or meaning.

Although Latin would have been spoken in Britain during the Roman occupation up to the 5th century by educated Britons, hardly any Latin words were passed on from this source to the Anglo-Saxon invaders. An exception was the *-caster*/*-chester* suffix for place-names like *Doncaster* and *Manchester*, from the Latin *castra*, meaning *camp*.

4.4.2 *Latin words adopted during the Anglo-Saxon period*

Other Latin words came into the language at different periods of the Anglo-Saxon settlement, many as a result of the conversion to Christianity and the establishment of the Church, because Latin was the language of the Bible and church services, and of learning and scholarship.

In the following selection of reflexes derived from Latin during this period, the date given is that of the earliest occurrence recorded in writing (taken from the *OED*). This is a 'no later than' date, and does not, of course, tell us at what earlier time the word had become common in the spoken language.

Activity 4.3

Divide the following list of words into sets according to the meanings, for example:

(a) religion and the Church;
(b) education and learning;
(c) household and clothing;
(d) plants, herbs and trees;
(e) foods.

You will also need (f) for miscellaneous words which do not fall into sets easily.

MnE	*OE*	*Date*	*Latin*	*MnE*	*OE*	*Date*	*Latin*
anchor	ancor	880	ancora	*master*	mægester	1000	magister
angel	engel	950	angelus	*mat*	matt	825	matta
apostle	apostol	950	apostolus	*minster*	mynster	900	monasterium
ark	arc	1000	arca	*mussel*	muscle	1000	muscula
balsam	balsam	1000	balsamum	*myrrh*	myrra	824	murra
beet	bete	1000	beta	*nun*	nunne	900	nonna
box (tree)	box	931	buxus	*organ*	organe	1000	organum
candle	candel	700	candela	*palm*	palma	825	palmum
cap	cæppe	1000	cappa	*pear*	pere	1000	pira
cedar	ceder	1000	cedrus	*pine*	pin	1000	pinus
chalice	celic	825	calix	*plant*	plante	825	planta
chest	cest	700	cista	*pope*	papa	900	papa
circle	circul	1000	circulus	*priest*	preost	805	presbyter
cook (n)	coc	1000	cocus	*psalm*	psealm	961	psalmus
coulter	culter	1000	culter	*radish*	rædic	1000	radicem
cowl	cugele	931	cuculla	*sabbath*	sabat	950	sabbatum
creed	creda	1000	credo	*sack*	sacc	1000	saccus
crisp	crisp	900	crispus	*school*	scol	1000	schola
disciple	discipul	900	discipulus	*shrine*	scrin	1000	scrinium
fan	fann	800	vannus	*silk*	sioloc	888	sericus
fennel	finugl	700	finuclum	*sock*	socc	725	soccus
fever	fefor	1000	febris	*sponge*	sponge	1000	spongia
font	fant/font	1000	fontem	*talent*	talente	930	talenta
ginger	gingiber	1000	gingiber	*temple*	templ	825	templum
lily	lilie	971	lilium	*title*	titul	950	titulus
lobster	lopustre	1000	locusta	*verse*	fers	900	versus
martyr	martyr	900	martyr	*zephyr*	zefferus	1000	zephyrus
mass	mæsse	900	missa				

These lists of words derived from Latin during the Anglo-Saxon period of English history show how in time loan-words become fully assimilated into the language.

4.5 ON loan-words in OE

There is little written evidence of ON words in OE. Here is a short list of some that have MnE reflexes, with their earliest recorded occurrences in writing.

MnE	*ON*	*Date*	*Quotation*
till (in the sense of *to*)	til	800	*Inscription, Ruthwell Cross, Dumfries*: Hweþræ þer fusæ fearran kwomu æþþilæ **til** anum
awe	agi	855	*A/S Chronicle* (AD 457): þa Brettas ... mid micle **eȝe** fluȝon
call	kalla	1000	*Battle of Maldon*: Ongan **ceallian** ofer cald wæter Byrhthelmes bearn
law	lagu	1000	*Laws of Ethelred*: ȝif he hine laðian wille ... do ðæt be ðam deopestan aðe ... on Engla **laȝe**, and on Dena **laȝe**, be ðam ðe heora **laȝu** si
fellow	felagc	1016	*A/S Chronicle*: Beȝen ða cyningas ... wurdon **feoluȝan** & wedbroðra
outlaw	utlagi	1023	*Wulfstan Homilies*: He scel beon **utlaȝa** wið me
haven	hofn	1031	*A/S Chronicle*: þa **hæfenan** on Sandwic
knife	knifr	1100	*Gloss on Latin word – Artauus*: **cnif**
take	taka	1100	*A/S Chronicle* (1076): Ac se kyngc ... hine let syððan **tacan**
their	ðeirra	1100	*A/S Chronicle* (AD 449): On **þeora** daȝum ȝelaðode Wyrtȝeorn Angelcin hider
wrong	wrangr	1100	*Wulfstan's Homilies*: þa unrihtdeman, þe ... wendaþ **wrang** to rihte and riht to **wrange**

4.6 Early French loan-words

There had been been close contact between the English court of Edward the Confessor (1042–1066) and Normandy, and some loan-words from Norman French appear in 11th-century documents, of which a few have survived into MnE.

MnE	*OF/ONF*	*Date*	*Quotation*
sot	*sot* (foolish)	1000	Ælfric, *Saints' Lives*, xiii: Ne bið se na wita þe unwislice leofað, ac bið open **sott**
capon	*capun*	1000	*Ælfric – Gloss on Latin words*: *Capo*, **capun**. *Gallinaccus*, **capun**
proud	*prud*	1050	Pryte heaȝe utawyrpð & wiþerwyrdnyss **prute** ȝenyerude
castle	*castel*	1075	*A/S Chronicle* (1048): þa hæfdon þa welisce men ȝewroht ænne **castel** on Herefordscire

MnE	*OF/ONF*	*Date*	*Quotation*
crown	*coroune*	1085	*A/S Chronicle*: Her se cyng bær his corona and heold his hired on Winceastre
arbalest	*arbaleste*	1100	*A/S Chronicle*, 1079: Mid anan **arblaste** of scoten (*cross-bow*)
chaplain	*capelain*	1100	*A/S Chronicle*, 1099: Se cyng Willím . . . Rannulfe his **capellane** þæt biscoprice on Dunholme geaf
tower	*tor/tur*	1100	*A/S Chronicle*, 1097: þurh þone weall þe hi worhton on butan þone **tur** on Lundenne

5. From Old English to Middle English

5.1 The evidence for linguistic change

The ways in which we have identified and described features of the language in the Old English texts in chapters 1–4 are those which we can systematically apply to any text of English. We look for:

- changes in **spelling** conventions, **letter forms** and the **alphabet** used; these are our only guide in OE and ME texts to the pronunciation of the language;
- changes in **pronunciation**, inferred from the written words;
- changes in **word-structure**, suffixes (inflections) and prefixes;
- changes in the **grammar** and word order;
- changes in the word-stock or **vocabulary** – new words appear, old ones are no longer used.

We call the language from about 1150–1450 **Middle English** (ME), because from our point of view in time it comes between the periods of Old and Modern English. The evidence for change and development in ME, before the first printing press was set up by William Caxton in 1476, lies in written manuscripts, just as for OE. Every copy of a book, letter, will, or charter had to be written out by hand, but only a few of the existing manuscripts in ME are originals, in the hand of their author. Many copies of a popular book like Chaucer's *Canterbury Tales*, for example, have survived, though Chaucer's original manuscripts have been lost. On the other hand, other works are known through a single surviving copy only.

As a result of the social and political upheaval caused by the Norman Conquest (see section 5.2 following), the West Saxon standard system of spelling and punctuation was in time no longer used. Writers used spellings that tended to match the pronunciation of their spoken dialect. Scribes often changed the spelling of words they were copying to match their own dialectal pronunciation. After several copies, the writing might contain a mixture of different dialectal forms. But for students of language today, the loss of the old OE standard writing system means that there is plenty of evidence for the different dialects of ME.

5.1.1 *The development of spelling and punctuation*

Today we are used to reading printed books and papers in Standard English which use a spelling and punctuation system that has been almost unchanged for over two hundred years. We are taught to use Standard English and standard spelling when we learn to write. MnE spelling is neutral to pronunciation, and written texts can be read in any regional accent. Misspelled words and non-standard forms look 'wrong'.

The writings of most authors from the late 15th century onwards, including the plays of Shakespeare and the King James Bible of 1611, are prepared for printing in modern editions by editors who almost always convert the original spelling and punctuation into modern standard forms. For example, an early edition of Shakespeare's *Henry IV Part 1* printed in 1598 contains these words spoken by Falstaff:

> If I be not ashamed of my soldiours, I am a souct gurnet, I haue misused the kinges presse damnablie. No eye hath seene such skarcrowes. Ile not march through Couentry with them, thats flat.

It contains several spellings that are now nonstandard – *soldiours, souct, presse, damnablie, seene, skarcrowes* – and lacks the 'apostrophe s' that is now used to mark elided sounds or possessive nouns – *Ile, thats, kinges presse* for present-day *I'll, that's* and *king's press. Souct* was an alternative spelling for *soused.*

The custom of modernising the punctuation of OE and ME texts, and both spelling and punctuation of authors from the 15th century onwards, leaves us unaware of the way modern spelling and punctuation developed. We read Chaucer's original 1390s spelling, but not Shakespeare's of the 1590s. The examples of historical English texts in this book are reproduced with their original spelling. Those texts transcribed from facsimiles have their original punctuation also, because this too is part of the development of written English. Where a facsimile is not available, an edited version has to be used, which may change some features of the original.

But all printed versions of old texts must compromise in reproducing the originals. Facsimiles are the nearest we can get to an authentic copy, although it needs experience to be able to decipher handwriting styles of the past.

5.2 The Norman Conquest and the English language

In chapters 2–4 we looked at Old English in the West Saxon dialect, which had become the standard form for writing by the first half of the 11th century in all dialect areas. A standard orthography (spelling system) means that changes in pronunciation tend not to be recorded. On the other hand, any differences or inconsistencies in spelling that do occur are a clue to changes in pronunciation and word-form which were taking place (see section 4.4.4). We can see this happening in the following 12th-century copy of a text that was originally written in the 11th century.

5.2.1 *Language in transition*

If you examine an ME text and compare the forms of words with their originals in OE, the evidence of changed spelling will suggest changes in pronunciation or word structure. When this is done systematically, knowledge of the probable dialectal area in which a text was written can be deduced. Building up the evidence for this in detail has been the work of ME scholars over many years. We can make use of their knowledge and examine some short texts for ourselves to see what we can find out about changes in the language after the OE period.

5.2.1.1 *Old English homilies, second half of the 12th century*

A homily is a sermon. The homilies in the manuscript from which the following text is taken were originally composed before the Conquest in the 11th century, but the manuscript was copied in the second half of the 12th century. So although it still has many features of the West Saxon literary standard language, there is evidence of 'a mixture of spelling traditions, West Saxon, Anglo-Norman and Latin, and also some spellings that reflect the scribe's West Midland regional dialect'. New spellings may indicate either changing pronunciation or a new spelling convention.

This short extract is the opening of a homily and consists of verses from St John's Gospel (chapter 12: 24–6) which the sermon itself expounds. It opens with a verse in Latin which is then repeated in English.

Text 30 – *Old English homily*, copied second half of 12th century (facsimile)

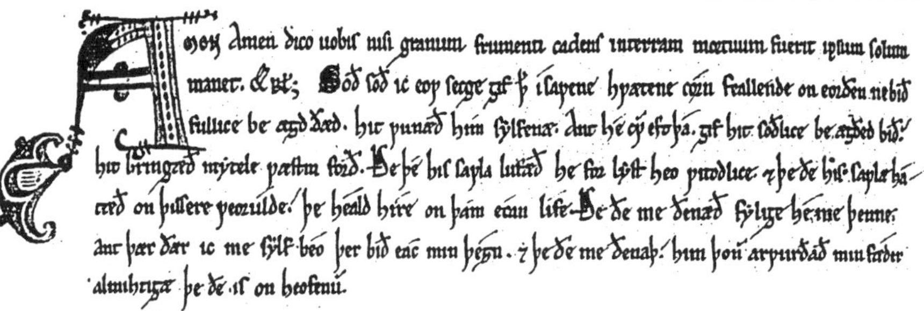

Transcription

Amen amen dıco uobıſ granum frumentı cadenſ ın terram mortuum fuerıt ıpſum ſolum manet. & Rl: Soð ſoð ıc eoƿ ſecge ȝıf þ́ ıſ aƿene hƿætene corn feallende on eorðen ne bıð fullıce be æȝdðæd. hıt wunæð hım ſẏlfenæ. ant he cƿ̄ eft þa. ȝıf hıt ſoðlıce be æȝðed bıð: hıt brıngæð mẏcele ƿæſtm forð. Đe þe hıſ ſaƿla lufæð he for lẏ́ſt heo ƿıtodlıce. 7 þe ðe hıſ ſaƿlæ ha tæð on þıſſere ƿeorulde: þe heald hıre on þam ecan lıfe. Đe ðe me ðenæð fẏ́lıȝe he me þenne ant þær ðær ıc me ſẏ́lf beo þer bıð eac mın þeȝn. 7 þe ðe me ðenaþ: hım þon̄ arƿurðað mın fæder almıhtıȝæ þe ðe ıſ on heofenū.

Modern printed version with punctuation

Amen amen dico uobis granum frumenti cadens in terram mortuum fuerit ipsum solum manet. et reliqua. Soð soð ic eow secge. Gif þæt isawene hwætene corn feallende on eorðen ne bið fullice beæʒdðæd, hit wunæð him sylfenæ; ant he cwæð eft þa: Gif hit soðlice beæʒðed bið, hit bringæð mycele wæstm forð. Ðe þe his sawla lufæð, he forlyst heo witodlice; and þe ðe his sawlæ hatæð on þissere weorulde, þe heald hire on þam ecan life. Ðe ðe me ðenæð, fyliʒe he me þenne; ant þær ðær ic me sylf beo, þer bið eac min þeʒn; and þe ðe me ðenaþ, him þonne arwurðað min fæder almihtiʒæ þe ðe is on heofenum.

Word for word translation

Soð soð ic eow secge; Gif þæt isawene hæwtene corn feallende on eorðen
truth truth I to you say if the sown wheaten corn falling on earth
ne bið fullice beæʒdðæd,
is not fully dead

hit wunæð him sylfenæ; ant he cwæð eft þa: Gif hit soðlice beæʒðed bið,
it remains to itself; and he spoke after then: If it truly dead is,
hit bringæð mycele wæstm forð.
it brings much growth forth.

Ðe þe his sawla lufæð, he forlyst heo witodlice; and þe ðe his sawlæ
He who his soul (=life) loves he loses it certainly: and he who his life
hatæð on þissere weorulde,
hates in this world

þe heald hire on þam ecan life. Ðe ðe me ðenæð, fyliʒe he me þenne;
he (will) hold it in the eternal life. He who me serves, follow he me then;
ant þær ðær ic me sylf beo,
and there where I myself am,

þer bið eac min þeʒn; and þe ðe me ðenaþ, him þonne arwurðað min
there is also my servant; and he who me serves, him then honours my
fæder almihtiʒæ þe ðe is
father almighty he who is

on heofenum.
in heaven.

Earlier West Saxon standard version

(*Words in Text 30 whose spelling appears to have changed are in bold type.*)

Soð soð ic eow secge; Gif þæt gesawene hæwtene corn feallende on **eorðan** ne bið fullice **beagod**, hit **wuniað** him **sylfum**; **and** he cwæð eft þa: Gif hit soðlice **beagod** bið, hit **bringað** mycele wæstm forð. Ðe þe his **sawle lufað**, he forlyst **hi** witodlice; and þe ðe his **sawle hatiað** on **þisre** weorulde, þe **healt** hire on am ecan life. Ðe ðe me **þegnað**, fyliʒe he me þenne; **and** þær ðær ic me sylf beo, þer bið eac min þeʒn; and þe ðe me **þegnaþ**, him þonne **arwurðiað** min fæder ælmihtiʒa þe ðe is on **heofonum**.

Text	*OE*	*Text*	*OE*	*Text*	*OE*
eorðen	eorðan	sawla	sawle	ðenæð	þegnaþ
beæʒdðæd	beagod	lufæð	lufað	ant	and
wunæð	wuniað	heo	hi	ðenaþ	þegnaþ
sylfenæ	sylfum	sawlæ	sawle	arwurðað	arwurðiað
ant	and	hatæð	hatiað	heofenum	heofonum
beæʒðed	beagod	þissere	þisre		
bringæð	bringað	heald	healt		

The differences are slight, but are evidence of the beginning of the loss of the West Saxon standard spelling system, and also of some possible changes of pronunciation.

📖 The vocabulary of Text 30 is listed in the *Word Book*.

5.2.2 *French – the prestige language after 1066*

After the conquest of England by William I in 1066, Norman French, not English, became the language of the ruling classes and their servants, because almost all the former English nobility were dispossessed of their lands. The chronicler Robert Mannyng, writing in 1338, refers to this:

NE Midlands dialect

To Frankis & Normanz for þare grete laboure
To Flemmynges & Pikardes þat were with him in stoure*
He gaf londes bityme of whilk þer successoure
Hold ȝit þe seyseyne with fulle grete honoure.

* in stoure = in battle.

† seyseyne = seisin = possession of land.

Here is another short account of the Conquest in an anonymous Chronicle, written in the 14th century, which still showed hostility to the Norman domination of England.

Text 31 – Anonymous short metrical chronicle, 14th century

SW Midlands dialect

	WW
Suþþe regnede a goude gome	After reigned a good man
Harold Godwynes sone	Harold Godwin's son
He was icluped Harefot	He was called Harefoot
For he was renner goud	For he was runner good
Bote he ne regnede here	But he ne-reigned here
Bot .ix. mones of a ȝere	But 9 months of a year
Willam bastard of Normandye	William bastard of Normandy
Hym cant þat was a vilanye	Him deposed that was a villainy
Harold liþ at Waltham	Harold lies at Waltham
& Willam bastard þat þis lond wan	& William bastard that this land won
He regnede here	He reigned here
On & tuenti ȝere	One & twenty years
Suþþe he deide at þe hame	Then he died at (the) home
At Normandye at Came	In Normany at Caen

📖 The vocabulary of Text 31 is listed in the *Word Book*.

William's policy of dispossessing the Anglo-Saxon nobility held in the Church also. French-speaking bishops and abbots were in time appointed to the principal offices, and many French-speaking monks entered the monasteries. Latin remained the principal language of both Church and State for official writing in documents, while French became the 'prestige language' of communication. We can compare the status of French in England from 1066 onwards with that of English in the British Empire in the 19th and early 20th centuries. The situation which developed is described by another verse chronicler, known as Robert of Gloucester, writing about 1300. His attitude towards Harold and William I is different from that of the anonymous chronicler of Text 31.

Text 32 – Robert of Gloucester's *Chronicle*, *c.* 1300

ME (southern dialect)

þus lo þe englisse folc. vor noȝt to grounde com.
vor a fals king þat nadde no riȝt. to þe kinedom.
& come to a nywe louerd. þat more in riȝte was.
ac hor noþer as me may ise. in pur riȝte was.
& þus was in normannes hond. þat lond ibroȝt iwis...
þus com lo engelond. in to normandies hond.
& þe normans ne couþe speke þo. bote hor owe speche.
& speke french as hii dude at om. & hor children dude also teche.
so þat heiemen of þis lond. þat of hor blod come.
holdeþ alle þulk speche. þat hii of hom nome.
vor bote a man conne frenss. me telþ of him lute.
ac lowe men holdeþ to engliss. & to hor owe speche ȝute.
ich wene þer ne beþ in al þe world. contreyes none.
þat ne holdeþ to hor owe speche. bote engelond one.
ac wel me wot uor to conne. boþe wel it is.
vor þe more þat a mon can. þe more wurþe he is.
þis noble duc willam. him let crouny king.
at londone amidwinter day. nobliche þoru alle þing.
of þe erchebissop of euerwik. aldred was is name.
þer nas prince in al þe world. of so noble fame.

WW

Thus lo the English folk for nought to ground came (= *were beaten*)
For a false king that ne-had no right to the kingdom
& came to a new lord that more in right was
But their neither (= *neither of them*) as one may see in pure right was
& thus was in Norman's hand that land brought certainly...
Thus came lo England into Normandy's hand
& the Normans ne-could speak then but their own speech
& spoke French as they did at home & their children did also teach.
So that high-men of this land that of their blood come
hold all the-same speech that they from them took.
For but a man knows French one counts of him little.
But low men hold to English & to their own speech yet.
I believe there ne-are in all the world countries none
that ne-hold to their own speech but England alone.
But well one knows for to know both well it is
for the more that a man knows the more worthy he is.
This noble duke William him(*self*) caused to crown king
at London on mid-winter's day nobly through all things
by the Archbishop of York. Aldred was his name.
There ne-was prince in all the world of so noble fame.

The vocabulary of Text 32 is listed in the *Word Book* as Text 56.

5.3 The earliest 12th-century Middle English text

The manuscript of *The Anglo-Saxon Chronicle* which was written in the abbey at Peterborough is of special interest for two reasons, one historical and the other linguistic:

- it is the only copy of the *Chronicle* which describes events up to the middle of the 12th century, nearly one hundred years after the Conquest;
- it gives us the first direct evidence of the changes in the language that had taken place by the 1150s.

We know that a disastrous fire at Peterborough destroyed most of the monastery's library in 1116, including its copy of the *Chronicle*. Later, another *Chronicle* was borrowed and copied. This re-written copy has survived and is the one known as *The Peterborough Chronicle*. The entries for the years up to 1121 are all in the same hand, and copied in the 'classical' West Saxon OE orthography. But there are two 'continuations' of the annals, probably written down by two scribes, one recording events from 1122 to 1131, and the other from 1132 to 1154, where the *Chronicle* ends.

The importance of the continuations is that the language is not the classical West Saxon OE of the older *Chronicle* to 1121, but is markedly different. It is good evidence of current English usage of that area in the first half of the 12th century. The monks of Peterborough were probably local men, and so spoke the East Midland dialect of English. Peterborough was within the Danelaw (see section 3.3.1.1), and some influence of Old Norse might be expected too. The tradition of writing in classical OE spelling was by now lost, and as the continuations of the annals were probably written from dictation, the scribe would tend to spell English as he heard and spoke it. Scribes were also now trained in the writing of French as well as Latin, and some conventions of writing French would influence their spelling of English words, like using ⟨th⟩ for ⟨þ⟩ and ⟨qu⟩ for ⟨cw⟩.

Activity 5.1

Text 33 is part of the annal for 1140 in the second continuation of the *Peterborough Chronicle*.

(i) Read through the text to see whether you can understand the gist of it without referring to the translation.
(ii) Use the literal translation following to make a MnE version.
(iii) List any differences between the language of the text, and that of the *Chronicle* annals in Texts 1–26, which you immediately notice.
(iv) Comment on the words of French derivation in the text: *uuerre*, *castel*, *prisun*.

📖 There is a detailed commentary in the *Text Commentary Book*.

Text 33 – Part of *Peterborough Chronicle* for 1140

.mc.xl. On þis gær wolde þe king Stephne tæcen Rodbert eorl
of gloucestre þe kinges sune Henries. ac he ne myhte for he
wart it war. þer efter in þe lengten þestrede þe sunne ⁊ te
dæi. abuton nontid dæies. þa men eten. ð me lihtede candles
to æten bi . . . wæron men suythe of wundred . . .
þer efter wæx suythe micel uuerre betuyx þe king ⁊ Randolf
eorl of cæstre noht for þi ð he ne iaf him al ð he cuthe axen
him. alse he dide all othre. oc æfre þe mare he iaf heom. þe
wærse hi wæron him. þe eorl heold lincol agænes þe king ⁊
benam him al ð he ahte to hauen. ⁊ te king for þider ⁊
besætte him ⁊ his brother Willelm de Romare in þe castel. ⁊
te æorl stæl ut ⁊ ferde efter Rodbert eorl of gloucestre. ⁊
brohte him þider mid micel ferd. ⁊ fuhten suythe on
Candelmasse dæi agenes heore lauerd. ⁊ namen him for his men
him suyken ⁊ flugæn. ⁊ læd him to Bristowe ⁊ diden þar in
prisun ⁊ in feteres. þa was al Engleland styred mar þan ær
wæs. ⁊ al yuel wæs in lande . . .
þa ferde Eustace þe kinges sune to france ⁊ nam þe kinges
suster of france to wife. wende to bigæton normandi þæþurh.
oc he spedde litel ⁊ be gode rihte for he was an yuel man.
for ware se he com he dide mar yuel þanne god. he reuede þe
landes ⁊ læide micele geldes on. He brohte his wif to
engleland. ⁊ dide hire in þe castel in cantebyri. God wimman
scæ wæs. oc scæ hedde litel blisse mid him. ⁊ Crist ne wolde
ð he sculde lange rixan. ⁊ wærd ded ⁊ his moder beien . . .

WW

1140. In this year wished the king Stephen take Robert earl of
Gloucester the king's son Henry's. but he ne was-able for he became
it aware. there after in the lent darkened the sun & the day.
about noontide day's. when men eat. that one lighted candles to
eat by . . . were men very amazed . . .
thereafter waxed violently much war between the king & Randolph
earl of chester (not) because he ne gave him all that he (could) demand
from-him. as he did all others. but ever the more he gave to-them. the
worse they were to-him. the earl held lincoln against the king &
took from-him all that he ought to have. & the king fared thither &
beseiged him & his brother William de Romare in the castle. &
the earl stole out & went after Robert earl of gloucester. &
brought him thither with great army. & fought violently on
Candlemass day against their lord. & captured him for his men
him betrayed & fled. & led him to Bristol & put there in
prison & in fetters. then was all England disturbed more than before
was. & all evil was in land . . .
Then went Eustace the king's son to France & took the king's
sister of France to wife. hoped to obtain normandy there-through.
but he sped little & by good right, for he was an evil man.
for where so he came he did more evil than good. he robbed the
lands & laid great taxes on. He brought his wife to
england. & put her in the castle in canterbury. Good woman
she was. but she had little bliss with him. & Christ ne wished
that he should long reign. & became dead & his mother both . . .

The vocabulary of Text 33 is listed in the *Word Book*.

The final paragraph of Text 33 is recorded on the cassette tape. Here is a broad phonetic transcription.

θaː fɛːrdə ɜstas θə kɪŋgəs sʊnə tɔː fraːns ənd naːm θə kɪŋgəs sʏstər ɔf fraːns tɔː wiːvə. weːndə tɔː bɪjætən nɔrmandɪ θæːrθʊrx. ɔk heː spɛdːə lɪtəl ənd bɛ goːde rɪçtə fɔr heː was aːn ʏvəl man. fɔr warəse heː coːm heː dɪdə maːr ʏvəl θanːə goːd. heː rɛːvədə θə laːndəs ənd læɪdə mɪtʃələ jeːldəs ɔn. heː brɔxtə hɪs wiːf tɔː ɛŋgləland. ənd dɪdə hir ɪn θə kastəl ɪn kantəbʏri. goːd wɪmːən ʃæː wæs. ɔk ʃæː hɛdːə lɪtəl blɪsːə mɪd hɪm. ənd kriːst nɛ wɔlsə θæt heː ʃʊldə laːŋgə riːksən. ənd wærd dɛːd ənd hɪs moːdər beɪən

5.3.1 *Loss of inflections*

The most important change is the beginning of the loss of most of the inflections of OE, mainly by their reduction in sound. This leads to a greater reliance on **word order**, and the more frequent use of **prepositions** to show the meanings that formerly might have been signalled by inflections. Consequently, the *Chronicle* text reads much more like MnE to us than the OE texts. There is also the beginning of the great influx of French words into the language.

Text 34 consists of three very short extracts from the *Peterborough Chronicle* annal for 1137. It is followed by a reconstructed version in West Saxon OE, so that you can study further evidence of the changes in the language.

Text 34 – *Peterborough Chronicle* for 1137, written *c.* 1154 (facsimile)

A note on the handwriting

Book-hand with the following features:

- 'continental' forms of ⟨g⟩, e.g. *king, hungær*;
- insular and continental forms of ⟨r⟩, cf. *ƿunder* and the '2-form' of ⟨r⟩ after ⟨o⟩ in *corn* and *fordon*;
- insular and continental forms of ⟨d⟩, cf. *land, dære* and *diden, sæden*, with both forms in *dædes*;
- mainly 'long s' ⟨ſ⟩, but two forms in *ſinnes*;
- ⟨ð⟩, ⟨þ⟩ and ⟨th⟩ used – ð for *ðæt, þolenden, erthe*;
- ⟨ƿ⟩ used for ⟨w⟩ – *ƿunder*, (but ⟨uu⟩ is written elsewhere in the MS);
- ⟨æ⟩ used for [ɛ] – *dædes, hungær*.

Ine cannei ne mai tellen alle þe
ƿunder ne alle þe pineſ ð hi diden ƿreccemen on þiſ land. 7 ð laſte
de þa .xıx. ƿintre ƿile Stephne ƿaſ king 7 æure it ƿaſ uuerſe 7
uuerſe.

Þa ƿaſ corn dære. 7 flec 7 cæſe 7 butere. for nan ne ƿæſ o þe land.
ƿreccemen ſturuen of hungær.

par ſæmetılede. þe erthe ne bar nan corn. for þe land paſ al
fordon. mıd ſuılce dædeſ. 7 hı ſæden openlıce ð xpıſt ſlep 7 hıſ ha
lechen. Suılc 7 mare þanne pe cunnen ſæın. pe þolenden .xıx. pıntre
for ure ſınnes.

I ne can ne ı ne maı tellen alle þe
punder ne alle þe pıneſ ð hı dıden preccemen on þıſ land. 7 ð laſte
de þa .xıx. pıntre pıle Stephne paſ kıng 7 æure ıt paſ uuerſe 7
uuerſe.

þa paſ corn dære. 7 flec 7 cæſe 7 butere. for nan ne pæſ o þe land.
preccemen ſturuen of hungær.

par ſæ me tılede. þe erthe ne bar nan corn. for þe land paſ al
fordon. mıd ſuılce dædeſ. 7 hı ſæden openlıce ð crıſt ſlep 7 hıſ ha
lechen. Suılc 7 mare þanne pe cunnen ſæın. pe þolenden .xıx. pıntre
for ure ſınnes.

Version in the former OE standard written form

ic ne cann ne ic ne mæg tellan ealle þa
wundor ne ealle þa pinas þe hie dydon wreccum mannum on þissum lande. 7 þæt læste
de þa .xix. wintra þa hwile þe Stephne cyning wæs 7 æfre hit wæs wyrsa 7
wyrsa.

þa wþs corn deore. 7 flesc 7 cese 7 butere. for nan ne wæs on þæm lande.
wrecce menn sturfon of hungre.

swa hæwr swa man tilode. seo eorþe ne bær nan corn. for þæt land wæs eall fordon. mid
swilcum dædum. 7 hie sædon openlice þæt crist slep 7 his ha
lgan. swilc 7 mare þanne we cunnon secgan. we þolodon .xix. wintra
for ure synna.

WW I ne can ne I ne may tell all the horrors ne all the pains that they caused
wretched-men in this land. & that lasted the 19 winters while Stephen was
king & ever it was worse & worse.

then was corn dear. & flesh & cheese & butter. for none ne was in the land.
Wretched-men died of hunger.

Where so one tilled. the earth ne bore no corn. for the land was all ruined.
with such deeds. & they said openly that Christ slept & his saints. Such &
more than we can say. we suffered 19 winters for our sins.

The vocabulary of Text 34 is listed in the *Word Book*.

Activity 5.2

Use the OE version to make a study of the changes that you can observe in the language. Look particularly at the following words or phrases:

OE	*Chronicle*	*OE*	*Chronicle*
NPs and PrepPs		**Verbs**	
ic	**I**	ic ne mæg tellen	**I ne mai tellen**
hit	**it**	hie dydon	**hi diden**
we	**we**	þæt læstede	**ðat lastede**
		Stephne wæs	**Stephne was**
hi/hie	**hi**	hit wæs	**it was**
man	**me**	corn wæs	**corn was**
		nan ne wæs	**nan ne wæs**
nan	**nan**	menn sturfon	**men sturuen**
nan corn	**nan corn**	man tilode	**me tilede**
ealle þa wundor	**alle þe wunder**	seo eorþe ne bær	**þe erþe ne bar**
ealle þa pinas	**alle þe pines**	þæt land wæs fordon	**þe land was fordon**
on þæm lande	**o þe land**	hie sædon	**hi sæden**
seo eorþe	**þe erþe**	Crist slep	**Crist slep**
þæt land	**þe land**	we cunnon secgan	**we cunnen sæin**
þa xix wintra	**þa xix wintre**	we þolodon	**we þolede**
on þissum lande	**on þis land**		
his halgan	**his halechen**		
for ure synna	**for ure sinnes**		
wreccum mannum	**wrecce men**		
wrecce men	**wrecce men**		
mid swilcum dædum	**mid suilce dædes**		
xix wintra	**xix wintre**		
cyning	**king**		
corn (deore)	**corn (dære)**		
flæsc/flesc	**flec**		
cyse/cese	**cæse**		
butere	**butere**		
Crist	**crist**		
of hungre	**of hunger**		

5.4 The book called *Ormulum*

Another early text dating from the late 12th century is an important source of information about the state of the language. It was written by a monk called Orm (a Danish name, as we have seen in section 3.4.1). He lived in northern Lincolnshire and wrote in an East Midland dialect of English like the *Peterborough Chronicle* continuations.

His object was to teach the Christian faith in English, and the verses were to be read aloud. So he devised his own system of spelling, in order to help a reader to pronounce the words properly. What is specially noticeable is the number of double consonant letters. He wanted his readers and listeners to distinguish clearly between long and short vowels in closed syllables (see section 5.4.2 following), because long or short vowels could mark differences in the meaning of words. So he wrote two consonant letters (*an bocstaff write twiȝȝess*) after the short vowels. Consequently he wanted any later copier of *Ormulum* to follow his spelling system exactly.

The following transcription of Orm's description of his book sets the text in its verse lines, which were not shown in this way in the manuscript (compare the facsimile of Text 36).

Text 35 – *Ormulum* (i)

þiss boc iss nemmned Orrmulum	this book is called Ormulum
forrþi þatt Orrm itt wrohhte...	because Orm it wrought (made)...
Icc hafe wennd inntill ennglissh.	I have turned into English
goddspelles hallȝhe lare.	(*the*) gospel's holy lore,
Affterr þatt little witt þatt me.	after that little wit that me
min Drihhtin hafeþþ lenedd...	my Lord has lent (=*granted*)...
annd wha-se wilenn shall þiss boc.	And whoever intend shall this book
efft oþerr siþe writenn.	again another time write,
himm bidde icc þat he't write rihht.	him ask I that he it copy right,
swa-summ þiss boc himm tæcheþþ.	in the same way (*that*) this book him teaches,
all þwerrt-ut affterr þatt itt iss.	entirely after (*the way*) that it is,
uppo þiss firrste bisne.	according to this first example,
wiþþ all swillc rime alls her iss sett.	with all such rhyme as here is set (*down*),
wiþþ all þe fele wordess.	with all the many words.
annd tatt he loke wel þatt he.	And (*I ask*) that he look well that he
an bocstaff write twiȝȝess.	a letter writes twice.
eȝȝwhær þær itt uppo þiss boc	Everywhere it in this book
iss writenn o þatt wise.	is written in that way.
loke he well þatt he't wrote swa.	(*Let him*) Look well that he it wrote so,
forr he ne maȝȝ nohht elless.	for he must not else (=*otherwise*)
onn Ennglissh writenn rihht te word.	in English write correctly the word.
þatt wite he wel to soþe.	That (*should*) know he well for sure.

📖 The vocabulary of Text 35 is listed in the *Word Book*.

Here is a broad phonetic transcription of Text 35, recorded on the cassette tape.

θɪs boːk ɪs nɛmnəd ɔrmʊluːm, fɔrðiːðat ɔrm ɪt wrɔxtə
ɪk haːvə wɛnd ɪntɪl ɛŋglɪʃ gɔdspɛləs halɣə laːrə
aftər θat lɪtlə wɪt θat mɛː miːn drɪçtɪn havɛθ leːnəd
and hwaːse wiːlən ʃal θɪs boːk ɛft oːðər siːðə wriːtən
hɪm bɪd ɪk θat heːt wriːtə rɪçt, swasʊm θɪs boːk hɪm tæːtʃɛθ
al θwɛrtuːt aftɛr θat ɪt ɪs ʊpoː θɪs fɪrstə biːznə
wɪθ al swɪlk riːm als heːr ɪs sɛt, wɪθ al θə feːlə woːrdɛs
and tat heː loːkə wɛl θat heː aːn boksaf wriːtə twijəs
ɛjhwær θæːr ɪt ʊpoː θɪs boːk ɪs wriːtən ɔ θat wiːzə.
loːk heː wɛl θat heːt wroːtə swaː, fɔr heː nə maj nɪçt ɛləs
ɔn ɛŋglɪʃ wriːtən rɪiçt tə woːrd, θat wiːt heː wɛl toː soːðə

There are fifteen syllables to every line, without exception, and the metre is absolutely regular. Single unstressed (x) and stressed (/) syllables alternate, always with an initial and final unstressed syllable. Here is the text set out in metrical form:

x / x / x / x / x / x / x / x

þiss **boc** iss **nemm** ned **Orr** mu **lum**. forr **þi** þatt **Orrm** itt **wrohh** te.
Icc /**ha**-fe /**wennd** inn/**till** Enng/**lissh**. godd/**spell**-es /**hall**-ȝhe /**la**-re.
Aff/**terr** þatt /**litt**-le /**witt** þatt /**me**. min/**Drihh**-tin /**ha**-feþþ /**le**-nedd.
Annd /**wha**-se /**wil**-enn /**shall** þiss /**boc**. efft /**o**-þerr /**si**-þe /**wri**-tenn.
Himm /**bidd**(e) icc /**þat** he't /**wri**-te /**rihht**. swa-/**summ** þiss /**boc** himm /**tæ**-cheþþ.
All /**þwerrt**-ut /**aff**-terr /**þatt** itt /**iss**. upp/**o** þiss /**firr**-ste /**bis**-ne.
Wiþþ/**all** swillc /**rim**(e) alls /**her** iss /**sett**. wiþþ/**all** þe /**fe**-le /**wor**-dess.
Annd /**tatt** he /**lo**-ke /**wel** þatt /**he**. an /**boc**-staff /**wri**-te /**twi**-ȝȝess.
Eȝȝ/**whær** þær /**itt** upp/**o** þiss /**boc**. iss /**wri**-tenn /**o** þatt /**wi**-se.
Lok(e)/**he** wel /**þatt** he't /**wro**-te /**swa**. forr /**he** ne /**ma**ȝȝ nohht /**ell**-ess.
Onn /**Enng**-lissh /**wri**-tenn /**rihht** te /**word**. þatt /**wit**(e) he /**wel** to /**so**-þe.

The stops in the manuscript of the text mark the end of each half-line and line of verse.

Orm's spelling is consistent, and it is an attempt to reform the system and relate each sound to a symbol. For example, he used three symbols to differentiate between the three sounds that the OE letter yogh ⟨ȝ⟩ had come to represent, [g], [j] and [x] .You will notice his use of ⟨wh⟩ for OE ⟨hw⟩, e.g. *wha-se*, *whas* for OE *hwa swa*, *hwæs* (MnE *whoso*, *whose*); and ⟨sh⟩ for ⟨sc⟩, e.g. *shall*, *Ennglissh* for *sceal*, *Englisc*.

5.4.1 *Orm's writing as evidence of language change in early ME*

Orm's 20,000-odd lines of verse are important evidence for some of the changes which had taken place in the language by the late 12th century in his part of the country, just over a hundred years after the Norman Conquest. His lines are, however, monotonous to read, since they are absolutely regular in metre. Students of literature do not place Orm high on their list, but for students of language his writing is invaluable.

The following facsimile is the Dedication that begins the book. It includes part of the extract already discussed,

Icc hafe wennd inntill Ennglissh.
Goddspelles hallȝhe lare.

Although the book is in verse, the lines are run together in order to fill all the space on the parchment.

Text 36 – *Ormulum* (ii) (facsimile)

A note on the handwriting

A very compressed book-hand:

- letter ⟨a⟩ is insular (cf. the earlier facsimiles of OE);
- insular ⟨ȝ⟩ is used for for [j] – e.g. *ȝet'* (*yet*);
- continental ⟨g⟩ – e.g. *godess* (*God's*);
- insular ⟨r⟩ e.g. *broþerr* except for small superscript form, e.g. *broþer^r*;
- continental ⟨f⟩, e.g. *flæshess*;
- long and round s – ⟨ſ⟩ and ⟨s⟩;
- thorn ⟨þ⟩ and wynn ⟨ƿ⟩ used, clearly differentiated, not ⟨th⟩ or ⟨w ~ uu⟩.

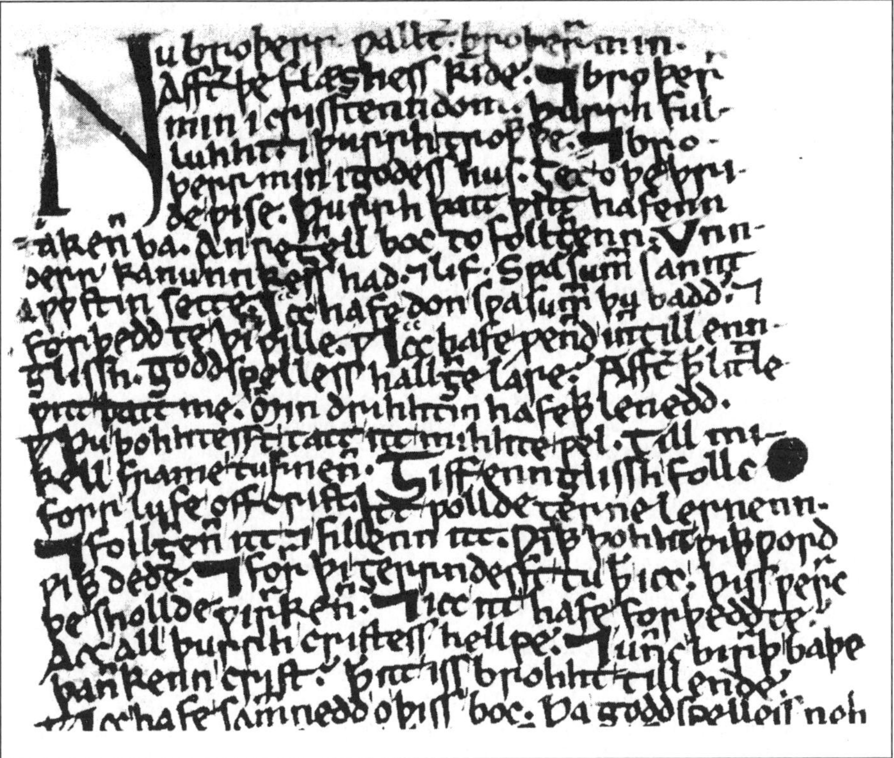

The following transcription reproduces the lineation of the text as written, with its abbreviations and with a few of the original letter forms.

Nu broþerr ƿalt^{r} · broþer^{r} mın ·
afft^{r} þe flæsheſſ kīde 7 broþer^{r}
mın ı crıſtenndom · þurrh fulluhht 7 þurrh trop^{p}e · 7 broþerr mın ı godeſſ huſ · ʒet^{t} o þe þrı-
de ƿıſe · þurrh þatt ƿıtt hafenn
taken^{n} ba · an reʒ^{h}ell boc to folʒ^{h}enn · Vnnderr kanunkeſſ had ·7 lıf · Spa ſum^{m} ſantt
appſtın ſette · Icc hafe don ſpa ſum^{m} þu badd · 7
forþedd te þı^{n} ƿılle · Icc hafe ƿen^{n}d intill ennglıſſh · goddſpelleſſ hallʒ^{h}e lare · Afft^{r} ꝥ lit^{t}le
ƿitt*tatt me · min drihhtin hafeþ^{þ} lenedd ·
Γ Þu þohteſſt tatt itt mihhte ƿel · till mikell frame tur^{r}nen^{n} · ʒiff ennglıſſh follc ●
forr lufe off crıſt · Itt ƿollde ʒerne lernenn ·
7 follʒ^{h}en^{n} ıtt 7 fıllenn ıtt · ƿıþ^{þ} þohht ƿıþ^{þ} ƿord
ƿıþ^{þ} dede · 7for^{r} þı ʒerrndeſſt tu ꝥ ıcc · þıſſ ƿer^{r}c
þe ſhollde ƿır^{r}ken^{n} · 7ıcc ıtt hafe forþedd te ·
acc all þurrh crıſteſſ hellpe · 7un^{n}c bır^{r}þ baþe
þan^{n}kenn crıſt · ꝥ ıtt ıſſ brohht tıll ende ·
Icc hafe ſam^{m}nedd o ıſſ boc · þa goddſpelleſſ neh
[*alle · þatt ſınndenn o þe meſſe boc ınn all þe ʒer att meſſe ·*]

* *Altered from* þatt.

If we write the text in its verse lines (14 syllables), with the words written out in full and using modern punctuation, the rhythmic pattern becomes clearer:

Nu broþerr walterr · broþerr min · afftr þe flæshess kinde ·
7 broþerr min i cristenndom · þurrh fulluhht 7 þurrh trowwþe ·
7 broþerr min i godess hus · ȝett o þe þride wise ·
þurrh þatt witt hafenn takenn ba · an reȝhell boc to follȝ^{he}nn ·
Vnnderr kanunkess had 7 lif · swa summ santt Awwstin sette ·
Icc hafe don swa summ þu badd · 7 forþedd te þin wille ·
Icc hafe wennd intill ennglish · goddspelless hallȝhe lare ·
Afftr þatt little witt tatt me · min drihhtin hafeþþ lenedd ·
Þu þohtesst tatt itt mihhte wel · till mikell frame turrnenn ·
ȝiff ennglissh follc forr lufe off crist · itt wollde ȝerne lernenn ·
7 follȝ^{h}en^{n} itt 7 fillenn itt · wiþþ þohht wiþþ word wiþþ dede ·
7 forrþi ȝerrndesst tu þatt icc · þiss werrc þe shollde wirrkenn ·
7 icc itt hafe forþedd te · acc all þurrh cristess hellpe ·
7 unnc birrþ baþe þann kenn crist · þatt itt iss brohht till ende ·
Icc hafe sammnedd o iss boc · þa goddspelless neh
[*alle · þatt sinndenn o þe messe boc · inn all þe ȝer att messe ·*]

WW

Now brother Walter · brother mine · after the flesh's nature ·
And brother mine in Christendom · through baptism and through faith ·
And brother mine in God's house · yet in the third way ·
Through that we have taken both · a rule book to follow ·
Under canon's order and life · as St Augustine set ·
I have done as you bade · and completed you your will ·
I have turned into English · (the) gospel's holy lore ·
After that little wit that me · my Lord has lent ·
You thought that it might well · to much benefit turn ·
If English folk for love of Christ · it would eagerly learn ·
And follow it and fulfil it · in thought in word in deed ·
And therefore desired you that I · this work (for) you should make ·
And I it have completed (for) you · but all through Christ's help ·
And us two (it) befits both (to) thank Christ · that it is brought to (an) end ·
I have gathered together in this book · almost all the gospels ·
[*That are in the mass-book · in all the year at Mass ·*]

Orm addresses Walter, who is his brother in three ways – firstly they are natural brothers with the same parents, 'affter þe flæshess kinde' – *after the nature of the flesh*; secondly, they are Christian brothers in faith who have both been baptised into the Church; thirdly, they are both monks, brothers in the monastery where they have taken vows to follow the rule.

The vocabulary of Text 36 is listed in the *Word Book*.

5.4.2 *Open and closed syllables*

If a syllable ends with a vowel (V) it is called an **open syllable**; if it ends with a consonant (C), it is a **closed syllable**. So one-syllable OE words like *he*, *swa*, *þe*, *hu*, *to*, *þa*, *ne* consist of open syllables, and those like *ðis*, *boc*, *is*, *þæt*, *wæs*, *gan*, of closed syllables.

In words of two or more syllables, if there was a sequence VCV, the consonant between the vowels was heard as part of the second syllable, as in *lare* (la-re), *ærende* (æ-rende), *siþe* (si-þe), *writen* (wri-ten), *oþer* (o-þer), *fela* (fe-la), *locaþ* (lo-caþ), *wise* (wi-se). In a sequence with two or more consonants, VCCV or VCCCV, the first consonant is heard as the end of the first syllable, which is therefore closed, as in *nemned* (nem-ned), *englisc* (en-glisc), *godspelles* (god-spel-les), *æfter* (æf-ter), *dryhten* (dryh-ten), *bocstæf* (boc-stæf).

5.4.3 *Orm's spelling*

Orm was anxious for his readers to read, and listeners to hear, the proper difference between long and short vowels (see section 3.1.3.1) in closed syllables, so he marked long vowels (or diphthongs) with a **single final consonant letter**, and short vowels with a **double final letter**. This is the reason why Orm wanted to be sure that his spelling was always copied correctly:

> Annd tatt he loke wel þatt he **an bocstaff write twiȝȝ ess**
> Eȝȝwhær þær itt uppo þiss boc iss writenn o þatt wise...

although there is no evidence that anyone ever did make another copy.

This is an example of using letters as **diacritics** in spelling. The doubled consonant letter did not mark the pronunciation of the consonant as double, but marked the preceding vowel as short. This convention has become a MnE spelling rule, e.g. *diner* and *dinner* are distinguished in spelling to mark the difference between the two vowels [aɪ] and [ɪ] by using ⟨-n-⟩ and ⟨-nn-⟩.

If a short vowel syllable was closed with two consonant sounds, as in the second syllable of ME *lauerd*/*laferd* (OE *hlaford* (*hla-ford*), then Orm doubled the first of the two letters – *laferrd*.

Activity 5.3

The following words are the OE originals of words from *Ormulum*, followed by Orm's spelling of the same words.

(i) Divide these OE words into syllables, and identify the syllables as open or closed.
(ii) Compare them with Orm's spelling and decide whether each word had a short or long vowel in its closed syllables. (There are also other changes in spelling and/or pronunciation which you could think about.)

OE spellings

ac	ceaster	heofones	þoht
anes	cild	hlæfdige	þus
and	eagum	milde	ure
anne	engel	modor	wencel
bliþe	findan	niht	wunden
boren	hæfdon	sum	wurdon

Orm's spellings

acc	chesstre	heffness	þohht
aness	child	laffdiȝ	þuss
annd	eȝhne	milde	ure
ænne	enngeln	moderr	wennchell
bliþe	findenn	nihht	wundenn
borenn	haffdenn	summ	wurrdenn

Orm's system of double consonant letters cannot be applied to open syllables, because they have no final consonants to be doubled. Open syllables, therefore, may be either long or short vowels in Orm's spelling, and are unmarked.

Activity 5.4

Explain why Orm spells an adverb meaning *together*, from OE *samen*, as *samenn*, but a related verb meaning *to gather*, from OE *samnian*, as *sammnenn*, when both ⟨a⟩ vowels are short.

5.4.4 *Evidence of changes in pronunciation*

The following list contains pairs of words, firstly in their OE spelling, and then in Orm's late 12th-century spelling. All these words had short vowels in closed syllables in OE.

ceaster/**chesstre**	heorte/**herrte**	þoht/**þohht**
cild/**child**	hlæfdige/**laffdiȝ**	**þus/þuss**
engel/**enngell**	milde/**milde**	wencel/**wennchell**
findan/**findenn**	niht/**nihht**	wunden/**wundenn**
hæfdon/**haffdenn**	sum/**summ**	wurdon/**wurrdenn**

Activity 5.5

Four of Orm's words in the list above have a single consonant letter marking a closed syllable: *child*, *findenn*, *milde* and *wundenn*. All the others have double letters, like *chesstre*, Orm was very consistent and accurate in his spelling, so

(i) What does the spelling tell us about the pronunciation of the vowels in these four words in Orm's Middle English? Are they long or short?
(ii) What do these words have in common that might help to explain the change?

Questions like these give you a glimpse into the problems which faced earlier students of the language. We have far too little evidence here to come to any conclusions, and must rely mostly on what generations of scholars have discovered for us, but it is a good idea to try to infer for ourselves, from historical texts, something about the changes that have taken place.

Activity 5.6

Divide the following words into two sets:

(i) those words spoken with long vowels in closed syllables in Orm's East Midland dialect (according to Orm's spelling); and
(ii) those spoken with short vowels in closed syllables.

Orm	*Meaning*	*OE source*
beldenn	encourage	beldan
birde	family	ge-byrd
childenn *fr* **child**	give birth	cild
erþe	earth	eorþe
faldess	(*sheep*)-folds	fald
goddspell	gospel	godspell
himmsellf	himself	him + self
hirdess	(*shep*)herds	hirde
kinde	kinsfolk	ge-cynd
land	land	land
mannkinn	mankind	manncynn
onn	in	on
reccnedd	reckoned = *paid*	gerecened
sammnenn	gather	samnian
þennkenn	think	þencan
wand	wound (*wrapped*)	wand (*past tense*)
wurrþenn	become	worden *fr* wurþan

5.4.5 *Commentary*

According to Orm's spelling, all the following words (taken from the preceding lists) have **long vowels**, because they are in closed syllables which he spells with a **single** consonant:

Orm	*Meaning*	*OE source*
beldenn	encourage	beldan
child	child	cild
childenn	give birth	(cild)
findenn	find	findan
kinde	kinsfolk	cynd
land	land	land/lond
milde	mild	milde
wand	wound (*past tense*)	wand/wond

It is known that in earlier OE these words had short vowels, therefore in Orm's dialect, by the later 12th century, they were being pronounced as long vowels, probably caused by the fact that [ld] and [nd] are **voiced** and relatively long, and so tend to lengthen the preceding vowel. This lengthening also occurred with other combinations of voiced consonants like [mb], but then shortened again. Sound changes in a language are seldom simple to describe and understand. They occur in some dialects and not in others, and even in some words and not in others, but here is a short list of words of this kind which have survived into MnE.

5.4.5.1 *Lengthening of OE short vowels before -ld, -nd and -mb*

Compare the present-day pronunciation of the following words, which all had short vowels in early OE, with their late OE and ME pronunciations

	Early OE	*Late OE*	*ME*	*MnE*
1	eald [æə]	āld [aː]	old [ɔː]	old [əʊ] RP
	camb [a]	cāmb [aː]	comb [ɔː]	comb [əʊ] RP
	ceald]cald [æə]]a]	cāld [aː]	cold [ɔː]	cold [əʊ] RP
	healdan [æə]	hāldan [aː]	holden [ɔː]	hold [əʊ] RP
	wamb [a]	wāmb [aː]	womb [ɔː]	womb [uː]
2	feld [e]	fēld [eː]	feld [eː]	field [iː]
	sceld [e]	scēld [eː]	scheld [eː]	shield [iː]
3	bindan [i]	bīndan [iː]	binden [iː]	bind [aɪ]
	blind [i]	blīnd [iː]	blind [iː]	blind [aɪ]
	cild [i]	cīld [iː]	child [iː]	child [aɪ]
	climban [i]	clīmban [iː]	climben [iː]	climb [aɪ]
	findan [i]	fīndan [iː]	finden [iː]	find [aɪ]
4	cynde [y]	cȳnde [yː]	kinde [iː]	kind [aɪ]
5	bunden [u]	būnden [uː]	bounden [uː]	bound [aʊ]
	funden]u]	fūnden [uː]	founden [uː]	found [aʊ]
	grund]u]	grūnd [uː]	ground [uː]	ground [aʊ]
	hund [u]	hūnd [uː]	hound [uː]	hound [aʊ]
	pund [u]	pūnd [uː]	pound [uː]	pound [aʊ]
	wunden [u]	wūnden [uː]	wounden [uː]	wound [aʊ]
				(*past participle of* to wind)

There are two points to notice:

- MnE pronunciation is different from ME. This is a result of the later sound changes to long vowels which began in the 15th century, called the Great Vowel Shift (see section 15.5).
- The vowels of the first group had also changed in quality, from [ɑː] to [ɔː].

If a third consonant followed [ld], [nd] or [mb] after a short vowel, the vowel did not lengthen. This explains our MnE pronunciation of *child* as [tʃaɪld], and *children* as [tʃɪldrən]. OE *cild* had a short vowel which became long. The ME long vowel later gradually changed from [iː] to [aɪ]. But the plural of *cild* was *cildru*, so the third [r] consonant prevented the [i] from lengthening.

Similarly, the vowel in OE *hund* (*hound*) became long, and later changed from [uː] to [aʊ], whereas the vowel of the numeral *hundred* stayed short:

5.4.5.2 *Shortening of long vowels before two consonants*

Whereas short vowels lengthened before [ld], [nd] or [mb] in late OE and early ME, long vowels which came before two consonants or a double consonant tended to become short. The clearest evidence comes from pairs of words which had the same long vowels in OE, but which are pronounced differently in MnE:

OE – all long vowels	***MnE***
blēde/blēdde	bleed/bled
fēde/fēdde	feed/fed
mēte/mētte	meet/met

Other pairs which show similar vowel changes are:

OE – all long vowels	***MnE***
cēpe/cēpte	keep/kept
clǣne (*adj*)/clǣnsian	clean/cleanse
hȳde/hȳdde	hide/hid
wīs/wīsdōm	wise/wisdom

The contrast of vowels in MnE can be explained only if the second of each pair became short, because the long vowels were all affected in the later Great Vowel Shift. The feature which they all had in common was the two following consonants. There were many other words whose long vowel in OE shortened before two consonants, but which cannot be illustrated by using minimal pairs, e.g. OE *dūst* is MnE *dust*, not **doust* (compare OE hūs, MnE *house*).

The same shortening took place in a first long syllable in words of three syllables, so that OE *sūþ* is MnE *south*, but *sūþerne* now has a short vowel in MnE *southern*; an OE *hāligbut* is today a *halibut*, not a **holybut*.

Activity 5.7

What might the pronunciation of the following MnE words have been if their long vowels in OE had not shortened in early ME?

OE	MnE	OE	MnE
blēdde	bled	hāligdæg	holiday
clǣnsian	cleanse	cēpte	kept
fēdde	fed	mētte	met
Hāligfeax	Halifax	ūttera	utter
hȳdde	hid	wīsdōm	wisdom

5.5 12th-century loan-words

5.5.1 *French*

We have seen in the course of these first five chapters that most of the English word-stock in the mid-11th century came from the Germanic language developed from those dialects spoken by the Angles, Saxons and Jutes in the 5th century. But there were also assimilated Latin words (see section 4.4), and a few early borrowings from French during the 10th and 11th centuries.

One of the results of the conquest of England by the Norman-French-speaking William I in 1066 was the absorption of hundreds of French words into English, and the loss of many OE words. The core vocabulary of present-day English has a large number of words that were originally French but which have been completely assimilated into English in their pronunciation, structure and spelling, as we shall see in the following chapters.

Three loan-words in Text 33 from the *Peterborough Chronicle* were from Anglo-Norman, the form of Old Northern French spoken by the Normans in England – *castel* (1075), *prisun* (1123), *uuerre* (1154). Written loan-words from the Anglo-Norman dialect of French during the 12th century that have survived include the following.

MnE	ONF	Date	MnE	ONF	Date
saint	*saint*	1122	peace	*pais*	1154
abbot	*abbat*	1123	rent	*rente*	1154
prison	*prisun*	1123	standard	*estandard*	1154
prior	*prior*	1123	treasure	*tresor*	1154
cardinal	*cardinal*	1125	charity	*charité*	1175
council	*cuncile*	1125	fruit	*fruit*	1175
clerk	*clerc*	1129	grace	*grace*	1175
duke	*duc*	1129	juggler	*jouglere*	1175
chancellor	*canceler*	1131	mercy	*merci*	1175
countess	*cuntesse*	1154	oil	*olie*	1175
war	*werre*	1154	palfrey	*palefrei*	1175
court	*cort/curt*	1154	paradise	*paradis*	1175
empress	*emperice*	1154	passion	*passiun*	1175
justice	*justice*	1154	prove	*prover*	1175
legate	*legate*	1154	sacrament	*sacrement*	1175
market	*market*	1154	table	*table*	1175
miracle	*miracle*	1154			

Activity 5.8

Is there any significance in the meanings of the earliest French words in the *Chronicle* and in the list which might explain why these particular words were adopted?

5.5.2 *Old Norse*

There is no evidence, other than in the surviving written manuscripts, of the number and distribution of loan-words taken from the ON dialects spoken by the Danes and Norwegians of the Danelaw, and their descendants after the 9th century. We have seen that dozens of OE and ON words were similar enough to be understood by speakers of both languages. We can imagine social situations in which OE and ON speakers regularly mixed, so that one language was infiltrated by the other. In the end, ON words were assimilated into English, with many now nonstandard and confined to the regional dialects in areas of the former Danelaw. Here is a selection of ON words recorded in writing during the 12th century.

sister	*systir*	1122	both	*baðar*	1175
tidings	*tiðendi*	1125	skill	*skil*	1175
die	*deyja*	1135	thrust	*ðrysta*	1175
low (*adj*)	*lagr*	1150	wing	*vængir*	1175
swain	*sveinn*	1150			

6. Early Middle English – 12th century

Standard English today is not a regional variety of English but linguists classify it as a dialect in the sense that it is one variety, among many, of the English language. It is the 'prestige dialect' of the language with a unique status (see section 1.1).

All present-day dialects of English in England, including Standard English, can be traced back to the dialects of the Middle English period (*c.* 1150–1450) in their pronunciation, vocabulary and grammar. Differences of spelling, vocabulary and grammar in the manuscripts are first-hand evidence of differences of usage and pronunciation, and of the changes that took place over the ME period.

We shall now look more closely at some of the evidence for change and development in the dialects of ME that a detailed analysis of a single short text provides.

6.1 Evidence of language change from late OE to early ME in Laȝamon's *Brut*

A chronicle history of Britain was written towards the end of the 12th century. The writer was called Laȝamon – 'Laȝamon wes ihoten' – and all we know about him is contained in the opening lines of the chronicle. He lived at *Ernleȝe* (now Areley Kings) in Worcestershire, 'at a noble church upon Severn's bank'. So we may assume that he was a priest and wrote in a West Midlands dialect.

He decided to write a history of the Britons and quotes three histories as his sources:

- the late 9th-century Old English translation of Bede's 8th-century Latin *Historia*;
- a Latin book by Albinus and Augustine; and
- Wace's French metrical *Roman de Brut*, finished in 1155, which was Laȝamon's principal source and expanded and edited by him.

The title *Brut* derives from the legendary story that Brutus, a great-grandson of the Trojan Aeneas (the hero of Virgil's Latin *Aeneid*), came to an uninhabited

Britain with a small company of the Trojans and founded Troynovant (New Troy – later known as Londinium, London). He was thus said to have been the first king of Britain.

Laȝamon's *Brut* includes the first telling in English of the story of King Arthur – later to be more fully told in Malory's 15th-century *Le Morte Darthur* (see Texts 95 and 96 in section 14.5) – and of King Lear. It was written in alliterative verse, but in a later popular style that is different from the classical OE poetry described in chapter 4. There is some rhyme and assonance, little poetic vocabulary, and sometimes the rhythm is counted in syllables rather than stresses. From our point of view, this an early transitional stage of verse-writing between OE poetry and Chaucer's regular metrical rhyming couplets in the later 14th century.

The following facsimile is of one of the two surviving manuscripts, copied fifty or more years after Laȝamon wrote it. (The first page of the manuscript is given on p. 100.)

A note on the handwriting

A style of book-hand called Gothic, with heavy, rounded strokes:

- long ⟨ſ⟩ and ⟨t⟩ ligatured (tied), e.g. *preoſt*, *ſtaþe*;
- round ⟨s⟩ generally word-final, otherwise long ⟨ſ⟩, but not consistently;
- 2-form of ⟨r⟩ after ⟨o⟩, e.g. *historia, weoren*;
- ⟨ð⟩ still used, e.g. *liðe*, *æðelen*;
- ⟨ȝ⟩ used for [j], e.g. *Laȝamon, ȝond* (*yon*) and ⟨g⟩ for [g], e.g. *engle* (*English*), *gon* (*go*);
- Insular ⟨d⟩, e.g. *leoden, drihten*.
- ⟨w⟩ used, not wynn ⟨ƿ⟩, and letter thorn written like wynn.

Activity 6.1

The words of the first paragraph of Text 37 are listed below in alphabetical order, together with their OE sources. Examine the spelling and structure of the words and identify any that you judge to be examples of:

(i) words that have not changed from their OE forms;
(ii) grammatical changes;
(iii) changes in spelling conventions that are not the result of changes in pronunciation;
(iv) words whose spelling suggests changes in pronunciation, for example:

  (a) the reduction to the mid-central vowel [ə] of the unstressed vowels of inflections,
  (b) the reduction or elision of vowels,
  (c) changes in consonants.

Text 37 – The opening of Laȝamon's *Brut* (facsimile)

Transcription of the first paragraph to line 13, column 2

Incipit hyſtoria Brutonum.

AN preoſt wes on
leoden: Laȝamon
wes ıhoten. **h**e we^{s}
leouenaðes ſone:
lıðe hım beo drıhtē.
he wonede at Ernleȝe: at æðelen
are chırechen. vppen ſeuarne ſta
þe: sel þar hım þuhte. on feſt
Radeſtone: þer he bock radde. **h**ıt
com hım on mode: ⁊ on hıs mern
þonke. þet he wolde of engle þa
æðelæn tellen. wat heo ıhoten
weoren ⁊ wonene heo comen.
þa englene londe: æreſt ahten.
æfter þan flode: þe from drıhtene
com. þe al her a quelde: quıc þat
he funde. buten noe ⁊ sem: japhet
⁊ cham. ⁊ heore four wıues: þe mıd
heom weren on archen. laȝamō
gon lıðen wıde ȝond þaſ leode
bı won þa æðela boc: þa he to bıſ
ne nom. **h**e nom þa englıſca boc:
þa makede seınt Beda. an oþer he
nom on latın: þe makede seınte
albın. ⁊ þe feıre auſtın: þe fulluht
broute hıder ın. Boc he nom þe
þrıdde: leıde þer amıdden. þa ma
kede a frenchıs clerc: wace wes
ıhoten. þe wel couþe wrıten. ⁊
he hoe ȝef þare æþelen alıenor
þe wes henrıes quene: þes heȝe^{s}
kınges. Laȝamon leıde þeos boc:
⁊ þa leaf wende.he heom leoflıche

(*2nd column*)

be heold: lıþe hım beo drıhten . fe
þeren he nom mıd fıngren: fıe
de on boc-felle. ⁊ þa ſoþe word: ſet
te togadere. ⁊ þa þre boc: þrumde
to ane. Nu bıddeð laȝamon alcne
æðele mon. for þene almıtē godd:
þet þeoſ boc rede. ⁊ leornıa þeos ru
nan: þ^{t} he þeos ſoðfeſte word: ſeg
ge to ſumne. for hıs fader ſaule:
þa hıne forð brouhte. ⁊ for hıs mo
der ſaule: þa hıne to monne ıber.
⁊ for hıs awene ſaule: þat hıre
þe ſelre beo. ameN.

Translation

The lines in the following transcription are set out as verse, not as in the manuscript, and abbreviations are filled out.

ME	WW
Incipit hystoria Brutonum.	Here begins the history of Britain
AN preost wes on leoden: Laȝamon wes ihoten.	(There) was a priest in (the) land, Laȝamon (who) was named;
he wes leouenaðes sone: liðe him beo drihten.	he was Leovenath's son, gracious to him be (the) Lord
he wonede at Ernleȝe: at æðelen are chirechen.	he dwelt at Areley, at a noble church
vppen seuarne staþe: sel þar him þuhte.	upon Severn's bank – good there (to) him (it) seemed –
on fest Radestone: þer he bock radde.	near Radestone, where he books read.
hit com him on mode: 7 on his mern . þonke	It came to him in mind, and in his chief thought,
þet he wolde of engle þa æðelæn tellen.	that he would (of' the) English the noble deeds tell –
wat heo ihoten weoren 7 wonene heo comen.	what they named were, and whence they came,
þa englene londe: ærest ahten.	who (the) English land first possessed,
æfter þan flode: þe from drihtene com.	after the flood that from (the) Lord came,
þe al her a quelde: quic þat he funde.	that all here destroyed alive that he found,
buten noe 7 sem: japhet 7 cham.	except Noah and Shem, Japhet and Ham,
7 heore four wiues: þe mid heom weren on archen.	and their four wives, who with them were in (the) ark.
laȝamon gon liðen wide ȝond þas leode	Laȝamon began to journey wide over this land,
bi won þa æðela boc: þa he to bisne nom.	he obtained the noble books which he for authority took.
he nom þa englisca boc: þa makede seint Beda.	He took the English book that made saint Bede;
an oþer he nom on latin: þe makede seinte albin.	another he took in Latin, that made Saint Albin
7 þe feire austin: þe fulluht broute hider in.	and the fair Austin, who baptism brought hither in;
boc he nom þe þridde: leide þer amidden.	(a) book he took the third, laid there in (the) midst,
þa makede a frenchis clerc: wace wes ihoten.	that made a French clerk, (who) Wace was called,
þe wel coue writen. 7 he hoe ȝef þare æþelen alienor	who well could write; and he it gave to the noble Eleanor,
þe wes henries quene: þes heȝes kinges.	who was Henry's queen the high King.
Laȝamon leide þeos boc: 7 þa leaf wende.	Laȝamon laid (down) these books, and the leaves turned (over)
he heom leofliche be heold: liþe him beo drihten.	he them lovingly beheld – merciful (to) him be (the) Lord –
feþeren he nom mid fingren: fiede on boc-felle.	pens he took with fingers, wrote on parchment,
7 þa soþe word: sette togadere.	and the true words set together,
7 þa þre boc: þrumde to ane.	and the three books compressed into one.
Nu biddeð laȝamon alcne æðele mon. for þene almiten godd:	Now prayeth Laȝamon each good man, for the Almighty God,
þet þeos boc rede. 7 leornia þeos runan:	that this book shall read and leam this counsel,
þat he þeos soðfeste word: scgge to sumne.	that he these true words say together,
for his fader saule: þa hine forð brouhte.	for his father's soul, who brought him forth,
7 for his moder saule: þa hine to monne iber.	and for his mother's soul, who him to man bore,
7 for his awene saule: þat hire þe selre beo. amen.	and for his own soul, that it the better be. Amen.

In the OE column, words are given inflections corresponding to those of the ME words in the *Brut* text. Words in brackets are the base forms of nouns and adjectives or the infinitives of verbs.

A transcription and translation of the rest of the facsimile are in the *Text Commentary Book*.

Laȝamon	***Old English***	***Laȝamon***	***Old English***
a quelde	acwealde (acwellan)	hine	hine
æfter	æfter	hoe	hi/hie/heo (*feminine acc*)
ærest	ærest	iber	ȝebær (ȝeberan)
æþelen	æþelan	ihoten	ȝehaten
æðelen + æðelæn	æþelum	leaf	leaf
ahte/ahten	ahte/ahton (aȝan)	leide	ȝeleȝd (lecȝan)
alcne (alc)	æȝhwylcne (æȝhwylc)	leoden	leodum
almiten	ælmihtiȝan (ælmihtiȝ)	leofliche	leoflice
amidden	onmiddan	leornia	leorna (leornian)
ane	anne (an)	leouenaðes	Leofnoþes
archen	OF arche	liþe/liðe	liþe
are = anre	anre (an = *def art*)	liðen	liþan
awene	aȝene (aȝen)	lond/londe	land/lond
beo	beo (beon)	makede	macode (macian)
bi heold	beheold (beheoldan)	mern	mæran
bi won	be + wan (winnan)	mid	mid
biddeð	biddað (biddan)	mode	mode (mod)
bisne	bisne (bisen)	moder	modor
boc	boc (*pl* bec)	mon/monne	mann/monn
boc-felle	boc + fell	nom	nam (niman)
bock	boc	on fest	on fæst
boten/buten	butan	oþer	oþer
brouhte	broȝhte (brinȝan)	preost	preost
broute	broȝhte (brinȝan)	quene	cwene (cwen)
chirechen	cyrican (*dative*)	quic	cwic
clerc	clerc	radde	ræd (rædan)
com/comen	com/comon (cuman)	rede	rætt (rædan)
couþe	cuþe (cunnan)	runan	runan (run)
drihten/drihtene	dryhten	saule	sawol
engle	enȝle	seið	sæȝþ (secȝan)
englene	enȝlena	sel/selre	sel/selra
fader	fæder	set	sette (settan)
feire	fæȝer	sone	sunu
feþeren	feþera (feþer)	soþe	soþ
fiede	feȝde (feȝan)	soðfeste	soþfæst
fingren	finȝrum (finȝer)	staþe	stæþe (stæþ)
flode	flode (flod)	tellen	tellan
forð	forþ	to sumne	to sumne (sum)
four	feower	togadere	toȝædere
frenchis	frencisc	þa	þa
funde	fand (findan, *pp funden*)	þan	þam
gon	ȝan	þare	þære
heo	hi/hie/heo	þas	þis
heom	him/heom	þat	þæt
heore	hire/hira/heora	þe	þe
her	her	þene	þone
heȝe[s]	hean (heah)	þeos	þas

Laȝamon	Old English	Laȝamon	Old English
þer	þær	wide	wide
þet	þæt	wif/wiues	wif/wifa
þonke	þanc/þonc	wolde	wolde
þridde	þridda	wonede	wunode (wunian)
þuhte	þuhte (þyncan)	wonene	hwanon/hwonon
vppen	uppon	word	word
wat	hwæt	writen	writan
wende	wende (wendan)	ȝef	ȝeaf (ȝiefan)
weoren/weren	wæron	ȝond	ȝeond
wes	wæs		

The aim of this chapter is to assemble evidence for changes and developments in spelling, pronunciation and grammar in early ME that can be found by using as data these words from the first paragraph of Text 37.

6.1.1 Vocabulary that has not changed from OE

Most of the following words are unchanged from OE, except for the pronouns *þa*, *þas*, *þe*, *þene*, *þeos*, *þet*, normally unstressed and so subject to the irregular spelling of vowels that is evidence for reduction to [ə].

(*The vocabulary discussed in the following sections is listed in three columns: 1 OE source, 2 Laȝamon, 3 MnE, with the Laȝamon vocabulary in bold type.*)

OE source	Laȝamon	MnE	OE source	Laȝamon	MnE
æfter	**æfter**	*after*	liþe	**liþe/liðe**	*= gracious*
ærest	**ærest**	*= first*	mid	**mid**	*= with*
anne (an)	**ane**	*one*	mode (mod)	**mode**	*= mind*
OF arche	**archen**	*ark*	oþer	**oþer**	*other*
anre (*indefinite art*)	**are = anre**	*= a, an*	preost	**preost**	*priest*
beo (beon)	**beo**	*be*	runan (run)	**runan**	*runes = writings*
beheold (beheoldan)	**bi heold**	*beheld*	sette (settan)	**set**	*set = wrote down*
			soþ	**soþe**	*sooth = true*
bisne (bisen)	**bisne**	*= as an example*	to sumne (sum)	**to sumne**	*= together*
boc + fell	**boc-felle**	*book-skin = parchment*	þa	**þa**	*then, when, etc.*
			þis	**þas**	*= this*
boc (*pl* bec)	**boc**	*book/books*	þe	**þe**	*that (relative pn)*
clerc	**clerc**	*cleric = scholar*	þone	**þene**	*the*
flode (flod)	**flode**	*flood*	þas	**þeos**	*these*
forþ	**forð**	*forth*	þæt	**þet**	*that*
fulluht	**fulluht**	*= baptism*	(?)	**þrumde**	*= compressed*
hi/hie/heo	**heo**	*= they*	þuhte (þyncan)	**þuhte**	*= seemed*
him/heom	**heom**	*= them*	wende (wendan)	**wende**	*= turned*
her	**her**	*here*	wide	**wide**	*widely*
hine	**hine**	*him (accusative)*	wolde	**wolde**	*would = wished*
hi/hie/heo (*fem*)	**hoe**	*= it*	word	**word**	*words*
leaf	**leaf**	*leaves*			

6.1.2 *Changes in the grammar*

6.1.2.1 *Loss of prefixes and suffixes*

Change in pronunciation may also produce change in the grammar. The comparative lack of grammatical inflections in present-day English is partly the result of the phonetic reduction of unstressed vowels described in section 5.3.1 which eventually led to the loss of suffixes. For example:

ʒehaten	**ihoten**	= *called*
ʒebær (ʒebcran)	**iber**	*bore*
ʒeleʒd (lecʒan)	**leide**	*laid*

The ⟨ʒe-⟩ prefix marking the past participle is reduced to ⟨i⟩ in *ihoten* and *iber*, and is elided in *leide*.

But there are some grammatical changes that are caused by other processes.

Regularisation of plural suffixes

For example, in OE, nouns formed their plurals in different ways. The following nouns are paired in their singular/plural forms:

OE	*MnE*
cyning/cyningas	king/kings
scip/scipu	ship/ships
cild/cildru	child/children
land/land	land/lands
andswaru/andswara	answer/answers
nama/naman	name/names
gos/ges	goose/geese

OE plurals were marked with a variety of different inflections, ⟨-as, -u, -ru, -a, -an⟩, or with a zero inflection, or by a change of vowel. Today almost all plural nouns take the ⟨-s⟩ suffix, from the OE ⟨-as⟩. A few take ⟨en⟩, from the very common OE ⟨-an⟩ plurals, and a small set, including *goose/geese*, are irregular, where a change of vowel signals plural number.

The OE plural of *cild* was *cildru*, which became ME *childre* or *childer*. In one dialect *childer* was given an additional ⟨-en⟩ suffix – *childeren* – which has become the Standard English *children*.

This historical process of 'making regular' – reducing a variety of forms to one – is called **regularisation**, and can be seen in several other features of the development of English. It proceeds at variable rates of change within different dialects of a language. The two changed plurals in our data are evidence of a stage in the development of regular ⟨s/-es⟩ and ⟨-en⟩ plurals in the West Midland dialect:

⟨-en⟩ *plural suffix*

feþera (feþer)	**feþeren**	*feathers = pens*

⟨-es⟩ *plural suffix*

wifa	**wiues**	*wives*

There are two other examples of regularisation. The first also shows that adjectives were still inflected to agree with their head nouns in this late 12th century text,

⟨-es⟩ *inflection*

hean (heah)	**heȝe**[s]	*high, noble*

The ⟨-es⟩ suffix marks agreement with the possessive noun *henries* in the line

þe wes henries quene: þes heȝes kinges.

Vowels of strong verbs

The second example shows how the vowels of strong verbs (see section 4.4.3) came to be interchanged,

fand (findan, *pp funden*)	**funde**	*found*

The vowel [u] of OE past participle *funden* is here used for the ME past tense, *funde*, not OE *fande*. The vowels of strong verbs interchanged in the dialects of ME, and continue to do so in present-day dialects as, for example, when *come* is used for the past tense – *I come home yesterday* instead of Standard English *came*.

6.1.3 *Changes in spelling*

6.1.3.1 *French spelling conventions*

The usage of French scribes can be seen in the introduction of certain French spelling conventions into English.

⟨ch⟩ replaces OE ⟨c⟩ for [tʃ] & ⟨k⟩ or ⟨ck⟩ for [k]

The digraph ⟨ch⟩ was a very useful convention taken from Anglo-Norman. In OE, letter ⟨c⟩ clearly represented [k] in words like *camp*, *candel*, *cocc*, *cot* and *cuppe* – that is, before back vowels. But it had come to be pronounced [tʃ] before front vowels, as in *cese* and *cild* (*cheese*, *child*). So using ⟨ch⟩ and ⟨k⟩ or ⟨ck⟩ helped to clarify the ambiguous OE letter ⟨c⟩.

cyrican (*dative*)	**chirechen**	*church*
frencisc	**frenchis**	*French*
leoflice	**leofliche**	*= lovingly*

macode (macian)	**makede**	*made*
boc	**bock**	*book*

⟨qu⟩ replaces OE ⟨cw⟩

There were not many OE words beginning with ⟨cw⟩, and the French ⟨qu⟩ eventually replaced the OE. *Quake*, *quell*, *queen*, *quick*, from OE *cwacian*, *cwellan*, *cwen*, *cwic*, are surviving reflexes. Two of them are in Text 37:

cwene (cwen)	**quene**	*queen*
cwic	**quic**	*quick = alive*

⟨ou⟩ replaces OE ⟨u⟩

The use of ⟨ou⟩ for the long vowel [uː] spelt ⟨u⟩ in OE was French in origin. The spelling *couþe* in Text 37 is an early example of a change that was established over the next two centuries. In early ME letter ⟨u⟩ was used for:

- back vowels [uː] (long) and [ʊ] (short) – *hus*, *tunge* (MnE *house*, *tongue*);
- the front vowel [y] in South West dialects, *hull* (MnE *hill*);
- the consonant [v], because letters ⟨u⟩ and ⟨v⟩ were variants of the same letter until the 17th century and used both for the vowel [u] and the consonant [v] – *uertu* (*virtue*);
- the consonant [w] in the form ⟨uu⟩, and also in the new spelling ⟨qu⟩ for ⟨cw⟩.

And the ME convention of marking a long vowel by doubling the letter (e.g. *estaat*, *theef*, *goos*) would mean that ⟨uu⟩ as a long vowel would have been confused with [w] [uv] and [vu]. So the adoption of French ⟨ou⟩ (*mouse*, *out*) or its alternative form ⟨ow⟩ as in *cow*, *now*, was practical and useful:

cuþe (cunnan)	**couþe**	= *knew* (*how to*)

6.1.3.2 *The influence of Latin spelling*

Because so much copying by scribes was from Latin, the spelling of Latin also had some effects on the spellings of ME.

Letter ⟨o⟩ for [ʊ]

The short vowel [ʊ] in OE words like *cuman*, *sum*, *munuc*, *sunu*, *wulf* came to be spelt with letter ⟨o⟩, which has survived into MnE spelling – *come*, *some*, *monk*, *son*, *wolf*. Letter ⟨u⟩ in bookhand writing could be confused with the 'minim' letters ⟨n⟩ and ⟨m⟩, as the following facsimile shows, and the letter ⟨o⟩ was clearer to read.

dū sperauimus in te.
In te domine spera
ui non confundar in
eternū

D eus in ad
iutorium
meum in
tende Domine ad adiu-

There is one example of the spelling ⟨o⟩ for ⟨u⟩ in Text 37:

sunu	**sone**	*son*

6.1.3.3 *Other changes in spelling*

⟨a⟩ replaces ⟨æ⟩

The useful OE letter ⟨æ⟩, which distinguished the front vowel [æ] from the back vowel [ɑ], ceased to be used in ME writing There were two linked reasons for the loss of the letter. Firstly it was not used in French spelling, and was one of the casualties of the changes brought about in the aftermath of the Norman Conquest. Secondly the sound of the long vowel [æː] shifted towards [ɛː], and came to be spelt ⟨e⟩. (This is a simplified explanation for a complex area of sound change.)

Some examples of OE words with short [æ] which were spelt with ⟨a⟩ in ME are, *æfter*, *æsc*, *cræft*, *græs*, which became *after*, *ash*, *craft*, *grass*. The following examples are from Text 37:

æʒhwylcne (æʒhwylc)	**alcne (alc)**	*each*
ælmihtiʒan (ælmihtiʒ)	**almiten**	*almighty*
fæder	**fader**	*father's (possessive)*
ræd (rædan)	**radde**	*read (past tense)*
stæþe (stæþ)	**staþe**	*= bank*
toʒædere	**togadere**	*together*
þære	**þare**	*= the*
þæt	**þat**	*that*

New letter ⟨g⟩ introduced

The 'open' form of OE letter yogh, ⟨ʒ⟩ belongs to the 'insular script' used in writing up to the 12th century. In OE, it had come to represent three sounds, according to its environment in a word – [g], [j] and [ɣ]. Text 37 shows how the 'carolingian' letter ⟨g⟩ was introduced for [g], while letter ⟨ʒ⟩ represented [j].

enʒle	**engle**	= *the English*
enʒlena	**englene**	= *of the English*
ʒod	**godd**	*God*
ʒeond	**ʒond**	= *throughout*

Variant spellings for [ʃ]

The digraph ⟨sc⟩ was pronounced [sk] in early OE, but changed to [ʃ]. It was not ambiguous like ⟨c⟩ because there were no late OE words pronounced with [sk]. But the influence of Old Norse words with ⟨sk⟩ (see section 3.4.1) led to a spelling change, with several letters or digraphs for [ʃ]:

- ⟨sc⟩ became rare after the 12th century. As the sound [ʃ] did not exist in early OF, ME texts written by French-educated scribes show a wide variety of attempts to find a symbol for it.
- ⟨s⟩ was used in the 12th & 13th centuries initially and finally, as in the final letter of the single example in Text 37,

  frencisc **frenchis** *French*

- ⟨ss⟩ was more frequent than ⟨s⟩ in all positions.
- ⟨sch⟩ was the commonest form from the end of the 12th century to the end of the 14th century (end of the 16th century in the North).
- ⟨ssh⟩ was common from the 13th to the 16th century in medial and final positions.
- ⟨sh⟩ (perhaps a simplification of ⟨sch⟩) is regularly used in the *Ormulum* (see section 5.4). It is the usual symbol in the London documents of the 14th century and in Chaucer, and from the time of Caxton onwards (*c*. 1480) it has been the established symbol for [ʃ] in all words except those like *machine*, *schedule*, *Asia* and words ending in *-tion*, etc., which are spelt unphonetically in order not to lose the evidence of their derivation.

The *OED* lists these variant spellings for *shield*, including initial ⟨ch⟩, from OE to MnE:

scild scyld sceld
seld sseld sheld cheld
scheld sceild scheeld cheeld schuld
scelde schulde schylde shilde
schelde sheeld
schield childe scheild shild shylde sheelde
schielde sheild
shield

⟨gg⟩ replaces ⟨cʒ⟩

The single example in Text 37 shows ⟨gge⟩ replacing OE⟨cʒ⟩ for [dʒ], as in *hegge* (*hedge*). The spelling ⟨dge⟩ was introduced in the 15th century.

secʒe (secʒan)	**segge**	= *say*

6.1.4 *Changes in pronunciation*

6.1.4.1 *Reduction of unstressed vowels*

We can now apply the same methods of observation and description that began in section 4.4.4 and that were continued throughout chapter 5. The phonetic 'reduction' of vowels in unstressed syllables is so normal today that the mid-central vowel *schwa*, [ə] is the commonest vowel in speech. In the late OE and early ME texts we are studying, we can see the change recorded. We assume that the vowels in OE suffixes originally spelt *-on*, *-an*, *-am*, *-um*, *-a*, *-u* and so on, were originally pronounced fully as [ɔ], [a] or [ʊ], and that when we find them spelt inconsistently or with ⟨e⟩, then a change has taken place. Here is evidence from the opening of the *Brut*.

⟨a⟩ ⇒ ⟨e⟩ = pronunciation [ə]

biddað (biddan)	**biddeð**	= *prays*
hire/hira/heora	**heore**	= *their*
sel/selra	**sel/selre**	= *good/better*
þridda	**þridde**	*third*

⟨or⟩ ⇒ ⟨er⟩ = pronunciation [ɔr] [ər]

modor	**moder**	= *mother's*

⟨u⟩ ⇒ ⟨e⟩ = pronunciation [ʊ] ⇒ [ə]

sunu	**sone**	*son*

⟨an⟩ ⇒ ⟨en⟩ = pronunciation [ən]

æþelan	**æþelen**	= *noble, excellent*
onmiddan	**amidden**	= *in the midst*
butan	**boten/buten**	*but* = *except*
cyrican (*dative*)	**chirechen**	*church*
liþan	**liðen**	= *go, journey*
tellan	**tellen**	*tel*
writan	**writen**	*write*

⟨an⟩ ⇒ ⟨n⟩ = elision of unstressed vowel

mæran	**mern**	= *splendid, chief*

⟨-on⟩ ⇒ ⟨en⟩ = pronunciation [ən]

ahte/ahton (aʒan)	**ahte/ahten**	= *owned, possessed*
com/comon (cuman)	**com/comen**	*came*
uppon	**vppen**	*upon*

⟨-um⟩ ⇒ ⟨-en⟩ = pronunciation [ən]

æþelum	**æþelen** **æðelæn**	= *noble, excellent*
finʒrum (finʒer)	**fingren**	*fingers*
leodum	**leoden**	= *country, nation*

⟨-ode⟩ ⇒ ⟨-ede⟩ = pronunciation [ədə]

macode (macian)	**makede**	*made*
wunode (wunian)	**wonede**	= *dwelt, lived*

6.1.4.2 *Other reductions and elisions*

[ɛj] ⇒ [ɛɪ] ⇒ [ɪɛ]

feʒde (feʒan)	**fiede**	= *wrote*

The transposition of the two vowels is an example of *metathesis* (see section 4.4.4).

OE æʒhwylcne [æjhwʏlknə] ⇒ [ælknə]

æʒhwylcne (æʒhwylc)	**alcne (alc)**	*each*

6.1.4.3 *Formation of new diphthongs*

These examples in Text 37 show the beginnings of the establishment of new diphthongs in ME, the semi-vowels [w] and [j] tending to become the vowels [ʊ] and [ɪ].

[aw] ⇒ [aʊ]

sawol	**saule**	*soul*

[ɛj] ⇒ [ɛɪ]

ʒeleʒd (lecʒan)	**leide**	*laid*

[æj] ⇒ [ɛɪ]

fæʒer	**feire**	*fair*
sæʒþ (secʒan)	**seið**	***says***

[aɣ] ⇒ [aw] (= first stage of diphthongisation)

aʒene (aʒen)	**awene**	*own*

6.1.4.4 *Long vowel [æː] ⇒ [ɛː]*

ʒebær (ʒeberan)	**iber**	*bore*
mæran	**mern**	*= splendid, chief*
ræde (rædan)	**rede**	*reads (present tense)*
wæron	**weoren/weren**	*were*
þær	**þer**	*there*

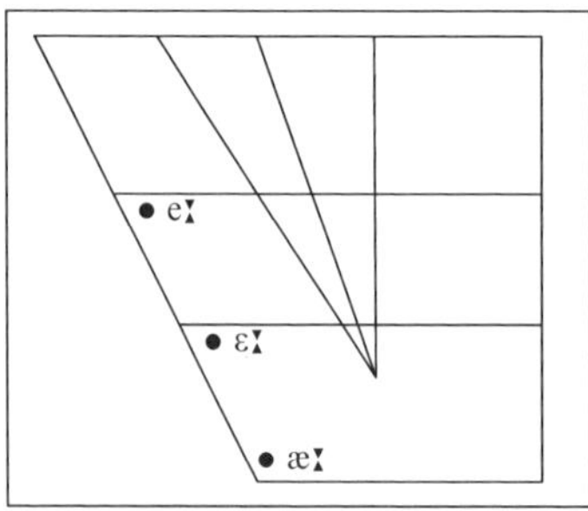

Vowel chart 4 [æː] to [eː]

The development of this vowel will not be discussed in detail here. Briefly, there were two sources of the long OE vowel [æː], and different pronunciations in OE dialects. One tended to develop into a half-close vowel [eː], and the other into a half-open vowel [ɛː], and both were spelt in ME with letter ⟨e⟩.

The difference between these two pronunciations of ⟨e⟩ is not contrastive in MnE RP, and is, very roughly, similar to the pronunciation of *get* and the Northern pronunciation of *gate* with a single vowel [geːt]. But the two contrastive vowels continued through ME into the 17th century. An attempt in the 16th century to spell the close vowel ⟨ee⟩ and the open vowel ⟨ea⟩ was made, but was not applied consistently.

6.1.4.5 *Smoothing of OE diphthongs*

All four OE diphthongs, long and short vowels spelt ⟨ea⟩ and ⟨eo⟩ were 'smoothed' – that is, they became single vowels – during the late OE. Text 37 has only two examples, the long [ɛːə] of *geaf* and short [æə] of *acwealde*.

OE diphthong [ɛːə] smoothed to [ɛː]

ʒeaf (ʒiefan)	**ʒef**	*gave*
acwealde (acwellan)	**a quelde**	*= destroyed*

Here is a summary of the smoothing of the OE diphthongs (the examples are not from the *Brut*).

- **OE short ⟨ea⟩.** The short diphthong pronounced [æə], became [æ], and so 'fell together' or merged with OE [æ]. Therefore it also became [a] in early ME, for example (not in Text 37):

OE	*ME*	*MnE*
heard	**hard**	*hard*
scearp	**scharp**	*sharp*

- **OE long ⟨ea⟩.** The long diphthong pronounced [ɛːə] or [æːə] fell together with [æː] and so came to be spelt ⟨e⟩ and pronounced either [ɛː] or [eː]. Together with other later changes, OE [æː] words have a variety of pronunciations in their MnE reflexes, for example (not in Text 37),

OE	*ME*	*MnE*		*OE*	*ME*	*MnE*	
beam	**bem**	*beam*	[iː]	great	**gret**	*great*	[ɛɪ]
bread	**bred**	*bread*	[ɛ]	heafod	**heved/hed**	*head*	[ɛ]
deaf	**def**	*deaf*	[ɛ]	hleapan	**lepen**	*leap*	[iː]
deaw	**dew**	*dew*	[juː]	read	**red**	*read*	[iː]
dream	**drem**	*dream*	[iː]	sceap	**schep**	*sheep*	[iː]
eage	**eie**	*eye*	[aɪ]	sceaþ	**schethe**	*sheath*	[iː]
eare	**ere**	*ear*	[ɪə]	slean	**sle**	*slay*	[ɛɪ]
feawe	**fewe**	*few*	[juː]	stream	**strem**	*stream*	[iː]

- **OE short ⟨eo⟩.** The short OE diphthong [eə] was smoothed and then fell together with the short vowel [e].
- **OE long ⟨eo⟩.** The long OE diphthong [eːə] was smoothed and fell together with the long close [eː] vowel or sometimes with [ɔː], depending upon which of the two vowels of the OE diphthong was more prominent. So that the MnE reflex of *ceosan* is *choose*, but the reflex of *freosan* is *freeze*.

[ɛːəw] ⇒ [uː]

feower	**four**	*four*

The different development of long ⟨eo⟩ in OE *feower* was conditioned by the [w] following the vowel. It had the effect of smoothing the long diphthong [eːə] to the close back vowel [uː].

6.1.4.6 *Shifting of OE [y] and [yː]*

The OE short and long vowels were high, rounded front vowels, now heard only in a few regional accents. During the ME period they changed, but at different times and in different ways in the dialects. The result is complex, either

(i) they became unrounded, and were pronounced [ɪ] and [iː] (close front vowels) (*Northern and East Midland dialects*); or
(ii) they became unrounded and shifted to [e] and [eː] (half close front vowels) (*Southern and South East dialects*); or
(iii) at first they remained as [y] and [yː], (close rounded front vowels) but as a result of the influence of French spelling were spelt ⟨u⟩. Then they retracted and were pronounced [ʊ] and [uː] (close rounded back vowels) (*West Midland and South West*).

Here are a few examples (not in Text 37). Notice how *busy* and *bury* today have the West Midland and South West spelling, but *busy* has the Northern and *bury* the Southern pronunciation – good examples of the irrational side of present-day English spelling.

OE short vowel /y/	***Some ME spellings***
byrigean	*bury/biry/bery*
bysig	*bisy/besy/busy*
cyssan	*kissen/kessen/kussen*

OE long vowel /y:/	***Some ME spellings***
hydan	*hiden/heden/huden/huiden*
hyran	*hire/here/hure/huire*

There are two examples in Text 37, but both of them have ⟨i⟩ (high front vowel [i]) instead of the expected West Midland ⟨u⟩.

⟨y⟩ ⇒ ⟨i⟩ = pronunciation [ʏ] ⇒ [ɪ]

dryhten	**drihten/drihtene**	= *God, Lord*
cyrican (*dative*) (cyrice)	**chirechen**	*church*

6.1.4.7 *[a] before nasal consonant*

OE spelling and pronunciation of the low back vowel before [n] varied between ⟨*an*⟩ and ⟨*on*⟩. In late OE it was ⟨an⟩ except in the West Midland dialect, which is that of the *Brut*. Chaucer, in the late 14th century, has *lond*, like the *Brut*, but *land* eventually became standard.

[an] ⇒ [ɔn]

hwanon/hwonon	**wonene**	*whence*
þanc/þonc	**þonke**	*= thought, favour*

[and] ⇒ [ɔnd]

land/lond	**lond/londe**	*land*
mann/monn	**mon/monne**	*man*

6.1.4.8 *OE low back vowel [ɑː] rounded ⇒ [ɔː]*

In the four examples from Text 37, the long vowel [ɑː] in OE has become [ɔː] according to the evidence of the spelling.

ȝan	**gon**	*= did (marks past tense)*
ȝehaten	**ihoten**	*= called*
nam (niman)	**nom**	*= took*
be + wan (winnan)	**bi won**	*won = acquired*

In present-day English the word *home* (OE *ham* [hɑːm]) is pronounced with a variety of vowels in England according to the dialectal area in which it is spoken or the social and educational background of the speaker. For example Northern [hoːm], RP [həʊm], London [haʊm], and so on. In ME, we assume that the spelling with ⟨o⟩ originally represented the pronunciation of a back rounded vowel in the region of [ɔ] or [o], in contrast with its neighbours like [ɑ] and [u]. We can never know what the dialectal and local variations in pronunciation were.

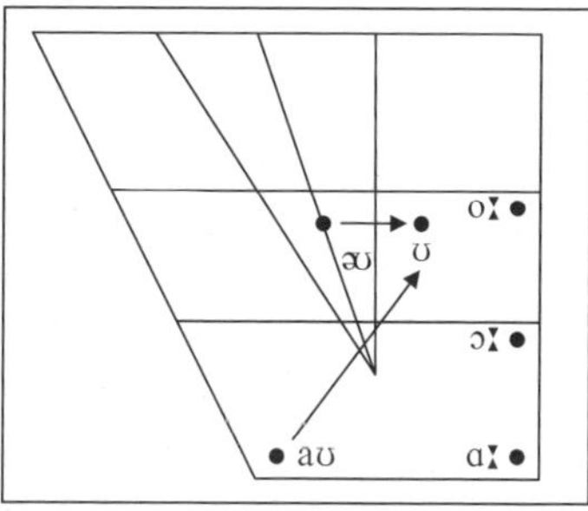

Vowel chart 5 MnE home

In Scots and some Northern dialects, however, *home* is pronounced [heːm] (spelt *hame*). Both *home* and *hame* are derived from OE *ham*, but [eː] is a *front* half-close vowel and [oː] a *back* half-close vowel.

How did this happen, and is it restricted to OE *ham*, or an example of a widespread change of the vowel [ɑː]?

Here are some short early ME texts. The words in bold type derive from OE words containing the low back vowel [ɑː].

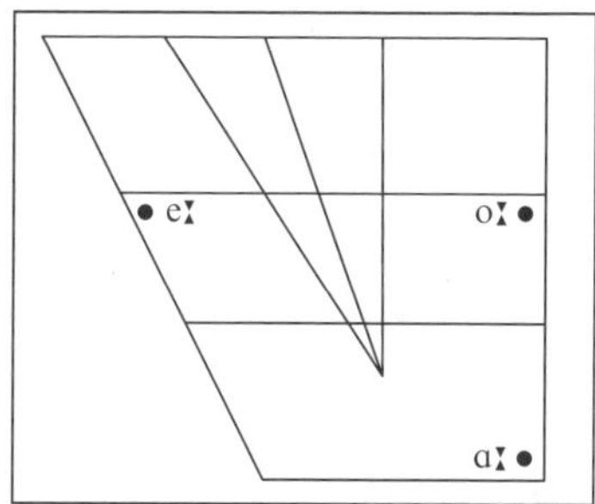

Vowel chart 6
[ɑː], [oː] and [eː]

OE **ahte**	þe nobeleste relike it is on þarof þat is in þe churche of Rome. So it **ouȝte** wel, hoso it understode fram ȝwanne it come. (*South West 13th C: St Kenelm*)
OE **agen**	(She) ledde hym to anoþer stede To hire **owen** chaumbre þat was... (*South East/London late 12th C: Kyng Alisaunder*)
OE **ban**	Alle þine **bones** he wolde tobreke (*South/South West Midland 13th C: Fox & the Wolf*)
OE **cnawan**	Trewer womon ne mai no mon **cnowe** þen Ich am (*East Midland 13th C: Dame Sirith*)
OE **ham**	Hauelok was war þat Grim swank sore For his mete, and he lay at **hom**... (*East Midland late 13th C: Havelok*)
OE **stan**	Gold and silver and preciouse **stones**... (*South East/London late 12th C: Kyng Alisaunder*)

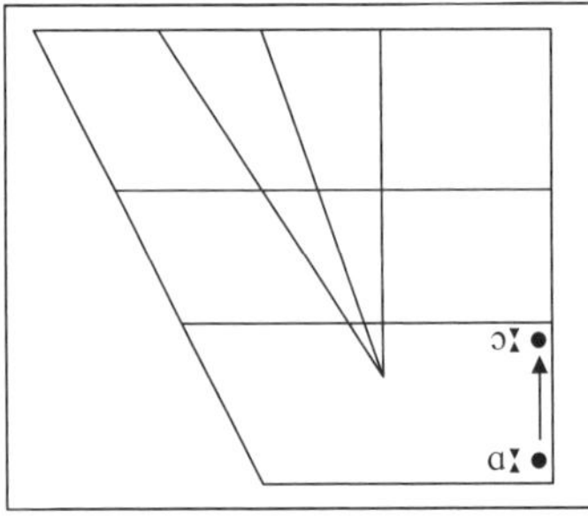

Vowel chart 7
OE [ɑː] to [ɔː]

The evidence of these texts suggests that in these dialect areas (South West, South East, East Midland), the long OE vowel [ɑː] had shifted, becoming sufficiently rounded and raised to cause writers to use the letter ⟨o⟩ to represent a sound like [ɔː]. The later development of this ME long half-open vowel [ɔː] spelt ⟨o⟩ or ⟨oa⟩ or ⟨oo⟩, to MnE [oː] or [əʊ] and its variants is part of the later Great Vowel Shift (see section 16.5).

The following texts contain the same words as those in the preceding quotations.

OE **ahte**	(He) bead to makien hire cwen of al þet he **ahte**. (*W. Midland late 12th C: Ancrene Wisse*)
OE **agan**	Ich æm þin **aȝen** mon, and iseh þisne swikedom... (*W. Midland late 12th C: Layamon*)
OE **ban**	Ich cwakie of grisle ant of grure, ant euch **ban** schekeð me (*W. Midland late 12th C: Sawles Warde*)
OE **cnawan**	For be þe thyng man drawes till Men schal him **knaw** for god or ill. (*Northern late 13th C: Cursor Mundi*)
OE **ham**	for hwon þet he slepe oðer ohwider fare from **hame**... (*W. Midland late 12th C: Sawles Warde*)
OE **stan**	and (hi) dide scræpe **stanes** þerinne... (*East Midland mid 12th C: Peterborough Chronicle*)

The use of the same spelling, ⟨a⟩, in these words could mean that

- the vowel had not yet shifted at the time when the texts were written; or
- the shift did not occur at all in these areas; or
- the vowel shifted in pronunciation, but writers kept the same spelling in the Northern texts.

In fact, in dialects north of the Humber and in the West Midlands, the long low vowel spelt ⟨a⟩ remained until the early 14th century, when it began to shift in a different direction and eventually became front half-close vowel [eː], as in Scots *hame*. The spelling, however, remained ⟨a⟩ or ⟨ai⟩ (letter ⟨i⟩ marking ⟨a⟩ as long), and so does not give us direct evidence. This frontward and upward shift suggests that the Northern low vowel was perhaps a more fronted [aː] rather than [ɑː]

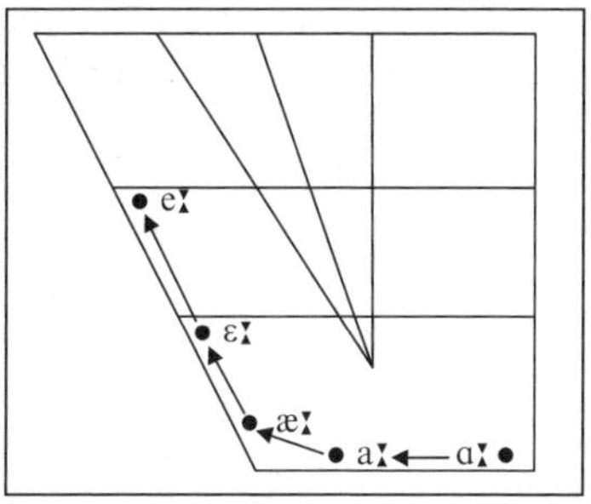

Vowel chart 8
Scots [ɑː] to [eː]

This is a warning that we cannot take the evidence of spelling only. It may not be an accurate marker of pronunciation.

We see from these examples that shifts of vowel pronunciation do not necessarily apply to a whole language, but to dialects of a language. Dialects differ from each other because the communities that speak them are in some way cut off from other communities and their ways of speech. The 'split' in the shift of OE long [ɑː] was probably a result of the clear geographical and political boundary marked by the rivers Humber and Lune, which prevented much direct communication between Northumbria and 'Southumbria'. The differences are still marked in present-day dialectal speech.

New words with the long low back vowel

The rounding of OE [ɑː] to [ɔː] was not the only change which we can observe between OE and ME long vowels, but it was the one in which the most marked shift took place. Most of the other vowels stayed as they were. But because the long vowel [ɑː] shifted to [ɔː] in Southern and Western dialects, we would expect there to be a gap in the vowel system. However, this gap did not occur, for two reasons.

Firstly, as we have seen, French words had begun to be used in English both before and after the Norman occupation of the country, (see sections 4.6 and 5.5.1). Here are some examples of adopted French words with the their first known occurrence in writing taken from the *Oxford English Dictionary*. This must be later than their use in the spoken language, but serves as a useful confirmation of a word's early assimilation into English:

age	OF eage	1325	I watʒ ful ʒong & tender of **age**
blame (v)	OF blâmer	1200	swiche men **blameð** þe prophete on þe sealm boc
cape	ONF cape	1205	A cniht mid his **capen**
cave	OF cave	1220	**Caue** ʒe [*the ant*] haueð to crepen in
chase (n)	OF chace	1297	Mest plente of fysch . . . And mest **chase** . . . of wylde bestes
dame	OF dame	1225	Almihti God . . . ʒiue ure **dame** his grace, so lengre so more
face	OF face	1290	More blod þar nas in al is **face**
grape	OF grape	1290	A luytel foul . . . brouʒte a gret bouʒ fol of **grapus** swyþe rede
lake	OF lac	1205	Ouer þen **lac** of Siluius & ouer þen **lac** of Philisteus
plate	OF plate	1290	He let nime **platus** of Iren sum del þunne and brode. . . . And on þe berninde **plates** him casten

These words all contained a long low (open) vowel [aː] in French, and would have been assimilated with a similar, but English, pronunciation. It began to shift to its MnE pronunciation [eː] or [ɛɪ]) later, in the Great Vowel Shift, which suggests that it was pronounced as a front low vowel [aː] rather than the back vowel [ɑː]. The French words must therefore have been adopted after the shift of OE [ɑː] and began to provide new English words with a similar low vowel.

The second reason why ME continued to have words with the vowel [ɑː] after the earlier shift to [ɔː] needs a separate section.

6.1.4.9 *Lengthening of short vowels in open syllables of two-syllable words*

OE short [ɑ] lengthens to ME long [ɑː]

In the following list, the ME words had the long vowel [ɑː] in their stem syllables:

Set 1 (not in Text 37)

OE	*ME*	*MnE*	*OE*	*ME*	*MnE*	*OE*	*ME*	*MnE*
bacan	**baken**	*bake*	lana	**lane**	*lane*	spade	**spade**	*spade*
baþian	**bathien**	*bathe*	manu	**mane**	*mane*	tacan	**taken**	*take*
crafian	**craven**	*crave*	nacod	**naked**	*naked*	talu	**tale**	*tale*
draca	**drake**	*drake*	nama	**name**	*name*	tapor	**taper**	*taper*
cnafa	**cnave**	*knave*	cwacian	**cwacien**	*quake*	wafian	**waven**	*wave*

So why had the OE vowel of these and other words, spelt with ⟨a⟩, not shifted to [ɔː] in early ME, like those just described in section 6.1.4.7? You will find that the original OE words have in common:

- **two** syllables (i.e. they are *disyllabic*);
- **open** stem syllables (see section 5.4.3), *ba-can*, etc.;
- **short** stem vowels.

The OE words in the following set have

- **one** syllable (monosyllabic);
- **closed** stem syllables;
- **short** stem vowels.

Set 2

and	dranc (*drank*)	hand	ram
batt (*bat*)	hamm (*ham*)	man	sac (*sack*)

and a third set,

- **two** syllables
- **closed** stem syllables
- **short** stem vowels.

Set 3

asse (*ass*)	catte (*cat*)	stagga (*stag*)
castel (*castle*)	mattoc (*mattock*)	thankien (*to thank*)

We now pronounce the MnE reflexes of Set 1 words with the long vowel or diphthong [eː] or [ɛː], but Sets 2 and 3 are still pronounced with a short vowel [æ], more or less unchanged from OE. In OE, the vowels of all three sets were short. Some feature of the Set 1 words must have caused the vowel to become long.

The evidence for this lengthening is not in the spelling of the ME words, which still used letter ⟨a⟩ and did not mark vowel length, but in their later MnE pronunciation [eː].

The significant features that all Set 1 words have in common are (a) they are **disyllabic** and (b) the stem vowel is in an **open** syllable. The short [ɑ] vowels in open syllables of disyllabic words must have lengthened to [ɑː], otherwise they would still have been pronounced as the short vowel [æ] today.

Lengthening of [e] and [o]

This lengthening of short vowels in open syllables of disyllabic words also affected OE words with [e] and [o], as you can see from the following lists (not in Text 37):

OE	*ME*	*MnE*	*OE*	*ME*	*MnE*	*OE*	*ME*	*MnE*
bera	**bere**	*bear* (*n*)	peru	**pere**	*pear*	hopian	**hopien**	*hope*
beran	**beren**	*bear* (*v*)	specan	**speken**	*speak*	losian	**losien**	*lose*
brecan	**breken**	*break*	spere	**spere**	*spear*	nosu	**nose**	*nose*
cnedan	**cneden**	*knead*	stelan	**stelen**	*steal*	open	**open**	*open*
etan	**eten**	*eat*	swerian	**swerien**	*swear*	smoca	**smoke**	*smoke*
melu	**mele**	*meal*	wefan	**weven**	*weave*	þrote	**throte**	*throat*
mete	**mete**	*meat*						

The evidence for the same lengthening is clear, although the pronunciation of the MnE reflexes, spelt with ⟨ea⟩, of ME words spelt with ⟨e⟩, is variable, e.g. *bear*, *break*, *speak*. The reasons for this variation are in later sound changes (see section 15.5.1.4).

The conclusion is, therefore, that the OE vowels [ɑ], [e] and [o] in open syllables of disyllabic words lengthened in the dialects of ME in the 12th and 13th centuries. It started earlier in Northern dialects, but was complete by *c.* 1250 everywhere.

Lengthening of [ɪ] and [ʊ]

Lengthening of the two short high vowels [ɪ] and [ʊ] only happened later in Northern and some Midland dialects, and is complicated by the fact that the vowel tended to shift lower, so that [ɪ] became [eː] and [ʊ] became [oː]. However, only limited evidence of this remains in MnE pronunciation or spelling, e.g.

OE	Northern ME	MnE
wice	**weke**	*week*
bitol (=*mallet*)	**betel**	*beetle*
duru	**dore**	*door*

The lengthening of short open vowels in disyllabic words was probably caused by the fact that the stem vowels were stressed, and so they lengthened with the loss of the second syllable.

6.1.4.10 *Consonant changes*

Consonants were much less subject to change than vowels, so there are only a few features to note.

Loss of initial [h]

After the Conquest and the establishment of French-speaking government and law, English ceased to be used in most official documents. The dialect of French we call Anglo-Norman was dominant in England until the mid-14th century. There is some possible evidence in Text 37 that words with initial ⟨h⟩ were beginning to lose it.

hwæt	**wat**	*what*
hwanon	**wonene**	*whence*

though these particular words from the set of ⟨hw-⟩ words are not conclusive. The now familiar spelling ⟨wh-⟩ and the 'aspirated' pronunciation [ʍ] for some speakers suggests an assimilation of [h] and [w] rather than the loss of [h].

Word-initial ⟨h⟩ was not pronounced in French, and the borrowing of numbers of French words beginning with ⟨h⟩ has led to its irregular pronunciation in present-day English.

> All the regional dialects of Southern English lost the phoneme /h/ during the Middle English period.
>
> (D. G. Scragg, *A History of English Spelling*, 1974)

There are three possibilities in MnE:

- A few borrowed French words have lost initial ⟨h⟩ in both spelling and pronunciation, like *able*, for example:

  > OF *hable* (modern French *habile*). The initial silent *h* has been generally dropped in English from the first, though many classical scholars tried to restore it in the 16th & 17th centuries.
  >
  > 1678 Marvell – Apt and **habile** for any congenerous action.

- A few others are spelt with an initial ⟨h⟩ which is not pronounced: like *heir*, *hour*, *honest*, *honour*.
- In the majority, the ⟨h⟩ is now pronounced in RP (though not in many dialects), 'spelling-pronunciation' having been adopted – *harmony*, *herb*, *heredity* (but not *heir*), *hospital*, and so on, and in England there is divided usage over *hotel* – [ə həʊtɛl] versus [ən əʊtɛl].

[ɣ] to [h] or elision of [ɣ]

broȝhte (brinȝan)	**brouhte**	*brought*
broȝhte (brinȝan)	**broute**	*brought*

The spelling ⟨h⟩ for ⟨ȝ⟩ may or may not represent a change from the velar fricative [ɣ] to the glottal fricative [h]. The fact that the same word is spelt both *brouhte* and *broute* presents a problem that we cannot resolve without more evidence.

The change of [m] to [n] in unstressed suffixes is part of the general reduction and final loss of most inflections.

⟨-am⟩ ⇒ ⟨-an⟩

þam **þan** = *the*

6.1.4.11 *Variations in ME spelling*

In the preceding lists, only one ME spelling is usually quoted, which may give the impression of a fairly fixed spelling system. This was not so. The following list of words derived from OE short and long ⟨eo⟩ illustrates the variety of spellings which occur in ME manuscripts. Notice that the spelling ⟨eo⟩ persisted although the sound had changed – another illustration of the danger of accepting spelling as an accurate guide to pronunciation.

short ⟨eo⟩

OE	*ME*	*MnE*
ceorfan	**keruen/keoruen/keorfen/cerue/kerue/kerve/karve**	*carve*
deorc	**dearc/derc/dorc/dorck/darc/darck/deork/durc/derk/deorke/duerke/derke/dirk(e)/dyrk/derck/dyrke/dork/darke**	*dark*
geolo	**ȝeolu/ȝeolo/ȝiolu/ȝeolew/ȝeoluw/ȝeolew/ȝeluw/ȝeleu/ȝelew/ȝelugh/ȝelogh/ȝelowȝ/ȝelȝ/ȝelw/ȝealwe/ȝelwe/yelwe/ȝelou/ȝelow/yelu/ȝelwhe/ȝelhewe**	*yellow*
heofon	**heofone/hefene/heofene/heouene/houene/heauene/heofne/heoffne/heffene/heuone/heuene/hefen/heyuen/heiuen/hevyn/hewyn/hewin/heven/heuin/heuon/heuun**	*heaven*

long ⟨eo⟩

OE	*ME*	*MnE*
ceosan	**ciose/ceose/cese/cheose/chese/chyese/chiese/chise/cheese/chees/ chess/schese/cheyss/cheise**	*choose*
freosan	**freosen/frosen/freese(n)/frese(n)/frise/freys/freis/freze/frieze**	*freeze*
freond	**friond/frynd/friend/vriend/frend(e)/vrend(e)/freond/vreond/freind(e)/ vrind/vryend/freend(e)/freynd/frind(e)/frynd(e)/freyind**	*friend*

6.1.4.12 *Summary of changes to vowels from late OE to early ME*

Chapter 5

- Reduction of vowels in unstressed syllables to [ə] leading to the eventual loss of most inflections (section 5.3 *passim*).
- Lengthening of short vowels before [ld], [nd] and [mb] (section 5.4.6.1).
- Shortening of long vowels before two consonants (section 5.4.6.1).

Chapter 6

- OE long [æː] shifted to [ɛː] or [eː] and short [æ] merged with [a] (section 6.1.4.4).
- OE diphthongs were smoothed and merged with other vowels (section 6.1.4.5).
- OE long [yː] and short [y] shifted, but differently in dialectal areas (section 6.1.4.6).
- OE long [ɑː] shifted to [ɔː] in dialect areas south of the Humber (section 6.1.4.8).
- In early ME some short vowels lengthened if they were in open syllables of disyllabic words, mainly [a], [e] and [o] (section 6.1.4.9).

All other vowels, long and short, remained virtually unchanged in the ME period.

6.1.5 *Vocabulary*

In the first paragraph of Laȝamon's *Brut*, which has been used to exemplify changes in the language in this chapter, all the words are derived directly from OE except one – *archen* (ark) from OF *arche*:

> From OF. *arche*: It is possible that the OE. *arc*, *arce* may itself have become *arch* in some dialects, but the use of this form down to the 16th c. is clearly from French (*OED*)

We must not draw firm conclusions from the tiny amount of data that has been studied, but it seems likely that the adoption of French words was very limited in the late West Midland dialect in which Laȝamon wrote at the end of the 12th century.

6.2 *The Owl & the Nightingale*

A poem described as 'witty and sophisticated' was written towards the end of the 12th century. It is an early example of metrical verse, in which the underlying pattern of the lines is a regular number of syllables, ending in rhyming words. *The Owl & the Nightingale* has 8-syllable lines in pairs of rhyming couplets. It contrasts with traditional alliterative Old English verse. Two lines,

þat underyat þe king Henri	*King Henry learnt about that –*
Iesus his soule do merci...	*(Jesus have mercy on his soul)*...

refer to the recent death of King Henry II in 1189, and so the poem can be fairly accurately dated to the 1190s. The original has not survived, but the facsimile Text 38, consisting of the opening lines, was probably copied after the mid-13th century. According to a consensus of scholarly opinion, the poem was written in a south-eastern dialect, but 'with a south-west-midland colouring'.

A note on the handwriting

Similar style to Layamon's *Brut* (Text 37) but with some peculiarities:

- Letter wynn is used, written with a dot over it, ⟨ṗ⟩, e.g. *ṗas* (*was*).
- Letter thorn is written like wynn without a dot ⟨p⟩ (but with some confusion, e.g. line 2).
- Letter yogh is used for [ç], e.g. *niȝtingale*, and [j], e.g. *diȝele*.
- The 2-form of ⟨r⟩ is written after ⟨o⟩, e.g. *ṗorste* (*worst*).
- Long ⟨ſ⟩ normal, *ſtif*, *ſtarc*, *ſtrong*, with round ⟨s⟩ word-final, *ṗas* (*was*) and sometimes initial, *sval*.
- Letter ⟨a⟩ is closed.

Here is a transcription of the first 18 lines:

	Edited version	**Literal translation**
Ich‾ṗas ın one ſum̃e dale·	Ich was in one sumere dale,	I was in a summery dale
In one ſuṗe dıȝele hale·	In one suþe diȝele hale;	In a very hidden nook
Iherde Ich holde grete tale·	Iherde Ich holde grete tale	Heard I hold great debate
An hule and one nıȝtıngale·	An hule and one niȝtingale·	An owl and a nightingale
þat plaıt waſ ſtıf 7 ſtarc 7 ſtrõg·	Þat plait was stif an starc an strong,	The pleading was stiff & fierce & strong
sumṗıle softe 7 lud among·	Sumwile softe an lud among;	Sometimes soft & loud now & then
An asþer* aȝen oþer sval·	An eiþer aȝen oþer sval	And each against other swelled
7 let þat wole mod ut al·	An let þat vuele mod ut al;	And let out that evil mood completely
7 eıþer ſeıde of oþeres cuſte·	An eiþer seide of oþeres custe	And each said of the other's character
þat alere ṗorſte þat hı ṗuſte·	Þat alreworste þat hi wuste;	All the worst that she kmew
7 hure 7 hure of oþere ſonge·	An hure an hure of oþeres songe	And especially if the other's song
hı holde plaıdıng ſuþe ſtronge·	Hi holde plaiding suþe stronge·	They held pleas very strong.
Þe nıȝtıngale bıgon þe ſpeche·	Þe niȝtingale bigon þe speche	The nightingale began the speech
In one hurne of one breche·	In one hurne of one breche,	In a corner of a clearing
7 sat upone vaıre boȝe·	An sat up one vaire boȝe	And sat upon a fair bough
þar ṗere abute bloſme ınoȝe·	Þar were abute blosme inoȝe,	Around which were blossoms enough
In ore ṗaſte þıcke hegge·	In ore waste þicke hegge	In a secure thick hedge
Imeınd mıd ſpıre 7 grene ſegge·	Imeind mid spire an grene segge·	Mingled with reeds & green sedge...

* asþer – *probably a scribal error for* eiþer

🕮 The vocabulary of Text 38 is listed in the *Word Book*.

🕮 A transcription and translation of the whole facsimile, with a complete vocabulary, is in the *Text Commentary*.

Text 38 – *The Owl & the Nightingale* (facsimile)

Ich was in one sumere dale.
in one suþe diȝele hale.
iherde ich holde grete tale.
an hule and one niȝtingale.
þat plait was stif & starc & strong.
sum wile softe & lud among.
an aiþer aȝen oþer sval.
& let þat vole mod ut al.
& eiþer seide of oþeres custe.
þat alre worste þat hi wuste.
& hure & hure of oþeres songe
hi holde plaiding suþe stronge.
Þe niȝtingale bigon þe speche.
in one hurne of one breche.
& sat up one vaire boȝe.
þar were abute blosme inoȝe.
in ore waste þicke hegge.
imeind mid spire & grene segge.
Ho was þe gladur vor þe rise.
& song auele cunne wise.
bet þuȝte þe dreim þat he were.
of harpe & pipe þan he nere.
bet þuȝte þat he were ishote.
of harpe & pipe þan of þrote.
Þo stod on old stoc þarbiside.
þar þo vle song hire tide.
& was mid iui al bigrowe.
hit was þare hule earding stowe.
Þe niȝtingale hi isez.
& hi bihold & ouersez.
& þuȝte wel vl of þare hule.
for me hi halt lodlich & fule.
Vnwiȝt ho sede awei þu flo.
me is þe wrs þat ich þe so.

Iwis for þine vule lete.
wel oft ich mine song forlete.
min horte atflip & falt mi tonge.
wonne þu art to me iþrunge.
me luste bet speten þane singe.
of þine fule ȝoȝelinge.
Þos hule abod fort hit was eve.
ho ne miȝte no leng bilene.
vor hire horte was so gret.
þat wel neȝ hire fnast at schet.
& warp a word þar aft longe.
hu þincþe nu bi mine songe.
wenst þu þat ich ne cunne singe.
þeȝ ich ne cunne of writelinge.
ilome þu dest me grame.
& seist me boþe tone & schame.
ȝif ich þe holde on mine note.
so hit bitide þat ich mote.
& þu were vt of þine rise.
þu sholdest singe an oþer wise.
Þe niȝtingale ȝaf answare.
ȝif ich me loki wit þe bare.
& me schilde wit þe blete.
ne reche ich noȝt of þine þrete.
ȝif ich me holde in mine hegge.
ne recche ich neu what þu segge.
Ich wot þat þu art un milde.
wiþ hom þat ne muȝe fro þe schilde.
& þu tukest wroþe & vuele.
whar þu miȝt over smale fuȝele.
vorþi þu art loþ al fuel kunne.
& alle ho þe driueþ honne.
& þe bi schricheþ & bi gredet.
& wel narewe þe bi ledet.

Very few ON or OF words occur in the text. A south-east dialect would have very little contact with the east midlands and north, the area of the Danelaw, and a hundred years or so after the Norman Conquest appears to be insufficient time for more than a few French words to have been assimilated for use in the poem by a 'sophisticated' writer.

It is relatively difficult to read 12th-century ME texts. This is partly because they contain numbers of OE words that have since dropped from the language or, if a word has a MnE reflex, because the spelling does not match the MnE spelling sufficiently to make it easily recognisable. The first lines of Texts 37 and 38 illustrate the problem:

> **AN** preoft wes on leoden: Laȝamon wes ihoten.
> he wes leouenaðes sone: liðe him beo drihten.
> he wonede at Ernleȝe: at æðelen are chirechen.
> vppen seuarne staþe: sel þar him þuhte.
> Ich was in one sumere dale,
> In one suþe diȝele hale;
> Iherde Ich holde grete tale
> An hule and one niȝtingale

The words *leoden*, *ihoten*, *liðe*, *drihten*, *wonede*, *æðelen*, *staþe* and *sel* (Text 37) and *suþe*, *diȝele*, *hale* (Text 38) have since dropped from the language, and someone unfamiliar with OE and early ME might not recognise *are chirechen* as *a church* (Text 37) or *hule* as *owl* and *an*, *one* as the indefinite article *a*, *an* (Text 38). And the syntax of *him þuhte – it seemed to him* (Text 37) – is now archaic. It is not surprising therefore that Chaucer, writing in the late 14th century, is generally the earliest writer studied in many English literature courses. He wrote in a London dialect which resembles MnE sufficiently well in its vocabulary and structure to be relatively easily readable – if not without some need of help from a glossary. The following chapters should help in plotting the development of the language towards a greater ease of readability and familiarity.

7. Early Middle English – 13th century

7.1 *The Fox and the Wolf*

Below is the opening of a poem called *The Fox and the Wolf*, dating from the early part of the 13th century.

Activity 7.1

Use the word-list following the text to compare the forms of the ME words and their OE sources, and comment on:

(i) the use of the letters ⟨v⟩ ⟨w⟩ and ⟨u⟩ in the words *vox*, *wox*, *neuere*, *leuere*, *oueral*, *wous*;
(ii) the use of letter ⟨e⟩ for the main vowel in *neuere*, *wes*, *nes*, *erour*, *strete*, *þen*;
(iii) the spelling ⟨ou⟩ for the vowel in *out*, *oundred*, *hous*, *wous*, *hounger*;
(iv) the spellings ⟨qu⟩ and ⟨ch⟩ in *aquenche*;
(v) the spelling ⟨o⟩ for the long vowels of *go*, *wo*, *none*, *so*, *loþ*, *one*, *strok*;
(vi) the spelling and possible pronunciation of *drunche* (it rhymes with *aquenche*);
(vii) the spelling of the vowels of *half*, *oueral*, *wal/walle*, *leuere*.

Text 39 – ***The Fox and the Wolf*, early 13th century**

Southern dialect (the text is edited)

ME	WW
A vox gon out of þe wode go	A fox went out of the wood (*gon . . . go* = *went*)
Afingret so þat him wes wo	Hungered so that to-him was woe
He nes neuere in none wise	He ne-was never in no way
Afingret erour half so swiþe.	Hungered before half so greatly.
He ne hoeld nouþer wey ne strete	He ne held neither way nor street
For him wes loþ men to mete.	For to-him (*it*) was loathsome men to meet.

Him were leuere meten one hen	To-him (*it*) were more-pleasing meet one hen
þen half an oundred wimmen.	Than half a hundred women.
He strok swiþe oueral	He went quickly all-the-way
So þat he ofsei ane wal.	Until he saw a wall.
Wiþinne þe walle wes on hous.	Within the wall was a house.
The wox wes þider swiþe wous	The fox was thither very eager (*to go*)
For he þohute his hounger aquenche	For he intended his hunger quench
Oþer mid mete oþer mid drunche.	Either with food or with drink.

OE	***Text***	***MnE***	***OE***	***Text***	***MnE***
acwencan	**aquenche**	*quench*	an	**one**	*one*
dryne	**drunche**	*drink* (*n*)	ofer eall/all	**oueral**	*= all the way*
æror	**erour**	*= before* (*ere*)	hundred	**oundred**	*hundred*
gan	**go**	*go*	ut	**out**	*out*
healf	**half**	*half*	swa	**so**	*so*
hungor	**hounger**	*hunger*	stræt	**strete**	*street*
hus	**hous**	*house*	strac *fr* strican	**strok**	*= went*
leof/leofra	**leuere**	*liefer = more pleasing*	fox	**vox/wox**	*fox*
			weall/wall	**wal/walle**	*wall*
laþ	**loþ**	*loth*	wæs	**wes**	*was*
næs = ne wæs	**nes = ne wes**	*was not*	wa	**wo**	*woe*
næfre	**neuere**	*never*	fus	**wous**	*= eager, ready*
nan	**none**	*no*	þænne	**þen**	*than*

The complete vocabulary of Text 39 is listed in the *Word Book*.

There is only one copy of the poem, and it is not the original. It must have been written and copied in the south of England, but it cannot be identified more closely with a particular dialectal area.

But even in these few lines we find clear indications of some of the changes discussed in chapter 6; for example, the rounding of OE [ɑː] to [ɔː], in words like *go*, *wo* and *loþ*, which had developed from OE *gan*, *wa* and *laþ*, points to a southern dialectal form because the vowel had not changed in Northern dialects. There are no words of ON derivation in the complete poem of *c*. 300 lines, which is further evidence that it was written outside the boundaries of the former Danelaw.

For a detailed description see the *Text Commentary Book*.

7.2 The South English Legendary

The South English Legendary is a manuscript containing verse legends of saints and the miracles they were said to have achieved in southern England. It includes a life of St Kenelm. There is no recorded historical evidence about him, but the legend tells of a seven year-old boy murdered in 819, whose body was recovered and buried in a shrine at Winchcombe in Gloucester. (The story of St Kenelm is printed in Bennett and Smithers, *Early Middle English Prose & Verse*.)

The facsimile is from one of several surviving manuscripts, and is part of the introduction to the legend, which begins with a review of the state of England in the early 9th century with its 'five kings'. There follows a transcription that reproduces the facsimile with its handwriting abbreviations, and also an edited version. The introductory lines in italics provide a suitable beginning to the facsimile. The full text is rather repetitive, so only a dozen lines are reproduced. The verse inclines to doggerel, with numbers of fillers like *iwis* and *þerto* used to make up the metre or provide a rhyme.

Text 40 – Introduction to the *Life of St Kenelm* (facsimile)

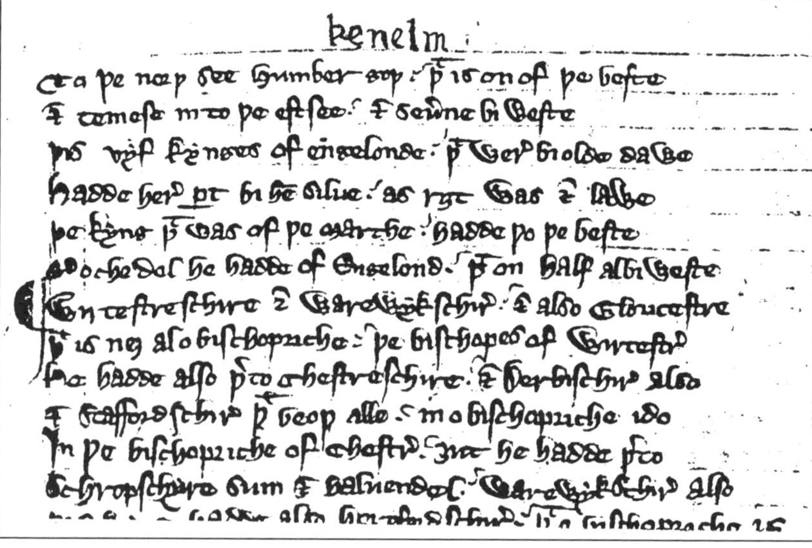

📖 The complete 38-line folio of the MS is reproduced with a transcription in the *Commentary Book*.

(Preceding lines)

Vif kinges þere were þulke tyme · in Engelond ido
For Engelond was god and long · & somdel brod þerto
Aboute eiȝte hondred mile · Engelond long is
Fram þe souþ into þe norþ · and to hondred brod iwis
Fram þe est into þe west · and also þere inne beoþ
Manie wateres god inou · as ȝe alday iseo
Ac þreo wateres principals · þer beoþ of alle iwis
Homber and Temese · Seuerne þe þridde is

Transcription

To þe norþ see humber goþ : þ^{t} ıs on of þe beſte
7 temeſe ınto þe eſt ſee : 7 seũne bı weſte
þıs vẏf kẏnges of engelond : þ^{t} wer̃ bı olde dawe
hadde her̃ pt bı hē sılue : as rȝt was 7 lawe
Þe kẏng þ^{t} was of þe marche : hadde þo þe beſte
Mochedel he hadde of Engelond : þ^{t} on half al bı weſte
Wnceſtreſchıre and Warewẏkſchır^{e} : 7 also Glouceſtre
þ^{t} ıs neȝ al o bıſchoprıche : þe bıſchopes of Wırceſtr^{e}
he hadde alſo þ^{r}to cheſtreſchıre : 7 Derbıſchır^{e} also
7 Staffordſchır^{e} þ^{t} beoþ alle : ın o bıſchoprıche ıdo
In þe bıſchoprıche of cheſtr^{e} : ant ȝute he hadde þ^{r}to
Schropſchyre sum 7 haluendel : Warewẏkschır^{e} alſo

Edited version

To þe norþ see Humber goþ · þat is on of þe beste
And Temese into þe est see · and Seuerne bi weste
Þis vyf kynges of Engelond : þat were bi olde dawe
Hadde here part bi hem silue : as riȝt was & lawe
Þe kyng þat was of þe Marche : hadde þo þe beste
Mochedel he hadde of Engelond : þat on half al by weste
Wircestreschire and Warewykschire : and also of Gloucestre
Þat is nei al o bischopriche : þe bischopes of Wircestre
He hadde also þerto Chestreschire : and Derbischire also
And Staffordschire þat beoþ alle : in o bischopriche ido
In þe bischopriche of Chestre : and ȝute he hadde þerto
Schropschire sum and haluendel : Warewykschire also

Translation

There were five kings in England at that time
For England was good and long and somewhat broad as well.
England is about eight hundred miles long
From south to north, and two hundred wide
From east to west, and therein also are
Many good rivers, as you can see any day,
But there are three principal rivers of all,
Humber and Thames, and Severn is the third.
The Humber, one of the best, flows into the north sea,
And Thames into the east sea, and Severn to the west.
These five English kings that there were in olden days
Had each their own part, as was right and lawful.
The king of the Welsh Marches then had the best.
He had a great part of England, in the west half
Worcestershire and Warwickshire and also of Gloucester
That is nearly all one bishopric, the bishop of Worcester's
He also had Chestershire and Derbyshire also
And Staffordshire, that are all in one bishopric,
The bishopric of Chester, and he had as well
Part of Shropshire and a half of Warwickshire also....

The vocabulary of Text 40 is listed in the *Word Book*.

A narrative poem dealing with the Passion, Resurrection and Ascension of Christ is another of the texts in the *South English Legendary*. Like Text 40, it is written in a South West dialect. The following facsimile is not from the late 13th-century original, but was probably copied in the early 14th century. It forms part of the story of Mary Magdalene's early morning visit to the tomb of Christ the day after the Crucifixion, and is based on St Matthew's Gospel, chapter 28, but with omissions and additions.

> In the end of the sabbath, as it began to dawn toward the first day of the week, came Mary Magdalene and the other Mary to see the sepulchre. And, behold, there was a great earthquake; for the angel of the Lord descended from heaven, and came and rolled back the stone from the door, and sat upon it. His countenance was like lightning, and his raiment white as snow. And for fear of him the keepers did shake, and became as dead men. . . . Now when they were going, behold, some of the watch came into the city, and shewed unto the chief priests all the things that were done.
>
> (*King James Bible*, 1611)

Text 41 – *The Southern Passion* (facsimile)

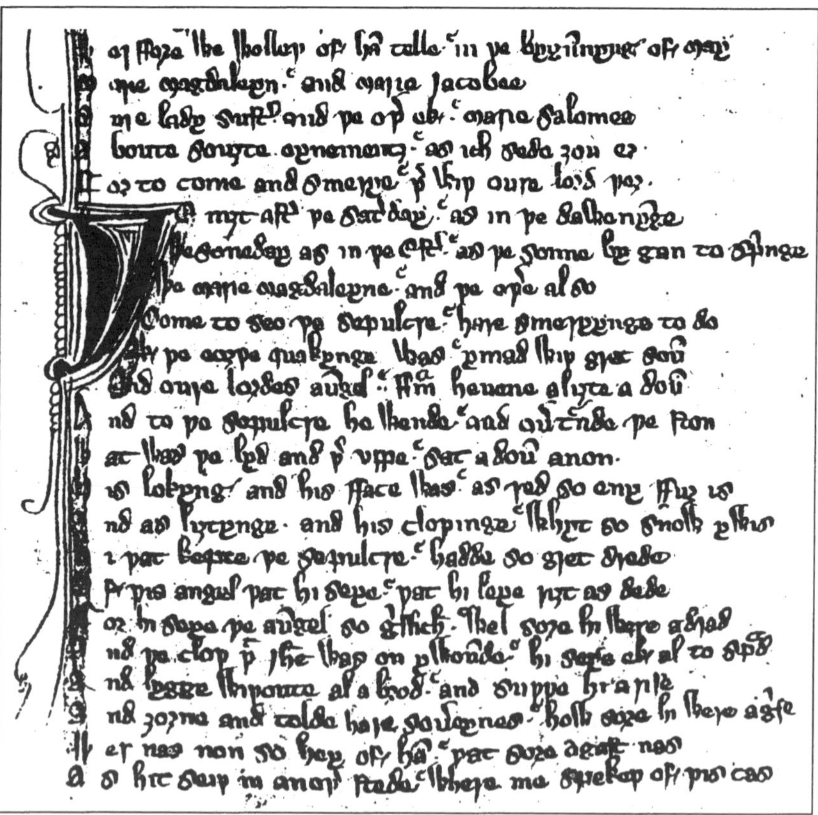

Transcription

þ er ffore we wolleþ of hā telle: ın þe bygūnyng of May
M arıe Magdaleyn: and Marıe Iacobee
O ure lady suſte^{r} and þe oþ^{r} ek: Marıe Salomee
a boute souȝte oynementȝ : as ıch sede ȝou er
ff or to come and smerye: þ^{r} wıþ oure lord þer
þe nıȝt aft^{r} þe sat^{r}day: as ın þe dawenȳge
þ e soneday as ın þe eſt^{r} : as þe sonne by gan to sp^{r}ınge
þ o Marıe Magdaleyne: and þe oþ^{r}e al so
c ome to seo þe sepulcre: hare smeryynge to do
A k þe eorþe quakynge was: ymad wı gret soū
A nd oure lordes aūgel: ff^{a}m heuene alıȝte a doū
A nd to þe sepulcre he wende: and ou^{r}t^{r}nde þe ſton
Þ at was þe lyd and þ^{r} vppe: sat a doū anon
hı s lokyng and hıs fface was: as red so eny ffur ıs
a nd as lıȝtynge and hıs cloþınge: whyt so snow ywıs
h ı þat kepte þe sepulcre: hadde so gret drede
O f þıs angel þat hı seye: þat hı leye rıȝt as dede
ff or hı seye e aūgel so g^{r}ıſlıch: wel sore hı were a drad
a nd þe cloþ þ^{t} Ihe was on ywoūde: hı seye ek al to sp^{a}d
a nd lygge wıþoute al a brod: and suþþe hı arıſe
a nd ȝorne and tolde hare ſou^{r}eyneſ: how ſore hı were ag^{r}ıſe
Þ er naſ non ſo hey of hā: þat ſore agaſt nas
a s hıt seıþ ın anoþ^{r} ſtede: where me spekeþ of þıs cas

(Initial letters of the lines of the MS are concealed in the margin.)

Edited text

...þer ffore we wolleþ of ham telle. In þe bygnnyng of May
Marie Magdaleyn and Marie Iacobee
Oure lady suster and þe oþer ek: Marie Salomee
aboute souȝte oynementȝ: as ich sede ȝou er
ffor to come and smerye: þerwiþ oure lord þer
þe niȝt after þe saterday: as in þe dawenynge
þe soneday as in þe ester: as þe sonne bygan to springe
þo Marie Magdaleyne: and þe oþere also
come to seo þe sepulcre: hare smeryynge to do
Ak þe eorþe quakynge was: ymad wi gret soun
And oure lordes aungel: ffram heuene aliȝte a doun
And to þe sepulcre he wende: and ouerturnede þe ston
Þat was þe lyd and þervppe: sat adoun anon
his lokyng and his fface was: as red so eny ffur is
and as liȝtynge and his cloþinge: whyt so snow ywis
hi þat kepte þe sepulcre: hadde so gret drede
Of þis angel þat hi seye: þat hi leye riȝt as dede
ffor hi seye þe aungel so grislich: wel sore hi were adrad
and þe cloþ þat Ihesus was on ywounde: hi seye ek al to sprad
and lygge wiþoute al a brod: and suþþe hi arise
and ȝorne and tolde hare souereynes: how sore hi were agrise
Þer nas non so hey of ham: þat sore agast nas
as hit seiþ in anoþer stede: where me spekeþ of þis cas

7.2.1 Vocabulary

In the South West dialect of this text the majority of lexical words (nouns, verbs, adjectives, adverbs) are derived from OE. The area is distant from the Danelaw, but there are two words of ON derivation, and some from French.

ON daga	**dawenynge**	dawning
ON systir	**suster**	sister
OF angele (cf. OE engel)	**angel/ aungel**	angel
OF cas	**cas**	case, occurrence
OF face	**fface**	face
OF oignement	**oynementȝ**	ointments
OF sepulcre	**sepulcre**	sepulchre
OF soverain	**souereynes**	sovereigns – rulers
AF soun (OE son)	**ȝoun**	sound

📖 The complete vocabulary of Text 41 is listed in the *Word Book*.

7.3 A guide for anchoresses

In the early 13th century, about 1230, a book was written for three sisters who had become anchorites (or *anchoresses*, the feminine form of the noun). The word *anchorite* derives from the Greek *anachoretes*, which mean 'one who has withdrawn' – that is, withdrawn from what we would regard as a normal way of life. In medieval times monks and nuns withdrew from society into their closed communities in monasteries and nunneries, and hermits and anchorites withdrew to lead solitary lives. But the difference between a hermit and an anchorite was that an anchorite was committed to living in a single place for life, enclosed in a small cell which was often attached to a church.

Ancrene Wisse is a book of devotional advice, written in a West Midland dialect, by a canon of Wigmore Abbey in northern Herefordshire, it is believed. The three anchorite sisters were enclosed nearby. Text 42 is from a section on 'fleshly and spiritual temptations' and follows a descripion of the 'unity of love'. Transcriptions and a word-for-word translation follow the facsimile, so that you can make your own study of the language.

Text 42 – *Ancrene Wisse* (facsimile)

Al þıſ ıſ ıſeıd mıne leoue ſuſtren · ꝥ oper leoue
nebbeſ beon eauer ıpent ſomet pıð luueful ſemblant : 7
pıð ſpote chére · ꝥ ʒe beon aa pıð anneſſe of an heorte 7
of a pıl ılımet togedereſ · aſ hıt ıprıten ıſ bı ure lau^{r}des
deore decıpleſ · Multıtudınıſ credentıum erat cor unum
7 anıma una · Pax uoƀ · þıſ peſ godeſ gretunge to hıs
deore decıpleſ · Grıð beo bımong op · ʒe beoð þe ancren of
englond ſpa feole togedereſ · tpentı nuðe oðer ma · godd
ı god op mutlı : ꝥ meaſt grıð ıſ among · Meaſt anneſſe 7
anredneſſe · 7 ſometreadneſſe of anred lıf after a rıple ·
Spa ꝥ alle teoð an · alle ıturnt aneſpeıſ : 7 nan frõmard
oðer · efter ꝥ pord ıſ · for þı ʒe gað pel forð 7 ſpedeð ın op
er peı : for euch ıſ pıðpard oþer ín an manere of lıflade ·
aſ þah ʒe peren an cuuent of lundene 7 of oxnefort · of

ſchreobſburı : oðer of cheſter · þear aſ alle beoð an ƿıð
an ımeane manere · ant ƿıð uten ſıngularıte · ꝥ ıſ anful
frommardſchıpe · lah þíng ı relıgıun · for hıt to ƿarpeð
anneſſe ⁊ manere ımeane : ꝥ ah to beon ın ordre · þıs
nu þenne ꝥ ʒe beoð alle aſ an cuuent · ıſ oþer hehe fa
me · þıſ ıſ godd ıcƿeme · þıſ ıſ nunan ƿıde cuð · ſƿa þet
oþer cuuent bıgınneð to ſpreaden toƿard englondeſ
ende · Ʒe beoð aſ þe moderhuſ heo ꝥ beoð of ıſtreonet ·

Edited version with modern punctuation and translation:

Al þis is iseid mine leoue sustren, þet ower leoue nebbes beon eauer
All this is said my beloved sisters, so that your dear faces should be always

iwent somet wið luucful semblant ant wið swote chere, þet ʒe beon
turned together with loving expressions and with sweet looks; so that you should be

aa wið annesse of an heorte ant of a wil ilimet togederes, as hit iwriten is
always with unity of one heart and of one will, joined together as it written is

bi ure lauerdes deore deciples:
about Our Lord's dear disciples:

Multitudinis credentium erat cor unum ant anima una; pax uobis.
And the multitude of them that believed were of one heart and of one soul; peace be unto you.

Þis wes Godes gretunge to his deore deciples: 'Grið beo bimong ow'. Ʒe beoʒ,
This was God's greeting to his dear disciples 'Peace be among you'. You are,

þe ancren of Englond, swa feole togederes – twenti nuðe oðer ma. Godd i
the anchoresses of England, so many together – twenty now or more; God in

god ow mutli þet meast grið is among, meast annesse, ant anrednesse, ant
good you increase that most peace is among, most unity and singleness and

sometreadnesse of anred lif, after a riwle, swa þet alle teoð
agreement of united life according to one rule, so that all pull

an, alle iturnt anesweis ant nan frommard oðer, efter
one way, all turned in one way and no one different from the others, as

þet word is. Forþi ʒe gað wel forð ant spedeð in ower wei, for
the word is. Therefore you go well forth and succeed on your way, for

euch is wiðward oþer in an manere of liflade, as þah ʒe
everyone is together with the others in one manner of living, as though you

weren an cuuent of Lundene ant of Oxnefort, of Schreobsburi, oðer of
were a community of London or of Oxford, of Shrewsbury or of

Chester, þear as alle beoð an wið an imeane manere ant wið uten
Chester, where all are one with a common manner and without

singularite þet is anful frommardschipe – lah þing i religiun, for
singularity – that is, individual difference – base thing in religion, for

hit towarpeð annesse ant manere imeane þet ah to beon in
it destroys unity and the manner shared that ought to be in

ordre. þis nu þenne þet ȝe beoð alle as an cuuent is ower
an order. this now, then, that you are all as one community, is your

hehe fame. þis is Godd icweme, þis is nunan wide cuð, swa þet
high fame. This is to God pleasing. This is already widely known, so that

ower cuuent biginneð to spreaden toward Engelondes ende. Ȝe beoð
your community begins to spread towards England's end. You are

as þe moderhus þet heo beoð of istreonet.
like the motherhouse that they are sprung from.

📖 The vocabulary of Text 42 is listed in the *Word Book*.

7.4 Lyric poems

7.4.1 *Court-hand*

In the book-hand style of all the preceding facsimiles the letters are formed separately. When thay are joined together, for greater speed in writing, a 'cursive script' is produced, and this style, developed in England in the 13th century for business transactions, is called **court-hand**, because it was the style in use in the English law-courts until the 18th century.

Here are three short extracts in facsimile from the best known collection of ME lyric poems in a manuscript called Harley 2253, which were written in court-hand. The dialect is West Midland. The poems were copied in the 1320s, but they were probably written in the later 13th century.

Text 43 – *Blow northerne wynd* (facsimile)

A note on the handwriting
Court-hand with elaborated ⟨þ⟩, long ⟨ſ⟩ and ⟨d⟩

- ⟨a⟩ is closed.
- Closed form of ⟨s⟩ also used – ⟨σ⟩, e.g. *σẏht* (*syht*).
- ⟨y⟩ is usually dotted – ⟨ẏ⟩.
- ⟨ȝ⟩ for [j], e.g. ȝ*ete* (*yet*). ⟨*g*⟩ for [g], e.g. *suetẏng*.
- wynn ⟨ƿ⟩ and eth ⟨ð⟩ not used.

There are ten verses altogether. The refrain *Blow northerne wynd* is repeated after each of them. The refrain and first verse are here reproduced:

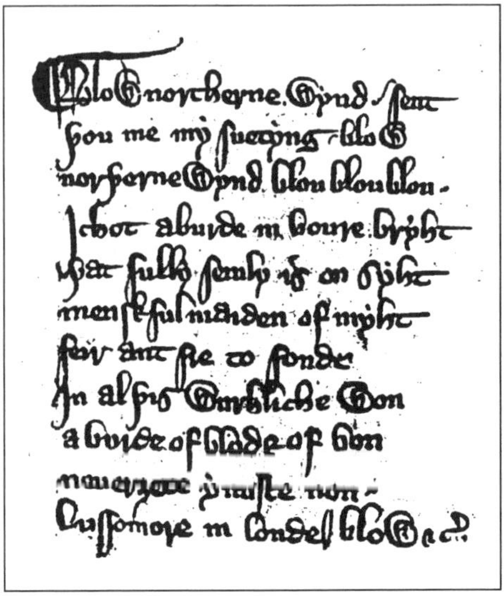

Blow northerne wẏnd / ſent
þou me mẏ ſuetẏng / blow
norþerne wẏnd blou blou blou.
Ichot a burde ın boure brẏht
þat ſullẏ ſemly ıs on ſẏht
menſkful maıden of mẏht
feır ant fre to fonde
In al þıs wurhlıche won
a burde of blod (*ant*) of bon
neuer ȝete ẏ nuſte non
luſſomore ın londe || blow (etc.)

Set out in conventional verse form

Blow northerne wynd
Sent þou me my suetyng
Blow norþerne wynd
Blou blou blou.
Ichot a burde in boure bryht
Þat sully semly is on syht
Menskful maiden of myht
Feir ant fre to fonde.
In al þis wurhliche won
A burde of blod (*ant*) of bon
Neuer ȝete y nuste non
Lussomore in londe
Blow (etc.)

The vocabulary of Text 43 is listed in the *Word Book*.

Text 44 – *Wiþ longẏng y am lad* (facsimile)

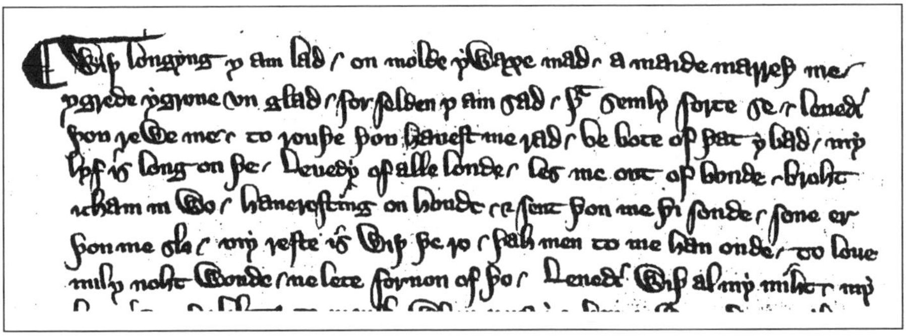

Transcription of the first stanza

Wıþ longẏng y am lad / on molde ẏ waxe mad / a maıde marreþ me/
ygrede ẏgrone vn glad / for ſelden y am sad / þ^{t} semly forte se / leuedı
þou rewe me / to rouþe þou haueſt me rad / be bote of þat ẏ bad / mẏ
lıf ıs long on þe / . . .

Here is the stanza in conventional modern printing, with lineation to mark verse patterning, metre and rhyme. The lyric has a rising duple rhythm with 3-stress lines. There are two rhymes, a = [ad], b = [eː]

	rhyme
Wiþ longyng Y am lad	a
On molde Y waxe mad	a
A maide marreþ me.	b
Y grede Y grone vnglad	a
For selden Y am sad	a
Þat semly forte se.	b
Leuedi þou rewe me!	b
To rouþe þou hauest me rad –	a
Be bote of þat Y bad!	a

📖 The vocabulary of Text 44 is listed in the *Word Book*.

Text 45 – *Lenten ys come wiþ loue to toune* (facsimile)

Lenten ẏs come wıþ loue to toune
wıþ bloſmen & wıþ brıddes roune
þ^{t} al þıs blıſſe brẏngeþ
daẏes eȝes ın þıs dales
notes ſuete of nẏhtegales
vch foul ſong ſıngeþ
þe þreſtelcoc hım þreteþ oo
awaẏ ıs huere wynter wo
when woderoue sprıngeþ
þıs foules ſıngeþ ferly fele
ant wlyteþ on huere wynter* wele
þat al þe wode rẏngeþ

**wynter* is said to be a scribal error for *wynn*.

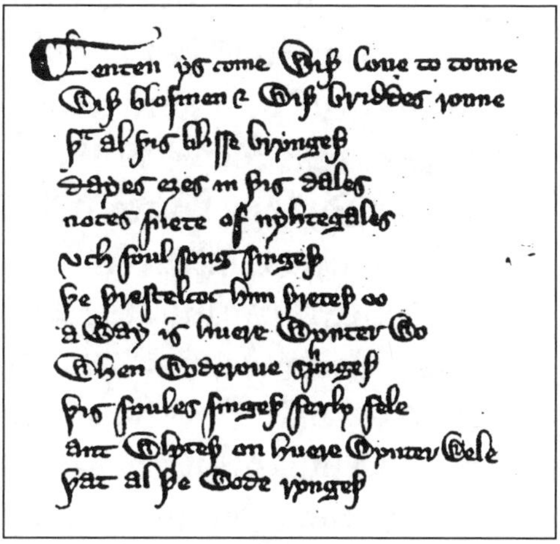

This poem is written in stanza form.

📖 The vocabulary of Text 45 is listed in the *Word Book*.

7.5 *The Bestiary*

The Bestiary, or *Book of Beasts*, was a medieval collection of descriptions of the animal world, written in a variety of verse forms.

It was believed that the animal and plant world was symbolic of religious truths – 'the creatures of this sensible world signify the invisible things of God'. Later scientific knowlege shows that some of the descriptions are inaccurate, for example the description of the eagle's flight in Text 47. Some of the animals in *The Bestiary*, like the unicorn, phoenix and basilisk, are imaginary or fabulous.

There is only one surviving manuscript, written in the East Midland dialect in the second half of the 13th century. The following facsimile of a page of the MS is a description of the Lion and its religious significance, followed by the first lines of the Eagle.

Text 46 – *The Bestiary* – The Lion (facsimile)

A note on the handwriting

- An unusual open form of letter wynn ⟨ƿ⟩ is used, made in three strokes.
- eth ⟨ð⟩ used throughout – thorn ⟨þ⟩ or ⟨ȝ⟩ not used.

- ⟨g⟩ used for both [g], e.g. *drageð* (*drags*), and [j], e.g. *negge* (*nigh* = *draw nigh*).
- 2-form of ⟨r⟩ after ⟨o⟩, e.g. *for*, *nopor* (*nowhere*).

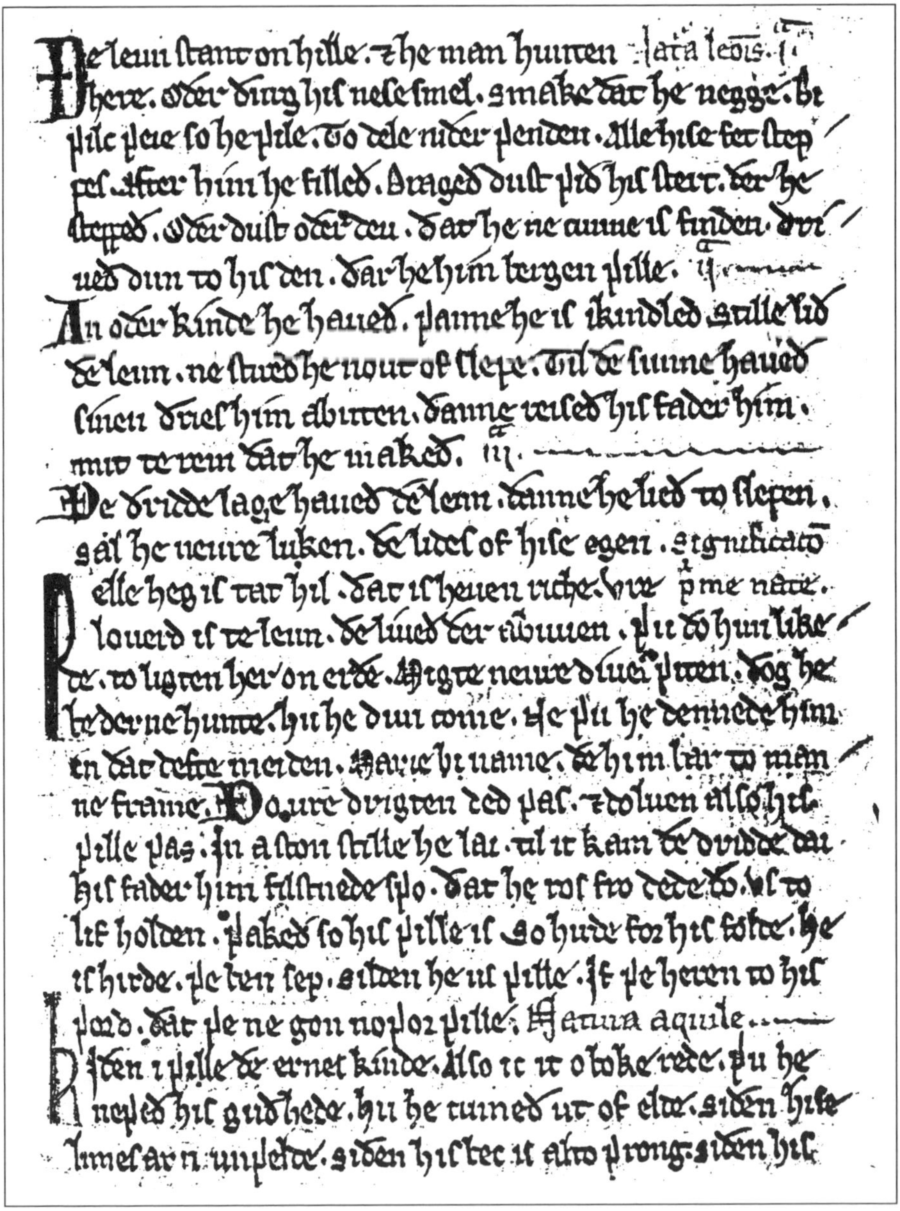

Transcription

Ð e leun ſtant on hılle . 7 he man hunten **Nat'a leōıs . 1[a] .**
here . Oðer ðurg hıſ neſe ſmel . Smake ðat he negge . Bı
pılc peıe ſo he pıle . To dele nıðer penden . Alle hıſe fet ſtep/
peſ . After hım he fılleð . Drageð duſt pıð hıſ ſtert . ðer he
ſteppeð . Oðer duſt oðer deu . ðat he ne cunne ıſ fınden . drí/

ueð dun to hıſ den . ðar he hím bergen pılle . ıj[a] ———
An oðer kínde he haueð . panne he ıſ ıkındled . Stılle lıð
ðe leun . ne ſtıreð he nout of ſlepe . Tıl ðe ſunne haueð
ſínen ðrıeſ hím abuten . ðanne reiſeð hiſ fader hím .
mit te rem ðat he makeð . **iij[a] .** ———
Ðe ðridde lage haueð ðe leun . ðanne he lieð to ſlepen .
Sàl he neure luken . ðe lideſ of hiſe egen . **significacō**
Þelle heg iſ tot hil . ðat iſ heuen riche . Vre **p[i]me nat[a]e**
louerd iſ te leun . ðe lıueð ðer abuuen . pu ðo him like/
de . to ligten her on erðe . Migte neure díuel piten . ðog he
be derne hunte . hu he dun come . Ne pu he dennede him
in ðat defte meiden . Marie bi name . ðe him lar to man/
ne frame . Ðo ure drigten ded paſ . doluen alſo hiſ **.ij[a] . .** ⁊ **iij[a]**
pille pas . In a ſton ſtılle he laı . tıl ıt kam ðc drıdde daı .
Hıſ fader hım fılſtnede ſpo . ðat he roſ fro dede ðo . Vſ to
lıf holden . pakeð ſo hıſ pılle ıſ So hırde for hıſ folde . he
ıſ hırde . pe ben ſep . Sılden he uſ pılle . If pe heren to hıſ
pord . ðat pe ne gon nopor ılle . **Natura aquıle .** ———
K ıðen ı pılle ðe erneſ kínde . Alſo ıc o boke rede . pu he
nepeð hıſ guðhede . Hu he turneð ut of elde . Sıðen hıſe
lımeſ arn unpelde Sıðen hıſ bec ıſ alto prong . ſıðen hıſ...

Text 46 set out in conventional verse form and printing

ME

Natura leonis:
Ðe leun stant on hille and he man hunten here
Oðer ðurg his nese smel smake ðat he negge
Bi wilc weie so he wile to dele niðer wenden
Alle hise fetsteppes after him he filleð
Drageð dust wið his stert ðer he steppeð
Oðer dust oðer deu ðat he ne cunne is finden
Driueð dun to his den ðar he him bergen wille.
An oðer kinde he haueð. Wanne he is ikindled
Stille lið ðe leun ne stireð he nout of slepe
Til ðe sunne haueð sinen ðries him abuten
Ðanne reiseð his fader him mit te rem ðat he makeð.
Ðe ðridde lage haueð ðe leun ðanne he lieð to slepen
Sal he neure luken ðe lides of hise egen.
Significacion:
Welle heg is tot hil ðat is heuen riche.
Vre louerd is te leun ðe líueð ðer abuuen.
Hu* ðo him likede to ligten her on erðe
Migte neure díuel witen ðog he be derne hunte
Hu he dun come ne hu* he dennede him
In ðat defte meiden, Marie bi name
Ðe him bar† to manne frame.
Ðo ure drigten ded was and doluen also his wille was
In a ston stille he lai til it kam ðe ðridde dai.
His fader him filstnede swo ðat he ros fro dede ðo
Vs to lif holden.
Wakeð so his wille is so hirde for his folde
He is hirde, we ben sep. Silden he us wille
If we heren to his word . ðat we ne gon nowor wille .

* MS *pu* (*wu*). *pu* and *hu* are alternative forms, from OE *hu* or *hwu*.

† MS lar.

Literal translation

The nature of the lion:
The lion stands on a hill. If he man hunts here
Or through (the) smell (with) his nose scents that they approach
By whichever way he wishes to (the) dale wend down.
All his footsteps after him he fills
Drags dust with his tail where he steps
Either dust or dew (so) that they cannot find him
Drives down to his den where he will protect them.
Another nature he has. When he is born
Still lies the lion nor stirs he not from sleep
Till the sun has shone thrice about him
Then his father raises him with the cry that he makes.
The third law has the lion when he lies (down) to sleep
Shall he never lock (close) his eye-lids.
Significacion:
Very high is the hill that is the kingdom of heaven.
Our Lord is the lion that lives there above.
How then it pleases him to lighten here on earth
Might never (the) devil know though he in secret hunts
How he came down nor how he lodged himself
In that gentle maiden, Mary by name
Who bore him to man's advantage.
When our Lord was dead and buried as his will was
In a grave still he lay till the third day came
His father him helped so that he rose from the dead then
To hold us to life.
(He) watches so his will is as shepherd for his fold
He is (the) shepherd, we are sheep. He will shield us
If we listen to his word so that we go nowhere wrongly.

The vocabulary of Text 46 is listed in the *Word Book*.

The last three lines of the Text 46 facsimile are the beginning of *The Bestiary* account of the Eagle. John Milton used the image of the eagle 'muing her mighty youth, and kindling her undazl'd eyes at the full midday beam...' in his *Areopagitica* (see Text 130 in chapter 17).

Text 47 – *The Bestiary* – The Eagle

(edited text)

ME	WW
Kiþen I wille þe ernes kinde	Show I wish the eagle's nature
Also Ic o boke rede:	As I it in book read
Wu he neweþ his guþhede	How he renews his youth
Hu he cumeþ ut of elde	How he comes out of old age
Siþen hise limes arn unwelde	When his limbs are weak
Siþen his bec is alto wrong	When his beak is completely twisted
Siþen his fligt is al unstrong	When his flight is all weak
And his egen dimme.	And his eyes dim.
Hereþ wu he neweþ him:	Hear how he renews himself:

A welle he seke þat springeþ ai	A spring he seeks that flows always
Boþe bi nigt and bi dai	Both by night and by day
Þerouer he flegeþ and up he teþ	Thereover he flies and up he goes
Til þat he þe heuene seþ	Till that he the heaven sees
Þurg skies sexe and seuene	Through clouds six and seven
Til he cumeþ to heuene.	Till he comes to heaven.
So rigt so he cunne	As directly as he can
He houe in þe sunne.	He hovers in the sun.
Þe sunne swideþ al his fligt	The sun scorches all his wings
And oc it makeþ his egen brigt.	And also it makes his eyes bright.
His feþres fallen for þe hete	His feathers fall because of the heat
And he dun mide to þe wete.	And he down then to the water
Falleþ in þat welle grund	Falls in the well bottom
Þer he wurdeþ heil and sund	Where he becomes hale and sound
And cumeþ ut al newe...	And comes out all new...

📖 The complete vocabulary of Text 47 is listed in the *Word Book*.

Text 48 – *The Bestiary* – The Whale

Two later 17th-century texts have the whale as their subject: Sir Thomas Browne on the subject of spermaceti, from his *Vulgar Errors* (1646), section 8.2.2, and an extract from John Evelyn's *Diary* in 1658, section 17.5, in which he describes the beaching of a whale at Greenwich. So it would be interesting to compare three different texts on the same topic. Here is part of *The Bestiary* account:

Edited text

Cethegrande is a fis
Þe moste ðat in water is...
Þis fis wuneð wið ðe se grund
And liueð ðer eure heil and sund
Til it cumeð ðe time
Þat storm stireð al ðe se
Þanne sumere and winter winnen
Ne mai it wunen ðerinne
So droui is te sees grund
Ne mai he wunen ðer ðat stund
Oc stireð up and houeð stille
Wiles ðat weder is so ille
Þe sipes ðat arn on se fordriuen
Loð hem is ded and lef to liuen
Biloken hem, and sen ðis fis
A neilond he wenen it is
Þerof he aren swiðe fagen
And mid here migt ðarto he dragen
Sipes on festen and alle up gangen
Of ston mid stel in ðe tunder
Wel to brennen one ðis wunder
Warmen hem wel and heten and drinken
Þe fir he feleð and doð hem sinken
For sone he diueð dun to grunde
He drepeð hem alle wiðuten wunde

Significio

Þis deuel is mikel wið wil and magt
So witches hauen in here craft
He doð men hungren and hauen ðrist
And mani oðer sinful list
Tolleð men to him wið his onde
Woso him folegeð he findeð sonde
Þo arn ðe little in leue lage
Þe mikle ne maig he to him dragen
Þe mikle I mene ðe stedefast
In rigte leue mid fles and gast
Woso listneð deueles lore
On lengðe it sal him rewen sore
Woso festeð hope on him
He sal him folgen to helle dim

📖 The complete vocabulary of Text 48 is listed in the *Word Book*.

WW translation

Cethegrande is a fis
Whale is a fish

Þe moste ðat in water is
the biggest that in water is

Þis fis wuneð wið ðe se grund
thus fish lives on the sea bottom

And liueð ðer eure heil and sund
and lives there ever healthy and sound

Til it cumeð ðe time
till it comes the time

Þat storm stireð al ðe se
that storm stirs up all the sea

Þanne sumere and winter winnen
when summer and winter contend

Ne mai it wunen ðerinne
ne may it dwell therein

So droui is te sees grund
so troubled is the sea bottom

Ne mai he wunen ðer ðat stund
ne may he live there that time

Oc stireð up and houeð stille
but moves up and stays still

Wiles ðat weder is so ille
while the weather is so bad

Þe sipes ðat arn on se fordriuen
the ships that are on sea driven about

Loð hem is ded and lef to liuen
hateful to them is death and pleasing to live

Biloken hem, and sen ðis fis
they look about and see this fish

A neilond he wenen it is
an island they think it is

Þerof he aren swiðe fagen
thereof they are very pleased

And mid here migt ðarto he dragen
and with their might thereto they draw

Sipes on festen and alle up gangen
ships on (it) fasten and all up go

Of ston mid stel in ðe tunder
of flint with steel in the tinder

Wel to brennen one ðis wunder
well to burn on this wonder

Warmen hem wel and heten and drinken
warm them wel and eat and drink

Þe fir he feleð and doð hem sinken
the fire he feels and makes them sink

For sone he diueð dun to grunde
for soon he dives down to bottom

He drepeð hem alle wiðuten wunde
he kills then all without wound

Significio (meaning)

Þis deuel is mikel wið wil and magt
this devil is great in deceit and strength

So witches hauen in here craft
as witches have in their sorcery

He doð men hungren and hauen ðrist
he makes men hunger and have thirst

And mani oðer sinful list
and many other sinful desire

Tolleð men to him wið his onde
entices men to him with his breath

Woso him folegeð he findeð sonde
whoso him follows (he) finds disgrace

Þo arn ðe little in leue lage
those are the little in faith weak

Þe mikle ne maig he to him dragen
the great ne may he to him draw

Þe mikle I mene ðe stedefast
the great I mean the steadfast

In rigte leue mid fles and gast
in true faith in body and spirit

Woso listneð deueles lore
whoso listens to the devil's teaching

On lengðe it sal him rewen sore
at length it shall him grieve sorely

Woso festeð hope on him
whoso fastens hope on him

He sal him folgen to helle dim
he shall him follow to hell dark

7.6 The Lay of Havelok the Dane

The Lay of Havelok is a poem of 3000 lines in rhyming couplets of 8-syllable lines, written in the late 13th century. The surviving, almost complete manuscript was copied in the early 14th century, and like most copies, shows evidence of modifications by the scribe. The poem was written in Lincolnshire in the East Midland dialect. It tells the story of Havelok, a prince of Denmark dispossessed of his rightful Danish inheritance by the wicked Godard, and Goldborough, a princess of England, similarly dispossessed of her succession by the wicked Godrich. All ends well, with Havelok and Goldborough married and king and queen of both England and Denmark jointly.

The short extract in facsimile is part of the story of Havelok's rescue, as a child, from being killed. The fisherman Grim has disobeyed his orders to drown the child and released him from being tied up and gagged. He and his wife Leve decide to raise Havelok with their family and flee to England. The town of Grimsby is said to be named after him in the legend.

Text 49 – *Havelok the Dane* (facsimile)

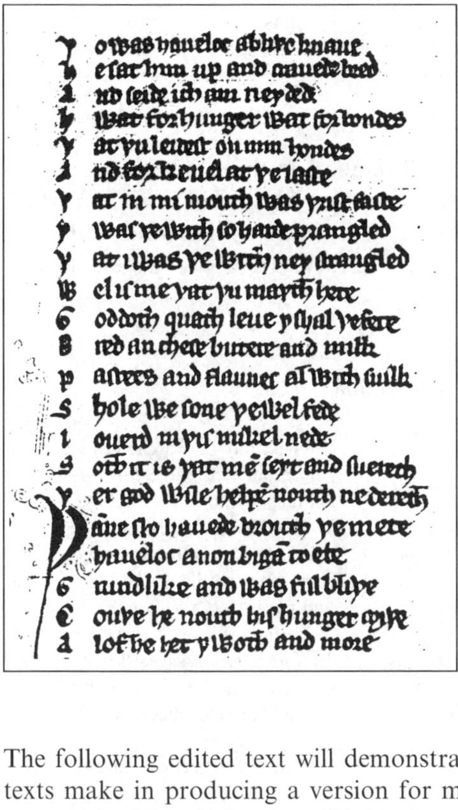

þ o was havueloc a blıþe knaue
h e ſat hım up and crauede bred
a nd ſeıde ıch am ney ded
h wat for hunger wat for bondes
þ at þu leıdeſt on mın hondes
a nd for keuel at þe laſte
þ at ın mı mouth was þrıſt faſte
ẏ waſ þewıth ſo harde prangled
þ at ı was þewıth ney ſtrangled
w el ıſ me þat þu mayth hete
G oddoth quath leue y ſhal þe fete
B red an cheſe butere and mılk
p aſtees and flauneſ al with ſuılk
s hole we ſone þe wel fede
l ouerd ın þıſ mıkel nede
s oth ıt ıs þat mē ſeyt and ſuereth
þ er god wıle helpē nouth ne dereth
þ āne ſho hauede brouth þe mete
haueloc anon bigā to ete
G rundlıke and was ful blıþe
C ouþe he nouth hıſ hunger mıþe
a lof he het y woth and more

The following edited text will demonstrate the decisions that editors of old MS texts make in producing a version for modern readers. Copyists' 'mistakes' are corrected, abbreviations are filled out and modern punctuation is added. Words are inserted to make up the scansion of the verse line. The words that have been modified or added are in bold type:

Þo was Havueloc a bliþe knaue.
He sat him up and crauede bred
And seide, 'Ich am **wel** ney ded,
Hwat for hunger, **hwat** for bondes
Þat þu leidest on min hondes.
And for **þe** keuel at þe laste
Þat in mi mouth was þrist **so** faste.
Y was **þerwith** so harde prangled
Þat I was **þerwith** ney strangled.'
'Wel is me þat þu **maght ete.**
Goddot ,' quath Leue, 'y shal þe fete
Bred **and** chese, butere and milk,
Pastees and flaunes, al with suilk
Shole we sone þe wel fede,
Louerd, in þis mikel nede.
Soth ø is þat **men seyth** and suereth,
Þer God wile helpen, **nouht** ne dereth.'
Þanne sho hauede **brouht** þe mete
Haueloc anon bigan to ete
Grundlike and was ful bliþe.
Couþe he **nouht** his hunger miþe.
A lof he **et**, y wot, and more,
For him hungrede swiþe sore.

The text has three words each of ON and OF origin:

ON band	**bondes**	bond	OF flaon	**flaunes**	cakes
ON kefli	**keuel**	gag	OF pastee	**pastees**	pasties
ON þrysta	**þrist**	thrust	OF strangler	**strangled**	strangled

which may be proportionately less than the numbers in the whole poem. Words from ON are to be expected because the poem was written in an area of high Danish settlement, and from OF because of the steady assimilation of French words into the language during the 13th century. Here are a few further examples.

Other Old Norse and Old French words in *Havelok*

Þet oþer day he kepte **ok**	*ON auk*	The next day he watched out **also**
Swiþe yerne þe erles kok		Very eagerly (for) the earl's cook
Til þat he say him on þe **brigge**	*ON bryggja*	Till he saw him on the **bridge**
And bi him mani fishes **ligge**...	*ON lyggja*	And by him many fishes **lie**...
Þe laddes were **kaske** and **teyte**	*ON kaskr/teitr*	The men were **active** and **eager**
Soth was þat he wolden him bynde		Truth was that he wanted to bind him
And **trusse** al þat he mihten fynde	*OF trousser*	And **pack** all that he might find
Of hise in arke or in **kiste**	*ON kista*	Of his in coffer or in **chest**
Þat he mouhte in **seckes þriste**	*ON sekkr/ðrysta*	*That he might in* **sacks thrust**
Wiþ **poure** mete and **feble** drink	*OF povre/feble*	With **poor** food and **feeble** drink
And dide **greyþe** a **super riche**	*ON greiða* *OF soper/riche*	And **prepared** a **supper rich**
Also he was no wiht **chiche**...	*OF chiche*	As if he was in no way **mean**...

📖 The complete vocabulary of Text 49 is listed in the *Word Book*.

7.7 Early 13th-century loan-words 1200–1249

7.7.1 *Old French*

Hundreds of French loan-words were taken into English speech and writing from the 13th century onwards, and lists of common words, with their MnE reflexes and dates of their earliest recorded occurrence are printed at the end of the following chapters. Most French loan-words from the 12th to the 14th centuries fall into one or other of the following semantic categories, which are related to the political, social and economic affairs of the time:

- art;
- architecture and building;
- church and religion;
- entertainment;
- fashion;
- food and drink;
- government and administration;
- home life;
- law and legal affairs;
- scholarship and learning;
- literature;
- medicine;
- military;
- riding and hunting;
- social ranks.

7.7.1.1 *Choice of examples of loan-words*

In the lists of loan-words only one spelling of the each word is given, though there are often several alternatives from Anglo-French (AF) and/or Old French (OF), with different dialectal English spellings also. Refer to the *Oxford English Dictionary* or a good etymological dictionary for details.

The lists do not give examples of loan-words that have not survived into MnE as reflexes of the originals.

7.7.1.2 *The dating of loan-words*

- The earliest written source that has been identified gives us a 'no later than' date, and the word would almost certainly have been in the spoken language long before it appeared in writing. The exceptions are the learned 'ink-horn terms' from Latin and Greek created by scholars and writers from the 16th century onwards.
- Large numbers of ME manuscripts have been destroyed or lost, and with them the evidence for the appearance of many words in writing.

- Very few manuscripts can be accurately dated, and many are copies of earlier originals, so that most of the dates given with quotations in the *Oxford English Dictionary* can only be approximate.
- It is a matter of chance that a manuscript contains a particular word, which lessens even further the accuracy of dating a word's adoption.

If you compare loan-words that begin with ⟨ch⟩ in the following list of 13th-century loan-words with those of later centuries, you will notice that their MnE pronunciation is [tʃ], the OF pronunciation when they were taken into English – *champion, change*, etc. Later borrowings, e.g. *chevron*, are pronounced with [ʃ], because the French pronunciation had changed. Only *chivalry*, which was originally pronounced with [tʃ], but now with [ʃ] like later loan-words, is an exception.

MnE	*OF*	*Date*
absolution	*absolution*	**1200**
baron	*barun*	**1200**
blame	*blasmer*	**1200**
ermine	*hermine*	**1200**
feast	*feste*	**1200**
fine (n)	*fin*	**1200**
lamp	*lampe*	**1200**
obedience	*obédience*	**1200**
olive	*olive*	**1200**
penitence	*pénitence*	**1200**
poor	*poure*	**1200**
religion	*religiun*	**1200**
rime	*rime*	**1200**
saffron	*safran*	**1200**
sergeant	*sergent*	**1200**
sermon	*sermun*	**1200**
service	*serfise*	**1200**
virgin	*virgine*	**1200**
wait	*waitier*	**1200**
arm (vb)	*armer*	**1205**
cape (cloak)	*cape*	**1205**
catch	*cachier*	**1205**
duke	*duc*	**1205**
hermit	*hermite*	**1205**
poor	*poure*	**1205**
prelate	*prélat*	**1205**
balm	*basme*	**1220**
basin	*bacin*	**1220**
art	*art*	**1225**
boil	*boillir*	**1225**
brooch	*broche*	**1225**
cellar	*celier*	**1225**
champion	*champiun*	**1225**
chapel	*chapele*	**1225**
chapter	*chapitre*	**1225**
chaste	*chaste*	**1225**
chattel	*chatel*	**1225**
clause	*clause*	**1225**
convent	*covent*	**1225**
crucifix	*crucefix*	**1225**
dame	*dame*	**1225**
devotion	*devocion*	**1225**
devout	*devot*	**1225**
dignity	*digneté*	**1225**
estate	*estat*	**1225**
fig	*fige*	**1225**
gentle	*gentil*	**1225**
habit	*habit*	**1225**
haunch	*hanche*	**1225**
heresy	*heresie*	**1225**
heritage	*heritage*	**1225**
image	*image*	**1225**
image	*image*	**1225**
largesse	*largesse*	**1225**
lesson	*lecon*	**1225**
letter	*letter*	**1225**
medicine	*medecine*	**1225**
messenger	*messagier*	**1225**
minstrel	*menestral*	**1225**
noble	*noble*	**1225**
ornament	*ornement*	**1225**
parlour	*parlur*	**1225**
physician	*fisicien*	**1225**
pillar	*piler*	**1225**
pity	*pitet*	**1225**
place	*place*	**1225**
preach	*prechier*	**1225**
prince	*prince*	**1225**
proof	*prueve*	**1225**
ransom	*rançon*	**1225**

MnE	OF	Date	MnE	OF	Date
remedy	*remedie*	**1225**	trinity	*trinite*	**1225**
remission	*remission*	**1225**	veil	*veile*	**1225**
salvation	*sauvacion*	**1225**	warden	*wardein*	**1225**
servant	*servant*	**1225**	warrant	*warant*	**1225**
siege	*sege*	**1225**	acquit	*aquiter*	**1230**
simony	*simonie*	**1225**	assail	*asalir*	**1230**
spice	*espice*	**1225**	banner	*banere*	**1230**
state	*estat*	**1225**	change	*changer*	**1230**
story	*estorie*	**1225**	poison	*puison*	**1230**
temptation	*temptaciun*	**1225**	service	*servise*	**1230**
tournament	*torneiement*	**1225**	constable	*cunestable*	**1240**
traitor	*traitre*	**1225**	ribald	*ribauld*	**1240**
treason	*treison*	**1225**			

7.7.2 Old Norse

MnE	ON	Date	MnE	ON	Date
aloft	*a lopt*	**1200**	skin	*skinn*	**1200**
aye (always)	*ei*	**1200**	they	*ðei-r*	**1200**
band	*band*	**1200**	though	*ðo*	**1200**
bank	*banki*	**1200**	thrive	*ðrifask*	**1200**
birth	*byrðir*	**1200**	hit	*hitta*	**1205**
bull	*bole*	**1200**	hap	*happ*	**1205**
clip	*klippa*	**1200**	scale(s)	*skal*	**1205**
egg (vb)	*eggja*	**1200**	gape	*gapa*	**1220**
flit	*flytja*	**1200**	sky	*sky*	**1220**
fro	*fra*	**1200**	crook	*krokr*	**1225**
get	*geta*	**1200**	crooked	*krokr + -ed*	**1225**
ill	*illr*	**1200**	loose (vb)	*louss*	**1225**
kid	*kið*	**1200**	rotten	*rotinn*	**1225**
kindle	*kynda*	**1200**	seemly	*sœmiligr*	**1225**
meek	*miukr*	**1200**	trust (vb)	*treysta*	**1225**
raise	*reisa*	**1200**	want	*vanta*	**1225**
rid	*ryðja*	**1200**	window	*vindauga*	**1225**
root	*rot*	**1200**	cast	*kasta*	**1230**
same	*same*	**1200**	loan	*lan*	**1240**
scare	*skirra*	**1200**			

7.7.3 Low German

The term *Low German* is used to identify early dialects of Dutch, Flemish and northern Germany. Words from these languages begin to be recorded in the 13th century, and include the following:

bounce	*bunsen*	**1225**	*Ancrene Riwle* – þer ʒe schulen iseon **bunsen** ham mit tes deofles bettles
snatch	*snacken*	**1225**	*Ancrene Riwle* – Ase ofte ase þe hund of helle keccheð ei god from þe . . . smit hine so luðerliche ˛et him loðie to **snecchen** eft to þe
tackle	*takel*	**1250**	*Genesis & Exodus* – And tol and **takel** and orf he [Abram] dede Wenden hom to here oʒen stede
poll (head)	*polle*	**1290**	*South English Legendary* – þe deuel . . . wolde fain henten heom bi þe **polle**
boy	*boi*	**1300**	*Beket* – ʒunge childerne and wylde **boyes** also . . . scornede hire

7.7.4 *Arabic*

New words may be adopted and then passed on to other languages. Numbers of Middle English loan-words from French were, in fact, ultimately derived from Arabic. For example, the word *saffron* was borrowed from OF *safran* and first recorded about 1200,

> *Trinity College Homilies* – Hire winpel wit oðer maked ʒeleu mid **saffran**.

but the ultimate source is Arabic *za faran*.

Similarly, the word *admiral* is first recorded about 1205,

> *Layamon* – þat on **admiral** of Babiloine he wes ældere.

The word's etymology is complex, and it might have been borrowed from OF, or directly from Arabic *amir al* (= *commander of* . . .).

Loan-words taken directly into English from Arabic are not in evidence until the late 16th century (see section 16.4.9).

8. Northern and Southern texts compared

Old English and Old Norse in the Danelaw

The Danish and Norwegian settlers in the Danelaw (see sections 3.3.1 and 3.4.1) at first spoke dialects of Old Norse, but living with or close by the Angles and Saxons of the North and East Midlands of England, their language was in time assimilated into English. No written record of the Old Norse spoken by them has survived. We believe that Old Norse and Old English were 'mutually intelligible' – much of the vocabulary was similar enough to be understood by either Danes or English. A principal difference lay in the inflections used in OE and ON to mark grammatical categories like singular/plural, past/present, and so on.

Loss of inflections in ME

The loss of inflections is called **levelling**. We have already seen that the variety of the inflections of OE began to be reduced in early ME by the process we call regularisation (see section 6.2.2.1). This took place more quickly in the Northern and Midland dialects spoken in or close to the Danelaw. Consequently, we find that these dialects show marked differences from the other Southern and Western dialects, with a much earlier reduction and loss of the OE inflections. The effect of the Viking settlement in the Danelaw was therefore not only an influx of Scandinavian words, but the kinds of simplification that are known to take place when people speaking similar languages communicate together, or when a pidgin language begins to be spoken.

8.1 *Cursor Mundi* – a history of the world

Cursor Mundi was written in the north of England towards the end of the 13th century. It consists of almost 24,000 lines of verse, retelling Christian legends and the stories of the Bible from the Creation to Doomsday (*cursor* is Latin for *runner* or *messenger*; *mundi* for *of the world*). The original manuscript by the unknown author has been lost, but it was copied many times and nine manuscript copies have survived. The version transcribed below is believed to be the closest to the original poem.

Late in the 14th century another copy was written in the south of England. The writer revised the poem systematically, changing word structure, rhyme, vocabulary and spellings to match his pronunciation. It therefore provides us with some good linguistic evidence about Northern and Southern dialectal differences in the 14th century.

Here are the opening lines from the Northern and Southern versions, with a literal translation of the Northern text. The author tells how people desire to read old romances and stories about princes, prelates and kings. They want to hear the things that please them best – wise men to hear wisdom, fools folly. A tree is known by its fruit, and in the present times men are esteemed only if they love 'paramours'. But bought love is false and the Virgin Mary is man's best lover – her love never fails.

Activity 8.1

(i) Examine the two texts for evidence of the changes in the language described in chapters 4–6 and summarised in section 6.4.12.

(ii) List some of the features by which we might identify the dialect of a text as either Northern or Southern early Middle English.

The etymological origins of the words are listed in the *Word Book*.

Text 50 – *Cursor Mundi* – Northern and Southern texts (i)

Translation	Northern version	Southern version
Man yearns to hear poems	Man yhernes rimes forto here	Men ȝernen iestes for to here
And (to) read romances in various styles	And romans red on manere sere	And romaunce rede in dyuerse manere
Of Alexander the conqueror	Of Alisaundur þe conquerour	Of Alisaunder þe conqueroure
Of Julius Caesar the emperor	Of luly Cesar þe emparour	Of lulius cesar þe emperoure
Of the strong strife of Greece and Troy	O Grece and Troy þe strang striif	Of grece & troye þe longe strif
Where many thousand lose their life	Þere many thosand lesis þer liif	Þere mony mon lost his lif
Of Brutus that warrior bold of hand	O Brut þat bern bald of hand	Of bruyt þat baroun bolde of honde
The first conqueror of England	Þe first conquerour of Ingland	Furste conqueroure of engelonde
King Arthur that was so great	Kyng Arthour þat was so rike	Of kyng Arthour þat was so riche
Whom none in his time was like	Quam non in hys tim was like	Was noon in his tyme him liche
Of marvels that befell his knights	O ferlys þat hys knythes fell	Of wondris þat his knyȝtes felle
That I hear tell of various adventures	Þat aunters sere I here of tell	And auntres duden men herde telle
Like Gawain Kay & other strong men	Als Wawan Cai and oþer stabell	As Wawayn kay & oþre ful abul
To defend the Round Table	Forto were þe Ronde Tabell	For to kepe þe rounde tabul
How Charlemagne & Roland fought	How Charles kyng and Rauland	How kyng charles & rouland fauȝt
With Saracens they wished no peace	Wit Sarazins wald þai na saght	Wiþ Sarazines nolde þei be sauȝt
Of Tristan and his beloved Isolde	O Tristrem and hys leif Ysote	Of tristram & of Isoude þe swete
How he for her became a fool	How he for here becom a sote	How þei wiþ loue firste gan mete

Of Yonec and of Isumbras	19.	O Ioneck and of Ysambrase	Of kyng Ion and of Isombras
Of Ydoine and of Amadas	20.	O Ydoine and of Amadase	Of Idoyne & of amadas
Stories of diverse things	21.	Storis als o serekin thinges	Storyes of dyuerse þinges
Of princes prelates and of kings	22.	O princes prelates and o kynges	Of princes prelatis & of kynges
Various songs of different rhyme	23.	Sanges sere of selcuth rime	Mony songes of dyuerse ryme
English French and Latin	24.	Inglis Frankys and Latine	As englisshe fransshe & latyne
Everyone is eager to read and hear	25.	To rede and here ilkon is prest	To rede & here mony are prest
The things that please them best	26.	Þe thynges þat þam likes best	Of þinges at hem likeþ best
The wise man will hear of wisdom	27.	Þe wisman wil o wisdom here	þe wise man of wisdome here
The fool draws near to folly	28.	Þe foul hym draghus to foly nere	þe fool him draweþ to foly nere
The wicked man is loth to hear of right	29.	Þe wrang to here o right is lath	þe wronge to here rit is looþ
And pride is angry at obedience	30.	And pride wyt buxsumnes is wrath	And pride wiþ buxomnes is wrooþ
(The) lecher has hatred of chastity	31.	O chastite has lichur leth	Of chastite þe lecchoure haþ lite
Anger always wars on compassion	32.	On charite werrais wreth	Charite aȝeyn wraþþe wal flite
But by the fruit may the discerning see	33.	Bot be þe fruit may scilwis se	But bi þe fruyte may men ofte se
Of what virtue is each tree	34.	O quat vertu is ilka tre	Of what vertu is vche a tre
Of every kind of fruit that man finds	35.	Of fruit þat man schal fund	And vche fruyt þat men may fynde
It derives from the root its nature	36.	He fettes fro þe rote his kynd	He haþ from þe rote his kynde
Of good pear tree come good pears	37.	O gode per tre coms peres	Of good pire com gode perus
Worse tree worse fruit it bears	38.	Wers tre vers fruit it beres	Werse tre wers fruyt berus
That (which) I speak of this same tree	39.	Þat I speke o þis ilke tre	Þat i saye þus of þis tre
Symbolizes man both me and thee	40.	Bytakens man both me and þe	Bitokeneþ mon boþe þe & me
This fruit symbolizes all our deeds	41.	Þis fruit alle our dedis	Þis fruyt bitokeneþ alle oure dedes
Both good and ill who rightly reads	42.	Both gode and ille qua rightly redis	Boþe gode & euel who so riȝte redes
Our deeds from our heart take root	43.	Ovr dedis fro vr hert tas rote	Oure dedes fro oure herte take rote
Whether they deserve pain or reward	44.	Quedur þai be worth or bale or bote	Wheþer þei turne to bale or bote
For by the thing that a man is drawn to	45.	For be þe thyng man drawes till	For bi þat þing mon draweþ tille
Men shall know him for good or ill	46.	Men schal him knaw for god or ill	Men may him for good or ille
An example about them here I say	47.	A saumpul her be þaem I say	Ensaumpel herby to hem I sey
That rage in their debauchery always	48.	Þat rages in þare riot ay	þat rage in her riot al wey
In riot and loose living	49.	In riot and in rigolage	In ryot & in rigolage
They spend the period of all their life	50.	Of all þere liif spend þai þe stage	Spende mony her ȝouþe & her age
For now none is held in fashion	51.	For now is halden non in curs	For now is he holden nouȝt in shouris
But (him) who can love passionately	52.	Bot qua þat luue can par amurs	But he con loue paramouris
That folly love, that vanity	53.	Þat foly luue þat uanite	þat foles lif þat vanite
No other pleasure pleases them now	54.	Þam likes now nan oþer gle	Him likeþ now noon oþere gle
It is but illusion to say	55.	Hit ne ys bot fantum forto say	Hit is but fantom for to say
Today it is tomorrow away	56.	Today it is tomoru away	Today hit is tomorwe away
With chance of death or change of heart	57.	Wyt chaunce of ded or chaunge of hert	Wiþ chaunce of deþ or chaunge of hert
What began in comfort has painful end	58.	Þat soft began has endyng smert	þat softe bigan endeþ ful smert
For when you most secure think to be	59.	For wen þow traistest wenis at be	For whenne þu wenest hit trewest to be
From her shall you or she from thee	60.	Fro hir schalt þou or scho fro þe	Þou shalt from hit or hit from þe
He that most firmly hopes to stand	61.	He þat tiithest wenis at stand	He þat weneþ stiffest to stonde
Let him take care his fall is very close	62.	Warre hym his fall is nexst his hand	War him his fal is nexte at honde
Ere he so violently down is brought	63.	Ar he sua brathly don be broght	Whenne he so soone doun is brouȝt
Where to go he knows not	64.	Wydur to wende ne wat he noght	Whider to wende woot he nouȝt
Until his love has led him	65.	Bytuixand his luf haf hym ledd	But to whom his loue haþ him led
To such reward as he him ??	66.	To sli mede als he him forwit	To take suche mede shal he be sted
For then shall reward without hindrance	67.	For þann sal mede witoten mer	For þere shal mede wiþouten let

Be allotted for deeds either better or worse	68. Be mette for dede or bettur or wer	Be sett to him for dew dett
Therefore I bless that loved one	69. Forþi blisce I þat aramour	Þerfore blesse we þat paramoure
(Who) when I have need helps me	70. Quen I haue nede me dos socure	Þat in oure nede doþ vs socoure
That saves me from sin first in the world	71. Þat saues me first in herth fra syn	Þat saueþ vs in erþe fro synne
And helps me to win heaven's bliss	72. And heuen blys me helps to wyn	And heuen blisse helpeþ to wynne
For though I have been untrue at times	73. For þof I quilum haf ben untrew	For þouȝe I sumtyme be vntrewe
Her love is always constantly new	74. Hir luue is ay ilik new	Hir loue is euer I liche newe
She holds her love true always	75. Hir luue sco haldes lele ilike	Hir loue is euer trewe and lele
That is sweeter than honey from a hive	76. Þat suetter es þan hony o bike	Ful swete hit is to monnes hele
Such (a one) on earth is not (to be) found	77. Suilk in herth es fundun nan	Suche oþere in erþe is founden none
For she is mother and maiden	78. For scho es modur and maiden	For she is modir & mayden alone
Mother and maiden never the less	79. Modur and maiden neuer þe lesse	Modir & mayden neuer þe les
Therefore Christ took flesh from her	80. Forþi of hir tok Crist his flesse	Þerfore of hir toke ihesu flesshe
Who truly loves this mistress	81. Qua truly loues þis lemman	Who þat loueþ trewely þis lemmon
This is the love that is never past	82. Þis es þe loue bes neuer gan	He shal haue loue þat neuer is woon
For in this love she never faile	83. For in þis loue scho failes neuer	For in þis lif she faileþ neuer
And in that other she lasts for ever	84. And in þat toþer scho lastes euer	And in þat oþer lasteþ euer

8.1.1 *Commentary*

(The Northern text word is first when pairs of words or phrases are quoted. Figures refer to line numbers.)

8.1.1.1 *Grammar*

Verb inflections

Present tense 3rd person singular (OE -eþ, -aþ or -þ)

þam likes/hem likeþ 26 draghus/draweþ 28 bytakens/bitokeneþ (2) 40, 41
drawes till/draweþ tille 45 likes/like 54 wenis/weneþ 61
saues/saueþ 71 helps/helpeþ 72 loues/loueþ 81
scho failes/she faileþ 83 lastes/lasteþ 84

The OE suffix is unchanged as [əθ] in the Southern text, but has become [əs], spelt ⟨-es⟩, ⟨-is⟩ or ⟨us⟩ in the Northern text. The elision of the vowel leaves the familiar ⟨s⟩ inflection of MnE 3rd person singular present tense verbs – *likes*, *draws*, *saves*, *fails*, etc. This is evidence of the swifter 'modernisation' of the language in the north, and of the linguistic conservatism of the south, relative, that is, to Old English.

Present tense 3rd person plural (OE -aþ)

yhernes/ȝernen 1

The evidence is minimal, but we notice that both inflections have changed, and that the Northern plural inflection ⟨es⟩ is identical to the singular.

Present tense 2nd person singular (OE -est, -ast, -st)

wenis/wenest 59 tiithest/stiffest 61

Noun inflections

The variety of OE inflections marking plural nouns – ⟨-as⟩, ⟨-u⟩, ⟨-ru⟩, ⟨-a⟩, ⟨-an⟩ and zero – was discussed in section 6.2.2.1. The evidence of both texts shows a regularisation to a common [əs] or [s], the MnE inflection, with the usual variants in spelling, ⟨-es⟩, ⟨-is⟩ and ⟨-us⟩, but we would need to examine much more data to be able to confirm this as the norm.

rimes/iestes 1	ferlys/wondris 11	knythes/knyȝtes 11
Sarazins/Sarazines 16	storis/storyes 21	princes/princes 22
prelates/prelatis 22	kynges/kynges 22	sanges/songes 23
thynges/þinges 26	peres/perus 37	dedis/dedes 41, 43

Many ME noun plurals retained the [ən] suffix.

Pronouns – 3rd person plural

Nominative (*OE hi/hie*)

wald þai na saght/nolde þei be sauȝt 16 -/þei 18
spend þai þe stage/-50

Possessive (*OE hira/heora*)

þer liif 6 Of all þere liif/her ȝouþe & her age 50

Dative (*OE him, heom*)

þam likes/hem likeþ 26

We are unlikely to notice the use of *þai*, *þer* or *þam* (*they*, *their*, *them*) unless we remember that the OE plural 3rd person pronouns were *hi*, *hira* and *him*. This borrowing from ON of distinctive forms, all beginning with ⟨th-⟩, began early on in the Northern dialects of ME. It spread southwards, but was not completed there even at the beginning of the 15th century. In Text 50 the Southern version has the ON *þei* as subject of a clause, but retains the older forms *her* and *hem* for the possessive and object cases. Chaucer, writing in the 1390s in the London dialect, used the new form for the subject pronoun,

And thus **they** been accorded and ysworn...

but the older forms for the others,

And many a louely look on **hem** he caste...
Men sholde wedden after **hir** estaat...

Feminine pronouns

The OE feminine subject pronoun was *heo*, beginning with ⟨h⟩ like all the personal pronouns, and therefore probably easily confused with the other pronouns. The development of MnE *she* began during the early ME period, but with a variety of transitional forms, illustrated in section 9.1.1 in the next chapter, in different dialectal areas. From the limited evidence of Text 50, the Northern text form was pronounced [ʃoː] and the Southern [ʃeː].

Subject (*OE heo*)

scho es/she is 78   scho failes/she faileþ 83
sco haldes 75

Object (*OE hi/hie*)

here/-18

Possessive and dative (*OE hire, hiere*)

hir luue/hir loue 74, 75   of hir/of hir 80

8.1.1.2 *Pronunciation*

Shifting and rounding of OE long open back vowel [ɑː] to [ɔː]

In section 6.1.4.8 it was said that this vowel change took place only south of the Humber, and the evidence of Text 50 confirms this:

wald/nolde 16	lath/looþ 29	wrath/wrooþ 30
bytakens/bitokene 40, 41	knaw/knowe 46	halden/ holden 51
nan/noon 54	fra/fro 71	nan/none 77
qua/who 81		

OE [y]

(See section 6.1.4.6.)

first/furste 8 (*OE fyrsta*)   -/duden 12 (*OE dydon*)

o/a before nasal consonant

(See section 6.1.4.7.)

many/mony 6	hand/honde 7, 62	sanges/songes 23
wrang/wronge 29	man/mon 40	stand/stonde 61
lemman/lemmon 81		

⟨k⟩ from ON and ⟨ch⟩ from OE

The contrast here comes from the Northern use of words derived from ON or from Northern pronunciation with [k] of OE words with [tʃ]:

rike/riche 9	ON rikr/OE rice & OF riche
like/liche 10 & ilik/I liche 74	ON likr/OE (ge)lice
serekin 21/-	ON ser + ON kyn or OE cynn
suilk/suche 77	Northern form of OE swilc/OE swilc, swelc
ilkon/-25, ilka/vche 34 & alkyn/vche 35	Northern forms of *ilch* from OE *ælc + an*.

8.1.1.3 *Spelling*

Double letters for long vowel

In order to distinguish long vowels from short, some scribes doubled the vowel letter. This accounts for most of the ⟨ee⟩ and ⟨oo⟩ spellings in MnE, but ⟨ii⟩ and ⟨aa⟩ dropped out of fashion, and ⟨uu⟩ was rarely used (see section 6.1.3.1). In Text 50 this is a feature of the Southern text only:

striif 5 fool 28 looþ 29
wrooþ 30 noon 54 woot 64

⟨qu-⟩ for ⟨wh-⟩

This ⟨qu-⟩ spelling is not the French convention for spelling OE ⟨cw⟩ (section 6.1.3.1) but a representation of a heavily aspirated fricative consonant, [xw]. ⟨qu-⟩ or ⟨quh-⟩ was in fact retained in Scots spelling through to the 17th century, e.g. *quhairunto*, *quhole* for *whereunto*, *whole* from a letter by King James VI in 1586.

quam/-10 (=whom) quat/what 34 quedur/wheþer 44
qua/who 81

⟨gh⟩

In OE, letter yogh ⟨ʒ⟩ had come to represent three sounds, [g] [j] [ɣ] (see section 3.1.2.3). With the adoption of the continental letter ⟨g⟩ for [g], ⟨ʒ⟩ tended to be used for [j]. Two related sounds that occurred after a vowel, [ç] and [x], caused problems of spelling, and among different choices, ⟨gh⟩ became common. [ç] and [x] are fricative consonants, as in Scots *licht*, *ocht*, *nicht*).

faght/fauʒt 15 saght/sauʒt 16 broght/brouʒt 63
noght/nouʒt 64
draghus/draweþ 28
right/rit 29

The consonants [x] and [ç] came to be elided in many words eventually, e.g. *brought*, *sought*, *right*, *bough* (though the spelling has been retained). In others it became the fricative consonant [f] as in *cough*, *tough*, *laugh*. The single example in Text 50 helps to show how the irregularity of the MnE pronunciation of ⟨gh⟩ is the result of a fairly random choice between different dialectal pronunciations.

þof/þouʒe 73

⟨s⟩, ⟨sse⟩ and ⟨sshe⟩ for word-final [ʃ]

(See section 6.1.3.3.)

Inglis/englisshe 24 Frankys/fransshe 24 flesse/flesshe 80

8.1.1.4 *Vocabulary*

Core vocabulary

MnE 'core vocabulary' – those words that are the most basic to the language and common in everyday use in speech – has two principal sources:

- OE words that have reflexes in the language today, which include words of ON origin; these form the basic 'Germanic' elements of the language.
- OF words that were adopted during the three to four centuries after the Norman Conquest of 1066, and which have been fully assimilated to English in their pronunciation, morphology and spelling.

If we therefore discover the proportion of OE to ON and OF words in a ME text, we have some evidence which may help in assessing its possible date and dialectal area. A text with a significantly large number of ON words is likely to be in a Northern or East Midland dialect, the area of Danish settlement. The higher the proportion of OF words, then the later the text's composition. This, of course, needs to be done with complete texts in order to obtain any statistically significant figures, and a whole range of evidence must be studied, including spelling and pronunciation, word-forms and grammar as well as etymological derivation. The figures for OE, ON and OF derivation for the two *Cursor Mundi* texts are:

	OE	*ON*	*OF/AN*
Northern text	76%	9%	15%
Southern text	78.5%	4.5%	17%

The ON and OF vocabularies of the two texts are:

Northern text – Old Norse

ai/ay	ON ei = always	sli	ON slikr = such
both	ON baðir	tas	ON taka
brathly	ON braðliga = violently	tiithest stiithest?	ON tiðast/?OE stiþe?
ferlys	ON ferligr	till	ON til
fra/fro	ON fra	tok	ON taka, tok
ill/ille	ON illr	traistest	ON treystr = most secure
rike	ON rikr	þai	ON þeir
rote	ON rot	þare	ON þeirra
saght	ON saht = settlement	þof	ON þo
scilwis	ON skilviss = discerning	wrang	ON wrang
sere	ON ser = various		
serekin	ON ser + kyn	**23 types**	

Northern text – Old French/Anglo-Norman

amurs	OF amur = love	chaunce	OF cheaunce
aunters	OF aventure	conquerour	AF conquerour
charite	OF charité	emparour	AN empereur
chastite	OF chasteté	failes	OF faillir

fantum	OF fantosme	romans	OF romans
foly	OF folie	ronde	AN rund
foul	OF fol = fool	saues	AN sauver
fruit	OF fruit	saumpul	AN essaumple
lele	OF leel	socure	AN sucurs
lichur	AN lechur, lichur	sote	OF sot = fool
manere	AN manere	stabell	OF stable = sturdy
par amurs/paramour	OF par amurs	stage	OF stage
prelates	OF prelat	storis	AN storie
princes	OF prince	striif	OF strif
rages	OF rager = live wantonly	tabell	OF table
rigolage	OF rigolage	uanite	OF vanité
rime/rimes	OF rime	vertu	OF vertu
riot	OF riote	werrais	AN werreier
		37 types	

Southern text – Old Norse

boþe	ON baðir	rote	ON rot	þei	ON þeir
ille	ON illr	sauȝt	ON saht = settlement	þouȝe	ON þo
liche	ON likr	tille	ON til	**10 types**	
nere	ON nær	wronge	ON wrangr		

Southern text – Old French/Anglo-Norman

abul	OF hable, able	lecchoure	AN lechur, lichur
age	OF eage	lele	OF leel
auntres	OF aventure	manere	AN maniere
baroun	OF barun	paramoure/-is	OF par amurs
charite	OF charité	prelatis	OF prelat
chastite	OF chasteté	princes	OF prince
chaunce	OF cheance	rage	OF rager
chaunge	AF chaunge	rigolage	OF rigolage
conqueroure	AF conquerour	riot/ryot	OF riote
dett	OF dete, dette	romaunce	OF romans
dew	OF deu	rounde	AN rund
dyuerse	OF divers	ryme	OF rime
emperoure	AN empereur	saueþ	AN sauver
ensaumpel	AN essaumple	socoure	AN sucurs
faileþ	OF faillir	storyes	AN storie
fantom	OF fantosme	strif	OF strif
foles/fool	OF fol = fool	tabul	OF table
foly	OF folie	vanite	OF vanité
fruyt/fruyte	OF fruit	vertu	OF vertu
iestes	OF geste = story	**39 types**	

8.1.1.5 *Summary – identifying Northern and Southern dialects of ME*

We have found the following differences between the two short extracts from the *Cursor Mundi* texts. No firm conclusions can be drawn from such a little data, but there is evidence of levelling and regularisation in both dialects.

	Northern text	*Southern text*	*Old English*
Verb inflections:			
Present 2nd person singular	-is, -est	-est	-est, ast, -st
Present 3rd person singular	-es, -is, -s	-eþ	-aþ
Present 3rd person plural	-es	-en	-aþ
Nouns:			
Plural inflections	-es, -s, -is	-es, -is, -uȝ	-as, -an, -u, -ru, -a
Pronouns:			
Feminine subject	scho/sco	she	heo
Feminine object	here	*no evidence*	hi/hie
Feminine possessive	hir	hir	hire/hiere
3rd person plural subject	þai	þei	hi/hie
3rd person plural possessive	þer	her	hira/heora
3rd person plural object/dative	þam	hem	him/heom
Pronunciation/spelling			
OE long vowel [ɑː] rounded to [ɔː]	*no*	*yes*	
OE close front vowel [y]	⟨i⟩	⟨u⟩	
o or a before nasal consonant	⟨a⟩	⟨o⟩	
ON ⟨k⟩ or OE ⟨ch⟩	⟨k⟩	⟨ch⟩ & ⟨k⟩	
⟨qu-⟩ or ⟨wh-⟩?	⟨qu-⟩	⟨wh-⟩	
spelling of [ʃ]	⟨-s/ss⟩	⟨ssh⟩	

You should be able to check these findings in later chapters on the dialects of the language in the 14th century.

Another MS of* Cursor Mundi *(facsimile)

The following facsimile of the first eleven lines of *Cursor Mundi* is from one of the other Northern manuscripts, probably copied about 1400.

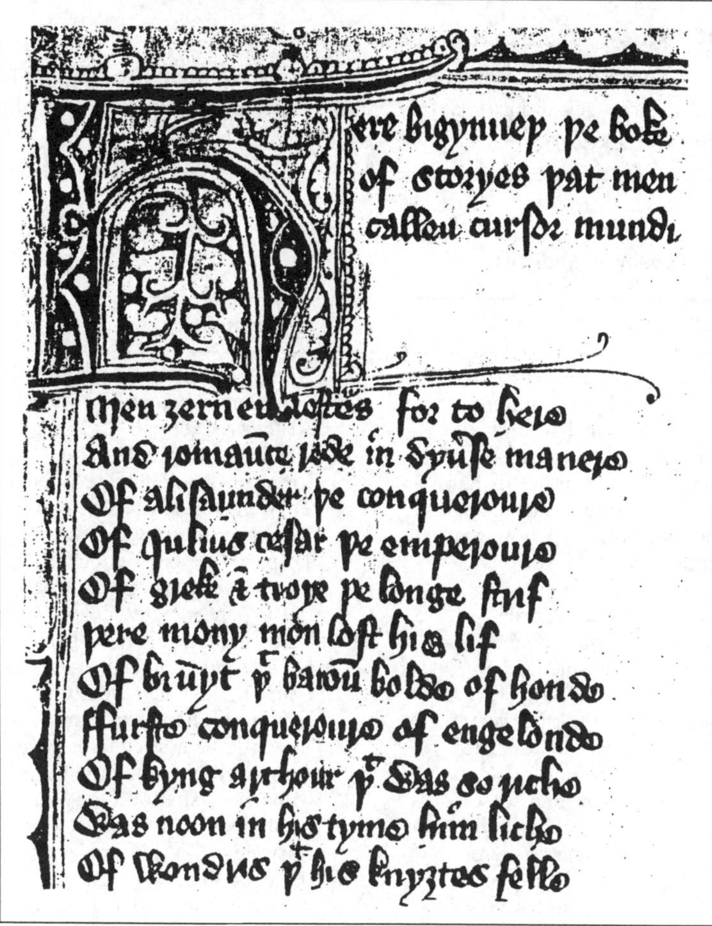

here bıgynneþ þe boke
of storyes þat men
callen curſor mundı

Men ȝernen ıeſtes for to here
And romaūce rede ın dyūſe* manere
Of alıſaunder þe conqueroure
Of ȷulıus ceſar þe emperoure
Of greſe 7 troye þe longe ſtrıf
Þere mony mon loſt hıs lıf
Of bruyt þ^{t} barōu bolde of honde
ffurſte conqueroure of engelonde
Of kyng arthour þ^{t} was so rıche
Was noon ın hıs tyme hım lıche
Of wondrıs þ^{t} hıs knyȝtes felle

* *dyuerse.*

Activity 8.2

Examine the next extract from *Cursor Mundi* in its Northern and Southern dialect forms and use the vocabulary lists to find evidence of change and difference in the language of the texts.

Text 51 – *Cursor Mundi* (ii)

Northern dialect	*Southern dialect*
Adam had pasid nine hundret yere	Adam past nyne hundride ȝere
Nai selcut þof he wex unfere	No wonder þei he wex vnfere
Forwroght wit his hak and spad	Al forwrouȝte wiþ his spade
Of himself he wex al sad.	Of his lyf he wex al mate
He lened him þan apon his hak	Vpon his spade his breste he leyde
Wit Seth his sun þusgat he spak	To seeth his son þus he seyde
Sun he said þou most now ga	Sone he seide þow moste go
To Paradis þat I com fra	To paradyse þat I coom fro
Til Cherubin þat þe yate ward.	To cherubyn þat ȝate warde
Yai sir, wist I wyderward	Þat kepeþ þo ȝates swyþe harde
þat tat vncuth contre ware	Seeth seide to his fadir þere
þou wat þat I was neuer þare.	How stondeþ hit fadir and where
þus he said I sal þe sai	I shal þe telle he seyde to sey
Howgate þou sal tak þe wai.	How þow shalt take þe riȝte wey
Toward þe est end of þis dale	Towarde þe eest ende of þe ȝonder vale
Find a grene gate þou sale	A grene way fynde þow shale
In þat way sal þou find forsoth	In þat wey shaltou fynde and se
Þi moders and mine our bather slogh	Þe steppes of þi modir and me
Foluand thoru þat gresse gren	Forwelewed in þat gres grene
Þat euer has siþen ben gren	Þat euer siþen haþ ben sene
Þat we com wendand als vnwis	Þere we comen goyinge as vnwyse
Quen we war put o paradis	Whenne we were put fro paradyse
Vnto þis wretched warld slade	Into þis ilke wrecchede slade
Þar I first me self was made	Þere myself firste was made
Thoru þe gretnes of our sin	For þe greetnes of oure synne
Moght na gres groue siþen þarin	Miȝte siþen no gras growe þerynne
Þe falau slogh sal be þi gate	Þat same wole þe lede þi gate
O paradis right to þe yate	Fro heþen to paradise ȝate

ON and OF Vocabulary

Northern text

ON baðir	**bather**	both
ON frā	**fra**	from
ON gata	**gate**	way, path
ON sloð	**slogh**	
ON taka	**tak**	take
ON til	**til**	to
ON þō	**þof**	though
ON ufoerr	**unfere**	weak, inform

Southern text

ON fra	**fro**	from
ON gata	**gate**	way, path
ON sama	**same**	same
ON taka	**take**	take
OF mat	**mate**	= downcast
OF paradis	**paradise**	paradise
OF passer	**past**	passed

ON and OF Vocabulary (*continued*)

Northern text			*Southern text*
OF contree	**contre**	country	
OF paradis	**paradis**	paradise	
OF passer	**pasid**	passed	
OF sire	**sir**	sir	
Northern dialect: ON words 8, OF 4			Southern dialect: ON words 4, OF 3

The complete vocabulary of both versions of Text 51 is listed in the *Word Book*.

8.2 Later 13th-century loan-words 1250–1299

8.2.1 *Old French*

abbey	*abaie*	**1250**	sugar	*çucre*	**1289**
attire	*atirer*	**1250**	amethyst	*ametiste*	**1290**
censer	*censier*	**1250**	colour	*color*	**1290**
defend	*defendre*	**1250**	courtier	*corteour*	**1290**
falcon	*faucon*	**1250**	creator	*creatour*	**1290**
figure (n)	*figure*	**1250**	cruet	*cruete*	**1290**
leper	*lepre*	**1250**	date (fruit)	*date*	**1290**
malady	*maladie*	**1250**	friar	*frere*	**1290**
music	*musique*	**1250**	fry	*frire*	**1290**
parson	*persone*	**1250**	gout	*goute*	**1290**
plead	*plaidier*	**1250**	grape	*grape*	**1290**
sacrifice	*sacrifice*	**1250**	herb	*erbe*	**1290**
scarlet	*escarlate*	**1250**	homage	*ommage*	**1290**
spy (vb)	*espier*	**1250**	incense	*encens*	**1290**
stable	*estable*	**1250**	inquest	*enqueste*	**1290**
virtue	*vertu*	**1250**	jewel	*juel*	**1290**
marshal	*mareschal*	**1258**	judge	*juger*	**1290**
dais	*deis*	**1259**	judgement	*jugement*	**1290**
park	*parc*	**1260**	lance	*lance*	**1290**
reign	*regne*	**1272**	manor	*manoir*	**1290**
sapphire	*safir*	**1272**	marble	*marbre*	**1290**
beauty	*bealte*	**1275**	melody	*melodie*	**1290**
clergy	*clergie*	**1275**	minister	*menestre*	**1290**
cloak	*cloke*	**1275**	mutton	*moton*	**1290**
country	*cuntrée*	**1275**	ointment	*oignement*	**1290**
fool	*fol*	**1275**	ordain	*ordener*	**1290**
goal/jail	*gaiole/jaiole*	**1275**	painting	*peindre*	**1290**
heir	*heir*	**1275**	palace	*palais*	**1290**
hue and cry	*hu/cri*	**1275**	pardon	*pardon*	**1290**
pillory	*pellori*	**1275**	parliament	*parlement*	**1290**
robe	*robe*	**1275**	partridge	*perdriz*	**1290**
russet	*rousset*	**1275**	penance	*peneance*	**1290**
supper	*soper*	**1275**	perch (stick)	*perche*	**1290**
executor	*executour*	**1280**	plate	*plate*	**1290**
mustard	*moustarde*	**1289**	porch	*porche*	**1290**

pork	*porc*	**1290**	assign	*asigner*	**1297**
pray	*preier*	**1290**	bailiff	*baillif*	**1297**
quilt	cuilte	**1290**	battle	*bataille*	**1297**
realm	*realme*	**1290**	cathedral	*cathédral*	**1297**
repent	*repentir*	**1290**	chamberlain	*chamberlain*	**1297**
reverence	*reverence*	**1290**	chance	*cheance*	**1297**
safe	*sauf*	**1290**	charge (vb)	*charger*	**1297**
seize	*saisir*	**1290**	chief	*chef/chief*	**1297**
sentence	*sentence*	**1290**	choice	*chois*	**1297**
slander	*esclaundre*	**1290**	choir	*cuer*	**1297**
slave	*esclave*	**1290**	collar	*coler*	**1297**
solace	*solas*	**1290**	dinner	*dîner*	**1297**
sovereign	*souversain*	**1290**	empire	*empire*	**1297**
squire	*esquier*	**1290**	feign	*feignant*	**1297**
statute	*statut*	**1290**	felon	*felon*	**1297**
sue	*suer*	**1290**	forest	*forest*	**1297**
summons	*sumunse*	**1290**	garrison	*garison*	**1297**
surplice	*surpliz*	**1290**	govern	*governer*	**1297**
sustenance	*sustenaunce*	**1290**	imprison	*emprisoner*	**1297**
taste	*taster*	**1290**	libel	*libel*	**1297**
tax (vb)	*taxer*	**1290**	madam	*ma dame*	**1297**
tyrant	*tyrant*	**1290**	mayor	*maire*	**1297**
venison	*venesoun*	**1290**	pain	*peine*	**1297**
joist	*giste*	**1294**	pavilion	*paveillun*	**1297**
wicket	*wiket*	**1296**	rebel (n)	*rebelle*	**1297**
abbess	*abbesse*	**1297**	roast	*rostir*	**1297**
accuse	*acuser*	**1297**	second	*second*	**1297**
alliance	*aliance*	**1297**	sir	*sire*	**1297**
archer	*archer*	**1297**	suite	*siwte*	**1297**
assault (n)	*asaut*	**1297**	verdict	*verdit*	**1297**

8.2.2 *Old Norse*

anger	*angr*	**1250**
rake	*raka*	**1250**
ransack	*rannsaka*	**1250**
scab	*skabbr*	**1250**
leg	*leggr*	**1275**

8.2.3 *Arabic*

The word *mattress* was recorded about 1290. It derived directly from OF *materas*, ultimately from Arabic *al-matrah.*

9. The 14th century – Southern and Kentish dialects

9.1 The dialect areas of Middle English

There were four main dialect areas of Old English – West Saxon, Kentish, Mercian and Northumbrian (see section 3.2). In Middle English, they remain roughly the same, except that the Mercian Midlands of England show enough differences between the eastern and western parts for there to be two distinct dialects, because the eastern Midlands were part of the Danelaw. So the five principal dialects of ME are usually referred to as:

- Southern
- Kentish (or South East)
- East Midland
- West Midland
- Northern

When a more accurate knowledge of where a manuscript was written is known, you will often find terms like *North West Midlands* which identify the area of the dialect more narrowly. Dialects have no boundaries, but merge one into the other. The dialect of Northern English spoken in what is now southern Scotland was known as *Inglis* until about 1500, when writers began to call it *Scottis*, present-day *Scots*.

French the prestige language until the mid-14th century

In the ME period no single dialect of the language was used for writing throughout the country in the way that the West Saxon dialect had become an OE written standard in the 10th and 11th centuries. After the Conquest, the language of the Norman ruling class was Old Northern French (ONF). The language of the English court in the 12th century was Parisian French, which carried more prestige than Anglo-Norman and other varieties – remember Chaucer's ironical

Map 5 ME dialects

comment in the 1390s on the Prioress's French, learned in a nunnery in east London:

> And Frenssh she spak ful faire and fetisly
> After the scole of Stratford-at-the-Bowe...

The language of instruction in English schools was French until the second half of the 14th century. John of Trevisa wrote in 1385:

> For Iohan Cornwal, a mayster of gramere, chayngede þe lore in gramerscole and construccion of Freynsch into Englysch, so þat now, in al the gramerscoles of Engelond childern leueþ Frensch, and construeþ and lurneþ an Englysch...

Not until 1362 was English used in the law courts and Parliament instead of French.

'Gret diversitee' in English

By the end of the 14th century the educated language of London was beginning to become a standard form of writing throughout the country, although the establishment of a recognised Standard English was not completed for several centuries. In Middle English there were only dialects, and writers or copyists used the forms of speech of their own region. Chaucer implied the lack of a standard and the diversity of forms of English at the end of his poem *Troilus and Criseyde*, written about 1385,

> Go, litel bok, go, litel myn tragedye...
> And for ther is so gret diversite
> In Englissh and in writyng of oure tonge,
> So prey I God that non myswrite the,
> Ne the mysmetre for defaute of tonge.

as did John of Trevisa also in the same year, 'þer buþ also of so meny people longages and tonges' (see Text 57 in this chapter).

Here are some other examples of the 'diversity of tongues', taken from writings from different parts of the country in the ME period and focussing on the use of pronouns. They show some of the variations of spelling and form in the same words. Notice how there is inconsistency within a dialectal area, and even within the same manuscript sometimes. It is difficult to know whether some of the differences are simply variations in the spelling or in the form and pronunciation of a word. As always, spelling tended to remain the same even though the pronunciation of a word had altered.

(WW translations follow each text. References are to text and line numbers in Bennett and Smithers, *Early Middle English Verse & Prose*, 1968.)

9.1.1 *Diversity of pronouns*

1st person singular pronoun (MnE I***)***

Also Ic it o boke rede *As I it in book read*	**Ic**	(East Midland) XII.2
Forr Icc amm sennd off heffness ærd *For I am sent from heaven's land*	**Icc**	(Orm, East Midland) XIII.81
Weste Hic hit miȝtte ben forholen *Knew I it might be hidden (=If I knew...)*	**Hic**	(East Midland) VI.237
Gode þonk nou hit is þus þat Ihc am to Criste vend. *God thank now it is thus* *That I am to Christ gone*	**Ihc**	(Southern) V.159
'Darie,' he saide, 'Ich worht ded But Ich haue of þe help and red.' 'Leue child, ful wel I se þat þou wilt to deþe te.' *'Darie,' he said, 'I were dead (=shall die)* *Unless I have of thee help and advice'* *'Dear child, full well I see* *That thou wilt to death draw.' (=you will die)*	**Ich** **I**	 (East Midland) III.75
Certes for þi luf ham Hi spilt. *Certainly for thy love am I spilt. (=ruined)*	**Hi**	(Northern) XV.22

3rd person singular feminine pronoun (MnE she)

The variant forms for *she* are evidence of a different evolution in different areas. Both the initial consonant and the vowel varied. In the Southern and West Midlands dialects the initial [h] of OE *heo* was retained, but with a variety of vowel modifications and spellings illustrated in the first group of quotations below.

The form *scho* with initial [ʃ] and vowel [o] developed in the Northern dialect, and probably evolved from the feminine personal pronoun *heo*, perhaps influenced also by the initial consonant of the feminine demonstrative pronoun *seo* in these sequences:

- from OE *seo*, [s'eo] > [s'io] > [si'o] > [sj'o] > [ʃo] and/or
- from OE *heo*, [h'eo] > [h'io] > [hjo] > [ʃo].

In the East Midland dialect the origin of the form *sche*, with initial [ʃ] and vowel [e], which became the standard *she*, is not known. Some of these forms are illustrated in the second group.

1st group

For þan heom þuhte þat heo hadde Þe houle ouercome... *Therefore to-them (it) seemed she had* *The owl overcome...*	**heo**	(South East late 12th C) I.619
Ho was þe gladur uor þe rise *She was the gladder for the branch*	**ho**	(South East late 12th C) I.19
And in eche manere to alle guodnesse heo drouȝ *And in every wayto all goodness she drew*	**heo**	(South West 13th C) VII.12
He song so lude an so scharþe... *She sang so loud and so sharp...*	**he**	(South East late 12th C) I.97
He wente him to þen inne þer hoe wonede inne *He went (him) to the inn* *Where she dwelled (in)*	**hoe**	(East Midland) VI.19
God wolde hue were myn! *God grant she were mine!*	**hue**	(West Midland) VIII.K.28
ha mei don wið Godd al þet ha eauer wule *she may do with God all that she ever wishes*	**ha**	(West Midland) XVIII.74
Nu ne dorste hi namore sigge, ure Lauedi; hac hye spac to þo serganz þet seruede of þo wyne *Now ne-dared she no more say, our Lady;* *but she spoke to the servants* *that served (of) the wine...*	**hi** **hye**	(Kentish 13th C) XVII.94

2nd group

þo he seghȝ hit nas nowth ȝhe... *When he saw it ne-was not she...*	**ȝhe**	(East Midland 13th C) III.197
Leiȝande sche saide to Blaunchflour... *Laughing she said to Blaunchflour...*	**sche**	(East Midland 13th C) III.241
She is my quene, Ich hire chalenge *She is my queen, I her claim*	**she**	(South East early 14th C) II.61
And te Lundenissce folc hire wolde tæcen and scæ fleh *And the London(ish) folk her wished (to) take and she fled*	**scæ**	(East Midland 12th C) XVI.262
Fro hir schalt þou or scho fro þe... *From her shalt thou or she from thee...*	**scho**	(Northern *c.* 1300) XIV.60
Hir luue sco haldes lele ilike *Hir love she holds true constantly*	**sco**	(Northern *c.* 1300) XIV.75
Yo hat mayden Malkyn Y wene *She is called maiden Malkin I believe*	**yo**	(Northern) XV.47
Annd tær ȝho barr Allmahhti Godd *And there she bore Almighty God*	**ȝho**	(East Midland 12th C) XIII.49

Some early ME dialects, as a result of certain sound changes, had come to use the word *he* for three different pronouns, MnE *he, she* and *they* (OE *he, heo* and *hi/hie*), which seems to us very confusing and ambiguous. For example:

Ambiguity of ME* he *in different dialects

He ne shulde nouȝth þe kyng ysee... *He was not allowed to see the king...*	**he = he**	(South East)
He schal ben chosen quen wiþ honur *She will be chosen queen with honour*	**he = she**	(East Midland)
þanne he com þenne he were bliþe For hom he brouhte fele siþe... *When he came then they were glad* *For to-them he brought many times...*	**he = he & they**	(East Midland)

The assimilation of the ON plural pronouns beginning with ⟨th⟩ has already been mentioned in section 8.1.1.1. Where there was a large Scandinavian population, in the North, all three forms *they, them* and *their* replaced the older OE pronouns beginning with ⟨h⟩. In the South, the OE forms remained for much longer. In the Midlands, *they* was used, but still with the the object and possessive pronouns *hem* and *hire*. The forms for *she* and *they* are therefore two of the clues which help to determine the dialect of a manuscript. Here are some examples of the variant forms for *they* and *them* in the dialects of ME:

***3rd person plural pronouns* (MnE they, them)**

Hi holde plaiding suþe stronge... *They held debate very strongly...*	**hi**	(South East) I.12

An alle ho þe driueþ honne... *And they all thee drive hence ...*	**ho**	(South East) I.66
þat þi dweole-song heo ne forlere. *That thy deceitful-song they (should) shun* (all three forms *hi, ho* and *heo* in one manuscript)	**heo**	(South East) I.558
And hie answerden and seyde *And they answered and said*	**hie**	(Kentish) XVII.185
Alle he arn off one mode *All they are of one mind*	**he**	(East Midland) XII.112
Nuste Ich under Criste whar heo bicumen weoren *Ne-knew I under Christ where they come were* (=*I didn't know where they had gone on earth*)	**heo**	(West Midland) X.33
þo þat hit com to þe time þat hoe shulden arisen ine ... *When that it came to the time* *That they should rise in...*	**hoe**	(Southern) V.263
And bispeken hou huy miʒten best don þe luþere dede *And plotted how they might best do the wicked deed*	**huy**	(South West) VII.38
...for na lickre ne beoþ ha *...for no more-like ne-are they*	**ha**	(West Midland) XVIII.66...
And þilke þat beþ maidenes clene þai mai hem wassche of þe rene. *And the-same that be maidens pure* *They may them(selves) wash in the stream*	**þai/hem**	(East Midland) III.53
For many god wymman haf þai don scam *For (to) many good women have they done shame*	**þai**	(Northern) XV.29
A red þei taken hem bitwene *A plan they made them between them*	**þei/hem**	(East Midland) IV.260
So hem charged þat wroþ þai were *So them burdened that angry they were*	**þai/hem**	(East Midland) III.178
And slæn heom alle clane... *And slain them all completely...*	**heom**	(West Midland) X.64
Hii sende to Sir Maci þat he þun castel ʒolde To hom and to þe baronie *They sent to Sir Maci that he the castle (should) yield* *To them and to the barons*	**hii/hom**	(South West) XI.27
Godd walde o sum wise schawin ham to men *God wished in some way (to) show them to men*	**ham**	(West Midland) XVIII.64

þe pipins war don vnder his tung þar ras o þam thre wandes yong *The seeds were put under his tongue* *There rose from them three young shoots*	**þam**	(Northern) XIV.281

9.2 How to describe dialect differences

Dialects are varieties of a single language which are 'mutually comprehensible', that is, speakers of different dialects can talk to and understand each other. An unfamiliar dialect may be difficult to understand at first because of its pronunciation or the use of unknown dialect words, but with familiarity, these difficulties disappear. This is not the case with a foreign language.

Dialects have most of their vocabulary and grammar in common, and we can therefore make a short list of features to look for when describing the differences between them.

Linguistic features marking ME dialectal differences

Spelling

- The alphabetical symbols used, and their relation to the contrasting sounds of the dialectal accent. We have to be careful not to assume that there is a one-to-one relation between sound and letter. Some differences of spelling in ME texts do not reflect differences of pronunciation, e.g. ⟨i ~ y⟩; ⟨u ~ v⟩; ⟨ȝ ~ gh⟩; ⟨ss ~ sch ~ sh⟩; ⟨þ ~ th⟩; ⟨hw ~ wh ~ qu⟩, etc. Remember that spelling tends to be conservative, and does not necessarily keep up with changed pronunciation.

Pronunciation

- Has the OE long vowel [ɑː] shifted to [ɔː] or not?
- Which vowel is used for the OE front rounded vowel [y]? For example, is *hill* (from OE *hyll*) spelt *hill*, *hell* or *hull*?
- Which vowels have developed from OE vowels spelt ⟨eo⟩, ⟨ea⟩ and ⟨æ⟩?

Word forms – pronouns

- What are the forms of personal pronouns? Have the ON 3rd person plural forms beginning with ⟨th-⟩ been adopted? What is the feminine singular pronoun?

Word forms – inflections

- On nouns, what suffixes are used to mark the plural?
- On verbs, what are:
  1. the present tense suffixes,
  2. the forms of past tense (strong or weak), past and present participles, and infinitive?
  3. the forms of the common verb *be*?

Grammar

- Examine word order within the phrase and the clause.
- How are negatives and questions formed?
- Find constructions which are no longer used in MnE.

Vocabulary

- Is the source of the words OE, ON, OF or another language, and in what proportion?

We can now use this list, or parts of it, to examine some ME texts which provide examples of the different dialects.

9.3 A South Eastern or Kentish dialect

The single manuscript of a book called *Ayenbyte of Inwit*, 'the remorse of conscience', is of great interest to students of the language for two reasons. Firstly because its author and exact date are both written on the manuscript. He writes in the preface,

> þis boc is dan Michelis of Northgate / ywrite an englis of his oȝene hand. þet hatte: Ayenbite of inwyt. And is of þe boc-house of saynt Austines of Canterberi.

oȝene = own; hatte = is called.

and towards the end of the book,

> þis boc is uolueld ine þe eue of þe holy apostles Symon an Iudas / of ane broþer of þe cloystre of sanynt Austin of Canterberi / Ine the yeare of oure lhordes beringe 1340.

uolueld = fulfilled, completed; þe eue of þe holy apostles Symon an Iudas = October 27; beringe = birth.

That is, Michael of Northgate, a monk of St Augustine's, Canterbury, finished the book (a translation from a French original) on 27 October 1340. The second quotation is included in the following facsimile of part of the manuscript towards its end:

Text 52 – Kentish dialect – Michael of Northgate's *Ayenbyte of Inwyt*, 1340 (i) (facsimile)

A note on the handwriting

An informal book-hand.

- ⟨ȝ⟩ used for [x] e.g. *berȝe* (=*protect*), *naȝt* (*not*) and [w] *halȝed* (*hallowed*)
- ⟨y⟩ is dotted ⟨ẏ⟩ and used for [ɪ], e.g. *ẏcome*, *ẏwẏte* and for [j], e.g. *man ẏere*, *ẏeue*, etc.
- ⟨g⟩ for [g], e.g. *god*, *engliss*.
- thorn ⟨þ⟩ still used e.g. *þe*, *þet*.
- ⟨w⟩ always, never wynn ⟨ƿ⟩, *wille*, *ywent*, etc.
- Long ⟨ſ⟩ almost always (only two examples of round ⟨s⟩ in the facsimile).

- Word-initial ⟨z⟩ and ⟨u⟩ for voiced fricatives [z] and [v] – *zende* (*send*), *yzed* (*said*), *uor* (*for*), *uram* (*from*).

Transcription

þıſ boc ıſ ẏcome to þe ende:
heuene blıſſe god ouſ zende: amen. Nou ıch wılle þet ẏe
ẏwtẏe hou hıt ıſ ẏwent: þet þıſ boc ıſ ẏwrıte mıd englıſſ of kent.
þıſ boc ıſ ẏmad uor lewede men / uor uader / and uor moder / and
uor oþer ken / ham uor to berȝe uram all manẏere zen / þet ıne
hare ınwẏtte ne bleue no uoul wen. huo aſe god ıſ hıſ name ẏzed /
þet þıſ boc made god hım yeue et bread / of Angleſ of heuene And
þerto hıs red / And onderuonge hıſ zaule huanne þet he ıſ d ẏad. Amen.
¶ ẏmende. þet þıſ boc ıſ uolueld ıne þe eue of þe holẏ apoſtleſ Sẏ -
mon and ıudaſ / of ane broþer of þe cloẏſtre of ſanẏnt auſtın
of canterberı / ıne þe ẏeare of oure lhordeſ berınge. 1340
¶ Vader oure þet Art ıne heueneſ / ẏ halȝed bẏ þı name. comınde þı rıche.
ẏworþe þı wıl / Aſe ıne heuene: and ın erþe. bread oure echedaẏeſ: ẏef
ouſ to daẏ . ẏ And uorlet ouſ oure ẏeldıngeſ: Aſe And we uorleteþ oure
ẏeldereſ. And ne ouſ led naȝt: ın to uondınge: AC vrı ouſ uram queade: zuo bẏ hıt.
hayl marıe / of þonke uol. lhord by mıd þe. ẏblêſſed þou ıne wẏmmen.
And ẏblıſſed þet ouet of þıne wombe. zuo by hıt

WW (set out in lines to show the rhymes)

þis boc is ycome to þe ende, heuene blisse god ous zende Amen.
this book is come to the end, heaven's bliss God us send Amen

Nou ich wille þet ye ywyte hou hit is ywent:
Now I wish that you know how it is went (*has happened*)

þet þis boc is ywrite mid engliss of kent.
That this book is written in English of Kent

þis boc is ymad uor lewede men
this book is made for common men

uor uader and uor moder and uor oþer ken
for father and for mother and for other kin

ham uor to berȝe uram all manyere zen
them for to protect from all kind of sin

þet ine hare inwytte ne bleue no uoul wen.
so that in their conscience ne remain no foul wen

huo ase god is his name yzed
who as God is his name said

þet þis boc made god him yeue þet bread of Angles of heuene and þerto his red
that this book made God to-him give the bread of angels of heaven and thereto his counsel

And onderuonge his zaule huanne þet he is dyad. Amen.
and receive his soul when that he is dead Amen

ymend þet þis boc is uolueld ine þe eue of þe holy apostles Symon and Iudas of ane broþer of þe cloystre of sanynt austin of canterberi ine þe yeare of oure lhordes beringe. 1340

Remember that this book was finished on the eve of the holy apostles Simon and Jude by a brother of the cloister of Saint Augustine of Canterbury in the year of Our Lord's birth 1340

Vader oure þet Art ine heuenes	*Our father which art in heaven*
y halȝed by þi name	*Hallowed be thy name*
cominde þi riche	*Thy kingdom come*
yworþe þi wil ase ine heuene and in erþe	*Thy will be done on earth as it is in heaven*
bread oure echedayes: yef ous to day	*Give us this day our daily bread*
and uorlet ous oure yeldinges	*And forgive us our trespasses*
ase and we uorleteþ oure yelderes	*As we forgive them that trespass against us*
and ne ous led naȝt in to uondinge	*And lead us not into temptation*
ac vri ous uram queade: zuo by hit.	*But deliver us from evil: so be it*

hayl marie of þonke uol	*Hail Mary full of grace*
lhord by mid þe	*The Lord be with thee*
yblissed þou ine wymmen.	*Blessed art thou among women*
and y blissed þet ouet of þine wombe	*And blessed be the fruit of thy womb*
zuo by hit	*So be it*

The complete vocabulary of Texts 52, 53 and 54 is listed in the *Word Book*.

The second reason for the manuscript's linguistic importance is that it is spelled consistently, and so provides good evidence for the South East dialect of Kent at that time.

Ayenbyte of Inwyt is therefore unique in providing an example of a Middle English dialect in an original copy whose date, author and place of writing are exactly known. It is as close to a 'pure' dialect that we can get, remembering that the written form of language can never provide a really accurate account of how a dialect was spoken.

The following texts from *Ayenbyte of Inwyt* are short exemplary tales which illustrate the virtue of showing mercy and generosity.

Activity 9.1

Before reading the commentary which follows, examine the language under the headings provided in Section 9.2. Here are some questions to consider:

(a) How far has the Kentish dialect of 1340 lost or changed the inflections of OE?
(b) Which vowel seems to be more frequent in Kentish than in other ME dialects?
(c) What can you say about the pronunciation of Kentish from the evidence of the spellings *uram, uor, þeruore, bevil, uol, zuo, mezeyse?*

Text 53 – Kentish dialect – Michael of Northgate's *Ayenbyte of Inwyt*, 1340 (ii)

Efterward Saint Gregori telþ þet Saint Boniface uram þet he wes child he wes zuo piteuous þet he yaf ofte his kertel and his sserte to þe poure uor God, þaȝ his moder him byete ofte þeruore. þanne bevil þet þet child yseȝ manie poure þet hedden mezeyse. He aspide þet his moder nes naȝt þer. An haste he yarn to þe gerniere, and al þet his moder hedde ygadered uor to pasi þet yer he hit yaf to þe poure. And þo his moder com and wyste þe ilke dede, hy wes al out of hare wytte. þet child bed oure Lhorde, and þet gernier wes an haste al uol.

WW

Afterward Saint Gregory tells that Saint Boniface from that he was child he was so piteous that he gave often his coat and his shirt to the poor for God, though his mother him beat often therefore. Then befell that that child saw many poor that had suffering. He espied that his mother ne-was not there. In haste he ran to the granary, and all that his mother had gathered for to last the year he it gave to the poor. And when his mother came and learned the same deed, she was all out of her wit. The child prayed our Lord, and the granary was in haste all full.

Here is a broad phonetic transcription of Text 53, recorded on the cassette tape.

ɛftərward zaɪnt grɛgɔrɪ tɛlθ ðɛt zaɪnt bonɪfas vram ðɛt heː wɛs tʃiːld heː wɛs zwɔː pitɛjus ðɛt heː jaf ɔftə hɪs kɛrtəl and hɪs ʃɛrtə tɔ ðə puːrə vor god, ðɑx hɪs moːdər hɪm bjɛːtə ɔftə ðɛːrvɔːrə. ðanə bɛvɪl ðɛt ðɛt tʃiːld ɪzeːj maniːə puːrə ðɛt hɛdən mɛzɛːjzə. heː aspiːdə ðɛt hɪs moːdər nɛs naxt ðəːr. an hɑːstə heː jarn tɔ ðə gɛrnɛːrə, and ɑl ðɛt hɪs moːdər hɛdə ɪgɑdərɛd vɔr tɔ pɑzɪ ðɛt jeːr heː hɪt jaf tɔ ðə puːrə. and ðɔː hɪs moːdər coːm and wɪstə ðə ɪlkə deːdə, heː wɛs ɑl ut ɔf harə wɪtə. ðɛt tʃiːld beːd urə hlɔːrdə, and ðɛt gɛrnɪɛːr wɛs ɑn hɑːstə ɑl vɔl.

9.3.1 *Commentary*

Grammar

The syntactic structures of MnE were present in Old English, and it is not surprising that the grammar of Middle English causes us few problems in conveying meaning. However, as we read older English, we are aware of phrases and combinations of words which are definitely 'old-fashioned', and which we would not use today. Sometimes the order of words is no longer acceptable, sometimes words appear to be missing, or to be superfluous when compared with English today. Sometimes particular combinations of words are no longer used. In addition, as Michael of Northgate was translating from the French, it is possible that some constructions were not genuine ME either, so we can observe differences, but not draw any final conclusions from them without further evidence. For example,

- uram þet he wes child   from that he was child

MnE requires *from when* or *from the time that*, and the addition of a determiner in the NP, e.g. *a child.*

- he yaf ofte his kertel   he gave often his coat

The adverb *often* in MnE either precedes the verb, *he often gave*, or follows the object, *he gave his coat often.*

- his moder him byete ofte   his mother him beat often
- he hit yaf to þe poure   he it gave to the poor

The direct object *him*, *it*, now follows the verb, *his mother beat him often*, *he gave it to the poor*.

- þanne bevil þet   then befell that

A MnE clause must contain a subject, and here the 'dummy subject' *it* would be used, *then it befell that*.

- þet hedden mezeyse   that had suffering

This is perhaps not ungrammatical in MnE, but it is a phrase that would sound strange.

- for to pasi þet yer   (in order) to last the year

The phrase *for to* in a structure like *I want for to go* is found in all ME texts, but is no longer Standard English, though still normal in some present-day dialects.

Double or multiple negatives

- his moder nes naȝt þer   his mother ne was not there

The OE negative *ne* preceded the verb, as in *ne wæs* (*was not*) and could be reinforced by other negatives like *næfre* (*never*),

ond hie **næfre** his banan folgian **noldon**
*and they **never** his murderer follow **ne-would***

In ME the emphatic *noȝt*, *naȝt* came to be used to reinforce the negative (it did not make it positive), as in Chaucer's

> Be wel auysed . . .
> That **noon** of us **ne** speke **noght** a word

In time, the older *ne* was dropped, leaving *not* as the Standard English negative word. However, the multiple negative remains the norm in most spoken dialects of England today – *There won't be no tradition left, will there*?

Word structure

A short text may not contain a sufficient variety of word-forms for us to come to any conclusions about the range of inflections. For example:

- There are no plural nouns in this text, so we cannot observe whether the *-es* or *-en* plurals are used. But the NP *þet gernier* shows the use of the older neuter OE pronoun *þæt* for MnE *the*, while the PrepP *to þe gerniere* has a dative case inflection *-e* on the noun, but the common form *þe* for the determiner. The NP *oure Lhorde* also has the inflection *-e* on the noun to mark dative case after *to*, *to our Lord.*
- There are no adjectives apart from possessive pronouns like *his* and *oure*, so there is no evidence here of the survival of inflections on adjectives.
- There is only one example of a present tense verb, *telþ*, with the 3rd person singular inflection *-(e)þ*. The past participle *ygadered* retains the prefix *y-*, from the OE *ge-*.
- The newer pronouns *she*, *they*, *them*, *their* are not used.

Even these limited observations, however, suggest that Kentish was a conservative dialect, that is, when compared to others it still retained more features of the OE system of inflections, even though greatly reduced. These features are very similar to those of South Western texts, and can be compared with John of Trevisa's in the next section. This fact is not surprising when we consider the geographical position of Kent, relatively cut off and distant from the Midlands and North of England, but accessible to the rest of the South.

Pronunciation and spelling

Words spelt with the vowel letter ⟨e⟩ are much in evidence because in the Kentish dialect:

- the OE vowel [æ] had shifted to [e], for example *þet* from *þæt*, *wes* (*wæs*), *hedden* (*hæfdon*), *þer* (*þær*), *dede* (*dæde*), *bed* (*bæd*) (see section 6.1.4.4);
- the OE vowel [y] unrounded and shifted to [e], as in *kertel*, *sserte* from OE *cyrtel*, *scyrte* (see section 6.1.4.6); and
- the OE diphthong, ⟨eo⟩ smoothed to [e] (see section 6.1.4.5).

The following spellings,

Kentish	uram	uor	eruore	bevil	uol	zuo	mezeyse
MnE	*from*	*for*	*therefore*	*befell*	*full*	*so*	*misease*

suggest that the consonants pronounced [f] and [s] in other dialects were **voiced** at the beginning of a word or root syllable in Kentish, and pronounced [v] and [z]. This **initial voicing of fricative consonants** is still a feature of South West dialects in Devon, Somerset, Dorset, Somerset, Wiltshire and Hampshire, though no longer in Kent (see P. M. Anderson, *A Structural Atlas of the English Dialects*, 1987, pp. 141–3). It applies equally to the consonant [θ], and must have done also in ME, but has never been recorded in spelling, because the letters ⟨þ⟩ or ⟨th⟩ are used for both the voiced and voiceless forms of the consonant, as in *thin* and *then*.

Activity 9.2

Find evidence in Text 54 following for changes in pronunciation, word-form and grammar from Old English, and of any special characteristics of the Kentish dialect in the 14th century.

(The French original of the text can be found in Kenneth Sisam, *Fourteenth Century Verse & Prose*, 1921, p. 213.)

Text 54 – Kentish dialect – Michael of Northgate's *Ayenbyte of Inwyt*, 1340 (iii)

Efterward þer wes a poure man, ase me zayþ, þet hedde ane cou; and yherde zigge of his preste ine his prechinge þet God zede ine his spelle þet God wolde yelde an hondreduald al þet me yeaue uor him. þe guode man, mid þe rede of his wyue, yeaf his cou to his preste, þet wes riche. þe prest his nom bleþeliche, and hise zente to þe oþren þet he hedde. þo hit com to euen, þe guode mannes cou com hom to his house ase hi wes ywoned, and ledde mid hare alle þe prestes ken, al to an hondred. þo þe guode man yseȝ þet, he þoȝte þet þet wes þet word of þe Godspelle þet he hedde yyolde; and him hi weren yloked beuore his bissoppe aye þane prest. þise uorbisne sseweþ wel þet merci is guod chapuare, uor hi deþ wexe þe timliche guodes.

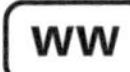

Afterward there was a poor man, as I am told, that had a cow; and heard say from his priest in his preaching that God said in his gospel that God would yield a hundredfold all that one gave for him. The good man, with the advice of his wife, gave his cow to his priest, that was rich. The priest her took blithely, and her sent to the others that he had. When it came to evening, the good man's cow came home to his house as she was accustomed, and led with her all the priest's kine, all to a hundred. When the good man saw that, he thought that that was the word of the Gospel that to-him* had restored (them); and to-him they were adjudged before his bishop against the priest. These examples show well that mercy is good trading, for it does increase the temporal goods.

* The obscure English is the result of a mistranslation of the French original.

9.4 An early South West dialect

Text 32 in chapter 5, from a verse chronicle by Robert of Gloucester (reproduced again in this section as Text 56) was written about 1300. The chronicle was first written late in the 13th century in the Gloucester dialect by a monk of Gloucester Abbey, and ended with the death of Henry I in 1136. Robert, a monk in the same abbey, revised and continued the text to 1272, the year of the death of Henry III. Here is a short extract from the *Chronicle* in facsimile.

Text 55 – Robert of Gloucester's *Chronicle* (i) (facsimile)

A note on the handwriting

Book-hand.

- Letter thorn written like wynn ⟨ƿ⟩
- Letter ⟨w⟩ used, not wynn.
- 2-form of ⟨r⟩ after ⟨o⟩.
- Letter yogh ⟨ȝ⟩ used for [j], *ȝonge* (*young*), [x], *fiȝte* and [*tz*] *fiȝ* (*Fitz*).

An vewe dropeſ of reine . þer velle grete inou .
Þis tokninge vel in þis lond . þo me þis men slou .
Vor þretti mile þanne . þis isei roberd .
Þat verst þis boc made . & was wel sore aferd .
Louerdingeſ þat were inome . at euesham manion .
As sir hunfrai de boun . sir ion le fiȝ ion .
& simondeſ sone de mountfort . sir gwy .
Sir baudewine de wake . sir ion de vescy .
Sir henri de hastinges . & sir nicole iwis .
Of segraue waſ þere inome . & al so sir peris .
& sir roberd þat sir peris . de mountfort soneſ were .
Þis & wel mo were inome . in þulke morþre þere .
Ac þe welsse fot men . þat þer were manion .
At þe biginninge of þe bataile . bigonne to fle echon .
& come þoru teukesburi . & þere men of þe toune .
Slowe hom al to grounde . þat þere hii leie þer doune .
So þicke in þe strete . þat reuþe it was to se .
& grace nadde non of hom . to fiȝte ne to fle .
Þo þe bataile waſ ido . & þe godemen aslawe were .
Sir simond þe ȝonge com . to mete is fader þere .

		Literal translation
A	n vewe dropeſ of reıne . þer velle grete ınou .	A few drops of rain there fell great enough
þ	ís toknınge vel ın þıs lond . þo me þıs men slou .	this portent fell in this land when these men were slain

v or þrettı mıle þanne . þıs ıſeı roberd .	for thirty miles then this saw Robert
þ at verſt þıs boc made . ⁊ was wel ſore aferd	that first this book made & was very sorely afraid
L ou^r^dıngeſ þ^t^ were ınome . at eueſham manıon .	gentlemen that were taken at Evesham many a one
a ſır unfraı de boun . Sır Jon le fıȝ Jon .	like Sir Humphrey de Boun, Sir John Fitzjohn
⁊ sımoneſ ſone . de moūtfort sır gwy .	& Sir Guy, son of Simon de Montfort
s ır baudewıne de wake . ſır Jon de veſcy .	Sir Baldwin de Wake, Sir John de Vescy
s ır henrı de haſtınges . ⁊ sır Nıcole ıwıs .	Sir Henry de Hastings & Sir Nicolas indeed
D e ſeg^a^ue waſ þere ınome . ⁊ al ſo sır perıs .	de Segrave was there captured & also Sir Peris
⁊ sır roberd þat sır perıs . de moūtfort ſoneſ were .	& Sir Robert who were Sir Peris de Montfort's sons
þ uſe ⁊ wel mo were ınome . ⁊ þulke morþre þere .	these & many more were taken & the same murdered there
A c þe welſſe fot men . þat þer were manıon .	but the Welsh footmen that there were many a one
a c þe bıgınnınge of þe bataıle . bıgonne to fle echon	at the beginning of the battle began to flee each one
⁊ come þoru teuſkeſburı . ⁊ þere men of þe toune	& came through Tewkesbury & there men of the town
S lowe hom al to groūde . þat þere hıı leıe þ^t^ doune	slew them all to the ground so that there they lay down
ſ o þıcke bıſtrete . þat reuþe ıt was to ſe .	so thickly strewn that pity it was to see
⁊ grace nadde non of hom . to fıȝte ne to fle .	& mercy had none of them to fight or to flee
þ o þe bataıle waſ ıdo . ⁊ þe godemen aslawe were .	when the battle was done & the good men slain were
s ır ſımond þe ȝonge come . to mete ıs fad' þere . . .	Sir Simon the young came to meet his father there . . .

📖 The complete vocabulary of Text 55 is listed in the *Word Book*.

Activity 9.3

Use the vocabulary of texts 55 and 56 to see whether you can find evidence for any of the following features by which southern dialects of ME are identified.

(i) The rounding of OE [ɑː] to [ɔː]; that is, OE words spelt with ⟨a⟩ now spelt with ⟨o⟩.

(ii) OE ⟨y⟩ now spelt with ⟨u⟩, though remaining the same sound.

(iii) OE ⟨eo⟩ now spelt ⟨o⟩; the diphthong has 'smoothed' and become a single vowel.

(iv) *Verb forms:*

Present tense plural and 3rd person singular suffix – ⟨-eþ⟩.
Present participle suffix – ⟨-inde⟩.
Past particle begins with ⟨i-⟩ and has lost its final ⟨-n⟩.
Infinitive has lost its final ⟨-n⟩.

(v) [f] at the beginning of a syllable is voiced [v], spelt ⟨v⟩ or ⟨u⟩.

(vi) 3rd person pronoun forms still begin with ⟨h-⟩.

Text 56 – Robert of Gloucester's *Chronicle* (ii)

þus lo þe englisse folc. vor noȝt to grounde com.
vor a fals king þat nadde no riȝt. to þe kinedom.
& come to a nywe louerd. þat more in riȝte was.
ac hor noþer as me may ise. in pur riȝte was.
& þus was in normannes hond. þat lond ibroȝt iwis . . .
þus com lo engelond. in to normandies hond.
& þe normans ne couþe speke þo. bote hor owe speche.
& speke french as hii dude at om. & hor children dude also teche.
so þat heiemen of þis lond. þat of hor blod come.
holdeþ alle þulk speche. þat hii of hom nome.
vor bote a man conne frenss. me telþ of him lute.
ac lowe men holdeþ to engliss. & to hor owe speche ȝute.
ich wene þer ne beþ in al þe world. contreyes none.
þat ne holdeþ to hor owe speche. bote engelond one.
ac wel me wot uor to conne. boþe wel it is.
vor þe more þat a mon can. þe more wurþe he is.
þis noble duc willam. him let crouny king.
at londone amidwinter day. nobliche þoru alle þing.
of þe erchebissop of euerwik. aldred was is name.
þer nas prince in al þe world. of so noble fame.

The vocabulary of Text 56 is listed in the *Word Book*.

9.5 A later 14th-century South West dialect

The following text, written in the 1380s by John of Trevisa, describes one man's view of the linguistic situation at that time. The complete work is a translation, with Trevisa's own additions, of a history called *Polychronicon* written in Latin earlier in the century. John of Trevisa was vicar of Berkeley near Gloucester when he translated *Polychronicon*.

It is a reminder to us of the historical origins of English and its dialects. Trevisa's attitude is not unlike that of some people today in his talk of the *apeyring* (*deterioration*) of the language, but the reasons he gives are different. He blames it on the fashion for speaking French. He is writing in the South West dialect of ME.

Text 57 – John of Trevisa on the English language in 1385 (i)

As hyt ys y-knowe houȝ meny maner people buþ in þis ylond þer buþ also of so meny people longages and tonges. Noþeles walschmen and scottes þat buþ noȝt ymelled wiþ oþer nacions holdeþ wel nyȝ here furste longage and speche

As it is known how many kinds (*of*) *people are in this island there are also of so many people languages and tongues. Nevertheless Welshmen and Scots that are not mingled with other nations hold well nigh* (*to*) *their native language and speech.*

Also englischmen þeyȝ hy hadde fram þe bygynnyng þre maner speche souþeron norþeron and myddel speche in þe myddel of þe lond, as hy come of þre maner people of Germania, noþeles by commyxstion and mellyng furst wiþ danes and afterward wiþ normans in menye þe contray longage ys apeyred and some vseþ strange wlaffyng chyteryng harryng and garryng, grisbittyng.

Also Englishmen though they had from the beginning three varieties of speech – Southern, Northern, and Middle speech in the middle of the land, as they came from three kinds of people from Germany, nevertheless by mixing and mingling first with Danes and afterward with Normans in many the language of the land is impaired and some use strange stammering, chattering, snarling and harsh gnashing.

This apeyring of þe burþ tonge ys bycause of twey þinges – on ys for chyldern in scole aȝenes þe vsage and manere of al oþer nacions buþ compelled for to leue here oune longage and for to construe here lessons and here þinges a freynsch, and habbeþ suþthe þe normans come furst into engelond.

This impairing of the native tongue is because of two things – one is that children in school, against the usage and custom of all other nations, are compelled to learn their own language and to construe their lessons and their tasks in French, and have (done so) since the Normans came first into England.

Also gentil men children buþ ytauȝt for to speke freynsch fram tyme þat a buþ yrokked in here cradel and conneþ speke and playe wiþ a child hys brouch. And oplondysch men wol lykne hamsylf to gentil men and fondeþ wiþ gret bysynes for to speke freynsch for to be more ytold of...

Also gentlemen's children are taught to speak French from (the) time that they are rocked in their cradle and can talk and play with a child's brooch. And country men want to compare themselves to gentlemen and seek with great industry to speak French in order to be more spoken about.

þys manere was moche y-used tofore þe furste moreyn* and ys seþthe somdel y-chaunged... now, þe ȝer of oure Lord a þousond þre hondred foure score and fyve, in al the gramerscoles of Engelond childern leueþ Frensch, and construeþ and lurneþ an Englysch...

This fashion was much followed before the first plague and is since somewhat changed.... Now, the year of our Lord one thousand three hundred four score and five, in all the grammar schools of England, children leave French, and construe and learn in English.

Also gentil men habbeþ now moche yleft for to teche here childern frensch. Hyt semeþ a gret wondur houȝ englysch, þat ys þe burþ-tonge of englyschmen and here oune longage and tonge ys so dyvers of soun in þis ylond, and þe longage of normandy ys comlyng of anoþer lond and haþ on maner soun among al men þat spekeþ hyt aryȝt in engelond.

Also gentlemen have now to a great extent stopped teaching their children French. It seems a great wonder how English, that is the native tongue of Englishmen and their own language & tongue, is so diverse in pronunciation in this island, and the language of Normandy is a newcomer from another land and has one pronunciation among all men that speak it correctly in England.

* *moreyn – a reference to the Black Death of the 1340s.*

The vocabulary of Texts 57 and 58 is listed in the *Word Book*.

The MS was written *c.* 1400. A version from another MS is given in Text 90, section 14.4.1, which illustrates the kinds of variation to be found in a different copy of a text.

9.5.1 Commentary

9.5.1.1 *Vocabulary*

All except one of the **function words** (prepositions, determiners, pronouns and conjunctions) are of OE origin. Such words form the 'framework' of sentences, and are a **closed class** of words which change very slowly, if at all. The only sign of French influence is the complex preposition *bycause of*, the origin of MnE *because* – *by cause of* being an English version of the French *par cause de*.

The adoption of words from French is much more evident in the **lexical words**, especially the nouns (see section 9.5.1.5 following), though there are no French-derived adverbs in this text.

9.5.1.2 *Spelling*

Trevisa's spelling illustrates some of the changes that had been generally adopted, although not consistently used. We have seen them all in texts of the 12th and 13th centuries and early 14th century:

- ⟨y⟩ – is interchangeable with ⟨i⟩, and represents the sound [i] – *bygynnyng, chyldern/childern, bysynes*.
- ⟨u⟩ and ⟨v⟩ – the familiar present-day relationship of letter ⟨u⟩ for vowel [u] and letter ⟨v⟩ for consonant [v] is still not established; ⟨u⟩ and ⟨v⟩ were variant shapes of the same letter. In Trevisa's text, ⟨u⟩ is generally written in the middle of a word, and ⟨v⟩ at the beginning, for either sound, [u] or [v], for example, *burþ, vseþ, vsage, leue, furst*. This practice continued for a long time, for although letter ⟨v⟩ was written for the consonant sound [v] by scriveners (professional copyists) in the 15th century, it was not taken up by printers regularly until the 18th century.
- ⟨ʒ⟩ and ⟨g⟩ – yogh, ⟨ʒ⟩, is retained for [j], [x] or [ɣ], as in *ʒer* [jɛr] (*year*) or *tauʒt* [taʊɣt] (*taught*). Letter ⟨g⟩ represents both [g], and also [ʒ] in borrowed French words like *vsage* [uzaʒ]:

engelond, garrying, grisbittyng, gret, gramer, þinges	[g]
usage, gentilmen, longages	[ʒ] and [g]
noʒt, niʒ, þeyʒ, aʒenes, tauʒt	[j] or [ɣ] or [x]

- ⟨ch⟩ – replaced OE ⟨c⟩ for the consonant [tʃ], as in *speche* and *teche* from OE, and *brouch* and *chaunged* from OF.
- ⟨sch⟩ – is Trevisa's spelling for the OE ⟨sc⟩, [ʃ], as in *englysch* and *oplondysch*.
- ⟨th⟩ – has not replaced ⟨þ⟩ in Trevisa, although he does also use ⟨th⟩ in *suþthe* and *seþthe* where the consonant is doubled. Letter ⟨þ⟩ survived into the 15th century.

9.5.1.3 *Word-forms and inflections*

We can see how spelling was related to pronunciation by the three functions of the word *a* in the text:

- as a reduced form of the preposition *an* meaning *in* or *on*, in the phrase *a freynsch, in French*;
- as a reduced form of the pronoun *hi* meaning *they* in *a buþ yrokked, they are rocked*; and
- as the indefinite article, as in MnE, in *a þousond.*

Nouns

- The regular plural inflection is ⟨-s⟩ or ⟨-es⟩. The OE plural *men* remains, but the variant forms for the plural of *child* are interesting. The OE plural *cildru* had developed into *childre* or *childer*. In Trevisa's and other dialects, this plural was doubled by a further ⟨en⟩ plural inflection, and Trevisa uses both *children* and *childern.*

Pronouns

- The ON 3rd person pronouns *they, them, their* have not yet reached the South West dialect. Trevisa uses *hy/here* for *they/their*, and *hamsylf* for *themselves.*

Verbs

- The 3rd person present tense plural inflection of verbs is ⟨-eþ⟩, from OE ⟨-aþ⟩, e.g. *conneþ, spekeþ* (*they speak, know*), and the 3rd person form of *be* is *buþ* (*they are*), derived from OE *beoþ.*
- Past participles still retain the prefix ⟨y-⟩ or ⟨i-⟩, which is a reduced form of the OE prefix ⟨ge-⟩.
- The infinitive inflection is reduced to ⟨e⟩ in spelling, *leue, playe, speke, teche*, and is probably not pronounced.
- Verbs adopted from French take the structure of English weak or regular verbs. For example, the past participle suffix is ⟨-ed⟩, *apeyred, ymelled, ychaunged*, as against the irregular forms of *yknowe, yleft* and *ytauȝt* derived from OE.

9.5.1.4 *Grammar*

- Many of the contrasts between older and present-day English are matters of style rather than significant grammatical differences. We can read Trevisa's text without much difficulty, but it does not transcribe word for word into colloquial MnE. For example, the phrases *meny maner people* and *þre maner speche* today require the preposition *of* – *many kinds of people, three varieties of speech.* In OE the words for *people* and *speche* would have been in the genitive case, and the ME form has a similar construction (see section 2.7.3).

- The phrase *a child hys broche, a child's toy*, is a new construction for the possessive, which survived for some time but has now been lost. It does not derive from OE.
- Infinitives which complement a main verb are marked by *for to*, e.g. *compelled for to leue . . . and for to construe, fondeþ wiþ gret bysynes for to speke frensch for to be more ytold of.*

This construction is still used in some MnE dialects, but is now nonstandard. Notice also that the last quotation is an example of 'preposition at the end of a sentence', centuries before prescriptive grammarians ruled that the construction was ungrammatical.

Activity 9.4

Make a similar study of the linguistic features of the following continuation of Trevisa's writing.

(i) *Spelling* – Identify and list some of the new combinations of letters and sounds.
(ii) *Inflections* – Do any suffixes remain from OE?
(iii) *Grammar* – Which constructions mark the text as ME and not MnE?
(iv) *Vocabulary* – What kinds of word have been taken into Trevisa's South West dialect of ME from French and Latin?

Text 58 – John of Trevisa on the English language (ii)

. . . also of þe forseyde saxon tonge þat is deled a þre and ys abyde scarslych wiþ feaw vplondyschmen and ys gret wondur, for men of þe est wiþ men of þe west, as hyt were vnder þe same party of heuene, acordeþ more in sounyng of speche þan men of þe norþ wiþ men of þe souþ.

þerfore hyt ys þat mercii, þat buþ men of myddel engelond, as hyt were parteners of þe endes, vndurstondeþ betre þe syde longages, norþeron and souþeron, þan norþeron and souþeron vndurstondeþ eyþer oþer.

Al þe longage of þe norþumbres and specialych at ȝork ys so scharp slyttyng and frotyng and vnschape þat we souþeron men may þat longage vnneþe vndurstonde. Y trowe þat þat ys bycause þat a buþ nyȝ to strange men and aliens þat spekeþ strangelych.

. . . also concerning the Saxon tongue that is divided into three and has barely survived among a few uneducated men (there) is great wonder. for men of the east with men of the west, as it were under the same part of heaven, agree more in (their) pronunciation than men of the north with men of the south.

Therefore it is that Mercians, who are men of Middle England, as it were partners of the extremes, understand better the languages on either side, Northern and Southern, than Northerners and Southerners understand each other.

All the language of the Northumbrians, and specially at York, is so shrill, cutting and grating and badly pronounced that we Southern men may that language hardly understand. . . . I believe that this is because they are close to foreign men and aliens that speak strangely.

9.5.1.5 *French vocabulary in Texts 57 and 58*

There are 32 lexical word types derived from OF in the two texts, which is a higher proportion than in the 12th- and 13th-century texts we have examined. The words with the dates of their first recorded occurrence in writing are:

acordeþ	1123	party	1290
normandy/normans	1205	strange/strangelych	1290
brouch	1225	apeyring/apeyred	1297
frotyng	1225	scarslych	1297
lessons	1225	soun(yng)	1297
ychaunged	1230	specialych	1297
vseþ/y-vsed	1240	vsage	1297
dyvers	1250	mellyng/ymelled	1300
contrary	1275	nacions	1300
gentilmen	1275	aliens	1330
maner(e)	1275	moreyn	1330
longage(s)	1290	people	1340
parteners	1290	gramer-scoles	1387

There are four words derived directly from Latin, a kind of borrowing that increases dramatically in the 16th and 17th centuries:

commyxstion (*Trevisa's is the first recorded use dated 1387*)
Germania
compelled
construe/construþ

9.6 Loan-words 1300–1319

Selected vocabulary adopted during the 14th century is listed at the end of chapters 9–13 by twenty year periods, in order to avoid over-long lists. The words are not related to the dialect topics of each chapter.

9.6.1 *French*

Large numbers of loan-words are dated 1300 because it is an approximate date standing for 'some time in the early 14th century', and also the date of long texts such as *Cursor Mundi*.

almond	*almande*	**1300**	carol	*carole*	**1300**
award (n)	*award*	**1300**	chair	*chaere*	**1300**
beef	*boef*	**1300**	chamber	*chambre*	**1300**
blanket	*blankete*	**1300**	chess	*esches*	**1300**
blue	*bleu*	**1300**	chivalry	*chevalerie*	**1300**
caitiff	*caitif*	**1300**	cloister	*cloistre*	**1300**

coat	*cote*	**1300**
condemn	*condemner*	**1300**
contrition	*contriciun*	**1300**
coverlet	*covrelit*	**1300**
curtain	*cortine*	**1300**
damnation	*dampnacion*	**1300**
dance (vb)	*dancer*	**1300**
demesne	*demesne*	**1300**
depose	*époser*	**1300**
duchess	*duchesse*	**1300**
emerald	*emeraude*	**1300**
enemy	*enemi*	**1300**
evidence	*évidence*	**1300**
exchequer	*eschequier*	**1300**
exile	*exil*	**1300**
expound	*espondre*	**1300**
faith	*feid*	**1300**
fashion	*façon*	**1300**
forfeit	*forfet*	**1300**
fur (n)	*forrer* (*vb*)	**1300**
garment	*garniment*	**1300**
garret	*garite*	**1300**
gender	*gendre*	**1300**
geometry	*géometrie*	**1300**
goblet	*gobelet*	**1300**
gown	*goune*	**1300**
idiot	*idiot*	**1300**
ivory	*yvoire*	**1300**
jollity	*jolivete*	**1300**
kennel	*kenil*	**1300**
lace	*las*	**1300**
lantern	*lanterne*	**1300**
leash	*lesse*	**1300**
mackerel	*makerel*	**1300**
majesty	*majesté*	**1300**
novice	*novisse*	**1300**
nutmeg	*nois mugue*	**1300**
orange	*orenge*	**1300**
page (boy)	*page*	**1300**
palsy	*paralisie*	**1300**
panel	*panel*	**1300**
pantry	*panetrie*	**1300**
parchment	*parchemin*	**1300**
pasty	*pastée*	**1300**
pearl	*perle*	**1300**
peer	*per*	**1300**
poet	*poete*	**1300**
prologue	*prologue*	**1300**
property	*proprieté*	**1300**
quail	*quaille*	**1300**
raisin	*reisin*	**1300**
record	*record*	**1300**
rein	*rene*	**1300**
retreat	*retret*	**1300**
romance	*romanz*	**1300**
sacrilege	*sacrilege*	**1300**
salmon	*samoun*	**1300**
saucer	*saussier*	**1300**
saviour	*sauveour*	**1300**
sceptre	*ceptre*	**1300**
skirmish	*escarmoche*	**1300**
soldier	*soudier*	**1300**
stomach	*estomac*	**1300**
study (vb)	*estudier*	**1300**
sturgeon	*esturgeoun*	**1300**
sulphur	*sulfere*	**1300**
surgeon	*surgien*	**1300**
tassel	*tasel*	**1300**
title	*title*	**1300**
towel	*touaille*	**1300**
tripe	*tripe*	**1300**
turret	*torete*	**1300**
vassal	*vassal*	**1300**
vestment	*vestement*	**1300**
vicar	*vicare*	**1300**
vinegar	*vyn egre*	**1300**
heron	*hairon*	**1302**
loin	*loigne*	**1302**
anoint	*enoint*	**1303**
assize	*asise*	**1303**
attorney	*atourné*	**1303**
chancel	*chancel*	**1303**
chronicle	*cronicle*	**1303**
culpable	*coupable*	**1303**
decree	*decré*	**1303**
enamour	*enamourer*	**1303**
horrible	(*h*)*orrible*	**1303**
indict	*enditer*	**1303**
jaundice	*jaunice*	**1303**
leisure	*leisir*	**1303**
marvel	*merveille*	**1303**
pestilence	*pestilence*	**1303**
single	*single*	**1303**
trespass (vb)	*trespasser*	**1303**
victual(s)	*vitaile*	**1303**
adore	*aorer*	**1305**
stallion	*estalon*	**1305**
porpoise	*porpeis*	**1309**
diamond	*diamant*	**1310**
garnet	*gernat*	**1310**
ruby	*rubi*	**1310**
plover	*plover*	**1312**
chase	*chacier*	**1314**
check	*eschec*	**1314**
dart (n)	*dart*	**1314**
encumbrance	*encombrance*	**1314**
mallard	*malart*	**1314**
equity	*equité*	**1315**
mirror	*mirrour*	**1315**
mystery	*misterie*	**1315**
solemn	*solempne*	**1315**

9.6.2 Old Norse

bait	*beit*	**1300**	sale	*sala*	**1300**
bark	*borkr*	**1300**	skirt	*skyrta*	**1300**
crawl	*krafla*	**1300**	slaughter	*slahtr*	**1300**
dirt	*drit*	**1300**	sly	*slægr*	**1300**
droop	*drupa*	**1300**	snare	*snara*	**1300**
girth	*gjorð*	**1300**	stack (n)	*stakkr*	**1300**
lift	*lypta*	**1300**	weak	*veikr*	**1300**

9.6.3 Low German

booze	*busen*	**1300**
hobble	*hobbelen*	**1300**
splint	*splinte*	**1300**

9.6.4 Latin

minor	*minor*	**1297**
limbo	*limbo*	**1300**
scripture	*scriptura*	**1300**

9.6.5 Arabic

hazard (a game)	OF *hasard* fr Arabic *az-zahr*	**1300**
camphor	OF *camfre* fr Arabic *kafur*	**1313**

9.6.6 Celtic

crag Celtic origin: cf. Irish and Gaelic *creag* **1300**

10. The 14th century – Northern dialects

The Northern dialects of ME came from the Northumbrian dialects of OE. The dialects of Scotland and the North of England today are still markedly distinct from Standard English and other dialects in features of the grammar and vocabulary, and from RP and Southern accents in pronunciation.

10.1 A 14th-century Scots English dialect

The Bruce is a verse chronicle of the life and heroic deeds of Robert Bruce (1274–1329), written by John Barbour about 1375 – *The Actes and Life of the Most Victorious Conqueror, Robert Bruce King of Scotland.* Barbour was archdeacon of Aberdeen and had studied and taught at Oxford and Paris. The first extract comes from Book I.

Text 59 – John Barbour on freedom, from *The Bruce* (i)

A fredome is a noble thing
Fredome mays man to haiff liking
Fredome all solace to man giffis
He levys at es yat frely levys
A noble hart may haiff nane es
Na ellys nocht yat may him ples
Gyff fredome failȝhe for fre liking
Is ȝharnyt our all oyer thing.
Na he yat ay has levyt fre
May nacht knaw weill the propyrte
Ye angyr na ye wrechyt dome
Yat is cowplyt to foule thyrldome
Bot gyff he had assayit it.

Scottish Text Soc, vol. II, 1980 (eds M. P. McDiarmid and J. A. C. Stevenson)

Once you have deciphered some unusual spellings, you will find that this Northern Scots dialect is closer to MnE than Southern dialects of England at that time. Rewriting the text in present-day standard spelling makes this clearer:

Ah freedom is a noble thing
Freedom makes man to have liking*
Freedom all solace to man gives

He lives at ease that freely lives
A noble heart may have no ease
Nor else nought that may him please
If freedom fails; for free liking
Is yearned over all other thing.
Nor he that aye has lived free
May not know well the property
The anger nor the wretched doom
That is coupled to foul thraldom
Unless he had assayed it.

*Liking = *free choice.*

Text 59 is recorded on the cassette tape.

aː freːdɔm ɪz a nɔːblə yɪŋg,
freːdɔm meːz man tɔ haːf likːɪŋg,
freːdɔm al sɔːlas tɔ man gɪvz
heː lɛvz at eːz yat freːlt lɛvz.
ə nɔːblə hart maɪ haːv naːn ɛːz
naː ɛlɪs nɔxt yat maɪ hɪm plɛːz
jɪf freːdɔm felj, fɔr freː likːɪŋg
ɪs jarnɪt uːr al ɔyər yɪŋg.
naː heː yat aɪ has lɛvɪt freː
maɪ naxt kna weːl yə prɔpərte
yɪ aŋgər na yə wrɛtʃɪt doːm
yat ɪz cuplɪt tɔ fuːl yɪrldoːm
bɔt jɪf heː had asaɪjɪt ɪt

10.1.1 *Commentary*

The text is too short to illustrate more than a few features of this dialect, but it is at an 'advanced' stage in its loss of the inflectional system of OE.

We might expect there to be words derived from Old Norse in a Northern dialect, but the text contains only two, *angyr* and *ay*, as against eight from Old French. Barbour was a scholar writing a literary romance, and it is therefore not surprising that he used words like *propyrte* and *solace*.

The vocabulary of Text 59 is listed in the *Word Book*.

10.1.1.1 *Spelling and pronunciation*

The metre of the verse is regular, an eight-syllable line rhyming in couplets. If you compare some of Chaucer's contemporary verses, you will see that some of Chaucer's words that end in a final ⟨e⟩ have to be pronounced to fit the metre of the verse, and some not. Perhaps this is what Chaucer was referring to when he hoped that no-one would 'mysmetre' his verse (see section 9.1). For example, the final ⟨e⟩ is pronounced in these lines from *The Book of the Duchess* as indicated:

For /nature /wold-**e** /nat suf /fys-**e**/
/To noon /erthly /crea /ture
Nat /long-**e** /tym-**e** /to en /dure
Wi /thout-**e** /slep and /be in /sor-**we**

But it is not always pronounced, and is always elided when it precedes a word beginning with a vowel, so that none of the final ⟨e⟩ spellings is pronounced in these lines:

/Purely /for de/faut(**e**) of /slep
That /by my /trouth(**e**) I /tak(**e**) no /kep...
/Pass(**e**) we /over /untill /eft;
That /wil not /be mot /ned(**e**) be /left.

The final ⟨e⟩ which was pronounced was all that was left of many of the former OE suffix inflections, and the fact that Chaucer could choose whether or not to pronounce them suggests that there was still variation between speakers.

In Barbour's verse, there is scarcely any evidence even of this remnant of the OE inflectional system. Check this in Text 60 which follows.

There are some spelling conventions to note in Barbour's writing:

- ⟨**ei**⟩⟨**ai**⟩ – Scots writers had adopted the convention of using ⟨i⟩ as a diacritic letter to mark a long vowel. In *haiff*, the ⟨ai⟩ represents [aː] and in *weill* the ⟨ei⟩ is [eː]. Not all uses of ⟨i⟩ following a vowel mark this feature, however. In *failʒhe* ⟨ai⟩ marks the diphthong derived from OF *faillir*; similarly the pronoun *thai*.
- ⟨**ʒh**⟩ – is written for ⟨ʒ⟩, representing the consonant [j], as in *failʒhe*, [faɪlj], and *ʒharnyt*, [jarnɪt].
- ⟨**ch**⟩ – is written for the ⟨ʒ⟩ or ⟨gh⟩ used in other dialect areas for the sound [x], as in *nocht*, as well as for the [tʃ] in *wrechyt*.
- ⟨**ff**⟩ – the doubled letters indicate unvoiced final consonants in *haiff* and *gyff*.
- ⟨**y**⟩ – from OE ⟨þ⟩ is used for ⟨th⟩ in some function words like *ye, yat* (*the, that*), as well as an alternative for ⟨i⟩.

10.1.1.2 *Word forms and inflections*

Nouns

None of the nouns is plural, but evidence of the plural inflection will be found in Text 60. The ⟨ing⟩ suffix on *liking* marks a noun which derives from a verb, sometimes called a gerund.

Verbs

The infinitive has no inflection – *haiff, knaw, pless. Present tense*: 3rd p sg inflection spelt ⟨is⟩ or ⟨ys⟩ – *giffis, levys*. Other verbs have only ⟨s⟩ – *has, mays*. Past participle: suffix spelt ⟨yt⟩ – *ʒharnyt, levyt, cowplyt* – and the OE prefix *ge-* has been lost.

Grammar

The word order of verse is often more marked and less normal than of prose, as in *Fredome all solace to man giffis*, in which the direct object *all solace* and adverbial *to man* precede the verb, and so cannot be reliable evidence of normal spoken usage. The relative pronoun is *that*, as in MnE, but spelt *yat*.

Activity 10.1

(i) See if any of the following linguistic features of ME Northern dialect are to be found in Texts 59 and 60.

(ii) Examine the proportion of words derived from OE, ON and OF.

- Words retaining the OE long back vowel [ɑː].
- Spelling words with ⟨i⟩ as a diacritic for a long vowel.
- Spelling ⟨s⟩ for [ʃ].
- Spelling ⟨quh⟩ for OE ⟨hw⟩.
- Present participle inflection of verbs ⟨-and⟩.
- Past tense 3rd p sg/pl and past participle inflections of weak verbs ⟨-it⟩ (or ⟨-yt⟩).
- Plural inflection of nouns ⟨-is⟩ or ⟨-ys⟩.
- ON form of 3rd person plural pronouns beginning with ⟨th-⟩.

Text 60 – John Barbour's *The Bruce* (ii)

The siege of Berwick, 1319 – the Scots are defending the town against the English.

	WW
Engynys alsua for to cast	Machines also for to throw
Yai ordanyt & maid redy fast	They set up & made ready fast
And set ilk man syne till his ward.	And set each man next to his post.
And schyr Walter ye gud steward	And Sir Walter the good Stewart
With armyt men suld rid about	With armed men had to ride about
And se quhar yat yar war mast dout	And see where that there was most doubt
And succour yar with his menȝe.	And bring help there with his company.
And quhen yai in sic degre	And when they in such state
Had maid yaim for defending	Had made them for defending
On ye Rud Ewyn in ye dawing	On the Rood Even* in the daybreak
Ye Inglis ost blew till assail.	The English host blew to attack.
Yan mycht men with ser apparaill	Then might men with various gear
Se yat gret ost cum sturdely	See that great host come resolutely
Ye toun enweround yai in hy	The town surrounded they in haste
And assailyt with sua gret will	And attacked with so great will
For all yar mycht yai set yartill	For all their might they set thereto
Yat thaim pressyt fast on ye toun.	Yet them† advanced fast on the town.
Bot yai yat gan yaim abandoun	But they that had them† resigned
To dede or yan to woundis sar	To death or else to wounds sore

Sa weill has yaim defendit yar	So well them† defended there
Yat leddrys to ye ground yai slang	That ladders to the ground they slung
And with stanys sa fast yai dan	And with stones so fast they struck
Yar fayis yat fele yar left liand	Their foes that many there stayed lying
Sum dede sum hurt and sum swonand.	Some dead some hurt and sum swooning.

* *Rood Even* – the eve of the Feast of the Exaltation of the Cross (Rood), that is, 13 September.

† *yaim/thaim* – the pronoun *them* used reflexively, meaning *themselves*.

The vocabulary of Text 60 is listed in the *Word Book*.

10.2 Another Northern dialect – York

The York Mystery Plays consist of a cycle of 50 short episodes which tell the story of the world according to medieval Christian tradition, from the Fall of the Angels and the Creation to the Last Judgement. Each trade gild of the city of York was responsible for the costs and production of a play, which was performed in procession on a pageant-wagon in the streets of York. Some of the plays were assigned to a gild whose occupation was reflected in the story. For example, the Bakers played *The Last Supper*, the Shipwrights *The Building of the Ark*, the Fishers and Mariners *The Flood*, and the Vintners *The Marriage at Cana.*

The cycle was produced each year at the feast of Corpus Christi, from the later 14th century into the early 16th century. Twelve 'stations' were set up in the streets, and each pageant-wagon moved in procession from one station to another to perform its play. They began the procession of wagons at 4.30 a.m., and the last play was probably finished after midnight. Banners were set up to mark the positions of the stations, and a proclamation was made.

Activity 10.2

Discuss the language and style of the Proclamation, e.g.

- the different functions of the word *þat*,
- verb inflections,
- noun inflections,
- forms of personal pronoun,
- the sources of the vocabulary – OE, ON or OF,
- spelling

Text 61 – The York Proclamation for the *Corpus Christi Plays*, 1415

Oiez &c. We comand of þe kynges behalue and þe mair & þe shirefs of þis Citee þat no man go armed in þis Citee with swerdes, ne with carlill axes, ne none othir defences in distourbaunce of þe kynges pees & þe play, or hynderyng of þe processioun of Corpore Christi; and þat þai leue þare hernas in þare ines, saufand knyghtes and squwyers of wirship þat awe haue swerdes borne aftir þame, of payne of forfaiture of þaire wapen &

inprisonment of þaire bodys. And þat men þat brynges furth pacentes, þat þai play at the places þat is assigned þerfore, and nowere elles, of the payne of forfaiture to be raysed þat is ordayned þerfore, þat is to say xl s.... And þat all maner of craftmen þat bryngeth furthe ther pageantez in order & course be good players, well arayed & openly spekyng, vpon payn of lesing of c s., to be paid to the chambre withoute any pardon. And that euery player that shall play be redy in his pagiaunt at convenyant tyme, that is to say at the mydhowre betwix iiijth & vth of the cloke in the mornyng, & then all oþer pageantes fast folowyng ilkon after oþer as þer course is, without tarieing...

10.2.1 Commentary

10.2.1.1 *Grammar*

As a proclamation it is written in a very formal style. The word *þat* is used frequently, and functions firstly as the marker of a noun clause [NCl], e.g.

We comand **þat** [no man go armed...]

and secondly as a relative pronoun in a relative clause [RelCl], e.g.

saufand knyghtes and squwyers of wirship [**þat** awe haue swerdes borne aftir þame]

Both uses of *þat* function to define precisely what is being commanded and to whom it applies. The formula *þat is to say*... is also used for this purpose, *þat* here functioning as a demonstrative pronoun. Another **formulaic** phrase is *of payne of* or *vpon payn of*, defining the penalties for not complying with the proclamation.

Verb forms

The evidence for a particular word-form in any one short text may be limited or non-existent, and this text contains few varieties of verb form. The two major classes of verb in OE, strong and weak (see section 4.4.3), continued through ME into MnE, but with many changes in individual verbs with, for example, some strong verbs becoming weak in their inflections. New verbs from French were inflected as weak, or regular verbs, with the ⟨-ed⟩ past tense and participle suffix, like *arayed*.

There were dialectal differences in verb inflections, but this text has few examples, and is also itself inconsistent, giving two different forms for the 3rd person plural present tense in the same verb, *brynges* and *bryngeth*. The common Northern inflection was ⟨-es⟩ or ⟨-is⟩, while ⟨-eth⟩ was used in the Midlands and South. York, which was a flourishing port in the 15th century, is situated on the river Ouse, or Humber, and so lies on the southern boundary of Northumbria. The people of York were therefore in direct contact with Midland dialectal speakers, and this may help to explain the use of both forms of inflection.

In John Barbour's Text 59 the inflection ⟨-ing⟩ was used in the Scots Northern dialect for a verb used as a verbal noun, or gerund, *liking*, and in Text 60 the inflection ⟨-and⟩ was used for present participles, *liand*, *swownand*. Similarly, in the York Proclamation, ⟨-and⟩ occurs on the verb *saufand* (*saving*), and ⟨-ing⟩ on the noun *hynderyng*. But ⟨-ing⟩ also occurs on other present participles – *spekyng*, *folowyng*, which was the form in other dialects. This is evidence of the 'mixed' dialect forms of the Proclamation.

Other verb forms are similar to those familiar to us in MnE, and include the passive voice with *be* and the past participle, and the use of the subjunctive mood to indicate what must or ought to be done.

	3rd p sg
no man	go (*subjunctive*)
þat	is to say
euery player that	shall play
	be redy (*subjunctive*)
as þer course	is
	1st p pl
We	comand
	3rd p pl
þai	leue (*subjunctive*)
knyghtes & squwyers þat	awe haue
men þat	brynges (furth)
þai	play (*subjunctive*)
all maner of craftmen þat	bryngeth (furthe)
	past participle
armed swerdes	borne
(well)	arayed
	passive voice
forfaiture þat	is ordayned
the places þat	is assigned
	to be raysed
	to be paid
	present participle
(openly)	spekyng
all oþer pageantes (fast)	folowyng

Noun forms

The plural inflection is ⟨-s⟩ or ⟨-es⟩, e.g. *knyghtes*, *shirefs*. This was so in all Northern dialects, sometimes spelt ⟨-is⟩, as we have seen in Barbour's *Bruce*. In Southern dialects, ⟨-en⟩ as the plural inflection was widespread in ME as well as ⟨-es⟩. It derived from the very common OE ⟨-an⟩ plural, but was eventually replaced by the regular ⟨s⟩ plural.

There is one example of the possessive inflection, also ⟨-es⟩, in *kynges*, MnE *king's*.

Pronoun forms

As we would expect, all the ON forms of 3rd person plural pronouns are used, *þai*, *þame* and *þaire*.

10.2.1.2 *Vocabulary*

There are 82 lexical word types: OE 51 = 62%; OF/AF 24 = 30%; ON 5 = 6%; Latin 2 = 2%

📖 The complete vocabulary of Text 61 is listed in the *Word Book*.

The sample is too small to be able to make any general inferences, but it suggests that by the end of the 14th century a large number of words of French derivation had been assimilated into English, certainly into formal written English. This is a hypothesis that can be tested by taking any historical text in English and looking up the derivation of its lexical words. Function words, as we have seen, are almost all of OE or ON derivation. Words from ON tended to be those of common speech, and many more of them survive, up to the present day, in dialectal rather than Standard English.

However, words derived from French are not necessarily specialised. Many of them are everyday words which have replaced the OE. For example, the word *city* is used, while OE *ceaster* only survives in place names like *Chester*, and *burh* in names like *Peterborough* or in the restricted meaning of *borough*. *Peace* has replaced *sibb* or *friþ*, *command* is more commonly used than *bid*, from OE *beodan*, and so on.

10.2.1.3 *Spelling*

Letter ⟨þ⟩ was still in use, but not consistently so in the text of the proclamation. The digraph ⟨th⟩ appears in the second half of the text in *that*, *bryngeth*, etc.

Typical of most ME writing is the general interchangeability of ⟨i⟩ and ⟨y⟩ for the vowel [i]; ⟨u⟩ and ⟨v⟩ were still variant forms of the same letter, and were to remain so for a long time yet. Scribes tended to write ⟨u⟩ in the middle of a word, as in *behalue*, *euery*, *course*, and ⟨v⟩ at the beginning, as in *vpon*, *vnwis*, *vertu*, *visage* for both the vowel [u] and the consonant [v]. Letter ⟨w⟩ was used similarly, as in *squwyers*, *awe*, *mydhowre*.

We are used to a system of 'correct spelling' in which all but a very few words have one standard spelling, to be found recorded in dictionaries. This was obviously not so for ME, as there are four different spellings for the word *pageant /pageants* in the York proclamation: *pagiaunt/pacentes/pageantes/pageantez*. But there are no other variants apart from *furth/furthe*, which is a reminder that words were often spelt with a redundant final ⟨-e⟩, like *mydhowre*, *cloke*. Again, this was to be a feature of English spelling for a long time to come.

The spelling *inprisonment* uses the prefix ⟨in-⟩ as in the phrase *in prison*. The spelling was later changed to match the spoken form [ɪm], which is conditioned by the following bilabial consonant [p].

10.3 The York Plays

The only copy of the York Plays to survive was written about 1470, and was originally the property of the corporation of the city. It was probably compiled from the various prompt copies belonging to each gild that performed a play, and the language may therefore be that of the late 14th century or early 15th century.

The dialect is Northern, but the scribes introduced a lot of modifications from the East Midland dialect, the evidence for which is in the variations of spelling of the same words. The use of some East Midland forms suggests the beginnings of a standardised system of spelling.

The plays are written in a variety of verse stanza patterns, with both rhyme and alliteration, so that they cannot be read as natural everyday speech, in spite of the liveliness of the dialogue dramatically. The following extract is from the Potters' *Pentecost Play*, which retells the story of the coming of the Holy Spirit at Pentecost, or Whitsuntide, after the Ascension of Christ. It fills out the story in *The Acts of the Apostles*, chapter 2.

The play does not attempt to portray the actual coming of the Spirit as it is told in the Bible,

> And when the day of Pentecost was fully come they were all with one accord in one place. And suddenly there came a sound from heaven as of a rushing mighty wind, and it filled all the house where they were sitting. And there appeared unto them cloven tongues like as of fire, and it sat upon each of them. And they were all filled with the Holy Ghost and began to speak in other tongues, as the Spirit gave them utterance.
>
> (*King James Bible*, 1611)

The following extract from the play spans the coming of the Holy Spirit, which is represented by the singing of the ancient hymn *Veni Creator Spiritus* (*Come Creator Spirit*). Two 'Doctors' speak contemptuously of the claim of the apostles that Jesus was alive again. After the hymn, Mary and Peter celebrate the coming of the Spirit.

Text 62 – From the York Potters' *Pentecost Play*, *c.* 1470 (facsimile)

i doctor

Harke maistir for mahoundes peyne
Howe þat þes mobbardis maddis nowe
þer maistir þat oure men haue slayne
Hase garte þame on his trifullis trowe

ij doctor

þe lurdayne sais he leffis agayne
þat mater may þei neuere avowe
For as þei herde his prechyng pleyne
He was away þai wiste noȝt howe

i doctor

They wiste noȝt whenne he wente
þerfore fully þei faile
And sais þam schall be sente
Grete helpe thurgh his counsaille

ij doctor

He myghte nowdir sende clothe nor clowte
He was neuere but a wrecche alway
But samme oure men and make a schowte
So schall we beste yone foolis flaye

i doctor

Nay nay þan will þei dye for doute
I rede we make no more deray
But warly wayte when þai come oute
And marre þame þanne if þat we may

ij doctor

Now certis I assente þer tille
Ȝitt wolde I noght þei wiste
Ȝone carles þan schall we kill
But þei liffe als vs liste
Angelus tunc cantare veni creator spiritus
Honnoure and blisse be euer nowe
With worschippe in þis worlde alwaye
To my souerayne sone Jesu
Oure lorde allone þat laste schall ay
Nowe may we triste his talis ar trewe
Be dedis þat here is done þis day
Als lange as ȝe his pase pursue
þe fende ne fendis yow for to flay
For his high halighaste
He lattis here on ȝou lende
Mirthis and trewthe to taste
And all misse to amende

Petrus

All mys to mende nowe haue we myght
þis is þe mirthe oure maistir of mente
I myght noȝt loke so was it light
A loued be þat lorde þat itt vs lente
Now hase he holden þat he vs highte
His holy goste here haue we hente
Like to þe sonne itt semed in sight
And sodenly þanne was itt sente

ij apostolus

Hitt was sente for oure sele
Hitt giffis vs happe and hele
Me thynke slike force I fele
I myght felle folke full feele

———————————————————————I doctor

Harke maiſtır for mahoundes peyne
Howe þat þes mobbardıs maddıs nowe
þer maiſtır þat oure men haue ſlayne
Haſe garte þame on hıs trıfullıs trowe

———————————————————————II doctor

Þe lurdayne ſaıs he leffıs agayne
Þat mater may þeı neuere avowe
For as þeı herde hıs prechyng pleyne
He was away þaı wiſte noȝt howe

———————————————————————I doctor

They wıſte noght whenne he wente
Þerfore fully þeı faıle
And ſaıs þam ſchall be ſente
Grete helpe thurgh hıs counſaılle

———————————————————————II doctor

He myghte nowdır ſende clothe nor clowte
He was neuere but a wrecche alway
But ſamme oure men and make a ſchowte
So ſchall we beſte yone foolıs flaye

———————————————————————I doctor

Nay nay þan wıll þeı dye for doute
I rede we make noȝt mekıll dray
But warly wayte when þaı come oute
And marre þame þanne ıf þat we may

———————————————————————II doctor

Now certıs I aſſente þer tılle
Yıtt wolde I noght þeı wıſte
ȝone carles þan ſchall we kıll
But þeı lıffe als vs lıſte
Angelus tunc cantare *venı creat^r ſp^tus**
Honnoure and blıſſe be euer nowe   Marıa
Wıth worſchıppe ın þıs worlde alwaye
To my ſouerayne ſone Ihu (*Jesu*)
Oure lorde allone þat laſte ſchall ay
Nowe may we trıſte hıs talıs ar trewe
Be dedıs þat here ıs done þıs day
Als lange as ȝe hıs paſe purſue†
Þe fende ne‡ fendıs yow for to flay§
For hıs hıgh halı gaſte
He lattıs here on ȝou lende
Mırthıs and trewthe to taſte
And all mıſſe to amende

———————————————————————Petrus

All mys to mende nowe haue we myght
Þıs ıs the mırthe oure maiſtır of mente
I myght noȝt loke, ſo was ıt lıght
A loued be þat lorde þat ıtt vs lente
Nowe haſe he holden þat he vs hıghte
Hıs holy goſte here haue we hente
Lıke to þe ſonne ıtt ſemed ın ſıght
And ſodenly þanne was ıtt ſente

———————————————————————II Apostolus

Hıtt was ſente for oure ſele
Hıtt gıffıs vs happe and hele
Me thynke ſlıke forſe I fele
I myght felle folke full feel

* Angel then to sing Come Creator Spirit.
† his pase pursue = follow in his steps.
‡ Written for he.
§ þe fende he fendis yow for to flay = he prevents the devil from frightening you.

The vocabulary of Text 62 is listed in the *Word Book*.

Phonetic transcription of part of Text 62 beginning *Honnoure and blisse* ..., recorded on the cassette tape.

ɔnuːr ænd blɪs be ɛvər nuː
wɪθ wɔrʃɪp ɪn θɪs wɔrld alwaɪ
tɔ mi sɔvəraɪn sʊn ʒeːzju
uːr lɔrd əlɔːn θæt læːst ʃæl aɪ.
nuː maɪ weː trɪst hɪs tɑːls ɑːr treʊ
bɛ deːds θæt hɛːr ɪs dʊn θɪs daɪ.
als læŋg as jeː hɪs pɑːs pʊrsuː
θə feːnd heː fɛnds juː for to flaɪ.
fɔr hɪs hiːç hɑːlɪ gɑːst
hɛː læts heːr ɔn juː lɛnd,
mɪrθs ænd treʊθ tɔ tɑːst,
ænd al mɪs tɔ ɑmɛnd
Petrus
al mɪs to mɛnd nuː hæv weː miːçt
θɪs ɪs θə mɪrθ uːr maɪstɪr ɔf mɛnt.
iː miːçt nɔxt loːk, sɔ wæs it liːçt,
ɑː lʊvd beː θæt lɔrd θæt ɪt θs lɛnt.
nuː hæs heː hɔːldən θæt heː ʊs hiːçt,
hɪs hɔlːɪ gɔːst heːr hæv we hɛnt.
liːk to θə sʊn ɪt seːmd ɪn siːçt,
ænd sudənlɪ θæn wæs ɪt sɛnt.
II Apostolus
hɪt wæs sɛnt fɔr uːr seːl,
hɪt gɪvz ʊs hæp ənd hɛːl,
mɛ θɪŋk slɪk fɔrs iː feːl,
iː miːçt fɛl fɔlk fʊl fɛːl

10.3.1 *Commentary*

10.3.1.1 *The verse*

Metre

This part of the play divides into patterned stanzas of twelve lines, the first eight having eight syllables and the last four having six, in a rising duple (or iambic) rhythm x / x / x / x /.

First stanza

x / x / x / x / 8 syllables, 4 stressed
Harke **mais** tir **for** ma **houn** des **peyne**
Howe þat þes mobbardis maddis nowe
Þer maistir þat oure men haue slayne
Hase garte þame on his trifullis trowe
Þe lurdayne sais he leffis agayne

Þat mater may þei neuere avowe
For as þei herde his prechyng pleyne
He was away þai wiste noȝt howe
x / x / x / 6 syllables, 3 stressed
They **wiste** noght **whenne** he **wente**
Þerfore fully þei faile
And sais þam schall be sente
Grete helpe thurgh his counsaille

Rhyme-scheme

The first eight lines of each stanza have two rhymes only, *abababab*, and the last four two rhymes *cdcd*:

Second stanza

He myghte nowdir sende clothe nor **clowte**
He was neuere but a wrecche **alway**
But samme oure men and make a **schowte**
So schall we beste yone foolis **flaye**
Nay nay þan will þei dye for **doute**
I rede we make noȝt mekill **dray**
But warly wayte when þai come **oute**
And marre þame þanne if þat we **may**
Now certis I assente þer **tille**
Yitt wolde I noght þei **wiste**
ȝone carles þan schall we **kill**
But þei liffe als vs **liste**

Alliteration

Each line has marked alliteration on some of the stressed syllables:

Third stanza

Hon[n]oure and blisse be euer [n]owe
With [w]orschippe in þis [w]orlde al[w]aye
To my [s]ouerayne [s]one Ihe[s]u
Oure [l]orde al[l]one þat [l]aste schall ay
Nowe may we [t]riste his [t]alis ar [t]rewe
Be [d]edis þat here is [d]one þis [d]ay
Als lange as ȝe his [p]ase [p]ursue
Þe [f]ende he [f]endis yow [f]or to [f]lay
For [h]is [h]igh [h]ali gaste
He [l]attis here on ȝou [l]ende
Mirthis and [t]rewthe to [t]aste
And all [m]isse to [m]aende

This sophisticated patterning of sound and rhythm combines the Old English tradition of alliterative verse with the newer French metrical rhymed verse (compare the *Owl and the Nightingale*, Text 38, section 6.2).

10.3.1.2 *Spelling and pronunciation*

We have seen that one of the principal changes in the language has been the gradual erosion of OE unstressed suffixes, for example [um] > [un] > [ən] > [ə] ~ Ø.

There were long periods when dialects varied in their progress towards an almost uninflected language, so that a word-final [ə] spelt ⟨e⟩ might still be pronounced as a grammatical inflection in one part of the country, but not in another. The evidence for this is very striking in verse writing, because poets would have a choice of current pronunciations with and without the final syllable to help in writing metrical verse (see section 10.1.1.1).

But none of the word-final letters ⟨e⟩ which might represent the unstressed vowel [ə] are pronounced in the last stanza of Text 62, and it is one part of the evidence that northern dialects changed more rapidly in this process of grammatical simplification than the midlands and south. The spelling of words with a redundant final letter ⟨e⟩ continued into the 17th century well after the letter was not pronounced in any dialect, as a glance as any of the later facsimiles will show.

10.3.1.3 *Word-forms and inflections*

Nouns

The plural suffix is spelt *-is* (*mobbardis*, *trifullis*, *dedis*, *mirthis*, *foolis*), except for the single occurrence of *-es* in *carles*. The evidence of the verse patterning suggests that the words were pronounced with a final [s] only – *mobbards*, *trifulls*, *deds*, *morths*, *fools*.

The one example of a possessive noun is *mahoundes*.

Verbs

There are by now considerably fewer verb inflections in this Northern dialect, with *is* common to both singular and plural 3rd person present tenses. All other inflections have been reduced to *-e*.

Present tense		
1st person singular	*-e*	(*I*) *rede, assente, wolde, myght, fele*
3rd person singular		
	-is	(*he*) *sais, leffis, fendis, lattis, giffis*
		(*he*) *hase, schall, myghte, is, thynke*
1st and 3rd person plural	*-is*	(*þei*) *maddis, sais,*
	-e	(*þei*) *haue, faile, will, ar, is*
		(*we*) *may, schall, haue*
singular subjunctive	*-e*	*liste, be, pursue*
plural subjunctive	*-e*	(*we*) *make, wayte, marre*
		(*þei*) *come, wiste, liffe*
Past tense		
singular	*-e*	(*he*) *was, wente, mente, lente, highte, semed*
plural	*-e*	(*þei*) *herde, wiste,*
Past participle		*slayne, garte, sente, done, loued, holden, hente, sente*
Imperative	*-e*	*harke, samme, make,*
Infinitive	*-e*	*trowe, avowe, be, sende, flaye, dye, kill, laste, triste, flay, lende, taste, amende, mende, loke, felle*

Personal pronouns

The Scandinavian 3rd person plural personal pronouns have been adopted in all forms, *þei*/*þai*, *þam*/*þame*, *þer*.

10.3.1.4 *Sources of vocabulary*

Word types: OE 140 = 77%; ON 14 = 8%; OF/AF 28 = 15%.

10.3.1.5 *Grammar*

We have examples of a number of developing grammatical features in text 62:

- The relative pronoun is *þat,* e.g. *þer maistir* ***þat*** *oure men haue slayne* (cf. OE *þe*).
- The passive verb construction with *be*, e.g. *was sente, schall be sente.*
- Perfective aspect with *have*, e.g. *haue slayne, hase garte, hase holden, haue hente.*
- Perfective aspect with *be*, e.g. *is done.*
- Northern form of present tense plural of *be* – *ar.*
- Modal verbs:

may	*may avowe, may triste*
might	*myghte sende, myght noȝt loke, myght felle*
shall	*schall be sente, schall kill, schall laste, schall flaye*
will	*will dye*
would	*wolde*

- Negative with *not* only, without the particle *ne*, e.g. *wiste noȝt, make noȝt, wolde noght.*
- Survival of dative pronoun without *to*, e.g. *þam schall be sente* (*to them shall be sent*).
- Impersonal verb construction, e.g. *as vs liste, me thynke* (*as it pleases us, it seems to me*).

Word order

The play is in verse, so we cannot draw conclusions about the word order of the everyday spoken and written language, but there is some variation from the unmarked *Subject – Predicator* (*Verb*) – *Object – Adverbial* order of clause constituents:

Od	***P=***	***S***	***A***	***=P***
Þat mater	may	þei	neuere	avowe

Oi	***P***	***S***	***A***
þam	schall be sente	Grete helpe	thurgh his counsaille

cj	***P=***	***S***	***A***	***Od***	***=P***
So	schall	we	beste	yone foolis	flaye

Od	***A***	***P=***	***S***	***=P***
ȝone carles	þan	schall	we	kill

cj	***Od***	***S***	***P=***	***A***	***A***	***=P***
For	his high hali gaste	He	lattis	here	on ȝou	lende

Od *P*
Mirthis and trewthe to taste

cj *Od* *P*
And all misse to amende

Od *P* *A* *P* *S* *Od*
All mys to mende nowe haue we myght

Od *A* *P*= *S* =*P*
His holy goste here haue we hente

10.4 Northern and Midland dialects compared

John de Thoresby became Archbishop of York in 1352. He found many of his parish priests ignorant and neglectful of their duties, and as one remedy for this he wrote a *Catechism* in Latin, setting out the basic doctrines of the faith. It was translated into English by a monk of St Mary's Abbey in York in 1357. This version is called *The Lay Folk's Catechism*. An extended version was written a little later by John Wyclif. He had been born in the North Riding of Yorkshire, but because he had lived and worked for a long time in Oxford and Leicestershire, his writings are in a variety of West Midlands dialect.

We can therefore clearly see some of the differences between Northern and West Midlands dialects by comparing the two versions of Archbishop Thoresby's *Catechism*.

Text 63 – *The York Lay Folks' Catechism*, 1357

This er the sex thinges that I have spoken of,
That the lawe of halikirk lies mast in
That ye er al halden to knawe and to kun*,
If ye sal knawe god almighten and cum un to his blisse:
And for to gif yhou better will for to kun tham,
Our fadir the ercebisshop grauntes of his grace
Fourti daies of pardon til al that kunnes tham,
Or dos their gode diligence for to kun tham...
For if ye kunnandly† knaw this ilk sex thinges
Thurgh thaim sal ye kun knawe god almighten,
Wham, als saint Iohn saies in his godspel,
Conandly for to knawe swilk‡ als he is,
It is endles life and lastand bliss,
To whilk§ blisse he bring us that bought us. amen

* to kun = to learn.
† kunnandly/conandly = clearly.
‡ swilk = such.
§ whilk = which.

Text 64 – *The York Lay Folks' Catechism*, Wyclif's version

These be þe sexe thyngys þat y haue spokyn of
þat þe law of holy chirche lys most yn.

þat þey be holde to know and to kunne;
yf þey schal knowe god almyȝty and come to þe blysse of heuyn.
And for to ȝeue ȝow þe better wyl for to cunne ham.
Our Fadyr þe archiepischop grauntys of hys grace.
forty dayes of Pardoun. to alle þat cunne hem
and rehercys hem . . .
For yf ȝe cunnyngly knowe þese sexe thyngys;
þorwȝ hem ȝe schull knowe god almyȝty.
And as seynt Ion seyþ in hys gospel.
Kunnyngly to know god almyȝty
ys endles lyf. and lastynge blysse.
He bryngge vs þerto. þat bowȝt vs
With hys herte blod on þe cros Crist Iesu. Amen.

📖 The vocabulary of Texts 63 and 64 is listed in the *Word Book*.

Activity 10.3

Compare the following words and phrases (line numbers in parentheses) from the two versions of *The Lay Folk's Catechism* and explain the differences.

- er / be (1)
- halikirk / holy chirche (2)
- mast / most (2)
- halden to knawe / holde to know (3)
- sal / schal (4)
- cum / come (4)
- til al / to alle (7)
- kunnes tham / cunne hem (7)
- kunnandly / cunnyngly (9) conandly / kunnyngly (12) lastand / lastynge (13)
- saies / seyþ (10)

📖 A commentary on Activity 10.3 is in the *Text Commentary Book*.

10.5 Chaucer and the Northern dialect

In Chaucer's 'The Reeve's Tale' are two undergraduate characters, 'yonge poure scolers',

Iohn highte that oon and Aleyn highte that oother
Of oon town were they born that highte Strother
Fer in the north, I kan noght telle where.

Chaucer makes their Northern origins clear by marking their speech with some of the features that his readers would recognise as different from the educated London dialect that he used (see chapter 13). Below is an extract from the 'Tale'. The Northern words are printed in ***bold italic*** type. Aleyn and Iohn have come to a mill and greet Symkyn, the miller. They intend to supervise the grinding of their corn, as millers were notorious for cheating their customers.

Activity 10.4

Discuss and explain the Northern features in the following text (words in ***bold italic***). Some are marked for pronunciation and some for different inflections. There are also some dialectal differences of meaning, listed in the table following the text.

A commentary on Activity 10.4 is in the *Text Commentary Book*.

Text 65 – from Chaucer's *The Reeve's Tale*

Aleyn spak first: Al hayl Symkyn in faith
How ***fares*** thy faire doghter and thy wyf?
Aleyn welcome, quod Symkyn, by my lyf
And Iohn also. How now what do ye here?
By god, quod Iohn, Symond, nede has ***na*** peere.
Hym ***bihoues*** serue hymself that has ***na*** swayn
Or ellis he is a fool, as clerkes sayn.
Oure maunciple, I ***hope*** he wol be deed,
Swa werkes ay the **wanges** in his heed.
And therfore **is** I come and eek Alayn
To grynde oure corn and carie it ***heem*** agayn…

It ***sal*** be doon, quod Symkyn, by my fay.
What wol ye doon whil that it is in hande?…

By god, right by the hoper wol I stande,
Quod Iohn, and se how the corn ***gas*** in.
Yet saw I neuere by my fader kyn
How that the hoper ***wagges til*** and ***fra***…

Aleyn answerde: Iohn, wiltow ***swa***?
Thanne wil I be byneth by my crown
And se how that the mele ***falles*** down
Into the trogh. That ***sal*** be my desport.
For, Iohn, in faith I may been of youre sort,
I ***is*** as ***ille*** a millere as ***ar*** ye.

OE feallan	**falles**	falls
OE faran	**fares**	fares
OE gan	**gas**	goes
OE ham	**heem**	home
OE hopian	**hope**	hope = believes
OE behofian	**hym bihouse**	= he must
OE is	**is**	is
OE nan	**na**	no
OE sceal	**sal**	shall
OE swa	**swa**	so
OE wagian	**wagges**	wags
OE wyrcan	**werkes**	works = aches
OE wang	**wanges**	= back teeth
OE *Northern*	**ar/arun**	are
ON fra	**fra**	fro

ON illr	**ille**	ill = bad
ON sveinn	**swayn**	swain = servant
ON til	**til**	till = to

This is only part of the dialogue between the miller and the two 'clerkes'. Other words in the *Tale* which give away their dialect are:

OE alswa	**alswa**	also
OE ban	**banes**	bones
not known	**fonne**	= fool
OE gan	**ga/gane**	go/gone
OE lang ON langr	**lang**	long
OE nan (ne + an)	**naan**	none
OE ra ON ra	**ra**	roe (deer)
OE sang	**sang**	song
OE sawol	**saule**	soul
OE wat fr witan	**waat**	= knows
OE hwa	**wha**	who
OEbaðir	**bathe**	both
ON illr ON heill	**il-hail**	bad luck

The vocabulary of Text 65 is listed in the *Word Book*.

10.6 Loan-words 1320–1339

10.6.1 *French*

button	*boton*	**1320**	broach (vb)	*brocher*	**1330**
mistress	*maistresse*	**1320**	chimney	*cheminée*	**1330**
pheasant	*fesant*	**1320**	dean	*deien*	**1330**
alum	*alum*	**1325**	dress	*dresser*	**1330**
arraign	*arainer*	**1325**	fraud	*fraude*	**1330**
array	*arayer*	**1325**	harness	*harneis*	**1330**
arrest	*arester*	**1325**	lay	*lai*	**1330**
baptism	*baptesme*	**1325**	marquess	*marchis*	**1330**
base	*base*	**1325**	mastiff	*mastin*	**1330**
boot	*bote*	**1325**	navy	*navie*	**1330**
brandish	*brandissir*	**1325**	petition	*peticiun*	**1330**
coroner	*coruner*	**1325**	pinnacle	*pinacle*	**1330**
enamel	*anamayller*	**1325**	portcullis	*porte coleice*	**1330**
lectern	*lettrun*	**1325**	prose	*prose*	**1330**
officer	*officier*	**1325**	remember	*remember*	**1330**
revel	*reveler*	**1325**	scullery	*escuelerie*	**1330**
tenant	*tenant*	**1325**	search	*cerchier*	**1330**
tenement	*tenement*	**1325**	sexton	*segerstain*	**1330**
usurp	*usurper*	**1325**	vanquish	*vencus*	**1330**
adjourn	*ajorner*	**1330**	latch	*lache*	**1331**
apparel	*aparail*	**1330**	cream	*creme*	**1332**
bacon	*bacon*	**1330**	sober	*sobre*	**1338**
biscuit	*bescuit*	**1330**			

10.6.2 *Old Norse*

flat	*flatr*	**1320**
race (n)	*ras*	**1325**

10.6.3 *Latin*

dirge	*dirige*	**1320**

11. The 14th century – West Midlands dialects

In the Anglo-Saxon invasion and settlement of Britain, the Angles occupied the Midlands and North of England, and what is now southern Scotland. Their dialect of OE is called Anglian as a general term, but its northern and southern varieties were different enough for two dialects to be recognised – Northumbrian (north of the river Humber) and Mercian (south of the Humber).

During the ME period, the Mercian (Midland) dialect itself developed in different ways. The East Midlands were part of the Danelaw (see section 3.3.1.1), the West Midlands were not, so the language of the East Midlands changed partly under the influence of the Danish Old Norse speakers who had settled there. As a result, OE Mercian became two ME dialects, East Midland and West Midland.

The two texts chosen to illustrate the West Midland dialect are sufficiently similar to be called the 'same dialect', but show differences which lead scholars to place one in the north and the other in the south of the West Midlands.

11.1 A North-West Midlands dialect – *Sir Gawayn and þe Grene Knyȝt*

A note on the use of letter ⟨ȝ⟩ in the poem

We think of MnE spelling as being irregular and inconsistent in the relationship of letters to sounds. This, however, began long before modern times, and the manuscript of Sir Gawayn provides a good example of the use of a single letter to represent several different sounds. The letter ⟨ȝ⟩ was used in writing this poem to represent several sounds, because it had developed from two sources, firstly from the OE letter ⟨ȝ⟩ (see section 3.1.3.4) and secondly as a form of letter ⟨z⟩. It was therefore used for all the following sounds (the words are from Texts 66 and 67):

- **[j]** ȝederly, *promptly*; ȝolden, *yielded*; ȝeres, *years*; ȝet, *yet*. (We use ⟨y⟩ in MnE.)

- **[ç]** Similar to the sound in German *ich*, [ɪç], and usually followed by [t] in ⟨ȝt⟩, e.g. knyȝt, *knight*; hyȝt, *height*; lyȝtly, *lightly*; lyȝt, *light*. (We use ⟨ght⟩ in MnE, though the sound of the ⟨gh⟩ has now been lost in these words.)

- **[x]** Similar to Scots *loch* [lox] or German *bach* [bax] after [a], [o] or [u]. e.g. þurȝ, *through*; raȝt, *reached*; laȝt, *laughed*; boȝeȝ, *boughs*; flaȝe, *fled*; laȝe, *laugh*. Again, ⟨gh⟩ is used in MnE, and the sound has changed either to [f], e.g. *cough*, or has been lost.

- **[w]** A developing sound change from OE [ɣ], e.g. þaȝ, *though*; also, elsewhere, arȝe, *arrow*; saȝe, *saw*; broȝeȝ, *brows*. Letter ⟨w⟩ is also used in the poem for this sound, e.g. *blowe*, *lawe*.

- **[s]** ⟨ȝ⟩ and ⟨tȝ⟩ were both used for letter ⟨z⟩. Letters ⟨z⟩ and ⟨tz⟩ had been used in Old French for the sound [ts], which changed to [s] and later to [z]. This French convention was used in the poem for the sound [s], e.g. hedleȝ, *headless*; resounȝ, *reasons*; hatȝ, *has*.

- **[z]** ⟨ȝ⟩ represented the voiced sound [z] in ⟨-es⟩ noun and verb suffixes, e.g. discouereȝ, lokkeȝ, renkkeȝ, boȝeȝ, cachcheȝ, steppeȝ, strydeȝ, haldeȝ, etc. However, letter ⟨s⟩ is also used in the text, e.g. houes, *hooves*; bones; schonkes, *shanks*, etc. yȝe-lyddeȝ, *eye-lids* illustrates the the use of letter yogh as [j] and[z].

The poem is written in 101 stanzas which have a varying number of unrhymed alliterative lines followed by five short rhymed lines. Like all OE and ME verse, it was written to be read aloud to an audience.

Text 66 – From *Sir Gawayn and þe Grene Knyȝt* (i) (facsimile)

The story so far: during the New Year celebrations at King Arthur's court a Green Knight rides in, carrying a battle axe, and challenges any knight to strike him a blow with the axe, provided that he can give a return blow a year and a day later. Gawain takes up the challenge.

Transcription

The grene knyȝt vpon groūde grayþely hȳ dreſſes
a lıttel lut w^{t} þe hede þe lere he dıſcoue^{r}ȝ
hıs longe louelych lokkeȝ he layd ou^{r} hıs croū
let þe naked nec to þe note ſchewe.
Gauan grıpped to hıs ax ⁊ gederes hıt on hyȝt
þe kay fot on þe folde he be fore ſette
Let hıt doū lyȝtly lyȝt on þe naked
þat þe ſcharp of þe ſchalk ſchyndered þe bones
⁊ ſchrāk þurȝ þe ſchyıre grece ⁊ ſcade hıt ī twȳne
þat þe bıt of þe broū ſtel bot on þe groūde.

þe fayre hede fro þe halce hıt to þe erþe
þat fele hıt foyned wyth her fete þere hıt forth roled.
þe blod brayd fro þe body þ[t] blykked on þe grene
⁊ nawþer falt[r] ed ne fel þe freke neu[r] þe helder
bot ſtyþly he ſtart forth vpon ſtyf ſchonkes
⁊ ruyſchly he raȝt out, þere as renkkeȝ ſtoden
laȝt to hıs lufly hed ⁊ lyft hıt vp ſone
⁊ ſyþen boȝeȝ to hıs blonk þe brydel he cachcheȝ
ſteppeȝ ĩto ſtelbawe ⁊ ſtrydeȝ alofte
⁊ hıs hede by þe here ĩ hıs honde haldeȝ
⁊ as ſadly þe ſegge hȳ ĩ hıs ſadel ſette ĩ ſtedde
as non vnhap had hȳ ayled þaȝ hedleȝ he were
he brayde hıs bluk aboute
þat vgly bodı þat bledde
monı on of hȳ had doute
bı þat hıs reſouȝ were redde

Edited version

The grene knyȝt vpon grounde grayþely hym dresses
A littel lut with þe hede, þe lere he discouereȝ
His longe louelych lokkeȝ he layd ouer his croun
Let the naked nec to þe note schewe.
Gauan gripped to his ax & gederes hit on hyȝt
Þe kay fot on þe fold he before sette
Let hit doun lyȝtly lyȝt on þe naked
Þat þe scharp of þe schalk schyndered þe bones
& schrank þurȝ þe schyire grece & scade hit in twynne,
Þat þe bit of þe broun stel bot on þe grounde.
Þe fayre hede fro þe halce hit to þe erþe
Þat fele hit foyned wyth her fete þere hit forth roled.
Þe blod brayd fro þe body þat blykked on þe grene
& nawþer faltered ne fel þe freke neuer þe helder
Bot styþly he start forth vpon styf schonkes
& runyschly he raȝt out, þere as renkkeȝ stoden,
Laȝt to his lufly hed & lyft hit vp sone
& syþen boȝeȝ to his blonk, þe brydel he cachcheȝ,
Steppeȝ into stelbawe & strydeȝ alofte
& his hede by þe here in his honde haldeȝ
& as sadly þe segge hym in his sadel sette
As non vnhap had hym ayled, þaȝ hedleȝ he were
in stedde.
He brayde his bluk aboute
Þat vgly bodi þat bledde
Moni on of hym had doute
Bi þat his resounȝ were redde.

WW

The green knight on (the) ground readily him(self) arranges
A little bend with the head the flesh he uncovers
His long lovely locks he laid over his crown
Let the naked neck in readiness show.
Gawain gripped (to) his axe & gathered it on high
The left foot on the ground he before set
Caused it (to) land swiftly down on the naked (flesh)
(So) that the sharp (blade) of the man sundered the bones
& cut through the fair flesh & severed it in two,

(So) that the blade of the bright steel bit on the ground
The fair head from the neck hit to the earth
That many it kicked with their feet where it forth rolled.
The blood spurted from the body that gleamed on the green
& neither faltered nor fell the man never the more
But stoutly he started forth upon sturdy shanks
& fiercely he reached out where men stood
Seized his lovely head & lifted it up at once
& then turns to his steed, the bridle he snatches,
Steps into (the) stirrup & strides aloft
& his head by the hair in his hand holds
& as steadily the man settled him(self) in his saddle
As (if) no mishap had troubled him though he headless were
in that place.
He twisted his trunk about
That ugly body that bled
Many (of them) of him had doubt
By (the time) that his reasons were declared,

Some re-ordering of words.

📖 The vocabulary of Text 66 with Text 67 is listed in the *Word Book*.

Phonetic transcription of recorded text.

ðə greːn kniːçt ʊpɔn gruːnd graɪðlɪ hɪm drɛsəs
ə lɪtəl luːt wɪð ðə hɛːd, ðə leːr heː dɪscʊvərɛz,
hɪs lɔŋg lʊvlɪç lɔkəs heː laɪd ɔːvər hɪs kruːn,
lɛt ðə nɑːkəd nɛk tɔ ðə noːt ʃɛwə.
gawan grɪpəd to hɪs æks ænd gɛdərəs hɪt ɔn hiːçt,
θə kaɪ foːt ɔn θə fɔːld heː bɛvɔːr sɛt,
lɛt hɪt duːn liːçtliɪ liːçt ɔn θə nɑːkɛd,
θæt θə ʃarp ɔv θə ʃælk ʃɪndərd θə bɔːnəs
ænd ʃrænk θʊrx θə ʃiːr grɛːs ænd ʃɑːd hɪt ɪn twɪn,
θæt θə bɪt ɔv θə bruːn steːl boːt ɔn θə gruːnd.
θə faɪr hɛːd frɔ θə hæls hɪt to θə ɛrθə,
θæt fɛːlə hɪt fɔɪnd wɪð hɛr feːt ðɛr hɪt fɔrθ rɔld.
θə bloːd braɪd frɔ θə bɔdɪ θæt blɪkɪd ɔn θə greːn
ənd nɑːʊðər faltərd nɛ fɛl θə freːk nɛvər θə hɛldər,
bʊy stiːθlɪ heː start fɔrθ əpɔn stɪf ʃɔŋkəs
ænd rʊnɪʃlɪ he: rɑːxt uːt, θɛr æs rɛŋkɛs stoːdən,
laxt tɔ hɪs lʊvlɪ hɛːd ænd lɪft hɪt ʊp soːn,
ænd sɪðən boːɣəz tɔ hɪs blɔŋk, θə briːdɛl heː cætʃɛs,
stɛpɛz ɪnto steːlbawə ænd striːdɛz əlɔft,
ænd hɪs hɛːd bɪ θə hɛːr ɪn hɪs hoːnd hɑːldəz,
ænd æs sædlð θə sɛdʒ hɪm ɪn hɪs sædəl sɛt
æs noːn ʊnhæp hæd hɪm aɪld, θɑx hɛːdlɛs heː weːr
ɪn stɛd.
heː braɪd hɪs blʊk əbuːt,
θæt ʊglɪ bɔdɪ θæt blɛdə.
mɔnɪ oːn ɔv hɪm hæd duːt,
bɪ θæt hɪz rɛːzunz wɛr rɛdə

📖 A commentary on the spelling and pronunciation of Text 66 is in the *Text Commentary Book*.

11.1.1 *Alliteration and rhyme*

The poem is evidence that the oral traditions of Old English alliterative verse were unbroken (see section 4.1.1). In *Sir Gawayn* each line divides into two, with a short break, or **cesura** in the middle. There are usually four stresses in a line, two in the first half and two in the second, three of which alliterate together, but this could vary, e.g.

/**G**auan /**g**ripped to his /ax   & /**g**ederes hit on /hyȝt
þe kay /**f**ot on þe /**f**old   he be/**f**ore /sette /
Let hit doun /**l**yȝtly   /**l**yȝt on þe /naked
Þat þe /**sch**arp of þe /**sch**alk   /**sch**yndered þe /bones
& /**schr**ank þurȝ þe /**sch**yire grece   & /**sc**ade hit in /twynne
Þat þe /**b**it of þe /**b**roun stel   /**b**ot on þe /grounde

Each stanza ends with a group of rhyming lines. The first short line was called the 'bob', which rhymed with two alternate lines of the following four, called the 'wheel' – ababa:

in **stedde**.
He brayde his bluk **aboute**
Þat vgly bodi þat **bledde**
Moni on of hym had **doute**
Bi þat his resounȝ were **redde**.

11.1.2 *Grammar*

Personal pronouns

A short extract from *Sir Gawayn* will not include all the pronouns, but Texts 66 and 67 provide the following:

			Singular		*Plural*
1st person	**subject**	I			
	object	me			
–	**genitive**				
			–		
2nd person	**subject**	þou			
	object	þe			
	genitive		–		
		Masculine	**Feminine**	**Neuter**	
3rd person	**subject**	he		hit	þay
	object	hym		hit	
	genitive	his		his	her
Relative pronoun		þat			

Activity 11.1

Complete the chart using the following lines from *Sir Gawayn* to identify the remaining pronouns (printed in bold type).

- **Scho** made hym so gret chere
  þat watʒ so fayr of face...
- **Ho** commes to þe cortyn & at þe knʒt totes.
  Sir Gawyn **her** welcumed worþy on fyrst
  And **ho** hym ʒeldeʒ aʒayn ful ʒerne of hir wordeʒ,
  Setteʒ *hir* softly by *his* syde & swyþely *ho* laʒeʒ...
  totes = peeps; ʒeldeʒ = replies; worþy = courteously; ʒerne = eager; swyþely = very much; laʒeʒ = laughs.
- He sayde, **ʒe** ar welcum to welde as **yow** lykeʒ;
  þat here is, al is **yowre** awen to haue at **yowre** wylle & welde...
  welde = use; þat here is = that which is here; welde = control.
- Where is now **your** sourquydrye & **your** conquestes?
  sourquydrye = pride.
- Where schuld I wale **þe**, quoþ Gauan, where is **þy** place?...
  wale = find.
- Bot **ʒe** schal be in **yowre** bed, burne, at **þyn ese**...
  burne = knight.
- I schal gif **hym** of my gyft þys giserne ryche...
  giserne = battle-axe; riche = splendid.
- To wone any quyle in þis won, hit watʒ not **myn** ernde...
  wone = remain; won = place; ernde = errand.
- And **we** ar in þis valay verayly **oure** one;
  Here ar no renkes **vs** to rydde, rele as **vus** likeʒ.
  oure one = on our own; renkes = men; rydde = separate; vus likeʒ = (it) pleases us.
- A comloker knyʒt neuer Kryst made **hem** þoʒt.
  comloker = comelier, nobler; hem þoʒt = (it) seemed to them.
- And syþen on a stif stange stoutly **hem** hanges...
  syen = afterwards; stange = pole.
- As fortune wolde fulsun **hom**...
  fulsun = help.
- How ledes for **her** lele luf **hor** lyueʒ han auntered...
  ledes = knights; her lele luf = their true love; lyueʒ = lives; han auntered = have risked.

Noun inflections

Plural nouns in the text are:

lokkeʒ bones fete schonkes renkkeʒ resounʒ

With the exception of *fete*, which still retains its OE vowel change to mark plural, they are marked by the ⟨s/ʒ⟩, or ⟨es/eʒ⟩ suffix. It derives from the former OE strong masculine ⟨-as⟩ plural, and is now the regular MnE plural suffix.

Verb inflections

We know that a principal feature of ME is the progressive change and eventual loss of most OE inflections, and also that one marker of ME dialects is the variety of verb inflections which was the result. Text 66 provides some information about verb inflections in the North West Midland dialect. Where it does not, other words from *Sir Gawayn* are listed in brackets:

Present tense			
1st person sing.	I	-e / Ø	bere, craue, telle, ask
2nd person sing.	þou	-es / -eȝ	redeȝ, hattes, hopes, deles
3rd person sing.	he ho hit	-es / -eȝ	dresses, gederes, discouereȝ, boȝeȝ, etc.
plural	we ȝe þay	-en	fallen; helden; ȝelden
Past tense			
1st person sing.	I	*weak vb* -ed	lakked, cheued = *got*
		strong vb	seȝ = *saw*
2nd person sing.	þou	-ed / es(t)	fayled; kyssedes = *kissed*
			gef = *gave*
3rd person sing.	he ho hit		**Strong verbs**; bot fel let schrank start
		-ed / -d	**Weak verbs**: blykked, faltered, foyned, gripped, roled, schyndered, brayde/brayd
		-t	hit, layd, laȝt, lyft, raȝt, scade, sette, bledde
plural	we ȝe þay	-en	stoden, maden
infinitive			schewe (tak gif prayse)
imperative			(gif = *give*; kysse; lepe; lach = *seize*)
present part.			sykande = *sighing*
			wreȝande = *denouncing*
past part.		-ed	lut, ayled, payed, hunted
		-(e)n	slayn

Several of these inflections are familiar in MnE, and the loss of many OE inflections is clear.

Inflections in ME

As a result of the Viking settlement in the Danelaw, levelling and regularisation (see section 6.1.2.1) – the loss or reduction of most of the OE inflections – took place earlier in the Northern and Midlands dialects than in the south.

The barrier to the easy reading of *Sir Gawayn* is not its grammar, but its poetic diction and the large number of West Midlands dialect words which have not survived into Standard English.

Activity 11.2

Text 67 is the next stanza of the poem and tells what happened when Gawain took up the Green Knight's challenge to strike a blow with the axe. Make some analysis of its language.

Text 67 – *Sir Gawayn and þe Grene Knyȝt* (ii)

For þe hede in his honde he haldeȝ vp euen
Toward þe derrest on þe dece he dresseȝ þe face
& hit lyfte vp þe yȝe-lyddeȝ & loked ful brode
& meled þus much with his muthe, as ȝe may now here:
Loke, Gawan, þou be grayþe to go as þou hetteȝ
& layte as lelly til þou me, lude, fynde,
As þou hatȝ hette in þis halle, herande þise knyȝtes.
To þe grene chapel þou chose, I charge þe, to fotte
Such a dunt as þou hatȝ dalt – disserued þou habbeȝ –
To be ȝederly ȝolden on Nw ȝeres morn.
Þe knyȝt of þe grene chapel men knowen me mony;
Forþi me for to fynde if þou fraysteȝ, fayleȝ þou neuer.
Þerfore com, oþer recreaunt be calde þe behoues.
With a runisch rout þe rayneȝ he torneȝ,
Halled out at þe hal dor, his hed in his hande,
Þat þe fyr of þe flynt flaȝe fro fole houes.
To quat kyth he becom knwe non þere,
Neuer more þen þay wyste fram queþen he watȝ wonnen.
What þenne?
Þe kyng & Gawen þare
At þat grene þay laȝe & grenne
Ȝet breued watȝ hit ful bare
A meruayl among þo menne.

📖 The complete vocabulary of Text 67 with Text 66 is listed in the *Word Book*.

11.2 A South-West Midlands dialect – *Piers Plowman*

Piers Plowman is one of the most famous medieval poems. It must have been a very popular work, because over fifty manuscripts have survived. The poem is an allegory of the Christian life, and of the corruption of the contemporary Church and society, written in the form of a series of dreams, or 'visions':

Ac on a May mornyng on Maluerne hulles (*hills*)
Me biful for to slepe . . .
And merueylousliche me mette, as y may telle. (mette = *dreamed*)

Piers Plowman, a humble poor labourer, stands for the ideal life of honest work and obedience to the Church.

The author was William Langland, but almost nothing is known about him except what can be inferred from the poem, though we must remember that the 'dreamer' of the visions is a character in the story, and may not always be identified with the author. For example, his name, *Will*:

A louely lady of lere in lynnene yclothed (lere = *face*)
Cam doun fro þe castel and calde me by name
And sayde '*Wille*, slepestou?' . . .
Ryht with þat ran Repentaunce and rehersede his teme
And made *Will* to wepe water with his eyes.

or William *Langland*:

> I haue lyued in *londe*, quod Y, my name is *Longe Wille*...

If his nickname is 'Long Will', he must have been a tall man, and unfit for hard physical work:

> Y am to wayke to worche with sykel or with sythe (*too weak*)
> And to long, lef me, lowe to stoupe (*too tall to stoop low*)
> To wurche as a werkeman eny while to duyren (*to last, endure*)

He lived in London, in Cornhill, with Kit and Calote (perhaps his wife and daughter, though there is no other evidence), and in the country:

> Thus y awakede, woet god, whan y wonede in Cornehull (*God knows*)
> Kytte and y in a cote... (*cottage*)
> And so y leue yn London and opelond bothe. (*in the country*)
> ...and riht with þat y wakede
> And calde Kitte my wyf and Calote my douhter.

He was sent to university (*scole*):

> When y ȝong was, many ȝer hennes (*many years ago*)
> My fader and my frendes foende me to scole... (*provided for*)

There are three versions of the poem, today called the A, B, and C texts, which show that Langland continually revised and extended the poem from the 1360s until the 1380s, when the C-text was probably completed. It is a fine 14th-century example of the tradition of alliterative verse in English. The dialect is of the South West Midlands, 'but rather mixed'. There are many variant spellings in the 50 different manuscripts, quite apart from the successive versions of the text itself.

In the Prologue the writer dreams of a 'fair field full of folk', the world of contemporary society:

Text 68 – *Piers Plowman* (i)

> In a somur sesoun whan softe was þe sonne
> Y shope me into shroudes as y a shep were
> In abite as an heremite vnholy of werkes,
> Wente forth in þe world wondres to here
> And say many sellies and selkouthe thynges.
> Ac on a May mornyng on Maluerne hulles
> Me biful for to slepe, for werynesse of-walked
> And in a launde as y lay, lened y and slepte
> And merueylousliche me mette, as y may telle.
> Al þe welthe of the world and þe wo bothe
> Wynkyng, as hit were, witterliche y sigh hit;
> Of treuthe and tricherye, tresoun and gyle,
> Al y say slepynge, as y shal telle
> Estward y beheld aftir þe sonne

And say a tour – as y trowed, Treuthe was there-ynne.
Westward y waytede in a while aftir
And seigh a depe dale – Deth, as y leue,
Woned in tho wones, and wikked spiritus.
A fair feld ful of folk fond y þer bytwene
Of alle manere men, þe mene and þe pore,
Worchyng and wandryng as þis world ascuth . . .
(*C-text*, ed. Derek Pearsall, Edward Arnold 1978.)

📖 The vocabulary of Text 68 is listed in the *Word Book*

The cassette tape contains a reading of the first nine lines:

ɪn ə sʊmər sɛːzun, hwæn sɔft wæs θə sʊnːə
iː ʃoːp meː ɪnto ʃruːdəs æz iː ə ʃeːp weːr
ɪn abiːt æz æn ɛrəmiːt ʊnhɔːlɪ əv wɛrks,
wɛnt fɔrθ ɪn ðə wɔrld wʊndrəs fɔr tɔ heːr,
ænd saɪ manɪ sɛlɪz ænd sɛlkuːθ θɪŋgəs.
ak ɔn ə maɪ mɔrnɪŋ ɔn malvɛrn hʏləs,
meː bifʏl fɔr to sleːp fɔr weːrɪnɛs ɔfwalkəd,
ænd ɪn ə land æs iː laɪ, lɛnəd iː ænd slɛpt,
ænd mɛrvɛɪlʊslɪç mɛː mɛtːə, æz iː maɪ tɛlːə

The printed text is edited, that is, it is based upon one of the C-text manuscripts, but uses other manuscript readings or makes changes where the manuscript does not make good sense. Abbreviations are also filled out, and modern punctuation put in. We are therefore not reading exactly what is in a manuscript.

Remember also that the manuscripts used by the editor are copies, and not the original, and so may include changes by the scribe. Consequently, any observations we make about either Langland's dialect, or the South West Midlands dialect in general, would need to be verified from much more evidence.

Activity 11.3

Refer to Section 9.2 on how to describe dialect differences, and comment on some linguistic features of Text 68.

📖 There is a descriptive commentary in the *Text Commentary Book*.

11.2.1 *Wrath and Patience in* Piers Plowman

Among the ME manuscripts which have come down to us, very many are in the form of sermons or homilies which set out the ideals of the Church and the Christian life. A typical example is contained in the Parson's Tale in Chaucer's *Canterbury Tales* (see section 13.1.2), in which the first prominent theme is sin and repentance for sin, or penitence,

Seint Ambrose seith that penitence is the plenynge of man for the gilt that he hath doon and namoore to doon any thyng for which hym oghte to pleyne.

The second theme is the Seven Deadly Sins, those sins which were thought to be the most offensive and serious,

> Now is it behouely thing to telle whiche ben dedly synnes, that is to seyn chieftaynes of synnes. . . . Now ben they clepid chieftaynes for as muche as they ben chief and sprynge of alle othere synnes.

The Seven Deadly Sins were pride, envy, wrath, sloth, covetousness, gluttony and lust. Chaucer's Parson defines wrath (*anger*, or *ire*) as,

> This synne of ire, after the discryuyng of seint Augustyn, is wikked wil to ben auenged by word or by ded.

In *Piers Plowman*, the dreamer vividly personifies each of the Seven Deadly Sins as men or women seeking repentance. In Text 69, Wrath appears:

Transcription of Facsimile,
Text 69 (p. 219)

Nau a waked wrathe : wıþ two whıte eyes
and wıþ a neuelyng noſe : nypped hıs lıppys
I am wraþ qd þat wy^{e} : wolde gladely smyte
boþ wıþ ſtone ⁊ wıþ ſtaf : ⁊ ſtel a pon my enemy
to sle hym ſleylıeſt : sleʒthes y þynke
þeʒth y ſıte ın þıs seuen ʒere : I schuld noʒt wel tel
þe harme þat I haue do : wıþ hand ⁊ wıþ tong . . .
I haue auntte to none : and an abbeſſe
hır wer leuer swoune or swolte : þan ſuffer ony payne
I haue be koke ın hır kechene : ⁊ þe couent ſerued
many monthes wıþ hem : and wıþ monkes boþe
I was þe pryoures potag^{er} : and oþer po^{r} ladıes
and made hem ıoutes of ıanglyng : how dā ıohān was baſtard
⁊ dam clarıce a kneʒthes doʒt^{er} : a kokowold was hyr syre
⁊ dam p̱nel a p^{r}ſtes fılıe : prıores worþ sche neuer
for scho had chıld ī a caponıs cort : scho worþe chalāget at þ^{e} elec(cıoun)
þus þaı ſetē softe : sū tyme and dıſputē
to þou lyyeſt ⁊ þou lıyeſt : be lady ouer hē all
and þan awaked I wrathe : ⁊ wold be a uenged
and þan I cry and I craſſe : wıþ my kene nayles
bıte ⁊ bete ⁊ bryng forþ : such þewes
þat al ladıes me loþeþ : þat loueþ ony wırchıp

Text 69 – *Piers Plowman* (ii) (facsimile)

Wrath, one of the Seven Deadly Sins

Edited version

Nau awaked Wrathe, wiþ two white eyes
And wiþ a neuelyng nose, and nypped his lippys.
'I am Wraþ,' quod þat weye, 'wolde gladely smyte,
Boþ wiþ stone and wiþ staf, and stel apon my enemy
To sle hym sleyliest sleʒthes Y þynke.
Þeʒth Y site in þis seuen ʒere I schuld noʒt wel tel
Þe harme þat I haue do wiþ hand and wiþ tong...
I haue auntte to none and an abbesse.
Hir wer leuer swoune or swolte þan suffer ony payne.
I haue be koke in hir kechene and þe couent serued,
Many monthes wiþ hem and wiþ monkes boþe.
I was þe pryources potager and oþer pore ladies
And made hem ioutes of ianglyng – how dame Iohan was bastard
And dame Clarice a kneʒthes doʒter, a kokowold was hyr syre,
And dame Purnel a prestes filie – priores worþ sche neuer,
For scho had child in a caponis cort scho worþe chalanget at þe eleccioun.
Þus þai seten softe sum tyme and disputen
To 'þou lyyest' and 'þou liyest' be lady ouer hem all.
And þan awaked I wrathe and wold be auenged.
And þan I cry and I crasse : wiþ my kene nayles
Bite and bete and bryng forþ such þewes
Þat al ladies me loþeþ þat loueþ ony wirchip.

Translation

Now awoke Wrath, with two white eyes
And with a snivelling nose, and nipped his lips.
'I am Wrath,' quoth that man, 'would gladly smite,
Both with stone and with staff, and steal upon my enemy
To slay him (with) slyest tricks I think (up).
Though I sit for seven years I should not well tell
The harm that I haue done with hand and with tongue...
I haue a nun, (who is) an abbess, for an aunt,
She would rather swoon or die than suffer any pain.
I have been cook in her kitchen and the convent served,
Many months with them and with monks both.
I was the prioress's and other poor ladies' cook
And made them soups of squabbling – how dame Iohan was a bastard
And dame Clarice a knight's daughter (her sire was a cuckold)
And dame Purnel a priest's daughter – prioress would she never be,
For she was challenged at the election that she had a child in a hen-yard.
Thus they sit softly some time and dispute
Till 'thou liest' and 'thou liest' be lady over them all.
And then awakened I, Wrath, and would be avenged.
And then I cry and I scratch with my keen nails,
Bite and beat and bring forth such manners
That all ladies that love any honour loath me.

📖 The lexical vocabulary of Text 69 is listed in the *Word Book*.

II.2.2 *Editing and printing a medieval text*

Modern printed books of older writers are all edited – that is, the surviving copies of a work are compared and a 'best' version is prepared by the editor for publication. This may be a version that does not correspond exactly to any of the originals, but draws on all of them. A typical heading in a printed text will read:

Edited from MS. Laud. Misc. 656
with variants from all other extant MSS.

To give you a short example of the problems of an editor, here are facsimiles of the same corresponding lines from two of the C-text manuscripts of *Piers Plowman* – Texts 70 and 71.

Activity 11.4

(i) Compare the facsimiles, Texts 70 and 71, and make your own edited version to produce a single text. Explain your choices.
(ii) Compare your version with that printed beneath as Text 72.

The editor of the version containing Text 72 used one 'base' MS, a second to correct the first where it was clearly faulty, and two more to supply better readings where both the others were unsatisfactory. None of the MSS were Langland's original.

Text 70 – *Piers Plowman* (iii) (facsimile)

(*MS Cotton Vespasian B XVI f. 64v*)

what ıs ꝑfut pacıence · quod actíua uíta ·
mekeneſſe and mẏlde ſpeche · and men of on wıl
þe whıche wıle loue lede · to oure lordes place
and þat ıs charıte chaumpıon · chef of all vertues——
and þat ıs pore pacıence · alle pereles to ſuffre
wheþer pouerte and pacıence · plece more god al mẏȝtí
þan so rıthful rıcheſſe · and reſonablelı to ſpende——
ȝe quıs eſt ılle quod concıence · quık laudabımus eū
þaw men reden of rıcheſſe · rıth to þe worldes ende
and whan he drou hım to þe deþ · þat he ne drat hym ſarre
þan enẏ pore pacıent · and þat ı preue bı reſoū——

Text 71 – *Piers Plowman* (iv) (facsimile)

(*MS Bodleian Douce 104*)

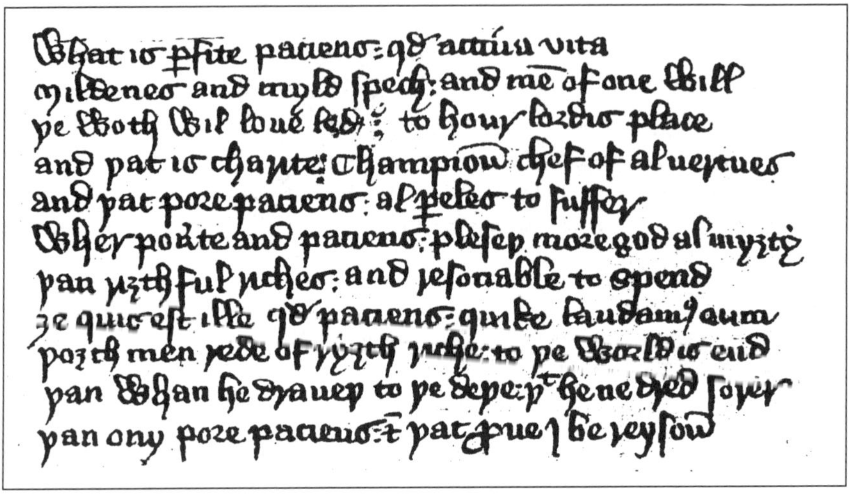

what ıs ꝑfıte pacıens : qd actíua uíta
mıldenes and myld ſpech : and mē of one wıll
þe woth wıl loue led : to hour lordıs place
and þat ıs charıte : chaumpıoū chef of all vertues
and þat pore pacıens : al ꝑeleſ to ſuffer
wher pou'te and pacıens : pleſeþ more god al myʒtẏ
þan rıʒthful rıches : and reſonable to spende
ʒe quıs eſt ılle qd pacıens : quıke laudamſ eum
þoʒth men rede of rẏʒth rıche : to þe worldıs end
þan whan he draueþ to þe deþe : þ^{t} he ne dyed ſorer
þan onẏ pore pacıens : ⁊ þat ꝑıue I be reyſoū

In the first line the question *What is parfit pacience?* is put to Patience by Activa Vita (Active Life). Patience answers, and a second question is put – *wheþer pouerte and pacience . plece more god al myʒti?* They are allegorical characters in the poem. Piers Plowman is seeking how to live a good life, and the next Passus (section) goes on to describe the life of Dowel – that is, how to do well. The text is from Passus XV, beginning at line 274.

Text 72 – *Piers Plowman* (v) – edited version of Texts 70 and 71

'What is parfit pacience?' quod Actiua Vita.
'Meeknesse and mylde speche and men of o will,
The whiche wil loue lat to our lordes place,
And þat is charite, chaumpion, chief of all vertues;
And þat is pore pacient, alle perelles to soffre.'
Where pouerte and pacience plese more god almyhty (where = whether)
Then rihtfullyche rychesse and resonableyche to spene?'
'ʒe, *quis est ille?*' quod Pacience, '*quik laudamus eum!*
Thogh men rede of rychesse rihte to the worldes ende

I wiste neuere renke þat riche was, þat whan he rekene sholde
Then when he drow to þe deth, that he ne dradd hym sarrore
Then eny pore pacient, and þat preue y be resoun.

(*C-text*, ed. Derek Pearsall, 1978)

📖 The lexical vocabulary of Text 72 is listed in the *Word Book*.

Activity 11.5

Examine any one or more of the texts in this chapter for evidence that they are West Midland dialects.

Typical markers of ME West Midland dialects include:

- OE long vowel [ɑː] has shifted; now spelt ⟨o⟩.
- OE vowel [y] remains, but spelt ⟨u⟩, e.g. *hull* for MnE *hill*.
- Suffix ⟨-ed⟩ sometimes 'devoiced' and spelt ⟨-et⟩.
- Pronouns: 3rd person feminine *ha* or *heo*; 3rd person plural possessive *hare*.
- Verbs: 3rd person plural present tense suffix ⟨-eþ⟩; present participle suffix ⟨-ende⟩.

11.3 Loan-words 1340–1359

11.3.1 *French*

advocate (n)	*avocat*	**1340**	patrimony	*patremoine*	**1340**
buckle	*boucle*	**1340**	redemption	*rédemption*	**1340**
closet	*closet*	**1340**	reward	*reward*	**1340**
conversation	*conversacion*	**1340**	sanctuary	*saintuarie*	**1340**
couch	*couche*	**1340**	subject (n)	*suget*	**1340**
cushion	*coissin, coussin*	**1340**	treacle	*triacle*	**1340**
dalliance	*dalliance*	**1340**	paper	*papir*	**1341**
embellish	*embellissir*	**1340**	sole (fish)	*sole*	**1347**
immortality	*immortalité*	**1340**	cherry	*cherise*	**1350**
innocent	*innocent*	**1340**	frock	*froc*	**1350**
mansion	*mansion*	**1340**	garter	*gartier*	**1350**
oppress	*oppresser*	**1340**	oyster	*oistre*	**1357**

11.3.2 *Old Norse*

snub	*snubba*	**1340**

11.3.3 *Latin*

discuss	*discutere*	**1340**
innumerable	*innumerabilis*	**1340**
reprehend	*reprehendere*	**1340**
solitary	*solitarius*	**1340**

12. The 14th century – East Midlands and London dialects

12.1 The origins of present-day Standard English

One of the reasons for learning about the development of the English language is to understand the relationship between dialects and Standard English in present-day English. In the conglomeration of different dialects that we call 'Middle English', there was no one recognised standard form. If we were to study the political, social and economic history of England in relation to the language, we would observe that the conditions for a standard language were beginning to emerge by the later 15th century. From the 16th century onwards, there is evidence that the need for a standard in spelling, pronunciation and grammar was being actively discussed. This naturally raised the question of which dialect or variety of the language was to be used for the standard.

What is a standard language?

One definition of a standard language, in modern sociological terms, is:

> The Standard is that speech variety of a language community which is legitimised as the obligatory norm for social intercourse on the strength of the interests of dominant forces in that society.
>
> (Norbert Dittmar, *Sociolinguistics*, 1976)

That is, the choice is made by people imitating those with prestige or power in their society, while the latter tend to prescribe their variety of the language as the 'correct' one to use. A standard language is not superior in itself as a language for communication – all dialects are regular and 'rule-governed' – but in its adoption and development it is the language of those with social and political influence, although advocates of a standard will often claim an intrinsic superiority for it.

In 1589 the poet George Puttenham published a book called *The Arte of English Poesie*. In it he gave advice to poets on their choice of language to use. It must be that of educated, not common people,

> neither shall he follow the speach of a craftes man, or other of the inferiour sort, though he be inhabitant or bred in the best towne and citie in this Realme. But he shall follow generally the better brought vp sort, . . . ciuill and graciously behauoured and bred;

The recommended dialect was therefore Southern, not Northern or Western;

> the usuall speach of the Court, and that of London and the shires lying about London within lx. myles, and not much aboue.

(Text 113, section 16.1.2 is a longer extract from Puttenham's book.)

This defines the literary language already in use in the 16th century, and clearly describes it as the prestigious language of the educated classes of London and the south-east. London was the centre of government, trade and commerce, and so the language of the 'dominant forces' in society would carry prestige, and others would seek to copy it.

This is a simplified explanation of a complex state of affairs, but it helps to explain why the educated London dialect formed the basis of the standard language as it developed. If the centre of government and commerce had been York, no doubt the Northern dialect would have formed the basis for Standard English today.

The London dialect in the later 14th century derived from a mixture of ME dialects, but was strongly influenced by the East Midlands dialect in particular. London naturally attracted large numbers of men and women and their families from other areas of the country to find work, bringing their own dialectal speech with them. Historians have identified a considerable migration of people from the East Midlands to London from the late 13th century to the mid-14th century, some of whom must have become the 'dominant social class' whose language carried prestige and was imitated by others. But because people migrated into London from other parts of the country also, there are features of Southern and Kentish also in the London dialect.

So present-day Standard English derives in its origins from the East Midland dialect of Middle English, and this explains why it is comparatively easy to read Chaucer's English of the late 14th century, and other East Midland texts. It will not be necessary, therefore, to examine the texts in this chapter in the detail given to those already described. You can apply the same principles of analysis to them, if you wish.

12.2 A South-East Midlands dialect – *Mandeville's Travels*

The Travels of Sir John Mandeville was one of the most popular books written in the 14th century, and over 300 manuscripts of it have survived, but its title is misleading. The original book was written in French in the 1350s by a doctor of Liège called Jehan de Bourgogne. He probably never travelled outside France, and based the stories on other men's travel writings, filling them out from his own imagination. It is believed that he adopted the name Sir John Mandeville, and wrote a preface claiming to be an Englishman born in St Albans, although the facts are not known for sure. The text in English is therefore a translation from the French by an unknown English writer using a South-East Midlands dialect. It cannot be a translation by the French author, because it is sometimes an inaccurate rendering.

Another version was written in verse form. The verse original was in a North-East Midlands dialect, but the only surviving manuscript is in a 'modernized version' of the 15th century. It gives us some idea of the standard literary language that had evolved and that writers were beginning to use. Unfortunately, part of the manuscript that corresponds to Text 73 is missing, but enough remains for comparison.

Text 73 – *The Travels of Sir John Mandeville* (i)

Now schall I seye ȝou sewyngly* of contrees and yles þat ben beȝonde the contrees þat I haue spoken of. Wherfore I seye ȝou, in passynge be the lond of Cathaye toward the high Ynde, and toward Bacharye, men passen be a kyngdom þat men clepen Caldilhe, þat is a full fair contre. And þere groweth a maner of fruyt, as þough it weren gowrdes; and whan þei ben rype, men kutten hem ato, and men fynden withinne a lytyll best, in flesch, in bon, and blode as þough it were a lytill lomb, withouten wolle. And men eten bothe the frut and the best: and þat is a gret mervueylle. Of þat frute I haue eten, allþough it were wondirfull: but þat I knowe wel, þat god is merueyllous in his werkes.

* sewyngly = 'followingly' = in what follows (fr OF suir/sewir, to follow).

Text 74 – *The Boke of Mawndevile*

...That bereth applis grete plente
And who þat cleueth an appul atwyn (*atwyn = apart, in two*)
A litille beest he fyndith thereyn.
To a litille lombe liche it ys
Of bloode and bone and eke of flessh
And welle shapen atte folle (*atte folle = at full, in every detail*)
In al thinge saufe it hath noo wolle (*saufe = save, except that*)
And men and women þere meest and leest (*meest and leest = most and least = greatest and lowliest*)
Eten of þat frute so with þat beest.

📖 The lexical vocabulary of Texts 73 and 74 is listed in the *Word Book*.

Here is part of a page in facsimile from one of the manuscripts of the *Travels*, with a transcription.

Text 75 – *The Travels of Sir John Mandeville* (ii) (facsimile)

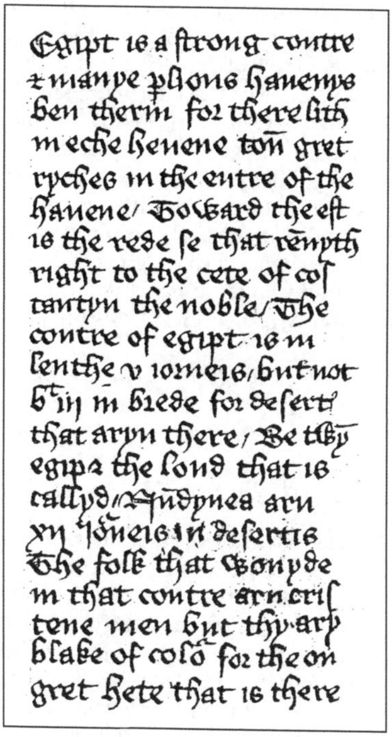

Egıpt ıs a ſtrong contre
& manye perılous hauenys
ben therın for there lıth
ın eche heuene toun gret
ryches ın the entre of the
hauene / Toward the eſt
ıs the rede ſe that rennyth
rıght to the cete of coſ
tantyn the Noble / The
contre of egıpt ıs ın
lenthe v ıorneıs but not
but ııj ın brede for deſert(ıs)
that aryn there / Betwyn
egıp & the lond that ıs
callyd / Nundynea arn
xıı ıourneıs ın deſertıs
The folk that wonyde
ın that contre arn crıſ
tene men but thy ary(n)
blake of color for the ou(er)
gret hete that ıs there
[*and brennynge of the ſonne*]

📖 The lexical vocabulary of Text 75 is listed in the *Word Book*.

12.3 The London dialect – Thomas Usk

From the late 14th century onwards we begin to find many more examples of everyday language surviving in letters and public documents than we do for earlier English. Literary language draws upon the ordinary language of its time, but in a special way, and we cannot be at all sure that the literature of a period tells us how people actually spoke.

London in Chaucer's day was, from time to time, the scene of violence and demonstration in the streets, and the following text describes one such series of incidents in the 1380s. Thomas Usk was involved with what turned out to be the wrong side in the political factions of his day, for he was unsuccessful in the appeal from which Texts 76 and 77 are taken, and later executed.

The *Appeal* is 'an example of the London English of a fairly well-educated man'. The original spelling is retained, but the punctuation is modern.

Text 76 – From Thomas Usk's *Appeal*, 1384 (i)

I Thomas Vsk . . . knowleched thes wordes & wrote hem with myn owne honde. . . . Also, that day that Sir Nichol Brembre was chose mair, a non after mete kom John

Northampton to John Mores hows, & thider kom Richard Norbury & William Essex, & ther it was accorded that the mair, John Northampton, sholde sende after the persones that thilk tyme wer in the comun conseil of craftes, and after the wardeyns of craftes, so that thei sholde kome to the goldsmithes halle on the morwe after, & ther the mair sholde speke with hem, to loke & ordeigne how thilk eleccion of Sir Nichol Brembre myght be letted; &, nad it be for drede of our lord the kyng, I wot wel eueri man sholde haue be in others top. And than sente he Richard Norbury, Robert Rysby, & me, Thomas Vsk, to the Neyte, to the duk of lancastre, to enforme hym in thys wyse: 'Sir, to day, ther we wolden haue go to the eleccion of the mair in goddes peas & the kynges, ther kom jn an orrible companye of criers, no man not whiche, & ther, with oute any vsage but be strength, chosen Sir Nichol Brembre mair, a yein our maner of eleccion to forn thys vsed; wher fore we preye yow yf we myght haue the kynges writ to go to a Newe eleccion.' And the duk seide: 'Nay, certes, writ shul ye non haue, auise yow amonges yowr selue.' & her of I appele John Northampton, John More, Richard Norbury, & William Essex.

(R. W. Chambers and Marjorie Daunt (eds), *A Book of London English 1384–1425*, 1931)

Text 77 – From Thomas Usk's *Appeal*, 1384 (ii)

Also, atte Goldsmithes halle, when al the people was assembled, the mair, John Northampton, reherced as euel as he koude of the eleccion on the day to forn, & seyde that truly: 'Sirs, thus be ye shape for to be ouer ronne, & that,' quod he, 'I nel noght soeffre; lat vs rather al be ded atones than soeffre such a vylenye.' & than the comunes, vpon these wordes, wer stered, & seiden truly they wolde go to a nother eleccion, & noght soeffre thys wrong, to be ded al ther for attones in on tyme; and than be the mair, John Northampton, was euery man boden gon hom, & kome fast a yein strong in to Chepe with al her craftes, & I wene ther wer a boute a xxx craftes, & in Chepe they sholden haue sembled to go to a newe eleccion, &, truly, had noght the aldermen kome to trete, & maked that John Northampton bad the poeple gon hoom, they wolde haue go to a Newe eleccion, & in that hete haue slayn hym that wolde haue letted it, yf they had myght; and ther of I appele John Northampton.

Selected vocabulary from Texts 76 and 77 is listed in the *Word Book*.

Activity 12.1

Two more extracts of texts in facsimile for study conclude the chapter. Choose any of the texts in this chapter and use the following check-list to find evidence of their being written in the East Midland or London dialect.

Features of East Midland and London dialects

Pronunciation and spelling

- OE long [ɑː] has rounded to [ɔː], spelt ⟨o⟩ or ⟨oo⟩.
- OE short [æ] written ⟨æ⟩ is now [a] and written ⟨a⟩.
- OE ⟨eo⟩ has smoothed and is now spelt ⟨e⟩.
- OE [y] has unrounded to [i], spelt ⟨i⟩, but there are inconsistencies in the London dialect, and some words originally with OE [y] use Kentish [e] or Southern [u].

Pronouns

- 3rd person plural, East Midland *he, here, hem* London *they, hir, hem.*

Verbs

- 3rd person singular present tense suffix ⟨-eþ⟩.
- 3rd person plural present tense suffix ⟨-en⟩.
- Past participle suffix ⟨-en⟩ retained, but prefix ⟨y-⟩ lost generally in East Midland, but not consistent in the London dialect, which sometimes retains prefix ⟨y-⟩ and drops the suffix ⟨-en⟩.
- Infinitive suffix ⟨-en⟩ generally retained (East Midland), but may be dropped in London dialect (Southern dialect influence).

12.4 Loan-words 1360–1379

12.4.1 *French*

oyster	*oistre*	**1357**	liberty	*liberté*	**1374**
grammar	*gramaire*	**1362**	royal	*roial*	**1374**
gruel	*gruel*	**1362**	tragedy	*tragedie*	**1374**
logic	*logique*	**1362**	treatise	*tretiz*	**1374**
moat	*mote*	**1362**	authority	*autorité*	**1375**
pastor	*pastour*	**1362**	banish	*banissir*	**1375**
pellet	*pelote*	**1362**	bonnet	*bonet*	**1375**
pullet	*poulet*	**1362**	captain	*capitaine*	**1375**
theology	*théologie*	**1362**	legacy	*legacie*	**1375**
trot	*troter*	**1362**	lieutenant	*lieutenant*	**1375**
adultery	*avouterie*	**1366**	literature	*littérature*	**1375**
apothecary	*apotecaire*	**1366**	question	*question*	**1375**
appetite	*apetite*	**1366**	retinue	*retenue*	**1375**
peach	*peche*	**1366**	scent	*sent*	**1375**
satin	*satin*	**1366**	season (vb)	*saisonner*	**1375**
squirrel	*esqirel*	**1366**	ague	*ague*	**1377**
taffeta	*taffetas*	**1373**	appurtenances	*apurtenance*	**1377**
adminster	*aminister*	**1374**	bill (document)	*bille*	**1377**
adorn	*aorner*	**1374**	galosh(es)	*galoche*	**1377**
complain	*complaindre*	**1374**	pen (writing)	*penne*	**1377**
divine	*devin*	**1374**	salary	*salarie*	**1377**
just	*juste*	**1374**	warren	*warenne*	**1377**

12.4.2 *Old Norse*

down (feathers)	*dun*	**1369**
glitter	*glitra*	**1375**
lug	*lugg*	**1375**
egg	*egg* (*cf.* Œ *æʒ*)	**1377**

12.4.3 *Low German*

wainscot *wagenschot* **1352**

12.4.4 *Latin*

submit	*submittere*	**1374**
remit (vb)	*remittere*	**1375**
scribe	*scriba*	**1377**

12.4.5 *Arabic*

alchemy OF *alquimie* fr Arabic *al-kimia* **1362**

12.4.6 *Celtic*

kern Irish *ceithern* – Irish foot-soldier **1351**

13. The London dialect – Chaucer, late 14th century

13.1 Chaucer's prose writing

Geoffrey Chaucer was born in the 1340s and died in 1400. He was acknowledged in his own day as the greatest contemporary writer, not only in poetry but also in the arts of rhetoric and philosophy. The following tribute to Chaucer after his death is from a poem by Thomas Hoccleve:

> Alas my worthy mayster honorable
> Thys landes verray tresouur and rychesse
> Deth by thy deth hath harme irriparable
> Vnto vs don; hir vengeable duresse
> Despoyled hath this land of the swetnesse
> Of rethorik, for vnto Tullius*
> Was nere man so lyk amonges vs.
> Also, who was hier in philosophy
> To Aristotle† in our tonge but thou?
> The steppes of Virgile‡ in poesie
> Thow filwedist eek, men wot wel enow . . .

*Marcus Tullius Cicero, d. 43 BC, Roman writer and orator.
†Greek philosopher, d. 322 BC.
‡Roman poet, d. 19 BC, author of the epic *The Aeneid*.

Chaucer wrote in the London dialect of the ME of his time, that is, the literary form of the language based on the speech of the educated class. The dialect of the mass of ordinary people living in London must have been as different from Chaucer's, both in form and pronunciation, as present-day Cockney is from educated RP and Standard English.

13.1.1 *'The Tale of Melibeus'*

The Canterbury Tales is Chaucer's best-known work, but some of the tales are much more widely read than others. Most of them are in verse, and it is unlikely that the two tales in prose will ever be popular, since their content and style are now out of fashion. The first prose tale is supposed to be told by Chaucer himself, after his comic satire on narrative romances, 'The Tale of Sir Thopas', has been interrupted by the Host:

> Namoore of this for goddes dignytee...

Chaucer agrees to tell 'The Tale of Melibeus',

> I wol yow telle a litel thyng in prose
> That oghte like yow as I suppose
> Or ellis certes ye be to daungerous*.
> It is a moral tale vertuous...

*Difficult to please, fastidious.

The tale is a translation from a French prose work which is itself based on a Latin original. Here are the opening paragraphs.

Text 78 – Chaucer's 'The Tale of Melibeus' (facsimile)

Here begynneth Chaucers tale of Melibee

A yong man called Melibeus myghty and riche
bygat vpon his wyfe that called was Prudence a doughter
which that called was Sophie Vpon a day byfell that he
for his disporte is went in to the feldes hym to play His wyfe
and eke his doughter hath he lafte wyth in his hous of
which the dores weren faste y shette Thre of his olde foes
han it espied and setten ladders to the walles of his hous
and by wyndowes ben entred and betten his wyfe and
wounded his doughter wyth fyue mortall woundes in
fyue places sondry that is to seyn in her fete in her handis
in her eres in her nose and in her mouthe and leften her for
dede and wenten away When Melibeus retorned was in
to his hous and sey all this myschefe he lyke a madde man
rentyng his clothes gan to wepe and crye Prudence his
wyfe as ferforth as she durste bysought hym of his wepyng
for to stynte but nought for thy he gan to crye and wepen
euyr the lenger the more

A yong man called Melıbeus myghty and rẏche
bygat vpon hıs wyfe that called was Prudnce a doughter
whıche that called was Sophıe vpon a day by fell that he
for hıs dıſporte ıs went ın to the ffeeldes hym to play hıs wẏfe
and eke hıs doughter hath he lafte wyth ın hıs houſe of
whıch the dores weren faſte ẏ ſhette thre of hıs olde foes
han ıt eſpıed and ſetten ladders to the walles of hıs houſe
and by wyndowes ben entred and betten hıs wyfe and
wounded hıs doughter wyth fyue mortall woundes ın
fyue places sondry that ıs to seyn ın her fete ın her handıs
ın hır heres ın her noſe and ın hır mouthe and leften her for
dede and wenten away / Whan Melıbeus retorned was ın
to hıs houſe and sey all thıs myſchefe he lyke a madde man
rentyng hıſ clotheſ gan to wepe and crye. Prudence hıs
wyfe as ferthforth as she durſte byſought hym of hıs wepẏg
for to stynte but nought* for thy he gan† to crye and wepen
euyr the lenger the more...

**nought for thy* meant 'nevertheless'.

†The verb *gan* in *he gan to wepe* was used as an auxiliary verb, to indicate past time – *he* ***wept***.

🕮 The lexical vocabulary of Text 78 is listed in the *Word Book*.

13.1.2 'The Parson's Tale'

The second prose tale has already been referred to in section 11.5 – 'The Parson's Tale'. It is a translation of two treatises in Latin, the first on penitence and the second on the Seven Deadly Sins. The following text is the commentary on gluttony in the second treatise.

Text 79 – Chaucer's 'The Parson's Tale' (facsimile)

After auarice comyth Glotenye which is expres a gayne the cōmaundemēt of god What Gloteny is Glotenye is vnmeſurable appetit to ete or to drinke or ellys to don ynogh to the vnmeſurable apetit and deſordeynee coueitiſe to ete or to drinke this synne corrumped all this world . as is wel shewd in the synne of adam and of Eue . . .

he þ^{t} is vſaunt to this synne of Glotenye he ne may noo synne w^{t}ſtonde he mote ben in servage of all vices ffor it is the deuell hoord there he hideth hym and reſteth him this synne hath manye speces Of sinnſe speces of Glo^{e} þ^{e} firſt is drōkenneſſe The firſte is dronkynneſse that is the horryble sepulture of mannes reſon and þ^{r}for whan a man is dronken . he hathe loſt is reſoun and this is dedly synne But sothely whan that a man ıs not wont to ſtronge drınke and peruenture ne knoweth not the strenght of the drınke or hathe ffebleſſe ın hıs hedd or hathe trauayled þorow the whıche he drınketh the moore al be he sodenly caught w[t] drınke, ıt ıs no dedly synne but venyall The [*end of page*]

....

The seconde spece of Glotenye ıs þ[t] the spırıt of a man wexeth all trouble for dronkeneſſe bıreueth hym the dıſcrecyoū of hıs wytte The ıȷ[de] spece of Glo[e] The therde spece of Glotenye ıs wh[a]nne a man deuoureth hıs mete and hathe no ryghtfull mane[re] of etynge. The ıııȷ[te] spıce of Glo[e] The ıııȷ[te] spece of Glotenye ıs whan thourgh the grete habundaunce of hıs mete the humo[ur]s of hıs body ben deſtemperyd The v spece of Glo[e] The fıfte ıs foryetylneſſe by to muchell drınkeynge ffor whıch som tyme a man forgeteth er the morwe what he ded at evyn or on the nyght before...

Theſe ben the v fyngers of the deueles hand by whıche he draweth folk to synne.

🕮 The vocabulary of Text 79 is listed in the Word Book.

Activity 13.1

Use the check-list in section 13.3.1 to describe some of the word-forms and grammar of Texts 78 and 79.

Here are facsimiles, from two manuscripts known as the Harley MS and the Hengwrt MS, of an extract from the Prologue to Chaucer's *Friar Tale*. It follows the *Summoner's Tale* about corrupt friars, so the friar is about to cap it with a story about a summoner.

13.2 Chaucer's verse

Text 80 – Chaucer's 'The Friar's Tale' (i) (facsimile from Harley MS 7334)

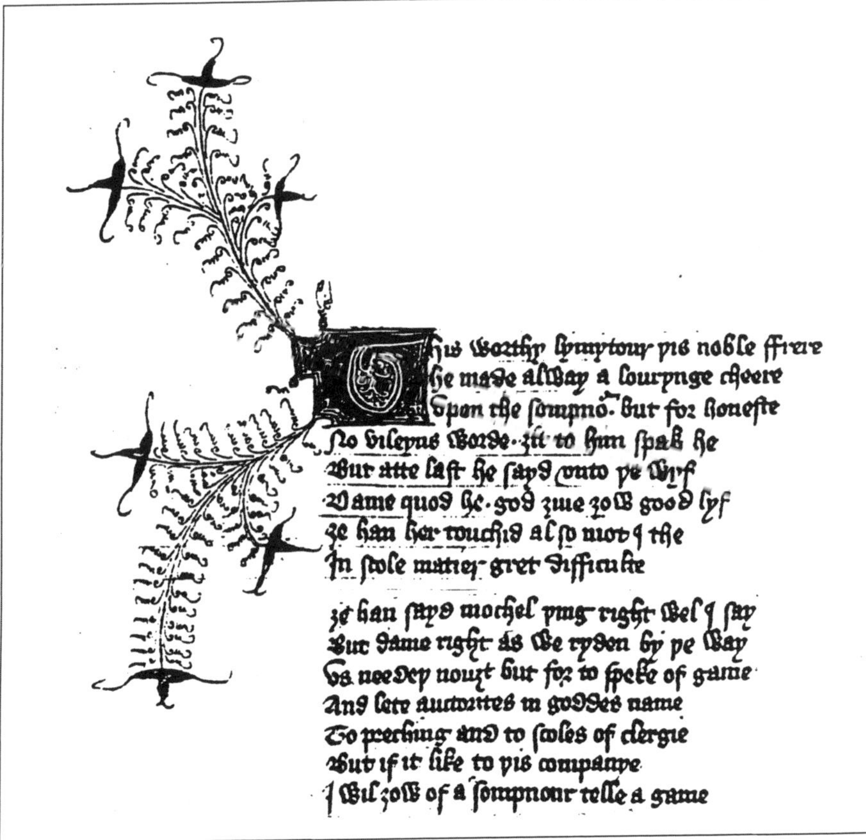

This worthy lymytour þıs noble ffrere
he made alway a lourynge cheere
upon the ſompnor. but for honeſte
No vıleyns worde. ʒıt to hım ſpak he
But atte laſt he ſayd unto þe wyf
Dame quod he. god ʒıue ʒow good lyf
ʒe han her touchıd alſo mot I the
In ſcole matter gret dıfficulte
ʒe han ſayd mochel þıng rıght wel I ſay
But dame rıght as we ryden by þe way
Us needeþ nouʒt but for to ſpeke of game
And lete auctorıtes ın goddes name
To prechıng and to ſcoles of clergıe
But ıf ıt lıke to þıs companye
I wıl ʒow of a ſompnour telle a game

Selected vocabulary from Text 80 is listed in the *Word Book*.

Text 81 – Chaucer's 'The Friar's Tale' (ii) (facsimile from the Hengwrt MS)

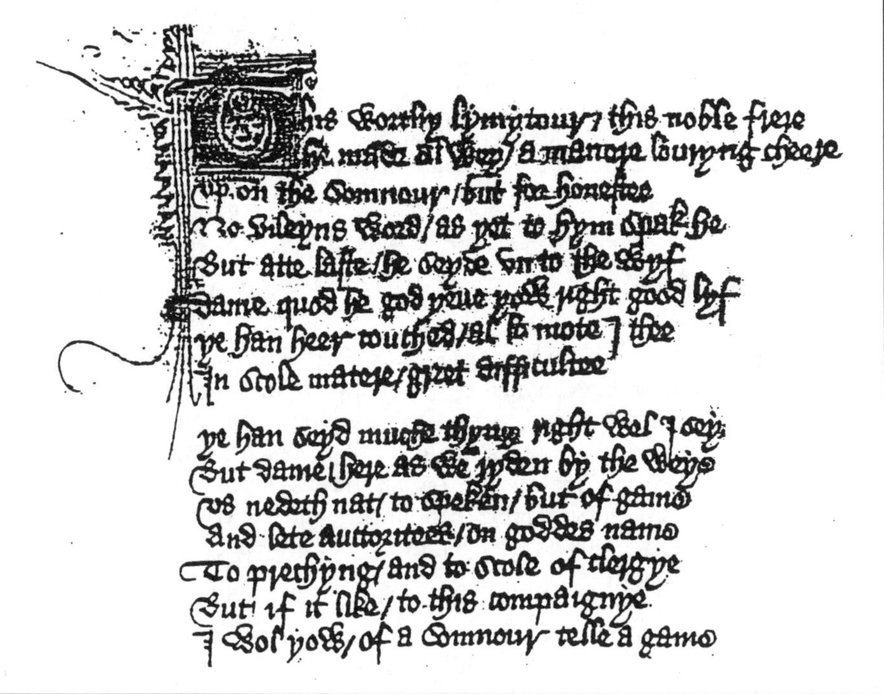

Thıs worthẏ lẏmẏtour / thıs noble frere
He made alweẏ / a manere lourẏng cheere
Vp on the Somnour / but for honeſtee
No vıleẏns word / as ẏet to hẏm spak he
But atte laſte / he seẏde vn to the wẏf
Dame quod he / god ẏeue ẏow rıght good lẏf
ẏe han heer touched / al ſo mote I thee
In scole matere / greet dıffıcultee
ye han seẏd muche thyng / rıght wel I seẏe
But dame / here as we rẏden by the weẏe
Vs nedeth nat / to speken / but of game
And lete auctorıtees / on goddes name
To prechẏng / and to scole of clergẏe
But ıf ıt lıke / to thıs compaıgnẏe
I wol ẏow / of a Somnour telle a game

A reading of the Hengwrt MS text is recorded on the cassette tape.

ðɪs wɔrði lɪmɪtuːr, ðɪs nɔːblə freːr
heː maːd alwɛɪ ə mænɛːr luːrɪŋg tʃeːr
ʊpɔn ðə sʊmnuːr, bʊt fɔr ɔnɛsteː,
nɔː vɪlɛɪnz wɔrd æz jɛt to hɪm spæk heː.
bʊt ætːə læst heː sɛɪd ʊnto ðə wiːf,
'daːmə' kwɔd heː 'gɔd jɛːv juː rɪçt goːd liːf,

jeː hæn heːr tʊtʃɛd, al sɔ moːt iː θeː,
ɪn scoːl mæteːrə grɛːt dɪfɪkʊlteː.
jeː hæn sɛɪd mʊtʃə θɪŋg, riçt wɛl iː sɛɪjə.
bʊt dɑːm, heːr æz weː riːdən bɪ ðe wɛɪjə,
ʊs neːdɛθ nat to spɛːkən bʊt ɔv gɑːmə,
ənd lɛːt aʊktɔriteːz, ɔn gɔdɛz nɑːmə,
tɑ prɛtʃɪŋg ænd tɑ skoːl(ə) ɔv klɛrdʒiːə.
bʊt ɪf ɪt liːkə tɑ ðɪs kɔmpaɪnjiə,
iː wɔl juː ɔv ə sʊmnuːr tɛl ə gɑːmə

13.2.1 *Verse form*

The verse form of the *Canterbury Tales* was what we now know as 'rhyming couplets' – each pair of lines rhymes – and in a metre traditionally called 'iambic pentameter'. The unit of rhythm is said to be a 'foot' containing an unstressed syllable (x) followed by a stressed syllable (/) – x /, which is called an **iamb**, and there are five of these in a line of verse (*penta* means *five* in Greek, hence **pentameter)**. Therefore a regular iambic pentameter line contains ten syllables of alternating unstressed and stressed syllables: x / x / x / x / x / . Here is a regular couplet from '*The Friar's Tale*':

He was if I shal yeuen* him his laude†
A theef and eek‡ a somnour and a baude
He **was** / if **I** / shal **ye** / uen **him** / his **laude**
A **theef** / and **eek** / a **som** / nour **and** / a **baude**

**yeuen = give.*
†laude = due honour.
‡eek = also.

Lines of verse are not always absolutely regular, but with this pattern in mind, we have plenty of evidence in Chaucer's verse about the number of syllables in words, their pronunciation and stress patterns. For example, if we assume that this couplet from 'The Friar's Tale' is metrically regular,

Thy body and this panne been myne by right
Thou shalt with me to helle yet to nyght

then it is clear that the word *panne* is pronounced as one syllable [pæn], but that *helle* has probably two syllables [hɛl – ə],

Thy **bo** / dy **and** / this **panne** / been **myne** / by **right**
Thou **shalt** / with **me** / to **hel** / le **yet** / to **nyght**

which is important evidence about the status of suffixes like ⟨-e⟩ in Chaucer's English. The final ⟨e⟩ was not pronounced in *panne*, but it was in *helle*. The probable reason in this case is that in the phrase *to helle*, the ⟨e⟩ of *helle* is a surviving inflection from Old English, marking the grammatical category called case.

What it shows is that in Chaucer's day, some final ⟨-e⟩ suffixes were pronounced, and some were not, varying from one dialect area to another as the last of the Old English suffixes finally disappeared in pronunciation, and so changed the grammar of the language. Chaucer had a choice which helped him in making his lines of verse flow easily. However, when reading his verse, remember that a final ⟨-e⟩ before a word beginning with a vowel or is elided, and not pronounced, as in the lines,

Thann(e) hau(e) I get(e) of yow maistri(e) quod she
Sith I may gouern and ches(e) as me list

In Text 82 following, the form *thest* for *the est* (l. 12) in the Harley MS demonstrates this kind of elision of a final ⟨e⟩ (though it is not a suffix in this case), but the form *the Est* in the Hengwrt MS shows an equally acceptable variation in pronunciation in which the vowel is not elided.

Today we pronounce words like *execution*, *fornication* and *defamation* as 4-syllable words, with the final syllable pronounced as [ʃən]. The evidence from Chaucer's verse is that these words were pronounced with 5 syllables, *ex-e-cu-ci-on*, as in line 68, *That boldely did execucion*. If you say this using present-day pronunciation, there are only 8 syllables *That / bold / ly / did / ex / e / cu / tion*. We can infer therefore that Chaucer's *boldely* had 3 syllables, and *execucion* 5, to make a regular 10-syllable line:

That	**bold**	e	**ly**	did	**ex**	e	**cu**	ci	**on**
1	2	3	4	5	6	7	8	9	10

13.3 Editing a text

Now follow transcriptions of two pages from each of the two manuscripts, Harley and Hengwrt, which include Texts 80 and 81.

Activity 13.2

Select a part of the texts, and write out your edited version, choosing what you think is the better text when there are differences between the two manuscripts. Add present-day conventions of punctuation. Discuss any problems you find.

Punctuation in the manuscripts

The Harley MS

The Harley MS has virtually no punctuation. Speech is not indicated by quotation marks, there are no commas or full-stops to mark off units of grammar, and capital letters mark the beginning of each line of verse, not of sentences. There are no apostrophes to mark the possessive of nouns – *the freres tale* (The Friar's Tale), *hir liues ende* (their lives' end), *in goddes name* (in God's name), *euery tounes eende* (every town's end). Apostrophes for this purpose were not introduced until the end of the 17th century.

The Hengwrt MS

Each line is divided into two by a *virgule*, the sign ⟨ / ⟩, which marks a **cesura**, or short pause in the line.

Text 82 – End of 'The Summoner's Tale' and beginning of 'The Friar's Tale'

Harley MS	**Hengwrt MS**
Thanne haue I gete of yow maistrie quod she	Thanne haue I gete / of yow maistrye / quod she
Sith I may gouern and chese as me list	Syn I may chese / and gouerne as me lest
Ȝe certis wyf quod he I hold it best	Ye c(er)tes wyf quod he / I holde it best
Kys me quod sche we ben no lenger wroþe	Kys me quod she / we be no lenger wrothe
ffor by my trouþe · I wol be to ȝow boþe	ffor by my trouthe / I wol be to yow bothe
This is to say ȝe boþe fair and good	This is to seyn / ye bothe fair and good
I pray to god þat I mot sterue wood	I pray to god / that I mote steruen wood
But I be to ȝow also good and trewe	But I to yow / be al so good and trewe
As euer was wyf siþþen þe world was newe	As euere was wyf / syn þ(*a*)t the world was newe
And but I be to morow as fair to seen	And but I be to morn / as fair to sene
As eny lady emp(*er*)esse or queen	As any lady / Emperice / or Queene
That is bitwixe thest and eek þe west	That is bitwix the Est / and eek the West
Doth by my lyf right euen as ȝow lest	Do with my lyf and deth / right as yow lest
Cast vp þe cortyns and look what þis is	Cast vp the Curtyn / looke how þ(*a*)t it is
And whan þe knyght saugh verrayly al þis	And whan the knyght / say verraily al this
That sche so fair was and so ȝong þerto	That she so fair was / and so yong ther to
ffor ioye he hent hir in his armes tuo	ffor ioye he hente hir / in his armes two
His herte bathid in a bath of blisse	His herte bathed / in a bath of blisse
A thousand tyme on rowe he gan hir kisse	A thousand tyme a rewe / he gan hir kisse
And sche obeyed him in euery þing	And she obeyed hym / in euery thyng
That mighte doon him pleisauns or likyng	That myghte do hym plesance / or likyng
And þus þay lyue vnto her lyues ende	And thus they lyue / vn to hir lyues ende
In parfyt ioye and ihū crist vs sende	In p(*ar*)fit ioye / and I(*es*)u crist vs sende
Housbondes meke ȝonge and freissche on bedde	Housbondes meke / yonge and fressh a bedde
And grace to ouer byde hem þat we wedde	And grace / tou(*er*)byde hem that we wedde
And eek I pray to Jhū schort her lyues	And eek / I praye I(*es*)u short her lyues
That wil nought be gouerned after her wyues	that nought wol be gou(*er*)ned /by hir wyues
And old and angry nygardes of despense	And olde / and angry nygardes of dispence
God sende hem sone verray pestilence	God sende hem soone / verray pestilence
There endith þe Wif of Bathe hire tale	Here endeth the Wyues tale of Bathe
There bygȳneth þe p(*ro*)log of þe ffreres tale.	The prologe of the ffreres tale.
This worthy lymytour þis noble ffrere	This worthy lymytour / this noble frere
he made alway a lourynge cheere	He made alwey / a manere louryng cheere
Vpon the sompno' · but for honeste	Vp on the Somnour / but for honestee
No vileyns worde · ȝit to him spak he	No vileyns word / as yet to hym spak he
But atte last he sayd vnto þe wyf	But atte last / he seyde vn to the wyf
Dame quod he · god ȝiue ȝow good lyf	Dame quod he god yeue yow right good lyf
Ȝe han her touchid al so mot I the	Ye han heer touched / al so mot I thee
In scole matter gret difficulte	In scole matere / greet difficultee
Ȝe han sayd mochel þing right wel I say	Ye han seyd muche thing / right wel I seye
But dame right as we ryden by þe way	But dame / here as we ryden by the weye
Vs needeþ nouȝt but for to speke of game	Vs needeth nat to speken / but of game
And lete auctorites in goddes name	And lete Auctoritees / on goddes name
To preching and to scoles of clergie	To prechyng / and to scole of clergye
But if it like to is companye	But if it like / to this compaignye
I wil ȝow of a sompnour telle a game	I wol yow / of a Somnour telle a game

Par de ȝe may wel knowe by þe name
That of a sompnour may no good be sayd
I pray ȝow þat noon of ȝow by euel a payd
A Sompnour is a renner vp and doun
Wiþ maundemētz for fornicaciū
And is y bete at euery tounes eende
Our oste spak a sir ȝe schold been heende
And curteys as a man of ȝour estaat
In company we wol haue no debaat
Telle ȝour tale and let þe sompno' be
Nay quod þe sompnour let him say to me
What so him list whan it comeþ to my lot
By god I schal him quyten euery grot
I schal him telle which a gret honour
Is to ben a fals flateryng lymytour

And his offis I schal him telle I wis
Oure host answerd and sayd þe sompno' is
And after þis he sayd vnto þe frere
Telleþ forþ ȝour tale my maister deere

Whilom þer was duellyng in my coñutre
An erchedeken a man of gret degre
That boldely did execucioñ
In punyschyng of fornicacioñ
Of wicchecraft and eek of bauderye
Of diffamacioun and auoutrie
Of chirchereues and of testamentes
Of contractes and of lak of sacraments
And eek of many anoþer cryme
Which neediþ not to reherse at þis tyme
Of vsur and of symony also
But certes lecchours did he grettest woo .

Pardee / ye may wel knowe by the name
That of a Somno(*ur*) / may no good be sayd
I praye / that noon of yow / be ypayd
A somnour / is a rennere vp and doun
With mandementz / for fornicacioun
And is ybet / at euery townes ende
Oure hoost tho spak / a sire ye sholde be hende
And curteys / as a man of your estaat
In compaignye / we wol no debaat
Telleth youre tale / and lat the Somno(*ur*) be
Nay quod the Somno(*ur*) / lat hym seye to me
What so hym list / whan it comth to my lot
By god / I shal him quyten euery grot
I shal him telle / which a gret honour
It is / to be a flaterynge lymytour
And of / many another maner(*e*) cryme
Which nedeth nat rehercen / for this tyme
And his office / I shal hym telle ywys
Oure hoost answerde / pees namoore of this
And after this / he seyde vn to the frere
Tel forth your tale / leeue maister deere

Here endeth the prologe of the Frere
and bigynneth his tale

Whilom/ther was duellynge in my contree
An Erchedekne / a man of hy degree
That boldely / dide execuciou(*n*)
In punysshyng of Fornicaciou(*n*)
Of wicchecraft / and eek of Bawderye
Of diffamaciou(*n*) / and auoutrye
Of chirche Reues / and of testamentz
Of contractes / and eek of lakke of sacramentz

Of vsure / and of Symonye also
But certes / lecchours / did he grettest wo

13.3.1 *Word-forms & grammar*

Activity 13.3

Use the following list to identify some of the differences in the word-forms and grammatical structures of Chaucer's English which contrast with modern Standard English.

Nouns

- What are the noun inflections for plural number and possessive case? Can you suggest a reason why some plural nouns in the texts are marked with ⟨-z⟩ rather than ⟨-s⟩?
- What forms of possessive structures can you find in the texts?

Pronouns

- What are the forms of the personal pronouns to be found in the texts, 1st, 2nd and 3rd person, singular and plural?
- What relative pronouns are used? Quote the examples in the texts.

Verbs

- Compare the forms of the infinitive in both MS texts.
- What other verb inflections are there in the texts? Compare them with present-day English verb inflections.
- Examine forms of the past tense for evidence of strong (irregular) and weak (regular) verbs and compare their MnE forms.
- Does *have* as an auxiliary verb mark perfective aspect in a verb phrase?
- Are there any examples of passive voice?
- Can you explain the constructions *as me list* (l.2) *what so him list* and *vs needeth nought* (l.42), when the MnE forms would be *as I please*, *whatever he pleases* and *we need not*?
- Identify the forms of the verb *be*.
- What is the meaning of *doon* (do) in *That mighte doon him pleisauns* (21) and of *did* in *lecchours did he grettest woo* (77)?

Grammar

- How is the negative formed?
- What is the meaning of *but* in:
  But I be to ȝow also good and trewe (l.8)
  And but I be to morrow . . . (l.10)
  Vs neede nouȝt but for to speke of game (l.42).
- Comment on word order.
- Are any constituents missing that would be expected in present-day English?

13.3.2 *Vocabulary*

Any text taken from Chaucer's writing will produce a fair proportion of words assimilated from French. This, of course, is not reliable evidence of the amount of French vocabulary in the common speech of uneducated men and women. The number of words of French origin in the present-day **core vocabulary** of English would be indirect evidence, and some knowledge of the loss of common Old English words would also help to indicate the extent of the infiltration.

Function words

Almost all function words derive from Old English. MnE *they*, *them*, *their* are important exceptions. They derive from the Old Norse dialects of Danish Viking settlers, adopted firstly in Northern England, and gradually moving south. Chaucer writes *they*, but still used OE *her* and *hem*.

Lexical words in Text 82

Word types: 229 (OE 156 = 68%, and ON 7 = 3%, total = 71%; OF 61 = 27%). Middle Dutch two words, Latin/Greek three words.

Loan-words in Text 82

Chaucer's vocabulary in Text 82 has just over a quarter of its lexical words derived from French. A list of the words derived from OF or ON and the very small number from Latin or Middle Dutch follows. The Harley MS words are in the left-hand column.

From Old Norse		dame	*dame*	host/oste	*hoost*
nygardes	*nygardes*	debaat	*debaat*	par de	*pardee*
angry	*angry*	degre	*degree*	parfyt	*p(ar)fit*
gete	*gete*	despense	*dispence*	payd	*ypayd*
housbondes	*housbondes*	diffamacioun	*diffamaciou(n)*	–	*pees*
cast	*cast*	empresse	*emperice*	pestilence	*pestilence*
meke (= meke)	meke	estaat	*estaat*	pleisauns	*plesance*
nay	*nay*	execucion	*execuciou(n)*	preching	*prechyng*
		flateryng	*flaterynge*	pray	*pray/praye*
From Latin or Greek		fornicacion	*fornicacioun*	p(*ro*)log	*prologe*
difficulte	*difficultee*	freissche	*fressh*	punyschyng	*punysshyng*
erchedeken	*erchedekne*	frere/ffrere/ffreres	*frere/fferes*	quyten	*quyten*
testamentes	*testamentz*	gouern(ed)	*gou(er)n(ed)*	reherse	*rehercen/reherse*
		grace	*grace*	sacraments	*sacramentz*
From Old French		honeste	*honestee*	symony	*symonye*
auctorites	*auctoritees*	honour	*honour*	sir	*sire*
auorite = adultery	*auoutrye*	ioye	*ioye*	sompnour	*somnour*
bauderye	*bawderye*	lecchours	*lecchours*	touchid	*touched*
certis/certes	*certes*	lymytour	*lymytour*	vsur	*vsur*
cheere	*cheere*	maister	*maister*	verray	*verray*
clergie	*clergye*	maistrie	*maistrye*	verrayly	*verraily*
company(e)	*compaignye*	manudements	*mandementz*	vileyns	*vileyns*
contractes	*contractes*	–	*manere*		
cortyns	*curtyn*	matter	*matere*	**From Middle Dutch**	
countre	*contree*	noble	*noble*	grot = fragment	*grot*
cryme	*cryme*	obeyed	*oneyed*	lak	*lakke*
curtys	*curteys*	offis	*office*		

📖 A complete word-list, including the OE vocabulary, is in the *Word Book*.

📖 A detailed commentary on Text 82 is in the *Text Commentary Book*.

13.4 Loan-words 1380–1399

13.4.1 *French*

ambush	*embusche*	**1380**	convert	*convertir*	**1382**
ceiling	*celer + -ing*	**1380**	crime	*crime*	**1382**
mitre	*mitre*	**1380**	desolation	*désolation*	**1382**
subsidy	*subsidie*	**1380**	homicide	*homicide*	**1382**
volume	*volum*	**1380**	lattice	*lattis*	**1382**
communion	*communion*	**1382**	plague	*plage*	**1382**

schism	*scisme*	**1382**
treaty	*treté*	**1382**
waiter	*weitteor*	**1382**
check	*eschec*	**1384**
flute	*fleute*	**1384**
magic	*magique*	**1384**
bay	*baie*	**1385**
alkali	*alcali (Arabic) al-qaliy*	**1386**
army	*armée*	**1386**
arsenic	*arsenic*	**1386**
bream	*brême*	**1386**
chant (vb)	*chanter*	**1386**
cinnamon	*cinnamone*	**1386**
confess	*confesser*	**1386**
contagion	*contagion*	**1386**
homily	*omelie*	**1386**
lute	*lut*	**1386**
mitten	*mitaine*	**1386**
oppose	*oposer*	**1386**
pledge (n)	*plege*	**1386**
poultry	*pouletrie*	**1386**
preface	*préface*	**1386**
spaniel	*espaignol*	**1386**
veal	*vel*	**1386**
confection	*confection*	**1387**
copy	*copier*	**1387**
perjury	*perjurie*	**1387**
prerogative	*prérogative*	**1387**
viscount	*viscounte*	**1387**
wardrobe	*warderobe*	**1387**
bar	*barre*	**1388**
lintel	*lintel*	**1388**
marjoram	*majorane*	**1390**
mince (vb)	*mincier*	**1390**
ordance	*ordenance*	**1390**
pigeon	*pijon*	**1390**
recreation	*récréation*	**1390**
salad	*salade*	**1390**
embroidery	*embroder*	**1393**
sanctity	*saintité*	**1394**
chevron	*chevron*	**1395**
arras	*Arras*	**1397**
blanch	*blanchir*	**1398**
noun	*noun*	**1398**
pleurisy	*pleurisie*	**1398**
thyme	*thym*	**1398**
toast (vb)	*toster*	**1398**
turquoise	*turqueise*	**1398**
allegiance	*ligeance*	**1399**
plume	*plume*	**1399**
secret	*secret*	**1399**

13.4.2 *Old Norse*

gap	*gap*	**1380**
calf (leg)	*khalfi*	**1386**
freckle	*freknur*	**1386**
keel	*kjoir*	**1397**
mire	*myrr*	**1387**
scrap	*skrap*	**1387**
gasp	*geispa*	**1390**
reef (sail)	*rif*	**1390**
bask	*baðask*	**1393**
odd	*odda*	**1398**

13.4.3 *Low German*

skipper *schipper* **1390** *Earl Derby's Expedition* – Item Herman, **skypper** de Dansk

13.4.4 *Latin*

complete	*completus*	**1380**
dissolve	*dissolvere*	**1380**
magnify	*magnificare*	**1380**
private	*privatus*	**1380**
suppress	*supprimere*	**1380**
temperate	*temperatus*	**1380**
temporal	*temporalis*	**1380**
commit	*committere*	**1386**
conspiracy	*conspiratio*	**1386**
intellect	*intellectus*	**1386**
rosary	*rosarium*	**1386**
promote	*promovere*	**1387**
history	*historia*	**1390**
equal	*aequalis*	**1391**

allegory	*allegoria*	**1382**	contempt	*contemptus*	**1393**
imaginary	*imaginarius*	**1382**	simile	*similis*	**1393**
lapidary	*lapidarius*	**1382**	testify	*testificare*	**1393**
necessary	*necessarius*	**1382**	incarnate	*incarnatus*	**1395**
quiet	*quies*	**1382**	index	*index*	**1398**
spacious	*spatious*	**1382**	rational	*rationalis*	**1398**
tributary	*tributarius*	**1382**	stupor	*stupor*	**1398**

13.4.5 *Italian*

There are very few loan-words from Italian before the 16th century, and all were borrowed via French:

alarm OF *alarme* < Italian *allarme – all arme! (to arms!)*
1325 *Early English Alliterative Poems* – Loude **alarom** vpon launde lulted was þenne

million OF *million* < Italian *millione*
1362 Langland, *Piers Plowman* – Mony **Milions** mo of Men and of Wymmen

13.4.6 *Celtic*

loch Gaelic *loch* **1375** Barbour's *Bruce* – In A nycht and In A day, Cummyn owt our the **louch** ar thai.

13.4.7 *Arabic*

Numbers of loans from originally Arabic words begin with *al- or el-*, incorporating the Arabic definite article *al-* (*the*).

camphor OF *camfre* < Medieval Latin *camphora* < Arabic *kafur*
1313 *Wardrobe Accounts 7 Edward II* – **Caumfre** 18*d*

lute OF *lut* < Arabic *al-ud*
1386 Chaucer, 'Manciple's Tale' – For sorwe of which he brak his minstralcye, Bothe harpe, and **lute**, and giterne, and sautrye.

alchemy OF *alquimie* < Arabic *al-kimia*
1362 Langland, *Piers Plowman* – Astronomye is hard þing.... Experimentis of **Alconomye**

elixir Medieval Latin *elixir* < Arabic *al-iksir*
1386 Chaucer, 'Canon's Yeoman's Tale' – The philosophre stoon, **Elixir** clept, we sechen fast echoon.

zenith OF cenit < Arabic *samt*
1387 *Trevisa Higden* – **Cinit**, þat is þe point þat is in þe welken euen aȝenst hem in þe oþer side of þe erþe.

almanac Medieval Latin *almanac* perhaps < Arabic *al-manakh*?
1391 Chaucer, *Astrolabe* – A table of the verray Moeuyng of the Mone from howre to howre, every day and in every signe, after thin **Almenak.**

amber OF *ambre* < arabic *anbar*
1398 *Trevisa* – The whale haþ gret plente of sperme ... and yf it is gaderid and dryeþ, it turneþ to þe substaunce of **ambra**.

syrup OF *sirop* < Arabic *sharab*
1398 *Trevisa* – Some drinke is medicinable as **surypes** ...

13.4.8 *Portuguese*

The first loan-words from Portuguese to appear in any number date from the 16th century. An exception is the word *strike*, meaning *hank*, *bundle*, which derives from the Portuguese word *estriga*, and was used by Chaucer in 'The Prologue' to *The Canterbury Tales*,

This Pardoner hadde heer as yelow as wex,
But smooth it heeng as dooth a **strike** of flex.

14. Early Modern English I – the 15th century

You will have seen that the 14th-century texts in chapters 12 and 13 are relatively easy to read without much help from a glossary – at least it is usually possible to make out the sense of late ME writing in the East Midland and London dialects. The following 15th century is for us, looking back, a period of transition to present-day English, and we talk of the **Early Modern English** period (**EMnE**), from about 1450, in the development of the language.

14.1 The beginnings of a standard language

Standard, official languages, with their rules of word-structure and grammar and choices of vocabulary, are all written in the same way, but may be spoken in a variey of dialectal accents. An agreed writing system has many advantages, and the consensus of educated opinion towards conformity in spelling and grammatical usage is part of social history.

> From 1066 to 1400, while Latin and French were the official written languages in England, there was no official English standard. English writing was regional and individual. During the 15th century an official standard began to emerge.
>
> (J.H. Fisher *et al.*, *An Anthology of Chancery English, 1984)*

It is important to remember that this does not entail standard speech, either in pronunciation or in vocabulary and grammar, although in contemporary England, certainly, there are social pressures towards conformity which ignore the continuing wide diversity of dialectal English.

In the 15th century, the City of Westminster, two miles distant and separate from London, had been the centre of government administration since the second half of the 12th century. The Chancery (originally *chancelery*) was the Court of the Lord Chancellor, and the written English that developed there in the 15th century was to become a standard, both in its style of handwriting ('Chancery hand') and in its vocabulary and grammar, because the use of English in administrative documents, rather than French, was re-established after about 1430.

14.1.1 *Chancery hand*

A continental business hand had developed in Italy and France from the 13th to the 14th centuries. It influenced the traditional cursive court-hand in England from the mid-14th century, and the resulting style is known either as **secretary hand** or **Chancery hand**. The following facsimile is an example of Chancery hand. It was dictated to a clerk called William Toly by King Henry V, who was with his army in France before Rouen, 'afore Roan', on 29 November 1418. It is the king's response to the breaking of a truce between him and the Duke of Brittany, and calls for 'reparation and restitution' for any violations of the truce.

Text 83 – Letter of King Henry V, 1418 (facsimile)

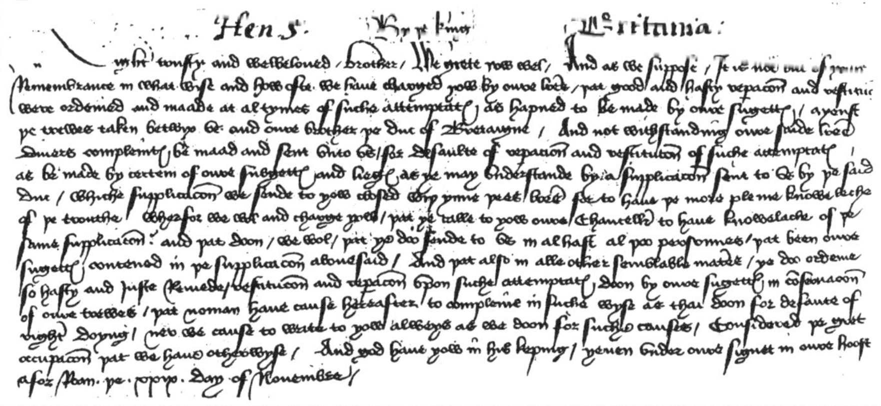

Transcription

Hen 5 By þe king **Britania**:

Rıght truſty and welbeloued / brother / We grete yow wel / And as we ſuppoſe / It ıs not
out of youre Remembrance ın what wıſe and how ofte we haue charged yow by oure
lres/þat good and haſty repacon and retıtucon were ordeıned and maade at altymes of
ſuche attemptates* as hapned to be made by oure ſugettes/ayenſt þe trewes taken betwıx
vs and oure brother þe duc of Bretaıgne / And not wıthſtandıng oure ſaıde ltres dıuers
compleıntes be maad and ſent vnto vs / for defaulte of repacıon and reſtıtucon of ſuche
attemptates as be made by certeın of oure ſubgettes and lıeges as ye may vnderſtand by a
ſupplıcacon ſent to vs by þe ſaıd duc / whıche ſupplıcacon we ſende to yow cloſed wıþ
ynne þees ltres for to haue þe more pleıne knoweleche of þe trouthe / wherfor we wol†
and charge yow / þat ye calle to yow oure Chancellr to haue knowelache of þe ſame
ſupplıccacon: and þat doon / we wol þat ye doo ſende‡ to vs ın al haſt al þoo perſonnes /
þat been oure ſugettes contened ın þe ſupplıcacon aboueſaıd / And þat alſo ın alle other
ſemblable§ mates / ye doo ordeıne ſo haſty and ıuſte Remede / reſtıtucon / and repcon
vpon ſuche attemptates doon by oure ſugettes ın cōſeruacon of oure trewes / þat noman
haue cauſe hereafter to complaıne ın ſuche wyſe as thaı doon for defaute of rıght doyng /
ner we cauſe to wrıte to yow alweys as we doon for ſuche cauſes / Conſıdered þe gret
occupacon þat we haue otherwyſe / And god haue yow ın hıs kepıng / yeuen vnder oure
ſıgnet ın oure hooſt afor Roan. þe .xxıx. day of Nouembre

* *attemptate* – 'a violent or criminal attempt; an attack, assault, outrage, raid, incursion'.

† *we wol* – we will, i.e. 'it is our will that . . .', 'we require . . .'

‡ *ye doo sende* – *doo* is a causative verb, i.e. 'that you cause to be sent . . .'.

§ *semblable* – similar.

Abbreviations

The scribe writes a final 'flourish' for ⟨-es⟩ in *atemptates*, *sugettes*, *compleintes*, *lieges*.

ltres	**lettres**	*letters*	*mates*	**materes**	*matters*
repacon	**reparacion**	*reparation*	*coseruacon*	**conservacion**	*conservation*
retitucon	**restitucion**	*restitution*	*occupacon*	**occupacion**	*occupation*
supplicacon	**supplicacion**	*supplication*			

Modernised spelling and punctuation

Right trusty and well beloved brother, we greet you well, and as we suppose it is not out of your remembrance in what wise and how often we have charged you by our letters that good and hasty reparation and restitution were ordained and made at all times of such attemptates as happened to be made by our subjects against the truce taken between us and our brother the Duke of Brittany. And notwithstanding our said letters, divers complaints [have] be[en] made and sent unto us for default of reparation and restitution of such attemptates as be made by certain of our subjects and lieges, as you may understand by a supplication sent to us by the said Duke. Which supplication we send to you [en]closed within these letters, for [you] to have the more plain knowledge of the truth. Wherefore we will and charge you that you call to you our Chancellor to have knowledge of the same supplication; and that done, we will that you *cause to be sent* to us in all haste all those persons that *are* our subjects contained in the supplication abovesaid. And that also in all other semblable matters you do ordain so hasty and just remedy, restitution and reparation upon such *violations* done by our subjects, in conservation of our truce, that no man have cause hereafter to complain in such *a way* as they do for default of right doing, nor [that] we *are compelled* to write to you always as we do for such causes, considered the great occupation that we have otherwise. And God have you in his keeping. Given under our signet in our host afore Rouen. the 29th day of November.

📖 The lexical vocabulary of Text 83 is listed in the *Word Book*.

14.1.2 *Chancery English*

14.1.2.1 *Spelling*

> The Chancery clerks fairly consistently preferred the spellings which have since become standard.... At the very least, we can say that they were trying to limit choices among spellings, and that by the 1440s and 1450s they had achieved a comparative regularization.
>
> (J. H. Fisher *et al.*, *An Anthology of Chancery English*, 1984)

14th-century spellings that conform to contemporary Standard English are unremarkable for readers today, so that we tend to be unaware of the choices that the Chancery clerks made. Here are some examples of spellings that are now standard, except for the persistent redundant final ⟨e⟩ which continued to be used for another two centuries:

Preferred Chancery spelling	***Other spellings less frequently used***
such(e)	sich, sych, seche, swich, sweche
much(e)	moch(e), mych(e)
which(e)/whych(e)	wich, wech
not/noght	nat
many	meny
any	eny, ony
but	bot
and	ond, ant
if/yf	yif, yef

This short selection of spellings recorded in the *Oxford English Dictionary* will illustrate the extent of spelling variation in the ME period:

realm	*reaume, reeaum, reawme, reome, reem(e), regm(e), rem(e), reame, reyme, reiem, reamme, reum(e), rewm(e), realme,*
poor	*pouere, povere, pouer, pover, poeuere, poeure, pouir, poer, powere, poyr, power, powar, poure, powre, pour, pore, poore*
people	*peple, pepule, pepul, pepull(e), pepille, pepill, pepil, pepylle, pepyll, peeple, poeple, poepul, peopel, peopull, puple, pupile, pupill, pupyll, pupul, peuple, pople*
receive	*rasawe, rassaif, rassave, recave, receave, receawe, receiuf, receive, receve, receyf, receyve, recieve, reciffe, recive, recyve, resaf, resaif, resaiff, resaive, resave, resawe, resayfe, resayff, resayve, resaywe, rescaive, rescayve, resceive, resceve, rescewe, resceyve, reschave, reschayfe, rescheyve, rescyve, reseve, reseyve, ressaif, ressaive, ressave, ressawe, ressayf, ressayve, resseve, resseyve, reycive*

We have seen how the spelling of the vowels in unstressed syllables varied in the OE period (in, for example, section 5.3.1), because the pronunciation of unstressed vowels was almost certainly [ə], the mid-central vowel *schwa*, for which there is no corresponding Roman letter. The same inconsistency of spelling is in early Chancery documents, alternating between *e, i, o and u*, with a 'drift towards standardisation' by using letter ⟨*e*⟩ more often. So *goodis* or *goodus* are in time consistently spelt *goodes*, before the final loss of the unstressed vowel in *goods*.

14.1.2.2 *Word-structure and grammar*

As Chancery English can be seen as the beginnings of Standard English, a survey of its grammatical structures will contain much that is common to present-day English, like the plural and the possessive markers ⟨s/es⟩, the pronouns *he/him/his* and *she/her/her* and the Northern plural subject pronoun *they* (although both *them* and *hem* are used for the object pronoun). Negatives are now marked by *not* only (or *nat*, *noght*, *nought*, *nowht*, etc.), and the older *ne has gone*.

When we read texts from the 15th century onwards, we have to compare an increasingly familiar language with its earlier stages of ME and OE in order to notice the changes taking place. There is still plenty that is not present-day English in spelling, vocabulary and grammar, but less and less as time progresses.

14.2 Early 15th-century East Midlands dialect – *The Boke of Margery Kempe*

Margery Kempe (*c.* 1373–*c.* 1439) was a woman from King's Lynn in Norfolk, who gave up married life as a result of her mystical experiences to devote herself to religion. She made many pilgrimages during her lifetime, and afterwards in the 1420s dictated a book describing her visions, temptations and journeys.

As the book was written down from Margery Kempe's own dictation, this is probably as close as we can get to ordinary speech of the early 15th century. The dialect is East Midlands, but we cannot tell how accurate was the scribe's reproduction of Margery's speech, or that of the only surviving manuscript, which was copied in the mid-15th century.

Here she describes her early marriage. Throughout the book she refers to herself as 'this creature':

Text 84 – *The Boke of Margery Kempe* (i)

Whan þis creatur was xx ȝer of age or sumdele mor sche was maryed to a worschepful burgeys of Lyn and was wyth chylde wyth in schort tyme as kynde wolde. And aftyr þat sche had conceyued sche was labowrd wyth grett accessys tyl þe chyld was born & þan what for labowr she had in chyldyng & for sekenesse goyng beforn she dyspered of hyr lyf, wenyng she mygth not leuyn.

MnE When this creature was 20 years of age or something more, she was married to a worshipful burgess of Lynn and was with child within short time as nature wills. And after (that) she had coneived she was in labour with great fevers till the child was born & then what for labour she had in childbirth & for sickness going before, she despaired of her life, thinking she might not live.

Here her first mystical vision is described:

Text 85 – *The Boke of Margery Kempe* (ii)

On a nygth as þis creatur lay in hir bedde wyth hir husbond she herd a sownd of melodye so swet & deletable hir þowt as she had ben in paradyse. And þerwyth she styrt owt of hir bedde & seyd Alas þat euyr I dede synne, it is ful mery in hevyn. Thys melodye was so swete þat it passyd alle þe melodye þat euyr mygth be herd in þis world wyth owtyn ony comparyson, & caused þis creatur whan she herd ony myrth or melodye aftyrward for to haue ful plentyuows & habundawnt teerys of hy deuocyon wyth greet sobbyngys & syhyngys aftyr þe blysse of heuen, not dredyng þe shamys & þe spytys of þe wretchyd world.

MnE On a night as this creature lay in her bed with her husband she heard a sound of melody so sweet & delectable to-her (it) seemed as she had been in Paradise. And therewith she started out of her bed & said 'Alas that ever I did sin, it is full merry in heaven'. This melody was so sweet that it passed all the melody that ever might be heard in this world without any comparison, & caused this creature, when she heard any mirth or melody afterward for to have full plenteous and abundant tears of high devotion with great sobbings & sighings after the bliss of heaven, not dreading the shames and the spites of the wretched world.

Text 85 is recorded on the cassette tape.

ɔn ə nɪxt as ðɪs krɛːtʊr læi ɪn hɪr bɛd wɪð hɪr hʊzbənd ʃiː heːrd ə suːnd ɒv mɛlɔdi sɔ sweːt ænd dɛlɛtabəl hɪr θot æz ʃiː hæd ben ɪn pærædiːs. ænd ðerwiɪθ ʃiː stiːrt ut ɒv hɪr bɛd ænd sæɪd, 'alæs ðæt ɛvər iː dɛd sɪn, ɪt ɪz fʊl mɛri ɪn hɛvən'. ðɪs mɛlɔdi wæs sɔ sweːt ðæt ɪt pasɪd al ðə mɛlɔdi ðæt ɛvər mɪçt bɛ herd ɪn ðɪs wɔrld wɪðutən ɔnɪ kɒmpærɪzon, ænd kɔʊzɪd ðɪs krɛːtʊr hwæn ʃiː herd ɔnɪ mɪrθ ɔr mɛlɔdi æftərward fɔr to hæv fʊl plɛntjus ænd æbʊndənt tiːrɪs ɒv hix dɛvosɪɔn wɪð greːt sɒiŋgz ənd siçɪŋgz æftər ðə blɪs ɒv hɛvən, nɒt drɛdɪŋ ðə ʃæːmɪs ənd ðə spiːtɪs ɒv ðə wrɛtʃɪd wɔrld

Here is the opening of the manuscript in facsimile:

Text 86 – *The Boke of Margery Kempe* (iii) (facsimile)

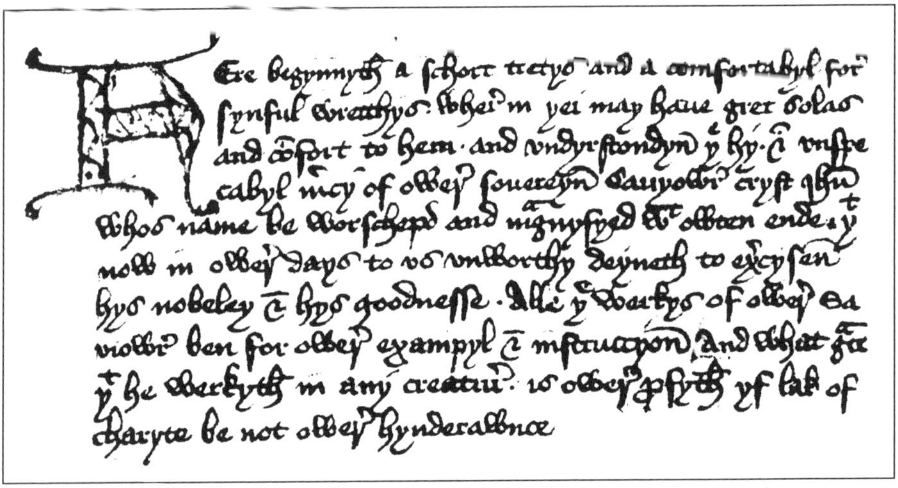

A note on the handwriting

- The forms of ⟨þ⟩ and ⟨*y*⟩ are written identically, both as ⟨*y*⟩.
- The digraph ⟨th⟩ is now normally used for [θ] and [ð]; ⟨*y*⟩ for ⟨þ⟩ is word-initial in a restricted number of function words, which are often abbreviated – *yei* (*they*), y^{e} (*the*), y^{t} (*that*), and in Text 87 *yā* (*than/then*), y^{u} (*thou*), y^{r} *for* (*therefore*), *yi* (*thy*).

H Ere begynnyth a ſchort tretys and a comfortabyl for
ſynful wrecchys. wher ɪn yeɪ may haue gret solas
and cōfort to hem. and vndyrſtondyn ye hy. & vnſpe
cabyl m^{r}cy of ower ſouereyn Sauyowr cryſt Ihū
whos name be worſchepd and m^{a}gnyfyed w^{t}owten ende. y^{t}
now ɪn ower days to vs vnworthy deyneth to ex^{r}cyſen
hys nobeley & hys goodneſſe. Alle ye werkys of ower Sa
vɪowr ben for ower exampyl & ɪnſtruccyon and what g^{a}ce
y^{t} he werkyth ɪn any creatur. ɪs ower pɪfyth yf lak of
charyte be not ower hynderawnce.

Edited version (using letter thorn)

Here begynnyth a schort tretys and a comfortabyl for
synful wrecchys. wher in þei may haue gret solas

and comfort to hem. and vndyrstondyn þe hy & vnspe
cabyl mercy of ower souereyn Sauyowr cryst Ihesu
whos name be worschepd and magnyfyed wythowten ende. þat
now in ower days to vs vnworthy deyneth to exercysen
hys nobeley & hys goodnesse. Alle þe werkys of ower Sa
viowr ben for ower exampyl & instruccyon and what grace
þat he werkyth in any creatur. is ower profyth yf lak of
charyte be not ower hynderawnce.

The next extract is typical of many descriptions of Margery Kempe's religious experiences, her tears of repentance and sense of sin and guilt.

Text 87 – *The Boke of Margery Kempe* (iv) – sin and God's forgiveness (facsimile)

As y^{ſ}s creatur lay ın cōtemplacyon ſor wepȳg
ın hır ſpıryt ſche ſeyde to owyr lord Ihū cryſt .
A lord maydenys dawnſyn now m^{r}yly ın heuyn :
xal not I don ſo. for be cawſe I am no mayden. lak of may
denhed ıs to me now gret sorwe. me thynkyth I wolde
I had ben ſlayn whan I was takyn fro ye funt ſton y^{t}
I xuld neu^{r} a dyſpleſyd ye. & yā xuldyſt y^{u} blyſſed lorde
an had my maydenhed w^{t} owtyn ende. A der God I haue not
lovyd ye alle ye days of my lyue & y^{t} ſor r^{e}wyth me. I haue
ronnyn a wey fro ye & yow haſt ronnyn aft^{r} me. I wold fal
lyn ın dyſpeyr & y^{u} woldyſt not ſuffer me. A dowt^{r} how

oftyn tymes haue I teld ye y^{t} thy ſynnes arn forȝoue
ye & y^{t} we ben onyd ın loue to gedyr w^{t} owtyn ende / y^{u} art to
me a ſynguler lofe dowt^{r}. & y^{r}for I behote ye y^{u} ſchalt
haue a ſynguler g^{a}ce ın hevyn. dowtyr & I be heſt ye y^{t} **I ſhal**
come to yın ende at yī deyng w^{t} my blyſſed modyr &
myn holy awngelys. & twelve apoſtelys. Seynt Katt^{r}yne.
ſeynt Margarete. Seynt Mary Mawdelyn. & many oyer
ſeyntyſ y^{t} ben ın hevyn. whech ȝevyn gret worſhep to me.
for ye g^{a}ce y^{t} I ȝeue to ye. thy God. yı lord Ihū

Edited text

As þis creatur lay in contemplacyon sor wepyng in hir spiryt sche seyde to owyr lord Ihesu cryst. A lord maydenys dawnsyn now meryly in heuyn : xal not I don so. for be cawse I am no mayden, lak of may denhed is to me now gret sorwe. me thynkyth I wolde I had ben slayn whan I was takyn fro þe funt ston þat I xuld neuyr a dysplesyd þe. & þan xuldyst þu blyssed Lorde an had my maydenhed wyth owtyn ende. A der God I haue not lovyd þe alle þe days of my lyue & þat sor rewyth me. I haue ronnyn a wey fro þe, & þow hast ronnyn aftyr me. I wold fallyn in dyspeyr & þu woldyst not suffer me. A dowtor how oftyn tymes haue I teld þe þat thy synnes arn forȝoue þe & þat we ben onyd in loue to gedyr wyth owtyn ende / þu art to me a synguler lofe dowtyr. & þerfor I behote þe þu schalt haue a synguler grace in hevyn, dowtyr & I be hest þe þat I shal come to þin ende at þi deyng wyth my blyssed modyr & myn holy awngelys. & twelve apostelys. Seynt Katteryne. Seynt Margarete. Seynt Mary Mawdelyn. & many oþer seyntys þat ben in Hevyn. whech ȝevyn gret worshep to me. for þe grace þat I ȝeue to þe. thy God. þi lord Ihesu /

📖 The lexical vocabulary of Texts 84–7 is listed in the *Word Book*.

Activity 14.1

Describe the linguistic features of these early 15th-century texts by Margery Kempe which contrast with the grammar of MnE. A check-list follows.

Word structure and grammar

- Forms and inflections of nouns.
- Forms of personal and demonstrative pronouns.
- What determines the choice of the pronouns *my/myn* and *þi/þin*, both used as determiners?
- Definite and indefinite articles.
- Prepositions and phrasal verbs, conjunctions.
- Strong and weak verbs and verb inflections for tense.
- Development of the verb phrase.
- Word order in clause and phrase.

Vocabulary

- Examine and comment on the derivation of the vocabulary in these texts.

Spelling

- Describe the principal features of the spelling which are to be contrasted with present-day spelling.

📖 A commentary on Activity 14.1 is in the *Text Commentary Book*.

14.3 Later 15th-century East Midlands dialect – the Paston letters

The Pastons were a prosperous Norfolk family, and a large collection of their letters written between the 1420s and 1500s has survived. The letters cover three generations of the family, and are a valuable source of evidence for historians as well as students of language. Much of the period was troubled by the political upheavals of the Wars of the Roses, and is reflected in the Pastons' letters.

The first letter, Text 88, is to the first-generation William Paston from his wife Agnes.

Text 88 – Letter from Agnes to William Paston, 1440

Agnes to her husband William Paston, probably written in 1440, 20 April.

Dere housbond I recomaunde me to yow &c blyssyd be god I sende yow gode tydynggys of þe comyng and þe brynggyn hoom of þe gentylwomman þat ye wetyn of fro Redham þis same nyght ~~ac~~ acordyng to poyntmen þat ye made þer for yowre self and as for þe furste aqweyntaunce betwhen John Paston and þe seyde gentilwomman she made hym gentil chere in gyntyl wyse and seyde he was verrayly yowre son and so I hope þer shal nede no gret trete be twyxe hym | þe parson of Stocton toold me yif ye wolde byin here a goune here moder wolde yeue ther to a godely furre þe goune nedyth for to be had and of coloure it wolde be a godely blew or ellys a bryghte sanggueyn | I prey yow do byen* for me ij pypys of gold | yowre stewes† do weel | the Holy Trinite have yow in gouernaunce wretyn at Paston in hast þe Wednesday next after Deus qui errantibus‡ for defaute of a good secretarye &c

Yowres
Agnes Paston

* do byen – the auxiliary *do* is used as a 'causative': 'get someone to buy for me…'

† stewes – fish-ponds.

‡ Deus qui errantibus – a day in the Church calendar, known by the Latin opening of a text used on that day.

MnE edited & punctuated

Dear husband, I recommend me to you &c. Blessed be God I send you good tidings of the coming and the bringing home of the gentlewoman that you know of from Redham this same night, according to (the) appointment that you made there for yourself. And as for the first acquaintance between John Paston and the said gentlewoman, she made him gentle cheer in gentle wise and said he was verily your son. And so I hope there shall need no great treaty between them.

The person from Stockton told me (that) if you would buy her a gown, her mother would give thereto a goodly fur. The gown needs to be had, and of colour it would be a goodly blue or else a bright sanguine.

I pray you, have bought for me two pipes of gold.

Your stews do well.

The Holy Trinity have you in governance. Written at Paston in haste the Wednesday next after Deus qui errantibus for default of a good secretarye &c

Yours
Agnes Paston

The next text is a Valentine letter from Margery Brews to the third generation John Paston, to whom she was engaged to be married.

Text 89 – Letter from Margery Brews to John Paston, February 1477

Edited version, not punctuated

Vn to my ryght welbelouyd voluntyn John Paston squyer be þis bill delyuered &c Ryght reuerent and wurschypfull and my ryght welebeloued voluntyne I recommaunde me vn to yowe full hertely desyring to here of yowr welefare whech I beseche almyghty god long for to preserve vn to hys plesure and ȝowr hertys desyre | and yf it please ȝowe to here of my welefare I am not in good heele of body ner of herte nor schall be tyll I here from yowe

For þer wottys no creature what peyn þat I endure
And for to be deede I dare it not dyscure

And my lady my moder hath labored þe mater to my fadure full delygently but sche can no more gete þen ȝe knowe of for þe whech god knowyth I am full sorry | but yf that ȝe loffe me as I trysto verely that ȝe do ȝe will not lette me þerfor. for if þat ȝe hade not halfe þe lyvelode þat ȝe hafe, for to do þe grettyst labure þat any woman on lyve myght I wold not forsake ȝowe

and yf ȝe commande me to kepe me true where euer I go
iwyse I will do all my myght ȝowe to love and neuer no mo
and yf my freendys say þat I do amys þei schal not me let so for to do
myn herte me byddys euer more to love ȝowe truly ouer all erthely thing
and yf þei be neuer so wroth I tryst it schall be bettur in tyme commyng

no more to yowe at this tyme but the holy trinite hafe yowe in kepyng and I besech ȝowe þat this bill be not seyn of non erthely creature safe only our selfe &c and thys lettur was ȝndyte at Topcroft wyth full heuy herte &c

be ȝour own M B.

The lexical vocabulary of Texts 88 and 89 is listed in the *Word Book*.

They were married later that year. Here is Margery's signature to a letter written two years later:

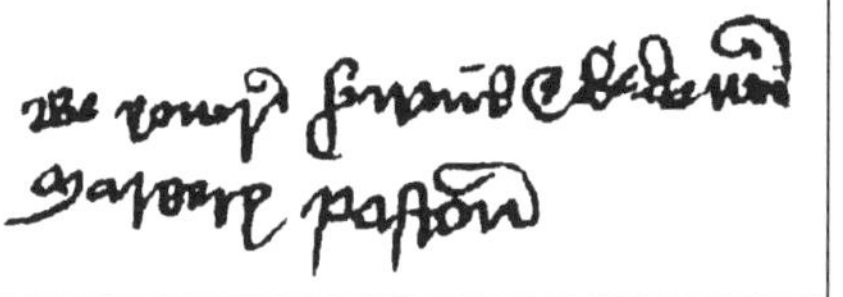

Be your^{e} s^{er}u^{au}nt & bedewom^{an} *
Margery Paston

* *A bedewoman is a woman who prays for another (OE (ge)bed) = prayer.*

The letter is recorded on the cassette tape.

ʊnto mi rixt wɛlbɛlʊvɪd vɔlʊntɪn, dʒɔn pæstən, skwijər, bi ðɪs bɪl dɛlɪvərd rixt rɛvərənt ænd wʊrʃɪpfʊl ənd mi rixt wɛlbɛlʊvɪd vɔlʊntin, iː rɛkɔmoʊnd mi ʊnto ju, fʊl hɛrtəlɪ dɛzirɪŋg to hiːr ɒv jur wɛlfæːr. hwɪtʃ i bɛsiːtʃ almixtɪ gɒd lɒŋg fɔr to prɛzɛrv ʊnto his pleːzjuːr ænd jur hɛrtɪs dɛzir, ænd ɪf ɪt pleːz ju to hiːr ɒv mi wɛlfær i æm nɒt ɪn guːd heːl ɒv bɔdɪ nɛr ɒv hɛrt nɔr ʃæl bi tɪl i hiːr frɒm juː

fɔr ðer wɒtɪs no kreːtjur hwæt pæɪn ðæt i ɛndjur
ænd fɔr to bi deːd i dæːd i dæːr ɪt nɒt dɪskjur

ænd mi læɪdɪ mi mʊdər hæθ læːbərd ðə mætər to mi fædʊr fʊl dɛlɪdʒəntlɪ bʊt ʃi kæn nɔ mɔr gɛt ðɛn ji knɔʊ ɒv, fɔr ðə hwɛtʃ gɒd knɔʊwɪθ i æm fʊl sɔri, bʊt ɪf ðæt ji lʊf mi æz i trɪst vɛrəlɪ ðæt ji doː, ji wɪl nɒt leːv mi ðerfɔr. fɔr ɪf ðæt ji hæd nɒt half ðə livlɔd ðæt ji hæv, fɔr to doː ðə greːtɛst læbʊr ðæt ænɪ wʊmən ɒn liv mixt, i wɒld nɒt fɔrsæːk ju.

ænd ɪf ji kɒmænd mi to kiːp mi tru hwer ɛvər i gɔː
ɪwɪs i wɪl doː al mi mixt ju tu lʊv ænd nɛvər no moː,
ænd ɪf mi freːndz sæɪ ðæt i doː əmɪs ðæɪ ʃæl nɒt mi lɛt so fɔr tɔ doː,
min hɛrt mɪ bɪdɪs ɛvər mɔr to lʊv ju trɪulɪ ovər al ɛrθlɪ θɪŋg,
ænd ɪf ðæɪ bi nɛvər so wroθ, i tirɪst ɪt ʃæl bi bɛtər ɪn tɪim cʊmɪŋg.

no mɔr to ju æt ðɪs tɪim, bʊt ðə holi trɪnɪti hæf ju ɪn kipɪŋg, ænd i bɛsitʃ ju ðæt ðɪs bɪl bi nɒt siːn ɒv noːn erθlɪ kreːtur sæːf onlɪ ur sɛlf, ænd ðɪs lɛtər wæs ɪndit æt tɔpkrɔft wɪð fʊl hɛvɪ hɛrt, bi jur oːn M B

14.4 Late 15th-century London English – William Caxton

William Caxton is known as the first English printer, and the setting-up of his printing press in London in 1476 was the beginning of a revolution in the production of books, which no longer had to be separately copied by hand. Copying did not, of course, die out immediately, and the professional scriveners were able to earn a living for some time. Caxton himself was, however, more than a printer of other people's writing. He himself translated into English and edited many of the books which he printed, and he provided a considerable number of prefaces and commentaries.

14.4.1 *Caxton's revision of* Polychronicon

In 1482 William Caxton printed a revised text of Trevisa's 1385 translation of Higden's *Polychronicon* (see Texts 57 and 58 in chapter 9). This provides an excellent example of some of the changes which had taken place in the language within a hundred years. Caxton evidently found Trevisa's English old-fashioned and out of date, as he said in an Epilogue:

> ...I William Caxton a symple persone have endeuoyred me to wryte fyrst overall the sayd book of Proloconycon and somwhat have chaunged the rude and old Englyssh, that is to wete certayn wordes which in these dayes be neither vsyd ne vnderstanden.

Caxton's 15th-century modernised version of John of Trevisa's description of the languages of Britain is printed below side by side with the 14th-century text. This Trevisa text is taken from a different manuscript and slightly expanded, and shows some interesting differences from Texts 57 and 58. This illustrates the lack of standardisation in Middle English and the way in which differences in the dialects of ME were reflected in writing. Some features of Caxton's punctuation, like his use of the virgule ⟨/⟩, are reproduced, but modern punctuation is added also.

Activity 14.2

(i) Describe the changes which Caxton has made to 'the rude and old Englyssh' of the 14th-century text.

(ii) Comment on the differences between the 14th-century text in this version and in Texts 57 and 58. Do they suggest significant differences in the pronunciation or grammar of the language, or simply of spelling conventions?

Text 90 – *Polychronicon*, John of Trevisa 1385

As it is i-knowe how meny manere peple beeþ in þis ilond þere beeþ also so many dyuers longages and tonges; noþeles walsche men and scottes þat beeþ nouȝt i-medled wiþ oþer naciouns holdeþ wel nyh hir firste longage and speche . . .

Also englische men þey þei hadde from þe bygynnynge þre maner speche norþerne sowþerne and middel speche in þe myddel of þe lond, as þey come of þre manere peple of Germania, noþeles by comyxtioun and mellynge firste wiþ danes and afterward wiþ normans in meny þe contray longage is apayred and som vseþ straunge wlafferynge chiterynge harrynge and garrynge grisbitynge.

This apayrynge of þe burþe tonge is bycause of tweie þinges; oon is for children in scole aȝenst þe vsage and manere of alle oþere naciouns beeþ compelled for to leue hire owne langage and for to construe hir lessouns and here þynges a frensche, and so þey haueþ seþ þe normans come first in to engelond.

Also gentil men children beeþ i-tauȝt to speke frensche from þe tyme þat þey beeþ i-rokked in here cradel and kunneþ speke and playe wiþ a childes broche; and vplondisshe men wil likne hym self to gentil men and fondeþ wiþ greet besynesse for to speke frensce for to be i-tolde of . . .

þis manere was moche i-vsed to for firste deth and is siþþe sumdel i-chaunged. For Iohn Cornwaile, a maister of grammer, chaunged þe lore in gramer scole, and construccioun of frensche into englische; and Richard Pencriche lerned þe manere techynge of hym and oþere men of Pencrich; so þat now, þe ȝere of oure Lorde a þowsand þre hundred and foure score and fyue, in alle þe gramere scoles of engelond children leueþ frensche and construeþ and lerneþ an englische . . .

Text 91 – *Polychronicon*, Caxton's version, 1482

As it is knowen how many maner peple ben in this Ilond ther ben also many langages and tonges. Netheles walshmen and scottes that ben not medled with other nacions kepe neygh yet theyr first langage and speche /

also englysshmen though they had fro the begynnyng thre maner speches Southern northern and myddel speche in the middel of the londe as they come of thre maner of people of Germania. Netheles by commyxtion and medlyng first with danes and afterward with normans In many thynges the countreye langage is appayred / ffor somme vse straunge wlaffyng / chytering harryng garryng and grisbytyng /

this appayryng of the langage cometh of two thynges / One is by cause that children that gon to scole lerne to speke first englysshe / & than ben compellid to constrewe her lessons in Frenssh and that have ben vsed syn the normans come in to Englond /

Also gentilmens childeren ben lerned and taught from theyr yongthe to speke frenssh. And vplondyssh men will counterfete and likene hem self to gentilmen and arn besy to speke frensshe for to be more sette by.

This maner was moche vsed to fore the grete deth. But syth it is somdele chaunged For sir Johan cornuayl a mayster of gramer chaunged the techyng in gramer scole and construction of Frenssh in to englysshe. and other Scoolmaysters vse the same way now in the yere of oure lord / M.iij/C.lx.v. the /ix yere of kyng Rychard the secund and leve all frenssh in scoles and vse al construction in englissh.

Text 90 *(continued)*

Also gentil men haueþ now moche i-left for to teche here children frensche. Hit semeþ a greet wonder houȝ englische, þat is þe burþe tonge of englissh men and her owne langage and tonge, ys so dyuerse of sown in þis oon ilond, and þe langage of normandie is comlynge of anoþer londe and haþ oon manere soun among alle men þat spekeþ hit ariȝt in engelond.

. . . also of þe forsaide saxon tonge þat is i-deled a þre and is abide scarsliche wiþ fewe vplondisshe men is greet wonder; for men of þe est wiþ men of þe west, as it were vndir þe same partie of heueneþ, acordeþ more in sownynge of speche þan men of þe norþ wiþ men of þe souþ.

þerfore it is þat mercii, þat beeþ men of myddel engelond, as it were parteners of þe endes, vnderstondeþ bettre þe side langages, norþerne and souþerne, þan norþerne and souþerne vnderstondeþ eiþer oþer.

Al þe longage of þe norþumbres and specialliche at ȝork is so scharp slitting and frotynge and vnschape þat we souþerne men may þat longage vnneþe vnderstonde. I trowe þat þat is bycause þat þey beeþ nyh to straunge men and aliens þat spekeþ strongliche.

Text 91 *(continued)*

And also gentilmen have moche lefte to teche theyr children to speke frenssh / Hit semeth a grete wonder that Englyssmen have so grete dyversyte in theyr owne langage in sowne and in spekyng of it / whiche is all in one ylond. And the langage of Normandye is comen oute of another lond / and hath one maner soune among al men that speketh it in englond . . .

Also of the forsayd tong whiche is departed in thre is grete wonder / For men of the este with the men of the west acorde better in sownyng of theyr speche than men of the north with men of the south /

Therfor it is that men of mercij that ben of myddel englond as it were partyners with the endes vnderstande better the side langages northern & sothern than northern & southern vnderstande eyther other.

Alle the langages of the northumbres & specially at york is so sharp slytyng frotyng and vnshape that we sothern men may vnneth vnderstande that langage I suppose the cause be that they be nygh to the alyens that speke straungely.

14.4.1.1 *Vocabulary change*

- About 14% of the words appear in one of the texts only (partly because of the omissions and additions that Caxton made to the Trevisa text).
- Forty-six pairs of words are identical in spelling, about 25%.
- More than half of the vocabulary has minor variants that indicate changes in spelling convention only, about 53%. For example:

  - ⟨*th*⟩/⟨þ⟩
  - ⟨*y*⟩/⟨*i*⟩
  - redundant ⟨*e*⟩
  - doubled letters
  - unstressed vowel variants
  - metathesis of ⟨*re*⟩/⟨*er*⟩
  - ⟨*ou*⟩/⟨*o*⟩
  - ⟨*-cion*⟩/⟨*-tion*⟩
  - ⟨*ssh*⟩/⟨*sch*⟩/⟨*sc*⟩
  - ⟨ȝ⟩/⟨*gh*⟩/⟨*y*⟩

- The only examples of the substitution of one word for another are:

  comlynge / comen
  holdeþ / kepe
  seþ – syn *(=since)*
  trowe / suppose

- There are two developments in the grammar, however – the loss of the 3rd person plural present tense inflection ⟨*-eþ*⟩, and of the past participle prefix ⟨*i-*⟩ (from the OE prefix ⟨*ge-*⟩):

Trevisa	*Caxton*	*Trevisa*	*Caxton*
beeþ	ben	i-deled	departed
haueþ	have	i-knowe	knowen
lerneþ	lerne	i-left	lefte
leue, leueþ	leve	i-medled	medled
vnderstonde (þ)	vnderstande	i-vsed	vsed
vseþ	use		

The lexical vocabulary of Texts 90 and 91 is in the *Word Book*.

14.4.2 *Caxton on 'dyuersite & chaunge of langage'*

A standard form of a language develops in a nation or society only at a particular time of its evolution, when the need becomes evident and pressing. We define the Middle English period partly by the fact that there was no one dialect which was accepted or used throughout the country as a standard in writing. The invention of printing was one factor, in the complex interaction of political and economic changes in England by the end of the 15th century, which led in time to the establishment of a written standard form of English.

One of Caxton's problems as printer and translator is clearly shown in a famous story which he tells in the Preface to his translation of a French version of Virgil's Latin poem *The Aeneid*, called *Eneydos*. A revolution in communications was brought about by the printing of books. A book might be bought and read anywhere in the country – which dialect of English should a printer use? For example, there were two words for *egg*, one derived from OE, the other from ON.

> From OE æȝ, aig, ey(e), ay(e), ȝey; *plural* æȝru, **eyren**(e), eyron, eyroun.
> From ON eg, egg, egge, ege, hegge – **egg**, **egges**.

The story in Text 92 is about the difficulty of asking for eggs for breakfast, but for Caxton it illustrates the problem of choice of language in translation,

> Loo what sholde a man in thyse dayes now wryte, egges or eyren?

This is just one of the problems which had to be overcome in the establishment of an agreed standard literary form of English over the next two hundred years.

If you were to examine Caxton's language in detail, you would find that he did not devise a consistent and regular spelling system, and that many of his decisions about spelling and grammatical form were already old-fashioned for the language of the 1480s.

Activity 14.3

(i) Examine Caxton's texts for evidence of his inconsistency of choice in spelling and word form.

(ii) Describe those features of Caxton's English by which we would describe it as 'archaic' in comparison with MnE.

A commentary on Caxton's spelling is in the *Text Commentary Book*.

Text 92 – Caxton on the diversity of English, 1490

Caxton has decided to translate Eneydos.

> And whan I sawe the fayr & straunge termes therin / I doubted that it sholde not please some gentylmen whiche late blamed me, sayeng that in my translacyons I had ouer curyous termes whiche coude not be vnderstande of comyn peple / and desired me to vse olde and homely termes in my translacyons. and fayn wolde I satisfye euery man / and so to doo, toke an olde boke and redde therin / and certaynly the englysshe was so rude and brood that I coude not wele vnderstande it. And also my lorde abbot of westmynster ded do shewe to me late, certayn euydences wryton on olde englysshe, for to reduce it in-to our englysshe now vsid / And certaynly it was wreton in suche wyse that it was more lyke to dutche than englysshe; I coude not reduce ne brynge it to be vnderstonden / And certaynly our langage now vsed varyeth ferre from that whiche was vsed and spoken whan I was borne / For we englysshe men / ben borne vnder the domynacyon of the mone, whiche is neuer stedfaste / but euer wauerynge / wexynge one season / and waneth & dyscreaseth another season / And that comyn englysshe that is spoken in one shyre varyeth from a nother. In so moche that in my dayes happened that certayn marchauntes were in a shippe in tamyse (*the river Thames*), for to haue sayled ouer the see into zelande (*Holland*) / and for lacke of wynde, thei taryed atte forlond (*Foreland*), and wente to lande for to refreshe them; And one of theym named sheffelde (*Sheffield*), a mercer, cam in-to an hows and exed for mete (*food*); and specyally he axyd after eggys; And the goode wyf answerde, that she coude speke no frenshe. And the marchaunt was angry, for he also coude speke no frenshe, but wolde haue hadde egges / and she vnderstode hym not / And thenne at laste a nother sayd that he wolde haue eyren / then the good wyf sayd that she vnderstod hym wel / Loo, what sholde a man in thyse dayes now wryte, egges or eyren / certaynly it is harde to playse euery man / by cause of dyuersite & chaunge of langage . . . but in my Iudgemente / the comyn termes that be dayli vsed, ben lyghter (*easier*) to be vnderstonde than the olde and auncyent englysshe /

📖 The lexical vocabulary of Text 92 is listed in the *Word Book*.

Here are two examples of Caxton's printing. The first is an advertisement, dating from about 1478, of Caxton's edition of the *Sarum Ordinal* (an ordinal is a book of church services; Sarum is the older name for Salisbury).

Text 93 – Caxton's advertisement, 1482 (facsimile)

If it plese ony man spirituel or temporel to bye ony
pyes of two and thre comemoraciōs of salisburi vse
enpryntid after the forme of this presēt lettre whiche
ben wel and truly correct, late hym come to westmo=
nester in to the almonesrye at the reed pale and he shal
haue them good chepe . . .

Supplico stet cedula

If it pleſe onẏ man ſpirituel or temporel to bẏe onẏ
pẏes of two and thre comemoraciōs of ſaliſburi uſe
enprẏntid after the forme of this preſēt lettre whiche
ben wel and trulẏ correct, late hẏm come to weſtmo
neſter in to the almoneſrẏ at the reed pale and he ſhal
haue them good chepe

Supplico ſtet cedula

📖 The lexical vocabulary of Text 93 is listed in the *Word Book*.

The second is one page from Caxton's own translation of a Dutch version of one of Aesop's fables, *Die Hystorie van Reynaert du Vos*, printed in Gouda in 1479. He completed the translation and printed it in 1481. This facsimile is from the second edition in 1489.

Text 94 – Caxton's *The Historye of Reynart the Foxe*, 1489 version (facsimile)

¶ How the lyon kynge of alle beſtys ſent out hys mau̅de
mentys that alle beeſtys ſholde come to hys feeſt and court/
¶ Capitulo Primo

IT was aboute yͤ tyme of penthecoſte or whytſontyde
that the wodes comynly be luſty and gladſom/And
trees clad with leuis & bloſſoms and yͤ grounde wyth
herbes & floures ſwete ſmellyng & alſo the fowles and byr:
des ſyngen melodyouſly in theyr armonye Thenne the lyon
the noble kynge of al beſtis wold in the holy dayes of this
feeſt holde an open court at ſtaden/whyche he dyde to knowe
ouer alle in his lande/¶ And commanded by ſtrayte com
myſſyons and mau̅dements that euery beeſt ſhold come thi
der in ſuche wyſe that alle the beeſtys grete and ſmale cam
to the courte ſauf Reynard the fox/For he knewe hym ſelf
fawty and gylty in many thynges ageynſt many beeſtys
that thyder ſhold comen that he durſte not auenture to goo
thyder/whan the kynge of alle beeſtys had aſſemblyd alle
hys court / Ther was none of them alle/ But that he had
compleyned ſore on Reynard the fox.
¶ The fyrſt complaynt made iſegrym the wulf on reynard
Capitulo ijº

ISegrym the wulf wyth hys lynage and frendes cam
and ſtode to fore the kynge. And ſayde hye & myghty
prynce my lord the kynge I beſeche yow that thurgh your
grete myght.ryght and mercy that ye wyl haue pyte on the
grete treſpas and the vnreſonable myſdedes that Reynart
the fox hath don to me and my wyf that is to wyte he is
comen in to myn hous ayenſt the wille of my wyf ¶ And
there he hath bepyſſed my chyldren where as they laye in
ſuche wyſe as they therof ben woxen blinde/wherupon was
a i

¶How the lyon kynge of alle beſtys ſent out hys maūde
mentys that alle beeſtys ſholde come to hys feeſt and court/
Capitulo Primo

IT was aboute þ[e] tyme of penthecoſte or whytſontyde
that the wodes comynly be luſty and gladſom/And
trees clad with leuis & bloſſoms and þ[e] ground wyth
herbeſ & floures ſwete ſmellyng & alſo the fowles and byr:
des ſyngen melodyouſly in theyr armonye Thenne the lyon
the noble kynge of al beſtis wold in the holy dayes of this
feeſt holde an open court at ſtaden/whyche he dyde to knowe
ouer alle in his lande/¶And commanded by ſtrayte com
myſſyons and maūdements that euery beeſt ſhold come thi
der in ſuch wyſe that alle the beeſtys grete and ſmale cam
to the courte ſauf Reynard the fox/For he knewe hym ſelf
fawty and gylty in many thynges ageynſt many beeſtys
that thyder ſhold comen that he durſte not auenture to goo
thyder/whan the kynge of alle beeſtys had aſſemblyd alle
hys court/Ther was none of them alle/But that he had
compleyned ſore on Reynard the fox.

¶The fyrſt complaynt made iſegrym the wulf on reynard
Capitulo ij°

ISegrym the wulf wyth hys lynage and frendes cam
and ſtode to fore the kynge. And ſayde hye & myghty
prynce my lord the kynge I beſeche yow that thurgh your
grete myght.ryght and mercy that ye wyl haue pyte on the
grete treſpas and the vnreſonable myſdedes that Reynart
the fox hath don to me and my wyf that is to wyte he is
comen in to myn hous ayenſt the wille of my wyf¶And
there he hath bepyſſed my chyldren where as they laye in
ſuche wyſe as they therof ben woxen blinde/wherupon was...

The lexical vocabulary of Text 94 is listed in the *Word Book*.

14.5 The medieval tales of King Arthur

In 1485 Caxton published a 'noble and joyous book entytled *Le Morte Darthur*'. He describes it in these words:

> ...a book of the noble hystoryes of the sayd Kynge Arthur and of certeyn of his knyghtes after a copye unto me delyvered. Whyche copye Syr Thomas Malorye dyd take oute of certeyn bookes of frensshe and reduced it into Englysshe.

We know that Sir Thomas Malory made his translations and adaptations from the French while he was in prison. He wrote at the end of one of the books which make up the collection,

> And I pray you all that redyth this tale to pray for hym that this wrote, that God sende hym good delyveraunce sone and hastely. Amen

but he died in prison in 1471.

Caxton's printed book was the only known source of Malory's version of the legends of King Arthur until 1934, when a manuscript was found in the Fellows' Library of Winchester College. It is not Malory's own hand, but more authentic than Caxton's book, which has many alterations, emendations and omissions.

Here is the opening of the fourth story, *The War with the Five Kings*, in the first of the books of the Winchester MS, *The Tale of King Arthur*.

Text 95 – Sir Thomas Malory's *Le Morte Darthur*, c. 1460–1470 (i) (facsimile)

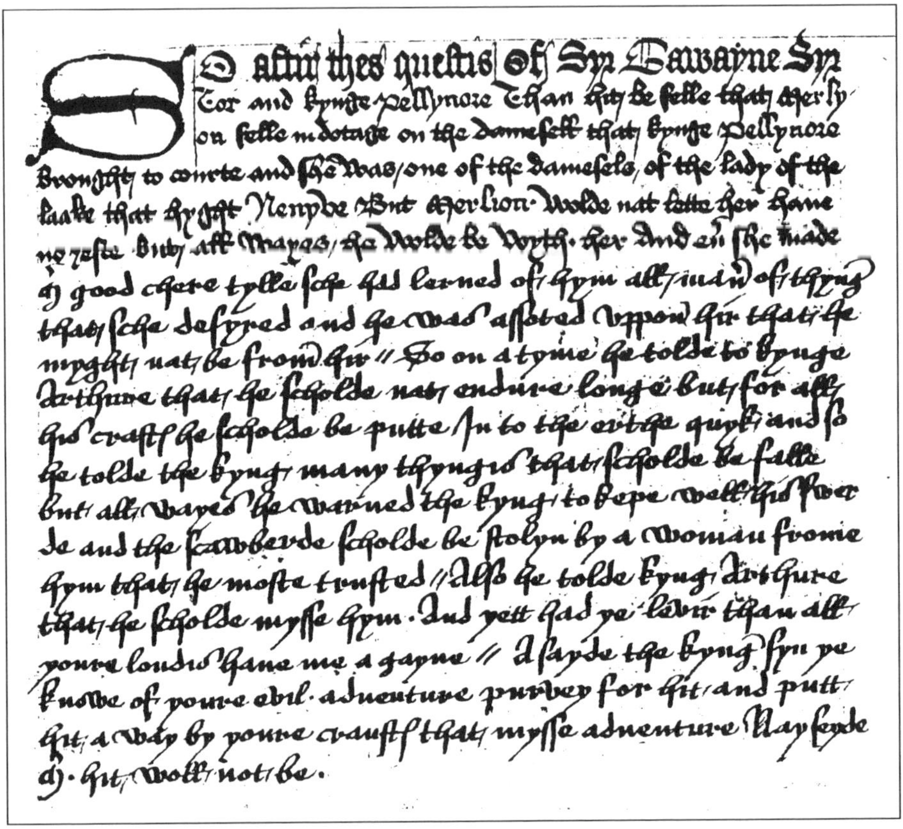

SO aftır thes queſtıs of Syr Gawayne Syr
Tor and kynge Pellynore Than hıt befelle that **Merly** /
on felle ın dotage on the dameſell that kynge **Pellynore**
brought to courte and ſhe was / one of the dameſels / of the Lady of the
laake that hyght Nenyve But **Merl**ıon wolde nat lette her have
no reſte but / all wayes / he wolde by wyth. her And ever ſhe made
M[erlıon] good chere tylle ſche had lerned of hym all maner of thyng
that ſche deſyred and he was aſſoted uppon hır that he
myght nat be from hır // So on a tyme he tolde to kynge
Arthure that he ſcholde nat endure longe but for all
hıs craftſ he ſcholde be putte ınto the erthe quyk / and ſo
he tolde the kyng many thyngıs that ſcholde be falle
but allwayes he warned the kyng to kepe well hıs ſwer //
de and the ſcawberde* ſcholde be ſtolyn by a woman frome
hym that he moſte truſted // Alſo he tolde kyng **Arthure**
that he ſcholde myſſe hym . And yett had ye levır than all
youre londıs have me agayne // A ſayde the kyng ſyn ye

knowe of youre evıl adventure purvey for hıt and putt
hıt a way by youre crauftſ that myſſeadventure / Nay ſeyde
M[erlıon] hıt woll not be .

* The scribe omitted: *for he told hym how the swerde and the scawberde.*

📖 The lexical vocabulary of Text 95 is listed in the *Word Book*.

Activity 14.4

The first six lines of Text 95 were written by the principal scribe, and the rest by a second scribe. The handwriting is clearly different. Does the second scribe's spelling differ from that of the first?

📖 A short commentary is in the *Text Commentary Book*.

The second extract from *Le Morte Darthur* comes from the final book in the Winchester MS, *The most piteous tale of the Morte Arthur saunz guerdon.* King Arthur has sustained a 'grevous wounde' in battle, and Sir Bedwere (Bedivere) has twice disobeyed the king's command to throw the jewelled sword Excalibur into the waters of the lake from which it first came.

Text 96 – Sir Thomas Malory's *Le Morte Darthur* (ii) (facsimile)

There are some small holes in the manuscript causing the loss of a few letters.

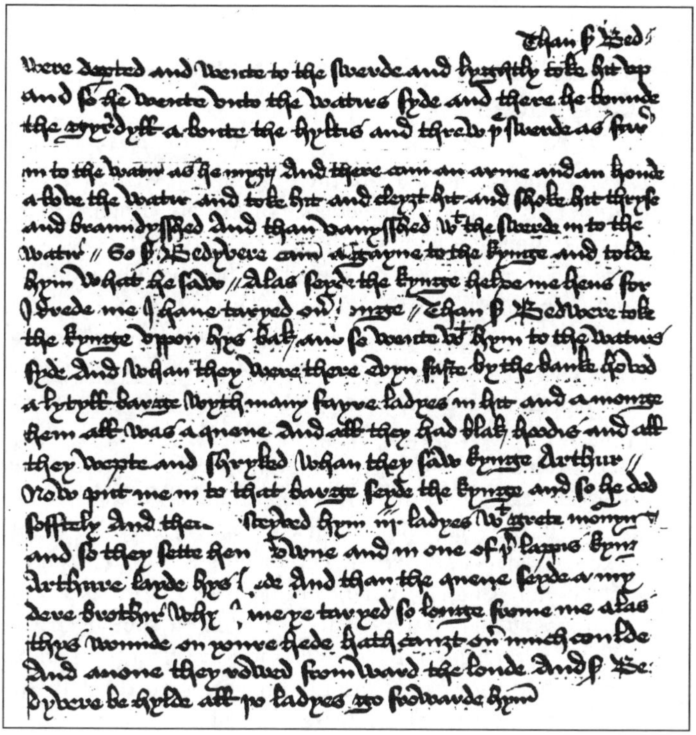

Than ſir Bed /
were dep(ar)ted and wente to the ſwerde and lyghtly toke hit vp
and ſo he wente vnto the watirs ſyde and there he bounde
the gyrdyll aboute the hyltes and threw þ[e] ſwerde as far
in to the watir as he myȝt / And there cam an arme and an honde
a bove the watir and toke hit and cleyȝt* hit and ſhoke hit thryſe
and braundyſſhed and than vanyſſhed w[t] the ſwerde into the
watir // So ſir Bedyvere cam agayne to the kynge and tolde
hym what he ſaw // Alas ſeyde the kynge helpe me hens for
I drede me I haue taryed ow[r] longe // Than ſir Bedwere toke
the kynge vppon hys bak and ſo wente w[t] hym to the wattirs
ſyde and whan they were there evyn faſte by the banke hoved
a lytyll barge wyth many fayre ladyes in hit and amonge
hem all was a quene and all they had blak hoodis and all
they wepte and ſhryked whan they ſaw kynge Arthur //
Now put me in to that barge ſeyde the kynge and ſo he ded
ſofftely and there [re]ſceyved hym iij. ladyes w[t] grete mo[r]nyng
and ſo they ſette hem [d]owne and in one of þ[r] lappis kyng
Arhure layde hys hede and than the quene ſeyde a my
dere brothir why [ha]ue ye taryed ſo longe frome me alas
thye wounde on youre hede hath cauȝt ou[er] much coulde
and anone they rowed from ward the londe and ſ[r] Be
dyvere be hylde all þo ladyeſ go frowarde hym . . .

* clyeȝt = clutched.

📖 The lexical vocabulary of Text 96 is listed in the *Word Book*.

14.6 Late 15th-century London dialect – the Cely letters

A collection of letters and memoranda of the Cely family, written in the 1470s and 1480s, gives us authentic handwritten evidence of London English a century after Thomas Usk's, and contemporary with the later Paston letters.

The Celys were wool merchants, or staplers. They bought woollen fleeces in England and sold them on the Continent in Calais and Bruges. The letters and accounts provide direct evidence for historians of the workings of a medieval English firm. They also give language students plenty of examples of late medieval commercial English, and are evidence of the speech and writing habits of middle-class Londoners of the period.

The collection contains letters by forty different people, but most are from two generations of the Cely family, father and sons. Like the Paston letters they show that there was as yet no fully standardised written English among private individuals (unlike scriveners and clerks). The spelling is not good evidence for the pronunciation of spoken English, partly because we do not know for certain the sounds given to particular letters, but also because spelling between different writers is somewhat irregular.There is comparatively little inconsistency of spelling by an individual, however. Variants are often to do with the addition of ⟨*e*⟩ or the choice of vowel letter in unstressed syllables:

afftyr/after	dewke/dwke	last/laste	trobellett/trobellytt
caleys/calles/callȝ *(Calais)*	frenche/frensche/frynche	lord/lorde	wryte/wrytt
com/come	gret/grete/grett	mche/meche	you/yow
dessesset/dessett *(deceased)*	hathe/hatth	non/none	

but the choice of some spellings does not seem to be based on any written standard, for example,

boshop	*bishop*	ordenons	*ordnance*	whas	*was*
dyssprowett	*disproved*	saffte	*safety*	whelcom	*welcome*
grasse	*grace*	trobellett	*troubled*	whisse	*wise*
hodyr	*other*	tytyng	*tiding*		

The following three texts consist of facsimiles and transcriptions, followed by versions in MnE spelling and punctuation.

Activity 14.5

List the principal lexical and grammatical features of the Celys' London English which mark its difference from MnE.

📖 A short commentary is in the *Text Commentary Book*.

Text 97 – George Cely in Calais to Richard Cely in London, 12 March 1478 (facsimile)

Transcription

Ryght rewerent and whorſhypffull ffadyr afftyr all dew recomen-
daſyon prtendyng I recomeavnd me vn to yow in the ~~mo~~ moſt lowly
eſt whiſſe that I con or may ffor dyr mor pleſythe ytt yow to
vndyr ſtond that I come vn to calles the thorſſeday afftyr my dep
tyng ffrom yow in ſaffte y thanke god and y whas whelcom vn
to my ffrendis ffor tyll my brodyr com to calles ther whas none
hodyr tydyng ther but I whas dede // etc // pleſythe ytt yow to vnd^{r}
ſtond ther ys now none m^{r}chants at callʒ nor whas but ffew thys
monythe / and as ffor any hodyr tydyngſ I con none wrytt vn to
yow as ʒett tyll y her mor and be the next wryttyng þt I
ſent ʒe ſhall vndyr the ſalle of yowr ffellis wt mor be the
graſſe of god ~~whah~~ who hawe yow and all yowrs in hys kepy^{n}g
amen wrytt at calles the xij th day of mche a lxxviij

p yowr ſon
G cely

MnE spelling and punctuation

Right reverent and worshipful father, after all due recommen-
dation pretending*, I recommend me unto you in the most lowliest wise that I can or may. Furthermore, pleaseth it you to
understand that I came unto Calais the Thursday after my dep(ar)-
ting from you, in safety I thank God, and I was welcome unto my
friends, for till my brother came to Calais there was none other
tidings there but† I was dead etc. Pleaseth it you to understand there is now none merchants at Calais nor was but few this
month, and as for any other tidings, I can none write unto
you as yet till I hear more, and by the next writing that I
send ye shall under(stand) the sale of your fells‡ with more, by the
grace of God, who have you and all yowrs in his keeping,
amen. Writ at Calais the 12th day of March, a(nno) 78.

per§ your son,
G Cely

* pretending = extended, having been given.
† but = except.
‡ fells = wool fleeces
§ per = by

The lexical vocabulary of Text 97 is listed in the *Word Book*.

Text 98 – Richard Cely (the father) in London to Agnes, Richard and George Cely in Essex, 12 August 1479 (facsimile)

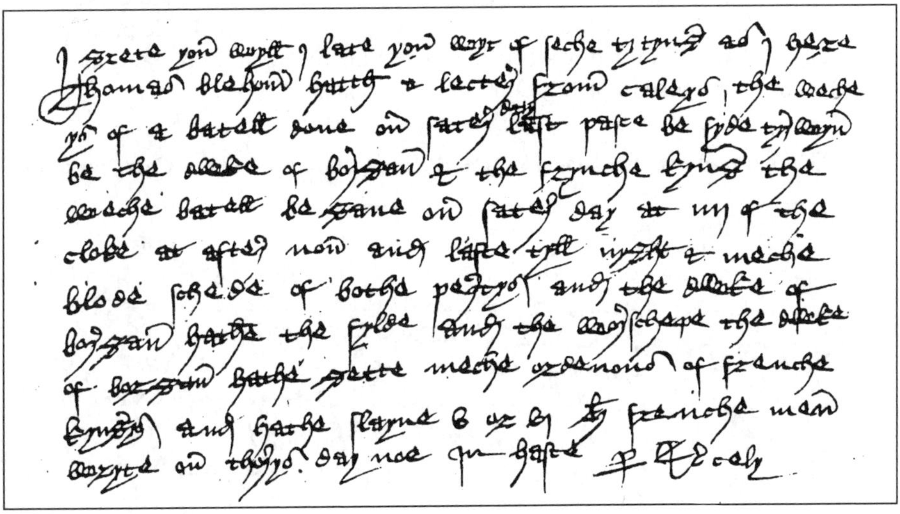

Transcription

I grete you wyll I late you wyt of ſeche tytyng as I here
Thomas blehom hatth a letter from caleys the weche
ys of a batell done on ſater^{day} laſt paſte be ſyde tyrwyn
be the dwke of borgan & the frynche kyng the
weche batell be gane on ſater day at iiij of the
cloke at after non and laſte tyll nyght & meche
blode ſchede of bothe pertys and the dwke of
borgan hathe the fylde and the worſchepe the dwke
of borgan hathe gette meche ordenons of frenche
kyngys and hathe ſlayne v or vj ml frensche men
wryte on thorys day noe in haſte

p Rc cely

Modern English spelling and punctuation

I greet you well. I let you wit of such tiding as I hear.
Thomas Blehom hath a letter from Calais, the which
is of a battle done on Saturday last past beside Tirwin
by the Duke of Burgundy and the French king, the
which battle began on Saturday at 4 of the
clock at afternoon, and lasted till night, and much
blood shed of both parties, and the Duke of
Burgundy hath the field, and the worship. The Duke
of Burgundy hath got much ordnance of (the) French
king's and hath slain 5 or 6 thousand Frenchmen.
Writ on Thursday now in haste.

per Richard Cely

📖 The lexical vocabulary of Text 98 is listed in the *Word Book*.

The following text is not a letter, but a jotted down note of political events and rumours in the troubled times preceding the deposing of Edward V and the accession of the Duke of Gloucester as Richard III. The first five items are written as facts, the rest, beginning with 'If', are rumours. The jottings were written on the back of an old memorandum, and are not always grammatically clear.

Lord Hastings, the Lord Chamberlain, had been executed in June 1483. The Chancellor was Thomas Rotherham, Archbishop of York. 'my lorde prynsse' was the Duke of York, Edward V's brother. The Earl of Northumberland and John Howard were supporters of the Duke of Gloucester.

Text 99 – Note of events (June 1483) and memoranda by George Cely (facsimile)

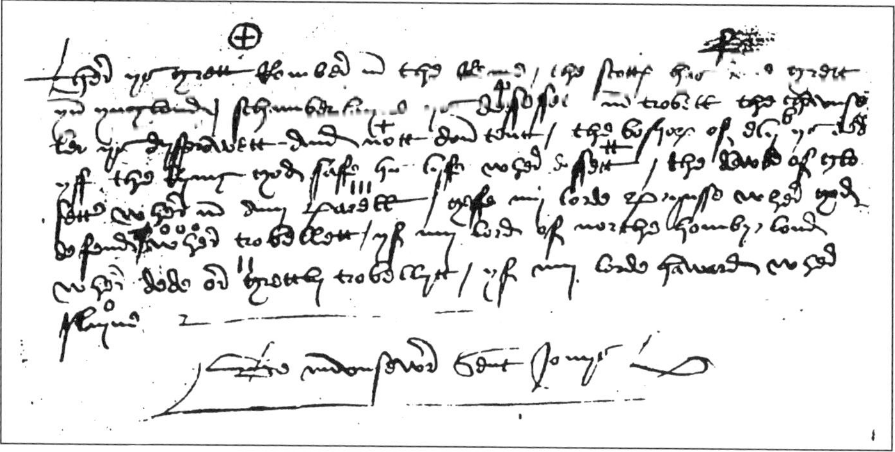

Ther ys grett romber ın the reme / the ſcottys has done gret
yn ynglond / ſchamberlayne ys deſſeſſet ın trobell the chavnſe
ler ys dyſſprowett and nott content / the boſhop of ely ys dede
yff the kyng god ſſaffe hıs lyffe wher deſſett / the dewke of glo
ſett wher ın any parell / geffe my lorde prynſſe wher god
defend wher trobellett / yf my lord of northehombyrlond
wher dede or grettly trobellytt / yf my lorde haward wher
ſlayne

De movnſewer sent jonys

'movnsewr sent jonys' (Monsieur St John) is a pseudonym, to disguise the name, for Sir John Weston, from whom George Cely presumably got the rumours.

Modern English spelling and punctuation

There is great romber* in the realm. The Scots has done great
in England. (The Lord) Chamberlain is deceased in trouble. The Chance
llor is disproved† and not content. The Bishop of Ely is dead.
If the King, God save his life, were deceased. (If) the Duke of Glou
cester were in any peril. If my Lord Prince were, God
defend, were troubled‡. If my Lord of Northumberland
were dead or greatly troubled. If my Lord Howard were
slain.

From monsieur Saint John

* romber = rumour, disturbance, upheaval.

† disproved = proved false.

‡ troubled = molested.

📖 The lexical vocabulary of Text 99 is listed in the *Word Book*.

The modernised versions of the letters help to clarify what are mainly difficulties of word recognition because of the spelling. A few phrases are listed below:

Text 97: George Cely

pretending	= extended = having been given
fells	= fells = wool fleeces
per (Latin)	= by

Text 98: Richard Cely

wit	= know

Text 99: George Cely

romber	= disturbance (obsolete meaning of 'rumour')
disproved	= proved false
troubled	= molested

14.7 15th-century loan-words

14.7.1 *French*

bail	*bail*	**1400**	compilation	*compilation*	**1426**
jury	*juree*	**1400**	guard (n)	*garde*	**1426**
lemon	*limon*	**1400**	umbrage	*umbrage*	**1426**
loyalty	*loialté*	**1400**	vellum	*velin*	**1430**
nitre	*nitre*	**1400**	public	*public*	**1436**
nutritive	*nutritif*	**1400**	terrier (dog)	*terrier*	**1440**
plaintiff	*plaintif*	**1400**	abhor	*abhorrer*	**1449**
sausage	*saussiche*	**1400**	enable	*en + hable*	**1460**
stew (vb)	*estuver*	**1400**	larceny	*larcin + -y*	**1460**
tart	*tarte*	**1400**	peasant	*paisant*	**1475**
retrieve	*retrouver*	**1410**	curb (n)	*courbe*	**1477**
assembly	*asemblee*	**1413**	manoeuvre	*manuvrer*	**1479**
punishment	*punisement*	**1413**	column	*columpne*	**1481**
condiment	*condiment*	**1420**	repeal	*repel*	**1483**
revenue	*revenu*	**1422**	virile	*viril*	**1490**
sable	*sable*	**1423**	resonance	*resonance*	**1491**

14.7.2 *Scandinavian*

reindeer	*hreindyri*	**1400**	steak	*steik*	**1420**
scant	*skamt*	**1400**	silt	cf. Danish *silt*	**1440**
score (cut)	*skora*	**1400**	link	*hlenkr*	**1450**

14.7.3 *Low German*

groove	*groeve*	**1400**	spool	*spoele*	**1440**
bulwark	*bolwerk*	**1418**	buoy	*boeie*	**1466**
pip	*pippe*	**1420**	deck	*dec*	**1466**
hop (plant)	*hoppe*	**1440**	luck	*luk*	**1481**
loiter	*loteren*	**1440**	excise	*excijs*	**1494**
pickle	*pekel*	**1440**			

14.7.4 Latin

juniper	*juniperus*	**1400**	subdivide	*subdividere*	**1432**
recipe	*recipe*	**1400**	subjugate	*subjugare*	**1432**
substitute (n)	*substitutus*	**1400**	summary	*summarius*	**1432**
tincture	*tinctura*	**1400**	testimony	*testimonium*	**1432**
ulcer	*ulcer*	**1400**	malefactor	*malefactor*	**1440**
gesture	*gestura*	**1410**	obdurate	*obduratus*	**1440**
superabundance	*superabundantia*	**1410**	lapse	*lapsus*	**1450**
incredible	*incredibilis*	**1412**	polite	*politus*	**1450**
interrupt	*interrumpere*	**1412**	prosody	*prosodia*	**1450**
lucrative	*lucrativus*	**1412**	querulous	*querulosus*	**1450**
moderate (adj)	*moderatus*	**1412**	scrutiny	*scrutinium*	**1450**
client	*clientem*	**1413**	solar	*solaris*	**1450**
distract	*distractem*	**1413**	seclude	*secludere*	**1451**
infinite	*infinitus*	**1413**	subordinate (adj)	*subordinatus*	**1456**
supplicate	*supplicare*	**1417**	frustrate	*frustra*	**1471**
immune	*immunis*	**1420**	gratis	*gratis*	**1477**
include	*includere*	**1420**	project (vb)	*projicere*	**1477**
innate	*innatus*	**1420**	tract	*tractus*	**1486**
picture	*pictura*	**1420**	extract (vb)	*extrahere*	**1489**
individual	*individualis*	**1425**	exhibit	*exhibere*	**1490**
subscribe	*subscribere*	**1425**	popular	*popularis*	**1490**
adjacent	*adjacere*	**1430**	conviction	*convictionem*	**1491**
inferior	*inferior*	**1432**	custody	*custodia*	**1491**
mechanical	*mechanicus*	**1432**	infancy	*infantia*	**1494**
ornate	*ornatus*	**1432**	legitimate	*legitimatus*	**1494**
prevent	*praevenire*	**1432**	reject	*rejicere*	**1494**
prosecute	*prosequi*	**1432**			

14.7.5 Spanish

cork	corcha	**1440**

14.7.6 Arabic

lemon	Fr *limion* fr Arabic *laimun*	**1400**	candy	Fr (*sucre*) *candi* fr Arabic *qandah*	**1420**
mosque	Fr *mosquı fr Arabic masgid*	**1400**	caraway	Fr *carvi* fr Arabic *al-karawiya*	**1440**

14.7.7 Celtic

clan	Gaelic *clann* – family, stock, race	**1425**	*bard*	Gaelic and Irish *bard*	**1450**
gull	Welsh *gwylan*, Cornish *guilan = Breton goelann*	**1430**	*glen*	Gaelic *gleann* – mountain-valley	**1489**

15. Early Modern English II – the 16th century (i)

In chapter 14 we saw how the private letters of the Pastons and the Celys in the 15th century give us some idea of everyday speech at the time. Another large collection, the *Lisle Letters*, from the early 16th century, provides us with examples of the language 50 years on.

The fact that writers at that time were not using a nationally standardised form of spelling does not mean that their spelling was haphazard, or that they simply 'wrote as they spoke'. There were some inconsistencies within an individual's spelling, especially in the use of a redundant final ⟨e⟩ on many words, but they had clearly learned a system. Variations occurred because there were no dictionaries or spelling books to refer to until later in the 16th century.

15.1 *The Lisle Letters*

These letters were written to and by Lord Lisle, his family, friends and staff, when he was Governor of Calais for King Henry VIII, from 1533 to 1540. The French town was at that time an English possession. The letters provide examples of a wide range of correspondence, both formal and informal, and are therefore first-hand evidence of the state of the language then.

15.1.1 *George Bassett to his parents*

Here is an example of a letter by a 14-year-old boy. George Bassett was Lady Lisle's son by her first marriage, and as part of his education he was 'put to service' in the household of Sir Francis Bryan. The letter is 'purely formal: the boy has nothing to say and he says it in the approved Tudor manner' (Muriel St Clare Byrne, editor of *The Lisle Letters*).

Text 100 – George Bassett to Lord and Lady Lisle, written 1 July 1539 (facsimile)

Ryht honorable and my moſt dere and ſıngler goode lorde
and ladye / ın my moſt humble man^{ner} I recõmaunde me unto yow
beſechynge to have yor daılye bleſſynge / and to here of yor goode
and proſpıus helth / fore the conſervatıone of whıche / I praye
daılye unto almyghty godde. I certıfye youe by theys my
rude l^{ett}res that my Maıſter and my Ladye be ın goode helthe /
to whome I am myche bounde. ffurthe^{r}more I beſeche
yor lordeſhıpe and ladıſhıpe to have me hertılye recõmẽdyde
unto my Brothe^{r} and Syſters. And thus I praye godde to conſerve
yor lordeſhıpe and ladıſhıpe eve^{r} ın goode / longe / and
proſperus helthe w^{t} hono^{r}. ffrom Woburn the
fırſte daye of Julye

By yor humble and
owne Son George
Baſſette

George Bassett's formal 'duty letter' to his parents does not tell us much about him, except that he can write very competently in beautiful handwriting. He uses the **strike** or **virgule** (/) as a mark of punctuation, and the occasional full-stop, then called a **prick**. There are some of the conventional abbreviations, similar to

those you will have noticed in the Cely and Paston letters and in all the MS facsimiles in the book, such as the **tilde** (~) over the vowel preceding one of the nasal consonants ⟨n⟩ or ⟨m⟩, especially if the consonant was double, and writing post-vocalic ⟨r⟩ and other combinations of letters as a superscript.

The lexical vocabulary of Text 100 is listed in the *Word Book*.

15.1.2 *Sir William Kingston to Lord Lisle*

The next letter is from Sir William Kingston, who was a member of the King's Privy Council and Constable of the Tower at the time. Sir William recommends a servant and, as there is no news to pass on, gossips about the King's activities and asks Lord Lisle to look out for some hawks for him. Notice the ironical reference to the usefulness of praying to St Loy (the saint whom Chaucer's Prioress swears by) – Lady Kingston's horse has been lame ever since she prayed for it. The letter is an example of an educated man's style of writing which, at first glance, would be unacceptable today in its presentation because there is no punctuation or paragraphing.

Activity 15.1

Examine the spelling of the words in the following letter, and discuss any that seem unusual to you. Is the spelling significantly irregular or inconsistent? How many words have more than one spelling?

The following words are names of birds used in hawking, or falconry:

goshawkes (*goshawks*)	*layners* (*lanners*)
sparhawkes (*sparrowhawks*)	*merlions* (*merlins*)
gerfawken (*gerfalcon*)	*yerkyn* (*jerkin = male gerfalcon*)

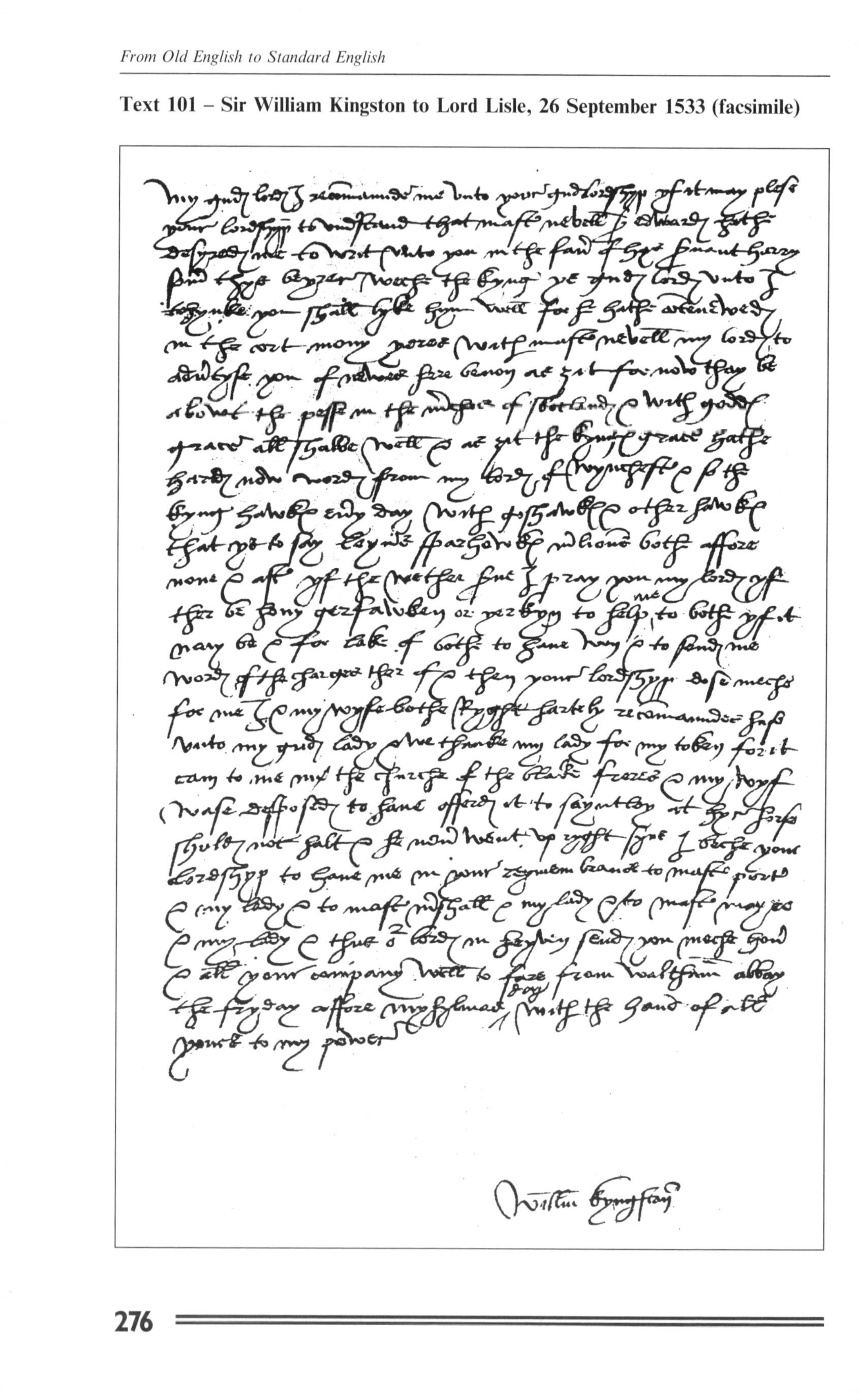

Text 101 – Sir William Kingston to Lord Lisle, 26 September 1533 (facsimile)

my gud lord I recõmaunde me vnto your gud lordſhyp yf ıt may pleſe
your lordſhyp to vnd^{er}ſtand that maſt^{er} nevell ſ^{ır} edward hath
deſyred me to wrıt vnto you ın the fau^{r} of hys ſ^{r}uant harry
ſom^{er} thys beyrer wech the kyng ys gud lord vnto I
thynke you ſhall lyke hym well for he hath cõtenewed
ın the cort mony yeres wıth maſte^{r} nevell my lord to
adv^{er}tyſe you of newes here be non as ȝıt for now thay be
abowt the peſſe* ın the m^{ar}ches of ſcotland & wıth godde^{s}
grace all ſhalbe well & as ȝıt the kynge^{s} grace hathe
hard now word from my lord of Wyncheſt^{er} & ſo the
kyng hawkes evry day wıth goſhawkes & other hawke^{s}
that ys to ſay layn^{er}s ſparhawke^{s} & m^{er}lıons both affore
none & aft^{er} yf the wether ſ^{er}ve I pray you my lord yf
ther be hony gerfawken or yerkyn to help $_{\wedge}^{me}$ to both yf ıt
may be & for lak of bothe to haue wun & to ſend me
worde of the charges ther of & then your lordſhyp doſe meche
for me I & my wyfe both ryght hartely recõmaunde huſ
vnto my gud lady & we thanke my lady for my token for ıt
cam to me ın the churche of the blake freres† & my wyf
waſe deſpoſed to haue offerd ıt to ſaynt loy‡ at hyr horſe
ſhuld not halt & he nev^{er} went vp ryght ſyne§ I beche your
lordſhyp to haue me ın your reymembrance to maſt^{er} port^{er}
& my lady & to maſt^{er} merſhall & my lady & to maſt^{er} mayes
& my lady & thus o^{ur} lord ın heyvın ſend you meche hon^{or}
& all your company well to fare from waltham abbay
the fryday affore myhylmas $_{\wedge}^{day}$ wıth the hand of all
yours to my power

Wıllm Kyngſton

* *pesse = peace*
† *freres = friars*
‡ *saynt loy = St Eligius (St Eloi in French)*
§ *syne = since*

MnE spelling and punctuation

My good lord I recommend me unto your good lordship.

If it may please your lordship to understand that Master Neville, Sir Edward, hath desired me to write unto you in the favour of his servant Harry Somer, this bearer, which the King is good lord unto. I think you shall like him well, for he hath continued in the Court many years with Master Neville.

My lord, to advertise you of news, here be none as yet, for now they be about the peace in the Marches of Scotland, & with God's grace all shall be well. And as yet the King's grace hath heard no word from my Lord of Winchester, & so the King hawks every day with goshawks & other hawks, that is to say lanners, sparrowhawks & merlins, both afore noon & after, if the weather serve.

I pray you my lord, if there be any gerfalcon or jerkin to help me to both, if it may be, & for lack of both to have one, & to send me word of the charges thereof, & then your lordship does much for me.

I & my wife both right heartily recommend us unto my good lady, & we thank my lady for my token, for it came to me in the church of the Black Friars & my wife was disposed to have offered it to Saint Loy that her horse should not halt, & he never went upright since.

I beseech your lordship to have me in your remembrance to Master Porter & my lady, & to Master Marshall & my lady, & to Master Mayes & my lady. And thus our Lord in heaven send you much honour & all your company well to fare.

From Waltham Abbey the Friday afore Michelmas Day, with the hand of all yours to my power

William Kingston

15.1.2.1 *Commentary*

The spelling is consistent. Most words when repeated are spelt identically, for example, *affore*, *gud*, *lordshyp*, *recommaunde*. The only exceptions are three pairs of words with and without an additional ⟨e⟩, a common feature in writing and printing up to the 18th century – *hath*/*hathe*, *word*/*worde* and *wyf*/*wyfe*.

The complete absence of punctuation makes an initial reading more difficult for us, but obviously was not regarded as a problem in private letters in the 1530s. The version printed above with present-day conventions of spelling, punctuation and paragraphing helps to remove much of the strangeness of the text. Idiom and style are also unfamiliar, but the letter is fully grammatical for its time.

📖 The lexical vocabulary of Text 101 is listed in the *Word Book*.

15.1.3 *The Bishop of Carlisle to Lord Lisle*

The Bishop of Carlisle, John Kite, was a contemporary of Lord Lisle's and an active statesman as well as churchman. He was a friend of Cardinal Wolsey and had been sent on several diplomatic missions in the 1510s and 1520s. This letter contains nothing of importance but is of interest as there is a postscript written in the bishop's own hand, which contrasts in penmanship with the main dictated part. He refers to Sir William Kingston, the writer of the previous letter (Text 101).

Text 102 – Letter from the Bishop of Carlisle to Lord Lisle, December 1533 (facsimile)

My lorde I co͡’mende me hertly vnto you ryght glad ye be ın good helth &c
Sr Rolland yor ſeru͡nt was wth me thıs day and gaue me comenda
cıons vppon yor byhalfe wherof I do moche hertly thanke you
And ferder he ſhewed me that yor Lordſhyp dıd not a lytle mervel
ſo many le͡ts as ye had ſende vnto me that ye herd nothynge
fro me agayne S^{r} I enſure you ſıth oure beyng togedre I receyvıd

no l͡re from you or oderwyſe but only comendacıon by yor
le͡ts ſent vnto Mr kyngeſton Ferder yor ſaıd ſeru͡nt ſhewıd
me that yor lordſhyp hath p^{ro}vıdıd for me ııj or ıj barells of heryng
I pray you hertly to cauſe the ſame to be co͡veyd vnto me . and I
ſhal conſıdere therof thr charge and pey ıt gladly at the ſyght
I prey you that I may be hertly co͡mended vnto my good lady
yor bedfelow Thus ffare you^{r} lordſhyp as wel as I wold my
ſelfe Ffrom carlıſle place the xvıjth of December

Syr Wıll^{yam} Kyngeſton and hıs goode wyffe reco͡men
deth them vnto you . & to yor goode hono^{r} . And
I p^{re}y you that thıs myn own hand wryggttyng
may be takyn ın p^{ar}ty of reco͡pense . for a lett^{er}
whıch I receyved from yor goode hono^{r}s ladyſhyp
thıs day / as above w^{rı}tten . by the hand of yors
wth hıs at comandement

Jo. Karlıol

Modernised spelling & punctuation

My lord I commend me heartily unto you right glad ye be in good health &c Sir, Roland your servant was with me this day and gave me commendations upon your behalf, whereof I do much heartily thank you. And further, he showed me that your Lordship did not a little marvel, so many letters as ye had sent unto me, that ye heard nothing from me again. Sir, I asssure you, since our being together I received no letter from you or otherwise, but only commendation by your letters sent unto Mr Kingston. Further. your said servant showed me that your lordship hath provided for me three or two barrels of herring. I pray you heartily to cause the same to be conveyed unto me, and I shal consider thereof the charge and pay it gladly at the sight. I pray you that I may be heartily commended unto my good lady your bedfellow. Thus fare your lordship as well as I would my self. From Carlisle Place, the 17th of December.

Sir William Kingston and his good wife recommendeth them unto you & to your good honour. And I pray you that this mine own handwriting may be taken in party of recompense for a letter which I received from your good honour's ladyship this day, as above written. By the hand of yours with his at commandment,

John Carlisle

📖 The lexical vocabulary of Text 102 is listed in the *Word Book*.

15.2 Formal prose in the 1530s

An example of formal written language contemporary with the Lisle Letters is Sir Thomas Elyot's *The boke named the Gouernour*, printed in London in 1531. Its 'proheme', or preface, dedicates the book to King Henry VIII.

Text 103 – Proheme to *The Gouernour*, 1531 (facsimile)

The Proheme.

The proheme of Thomas Elyot knyghte vnto the moste noble & victorious prince kinge Henry the eyght kyng of England and Fraunce / defender of the true faythe / and lorde of Irelande.

Elyot's purpose was 'to describe in our vulgare tunge/the fourme of a iuste publike weale' – for *weale* or *weal*, now an archaic word, we would use *welfare* or *prosperity*. He named it *The Gouernour* 'for as moch as this present boke treateth of the education of them/that hereafter may be demed worthy to be gouernors of the publike weale'. He wrote it in English, but in common with all educated men regarded Latin and Greek the essential languages of education and learning, as the following short extracts show.

The first chapter of the book deals with,

The firste boke.

¶ The significacion of a publike weale/and why it is called in latin *Respublica*.

Text 104 – Sir Thomas Elyot's *The Gouernour*, 1531 (i) (facsimile)

A publike weale is a body lyuyng/cõpacte or made of sondry astates and degrees of men/ whiche is disposed by the ordre of equite/and gouerned by the rule and moderation of reason. In the latin tonge hit is called Respublica/ of the whiche the worde Res/hath diuers significations/ & doth nat only betoken that/ that is called a thynge/ whiche is distincte from a persone / but also signifieth astate / condition / substance / and profite. In our olde vulgare/pfite is called weale: And it is called a welthy contraye/ wherin is all thyng that is profitable: And he is a welthy man / that is riche in money and substance. Publike(as Varro saith)is diriuied of people: whiche in latin is called Populus. wherfore hit semeth that men haue ben lõge abused in calling Rempublicã a cõmune weale. And they which do suppose it so to be called for that / that euery thinge shulde be to all men in cõmune without discrepance of any astate or condition/be ther to moued more by sensualite / than by any good reason or inclinatiõ to humanite. And that shall sone appere vnto them that wyll be satisfied either with autorite/or with naturall ordre and example.

Publyke weale.

Respublica.

Plebs.

Fyrst the ppre & trewe signification of the wordes publike & cõmune/whiche be borowed of the latin tonge for the insufficiẽcie of our owne lãgage/shal sufficiẽtly declare the blyndenes of them / whiche haue hitherto holden and maynteyned the sayde opiniõs.

Transcription with abbreviations filled out

A publike weale is a body lyuyng / compacte or made of ſondry aſtates and degrees of men / whiche is diſpoſed by the ordre of equite / and gouerned by the rule and moderation of reaſon. In the latin tonge hit is called Reſpublica / of the whiche the worde Res/ hath diuers ſignificacions / & dothe nat only betoken that / that is called thynge / whiche is diſtincte from a perſone / but alſo ſignifieth aſtate / condition / ſubſtance / and profite. In our olde vulgare / profite is called weale: And it is called a welthy contraye / wherin is all thyng that is profitable: And he is a welthy man / that is riche in money and ſubſtance. Publike (as Varro ſaith) is diriuied of people: whiche in latin is called Populus. wherfore hit ſemeth that men haue ben longe abuſed in calling Rempublicam a commune weale. And they which do ſuppoſe it ſo to be called for that / that euery thinge ſhulde be to all men in commune without diſcrepance of any aſtate or condition / be ther to moued more by ſenſualite / than by any good reaſon or inclination to humanite. And that ſhall ſone appere vnto them that wyll be ſatiſfied either with autorite / or with naturall ordre and example.

Fyrſt the propre & trewe ſignification of the wordes publike & commune / whiche be borowed of the latin tonge for the inſufficiencie of our owne langage / ſhal ſufficiently declare the blyndenes of them / whiche haue hitherto holden and maynteyned the ſayde opinions . . .

Elyot refers to 'the insufficiencie of our owne langage' when defining the words *publike* and *commune* 'whiche be borowed of the latin tonge'. Elyot's *commune* is MnE *common*, and is used in the sense of the word *commoner* as against *noble*. We know now that both words had been taken from Old French during the ME period, but their source was Latin *publicus* and *communis*, and Elyot, like other scholarly writers of the period, himself Englished many Latin and Greek words in order to express his meaning. Sir Thomas Elyot sets out a programme of education for young noblemen in which learning Latin begins before the age of seven:

The ordre of lernynge that a noble man
shulde be trayned in before he come
to thaige of seuen yeres. Cap.v.

Text 105 – Sir Thomas Elyot's *The Gouernour*, 1531 (ii) (facsimile)

But there can be
nothyng more conuenient/than by litle and
litle to trayne and exerciſe them in ſpekyng
of latyne: infourmyng them to knowe firſt
the names in latine of all thynges that cometh in ſyghte/and to name all the partes
of theyr bodies:

But there can be
nothyng more conuenient / than by litle and
litle to trayne and exerciſe them in ſpekyng
of latyne: infourmyng them to knowe firſt
the names in latine of all thynges that cometh in ſyghte / and to name all the partes
of theyr bodies:

It is clear that in Elyot's day just as today, strong feelings could be aroused over accent and pronunciation. Here he is recommending the kind of nurse and serving-woman that a young nobleman under seven should have:

Text 106 – Sir Thomas Elyot's *The Gouernour*, 1531 (iii) (facsimile)

But to retourne to my
purpoſe; hit ſhall be expedient/that a noble mannes ſonne in his infancie haue with
hym continually/onely ſuche/as may accuſtome hym by litle and litle to ſpeake pure
and elegant latin. Semblably the nouriſes
& other women aboute hym/if it be poſſi-
ble/to do the ſame: or at the leſte way/that
they ſpeke none engliſſhe but that/whiche
is cleane/polite/perfectly/and articulately
pronounced/omittinge no lettre or ſillable/
as foliſſhe women often times do of a wan-
tonneſſe/wherby diuers noble men/and gē-
tilmennes chyldren (as I do at this daye
knowe) haue attained corrupte and foule
pronuntiation.

But to retourne to my purpoſe: hit ſhall be expedient / that a noble mannes ſonne in his infancie haue with hym continually / onely ſuche / as may accuſtome hym by litle and litle to ſpeake pure and elegant latin. Semblably the nouriſes & other women aboute hym / if it be poſſible / to do the ſame: or at the leſte way / that they ſpeke none engliſſhe but that / whiche is cleane / polite / perfectly and articulately pronounced / omittinge no lettre or ſillable / as foliſſhe women often times do of a wantonneſſe / wherby diuers noble men / and gẽtilmennes chyldren (as I do at this daye knowe) haue attained corrupte and foule pronuntiation.

We can use these texts from *The Gouernor* not only for the interest of their subject matter and style, but to observe those features of grammar and lexis which clearly mark Elyot's language as still archaic in terms of MnE, but yet much closer to our Standard English than the earlier texts we have studied.

15.2.1 *Commentary*

15.2.1.1 *Spelling*

- There are only a few alternative spellings in the Elyot texts, which show a transitional stage in the development of a standard:

  1 words may or may not have a redundant letter ⟨e⟩ and use both ⟨i⟩ and ⟨y⟩ for the vowel: *latin/latine/latyne*; *onely/only*; *ther/there*; *thinge/thyng/thynge*; *which/whiche*;
  2 the OE neuter pronoun *hit* is beginning to lose its initial consonant: *hit/it*;
  3 nouns end in either ⟨-cio(u)n⟩ or ⟨-tio(u)n⟩; the alternative ⟨c⟩ or ⟨t⟩ derives from the dual source of such words, from OF with the spelling ⟨-cion⟩, or from the original Latin suffix ⟨-tio ~ -tion-(em)⟩: *significacions/signification*, *pronounced/pronuntiation*;
  4 *shal/shall*.

- Abbreviations used in the writing of manuscripts are carried over into printing, particularly the macron or tilde to mark a following nasal consonant ⟨n⟩ or ⟨m⟩, as in *cõpacte* (*compacte*), *lõge* (*longe*), *cõmune* (*commune*), *inclinatiõ* (*inclination*). A barred letter ⟨p⟩ – ⟨p̱⟩ marks a the omission of ⟨ro⟩, for example *p̱pre* for *propre*, *p̱fite* for *profite*.
- Long ⟨ſ⟩, continues in word-initial and medial positions; round ⟨s⟩ is word-final.
- Letters ⟨u⟩ and ⟨v⟩ are still alternative forms of the same letter, used for both the vowel [u] and the consonant [v] , their use depending upon their position in the word:

word-initial ⟨v⟩ – consonant *vulgare, vertue, violently*; vowel *vnto, vniuersall*
word-medial ⟨u⟩ – consonant *soueraigne, moreouer, haue*; vowel *naturall, studie, tunge*

This can be clearly seen in the spelling of *deuulgate*, a now obsolete form of *divulgate* or *divulge*.

- Letter ⟨j⟩ is not yet used for [dʒ] – *maiestie, iuge, subiectes, iuste.*

15.2.1.2 *Punctuation*

- Full-stops mark the end of sentences, which begin with capital letters.
- The virgule ⟨/⟩ is used where we would expect a comma ⟨,⟩.
- The colon ⟨:⟩ is occasionally written.
- The ampersand for *and* resembles the older OE form like figure seven, ⟨7⟩.

15.2.1.3 *Vocabulary*

There are 130 lexical words (nouns, verbs, adjectives, adverbs) in the three Texts 104–6. Their proportions by derivation are: OE/ON 58 = 44.6%; OF/AF 61 = 46.9%; Latin 11 = 8.5% If you compare these figures with those of any of the ME texts in earlier chapters, you will see that by the 16th century there is a much larger proportion of words from French and Latin in formal prose like Elyot's *The Gouernour* – roughly 55% to 45% from OE. In other words, there is a scholarly vocabulary of words which do not belong to the native **core vocabulary** of English, which generally consists of surviving reflexes from OE, and OF words that had been fully assimilated into English in spelling and pronunciation by the 14th century.

📖 The lexical vocabulary of Texts 103–6 is listed (i) alphabetically, and (ii) by derivation and date, in the *Word Book*.

15.2.1.4 *Grammar*

Verb inflections

The only significant difference from the present-day grammatical system in the texts is the 3rd person present tense inflection ⟨-eth⟩, *all thyngs that* ***cometh****, &* ***dothe*** *nat only betoken, but also* ***signifieth****, wherfore hit* ***semeth***. But the verbs in *that they* ***speke*** and ***do*** *suppose* are uninflected, and so we would need more data to establish the norm.

Other differences lie in the use of the system rather than in the system itself, for example, the choices made then and now in the selection of pronouns.

Relative pronouns

Today *who* is the relative pronoun used to refer to human subjects, and *which* for non-human referents only, but in Elyot's syntax *which* refers to both human and non-human:

a publike weale ... ***whiche*** *is disposed by ...*
a thynge ***whiche*** *is distincte from a persone*
And they ***which*** *do suppose it so to be called ...*
*the blyndenes of them/****whiche*** *haue hitherto ...*

Elyot also uses *that* as a relative pronoun for both human and non-human referents, as in present-day usage,

> *that/**that** is called...*
> *wherin is all thyng **that** is profitable*
> *he is a welthy man/**that** is riche in money and substance*
> *them **that** will be satisfied...*

Neuter pronouns

Elyot uses both the older form of neuter pronoun *hit*, surviving from OE, and *it*, which suggests that usage had not yet standardised:

> *and why **it** is called in latin Respublica*
> *In the latin tonge **hit** is called Respublica*
> ***hit** shall be expedient*
> *if **it** be possible*
> *And **it** is called a welthy contraye...*
> *wherfore **hit** semeth...*
> *they which do suppose **it** so to be called...*

15.3 A different view on new words

Sir Thomas Elyot expressed a scholar's view on the superiority of the resources of Latin and Greek, from which languages hundreds of words were 'Englished'. These words were disparagingly referred to as 'inkhorn terms' – words coming from the scholar's horn of ink and therefore pedantic – and there was a lot of controversy over this. For example, George Puttenham called the introduction of Latin and Greek words 'corruption' of language, the result of the 'peeuish affectation of clerks and scholers', because it introduced polysyllabic words into English.

Text 107 – George Puttenham on inkhorn terms, 1589 (facsimile)

> but now I muſt recant and confeſſe that our Normane Engliſh which hath growen ſince *William* the Conquerour doth admit any of the auncient feete, by reaſon of the many *polyſillables* euen to ſixe and ſeauen in one word, which we at this day vſe in our moſt ordinarie language: and which corruption hath bene occaſioned chiefly by the peeuiſh affectation not of the Normans them ſelues, but of clerks and ſcholers or ſecretaries long ſince, who not content with the vſual Normane or Saxon word, would conuert the very Latine and Greeke word into vulgar French, as to ſay innumerable for innombrable, reuocable, irreuocable, irradiation, depopulatiō & ſuch like, which are not naturall Normans nor yet French, but altered Latines, and without any imitation at all: which therefore were long time deſpiſed for inkehorne termes, and now be reputed the beſt & moſt delicat of any other.

auncient feete means the verse rhythms of the classical Latin and Greek poets. A foot is a unit of rhythm.
peeuish is here used as an adjective of dislike, 'expressing rather the speaker's feeling than any quality of the object referred to' (*OED*).

The lexical vocabulary of Text 107 is listed alphabetically and by derivation and date, in the *Word Book*.

But there were those who did not not accept Sir Thomas Elyot's view on 'the insufficiencie of our own langage', and who disliked any borrowing from other languages, not just the creation of 'inkhorn terms'. Richard Verstegan's view, published in 1605, is typical of many 16th-century writers.

Text 108 – Richard Verstegan's *A Restitution of Decayed Intelligence*, 1605 (facsimile)

Since the tyme of *Chaucer*, more Latin & French, hath bin mingled with our toung then left out of it, but of late wee haue falne to ſuch borowing of woords from, Latin, French, and other toungs, that it had bin beyond all ſtay and limit, which albeit ſome of vs do lyke wel and think our toung thereby much bettred, yet do ſtrangers therefore carry the farre leſſe opinion thereof, ſome ſaying that it is of it ſelf no language at all, but the ſcum of many languages, others that it is moſt barren, and that wee are dayly faine to borrow woords for it (as though it yet lacked making) out of other languages to patche it vp withall, and that yf wee were put to repay our borrowed ſpeech back again, to the languages that may lay claime vnto it; wee ſhould bee left litle better then dumb, or ſcarſly able to ſpeak any thing that ſhould bee ſencible.

Our toung diſcredited by our language-borrowing.

The lexical vocabulary of Text 108 is listed alphabetically and by derivation and date, in the *Word Book*.

However, if we compare the etymologies of the lexical words in these two texts, which are roughly equal in length, we find that a quarter of Puttenham's vocabulary derives directly from Latin, in spite of his attack on the 'peevish affectation' of inkhorn terms.

Puttenham			
Lexical word types: 56	OE	18	32.1%
	OF/AF	23	41.1%
	Latin	14	25.0%
	not known	1	1.8%
Verstegan			
Lexical word types: 49	OE/ON	35	71.5%
	OF/ONF	12	4.5%
	not known	2	4.00%

15.4 John Hart's *An Orthographie*

During the 16th century the first dictionaries, spelling-books and grammars of English were published. The writers were responding to a growing sense that the language needed an agreed form of spelling, grammar and vocabulary. People saw that the letters of the alphabet were too few to match the sounds of English, and that the spelling of many words did not match their pronunciation. Puttenham's view of the language as 'corrupted' was shared by many others.

One of the earliest books which advocated a reform of English spelling was John Hart's *An Orthographie*, published in 1569. In the following extract he is justifying the need for his new spelling system, 'the new maner'.

Text 109 – John Hart's *An Orthographie*, 1569 – howe euerye language ought to bee written (facsimile)

Which is vppon the conſideration of the
ſeuerall voices of the ſpeach, and the vſe
of their ſeuerall markes for them, which
we cal letters. But in the moderne & pre-
ſent maner of writing (aſwell of certaine
other languages as of our Engliſh) there
is ſuch confuſion and diſorder, as it may
be accounted rather a kinde of ciphring,
or ſuch a darke kinde of writing, as the
beſt and readieſt wit that euer hath bene,
could, or that is or ſhalbe, can or may, by
the only gift of reaſon, attaine to the ready and perfite reading thereof, without a
long and tedious labour, for that it is vn-
fit and wrong ſhapen for the proportion of
the voice. Whereas the new maner hereafter (thoughe it ſeeme at the firſt very
ſtraunge, hard and vnprofitable) by the
reading only therof, will proue it ſelfe fit,
eaſie and delectable, and that for whatſo-
euer Engliſh may be writtē in that order.

> Which is uppon the consideration of the seuerall voices of the speach, and the use of their seuerall markes for them, which we cal letters. But in the moderne & present maner of writing (as well of certaine other languages as of our English) there is such confusion and disorder, as it may be accounted rather a kinde of ciphring, or such a darke kinde of writing, as the best and readiest wit that euer hath bene, could, or that is or shalbe, can or may, by the only gift of reason, attaine to the ready and perfite reading thereof, without a long and tedious labour, for that it is unfit and wrong shapen for the proportion of the voice. Whereas the new maner hereafter (thoughe it seeme at the first very straunge, hard and unprofitable) by the reading only therof, will proue it selfe fit, easie and delectable, and that for whatsoeuer English may be writtẽ in that order.

Hart's argument begins with the 'fiue differing simple soundes or voyces' – that is, the five vowels written ⟨a e i o u⟩ and sounding, in stressed syllables, something like [æ/a ɛ ɪ ɑ/ɔ ʊ] as short vowels and [æː/aː eː/ɛː iː oː uː] as long vowels. They should, he says, each represent one sound, but 'they haue bene and are abused in diuers soundes'. He illustrates their proper pronunciation with this sentence:

> The pratling Hosteler hath dressed, curried, and rubbed our horses well.

and adds,

> none of the fiue vowels is missounded, but kept in their proper and auncient soundes.

As you read that sentence, remember two things. Firstly, that the present-day RP and Southern English pronunciation of *curried* and *rubbed*, with the short vowel [ʌ], did not exist then. The vowel was [ʊ]. Secondly, that the ⟨r⟩ in *horses* was pronounced, and the vowel in *Hosteler* and *horses* was the same. Also the ⟨h⟩ of *Hosteler* was probably not sounded. A possible phonetic version of the sentence reads,

> [ðə pɹætlɪŋ ɒstələɹ hæθ dɹɛst kʊɹɪd ænd ɹʊbd uːɹ hɒɹsɪz wəl]

Hart pointed out two spelling conventions which are still part of the modern English system, but which he did not use in his reformed spelling. The first was the use of a final ⟨e⟩ as a diacritic letter to mark a preceding long vowel, as in MnE *hate/hat, site/sit*. The second was the use of double consonants to mark a preceding short vowel, as in MnE *matting/mating* and *robbing/robing*. He preferred to use a dot under the letter to mark a long vowel, e.g. ⟨ị⟩:

> I leaue also all double consonants: hauing a mark for the long vowell, there is therby sufficient knowledge giuen that euerye unmarked vowell is that…

The interest of Hart's book for us is not so much in the reformed alphabet which he invented, but the authentic evidence it indirectly provides about changes in the pronunciation of English. Here is a facsimile of the opening of the first two pages of the second part of the book, which is printed in Hart's new spelling, followed by a transcription into MnE spelling:

Activity 15.2

Identify the sound changes that Hart describes in this extract from his book.

Text 110 – John Hart's new alphabet and spelling system (facsimile)

*An exersịz ov ðat huiʧ iz sẹd: huer-in iz de-
clard, hou ðe rest ov ðe consonants ar mad
bei ðinstruments ov ðe mouθ: huiʧ
uaz omited in ðe premisez, for ðat
ui did not muʧ abiuz
ðem. Cap. vij.*

*In ðis tịtl abuv-uritn, ei konsi-
der ov ðe ị, in exersịz, & ov ðe
u, in instruments: ðe leik ov ðe
ị, in tịtl, huiʧ ðe kómon man
and mani lernd, dụ sound in ðe
diphθongs ei, and iu: iet ei
uld not θink it mịt to ureit ðẹm, in ðọz
and leik ụrds, huẹr ðe sound ọv ðe voël ọn-
li, mẹ bi as uel álouëd in our spịʧ, as ðat ov
ðe diphθong iuzd ov ðe riud: and so fár ei álou
observasion for derivasions. ∾/ hierbei iu mẹ
persẹv, ðat our singl sounding and ius of letters, mẹ in proses ov teim, bring our họl nasion
tu ọn serten, perfet and ʒeneral ʃpẹking. ∾
/huer-in ʃi must bi rịuled bei ðe lernd from
teim tu teim. ∾/ and ei kan not blạm ani man
tu θink ðis maner ov niu ureiting ʃtranʒ, for
ei du konfés it iz ʃtranʒ tu mei self, ðoh befọr
ei hạv ended ðe ureiting, and iu ðe rịding ov
ðiz bụk, ei dout not bọð iu and ei ʃal θink
our lạburs uel bestoëd. ∾/ and not-uiθ-stan-
ding ðat ei hạv devịzd ðis niu maner ov ureiting for our /ingliʃ, ei miẹn not ðat /latin
ʃuld bi-uritn in ðez leters, no mọr ðen ðe
/grịk or /hebriu, nẹðer uld ei ureit t'ani
man ov ani ʃtranʒ nasion in ðez léters, but
huen az ei-uld ureit /ingliʃ. ∾/ and az ei-uld
gladli konterfet hiz ʃpịʧ uiθ mei tung, so-uld
ei hiz ureiting uiθ mei hand. ∾ / iet huo kuld
let mi t'iuz mei pén ðe best ei kuld, ðerbei t'-
átẹn ðe sụner tu ðe perfet pronunsiasion, ov a-
ni ʃtranʒ ʃpịʧ: but ureiting /ingliʃ, ui mẹ
(az is sẹd) iuz for evri ʃtranʒ ụrd, ðe sạm
marks or léters ov ðe voises huiʧ ui du feind in
ʃpịʧ, uiðout ani-uðer regard tu ʃiọ bei-urei-
ting huens ðe-ụrd iz boroëd, ðen az ui du-in
ʃpẹking. ∾/ for suʧ kuriozite in superflụz léters, for derivasion or diferens, and so furθ, iz
ðe disordring and konfounding, ov ani-urei-
ting: kontrari tu ðe lau-ov ðe perfeksion ðer-
of, and agenst ául rẹzon: huer-bei, it ʃuld bi o-
bedient untu ðe pronunsiasion, az tu hir lạdi-
and mistres: and so, ád or diminiʃ az ʃi ʃaul
in sukses ov teim kómaund. ∾/*

An exercise of that which is said: wherein is declared, how the rest of the consonants are made by th'instruments of the mouth: which was omitted in the premisses, for that we did not much abuse them. Chapter vii

In this title above-written, I consider of the ⟨i⟩ in exercise, & of the ⟨u⟩, in instruments: the like of the ⟨i⟩, in title, which the common man, and many learned, do sound in the diphthongs ⟨ei⟩, and ⟨iu⟩: yet I would not think it meet to write them, in those and like words, where the sound of the vowel only, may be as well allowed in our speech, as that of the diphthong used of the rude: and so far I allow observation for derivations. ~ / Whereby you may perceive, that our single sounding and use of letters, may in process of time, bring our whole nation to one certain, perfet and general speaking. ~ / Wherein she must be ruled by the learned from time to time. ~ / And I can not blame any man to think this manner of new writing strange, for I do confess it is strange to my self, though before I have ended the writing, and you the reading of this book, I doubt not but you and I shall think our labours well bestowed. ~ / And not-with-standing that I have devised this new manner of writing for our /English, I mean not that /Latin should be written in these letters, no more then the /Greek or /Hebrew, neither would I write t'any man of any strange nation in these letters, but whenas I would write /English. ~ / And as I would gladly counterfeit his speech with my tongue, so would I his writing with my hand. ~ Yet who could let me t'use my pen the best I could, thereby t' attain the sooner to the perfect pronunciation, of any strange speech: but writing /English, we may (as is said) use for every strange word, the same marks or letters of the voices which we do find in speech, without any other regard to show by writing whence the word is borrowed, then as we do in speaking. ~ / For such curiosity in superfluous letters, for derivation or for difference, and so forth, is the disordering and confounding, of any writing: contrary to the law of the perfection thereof, and against all reason: whereby, it should be obedient unto the pronunciation, as to her lady and mistress: and so, add or diminish as she shall in success of time command.

The opening lines of Text 110 are recorded on the cassette tape.

an ɛksɛrsiz ɒv ðat hwɪtʃ ɪz sɛːd hwerɪn ɪs dɛklard, həʊ ðə rɛst ɒv ðə kɒnsɒnants ɑr mad bəɪ ðɪnstrʊmɛnts ɒv ðə məʊθ, hwɪtʃ waz ɔmɪtɛd ɪn ðə prɛmɪsɛz, fɔr ðat wi dɪd nɒt mʊtʃ abjuz ðɛm.
tʃaptɛr sɛvən
ɪn ðɪs tiːtəl abʊv wrɪtən, əɪ kɒnsɪdər ɒv ðɪ iː ɪn *ɛksɛrsiz*, and ɒv ðə ʊ ɪn *ɪnstrʊmɛnts* ðə ləik ɒv ðə i ɪn tiː*təl hw*ɪtʃ ðə kɒmən man, and manɪ lernd, duː səʊnd ɪn ðə dɪphθɒŋgz əi and ju. jɛt əi wʊld nɒt θɪŋk ɪt miːt tʊ wrəit dɛm, ɪn ðoːz and ləik wuːrdz, hweːr ðə səʊnd θv ðə voɛl oːnlɪ, mɛː bi aswɛl ələʊɛd ɪn əʊr spiːtʃ, as ðat ɒv ðə dɪfθɒŋg juzd θv ðə rɪud, and so fɑr əi əəʊ ɒbsɛrvasɪɔn fɔr dɛrivasiɔns. hwerbəɪ ju mɛː pɛrseːv, ðat əʊr sɪŋgəl səʊndɪŋg and jus ɒv lɛtərz, mɛː ɪn prosɛs ɒv təɪm, brɪŋg əʊr hoːl nasɪɔn tu oːn sertɛn, perfɛt and dʒɛnɛral speːkɪŋg. hwerɪn ʃi mʊst bi rɪulɛd bəi ðə lɛrnɛd frɒm təim tə təim

15.4.1 *Commentary*

Hart apparently believed that a reformed spelling, in which there was only one letter for each sound, would in time put an end to social and regional dialectal accents, and

> ...bring our whole nation to one certain, perfet and general speaking.

Believing that writing 'should be obedient unto the pronunciation', he sets out some of his objections to the current spelling system:

- **superfluous letters** – some of the letters of the Roman alphabet are redundant and could be dropped.
- **derivation** – a 'strange word' (i.e. a loan-word from another language) should be written according to its English pronunciation, and not to match its foreign derivation.
- **difference** – he also rejects the use of different spelling for words which are pronounced alike. If there is no confusion when we speak them, then there can be none when we write them.

15.5 The Great Vowel Shift

Between the time of Chaucer in the late 14th century, and Shakespeare in the late 16th century, all the **long vowels** in English spoken in the Midlands and South of England shifted in their pronunciation. We don't know why it happened, and no similar shift is known to have taken place at other times. It has therefore been called the Great Vowel Shift (GVS).

The shift was not complete in 1569, and there was much variation between regional and social dialect speakers, but in time all the long vowels were either raised or became diphthongs. In spite of Hart and other reformers up to the present day, our spelling system has never been altered to fit the changed pronunciations.

John Hart published three books on spelling reform between 1551 and 1570, and is the chief authority for the pronunciation of the time. He was clear that the 'beste and moste perfite English' was the speech of educated Londoners, maintaining that they took the best features and left the worst of contemporary dialects. He is an authentic source of evidence for the shifting of the long vowels at a transitional stage.

15.5.1 *Evidence for the Great Vowel Shift in* An Orthographie

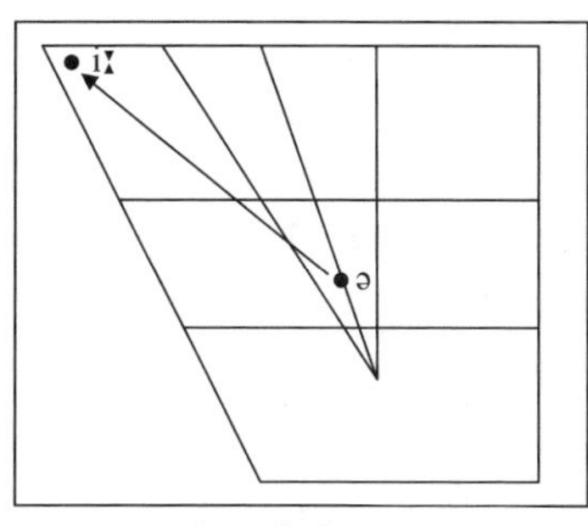

Vowel chart 9

Hart's statement,

> The sound of the vowel only, may be as well allowed in our speech, as that of the diphthong used of the rude.

means that there were two current pronunciations of the vowel spelt ⟨i⟩ in *exercise*. One was 'the vowel only', ME [iː], a simple or pure vowel. The other was a diphthong which Hart spells ⟨ei⟩. This diphthong was probably pronounced [əi].

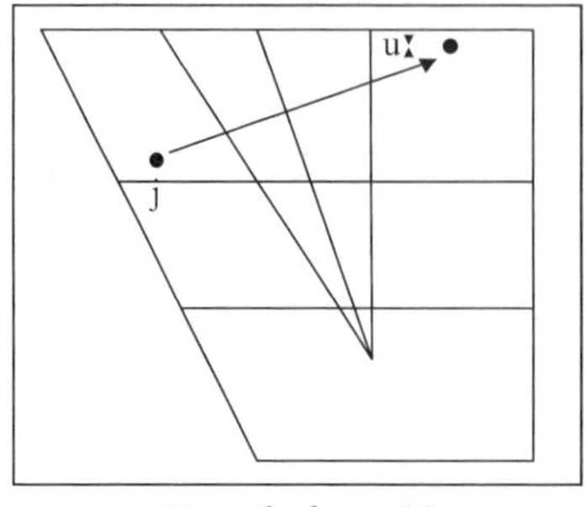

Vowel chart 10

There were also clearly two pronunciations of the ⟨u⟩ of *instruments* – [u], and the newer [ɪu] or [ju]. The changes had occurred among 'rude common men', and therefore marked a social dialect. What is interesting is that the 'vulgar' pronunciations have now taken over in prestigious speech – [əɪ] eventually shifted further to MnE RP [aɪ]. Similarly, [ju] is the RP pronunciation of many (but not all) words with ⟨u⟩, like *tune*, *music* and *fuel*.

This illustrates two of the problems of trying to make a spelling system that accurately represents pronunciation. Firstly, which of two alternatives do you select, the conservative or the new? Secondly, because pronunciation is continuously changing over time, is spelling to be altered when a new pronunciation has clearly taken over?

John Hart spelt words in his new alphabet according to his own interpretation of their current 1560s pronunciation. All the words in the following lists are taken from the section printed in Hart's new spelling in *An Orthographie*. There is sufficient evidence here to confirm the general movement of the long vowels which was taking place in the 16th century. The spelling of the words in the following lists is transcribed from Hart's new alphabet illustrated in Text 110.

15.5.1.1 *Words spelt with letter ⟨i⟩*

In ME, long vowels spelt with ⟨i⟩ were pronounced [iː]. Hart's spelling shows two pronunciations, already referred to. Some are conservative:

Hart's pronunciation [iː]

advertised	devised	reciteth	sight
aspiring	exercise	right	strikes
derived	high	rightly	title

others are pronounced with the diphthong [əɪ], which Hart spelt ⟨ei⟩:

Hart's pronunciation [əɪ]

describe	find	line	tie
desire	I	lively	time
devise	idly	mind	trifle
divers	life	mine	wise
divide	like	pipe	write

15.5.1.2 *Words spelt with letter ⟨y⟩*

The adverbial suffix ⟨-ly⟩ is today pronounced with a short [ɪ] in RP, an unstressed syllable. In Hart's book such adverbs, e.g. *diversely*, *especially* and *presently*, and the verb *crucify*, are spelt with ⟨ei⟩, pronounced [əɪ], which developed into [aɪ] (see section 18.3.2 on Dryden's rhymes at the end of the 17th century). Present-day pronunciation of the suffix as [ɪ] results from later sound changes in unstressed syllables. Hart spells *softly* with ⟨i⟩ however, which suggests that the change from [iː] to [əɪ] was not complete.

The single syllable words *by*, *my*, *thy* and *why* are spelt with ⟨ei⟩ and so pronounced [əɪ]. They were therefore beginning the shift of long [iː] to its present-day [baɪ], [maɪ], [aɪ] and [ʍaɪ].

15.5.1.3 *Words spelt with ⟨ee⟩*

More quotations from John Hart's book inform us about other changes in pronunciation.

> We call the e, in learning the A.B.C. in the sound of i, and do double the e, for that sound, as in see the Bee doth flee.

That is, the name of letter ⟨e⟩ is pronounced [iː], and the sound is often spelt ⟨ee⟩. The words *see*, *bee* and *flee* derive from OE *seon*, *beo* and *fleon*. The ⟨eo⟩ diphthongs 'smoothed' to [eː] in the ME period, and the spelling ⟨ee⟩ marked the long vowel [eː] at that time.

But by the mid-16th century, Hart tells us that the pronunciation was [siː], [biː] and [fliː], which it is today. Therefore, ME [eː] (a half close front vowel) had shifted and raised to the close vowel [iː].

In Hart's new spelling the vowels of *be*, *even*, *Hebrew*, *these* and *we* were spelt ⟨e⟩ and therefore pronounced [eː], the older ME sound. *She* was spelt with ⟨i⟩, however, which is evidence of the incomplete shifting of [eː] to [iː].

All the following words were written with ⟨i⟩ in Hart's new spelling and therefore pronounced [iː]:

chiz (*cheese*)	**mit** (*meet*)	**prosideth** (*proceedeth*)	**spidier** (*speedier*)
Grik (*Greek*)	**nid** (*need*)	**si** (*see*)	**switnes** (*sweetness*)
kip (*keep*)	**nidful** (*needful*)	**spich** (*speech*)	**tith** (*teeth*)

These words, all formerly pronounced with [eː] in ME and spelt ⟨e⟩ or ⟨ee⟩, had all raised to the close vowel [iː].

John Hart's evidence helps to explain also why the pronunciation of the ⟨i⟩ vowel in *exercise* and *title* was shifting to the diphthong [əɪ] in the mid-16th century. Both shifts were part of a general 'push-pull' movement of the long vowels. If [eː] vowels were raised far enough to be confused with [iː], which is a close vowel, and cannot be raised any higher, words with [iː] can only remain contrastive by using a glide to make a diphthong – at first probably [ɪiː], then [əɪ], which widened further

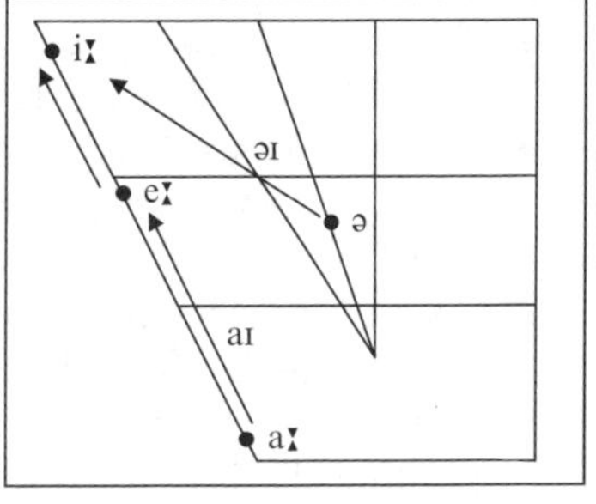

Vowel chart 11

to [aɪ], as it now is in MnE RP. These changes only happened within some speech communities, and slowly, by degrees, so that the older and newer pronunciations would be heard at the same time.

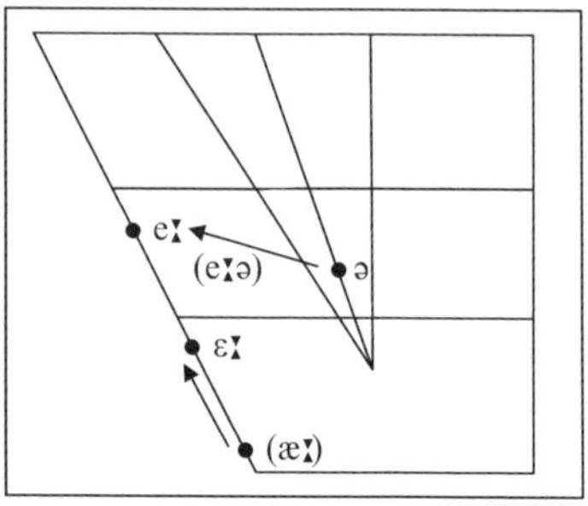

Vowel chart 12

15.5.1.4 *Spellings with* ⟨*ea*⟩

In some dialects of ME there had been two contrasting long front vowels, close [e:] and open [ɛ:], both spelt ⟨e⟩ or ⟨ee⟩. For example, in Chaucer's 'Prologue' we find the following contrasting rhymes. *Breeth* and *heeth* derived from words with OE [æː] which had raised to open [ɛː], but *seke* and *seeke* with close [eː] derived from OE [eː] and the smoothed diphthong [eːə]. The two front vowels [eː] and [ɛː] did not rhyme.

OE source	*ME rhyme*	*ME pronunciation*	*MnE reflex*
brǣþ	**breeth**	[brɛːθ]	breath
hǣþ	**heeth**	[hɛːθ]	heath
sēcan	**seke**	[seːk]	seek
sēoc	**seeke**	[seːk]	sick

During the 15th century, scribes had begun to use the spelling ⟨ea⟩ for words of French origin with open [ɛ:], so that, for example, *raison* came to be spelt *reason*. Letter ⟨a⟩ is here used as a diacritic. In the 16th century, the spelling was extended to words from OE with the same vowel; *mele* and *herte* were re-spelt *meal* and *heart*. Unfortunately for us, what might have been a very neat solution has been made complicated:

- The re-spelling was not used or applied consistently.
- Pronunciation of these two front vowels differed between regional and social dialects in ME. In some dialects the distinction was not made.
- ⟨ea⟩ words with [ɛ:] shifted to [eː] in the GVS, but were raised further to [iː] in some dialects, so that they came to be pronounced like ⟨ee⟩ words.
- There were therefore marked dialectal differences in the pronunciation of ⟨ea⟩ words in the 16th and 17th centuries.
- This variation in the pronunciation of ⟨ea⟩ words, with further changes, continued into the 18th century when present-day pronunciations were settled. RP derives from the prestige varieties of pronunciation.

Present-day English clearly reflects these variations and later changes, as in the words *leaf* [i:], *great* [ɛɪ], *dead* [ɛ], *heart* [ɑ:], *heard* [ɜː], *ear* [ɪə], *pear* [ɛə]. The vowels of *heart, heard, ear, pear* were affected by the later loss of post-vocalic ⟨r⟩, which tends to lower the vowel, but the differences can only be accounted for as a result of the fortuitous 'selection' from different social or regional dialectal accents.

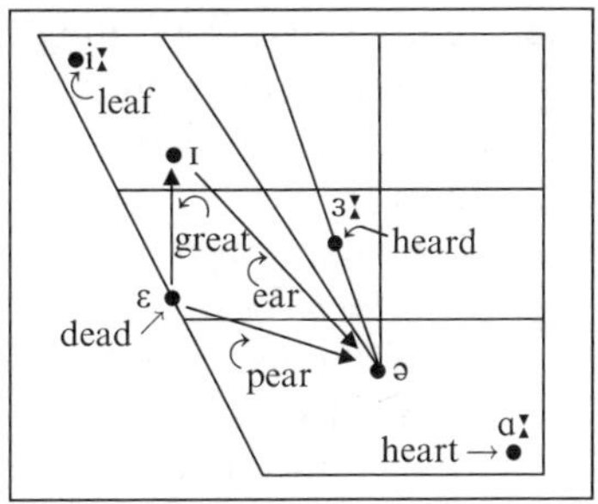

Vowel chart 13

Most words which we now spell with ⟨ea⟩ have letter ⟨e⟩ for the long vowel [e:] in Hart's spelling,

ber (*bear* – vb)	**brethd** (*breathed*)	**lev** (*leave*)	**redi** (*ready*)
brek (*break*)	**esi** (*easy*)	**meneth** (*meaneth*)	**rezon** (*reason*)
breth (*breath*)	**gret** (*great*)	**ner** (*near*)	**resonabl** (*reasonable*)
breth (*breathe*)	**lern** (*learn*)	**plez** (*please*)	**spek** (*speak*)

These words had probably shifted to [eː] from the open ME [ɛː], but Hart did not provide separate letters for the two vowels [eː] and [ɛː].

If you examine the pronunciation of these ⟨ea⟩ words today, you will see that there have been subsequent changes which have affected words selectively. Many now have the high vowel [iː], and there is evidence that this was already happening in Hart's day, because he spells a few words, including *read, reading* and *appear* with letter ⟨i⟩ – *rid, riding* and *apir*.

15.5.1.5 *Spellings with ⟨o⟩, ⟨oo⟩ or ⟨oa⟩*

Here is another quotation from Hart:

> . . . and o, single or double in the sound of u, as, they two come to do some good, which is the mere sound of the u.

That is, the vowel pronounced [u] is sometimes spelt with ⟨o⟩ or ⟨oo⟩, as in *two, come, to, do, some* and *good.* The explanation for these words, all pronounced alike according to Hart, is more complicated, and involves different sound changes or spelling conventions.

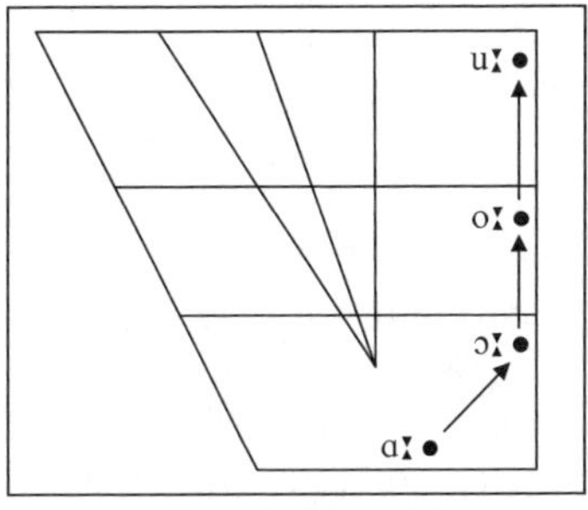

Vowel chart 14

- OE *twa* [twɑː] (low back vowel) had 'rounded' to *two* [twɔː] (half open back vowel) in early ME, and later to [twoː], (half close back vowel). The [w] was lost before the rounded back vowel, but letter ⟨w⟩ was retained in the spelling. In the GVS, the [oː] was raised to [uː], so that OE [twaː] had now changed to [tuː].

- *to* and *do* were long half close back vowels in OE and ME, [toː], [doː], and raised to close [uː] in the GVS – [tuː], [duː].
- The alternative spelling of, for example, OE *cuman* and *sum* with ⟨o⟩ was adopted in ME to avoid the confusion of ⟨u⟩ with minim letters – ⟨n ~ m ~ w⟩ – *comen* and *som*, but the pronunciation was unchanged. The GVS did not affect them, because they were short vowels, [kʊm] and [sʊm].

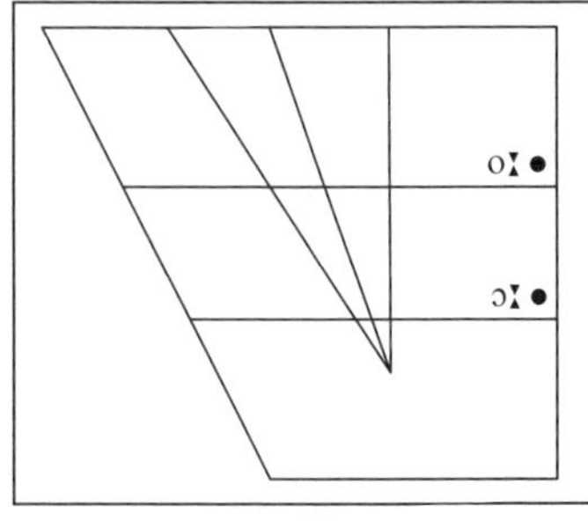

Vowel chart 15

- The vowel of ME *gōd* meaning *good* was long, so it shifted to [uː] in the GVS, together with *blōd* (*blood*) and *fōde* (*food*). Their different pronunciations today – RP [gʊd ~ blʌd ~ fuːd] are the result of later changes.

Just as in ME there were two mid long front vowels which were contrastive, close [eː] and open [ɛː], there were also two back vowels, close [oː] and open [ɔː], both spelt with letter ⟨o⟩ or ⟨oo⟩. In the 16th century, some writers and printers began to spell the vowel of long open [ɔː] with ⟨oa⟩, the letter ⟨a⟩ not representing a sound, but acting as a diacritic, like the ⟨a⟩ in ⟨ea⟩. But Hart does not provide different letters for these two vowels any more than he did for the two ME ⟨e⟩ vowels, and the evidence of pronunciation from his spelling is as follows.

[o] [o:]				[u] [u:]	
Hart	***MnE***	***Hart***	***MnE***	***Hart***	***MnE***
both	*both*	thoh	*though*	behuf	*behoof*
hop	*hope*	besto	*bestow*	buk	*book*
not	*note*	boro	*borrow*	fulish	*foolish*
on	*one*	kno	*know*	gud	*good*
onli	*only*	knoledg	*knowledge*	skul	*school*
voel	*vowel*	sho	*show*	suth	*sooth*
huo	*who*	aproch	*approach*	tuk	*took*
huoz	*whose*	brod	*broad*	understud	*understood*
oht	*ought*				

There is evidence of these two contrasting pairs of front and back vowels in other 16th-century orthoepists (writers on pronunciation). The next facsimile is a page from William Bullokar's *Boke at Large* (1580), showing another 'amendment of ortography' (revised alphabet) with separate letters proposed for the long vowels [eː], [ɛː], [oː] and [ɔː]. It is clear that in the late 16th century they were still separate phonemes.

Text 111 – William Bullokar's *Boke at Large*, 1580 (facsimile)

The names of the letters according to this amendment of ortography, appéere in this Table, by the which ye may name the letters in the written Copies following.

a / a	b / b	cé / c'	kæ / c	ché / ch	d / d	e:ea / e:æ	é / e'
f / f	gé / g'	ga / g turn a into e.	hé / h	i / i	k / k	l / l	yl / l'
m / m	ym / m'	n / n	yn / n'	o / o	betwe'n o:&:v / ꝏ	p / p	phé / ph
qué / q	r / r	er / r'	s / s	shé / sh	t / t	thé / th	thé'f / th
v / v	ou / v'	vé / v'	wé / w	whé / wh	x / x	yé / y	zé / z

The letters for the two mid-front vowels [ɛ] and [e] (short and long) are shown at the end of the top row as ⟨e:æ⟩ and ⟨e'⟩. Words containing these letters in Bullokar's text in his new spelling include, for example,

⟨e⟩	= [ɛ]	sent, qestion, terror *sent, question, terror*
⟨æ⟩	= [ɛː]	mæning, thærfore, encræse, decræse, whær, læu *meaning, therefore, increase, decrease, where, leave*
⟨e'⟩	= [eː]	bre'f, agre', be', be'ing, e'nglish, ke'p, we', ye'ld *brief, agree, be, being, English, keep, we, yield*

Letters for the mid-back vowels, approximately [ɔ] and [o] (short and long) are in the third row, ⟨o⟩ and ⟨ꝏ⟩. Letter ⟨ꝏ⟩ is glossed 'betwe'n o & u', which is evidence of the raising of long [oː] towards [uː]. Examples are,

⟨o⟩	=[ɔ]	qestion (*3 syllables*), prosody, diphthong, wrongd *question, prosody, diphthong, wronged*
⟨o⟩	=[ɔː]	wo, on *woe, one*
⟨ꝏ⟩	=[oː]~[uː]	untꝏ , tꝏ, dꝏth *unto, to/too*, doth

15.5.1.6 Spellings with ⟨ou⟩ or ⟨ow⟩

The digraph ⟨ou⟩, also spelt ⟨ow⟩, was originally taken from French spelling to represent the OE and early ME long close back [uː]. Hart's phonetic spelling with ⟨ou⟩ rather than ⟨u⟩ tells us that this vowel had become a diphthong, probably then pronounced [əʊ]. Examples from Hart's book are (in present-day spelling):

account	doubt	out	touch
bound	found	pound	without
brought	four	pronounce	allow
confound	mouth	round	down
counsel	noun	sought	how
counter	our	sound	now

15.5.1.7 *Spellings with ⟨a⟩*

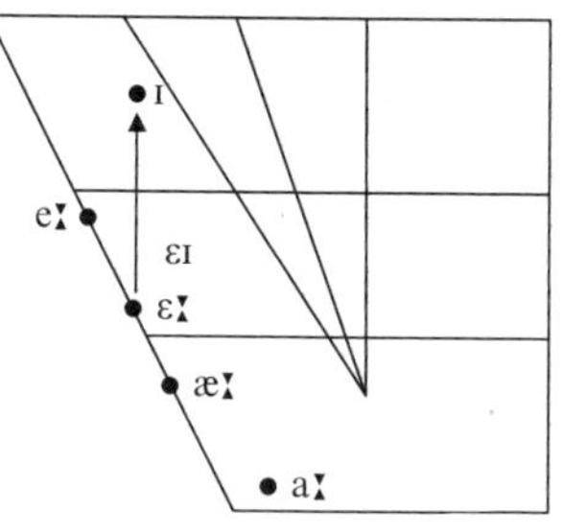

Vowel chart 16

The OE long vowel [ɑ:] had long before rounded and shifted to [ɔ:] in the South and Midlands, and words with this vowel were spelt with ⟨o⟩, e.g. OE *stan* and *ban* became *stone* and *bone*. The 'gap' in the system was filled in time with words of OF derivation like *grace* and *task*, and by OE disyllabic words whose short [a] vowels became long, e.g. OE *nama* and *lana* became *name* [naːmə] and *lane* [laːnə]. Words with a long vowel spelt with letter ⟨a⟩ in ME did not follow the pattern of the OE words which had earlier shifted to the back vowel [ɔː]. The ME vowel must have been, or shifted forwards to become, a front open vowel, [aː]~[æː], and then [ɛː]~[eː]. *Name*, for example, is now pronounced [nɛːm] or [neːm].

In Hart's new orthography, all the following words were spelt with letter ⟨a⟩, and were therefore still pronounced with [aː] or [æː]. This suggests that the shift upwards to [ɛ:] or [eː] was not yet evident in Hart's time.

any	labours	nation	spake
change	lady	observation	strange
blame	late	place	table
derivation	made	same	take
grace	many	shape	vary
have	name		

15.5.1.8 *Summary of changes to long vowels and diphthongs from ME to MnE*

A few examples of words with long vowels in the two pages of Hart's new spelling in Text 110 have been sorted into sets below. Hart's subscript dot or 'prick' to mark a long vowel has been used as a criterion (though he did not print it consistently).

Source (OE/OF)	*ME*	*Hart's spelling*	*MnE (RP)*
1		**⟨ei⟩**	
OE tīma [iː]	time [iː]	**teim = [əɪ]**	time [ai]
2		**⟨i⟩**	
OF exercīse [iː]	exercisen [iː]	**exersiz = [iː]**	exercise [ai]
3		**⟨i⟩**	
OE mē [eː]	me [eː]	**mi = [iː]**	me = [iː]
OE rǣdan [æː]	reden [eː]	**rid = [iː]**	read = [iː]
OE spēc[eː]	speche [eː]	**spich = [iː]**	speech = [iː]
4		**⟨e⟩**	
OE specan [ɛ]	speken [ɛː]	**spek = [eː]**	speak [iː]
OF perceivre [ɛ]	perceiven [ɛː]	**persev = [eː]**	perceive [iː]
		⟨e⟩	
OE mæg [æj]	mai [æɪ]	**me = [eː]**	may [eɪ]
5		**⟨a⟩**	
OF blamer [a]	blamen [aː]	**blam = [aː]**	blame [eɪ]
OE hlǣfdige [æː]	ladi [aː]	**ladi = [aː]**	lady [eɪ]
OE macode [a]	made [aː]	**mad = [aː]**	made [eɪ]
6		**⟨o⟩**	
OE ānlic [ɑː]	onli [ɔː]	**onli = [oː]**	only [oː] or [əʊ]
		⟨o⟩	
OE ān [ɑː]	on [ɔː]	**on = [oː]**	one [wʌn] or [wʊn]
7		**⟨u⟩**	
OE dōn [oː]	don [oː]	**du = [uː]**	do [uː]
		⟨u⟩	
OE bōc [oː]	bok [oː]	**buk = [uː]**	book [ʊ]
8		**⟨ou⟩**	
OE mūþ [uː]	mouth/muth [uː]	**mouth = [əʊ]**	mouth [aʊ]
OE ūre [uː]	oure/ure [uː]	**our = [əʊ]**	our [aʊ]

📖 A larger selection of words from Hart's *An Orthographie* is in the *Word Book*.

15.5.2 *The Great Vowel Shift – a summary*

There is still disagreement among scholars about the causes and precise development of the GVS. The sound changes were gradual, but sufficiently noticeable for men like John Hart and other writers on pronunciation and spelling in the 16th and

17th centuries to attempt to describe them. Their concern was often with social correctness and a concern to make the language perfect, but what they described is as near first-hand evidence as we can get.

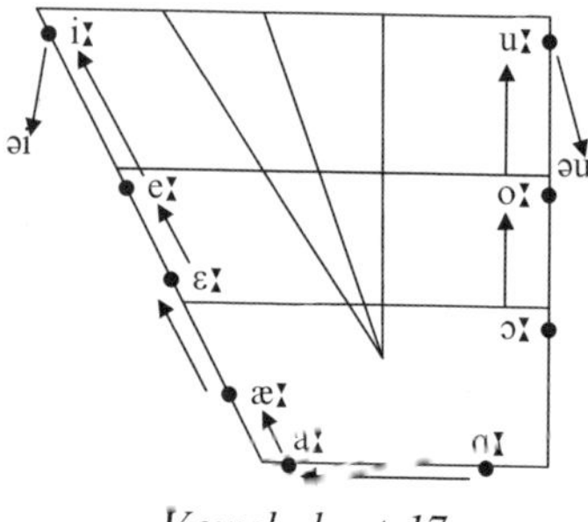

Vowel chart 17

We can summarise the GVS in terms of a 'drift upwards' of the long vowels, with the close or high vowels [iː] and [uː] becoming diphthongs, at first [əɪ] and [əʊ] and eventually (in RP) [aɪ] and [aʊ] – e.g. *ride, house*.

The diagram (Vowel chart 17) over-simplifies the process, because there are exceptions to the pattern of drift. To take one example, the ME long vowel [uː] of words like *cupe* (*coop, basket*), *drupen* (*droop*), *rum* (*room*), *wund* (*wound*, n), *tumbe* (*tomb*) did not diphthongise. They all have a labial consonant before or after the vowel – [p ~ m ~ w] – which had the effect of retaining the vowel [uː]. You will notice, however, that the vowel of the past participle *wound* of the verb *wind* did become the diphthong [aʊ], which warns us not to over-generalise in terms of rules of sound change.

Northern dialects of ME were not affected so immediately by the shift of long vowels. Present-day Scots, for example, still retains the old pronunciation of *house* [huːs].

15.6 Punctuation in 16th-century texts

The facsimiles of written and printed texts will have shown some differences from present-day conventions in punctuation, especially in the OE and ME texts. John Hart provides a useful summary of the situation in the 1560s in *An Orthographie*

> I will brieflye write of distinction or pointing. . . . For it sheweth us how to rest: when the sentence continueth . . .
>
> The first marked thus , the Greekes call comma , for which the Latines and other vulgares haue used a strike thus / . . . alwayes signifying the sentence unfinished.
>
> The second marked thus : the Greekes call colon. . . . And the last of these three is a pricke thus . to signifie the ende of a full and perfite sentence.

He also describes the *Parenthesis* ( ), the *interrogatiue* ?, and the *admiratiue* !

15.7 Loan-words 1500–1549

15.7.1 *French*

minion	*mignon*	**1501**	scene	*scène*	**1540**
trophy	*trophée*	**1513**	sally (n)	*saillie*	**1542**
pioneer	*pionnier*	**1523**	baton	*bâton*	**1548**
pilot	*pillotte*	**1530**	colonel	*coronnel*	**1548**
anatomy	*anatomie*	**1540**	machine	*machine*	**1549**

15.7.2 Scandinavian

scud	(*obscure*)	**1532**
scrag	(*obscure*)	**1542**

15.7.3 Low German

hawker	*hoker*	**1510**	cambric	*Kameryk*	**1530**
dock	*docke*	**1513**	snap (vb)	*snappen*	**1530**
wagon	*wagen*	**1523**	rove	*roven*	**1548**
uproar	*oproer*	**1526**			

15.7.4 Latin

legal	*legalis*	**1500**	dissident	*dissidentem*	**1534**
consolidate	*consolidare*	**1511**	imitate	*imitari*	**1534**
alienate	*alienatus*	**1513**	area	*area*	**1538**
genius	*genius*	**1513**	expectation	*expectationem*	**1538**
impersonal	*impersonalis*	**1520**	peninsula	*peninsula*	**1538**
appropriate	*appropriatus*	**1525**	gradual	*gradualis*	**1541**
habitual	*habitualis*	**1526**	malignant	*malignantem*	**1542**
insinuation	*insinuationem*	**1526**	mediate	*mediare*	**1542**
dexterity	*dexteritas*	**1527**	conspicuous	*conspicuus*	**1545**
digress	*digress-*	**1530**	extinguish	*extinguere*	**1545**
encyclopedia	*encyclopaedia*	**1531**	allusion	*allusionem*	**1548**
nervous	*nervus*	**1531**	denunciation	*denunciationem*	**1548**
resuscitate	*resuscitare*	**1532**	incumbent	*incumbentem*	**1548**
excrescence	*excrescentia*	**1533**	notorious	*notorius*	**1548**
folio	*folio*	**1533**	orbit	*orbita*	**1548**

15.7.5 Italian

From the 16th century onwards many loan-words were adopted from Italian, especially in the vocabulary of music and painting.

milliner	*Milan + -er*	**1529**	carnival	*carnevale*	**1549**
artichoke	*articiocco*	**1531**	cupola	*cupola*	**1549**
algebra	*allegro*	**1541**	gondola	*gondola*	**1549**
ballot	*ballotta*	**1549**			

15.7.6 Spanish

galleon	*galeon*	**1529**
armada	*armada*	**1533**
sherry	(*vino* de) *Xeres*	**1540**

15.7.7 Arabic

arsenal	It *arzenale* fr Arabic *dar accinakah*	**1506**
algebra	It *algebra* fr Arabic *al-jebr*	**1541**

15.7.8 Celtic

pillion	Irish *pillín*, Gaelic *pillin* – a saddle	**1503**
bog	Irish or Gaelic *bogach* – a bog	**1505**
plaid	Gaelic *plaide*	**1512**
caber	Gaelic *caber*	**1513**
slogan	Gaelic *sluagh-ghairm* (from *sluagh* host + *gairm* cry, shout); original meaning *war-cry*	**1513**
galloglass	Irish and Gaelic *gall-oglch*, from *gall* – foreigner, stranger + *oglch* – youth; a class of retainers formerly maintained by Irish chiefs	**1515**
metheglin	Welsh *meððyglyn* healing + *llyn* liquor, mead	**1533**
cairn	Gaelic *carn*	**1535**
coracle	Welsh *corwgl*	**1547**

16. Early Modern English III – the 16th century (ii)

16.1 The development of the standard language

We saw in earlier chapters that there was no ME standard language, but a number of inter-related dialects. English today consists of a much greater number of inter-related dialects, spread throughout the world, but in England people now tend to regard the Standard English dialect as 'the English language', and may look on the other regional and social dialects as substandard or inferior. Hence they talk of 'good English' or 'correct English', and devalue the status of the regional dialects.

This point of view is not new, of course, and we have seen evidence of concern over the differences between the dialects at least as far back as the 14th century, in John of Trevisa's discussion of the language (Texts 57 and 58). Both Chaucer in the 1380s and Caxton in the 1480s refer to the 'diversity' of the English language.

First to develop was a written standard. Educated men and women wrote in the standard but many continued to speak in the dialect of their region. John Aubrey, writing in the mid-17th century, says of Sir Walter Raleigh (1552–1618),

> Old Sir Thomas Malett, one of the Justices of the King's bench *tempore Caroli I et II*, knew Sir Walter, and I have heard him say, that notwithstanding his so great Mastership in Style and his conversation with the learnedest and politest persons, yet he spake broad Devonshire to his dying day.

Aubrey perhaps implies that this was unusual, and that gentlemen in his time did not speak in regional dialects at court. There is also the hint that dialect does not somehow fit with learning and polite behaviour.

We have already noted in chapter 14 how, by the end of the 15th century, there is less and less evidence in printed books and in manuscripts of the range of dialects of English. Regional and social varieties still flourished, as they do today, but the evidence for them is much more difficult to find. There are no written records of colloquial speech as authentic as sound-recording makes possible for present-day English. The language of informal letters or the dialogue of characters in prose drama are probably the nearest we can get to everyday speech of the time.

16.1.1 'The best and most perfite English'

John Hart in *An Orthographie* insisted that writing should represent speech, 'we must be ruled by our speech'. But he also recognised the problem that the diversity of dialects posed in using his new alphabet to write English as it sounded – whose dialect do you choose?

Text 112 – John Hart's *An Orthographie* – the speech of 'the learned sort'

Notwithstanding, he should haue a wrong opinion of me, that should thinke by the premisses, I ment any thing shoulde be printed in London in the maner of Northerne or Westerne speaches: but if any one were minded at Newcastell uppon Tine, or Bodman in Cornewale to write or print his minde there, who should iustly blame him for his Orthographie, to serue hys neyghbours according to their mother speach, yea, though he wrate to London, to whomsoeuer it were, he could be no more offended to see his writing so, than if he were present to heare him speake: and there is no doubt, but that the English speach, which the learned sort in the ruled Latin, togither with those which are acquainted with the vulgars Italian, French, and Spanish doe vse, is that speach which euery reasonable English man, will the nearest he can, frame his tongue therevnto: but such as haue no conference by the liuely voice, nor experience of reading, nor in reading no certaintie how euery letter shoulde be sounded, can neuer come to the knowledge and vse, of that best and moste perfite English: which by Gods grace I will the neerest I can follow, leauing manye an Inckhorne terme (which I could vse) bicause I regarde for whose sake I doe it.

This is clear evidence of Hart's advocacy of educated London speech as 'the best and most perfite', spoken by 'euery reasonable English man'.

16.1.2 'The vsuall speach of the Court'

George Puttenham's advice to writers about choosing the best variety of English was briefly quoted in section 12.1. Here is a longer extract which illustrates his awareness of the range of available regional and social varieties before Standard English was a fully accepted and defined variety.

Activity 16.1

(i) Describe the assumptions about language which are evident in the text. Comment particularly on:
   (a) his use of the word *corruptions* to describe changes in a language;
   (b) the reference to a language which is *naturall*, *pure* and *the most vsuall*;
   (c) his contrasting of *good townes and Cities* with other places;
   (d) his references to *the inferiour sort* of men and women;
   (e) the attitude implied in *any speach vsed beyond the riuer of Trent*.

(ii) Are Puttenham's attitudes still current today?

Text 113 – George Puttenham on the best language, from Book III, Chapter IIII, *Of the Arte of English Poesie*, 1589 (facsimile)

But after a ſpeach is fully faſhioned to the common vnderſtanding, & accepted by conſent of a whole countrey & natiō, it is called a language, & receaueth none allowed alteration, but by extraordinary occaſions by little & little, as it were inſenſibly bringing in of many corruptiōs that creepe along with the time: ....

This part in our maker or Poet muſt be heedyly looked vnto, that it be naturall, pure, and the moſt vſuall of all his countrey: and for the ſame purpoſe rather that which is ſpoken in the kings Court, or in the good townes and Cities within the land, then in the marches and frontiers, or in port townes, where ſtraungers haunt for traffike ſake, or yet in Vniuerſities where Schollers vſe much peeuiſh affectation of words out of the primatiue languages, or finally, in any vplandiſh village or corner of a Realme, where is no reſort but of poore ruſticall or vnciuill people: neither ſhall he follow the ſpeach of a craftes man or carter, or other of the inferiour ſort, though he be inhabitant or bred in the beſt towne and Citie in this Realme, for ſuch perſons doe abuſe good ſpeaches by ſtrange accents or ill ſhapen ſoundes, and falſe ortographie. But he ſhall follow generally the better brought vp ſort, ſuch as the Greekes call [*charientes*] men ciuill and graciouſly behauoured and bred. Our maker therfore at theſe dayes ſhall not follow *Piers plowman* nor *Gower* nor *Lydgate* nor yet *Chaucer*, for their language is now out of vſe with vs: neither ſhall he take the termes of Northern-men, ſuch as they vſe in dayly talke, whether they be noble men or gentlemen, or of their beſt clarkes all is a matter: nor in effect any ſpeach vſed beyond the riuer of Trent, though no man can deny but that theirs is the purer Engliſh Saxon at this day, yet it is not ſo Courtly nor ſo currant as our Southerne Engliſh is, no more is the far Weſterne mās ſpeach: ye ſhall therfore take the vſuall ſpeach of the Court, and that of London and the ſhires lying about London within lx. myles, and not much aboue. I ſay not this but that in euery ſhyre of England there be gentlemen and others that ſpeake but ſpecially write as good Southerne as we of Middleſex or Surrey do, but not the common people of euery ſhire, to whom the gentlemen, and alſo their learned clarkes do for the moſt part condeſcend, but herein we are already ruled by th'Engliſh Dictionaries and other bookes written by learned men, and therefore it needeth none other direction in that behalfe.

Condescend to meant adjust to – that is, gentlemen everywhere could speak 'good Southerne', but talked to the common people in dialect.

Puttenham was expressing a point of view which is probably common in all societies. There is evidence earlier in the 16th century in the books on spelling and grammar which Puttenham mentions, that 'diversity' in the language worried writers and scholars. The implications of this point of view are, however, more serious, because it is not limited simply to specifying a choice of language for writers:

- Varieties of the language are marked by social class and education. Social classes speak differently and can be recognised by their speech. Written and spoken English have prestige varieties.
- Once a written standard language also becomes the norm for speech in the educated class, the division between that class and regional dialect speakers is complete.

Such differences of language are a part of every society, but in different degrees. Standardisation of language is a necessary development in a society, but brings with it social consequences which are, therefore, the background to our continuing study of the development of Early Modern English in the 16th and 17th centuries.

16.2 Evidence for some 16th-century varieties of English

16.2.1 *National dialects*

The dialogue of characters in plays cannot be taken as completely authentic evidence of the spoken language, but may indicate the more obvious dialectal features of speech. In Shakespeare's *The Life of Henry the Fift* there are comic episodes involving four captains – Gower, Fluellen, Mackmorrice and Iamy. Their names give them away as an Englishman, a Welshman, an Irishman and a Scotsman.

Activity 16.2

Describe the dialectal features of the characters' speech which is indicated by the spelling, vocabulary and syntax of the dialogue.

📖 Activity 16.2 is discussed in the *Text Commentary Book*.

Text 114 – Shakespeare's *The Life of Henry the Fift* (facsimile)

Enter Gower.

Gower. Captain *Fluellen*, you muſt come preſently to the Mines; the Duke of Glouçeſter would ſpeak with you.

Flu. To the Mines? Tell you the Duke, it is not ſo good to come to the Mines: for look you, the Mines are not according to the Diſciplines of War; the Concavities of it is not ſufficient: for look you, th' athverſary, you may diſcuſs unto the Duke, look you, is digt himſelf four yards under the Countermines: by *Cheſhu*, I think a will plow up all, if there is not better directions.

Gower. The Duke of *Glouceſter*, to whom the Order of the Siege is given, is altogether directed by an Iriſh man, a very valiant Gentleman, I'faith.

Welch. It is Captain *Makmorrice*, is it not?

Gower. I think it be.

Welch. By *Cheſhu* he is an Aſs, as in the World, I will verifie as much in his Beard: he ha's no more directions in the true diſciplines of the Wars, look you, of the *Roman* diſciplines, than is a Puppy-dog.

Enter. Makmorrice, *and Captain* Jamy.

Gower. Here a comes, and the *Scots* Captain, Captain *Jamy*, with him.

Welch. Captain *Jamy* is a marvellous valorous Gentleman, that is certain, and of great expedition and knowledge in th'aunchiant Wars, upon my particular knowledge of his directions; by *Cheſhu* he will maintain his Argument as well as any Militarie man in the World, in the Diſciplines of the priſtine Wars of the *Romans*.

Scot. I ſay gudday, Captain *Fluellen*.

Welch. Godden to your Worſhip, good Captain *James*.

Gower. How now, Captain *Makmorrice*, have you quit the Mines? have the Pioners given o're?

Iriſh. By Chriſh, Law, tiſh ill done: the Work iſh give over, the Trompet ſound the Retreat. By my Hand I ſwear, and my father's Soul, The Work iſh ill done: it iſh give over: I would have blowed up the Town, ſo Chriſh ſave me, law, in an hour. O tiſh ill done, tiſh ill done: by my Hand tiſh ill done.

Welch. Captaine *Makmorrice*, I beſeech you now, will you vouchafe me, look you, a few diſputations with you, as partly touching or concerning the diſciplines of the War, the *Roman* Wars, in the way of Argument, look you, and friendly communication: partly to ſatisfie my Opinion, and partly for the ſatisfaction, look you, of my Mind, as touching the direction of the Military diſcipline, that is the Point.

Scot. It ſall be vary gud, gud feith, gud Captens bath, and I ſall quit you with gud leve, as I may pick occaſion: that ſal I marry.

Iriſh. It is no time to diſcourſe, ſo Chriſh ſave me: The day is hot, and the Weather, and the Wars, and the King, and the Duke: it is not time to diſcourſe, the Town is beſeech'd: and the Trumpet calls us to the Breach, and we talk, and by Chriſh do nothing, 'tis ſhame for us all: ſo God ſa'me 'tis ſhame to ſtand ſtill, it is ſhame by my hand: and there is Throats to be cut, and Works to be done, and there iſh nothing done, ſo Chriſt ſa'me law.

Scot. By the Mes, ere theiſe eyes of mine take themſelves to ſlomber, ayle de gud ſervice, or Ile ligge i'th' grund for it; ay, or go to death: and Ile pay't as valorouſly as I may, that ſal I ſurely do, the breff and the long; marry, I wad full fain heard ſome queſtion 'tween you tway.

16.2.2 Using thou/thee and ye/you

The grammatically singular forms *thou/thee* and plural *ye/you* were used as markers of social difference. A superior used *thou* to an inferior, who had to address his superior with *you.* A friendly relationship was also marked in this way. You began to use *thou* when you reached a more intimate relationship with a person. We have lost this distinction in most parts of England, although *tha/thee* is still used in West Yorkshire speech.

This social meaning of *thou* and *ye* had been established well before the 16th century. Here is an example from the 1390s in Chaucer's 'The Knight's Tale'. Arcite, in prison, addresses the gods Mars and Juno at first with *thow* as individuals, and then with *youre* as a pair. Immediately he goes on to address his absent love Emelye, whom he has seen but not yet met, with *ye*. He is the suppliant, and she is far above him in his estimation, so *thow* would be not be appropriate, as it would mark an established intimacy:

> Allas ***thow*** felle Mars, allas Iuno,
> Thus hath ***youre*** ire oure lynage al fordo...
> ***Ye*** sleen me with ***youre*** eyen, Emelye,
> ***Ye*** been the cause wherfore that I dye

Elsewhere in *The Canterbury Tales* the Host addresses the Cook with *thou*,

> Now tel on, gentil Roger, by ***thy*** name
> But yet I praye ***thee*** be nat wrooth for game...

but uses *ye* to the Monk, his social superior,

> Now telleth ***ye***, sire monk, if that ***ye*** konne...

In the following extract from Shakespeare's *Much Adoe About Nothing*, Don Pedro and Claudio are unaware that their friend Benedicke has been told to 'kill Claudio', so they indulge in witty cross-talk in which Benedicke does not join.

Activity 16.3

Discuss the evidence for the misunderstanding in the relationship between Claudio and Benedicke from their use of the pronouns *you* or *thee/thou*.

Text 115 – Shakespeare's *Much Adoe About Nothing*, Scene 14 (Act 5, Scene 1)

DON PEDRO	See see, heere comes the man we went to seeke.
CLAUDIO	Now signior, what newes?
BENEDICKE	(*to Don Pedro*) Good day my Lord.
DON PEDRO	Welcome signior, **you** are almost come to parte almost a fray.

CLAUDIO Wee had likt to haue had our two noses snapt off with two old men without teeth.

DON PEDRO Leonato and his brother what thinkst **thou**? had we fought, I doubt we should haue beene too yong for them.

BENEDICKE In a false quarrell there is no true valour, I came to seeke **you** both.

CLAUDIO We haue beene vp and downe to seeke **thee**, for we are high proofe melancholie, and would faine haue it beaten away, wilt **thou** vse thy wit?

BENEDICKE It is in my scabberd, shal I drawe it?

DON PEDRO Doest **thou** weare thy wit by thy side?

CLAUDIO Neuer any did so, though very many haue been beside their wit, I will bid **thee** drawe, as wee doe the minstrels, draw to pleasure vs.

DON PEDRO As I am an honest man he lookes pale, art **thou** sicke, or angry?

CLAUDIO What, courage man: what though care kild a catte, **thou** hast mettle enough in **thee** to kill care.

BENEDICKE Sir, I shall meete **your** wit in the careere, and **you** charge it against me, I pray **you** chuse another subiect.

CLAUDIO Nay then giue him another staffe, this last was broke crosse.

DON PEDRO By this light, he chaunges more and more, I thinke he be angry indeed.

CLAUDIO If he be, he knowes how to turne his girdle.

BENEDICKE (*aside to Claudio*) Shall I speake a word in **your** eare?

CLAUDIO God blesse me from a challenge.

BENEDICKE You are a villaine, I ieast not, I will make it good howe **you** dare, with what **you** dare, and when **you** dare: doe me right, or I will protest **your** cowardise: **you** haue killd a sweete Lady, and her death shall fall heauie on **you**, let me heare from **you**.

CLAUDIO Well I wil meet **you**, so I may haue good cheare.

DON PEDRO What, a feast, a feast?

CLAUDIO I faith I thanke him he hath bid me to a calues head & a capon, the which if I doe not carue most curiously, say my kniffe's naught, shall I not find a woodcoke too?

BENEDICKE Sir **your** wit ambles well, it goes easily.

DON PEDRO Ile tell **thee** how Beatrice praisd thy witte the other day: I said **thou** hadst a fine witte, true said she, a fine little one: no said I, a great wit: right saies she, a great grosse one: nay said I, a good wit, iust said she, it hurts no body: nay said I, the gentleman is wise: certaine said she, a wise gentleman: nay said I, he hath the tongues: that I beleeue said shee, for he swore a thing to me on munday night, which hee forswore on tuesday morning, theres a double tongue theirs two tongues, thus did shee an houre together trans-shape thy particular vertues, yet at last she cōcluded with a sigh, **thou** wast the properst man in Italy.

CLAUDIO For the which shee wept heartily and saide she cared not.

DON PEDRO Yea that she did, but yet for all that, and if she did not hate him deadly, she would loue him dearely, the old mans daughter told vs all.

CLAUDIO All all, and moreouer, God sawe him when he was hid in the garden.

DON PEDRO But when shall we set the sauage bulles hornes on the sensible Benedicks head?

CLAUDIO Yea and text vnder-neath, here dwells Benedick the married man.

BENEDICKE Fare **you** wel, boy, **you** know my minde, I wil leaue **you** now to **your** gossep-like humor, **you** breake iests as braggards do their blades, which God be thanked hurt not: (*to Don Pedro*) my Lord, for **your** many courtisies, I thanke **you**, I must discontinue **your** company, **your** brother the bastard is fled from Messina: **you** haue among **you**, kild a sweet and innocent lady: for my Lord Lacke-beard there, hee and I shal meet, and till then peace be with him. (*exit*)

DON PEDRO He is in earnest.

CLAUDIO In most profound earnest, and ile warrant **you**, for the loue of Beatrice.

DON PEDRO	And hath challengde **thee**.
CLAUDIO	Most sincerely.
DON PEDRO	What a pretty thing man is, when he goes in his dublet and hose, and leaues off his wit!

📖 A detailed commentary is in the *Text Commentary Book*.
(Section 17.3.4. discusses George Fox on *thee/thou* in the mid-17th century.)

16.2.3 *Regional dialects*

By the end of the 16th century the educated language of London was clearly established as the standard for writing in England, so that there is little evidence of the regional dialects apart from occasional references. Here is another extract from Richard Verstegan's *A Restitution of Decayed Intelligence* (see Text 108) which gives us just a little information. He is discussing 'alteration and varietie' in related languages like Danish, Norwegian and Swedish, and is saying that they do not borrow 'from any extrauagant language' (the word *extrauagant* here meant *outside the boundaries*, that is, *foreign*):

Text 116 – Richard Verstegan (1605) on regional dialects (facsimile)

This is a thing that eaſely may happen in ſo ſpatious a toung as this, it beeing ſpoken in ſo many different countries and regions, when wee ſee that in ſome ſeueral partes of *England* it ſelf, both the names of things and pronountiations of woords are ſomwhat different, and that among the countrey people that neuer borrow any woords out of the Latin or French, and of this different pronountiation one example in ſteed of many ſhal ſuffiſe, as this: for pronouncing according as one would ſay at *London*, **I would eat more cheeſe yf I had it**, the northern man ſaith, **Ay ſud eat mare cheeſe gin ay hadet**, and the weſterne man ſaith: **Chud eat more cheeſe an chad it.** Lo heer three different pronountiations in our own countrey in one thing, & heerof many the lyke examples might be alleaged.

Activity 16.4

Identify and describe the differences between the three dialectal sentences quoted in Text 116:

I would eat more cheese yf I had it.
Ay sud eat mare cheese gin ay had et.
Chud eat more cheese an chad it.

There is little evidence of contemporary regional dialect in Shakespeare's plays, but an example can be found in *The Tragedie of King Lear*. Edgar, the Duke of Gloucester's son, banished by King Lear, disguises himself as a madman – a Tom a Bedlam. The speech he assumes is often inconsequential but not obviously dialectal, for example,

> Away, the fowle fiend followes me, thorough the sharpe hathorne blowes the cold wind, goe to thy cold bed and warme thee.

but at one point, defending his blinded father, his speech becomes clearly dialectal for one short episode:

Activity 16.5

(i) Which of Richard Verstegan's examples of dialect in Text 116 does Edgar's speech resemble?

(ii) The scene of the play is set in Kent. The words *ice try* stand for *I sal try*. *Sal* for *shall* and *gate* for *way* are both Northern forms. Is Shakespeare accurately reproducing a regional dialect?

(iii) Describe the differences in Edgar's language, when he is talking to Gloster and the Steward, which mark it as a dialect.

(iv) Explain the changing use of the 2nd person pronouns *thou/thee/thine* and *ye/you/your.*

Text 117 – Shakespeare's *The Tragedie of King Lear* (facsimile)

Gloster does not recognise Edgar as his son, and cannot see him. The Steward believes Edgar to be a beggar.

Glou. Now good Sir, what are you?
Edg. A moſt poor man, made tame to fortunes blows
Who, by the Art of known, and feeling ſorrows,
Am pregnant to good pitty. Give me your hand,
I'le lead you to ſome hiding.
Glou. Hearty thanks:
The bounty, and the benizon of Heaven
To boot, and boot.

Enter Steward.

Stew. A proclaim'd prize: moſt happy:
That eyeleſs head of thine, was firſt fram'd fleſh
To raiſe my fortunes. Thou old, unhappy traitor,
Briefly thy ſelf remember: the Sword is out
That muſt deſtroy thee.
Glou. Now let thy friendly hand
Put ſtrength enough to't.
Stew. Wherefore, bold Peazant,
Darſt thou ſupport a publiſh'd traitor? hence,
Leſt that th'infection of his fortune take
Like hold on thee. Let go his Arm.
Edg. Chill not let go Zir,
Without vurther caſion.
Stew. Let go, Slave, or thou dy'ſt.
Edg. Good Gentleman go your gate, and let poor volk paſs: and'chud ha'been zwagged out of my life, 'twould ha'been zo long as 'tis, by a vortnight. Nay, come not near th'old man: keep out che vor'ye, or ice try whither your Coſtard, or my Ballow be the harder; chill be plain with you.
Stew. Out Dunghil.
Edg. Child pick your teeth Zir: come, no matter vor your foyns.
Stew. Slave thou haſt ſlain me: villain, take my purſe;
If ever thou wilt thrive, bury my body,
And give the Letters which thou find'ſt about me,
To *Edmud* Earl of *Gloſter*: ſeek him out
Upon the Engliſh party. Oh untimely death, death.
Edg. I know thee well. A ſerviceable Villain,
As duteous to the vices of thy Miſtris,
As badneſs would deſire.
Glou. What, is he dead?
Edg. Sit you down Father: reſt you.

16.2.3.1 *Commentary*

Edgar's dialect

Chill not let goe Zir without vurther casion
chill be plain with you
Chill* picke your teeth Zir

* Folio has *Child.*

The initial ⟨ch⟩ represents the 1st person singular pronoun (MnE *I*), and is the consonant /tʃ/ of OE *ic*, ME *ich*. The vowel has been elided, and the word is attached to its following verb in *chill*/*I will.*

and '**chud** ha' bin zwagged out of my life...

and here means *if*, a common usage in ME and EMnE; '*chud* is *I would/should*; *zwagged* is used to mean *forced by blustering language.*

keep out **che** vor'ye...

Che is the dialectal form of the pronoun *I.*

Zir, vurther, volk, zwagged, zo, vortnight, vor all show the same feature of pronunciation. The initial voiceless fricative consonants [s] and [f] of *Sir, further, folk, swagged, so, fortnight* are all voiced. This was the pronunciation in all the dialects of the South at the time, and is still to be heard in the South West of England in rural dialects. *Vor* is perhaps a reduced form of *warn*?

Casion is *occasion*; *Costard* originally meant *apple*, but was used jokingly for *head*. *Ballow* appears to be a misprint for *batton* or *baton*. The *Oxford English Dictionary* says,

> Only in the Shakespeare. Folio of 1623, and subsequent editions, where the Quartos have *battero*, and *bat* (*stick, rough walking-stick*); besides which, *batton, battoun*, (*stick, cudgel*) is a probable emendation.

The scene in the play is set in Kent, and the dialectal features described so far probably fit. But in *ice try*, *ice* presumably represents the pronunciation *I sal* for *I shall*, and *gate* means *way*. Both of these are Northern forms, so it looks as if Shakespeare was using a few easily recognisable conventions for indicating a 'rustic' character, and not accurately reproducing Kentish.

These Northern forms, using [s] for Southern [ʃ] in *shall* can be seen in Text 114 from *The Life of Henry the Fift* in the speech of the Scots Captain Iamy:

It **sall** be vary gud... I **sall** quit you... that **sall** I mary

whereas the Irishness of Captain Mackmorrice is marked by his use of [ʃ] for [s] or [z] in two words only, *Christ* and *is*:

By **Crish** Law **tish** ill done: the Worke **ish** giue ouer...

Thou/thee and you

The *Lear* text illustrates the supposed inferiority of Edgar, playing the part of a poor beggar, in relation to the Steward. Hence Edgar uses *you/your* as well as *Zir* and *good Gentleman* to show respect and an inferior social position, while the Steward addresses Edgar with *thou/thee/thine* to match the contemptuous *bould Pezant*, *Slaue* and *Dunghill*. On the death of the Steward, Edgar resumes his normal rank, and so addresses the body with 'I know *thee* well'. Speaking to Gloster, the Steward uses *thou*, in spite of Gloster's rank, as a form of insult in the circumstances in which he finds him and Edgar.

16.3 English at the end of the 16th century

Reading texts from the 16th century onwards, we find fewer and fewer features of vocabulary and grammar which are archaic and unfamiliar, and it becomes more difficult to specify exactly what differences there are between older and contemporary English. This is especially so if the spelling of older texts is modernised. Facsimiles or exact reproductions make the language look more unfamiliar than it really is. But it is worth trying to sum up the principal differences between English in 1600 and Standard English today. Many of them have already been described in relation to the printed texts.

16.3.1 *Spelling and punctuation*

OE and ME ⟨þ⟩ is no longer in use, except in the conventional abbreviations for *the* and *that*, ⟨y^{e}⟩ and ⟨y^{t}⟩. ⟨u⟩ and ⟨v⟩ are still used for both vowel [u] and consonant [v], determined by their position in the written or printed word. Similarly, long and short ⟨s⟩ continue to be written and printed according to their position in the word.

Letter ⟨j⟩ is not yet in general use for the consonant, only as a variant of letter ⟨i⟩. Letters ⟨i⟩ and ⟨y⟩, are generally interchangeable for the vowel [i]. The redundant final ⟨e⟩ is still added to many words, long after the unstressed vowel [ə] has disappeared. The comma ⟨,⟩, colon ⟨:⟩ and full-stop (prick) ⟨.⟩ are used, with question and exclamation marks ⟨?⟩, ⟨!⟩. The virgule or strike ⟨/⟩ was no longer in general use by 1600. The apostrophe ⟨'⟩ to mark the possessive has not yet appeared.

16.3.2 *Pronunciation*

The raising or diphthongisation of long vowels in the South and Midlands (the Great Vowel Shift) has taken place, but is not yet complete. For some time, until after the 16th century, there were no words with the long back vowel [ɑː]. ⟨ee⟩ words were generally pronounced [iː], ⟨ea⟩ words [eː] or [ɛː], ⟨oo⟩ words [uː] and ⟨oa⟩ words [oː], but there was considerable irregularity and variation. Many words spelt with ⟨ea⟩ and ⟨oo⟩ were pronounced with either a long or a short vowel in different dialects. This diversity led to a growing demand for **regularity** and **standardisation**.

16.3.3 *Vocabulary*

The assimilation of large numbers of classical Latin and Greek words into the written language had been made easy because of the previous borrowing of hundreds of French words. At the same time, numbers of new prefixes and suffixes were also taken into the language, and used with English words, for example,

prefixes		***suffixes***	
circum-	non-	-able	-ant}-ent
co-	pre-	-acy	ate
dis-	re-	-age	-ess
en-}em-	semi-	-al	-ician
inter-	sub-	-ance	-ise
	-ancy/-ency		-let

Words had been borrowed from several other languages, as the end-of-chapter lists of examples of loan-words show (see sections 15.7 and 16.4). Some were adopted through travel and exploration, others from foreign literature and culture. Many were borrowed indirectly, via another language.

16.3.4 *Grammar*

In general terms, the grammar of 16th-century English is that of Modern English, and only a few features mark it as an earlier form.

Personal pronouns

Both 2nd person pronouns, *thou/thee/thy/thine* and *ye/you/your*, and the neuter pronouns *hit/his* were still in use. The unstressed form *a*, written for *he* in Shakespeare's *The Life of Henry the Fift*, when Mistress Quickly describes Falstaff's death, probably reproduces a common spoken form.

> . . . ***a*** made a finer end, and went away and it had beene any Christome Childe: ***a*** parted eu'n iust betweene Twelue and One . . . and ***a*** babeld of greene fields . . . so ***a*** cryed out, God, God, God, three or foure times . . . so ***a*** bad me lay more Clothes on his feet . . .

Relative pronouns

That and *which* were most common, and *which* was used with a human subject – *Our Father* **which** *art in heaven . . .*, but *who/whom* began to be used in the late 16th century.

Verbs

- In the verb phrase, the **modal system** was established, with the verbs *will/would, shall/should, can/couthe ~ coude, dare/durst, may/might ~ mought* and *mote/must*.
- The **passive** was fully in use.

- **Perfect aspect** was expressed with *have*, and also with *be* when the verb was intransitive, e.g. *I **am** come*. Some complex verb phrases were recorded but they were still to develop in general use.
- The **3rd person singular present tense** was marked by both ⟨-eth⟩ (the Southern form) and ⟨-s⟩ (the Northern form), e.g.

> Beautie ***doth*** varnish Age, as if new borne,
> And ***giues*** the Crutch the Cradles infancie.
> O tis the Sunne that ***maketh*** all thinges shine.
>
> *Loues Labours Lost*, Act IV, Sc. 3

but ⟨-s⟩ eventually became standard. The *King James Bible* of 1611 kept the old-fashioned ⟨-eth⟩ suffix, as the translation was based upon the early 16th century translations of Tyndale and Coverdale. Poets continued to use both forms, because they provided different metrical and syllabic patterns. There is evidence in William Bullokars' *Booke at Large* (1570) that both the ⟨-eth⟩ and ⟨-s⟩ suffixes were acceptable:

> And, s, for, eth, may chaũged be
> to yield som vers his grace truly.

Interrogatives and negatives

The inversion of subject and verb in the simple present and past for the interrogative was still common – *knowest thou?, came he?* – *but the MnE form with do* had also come into use – *dost thou know?, did he come?*

Similarly, the negative *not* was still used with inversion – *I know not* – but was now also used with *do* – *I do not know*. It is at about this time that the multiple negative ceased to be standard usage, though it was and still is normal usage in the dialects.

There *and* it

The filling of the subject slot in a clause with the 'dummy' *there* or *it* had been established well before the beginning of the century, e.g. in Chaucer,

> With vs ***ther was*** a doctour of phisik
> In al this world ne was ther noon hym lik...
> ***It is nat*** honeste, ***it may noght*** auance
> For to deelen with no swich poraille...

and this led to the loss of the OE and ME **impersonal verb** constructions without a subject, such as,

> ***Me thynketh*** it acordant to resoun...
> A yeman he hadde and seruantz namo
> At that tyme for ***hym liste*** ryde so.

which were replaced with *It seems to me*... and *It pleased him to ride so*.

Nouns

The plural with ⟨-s⟩ or ⟨-es⟩ was the regular form, and most ⟨-en⟩ forms like *eyren* (*eggs*) and *shoon* (*shoes*) had gone, at least from literary language.

16.4 Loan-words 1550–1599

16.4.1 *French*

chamois	*chamois*	**1560**	vase	*vase*	**1563**
gauze	*gaze*	**1561**	combat	*combat*	**1567**
grotesque.	*crotesque*	**1561**	genteel	*gentile*	**1599**

16.4.2 *Scandinavian*

rug	*rogg*	**1551**	snag	*snag*	**1577**
simper	(*obscure*)	**1563**	scuffle	*skuff*	**1590**
skit	*? skytja*	**1572**	snug	(*obscure*)	**1595**
wad	(*obscure*)	**1573**	scrub	(*obscure*)	**1596**

16.4.3 *Low German*

spatter	*spatten*	**1582**	split	*splitten*	**1590**
reef (rocks)	*rif*	**1584**	frolic	*frolicken*	**1593**
snip	*snippen*	**1586**	muff	*mof*	**1599**

16.4.4 *Latin*

medium	*medium*	**1551**	strict	*strictus*	**1578**
demonstrate	*demonstrare*	**1552**	catastrophe	*Gk καταστροφή*	**1579**
denominate	*denominare*	**1552**	interregnum	*interregnum*	**1579**
prodigious	*prodigiosus*	**1552**	rostrum	*rostrum*	**1579**
superintendent	*superintendere*	**1554**	compendium	*compendere*	**1581**
external	*externus*	**1556**	omen	*omen*	**1582**
insane	*insanus*	**1560**	janitor	*janua + -tor*	**1584**
meditate	*meditari*	**1560**	expostulation	*expostulationem*	**1586**
urge	*urgere*	**1560**	emulate	*aemulari*	**1589**
eradicate	*eradicare*	**1564**	quarto	*quarto*	**1589**
dire	*dirus*	**1567**	critical	*criticus*	**1590**
decorum	*decorum*	**1568**	horrid	*horridus*	**1590**
calculate	*calculare*	**1570**	militia	*militia*	**1590**
nasturtium	*nasturtium*	**1570**	radius	*radius*	**1597**
excursion	*excursionem*	**1574**	sinus	*sinus*	**1597**
vast	*vastus*	**1575**	pathetic	*patheticus*	**1598**
hereditary	*hereditarius*	**1577**	delirium	*delirium*	**1599**
ignoramus	*ignoramus*	**1577**	excavate	*excavare*	**1599**
vagary	*vagari*	**1577**	stratum	*stratum*	**1599**

16.4.5 *Italian*

sonnet	*sonetto*	**1557**	madonna	*madonna*	**1584**
manage	*maneggiare*	**1561**	madrigal	*madrigale*	**1588**
tarantula	*tarantola*	**1561**	motto	*motto*	**1589**

scope	*scopo*	**1562**	duo	*duo*	**1590**
squadron	*squadrone*	**1562**	garb	*garbo*	**1591**
lottery	*lotteria*	**1567**	balloon	*ballone*	**1592**
argosy	*Ragusea*	**1577**	bandit	*bandito*	**1593**
mountebank	*montimbanco*	**1577**	belladonna	*bella donna*	**1597**
violin	*violino*	**1579**	bravo	*bravo* (*villain*)	**1597**
parapet	*parapetto*	**1583**	stucco	*stucco*	**1598**
piazza	*piazza*	**1583**	macaroni	*maccaroni*	**1599**

The following words from Italian are first recorded in Shakespeare's *Love's Labours Lost* (1588):

pedant	pedante	III. i. 179, I that haue beene.... A domineering **pedant** ore the Boy.
stanza	stanza	IV. ii. 107 Let me heare a staffe, a **stanze**, a verse, *Lege domine*...

16.4.6 *Spanish*

The number of loan-words from Spanish increases during the second half of the 16th century. A significant number from this time onwards are taken from American Spanish (Mexico and southern USA).

apricot	*albaricoque*	**1551**	sarsaparilla	*zarzaparrilla*	**1577**
cannibal	*canibales*	**1553**	corral	*corral*	**1582**
canoe	*canoa*	**1555**	mosquito	*mosquito*	**1583**
hammock	*hamaca*	**1555**	renegade	*renegado*	**1583**
hurricane	*huracan*	**1555**	maize	*maiz*	**1585**
iguana	*iguana*	**1555**	tobacco	*tabaco*	**1588**
Negro	*negro*	**1555**	peccadillo	*pecadillo*	**1591**
tornado	*tronada*	**1556**	mulatto	*mulato*	**1595**
brocade	*brocado*	**1563**	rusk (bread)	*rosca*	**1595**
potato	*patata*	**1565**	punctilio	*puntillo*	**1596**
alligator	*al lagarto*	**1568**	sombrero	*sombrero*	**1598**
armadillo	*armadillo*	**1577**	bravado	*bravada*	**1599**
bastinado	*bastonada*	**1577**	cedilla	*cedilla*	**1599**

The word *anchovy* (Spanish *anchova*) is first recorded in 1596 in Shakespeare's *1 Henry IV*, II.iv.588:

Item, **Anchoues**, and Sacke after Supper, ij*s*. vi*d*.

16.4.7 *Portuguese*

The number of loan-words directly from Portuguese is relatively small, but the dictionary lists many words as 'from Spanish or Portuguese', which are two closely related languages.

apricot	*albricoque*	**1551**	copra	*copra*	**1584**
flamingo	*flamengo*	**1565**	buffalo	*bufalo*	**1588**
molasses	*melaço*	**1582**	palanquin	*palanquim*	**1588**
			mandarin	*mandarim*	**1589**

One of the earliest written uses of the word *madeira* for the wine named after the island Madeira is in Shakespeare's *I Henry IV*, I.ii.128:

A Cup of **Madera**, and a cold Capons legge.

16.4.8 *Russian*

The first loan-words from Russian that are commonly known appear in the latter half of the 16th century. Most borrowings are used in a context that refers to or describes Russian affairs, and so remain relatively unassimilated in their reference.

kvass	*kvas* – a beer made from rye	**1553**
rouble	*ruble* – the unit of currency	**1554**
czar/tsar	*tsar*	**1555**
muzhik	*muzhik* – a Russian peasant	**1568**
boyar	*boy·rin* – a former order of Russian aristocracy	**1591**

The next Russian loan-words are recorded in the 18th century (section 19.10.8).

16.4.9 *Arabic*

magazine	Fr *magasin* fr Arabic *makhazin*	**1583**
monsoon	Du *monssoen* fr Arabic *mausim*	**1584**
jar (vessel)	Fr *jarre* fr Arabic *jarrah*	**1592**

Loan-words taken directly from Arabic:

sheikh	*shaikh*	**1577**
muezzin	*mu'aððin*	**1585**
mufti – Muslim priest	*mufti*	**1586**
coffee	*qahwah*	**1598**
hashish	*hashish*	**1598**
sash	*shash*	**1599**

16.4.10 *Celtic*

trews	Irish *trius*, Gaelic *triubhas* – trousers, breeches	**1568**
shamrock	Irish *seamrog*	**1571**
brogue	Irish and Gaelic *brog* – shoe	**1586**
gillie	Gaelic *gille* a lad, servant – an attendant on a Highland chief	**1596**

17. Early Modern English IV – the 17th century (i)

In chapters 14–16 we have been following the establishment of educated London English as a standard language. Although all varieties of 17th- and 20th-century writing are clearly contrasted in style, the underlying grammatical differences between 17th-century and present-day English are relatively small, so there are fewer developments in the grammar to record. As the spelling of words becomes more and more regular, the look of the printed page becomes more familiar, though we still find less conformity to a standard spelling and punctuation in handwriting until the mid-18th century. The vocabulary is, of course, always losing and gaining words according to the needs of communication.

The remaining chapters of the book therefore consist of a series of texts which provide some typical examples of the uses of the language – ordinary uses, letters and diaries for example, and examples of literary prose both colloquial and rhetorical, together with sections on some of the evidence for changes in pronunciation during the century.

17.1 Evidence for changes in pronunciation

All living languages are in a constant state of change in their grammar and vocabulary. The grammar of a standard language, however, changes slowly, because new forms tend to be resisted, and the very fact of its being standard means that it is regarded as fixed and unchangeable.

At the same time as the establishment of a standard in vocabulary and grammar, social standards of pronunciation are also set up, and the speech of those with prestige or authority is imitated by others. In this way there is a polarisation of opinion in attitudes to language use, which is derived from differences of social class and education. In the 17th and 18th centuries rural and artisan speech was referred to as *barbarous*, meaning *uncultured* or *unpolished* as against *polite* or *civilised*. The Dean of Canterbury in 1864 referred to 'persons of low breeding and inferior education' who 'leave out the aspirate' and are therefore below the mark in intelligence (see Text 182, section 21.2).

In England today, if a man or woman were said to have 'a good accent', we would understand that they spoke in Received Pronunciation (RP). It is sometimes asserted that such speech 'has no accent', and to say of someone that 'she speaks with an accent' is to imply a nonstandard or regional way of speaking.

The evidence for pronunciation in the 17th century is much less easy to interpret than that for the vocabulary, spelling and grammar, in spite of a series of books on spelling and pronunciation, because unlike today, there was no International Phonetic Alphabet (IPA) to provide an agreed reference for the relationship of sounds to letters. Other evidence comes from a study of the rhymes in poetry. Some of this evidence is discussed in section 18.3.2.

17.1.1 *Occasional spellings in handwritten sources*

Another indirect source of knowledge about changing pronunciation is in the spelling of written manuscripts. Printers in the 17th century tended to regularise spelling more and more, even though there were still variations and no fixed standard spelling yet. In letters, however, even educated writers sometimes used 'phonetic' spellings, and these provide some clues to their pronunciation. The concept of a 'spelling mistake' had not yet been established.

Here is a small selection of 'occasional spellings' which are evidence of differences in pronunciation. The range of differences in dialectal pronunciation would have been much greater then than now. People moved from all parts of the country into London, and their varieties of dialectal accent were in competition with each other for acceptability. Sometimes it was the 'vulgar' speech which eventually became the social standard.

The following activity is designed to show the kind of evidence which scholars draw upon in building up their knowledge of changes in the language. The words do not come from any one particular social class. The ME source, the spelling found in a written 17th-century source, and the MnE reflex are given for each word.

Activity 17.1 – vowels

What changes in the pronunciation of the vowels do the spellings of each group show?

ME	*17th-century writing*	*MnE reflex*
[aː]		[ei]
came	**ceme**	came
cradel	**credyll**	cradle
take	**teke**	take
[eː]		[iː]
semed	**symed**	seemed
stepel	**stypylle**	steeple
[ɛː]		[iː]
discrete	**discrate**	discreet
retrete	**retrate**	retreat

[ʊɪ] or [ɔɪ]		**[ɔɪ]**
joinen	**gine**	join
puisun/poisoun	**pyson**	poison
rejoissen	**regis**	rejoice
[iː]		**[ai]**
defiled/defyled	**defoyled**	defiled
[ɛr]		**[äː]**
certein	**sarten**	certain
derþe	**darth**	dearth
diuert	**divart**	divert
lernen	**larne**	learn
merci	**marcy**	mercy
persoun	**parson**	person/parson

Although consonants are more stable than vowels, there have been a number of changes for which there is evidence in written letters.

Activity 17.2 – consonants

Describe any changes of pronunciation in the consonants indicated by the spelling in these words:

ME	*17th-century writing*	MnE reflex
doughter	**dafter**	daughter
boght	**boft**	bought
fasoun	**fessychen**	fashion
instruccion	**instrocshen**	instruction
issu/issue	**ishu**	issue
suspecious	**suspishious**	suspicious
seute/siute	**sheute**	suit
morsel	**mosselle**	morsel
persoun	**passon**	person/parson
portion	**posshene**	portion
scarsliche	**skasely**	scarcely
excepte	**excep**	except
often	**offen**	often
wastcotte	**wascote**	waistcoat
linnene	**lynand**	linen
los	**loste**	loss
syns	**synst**	since
vermine	**varment**	vermin/varmint

There is a commentary on Activities 17.1 and 17.2 in the *Text Commentary Book*.

17.1.2 *Evidence of change from musical settings*

Sir Walter Raleigh's poem *What is our life?* was set to music by Orlando Gibbons in 1612. The first two lines are,

> What is our life? a play of passion,
> Our mirth the music of division . . .

The music sets *passion* to three syllables on separate notes, *pas/si/on*, and *division* to four, *di/vi/si/on*, so the pronunciation of the words must have been ['pæsi,on] and [dɪ'vɪzi,on], with secondary stress on the final syllable [on]. The reduction of the last two syllables led to today's pronunciation, ['pæʃən] and [dɪ'vɪʒən]. The loss of secondary stress in many words marks one of the differences between 16th- and 17th-century pronunciation and today's.

17.1.3 *Evidence of change from verse*

Hundreds of lines of verse were written in the late 16th and early 17th centuries by William Shakespeare, Ben Jonson and other dramatists, using the iambic pentameter line (see section 13.2.1), which in its regular form consists of ten syllables of alternating unstressed and stressed syllables, as in Raleigh's poem and in these lines of Shakespeare,

> What / **say** you, / **can** you / **loue** the / **Gen** tle / **man**?
> This / **night** you / **shall** be / **hold** him / **at** our / **feast**

This gives us the patterning of stressed syllables in words of two or more syllables, and shows whether the distribution of stress has since changed. For example, the word *proportion* in these lines,

> I thought King Henry had resembled thee,
> In Courage, Courtship, and Proportion:

must have four syllables to complete the second line:

> In / **Cour**- age / **Court**- ship / **and** Pro / **por**- ti- / **on**

and reinforces the musical evidence about the pronunciation of *passion* and *division*.

Activity 17.3

What is the stress pattern of the italicised words in the following lines from Shakespeare, and in present-day speech?

1 . . . I do *coniure* thee,
Who art the Table wherein all my thoughts
Are visibly *Character'd* . . .
2 Ay, and peruersly, she *perseuers* so:
3 Goe to thy Ladies graue and call hers thence,
Or at the least, in hers, *sepulcher* thine.
4 Madam: if your heart be so *obdurate*:
Vouchsafe me yet your Picture for my loue,
5 Nephew, what meanes this passionate *discourse*?
6 She beares a Dukes *Reuenewes* on her back,
And in her heart she scornes our Pouertie:
7 *Pernitious* Protector, dangerous Peere . . .
8 Away: Though parting be a fretfull *corosiue*,
It is *applyed* to a deathfull wound.
9 Close vp his eyes, and draw the Curtaine close,
And let vs all to *Meditation*.
10 Is it for him you do *enuie* me so?

17.2 Sir Thomas Browne

Sir Thomas Browne (1605–1682), after studying medicine on the Continent, practised as a physician in Norwich for the rest of his life, but he is remembered today as a writer. His first book *Religio Medici* ('the faith of a doctor') had been written as 'a private Exercise directed to myself', but a pirated edition had been published 'in a most depraved Copy', so he decided to publish his own version.

The book explores the tension that then existed between religious faith and new scientific ideas. This conflict had been expressed earlier by John Donne in 1611,

And new Philosophy calls all in doubt,
The Element of fire is quite put out;
The Sun is lost, and th'earth, and no mans wit
Can well direct him where to looke for it . . .
'Tis all in peeces, all coherence gone;
All just supply, and all Relation.
(*An Anatomy of the World*)

17.2.1 *Religio Medici*

The following short extract from *Religio Medici* expresses Sir Thomas Browne's religious faith:

Text 118 – Sir Thomas Browne's *Religio Medici*, 1642

As for those wingy Mysteries in Divinity, and airy subtleties in Religion, which have unhing'd the brains of better heads, they never stretched the *Pia Mater** of mine. Methinks there be not impossibilities enough in Religion for an active faith; the deepest Mysteries ours contains have not only been illustrated, but maintained, by Syllogism† and the rule of Reason. I love to lose my self in a mystery, to pursue my Reason to an *O altitudo*! 'Tis my solitary recreation to pose my apprehension with those involved Ænigma's and riddles of the Trinity, with Incarnations, and Resurrection. I can answer all the Objections of Satan and my rebellious reason with that odd resolution I learned of *Tertullian, Certum est quia impossibile est*‡.

* *Pia Mater* – a membrane in the brain.

† *Syllogism* – a logical argument consisting of two propositions and a conclusion.

‡ *Certum est quia impossibile est* – Latin for *It is certain because it is impossible.*

The lexical vocabulary of Text 118 is listed in the *Word Book*.

Students of literature today value Browne's writings for their style rather than for their content, and style is of interest to students of language too, in showing how a writer exploits and expands the resources of the language of the time.

17.2.2 *Vulgar Errors 1646*

Sir Thomas Browne's learning is illustrated in the volumes of *Pseudodoxia Epidemica, or Enquiries into very many received tenents and commonly presumed truths*, which are more popularly known as *Vulgar Errors* – *vulgar* in the sense of *common*. He examines a variety of beliefs which were commonly held, in the light of authority (what had been written about the subject), rational thought, and experience. The outcome is often, to a modern reader, quaint and amusing, but the book gives us valuable insights into the 'world view' of the early 17th century, still largely a late Medieval view in spite of the beginnings of scientific experiment at that time.

17.2.2.1 *Of Sperma-Ceti*

The following extract shows the alternation of direct observation and appeal to antiquarian authorities (now long since forgotten), which he applies to the problem, 'what is spermaceti?', a substance found in whales, and used both in medicine and the manufacture of candles. Notice also his literal acceptance of the Old Testament account of Jonah and the whale. (This is the second of three texts on the whale – see Text 48 from the medieval *Bestiary* and Text 133 from John Evelyn's *Diary*.)

Activity 17.4

(i) Divide the lexical words into two sets, formal and core vocabulary, using your own judgement. Then look up the derivation of the words and see if there is any correlation between formality and derivation.

(ii) Discuss how the grammatical structures that Browne uses tend to make the style of his writing formal and unlike ordinary speech.

Text 119 – Sir Thomas Browne's *Vulgar Errors*

Of Sperma-Ceti, and the Sperma-Ceti Whale.

What Sperma-Ceti is, men might justly doubt, since the learned *Hofmannus* in his work of Thirty years, saith plainly, *Nescio quid sit**. And therefore need not wonder at the variety of opinions; while some conceived it to be *flos maris*†, and many, a bituminous substance floating upon the sea.

That it was not the spawn of the Whale, according to vulgar conceit, or nominal appellation‡ Phylosophers have always doubted, not easily conceiving the Seminal humour of Animals§, should be inflamable; or of a floating nature.

That it proceedeth from a Whale, beside the relation of *Clusius*, and other learned observers, was indubitably determined, not many years since by a Sperma-Ceti Whale, cast upon our coast of *Norfolk*. Which, to lead on further inquiry, we cannot omit to inform. It contained no less then sixty foot in length, the head somewhat peculiar, with a large prominency over the mouth; teeth only in the lower Jaw, received into fleshly sockets in the upper. The Weight of the largest about two pound: No gristly substances in the mouth, commonly called Whale-bones; Only two short finns seated forwardly on the back; the eyes but small, the pizell large, and prominent. A lesser Whale of this kind above twenty years ago, was cast upon the same shore.

The discription of this Whale seems omitted by *Gesner*, *Rondeletius*, and the first Editions of *Aldrovandus*; but describeth the latin impression of *Pareus*, in the Exoticks of *Clusius*, and the natural history of *Nirembergius*; but more amply in Icons and figures of *Johnstonus*...

Out of the head of this Whale, having been dead divers days, and under putrifaction, flowed streams of oyl and Sperma-Ceti; which was carefully taken up and preserved by the Coasters. But upon breaking up, the Magazin of Sperma-Ceti, was found in the head lying in folds and courses, in the bigness of goose eggs, encompassed with large flakie substances, as large as a mans head, in form of hony-combs, very white and full of oyl... And this many conceive to have been the fish which swallowed *Jonas*. Although for the largeness of the mouth, and frequency in those seas, it may possibly be the *Lamia*.

Some part of the Sperma-Ceti found on the shore was pure, and needed little depuration¶; a great part mixed with fetid oyl, needing good preparation, and frequent expression, to bring it to a flakie consistency. And not only the head, but other parts contained it. For the carnous parts being roasted, the oyl dropped out, an axungious|| and thicker parts subsiding; the oyl it self contained also much in it, and still after many years some is obtained from it...

* *nescio quid sit* – Latin for *I do not know what it is.*

† *flos maris* – Latin for *a flower of the sea.*

‡ *nominal appellation* – a name given without reference to fact.

§ *Seminal humour* – sperm; *humour* meant *a body fluid.*

¶ *depuration* – purifying.

|| *axungious* – greasy, like lard.

17.2.2.2 *Commentary*

Formal vocabulary

Sir Thomas Browne's writing is highly 'literary' or 'formal'. Our judgement of the formality or informality of a text is subjective, and neither word can be precisely defined, but we can probably reach a consensus on most of the formal words in this text in terms of

- their unfamiliarity, or
- their relative infrequency of use, or
- the context in which they are usually used.

The following list of formal vocabulary from Text 119 is based on a personal reaction to the text, and is therefore open to any reader to discuss and amend or criticise. The list omits words like *men*, *work*, *saith*, *years*, *weight*, *mouth*, *shore*, *first*, *head*, *dead*, *taken*, *large*, *oil*, which are short, familiar and common and so belong to the 'core vocabulary'. We want to find out whether there is any linguistic evidence to explain a selection that is based only on intuitive judgement.

amply	Editions	humour	observers	putrifaction
Animals	encompassed	Icons	obtained	received
appellation	Exoticks	impression	omit	relation
axungious	expression	indubitably	peculiar	Seminal
bituminous	fetid	inflamable	Phylosophers	sockets
carnous	figures (*n*)	inform	preparation	spawn (*n*)
conceived	fleshly	inquiry	preserved	Sperma-Ceti
consistency	forwardly	learned (*adj*)	proceedeth	subsiding
contained	frequency	Magazin	prominency	substance
depuration	frequent (*adj*)	nominal	prominent	vulgar
describeth	gristly			

Only one word comes directly from OE (*flæsclic*). Three others are later ME or EMnE derivations from OE word-stems, *learned* (*adj*) (1340), *gristly* (1398) and *forwardly* (1552). Only two other words were recorded before the 14th century – *divers* and *socket*.

Thirty-three words are from French (62%) and sixteen from Latin or Greek (30%). The figures for the earliest occurrence of the words is as follows:

OE	1.8%	***15th C***	21.4%
13th C	3.6%	***16th C***	28.6%
14th C	33.9%	***17th C***	10.7%

We can therefore suggest a hypothesis, for which there is some evidence to support our intuitive classification of the formal words in the text: *that words classified as formal tend to be those which were taken into English from French, Latin or Greek from the 14th century onwards.*

All the formal vocabulary consists of lexical words – nouns, verbs, adjectives or adverbs. The complete text contains 442 words (tokens) , some of them occurring more than once, giving a total of total of 231 different words (types). The structure of a text is held together by the function words – pronouns, determiners, conjunctions, and prepositions – which almost all derive from Old English and form a small closed class of words. These function words make up about two-fifths of the vocabulary of the text.

📖 A complete list of the lexical vocabulary of Text 119 with dates and derivations is in the *Word Book*.

Formal syntax

Choice of vocabulary is important, but words alone do not make up language use. The way they are ordered into sentences in writing is an essential feature of the style of the writing, and is usually correlated with the lexical choices. Grammatical complexity is often a feature of formality of style. Clauses may be embedded into other clauses or phrases and made subordinate to another clause. Each level of the grammar – sentences, clauses, phrases and words – may be coordinated together. The normal, unmarked order of the elements of a declarative clause (one that makes a statement) is,

Subject (S) – Predicator (P) – Complement (C) or Object (O) – Adverbial (A).

If the normal order of a clause is changed, then this may be stylistically significant too, and the focus of information in the clause is altered. The potential for variety and complexity of style is great. We can take the first sentence as an example:

What Sperma-Ceti is, men might justly doubt, since the learned *Hofmannus* in his work of Thirty years, saith plainly, *Nescio quid sit*.

Main clause	**O – NCl**	**S**	**P=**	**A**	**–P**
	[What Sperma-Ceti is],	men	might	justly	doubt,
	theme				

The grammatical object of the verb in this opening main clause (MCl) is itself an embedded clause, *[What Sperma-Ceti is]* , functioning like a noun, and therefore a noun clause (NCl) and comes first, so the question *What Sperma-Ceti is* is made grammatically prominent and announces the theme of both the clause and the text. The 'unmarked order' of the clause constituents is:

S	**P**	**O = NCl**	**A**
Men	might doubt	[what Sperma-Ceti is]	justly

This main clause is followed by an adverbial clause which includes the Latin quoted clause *Nescio quid sit - I don't know what it is*, functioning as the object of *saith*.

	scj	**S**	**A**	**P**	**A**
AdvCl (quoting)	[since	the learned *Hofmannus*	in his work of Thirty years,	saith	plainly],
	O				
quoted clause	[*Nescio quid sit*].]]				

The grammar of the text is marked by similar kinds of complexity, with the re-ordering and embedding of clause elements.

A list of the lexical vocabulary of Text 119 is in the *Word Book*, and a more detailed grammatical analysis in the *Text Commentary Book*.

17.2.2.3 Of the Badger

It was a 'vulgar error' of the times that a badger's legs were longer on one side than the other. Sir Thomas Browne discusses this.

Activity 17.5

Discuss the distribution of words of OE, French and Latin derivation, and their effect upon the style of the writing.

Text 120 – Sir Thomas Browne's *Of the Badger*

The Third Book, Ch V.
Of the Badger

That a Brock or badger hath the legs on one side shorter then of the other, though an opinion perhaps not very ancient, is yet very general; received not only by Theorists and unexperienced believers, but assented unto by most who have the opportunity to behold and hunt them daily. And for my own part, upon indifferent enquiry, I cannot discover this difference, although the regardable side be defined, and the brevity by most imputed unto the left.

Again, It seems no easie affront unto reason, and generally repugnant unto the course of Nature; for if we survey the total set of Animals, we may in their legs, or Organs of progression, observe an equality of length, and parity of Numeration; that is, not any to have an odd legg, or the supporters and movers of one side not exactly answered by the other. Perfect and viviparous quadrupeds, so standing in their position of proneness, that the opposite points of Neighbour-legs consist in the same plane; and a line descending from their Navel intersects at right angles the axis of the Earth...

📖 There is a list of the lexical vocabulary of the text in the *Word Book*.

Text 120 is recorded on the cassette tape.

ɔv ðə bædʒər

ðæt ə brɔk ɔr bædʒər hæθ ðə lɛgz ɒn oːn səid ʃɔrtər ðɛn ɒv ðə ʊðər, ðoː ən ɔpɪnjɔn pərhæps nɒt vɛrɪ eːnsjənt, ɪz jɛt vɛrɪ dʒɛnərəl, rɪsiːvd nɒt ʊnlɪ bəi θiərɪsts ænd ʊnɛkspirɪənsd bɪliːvərz, bʊt asɛntɛd ʊntu bəi moːst hu hæv ðɪ ɒportjunɪti tu bɪhoːld ænd hʊnt ðəm deːli. ənd for məi oːn pɑrt, əpɒn ɪndɪfərənt ɛnkwəiri, əi kænɒt dɪskʊvər ðɪs dɪfərəns, ɔlðo: ðə rɪgɑrdəbəl səid bi dɛfəind, ænd ðə brɛvɪti bəi moːst ɪmpjutɪd ʊntu ðə lɛft. əgeːn, ɪt siːmz no izi əfrɒnt ʊntu rizən, ænd dʒɛnərəli rɪpʊgnənt ʊntu ðə kɔːrs ɒv netjur, fɔr ɪf wi sʊrve: ðə tɔtəl sɛt ɒv ænɪməlz, wi meː ɪn ðeːr lɛgz, ɔr ɔrgənz ɒv prɔgrɛsiən, ɒbsɛrv æn ɪkwalɪtɪ ɒv lɛŋθ, ænd pærɪtɪ ɒv njuməresiən, ðæt ɪz, nɒt æni tu hæv æn ɒd lɛg, or ðə səpɔrtərz ænd muːvərz ɒv oːn səɪd nɒt ɛgzæktli answərd bəi ðɪ ʊðər. pɛrfɛkt ænd vɪvɪparʊs kwadrʊpɛdz, so stændɪŋ ɪn ðeːr pɔzɪsɪən ɒv proːnːɛs, ðæt ðɪ ɒpəzɪt pɔɪnts ɒv neːbʊr lɛgz kɒnsɪst ɪn ðə seːm pleːn ænd ə ləin dɛsɛndɪŋ frɒm ðer neːvəl ɪntərsɛkts æt rəit æŋgəlz ðɪ æksɪs ɒv ðɪ ɛrθ.

17.3 George Fox's *Journal*

George Fox (1624–1691) was the son of a Leicestershire weaver. He experienced a religious conversion, an intense spiritual conviction of 'the Inner Light of Christ', and left home in 1643 to become a preacher and the founder of the Society of Friends, or Quakers. At this time, however, failure to conform to the doctrines and practice of the Church of England meant civil penalties and often persecution. He was imprisoned many times, and it was during his long stay in Worcester jail between 1673 and 1674 that he dictated an account of his experiences to his fellow prisoner Thomas Lower, who was Fox's son-in-law. The *Journal* is a moving account of his life but in addition, for students of language, an insight into everyday spoken language of the later 17th century.

17.3.1 The written Journal

Here is a short example in facsimile from the manuscript of the *Journal* in Thomas Lower's handwriting, describing events in 1663. Writing ⟨ye⟩ for ⟨the⟩ and ⟨y^{t}⟩ for ⟨that⟩ was common, the ⟨y⟩ representing the old letter ⟨þ⟩ in these conventional abbreviations.

Text 121 – George Fox's *Journal*, 1663 (facsimile)

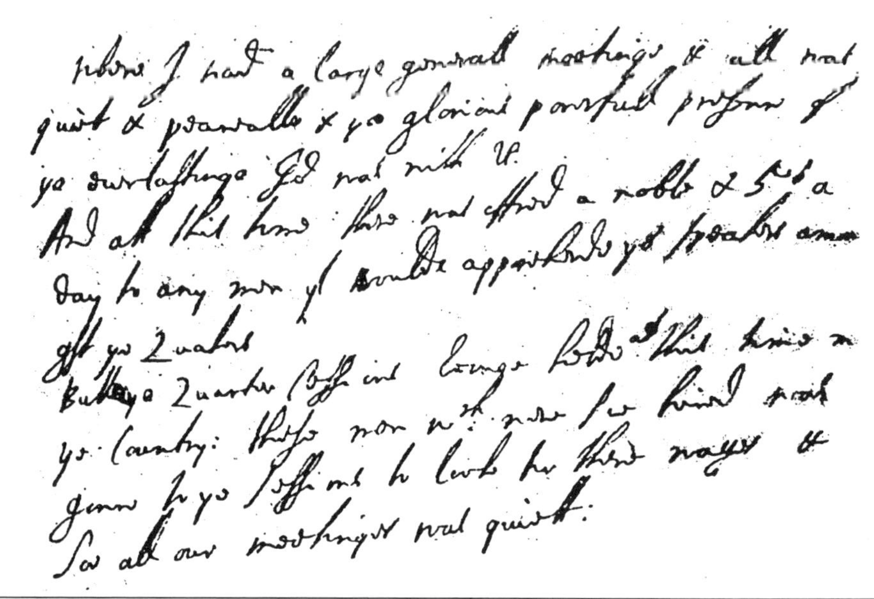

[And soe from Will: Pearsons I past through ye Countryes
visitinge freinds till I came to Pardsey Cragge]
where I had a large generall meetinge & all was
quiet & peaceable & ye glorious powerfull presence of
ye everlastinge God was with us.
And att this time there was offred a noble & 5s.a
day to any men y^{t} coulde apprehende ye speakers amon
gst ye Quakers
Butt ye Quarter Sessions beinge helde^{at}this time in
ye Country: these men wch were soe hired was
gonne to ye Sessions to looke for there wages: &
soe all our meetinges was quiett.

17.3.2 George Fox's own handwriting

The next facsimile is in Fox's own handwriting, from his account of his appearance at the Sessions in Lancaster in 1652, on a charge of blasphemy. The argument is theological, Fox often interpreting Scripture literally, and finding texts from the

Bible to support his point of view. Fox's own spelling is more individual and idiosyncratic than his son-in-law's. The references in the left margin are to New Testament texts (*Corinthians*, *Ephesians*, *2 Peter Galatians*). The letter **a** precedes Fox's answers to the charges against him – what he is alleged to have said:

Text 122 – George Fox's handwriting (facsimile)

	first that he did aferm that he had the devenety ecenshelly in him.—
Co^{rn} 6 16	**a** for the word esanshally it is a expreshon of ther one but that the seants ar the tempells of god
epef 4 6	+ god doeth dwell in them that i witnes & the criptuer doeth witnes: + if god doeth dwell in
2 Peter 1 4	them the devenety dwelleth in them + the criptuer seath ye seants shall be maed par takers of the devin nator this i witness
	2 boeth baptisme & the lords super ar unlowfull.
glash 3 27	**a** as for the word unlowfull it was not spoken by mee but the sprinkling of enfants i deny...

Some extracts follow in which Fox speaks of some of his many clashes with individuals and institutions.

17.3.3 *The origin of the name 'Quaker'*

The name 'Quaker' was at first a term of abuse, which has since been adopted by the Friends and its original connotations lost. Fox and his followers called themselves Children of the Light, Friends of Truth, or simply Friends. He described Quakers in a book called *Instructions for Right Spelling*, 1673 (see section 18.2.1):

> *Quakers*, they are in Derision so called by the Scorners of this Age; but their proper Name is, Children of the Light; and though they are accounted a Sect of Hereticks newly sprung up, by some who have rashly passed Judgment uppon them, yet upon a serious and diligent Search into their principles and Examples, they will appear to be led by a *Christian* Spirit.

George Fox explained in the *Journal* how the name Quaker came about,

> ...this was Justice Bennett of Darby y^{t} first called Us Quakers because wee bid y^{m} tremble att ye Word of God & this was in ye year 1650.

and referred to this in a letter addressed to Justice Bennett:

Text 123 – George Fox's *Journal*, 1650

Collonell Bennett that called the servants of the Lord Quakers
G.F. paper to him: Collonell bennett of darbe 1650.

...thou wast the first man in the nation that gave the people of god the name quaker And Called them quakers, when thou Examinest George in thy house att Derbey (which they had never the name before) now A Justice to wrong name people, what may the brutish people doe, if such A one A Justice of peace give names to men, but thou art Lifted upp proud and haughty and soe turnest Against the Just one given upp to misname the saints, and to make lyes for others to beeleve.

Thus saith the LORD, The heaven is my throne, and the earth is my footstool: where is the house that ye build unto me? and where is the place of my rest? For all those things hath mine hand made, and all those things have been, saith the LORD: but to this man will I look, even to him that is poor and of a contrite spirit, **and trembleth at my word.** (Isaiah Ch. 66, 1–2)

The spelling and punctuation of the written *Journal* are typical of the time in their lack of conformity to the developing printed standard, but if a transcription is made using present-day spelling and punctuation, it becomes easier to examine the features of vocabulary and grammar which mark the narrative style.

Transcription into modern spelling and punctuation

...Thou wast the first man in the nation that gave the people of God the name 'Quaker', and called them 'Quakers', when thou examine(d)st George (*Fox*) in thy house at Derby (which they had never the name before). Now, a Justice to wrong name people! What may the brutish people do, if such a one – a Justice of Peace – give names to men? But thou art lifted up proud and haughty, and so turnest against the just. (*Thou art*) one given up to misname the saints, and to make lies for others to believe ...

There can be no doubt that this is a record of speech, with its exclamation 'now A Justice to wrong name people', and the verb *wrong name*, but its only marked difference from MnE is the use of *thou* in addressing the Justice, which Fox insisted upon.

17.3.4 *Saying 'thou' to people*

The use of *thee*/*thou*/*thine* (see section 16.2.2) began to become old-fashioned and out of date in polite society during the 17th century. The grammarian John Wallis in 1653 considered that the use of *thou* was 'usually contemptuous, or familiarly caressing', and that 'custom' required the plural *you* when addressing one person. George Fox took a different view. He believed that the use of *thou* to address one person was a mark of equality between people, whereas it had long been used to mark social superiority or inferiority. So he published a pamphlet in 1660:

Text 124 – George Fox's *A Battle-Door for Teachers and Professors* (facsimile)

A

BATTLE-DOOR

FOR

TEACHERS and PROFESSORS

TO LEARN

Plural & Singular:

YOU to *Many*, and *THOU* to *One*; Singular *one*, *Thou*; Plural *many*, *You*.

AN

INTRODUCTION:

Which is, *a leading into the* BATTLE-DOOR which is, *The Entrance into* Learning.

FOr all you Doctors, Teachers, Schollars, and School-masters, that teach people in your *Hebrew*, *Greek*, *Latine*, and *English* Grammars, Plural and Singular; that is, *Thou* to one, and *You* to many, and when they learn it, they must not practiceit: what good doth your teaching do them? for he is a Novice, and an Ideot, and a fool called by *You*, that practises it; Plural, *You* to many; and Singular, *Thou* to one.

NOw People, What good doth all your giving money to these School-masters, Teachers, and Doctors, to teach your children Singular and Plural, in their Accidence, and Grammars? what good doth your learning do them, when you do not intend, that they should practice it, when they have learned it; that is, Thou *to one, and* You *to many, he is called clownish, and unmannerly, if your childe practice that which he hath learned at School, which you have paid for, he is called a Clown, and unmannerly, and ill bred.*

Fox practised what he preached, addressing Justices of the Peace as *thou*, and refusing to take off his hat in court – both of which were regarded as insulting behaviour.

Text 125 – George Fox's *Journal* – thee and thou (i)

> ...& before I was brought in before him ye garde saide It was well if ye Justice was not drunke before wee came to him for hee used to bee drunke very early: & when I was brought before him because I did not putt off my hatt & saide thou to him hee askt ye man whether I was not Mased or fonde: & I saide noe: Itt was my principle: & soe I warned him to repent & come to ye light y^{t} Christ had enlightened him withall y^{t} with it hee might see all his evill words & actions y^{t} hee had donne & acted & his ungodly ways hee had walked in & ungodly words hee had spoaken...

The next extract from the Journal describes events at Patrington in the East Riding of Yorkshire in 1651.

Text 126 – George Fox's *Journal*, 1651 – thee and thou (ii)

> ...And afterwards I passed away through ye Country & att night came to an Inn: & there was a rude Company of people & I askt ye woman if shee had any Meate to bringe mee some: & shee was somethinge strange because I saide thee & thou to her: soe I askt her if shee had any milke but shee denyed it: & I askt her if shee had any creame & shee denyed y^{t} also though I did not greatly like such meate but onely to try her.
>
> And there stoode a churne in her house: & a little boy put his hande Into ye churne & pulled it doune: & threw all ye creame In ye floore before my eyes: & soe Itt manifested ye woman to bee a lyar: & soe I walkt out of her house after ye Lord God had manifested her deceite & perversenesse: & came to a stacke of hay: & lay in ye hay stacke all night: beinge but 3 days before ye time caled Christmas in snowe & raine.

17.3.5 *The steeplehouse*

The use of a particular word may cause offence when its connotations are not shared. For George Fox, the *Church* meant *the people of God*, and he refused to use the word for the building in which religious worship took place. This, like much of Fox's preaching, his use of *thee* and *thou*, and his principled refusal to remove his hat before a magistrate, caused offence. Here is one of many references to this in his *Journal*:

Text 127 – George Fox's *Journal*, 1652 (i)

> (1652) ...And when I was at Oram before in ye steeplehouse there came a professor* & gave me a push in ye brest in ye steeplehouse & bid me gett out of ye Church: alack poore man saide I dost thou call ye steeplehouse ye Church: ye Church is ye people whome God has purchased with his bloode: & not ye house.

**professor – one who professes religion*, in Fox's view one who pretends to be religious, but is not truly so.

17.3.6 *George Fox persecuted*

The *Journal* is full of accounts of violent attacks on Fox and his followers for their faith and preaching. The following extract is typical. Barlby is about twelve miles south of York, and Tickhill about six miles south of Doncaster.

Activity 17.6

Examine the grammatical structure of the narrative, and describe those features which mark the text as written down from dictation, in contrast to, for example, Sir Thomas Browne's prose.

An analysis can be found in the *Text Commentary Book*.

Text 128 – George Fox's *Journal*, 1652 (ii)

. . . then we went away to Balby about a mile off: & the rude people layde waite & stoned us doune the lane but blessed be ye Lorde wee did not receive much hurte: & then ye next first day* I went to Tickill & there ye freinds† of y^{t} side gathered togeather & there was a meetinge‡.

And I went out of ye meetinge to ye steeplehouse & ye preist & most of ye heads of ye parish was gott uppe Into ye chancell & soe I went uppe to y^{m} & when I began to speake they fell upon mee & ye Clarke uppe with his bible as I was speakinge & hitt mee in ye face y^{t} my face gusht out with bloode y^{t} I bleade exceedingely in ye steeplehouse & soe ye people cryed letts have him out of ye Church as they caled it: & when they had mee out they exceedingely beate mee & threw me doune & threw mee over a hedge: & after dragged mee through a house Into ye street stoneinge & beatinge mee: & they gott my hatt from mee which I never gott againe.

Soe when I was gott upon my leggs I declared to y^{m} ye worde of life & showed to y^{m} ye fruites of there teachers & howe they dishonored Christianity.

And soe after a while I gott Into ye meetinge againe amongst freinds & ye preist & people comeinge by ye house I went foorth with freinds Into ye Yarde & there I spoake to ye preist & people: & the preist scoffed at us & caled us Quakers: but ye Lords power was soe over y^{m} all: & ye worde of life was declared in soe much power & dreade to y^{m} y^{t} ye preist fell a tremblinge himselfe y^{t} one saide unto him looke howe ye preist trembles & shakes hee is turned a Quaker alsoe.

* *first day* – Fox's term for *Sunday*.
† *freinds* – members of the Society of Friends.
‡ *meetinge* – the Quaker term for a religious service.

The lexical vocabulary of Texts 121–8 is listed in the *Word Book*.

17.4 John Milton

George Fox gave offence to the religious and civil authorities both during the Commonwealth under Oliver Cromwell in the 1650s, and the Restoration of Charles II after 1660. John Milton (1608–1674), on the other hand, devoted years of political activity to the Puritan cause in the 1640s and 1650s, writing books and pamphlets on behalf of, for example, religious liberty (against bishops), domestic liberty (for divorce) and civil liberty (against censorship).

One of his best-known pamphlets was *Areopagitica* (the *Areopagus* was the highest civil court of Ancient Athens), 'A Speech of Mr. John Milton for the Liberty of Vnlicenc'd Printing, to the Parlamant of England, Printed in the Yeare 1644.' It is called a speech though printed, and uses the rhetorical model of Greek and Latin oratory – as if it were written to be spoken. Its style is in complete contrast to the artless narrative of George Fox.

Text 129 – John Milton's *Areopagitica* (i) (facsimile)

be aſſur'd, Lords and Commons, there can no greater teſtimony appear, then when your prudent ſpirit acknowledges and obeyes the voice of reaſon from what quarter ſoever it be heard ſpeaking; and renders ye as willing to repeal any Act of your own ſetting forth, as any ſet forth by your Predeceſſors.

If ye be thus reſolv'd, as it were injury to thinke ye were not, I know not what ſhould withhold me from preſenting ye with a fit inſtance wherein to ſhew both that love of truth which ye eminently profeſſe, and that uprightneſſe of your judgement which is not wont to be partiall to your ſelves; by judging over again that Order which ye have ordain'd *to regulate Printing. That no Book, pamphlet, or paper ſhall be henceforth Printed, unleſſe the ſame be firſt approv'd and licenc't by ſuch*, or at leaſt one of ſuch as ſhall be thereto appointed. . . .

I deny not, but that it is of greateſt concernment in the Church and Commonwealth, to have a vigilant eye how Bookes demeane themſelves as well as men; and thereafter to confine, impriſon, and do ſharpeſt juſtice on them as malefactors: For Books are not abſolutely dead things, but doe contain a potencie of life in them to be as active as that ſoule was whoſe progeny they are; nay they do preſerve as in a violl the pureſt efficacie and extraction of that living intellect that bred them. I know they are as lively, and as vigorouſly productive, as thoſe fabulous Dragons teeth; and being ſown up and down, may chance to ſpring up armed men. And yet on the other hand unleſſe warineſſe be us'd, as good almoſt kill a Man as kill a good Book; who kills a Man kills a reaſonable creature, Gods Image; but hee who deſtroyes a good Booke, kills reaſon it ſelfe, kills the Image of God, as it were in the eye. Many a man lives a burden to the Earth; but a good Booke is the pretious life-blood of a maſter ſpirit, imbalm'd and treaſur'd up on purpoſe to a life beyond life.

Activity 17.7

Comment on the stage of development in spelling and grammar which has been reached in Text 129, in comparison with the 16th-century texts of chapters 15 and 16. Use the following examples:

Spelling and punctuation

(i) The distribution of letters ⟨u⟩ and ⟨v⟩, ⟨i⟩ and ⟨j⟩.
(ii) The distribution of long and short ⟨ſ⟩ and ⟨s⟩.
(ii) The use of ⟨-y⟩ in the spelling of *testimony*, *injury*, etc.
(iii) What does the spelling ⟨'d⟩ in *assur'd*, *treasur'd*, etc. imply about pronunciation?
(iv) What was the probable pronunciation of *armed*?
(v) Comment on these spellings:
  (a) *Bookes* and *Books*, *Booke* and *Book*;
  (b) *Dragons teeth* and *Gods Image*;
  (c) *potencie* and *efficacie*.

Grammar

(i) Comment on the grammar of,
  (a) *ye*;
  (b) *I know not* / *I deny not*;
  (c) *doe contain* / *do preserve*;
  (d) *who kills a Man kills a reasonable creature*;
  (e) *that order which ye have ordain'd* / *whose progeny they are* / *hee who destroyes*.
(ii) What is the inflection of the 3rd person singular present tense of verbs?

The second text from *Areopagitica* is often quoted as an example of the 'high style' of rhetorical writing, and for Milton's vision of an approaching Golden Age in England. Its content and imagery derive largely from the older Medieval world view.

The 'spirits' and the 'vital and rational faculties' refer to the belief that the human body contained both a 'vegetable soul', which conducted unconscious vital bodily processes, and a 'rational soul', which controlled understanding and reason.

The comparison of the Nation to an eagle depends upon an ancient 'vulgar error' which Sir Thomas Browne did not in fact discuss. The description of the eagle in a 13th-century bestiary can be found in section 7.5.

Text 130 – John Milton's *Areopagitica* (ii) (facsimile)

For as in a body, when the blood is freſh, the ſpirits pure and
vigorous, not only to vital, but to rationall faculties, and thoſe in
the acuteſt, and the perteſt operations of wit and ſuttlety,it argues
in what good plight and conſtitution the body is, ſo when the
cherfulneſſe of the people is ſo ſprightly up, as that it has,not only
wherewith to guard well its own freedom and ſafety, but to ſpare,
and to beſtow upon the ſolideſt and ſublimeſt points of controver-
ſie, and new invention, it betok'ns us not degenerated, nor droo-
ping to a fatall decay, but caſting off the old and wrincl'd skin of
corruption to outlive theſe pangs and wax young again, entring
the glorious waies of Truth and proſperous vertue deſtin'd to become great and honourable in theſe latter ages. Methinks I ſee in
my mind a noble and puiſſant Nation rouſing herſelf like a ſtrong
man after ſleep, and ſhaking her invincible locks: Methinks I ſee
her as an Eagle muing her mighty youth, and kindling her undazl'd
eyes at the full midday beam; purging and unſcaling her long abuſed ſight at the fountain it ſelf of heav'nly radiance; while the
whole noiſe of timorous and flocking birds, with thoſe alſo that
love the twilight, flutter about, amaz'd at what ſhe means, and in
their envious gabble would prognoſticat a year of ſects and ſchiſms.

Activity 17.8

Discuss the style and rhetoric of this extract.

📖 A stylistic analysis can be found in the *Text Commentary Book*.

📖 The lexical vocabulary of Texts 129 and 130 is listed in the *Word Book*.

17.5 John Evelyn's *Diary*

John Evelyn (1620–1706) travelled widely on the Continent and had a great variety of interests – he published books on engraving, tree-growing, gardening, navigation and commerce, and architecture, but is now best known for his *Diary*, which covers most of his life.

During the Civil Wars of the 1640s Evelyn was a royalist in sympathy. After the execution of King Charles I in 1649 a Commonwealth was set up, with Oliver Cromwell later named Lord Protector. One of the many ordinances or regulations imposed by the Puritan regime abolished the celebration of Christmas and other Church festivals. On Christmas Day 1657 John Evelyn went with his wife to the chapel of Exeter House in the Strand, London, where the Earl of Rutland lived. He recorded in his *Diary* what happened.

Text 131 – John Evelyn's *Diary* for 25 December 1657

I went with my Wife &c: to *Lond:* to celebrate *Christmas day*. Mr. *Gunning* preaching in *Excester* Chapell on *7: Micha 2*. Sermon Ended, as he was giving us the holy Sacrament, The Chapell was surrounded with Souldiers: All the Communicants and Assembly surpriz'd & kept Prisoners by them, some in the house, others carried away: It fell to my share to be confined to a roome in the house, where yet were permitted to Dine with the master of it, the Countesse of *Dorset*, *Lady Hatton* & some others of quality who invited me: In the afternoone came *Collonel Whaly*, *Goffe* & others from *Whitehall* to examine us one by one, & some they committed to the *Martial**, some to Prison, some Committed: When I came before them they tooke my name & aboad, examind me, why contrary to an Ordinance made that none should any longer observe the superstitious time of the *Nativity* (so esteem'd by them) I durst offend, & particularly be at *Common prayers*, which they told me was but the *Masse* in *English*, & particularly pray for *Charles stuard*, for which we had no Scripture: I told them we did not pray for *Cha: Steward* but for all *Christian Kings*, *Princes & Governors*: They replied, in so doing we praied for the K. of *Spaine* too, who was their Enemie, & a *Papist*, with other frivolous & insnaring questions, with much threatening, & finding no colour to detaine me longer, with much pitty of my Ignorance, they dismiss'd me: These were men of high flight, and above Ordinances: & spake spitefull things of our B: Lords nativity: so I got home late the next day blessed be God: These wretched miscreants, held their muskets against us as we came up to receive the Sacred Elements, as if they would have shot us at the Altar, but yet suffering us to finish the Office of Communion, as perhaps not in their Instructions what they should do in case they found us in that Action:

**Martial – Marshal*, the title of a senior Army officer.

The object of the raids on churches was political as well as religious, as the authorities were afraid of royalist plots against the government. A newspaper, *The Publick Intelligencer*, printed an account on 28 December 1657.

Activity 17.9

Compare the language of Evelyn's account of the events with that of the newspaper.

A descriptive analysis can be found in the *Text Commentary Book*.

Text 132 – *The Publick Intelligencer*, 28 December 1657

This being the day commonly called *Christmas*, and divers of the old Clergymen being assembled with people of their own congregating in private to uphold a superstitious observation of the day, contrary to Ordinances of Parliament abolishing the observation of that and other the like Festivals, and against an express Order of his Highness and his Privy-Council, made this last week; for this cause, as also in regard of the ill Consequences that may extend to the Publick by the Assemblings of ill-affected persons at this season of the year wherein disorderly people are wont to assume unto themselves too great a liberty, it was judged necessary to suppress the said meetings, and it was accordingly performed by some of the Soldiery employed to that end; who at *Westminster* apprehended one Mr *Thiss cross**, he being with divers people met together in private; In *Fleet street* they found another meeting of the same nature, where one Dr *Wilde* was Preacher; And at Exeter-house in the Strand they found the grand Assembly, which some (for the magnitude of it) have been pleased to term *the Church of England;* it being (as they say) to be found no where else in so great and so compact a Body, of which Congregation one Mr *Gunning* was the principal Preacher, who together with Dr *Wilde*, and divers other persons, were secured, to give an account of their doings: Some have since been released, the rest remain in custody at the White-Hart in the Strand, till it shall be known who they are:

**Thiss cross* was the paper's version of *Thurcross*. Timothy Thurcross was a Doctor of Divinity and priest.

The following entry in the *Diary* describes a whale that was stranded in the Thames Estuary, and is an interesting contrast to Sir Thomas Browne's account in Text 119, section 17.2.2, and that in the medieval *Bestiary* in Text 48, section 7.5.

Text 133 – John Evelyn's *Diary* for 2 and 3 June 1658

June 2. An extraordinary storme of haile & raine, cold season as winter, wind northerly neere 6 moneths.
3 A large *Whale* taken, twixt my Land butting on ye Thames & Greenwich, which drew an infinite Concourse to see it, by water, horse, Coach on foote from *Lon'd*, & all parts: It appeared first below *Greenwich* at low-water, for at high water, it would have destroy^e^d all ye boates: but lying now in shallow water, incompassd wth boates, after a long Conflict it was killed with the harping yrons, & struck in ye head, out of which spouted blood and water, by two tunnells like Smoake from a chimny: & after an horrid grone it ran quite on shore & died: The length was 58 foote: 16 in height, black skin'd like Coach-leather, very small ey^e^s, greate taile, small finns & but 2: a piked* snout, & a mouth so wide & divers men might have stood upright in it: No teeth at all, but sucked the slime onely as thro a grate made of yt bone wch we call Whale bone: The throate y^e^t so narrow, as woud not have admitted the least of fishes: The extreames of the Cetaceous bones hang downewards, from y^e^ upper jaw, & was hairy towards the Ends, & bottome withinside: all of it prodigious, but in nothing more wonderfull then that an Animal of so greate a bulk, should be nourished onely by slime, thrū those grates:

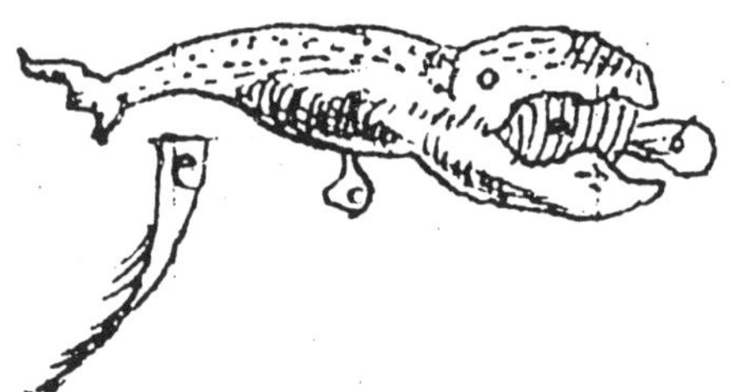

a) The bones making y^e^ grate.
b) The Tongue,c. y^e^ finn:d y^e^ Eye:
e) one of y^e^ bones making the grate (a) f y^e^ Tunnells thrı which shutting y^e^ mouth, the water is forced upward, at least 30 foote, like a black thick mist. &c:

* *piked – pointed.*

17.6 The Royal Society and prose style

The Royal Society of London for the Improving of Natural Knowledge, usually called just 'The Royal Society', was founded in 1662 under the patronage of King Charles II, who had been restored to the throne in 1660. Evelyn was a founder member of Society, whose members met regularly to present and discuss scientific papers. The poet John Dryden was also a member, and two verses of a poem called *Annus Mirabilis – The Year of Wonders 1666* contain what he called an 'Apostrophe to the Royal Society'. (An apostrophe is a term in rhetoric which means 'a figure in which a writer suddenly stops in his discourse, and turns to address some other person or thing'.)

This I fore-tel, from your auspicious care,
  Who great in search of God and nature grow:
Who best your wise Creator's praise declare,
  Since best to praise his works is best to know.
O truly Royal! who behold the Law,
  And rule of beings in your Makers mind,
And thence, like Limbecks, rich Ideas draw,
  To fit the levell'd use of humane kind.

Evelyn's diary entry on the whale shows his interest in the detailed scientific observation of natural phenomena, expressed obliquely in Dryden's poem as 'the Law and Rule of beings in your Makers mind'.

Members of the Royal Society like John Evelyn and John Dryden were dedicated to new ways of scientific thinking and experiment, and the style of writing which they began to adopt in the 1660s also changed. The following statement, about the prose style being developed by members of the Society in their scientific papers, was written by Thomas Sprat, Secretary of the Royal Society, in 1667.

Text 134 – Thomas Sprat's *The History of the Royal Society*, 1667 (facsimile)

Sect. XX. *Their manner of Diſcourſe.*

Thus they have directed, judg'd, conjectur'd upon, and improved *Experiments*. But laſtly, in theſe, and all other buſineſſes, that have come under their care; there is one thing more, about which the *Society* has been moſt ſollicitous; and that is, the manner of their *Diſcourſe*: which, unleſs they had been very watchful to keep in due temper, the whole ſpirit and vigour of their *Deſign*, had been ſoon eaten out, by the luxury and redundance of *ſpeech*. The ill effects of this ſuperfluity of talking, have already overwhelm'd moſt other *Arts* and *Profeſſions*; inſomuch, that when I conſider the means of *happy living*, and the cauſes of their corruption, I can hardly forbear recanting what I ſaid before; and concluding, that *eloquence* ought to be baniſh'd out of all *civil Societies*, as a thing fatal to Peace and good Manners.

For now I am warm'd with this juſt Anger, I cannot with-hold my ſelf, from betraying the ſhallowneſs of all theſe ſeeming Myſteries; upon which, *we Writers*, and *Speakers*, look ſo bigg. And, in few words, I dare ſay; that of all the Studies of men, nothing may be ſooner obtain'd, than this vicious abundance of *Phraſe*, this trick of *Metaphors*, this volubility of *Tongue*, which makes ſo great a noiſe in the World. But I ſpend words in vain; for the evil is now ſo inveterate, that it is hard to know whom to *blame*, or where to begin to *reform*.

They have therefore been moſt rigorous in putting in execution, the only Remedy, that can be found for this *extravagance*: and that has been, a conſtant Reſolution, to reject all the amplifications, digreſſions, and ſwellings of ſtyle: to return back to the primitive purity, and ſhortneſs, when men deliver'd ſo many *things*, almoſt in an equal number of *words*. They have exacted from all their members, a cloſe, naked, natural way of ſpeaking; poſitive expreſſions; clear ſenſes; a native eaſineſs: bringing all things as near the Mathematical plainneſs, as they can: and preferring the language of Artizans, Countrymen, and Merchants, before that, of Wits, or Scholars.

It is very clear from Thomas Sprat's attack on 'the luxury and redundance of speech' that he would have disapproved of a little book published by Joshua Pool four years before in 1663. Pool's *Practical Rhetorick* was a school text-book, and one in a long series on the subject published between the 16th and 18th centuries. Rhetoric in medieval times was the first of the three parts of a university education, with Grammar and Logic. It included *Invention* (finding new ways of expressing things) and *Disposition* (the art of ordering and interweaving themes, but the subject of Joshua Pool's book was *Elocution*, which was concerned with style, and especially with figures of speech called *tropes* and *figures*.

The first 33 pages of *Practical Rhetorick* are taken up with variations on a single short sentence – *Love ruleth all things* – which exhaustively illustrate the tropes and figures listed in the margins, as you can see from the facsimile of the first two pages below. Clearly, this is Sprat's 'superfluity of talking' which he sums up pejoratively as *eloquence* – 'this vicious abundance of *Phrase*, this trick of *Metaphors*, this volubility of *Tongue*, which makes so great a noise in the World'.

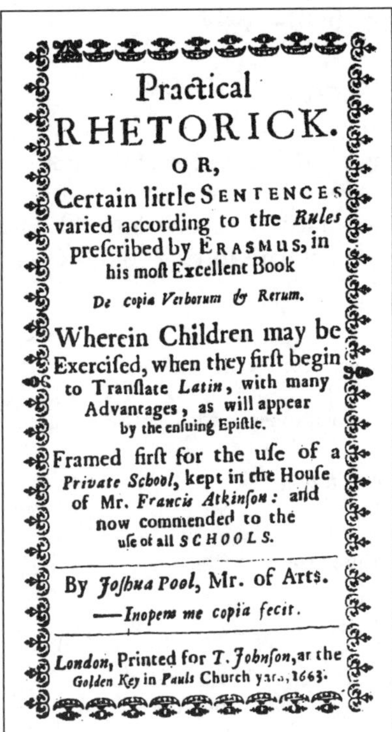

Practical
RHETORICK.
OR,
Certain little SENTENCES varied according to the *Rules* preſcribed by ERASMUS, in his moſt Excellent Book
De copia Verborum & Rerum.

Wherein Children may be Exerciſed, when they firſt begin to Tranſlate *Latin*, with many Advantages, as will appear by the enſuing Epiſtle.

Framed firſt for the uſe of a *Private School*, kept in the Houſe of Mr. *Francis Atkinſon*: and now commended to the uſe of all SCHOOLS.

By *Joſhua Pool*, Mr. of Arts.
—*Inopem me copia fecit.*

London, Printed for *T. Johnſon*, at the *Golden Key* in *Pauls* Church yard, 1663.

Text 135 – Joshua Pool's *Practical Rhetorick*, 1663 (facsimile)

2 *Practical Rhetorick.*

Love *ruleth* all things:
All things *are ruled* by love.
Love *maſtereth* all things:
All things *are maſtered* by love.
Heterôſis (ſeu Mutatio) Numeri. Love *throws down* all before it:
All things *are thrown down* before love.
Love *conquers* every thing:
Every thing *is conquered* by love.
CUPID *overcomes* every thing:
Every thing *is overcome* by CUPID.
Periphraſis. VENUS *Son* overcomes all things:
All things are overcome by VENUS *Son*.
The blind God conquers every thing:
Every thing is conquered by that *blind God*.
CYTHEREA's *Son* quells all things:
All things are quelled by CYTHEREA's *Son*.
The PAPHIAN *Prince* ruleth all things.
All things are ruled by the PAPHIAN *Prince*.
The

Practical Rhetorick. 3

The CYPRIAN *Queen's blind boy*, ſubdues all things:
All things are ſubdued by *the* CYPRIAN *Queens blind Boy*.
Love overcometh *many* things; *Meiôſis, Tapeinôſis, ſeu Diminutio.*
Love overcometh *great* things:
Love overcometh *no few* things;
Love overcometh *no ſmall* things. *Litotes.*
All things *yield* to love: *Heterôſis, ſeu mutatio affirmativorum negativis.*
There is *nothing*, that doth *not yield* to love.
There is *nothing*, that is *not overcome* by love:
There can be *nothing*, that love doth *not overcome*.
Love *triumphs over all* things:
There is *nothing*, over which Love doth *not triumph*.
Love *reigns as Lord and King* in *all* things:
There are no *things*, in which love doth *not reign as Lord and King*.
Love *is the Conquerour* of all things: *Mutatur Verbum Nomine.*
There is nothing, of which Love is *not the Conquerour*.
Love *exerciſeth his power* in all things:
B 2 There

17.7 Loan-words 1600–1649

17.7.1 Shakespeare's Latin and Greek

William Shakespeare (1564–1616) was among the first to use the following words derived from Latin or Greek. This briefly illustrates a process of adoption from the two languages that depended on scholarship and learning, rather than social, political and economic contact with foreign countries and speakers.

1588 *apostrophe* (*L apostrophe, Gk ἀποστροφή*)
Loves Labours Lost, IV. ii. 123:
You finde not the **apostraphas**, and so misse the accent.

1590 *premeditated* (*L praemeditare*)
A Midsummer Nights Dream, V. i. 96:
Great Clearkes haue purposed
To greete me with **premeditated** welcomes.

1593 *obscene* (*L obscenus*)
Richard II, IV. i. 131:
That in a Christian Climate, Soules refiníde
Should shew so heynous, black, **obscene** a deed.

1598 *frugal* (*L frugalis*)
Merry Wives of Windsor, II. i. 28:
I was then **Frugall** of my mirth.

1601 *dexterously/dexteriously* (*L dexter + -ous + -ly*)
Twelfth Night, I. v. 66:
OLIVIA Can you do it?
CLOWN **Dexteriously**, good Madona.

1604 *accommodation* (*L accommodationem*)
Othello, I. iii. 239:
Such **Accomodation** and besort As leuels with her breeding.

1605 *assassination* (*L assassinare*)
Macbeth, I. vii. 2:
If th' **Assassination**
Could trammell vp the Consequence, and catch
With his surcease, Successe.

1605 *dislocate* (*L dislocare*)
King Lear, IV. ii. 65:
These hands..are apt enough to **dislocate** and tear
Thy flesh and bones.

1606 *indistinguishable* (*L distinguere + in- + -able*)
Troilus & Cressida, V. i. 33:
You ruinous But, you whorson **indistinguishable** Curre.

1606 *submerged* (*L submergere*)
Antony & Cleopatra , II. v. 94:
So halfe my Egypt were **submerg'd** and made
A Cesterne for scal'd Snakes.

1607 *misanthrope* (*Gk μῑσάνθρωπος*)
Timon of Athens, IV. iii. 53:
I am **Misantropos**, and hate Mankinde

17.7.2 *French*

Shakespeare's use of the following words is the earliest recorded in the *Oxford English Dictionary*:

1588 *pedant* (*Fr pédant < Ital pedante*)
Loves Labours Lost, III. i. 179:
I that haue beene . . . A domineering **pedant** ore the Boy.

1607 *reliance* (*rely < OF relier, + -iance*)
Timon of Athens, II. i. 22:
My **reliances** on his fracted dates
Haue smit my credit . . .

Other adoptions from French included:

dessert	*dessert*	**1600**	repartee	*repartie*	**1645**
invalid	*invalide*	**1642**	mêlée	*meslee*	**1648**
reveillé	*reveillée*	**1644**			

17.7.3 *Scandinavian*

troll	*troll*	**1616**	keg	*kaggi*	**1632**
oaf	*alfr*	**1625**	skittles	*?skyttel*	**1634**

17.7.4 *Low German*

knapsack	*knapsack*	**1603**	onslaught	*aanslag*	**1625**
landscape	*landschap*	**1603**	easel	*ezel*	**1634**
brandy	*brandewijn*	**1622**	drill (bore)	*drillen*	**1649**
decoy	*de kooi*	**1625**			

17.7.5 *Latin*

antipathy	*antipathia*	**1601**
premium	*praemium*	**1601**
initiate	*initiare*	**1603**
torpor	*torpere*	**1607**
transient	*transiens*	**1607**
equilibrium	*aequilibrium*	**1608**
specimen	*specimen*	**1610**
adapt	*adaptare*	**1611**
series	*serere*	**1611**
spectrum	*spectrum*	**1611**
census	*census*	**1613**
fictitious	*ficticius*	**1615**
plus	*plus*	**1615**
vertebra	*vertebra*	**1615**
assassinate	*assassinare*	**1618**
amanuensis	*amanuensis*	**1619**
tenet	*tenet*	**1619**
urban	*urbanus*	**1619**
inclement	*inclementem*	**1621**
squalor	*squalor*	**1621**
affidavit	*affidavit*	**1622**
par	*par*	**1622**
vindicate	*vindicare*	**1623**
emancipate	*emancipare*	**1625**
jocular	*jocularis*	**1626**
arena	*harena*	**1627**
apparatus	*apparare*	**1628**
expensive	*expendere*	**1628**
jurisprudence	*jurisprudentia*	**1628**
agendum	*agendum*	**1629**
veto (n)	*veto*	**1629**
fiat	*fiat*	**1631**
intimate (adj)	*intimatus*	**1632**
curriculum	*curriculum*	**1633**
forceps	*forceps*	**1634**
query	*quaere*	**1635**
atmosphere	*atmosphaera*	**1638**
formula	*forma*	**1638**
autograph	*autographum*	**1640**
onus	*onus*	**1640**
crux	*crux*	**1641**
impetus	*impetus*	**1641**
incubate	*incubare*	**1641**
focus	*focus*	**1644**
compensate	*compensare*	**1646**
datum/data	*datum*	**1646**
insignia	*insignia*	**1648**

17.7.6 *Italian*

portico	*portico*	**1605**
ghetto	*getto*	**1611**
stiletto	*stiletto*	**1611**
volcano	*volcano*	**1613**
villa	*villa*	**1615**
grotto	*grotta*	**1617**
balcony	*balcone*	**1618**
fresco	*fresco*	**1620**
ditto	*ditto*	**1625**
gala	*gala*	**1625**
manifesto	*manifesto*	**1644**
opera	*opera*	**1644**
bulletin	*bullettino*	**1645**
miniature	*miniatura*	**1645**
recitative	*recitativo*	**1645**
granite	*granito*	**1646**
gusto	*gusto*	**1647**
incognito	*incognito*	**1649**
trill	*trillo*	**1649**

17.7.7 *Spanish*

llama	*llama*	**1600**
embargo	*embargo*	**1602**
alpaca	*al paco*	**1604**
chocolate	*chocolate*	**1604**
tomato	*tomate*	**1604**
desperado	*desperado*	**1610**
sierra	*sierra*	**1613**
guitar	*guitarra*	**1621**
junta	*junta*	**1623**
cockroach	*cucaracha*	**1624**
lime (fruit)	*lima*	**1638**
castanet	*castañeta*	**1647**

17.7.8 *Portuguese*

emu	*ema*	**1613**	tank (cistern)	*tanque*	**1616**
fetish	*feitiço*	**1613**	pagoda	*pagode*	**1634**

17.7.9 *German*

hamster	*hamster*	**1607**	sauerkraut	*sauerkraut*	**1633**
plunder (vb)	*plündern*	**1632**			

17.7.10 *Urdu and Hindi*

The first words from Urdu or Hindi to be recorded in writing date from the turn of the 16th and 17th centuries. The East India Company was spreading its influence across India, leading in time to British rule of the 'Empire of India' which did not end until independence was once more achieved in 1947. Many Urdu or Hindi words written by travellers in letters and books in English about their experiences have not become well known, though you will find them in the *Oxford English Dictionary*. Most of the examples here and in following chapters relate directly to Indian life and culture. Only a few have wider currency, like *bangle*, *bungalow*, *gymkhana*, *khaki*, *pyjamas*, *chitty*, *chutney*, *dinghy*, *dungarees*, *loot*, *thug*. With the rise in popularity of Indian cooking since the 1950s, related words like *tandoori*, *biryani*, *chupatti*, *samosa*, *tikka* are now familiar.

Hindi

Hindi is the vernacular language of Northern India, spoken in many dialectal forms. The earliest words that have remained reasonably familiar include the following.

sari	*sari*	**1598**
dungaree	*dungri* – originally, a coarse calico	**1613**
guru	*guru* – teacher, priest	**1613**
chintz	*chint*	**1614**
cot (bed)	*khat*	**1634**
juggernaut	1 *Jagannath* – lord of the world – Krishna	**1638**
	The meaning has subsequently developed:	
	2 a large heavy vehicle	**1841**
	3 a heavy lorry	**1927**

Urdu and Hindustani

Hindustani was the language of the Muslim conquerors of Hindustan, and was a form of Hindi with a large admixture of Arabic and Persian words. It was also called *Urdu* – *zaban-i-urdu,* meaning 'language of the camp', that is, of the Mogul conquerors. It later became a kind of *lingua franca* over all India, varying greatly in its vocabulary according to the locality and local language.

Urdu has since 1947 been distinguished from Hindustani (the *lingua franca*) and designated as the official language of Pakistan.

toddy 1	*tari* – from *tar, palm-tree*	**1609**
	1 The sap obtained from the wild date, coconut, and palmyra, drunk in tropical countries; also, the intoxicating drink produced by fermentation	**1786**
	2 A drink of whisky or other spirits with hot water and sugar	
rupee	*rupiyah* – monetary unit of India & Pakistan	**1612**
cummerbund	*kamar-band*	**1616**
begum	*begum* – a queen, princess, or lady of high rank in Hindustan	**1634**

17.7.11 *Arabic*

gazelle	Fr *gazelle* fr Arabic *ghazal*	**1600**
assassin	Fr *assassin* fr Arabic *hashshashin*	**1603**
sherbet	Turkish *sherbet* fr Arabic *sharbah*	**1603**
zero	Fr *zéro* fr Arabic *çifr*	**1604**
alcohol	Med Lat *alcohol* fr Arabic *al-kohl*	**1615**
sequin	Fr *sequin* fr Arabic *sikkah*	**1617**
sofa	Fr *sofa* fr Arabic *soffah*	**1625**
henna	*hanna*	**1600**
imam	*imam* – the officiating priest of a Muslim mosque	**1613**
salaam	*salam* – (*as*)*salam* (*alaikum*), Peace (be upon you)	**1613**
Muslim	*muslim*	**1615**
emir	*amir*	**1625**
fetwa/fatwa	*fetwa* – A decision given by a Mufti or other Muslim juridical authority	**1625**
Koran	*quran*	**1625**
harem	*harim* – the part of a Muslim dwelling-house appropriated to the women	**1634**

17.7.12 *Celtic*

leprechaun	Irish *lupracán*	**1604**
dun (n)	Irish and Gaelic *dun* – hill, hill-fort	**1605**
Tory	1 in the 17th century, dispossessed Irish outlaws, who plundered and killed the English settlers and soldiers; later, often applied to any Irish Papist or Royalist in arms	**1646**
	2 from 1689, the name of one of the two major political parties in England, and (later) in Great Britain	**1705**

17.7.13 *Japanese*

The slow 'opening-up' of Japan to the West began in the 17th century. Almost all the loan-words are used to refer to aspects of Japanese life, with many first occurring in books of travel. One word only – *tycoon* (1857) – seems to have lost its Japanese connotations.

shogun	*shogun*, short for *sei-i-tai shogun*, 'barbarian-subduing great general'; the hereditary commander-in-chief of the Japanese army, until 1867 the virtual ruler of Japan.	**1615**

17.7.14 *Chinese*

Chinese loan-words, like Japanese, are only partly assimilated, and occur in reference to a Chinese context – social life, cooking and so on. The first recorded loan-words belong to the late 16th and early 17th century:

lychee/litchi	*li-chi*; a fruit	**1588**
sampan	*san-pan*, boat	**1620**

18. Early Modern English V – the 17th century (ii)

18.1 John Bunyan

John Bunyan (1628–1688) was the son of a Bedfordshire brass-worker, and followed his father's trade after learning to read and write in the village school at Elstow. He served in the Parliamentary army during the Civil War in the 1640s, and joined a Nonconformist church in Bedford in 1653 and preached there. His first writings were against George Fox and the Quakers. But he too came into conflict with the authorities in 1660 for preaching without a licence, and spent twelve years in Bedford jail, during which time he wrote nine books. In 1672 he returned to the same church, and was again imprisoned for a short time in 1676, when he finished the first part of *The Pilgrims Progress*. The book was published in 1678, and a second part in 1684.

The Pilgrims Progress is an allegory, in which personifications of abstract qualities are the characters. The story is in the form of a dream, in which the narrator tells of Christian's progress 'from this World to that which is to come'.

The following text, reproduced in facsimile, is from the 1678 first edition of the book. Christian's

The Pilgrims Progreſs. 183

The Pilgrims now, to gratify the Fleſh,
Will ſeek its Eaſe; but oh how they afreſh
Do thereby plunge themſelves new Grief into!
Who ſeeks to pleaſe the Fleſh, themſelves undo.

religious doubts have caused him to lose hope and fall into despair. In the terms of the allegory he and his companion Hopeful have been caught by Giant Despair and thrown into the dungeon of Doubting Castle.

Bunyan's use of the language brings us close to hearing the colloquial, everyday speech of the 1670s. It is 'the language of artizans, countrymen and merchants', not of 'wits and scholars', that Thomas Sprat commended.

The text shows us that in printed books, spelling was by now standardised in a form which has hardly changed since. There are only a few conventions which are unfamiliar, like the use of long ⟨s⟩, the capitalising of some nouns and adjectives, and the use of italics to highlight certain words. And also the absence of an apostrophe in the title – *The Pilgrims Progress.*

Text 136 – John Bunyan's *The Pilgrims Progress*, Doubting Castle (facsimile)

They ſleep in the grounds of Giant Deſpair.

Neither could they, with all the skill they had, get again to the Stile that night. Wherefore, at laſt, lighting under a little ſhelter, they ſat down there till the day brake; but being weary, they fell aſleep. Now there was not far from the place where they lay, a *Caſtle*, called *Doubting Caſtle*, the owner whereof was *Giant Deſpair*, and it was in his grounds they now were ſleeping; wherefore he getting up in the morning early, and walking up and down

He finds them in his ground, and carries them to Doubting *Caſtle.*

in his Fields, caught *Chriſtian* and *Hopeful* aſleep in his grounds. Then with a *grim* and *ſurly* voice he bid them awake, and asked them whence they were? and what they did in his grounds? They told him, they were Pilgrims, and that they had loſt their way. Then ſaid the *Giant*, You have this night treſpaſſed on me, by trampling in, and lying on my grounds, and therefore you muſt go along with me. So they were forced to go, becauſe he was ſtronger then they. They alſo had but little to ſay, for they knew themſelves in a fault. The *Giant* therefore drove them be-

The Grievouſneſs of their Impriſonment

fore him, and put them into his Caſtle, into a very dark Dungeon, naſty and ſtinking to the ſpirit of theſe two men: Here then they lay, from *Wed-*

Pſ. 88. 18.

neſday morning till *Saturday* night, without one bit of bread, or drop of drink, or any light, or any to ask how they did. They were therefore here in evil caſe, and were far from friends and acquaintance. Now in this place, *Chriſtian* had double ſorrow, becauſe 'twas through his unadviſed haſte that they were brought into this diſtreſs.

Well, on *Saturday* about midnight they began to *pray*, and continued in Prayer till almoſt break of day.

Now a little before it was day, good *Chriſtian*, as one half amazed, brake out in this paſſionate Speech, *What a fool, quoth he, am I thus to lie in a ſtinking Dungeon, when I may as well walk at liberty?* I have a *Key* in my boſom, called *Promiſe*, that will, I am perſuaded, open any Lock in *Doubting Caſtle*. Then ſaid *Hopeful*, That's good News; good Brother pluck it out of thy boſom and try:

A Key in Chriſtians, *boſom called Promiſe, opens any Lock in* Doubting *Caſtle.*

Then *Chriſtian* pulled it out of his boſom, and began to try at the Dungion door, whoſe bolt (as he turned the Key) gave back, and the door flew open with eaſe, and *Chriſtian* and *Hopeful* both came out. Then he went to the outward door that leads into the *Caſtle yard*, and with his *Key* opened the door alſo. After he went to the *Iron* Gate, for that muſt be opened too, but that Lock went *damnable* hard, yet the Key did open it; then they thruſt open the Gate to make their eſcape with ſpeed, but that Gate, as it opened, made ſuch a creaking, that it waked *Giant Deſpair*, who haſtily riſing to purſue his Priſoners, felt his Limbs to fail, ſo that he could by no means go after them. Then they went on, and came to the Kings high way again, and ſo were ſafe, becauſe they were out of his Juriſdiction.

Bunyan was not a scholar of the universities in Latin and Greek. His own use of the language was influenced by his reading of the King James Bible of 1611, but at the same time reflects popular everyday usage. We can therefore use *The Pilgrims Progress* with reasonable confidence as evidence of ordinary language use in the 1670s.

Although there has been little change in the basic grammatical patterns of the language since the 17th century, there are recognisable features of vocabulary and grammar, part of the idiom and usage of that period, which date it.

Activity 18.1

Discuss the vocabulary and grammar of the following sets of sentences from *The Pilgrims Progress*.

Text 137 – The language of *The Pilgrims Progress*

1

- his reason was, for that the Valley was altogether without *Honour*;
- ... but he could not be silent long, because that his trouble increased.
- So the other told him, that by that he was gone some distance from the Gate, he would come at the House of the *Interpreter* ...
- ...all is not worth to be compared with a little of that that I am seeking to enjoy.

2

- ...by reason of a burden that lieth hard upon me:
- The shame that attends Religion, lies also as a block in their way:
- Why came you not in at the Gate which standeth at the beginning of the way? How stands it between God and your Soul now?

3

- ...but the ground is good when they are once got in at the Gate.
- I thought so; and it is happened unto thee as to other weak men.
- So when he was come in, and set down, they gave him something to drink;
- There was great talk presently after you was gone out...

4

- Then said *Pliable*, Don't revile;
- My Brother, I did not put the question to thee, for that I doubted of the truth of our belief my self...
- Well then, did you not know about ten years ago, one *Temporary*?
- Nay, methinks I care not what I meet with in the way...
- Why came you not in at the Gate which standeth at the beginning of the way?

5

- But my good Companion, do you know the way...?
- ...dost thou see this narrow way?
- Wherefore dost thou cry?
- But now we are by our selves, what do you think of such men?
- ...how many, think you, must there be?
- Know you not that it is written...?
- Whence came you, and whither do you go?

6

- Oh, did he light upon you?
- Know him! Yes, he dwelt in *Graceless*...
- I thought I should a been killed there...
- If this Meadow lieth along by our way side, lets go over into it.
- But did you tell them of your own sorrow? Yes, over, and over, and over.
- ...the remembrance of which will stick by me as long as I live.
- Joseph was hard put to it by her...
- ...but it is ordinary for those...to give him the slip, and return again to me.
- He said it was a pitiful low sneaking business for a Man to mind Religion.
- ...let us lie down here and take one Nap.

7

- I beshrow him for his counsel;
- ...and he wot not what to do.
- Who can tell how joyful this Man was, when he had gotten his Roll again!
- The Shepherds had them to another place, in a bottom, where was a door in the side of an Hill.
- He went on thus, even untill he came at a bottom...
- ...out of the mouth of which there came in an abundant manner Smoak, and Coals of fire, with hideous noises.
- And did you presently fall under the power of this conviction?
- But is there no hopes for such a Man as this?
- They was then asked, If they knew the Prisoner at the Bar?
- ...but get it off my self I cannot
- ...abhor thy self for hearkning unto him

8

- The hearing of this is enough to ravish ones heart.
- A Lot that often falls from bad mens mouths upon good mens Names.

📖 A commentary on these sentences is in the *Text Commentary Book*.

18.2 Spelling and pronunciation at the end of the 17th century

18.2.1 *George Fox and Ellis Hookes'* Instructions for Right Spelling, *1673*

Instructions for Right Spelling is one of many books on spelling, reading and writing which were regularly published throughout the 17th and 18th centuries. One section of the book lists pairs of words 'which are alike in Sound, yet unlike in their Signification' – *homophones* – and so give us data on pronunciation changes both before and after 1673. Here is a facsimile of the frontispiece and the first two pages of homophones, which are put into simple sentences in order to clarify their meaning:

Text 138 – Fox and Hookes' *Instructions for Right Spelling*, 1673 (facsimile)

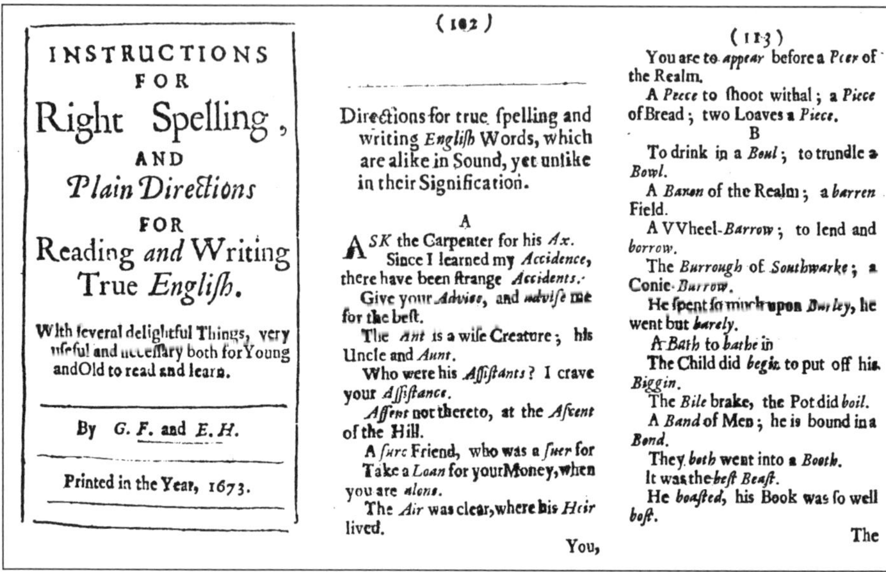

INSTRUCTIONS
FOR
Right Spelling,
AND
Plain Directions
FOR
Reading *and* Writing
True *Engliſh*.

With ſeveral delightful Things, very uſeful and neceſſary both for Young and Old to read and learn.

By *G. F.* and *E. H.*

Printed in the Year, 1673.

(102)

Directions for true ſpelling and writing *Engliſh* Words, which are alike in Sound, yet unlike in their Signification.

A

A*SK* the Carpenter for his *Ax*.

Since I learned my *Accidence*, there have been ſtrange *Accidents*.

Give your *Advice*, and *adviſe* me for the beſt.

The *Ant* is a wiſe Creature; his Uncle and *Aunt*.

Who were his *Aſſiſtants*? I crave your *Aſſiſtance*.

Aſſent not thereto, at the *Aſcent* of the Hill.

A *ſure* Friend, who was a *ſuer* for

Take a *Loan* for your Money, when you are *alone*.

The *Air* was clear, where his *Heir* lived.

You,

(113)

You are to *appear* before a *Peer* of the Realm.

A *Peece* to ſhoot withal; a *Piece* of Bread; two Loaves a *Piece*.

B

To drink in a *Boul*; to trundle a *Bowl*.

A *Baron* of the Realm; a *barren* Field.

A VVheel-*Barrow*; to lend and *borrow*.

The *Burrough* of *Southwarke*; a Conie-*Burrow*.

He ſpent ſo much upon *Barley*, he went but *barely*.

A *Bath* to *bathe* in

The Child did *begin* to put off his *Biggin*.

The *Bile* brake, the Pot did *boil*.

A *Band* of Men; he is bound in a *Bond*.

They *both* went into a *Booth*.

It was the *beſt Beaſt*.

He *boaſted*, his Book was ſo well *boſt*.

The

Here is a complete list (including those in Text 138) of the pairs of homophones in *Instructions for Right Spelling*.

Activity 18.2

(i) Identify those pairs of words that are still homophones.
(ii) Divide the data into sets according to the changes in pronunciation that have occurred.
(iii) Describe and explain the changes in each set.

A
ask / ax
accidence / accidents
advice / advise
ant / aunt
assistants / assistance
assent / ascent
sure / suer
a loan / alone
air / heir
appear / a peer
a peece / a piece

B
boul / bowl
baron / barren
barrow / borrow
burrough / burrow
barley / barely
bath / bathe
begin / biggin
bile / boil
band / bond
both / booth
best / beast
boasted / bost
bark / barque
Barbarie / barbara
bill'd / build
bald / baul'd
bad / bade
by / buy
bolt / boult
bow / bough
bore / boar
brows / browz
blew / blue
brute / bruit
bred / bread
bare / bear

C
copies / coppice
coughing / coffin
cough't / caught
chaps / chops
chare / chair / cheer
currents / corrants
cost / coast
causes / causeys
quoteth / coateth

cool'd / could
call / caul
cousin / cozen
council / counsel
cruel / crewel
crue / crew

D
deer / dear
dun / done
does / dose
device / devise
decease / disease
desert / desart

E
east / yeast
earn / yarn / yern
eat / ate
eminent / imminent

F
froise / phrase
fare / fair
fens / fence
fur / fir
form / fourm
flie / flee
feign / fain
feed / fee'd
find / fin'd
fold / foal'd
forth / fourth
furz / furs
foul / fowl
Francis / Frances
freez / freese
flower / flowr

G
guardian / garden
guess / guests
ghost / go'st
galls / gauls
gilt / guilt
glister / clyster

H
hare / hair
holy / wholy
hole / whole
hast / haste
hoop / whoop
hire / higher / hy her
here / hear
homely / homilie
hens / hence
holly / holy

I
idle / idol
eyes / ice
eye / I
ire / eyer
incite / in sight / insight

J
jet / jeat
jointer / joynture
jerking / jerkin

K
kennel / channel
knots / gnats

L
lines / loins
lane / lain
low / low (*vb*)
laught / loft
lead / led
leases / leasers
lothe / loth
lyes / lice
light (*vb*) / lite
Latine / latten
low'd / loud
least / lest
lesson / lessen
leapers / lepers
lo / low
lose (*the knot*) / loose (*his labour*)

M
meet / meat / mete
message / messuage
manner / manor
mote / moat
moan / mown
mouse / mows
mite / might
mower / more
mantle / mantil
millions / melons
Mary / marry
moles / moulds

N
neece / neese
needless / needles
neither / nether
nay / neigh
naught / nought

O
ore / oar / ower
ours / hours
of / off
own / one
ought / oft

P
pains / panes
plot / plat
principal / principle
place / plase
past / paste
price / prize
pare / pear / pair
palait? (=*palate*) / pallet
parson / person
princes / princess
praise / preys
pillars / *cater*-pillers
pride / pry'd
profit / prophet
power / pour

R
rain / reign / rein
raise / rayes
rancour / ranker
red / read
rear / rere
reason / raisin
rite / right
write / wright
rinde / Rhine
roe / row
rose (*vb*) / rose (*n*)
roes / rows
rower / roar
wrot / rot
rapt (=*rapped*) / wrapt
roads / Rhodes
room / Rome
rung / wrung / rough (*sic*)
rack / wrack
reed / read
wrought / wrote / rote
raze / raise
rasour / raiser
rest / wrest

S

savers / savors
seas / seize
ceasing / sessing
seller / cellar
centurie / centory
sheer (= *shear*) / Hampshire
cite / sight
sole / soul
sound / swoon
strait / straight
slight / sleight
succour / sucker
sum / some
sun / son
shoots / sutes / suits
sivs / sives
sithes / sighs
sower / sowr
sex / sects
steed / stead
slow / slough
seas / cease
shoes / shews
Stanes (= *Staines*) / stains
sheep / ship

T

tax / tacks
thyme / time
tide / ty'd
toe / towe
toad / toed / towed
too / two / to
treatise / treaties
then / than
thrown / throne
through / thorow
there / their
tongs / tongues
tail / tale
tomb / tome

V

vein / vain
viol / vial
vale / vail
vacation / vocation
victuals / vital

W

weight / wey / way
wait / weight
were / wear / ware
wast / waste
wrest / wrist
wist / wisht

Y

yew / you
ewer / ure
ye / yea
earn / yarn

There is a descriptive analysis in the *Text Commentary Book*.

18.2.2 *Christopher Cooper's* The English Teacher, *1687*

Christopher Cooper, 'Master of the Grammar School of Bishop-Stortford in Hartfordshire', published *The English Teacher or The Discovery of the Art of Teaching and Learning the English Tongue* in 1687. He has been described as 'the best phonetician and one of the fullest recorders of pronunciation that England (and indeed modern Europe) produced before the nineteenth century, the obscure schoolmaster of a country town' (E. J. Dobson, *English Pronunciation 1500–1700*, 1968). An examination of Christopher Cooper's book will therefore provide good evidence about the pronunciation of English in his time.

Cooper's description of the relationship of letters to sounds is, like that of all the orthoepists of the 16th and 17th century, not always easy to follow, because there was then no phonetic alphabet to act as a reference for the sounds. His first concern is the spelling of the vowels and consonants, to which he relates the variety of sounds which they represent. He made no proposals for spelling reform, but aimed at teaching the spelling system in general use at that time.

There was still a clear distinction of quantity between short and long vowels with the same quality, as in OE and ME, but this had become complicated as a result of the Great Vowel Shift (see section 15.5), which was not fully complete until round about the end of the 17th century. As the shift of the long vowels took place in the South of England, and not in the North, the educated speech of London and the Home Counties – the emerging standard language – was affected by it.

Activity 18.3

Examine the following lists from Cooper's *The English Teacher* in turn (Texts 139–44). Discuss the evidence they show of:

(a) Cooper's pronunciation in the 1680s and any change from Middle English as a result of either the shift of the long vowels, or other causes.
(b) Later changes which have taken place in the pronunciation of any of the words.

A commentary on Activity 18.3 is in the *Text Commentary Book*.

18.2.2.1 *'Of the Vowel a'*

Text 139 – Christopher Cooper's *The English Teacher*, 1687 (i) (facsimile)

34 *Of the Vowel* **a.**

CHAP. II.

Of the Vowel **a.**

A Hath three ſounds, which, for diſtinction ſake, I have expreſt in writing after this manner a *a* *a*. The firſt of theſe, for the moſt part, is pronounced long in its own ſound before *nch*, and *s* when another Conſonant follows, and before *r* unleſs *ſh* follows. But when *e* is put to the end, it is then pronounced in a more ſlender ſound, to wit, the lengthning of *e* ſhort; but it is to be obſerv'd that in all theſe words, except in *cane*, *wane*, *ſtrange-r*, *manger*, *mangye*, and before *ge*; as in *age*, *u* guttural is put after *a*; which *u* is nothing elſe but a continuation of a naked murmur after *a* is formed: for by reaſon of the ſlenderneſs, unleſs we more accurately attend, the tongue will not eaſily paſs to the next conſonant without *u* coming between. The difference will plainly appear to thoſe ears, that can diſtinguiſh ſounds, in the Examples placed in the following order.

a ſhort	a long	*a* ſlender
Bar	*Barge*	*Bare*
blab	*blaſt*	*blazon*
cap	*carking*	*cape*
car	*carp*	*care*
cat	*caſt*	*caſe*
daſh	*dart*	*date*
flaſh	*flasket*	*flake*
gaſh	*gaſp*	*gate*
grand	*grant*	*grange*
land	*lance*	*lane*
maſh	*mask*	*maſon*
pat	*path*	*pate*
tar	*tart*	*tares*

It is difficult for us to interpret Cooper's description because what we are trying to discover is precisely what he could assume his contemporary readers already knew. 'Short' and 'long' vowels present no problem, but 'slender' is not a term used in phonetic description today. He describes 'the Vowel a' as having three sounds, for which he uses three forms of the letter – ⟨a⟩, ⟨*a*⟩ and ⟨*α*⟩ – but he does not use the third letter in the examples in Text 139. He describes two realisations of ⟨a⟩, 'a short, a long', and one of ⟨*a*⟩, '*a* slender'. Their probable pronunciations were:

- a short: [a] or [æ]
- a long: [aː] or [æː]
- *α* slender: [ɛː]

We cannot know the precise realisation of 'a short' and 'a long', but know that they were front vowels. Remember that ⟨ar⟩, as in *bar*, *car*, *tar*, *barge*, *carking*, *carp*, *dart* and *tar*, was not yet a digraph for the low back vowel [ɑ] in RP and other English dialects. The ⟨r⟩ was pronounced like any other consonant, [aɹ], as it still is in rhotic dialects, which have kept the pronunciation of post vocalic [r].

He distinguishes between the ⟨a⟩ of *car* and *care*. The '*a* slender' of *care* is compared to a 'lengthening of *e* short', followed by '*u* guttural', what he calls 'a naked murmur after *a* is formed'. Cooper's 'u guttural' was the short vowel [ə], so this must be the evolution of a diphthong in the word, pronounced [kɛəɹ], and the origin of today's RP pronunciation of *care* as [kɛə].

Cooper differentiated the vowels in certain pairs of words which today are identical homophones in RP and other dialects. These words have remained different in parts of the North of England and in East Anglia. For example, *pane* with a pure vowel [peːn] and *pain* with a diphthong [pɛɪn] (see J. C. Wells, *Accents of English*, 1, chapter 3, section 3.1.5, Cambridge University Press, 1982).

The contrast is not the same as that in Cooper's speech, however, where the spelling ⟨ai⟩ represents '*a* pure' and ⟨a-e⟩ is a diphthong. He describes the difference in this way:

Text 140 – Christopher Cooper's *The English Teacher*, 1687 (ii) (facsimile)

let him conſider the following Examples, in which *ai* pronounced gently hath the ſound of *a* pure, as in *cane*, but where *a* onely is written *u* guttural is ſounded after it; as

Bain	*Hail*	*Maid*
bane	*hale*	*made*
main	*lay'n*	*pain*
mane	*lane*	*pane*
plain	*ſpaid*	*tail*
plane	*ſpade*	*tale*

18.2.2.2 'Of the Vowel e'

The original purpose of the digraph ⟨ea⟩ was to distinguish the more open of the two long front vowels [ɛː] from the closer vowel [eː], usually spelt ⟨ee⟩ (see section 15.5.1.4). Cooper's description is:

> That sound which is taken for the long e is exprest by putting *a* after it; as *men*, *mean*

His 'long e' was the vowel [ɛː].

18.2.2.3 'Of the Vowel o'

The following facsimile from *The English Teacher* lists some words pronounced with the vowel [u] or [uː], spelt either ⟨o⟩ or ⟨oa⟩ or ⟨oo⟩.

Activity 18.4

Consider the contemporary pronunciation of the words in Cooper's list, some of which have changed from [u] or [uː] in the 1680s. Do they have any feature in common which might explain the change?

Text 141 – Christopher Cooper's *The English Teacher*, 1687 (iii) (facsimile)

Rule 2.

o oa ou in theſe following is ſounded *oo*.

A-board	*con-courſe*	*court-ſhip*	*ſourſe*	*whom*
ac-cou-tred	*could*	*force*	*ſword*	*whore*
af-ford	*courſe*	*forces*	*ſworn*	*who-ſo-e-ver*
be-hoves	*courſes*	*move*	*tomb*	*womb*
boar	*court*	*mourn*	*two*	*worn*
born	*cour-ti-er*	*ſcourſe*	*un-couth*	*would*
bourn	*court-li-neſs*	*ſhould*	*who*	

In all others this ſound is written *oo*; as *look*, *roof*. But *Board*, *forth*, *prove*, *ſloup*, are better written *boord*, *foorth*, *proove*, *ſloop*.

Blood-i-ly, *good-ly-neſs*, *flood*, *hood*, *brother-hood*, *ſiſterhood*, *neighbourhood*, *falſehood*, *ſoot*, *flood*, *wood*, *wool*; have the ſound of *o* labial ſhort. *O* in *women* is ſounded as *i*. in *Damoſel* not at all.

See *o* for *u* guttural, Ch. 6. Rule 6. *O* for *ou* labials, Ch. 7. Rul. 4.

Commentary

These words are still pronounced with the short [ʊ] or long [uː]:

accoutred	uncouth
behoves (*or* [əʊ])	who
could	whom
move	whosoever
should	womb
tomb	would
two	

All the others are now pronounced with the vowel [ɔː] in RP and most English dialects. In each word the vowel was followed by post-vocalic [r] which had the effect of lowering the vowel, which either lengthened or became a diphthong when [r] ceased to be pronounced.

18.2.2.4 *'Improper diphthongs'*

Cooper differentiated diphthongs in pronunciation from digraphs in writing. He did not, however, use the word *digraph* but the phrase *improper diphthong* for pairs of letters which represented only one sound. In Text 142 he describes the different current pronunciations of words with ⟨ea⟩, which we have already seen as a feature of con-temporary spelling. Cooper's 'e short' meant [ɛ], 'e long' [ɛː], 'ee' [iː], '*α*' [ɛː] and 'a' [æː].

18.2.2.5 *'Barbarous speaking'*

The pronunciation of rural and urban dialects has always been regarded as inferior by those who consider themselves to be in a superior social class. Cooper, as a teacher, shows this in his chapter 'Of Barbarous Speaking', in which he implies that a person's pronunciation will determine his spelling:

Activity 18.5

(i) Read pages 77 and 78 from *Of Barbarous Dialects* (reproduced in Text 143).
(ii) Are any of the 'barbarous' pronunciations to be heard today, in: (a) Received Pronunciation; (b) any of our regional dialects?
(iii) Does this provide any evidence that some features of Received Pronunciation, the socially prestigious accent of English today, have derived from regional accents?

Text 142 – Christopher Cooper's *The English Teacher*, 1687 (iv) (facsimile)

CHAP. VIII.

Of the improper Dipthongs ea, oa, eo, ie. *In which one Vowel alone is pronounced; to which may be added* ui, *as it is commonly taken.*

Rule 1. *Of* ea.

EA is put 1. For *e* ſhort. 2. For *e* long. 3. For *u*. 4. For *a* and a.

(*e*) ſhort			
Al-rea-dy	*en-dea-vor*	*Pa-ge-ant*	*Wealth*
Be-head	*Fea-ther*	*plea-ſant*	
bread	*Head-y*	*Reach-les*	
breadth	*Head-long*	*rea-dy*	
break-faſt	*head-ſtal*	*realm*	
breaſt	*head-ſtrong*	*ſhred*	
breath	*health*	*Shread*	
Cleanſe	*hea-ven*	*ſpread*	
Dead-ly	*hea-vy*	*ſtead-y*	
dearth	*Lea-ther*	*ſtead-faſt*	
death	*lead*	*ſtealth*	
dread	*lea-ven*	*Threat-ning*	
Earth	*lea-ver*	*trea-che-ry*	
	lea-ver-et	*tread*	

for (*ee*)	
Ap-pear	*Gear*
ar-rear	*Hear*
Beach	*Near*
be-ſmear	*Sear*
blear-eyd	*ſhears*
Chear	*ſpear*
clear	*ſphear*
Dear	*ſteam*
Ear-wig	*Tear*
ears	*Weary*
Fear	*Year*

(*e*) long				
Ap-peal	*clea-vers*	*feat*	*plea-der*	*Teach*
ap-peaſe	*con-ceal*	*for-ſwear*	*plea-ſing*	*teal*
Bea-con	*con-geal*	*freak*	*peach*	*team*
bead	*creak*	*Glean*	*pea-cock*	*trea-tiſe*
bea-dle	*cream*	*greaſe*	*peal*	*Veal*
bea-gle	*crea-ture*	*great*	*preach*	*Weak-nes*
beak-er	*Dea-con*	*greave*	*Quean*	*weal*
beam	*deal*	*grea-vy*	*quea-ſy*	*wean*
bean	*dean*	*Heal*	*Reach*	*weave*
beaſt	*de-ceaſe*	*heap*	*ream*	*wheal*
beat	*de-creaſe*	*heat*	*reap*	*wheat*
bea-ver	*de-feat*	*heath-cock*	*reave*	
be-lea-guer	*de-mean-our*	*hea-then*	*re-leaſe*	
be-neath	*diſ-eaſe*	*heave*	*re-peal*	
be-queath	*dream*	*Im-peach*	*re-peat*	
be-reave	*Each*	*im-plead*	*re-treat*	
bleach	*ea-ger*	*in-creaſe*	*re-veal*	
bleak	*ea-gle*	*Leach*	*Sea*	
breach	*ea-glet*	*leaf*	*ſeam*	
break	*ean*	*leam*	*ſeal-ing*	
bream	*eaſe-ment*	*lean-ing*	*ſeat*	
Ceaſe	*ea-ſi-nes*	*lean-nes*	*ſheaf*	
cheap	*eaſt*	*leap*	*ſheat*	
cheat	*ea-ſter*	*leaſt*	*ſheath*	
clean	*eat*	*leave*	*ſneak*	
cleav-er	*en-creaſe*	*Mead*	*ſpeak*	
	en-treat	*meal*	*ſqueak*	
	eſ-cheat	*mean*	*ſqueal*	
	e-ſtreat	*meat*	*ſquea-miſh*	
	ex-tream	*Neat*	*ſteal*	
	Fe-al-ty	*Steak*	*ſtrea-mer*	
	feaſt	*Plea*	*ſweat*	

for (*a*)
Bear
beard
Earl
ear-ly
earn
ear-neſt
Learn
Re-hearſe
Scream
ſcarce
ſearch
ſheard
ſwear
Tear [*rend*]
Wear
wea-riſh

for (a)
Diſ-hear-ten
Heart
hear-ten
hearth
hear-ty
heart-leſs

Some of this kind are written otherwiſe, and perhaps better; as *breſt*, *bever*, *ech*, *eger*. *Appeer*, *beech*, *cleer*, *cheer*, *yeer*, *ſphere*.

Text 143 – Christopher Cooper's *The English Teacher*, 1687 (v) (facsimile)

Of Barbarous Dialect. 77

CHAP. XIX.

Of Barbarous Speaking.

HE, that would write more exactly, muſt avoid a Barbarous Pronunciation; and conſider for facility, or thorow miſtake, many words are not ſounded after the beſt dialect: Such as

A.

E.
Ex-tre, axle-tree
eend, end
e'nt, is it not

I.
Im-poſſable, im poſſible;

B.
Buſhop, Biſhop
Bellis, bellows

F.
Frankamcenſe, —incenſe
Firmity, frumenty
Fut, foot
Fâw, few

K.

C.
Chimly, Chimney
Chorles, Charles

G.
Gurgians, *gurgions*, grudgings; *gem me*, *gim me*, give me; *gove*, *gov*, gave; *griſt*, graſt, graff; *git*, get.

L.
Lat, let; *leece*, lice

D.
Dud, did
Dander, *dandruffe*, dandraffe

H.
Hundurd, hundred
howſomever, *howzever*, howſoever; *Hild*, held; *hankecher*, handkerchief.

M.
Mought, *med*, might; *Maracle*, miracle; *meece*, mice;

78 *Of Barbarous Dialect.*

N.
Nother, neither

R.
Reddiſh, Raddiſh

V.
Vitles, Victuals.

O.
Ommoſt, almoſt
Wuts, Oats
Op, up
Wun, one.

S.
Sez, ſayes; *ſed*, ſaid; (*ſh*) for (*ſ*) before (*u*) as *Shure*, *Shugar*, &c. *Stomp*, Stamp; *skim-mer*, ſcummer; *ſcurge*, ſcourge. *ſcru-pe-lous*, ſcrupulous; *ſhet*, ſhut; *ſarvice*, ſervice.

W.
Widſt, *wudſt*, wouldſt; *wull*, will; *wuth*, with; *wumme*, *wuth me*, with me; *whutter*, hotter; *whuther*, whether; *wuſted*, worſted; *warry*, weary; *wont*, will not.

P.

Q.
Quawm, qualm

T.
Terrable, terrible; *Tunder*, tinder; *Thraſh*, threſh; *Their*, *there*, thare; *Truel*, trowel;

Y.
Yerb, herb; *yerth*, earth; *yau*, you; *yeuſleſs*, *yeuſary*, &c. uſeleſs, &c.

18.2.2.6 'Words that have the same pronunciation'

Other lists in Cooper's book are useful to us in our study of changing pronunciation. For example, there are several pages of 'Words that have the same pronunciation, but different signification and manner of writing', as in Fox and Hookes's *Instructions for Right Spelling*. Most of them are pronounced alike today, though not necessarily with the same vowels as in the 1680s. For example, *seas* and *seize* are homophones today, [siːz], but would have been pronounced [sɛːz] or [seːz] in Cooper's time, the final raising to [iː] not yet having taken place.

Some of the words confirm changes since ME. For example, the pairing of *rest/wrest*, *right/wright* and *ring/wring* shows the loss of ⟨w⟩ from the OE and ME initial consonant group ⟨wr⟩ to be complete. John Hart's *An Orthographie* showed that the ⟨w⟩ was still pronounced in the 16th century.

Here are a few of the pairs which have remained homophones.

altar / alter	chewes / chuse	in / inn
assent / ascent	dear / deer	lesson / lessen
bare / bear	hair / hare	pair / pare / pear

Others show that at least one word in each pair or group has changed since the 1680s, for example, the pronunciation of *are*, *one*, the *-ure* of *censure*, *gesture* and *tenure*, the *oi* of *oil* and *loin*, and the *ea* of *flea*, *heard*, *least*, *rear*, *reason*, *shear* and *wear*.

Activity 18.6

Compare Cooper's list with Fox and Hookes' in section 18.2.1.

Text 144 – Christopher Cooper's *The English Teacher*, 1687 (vi)

are / air / heir / ere
ant / aunt
bile / boil
censer / censor / censure
coat / quote
comming / cummin
cool'd / could
coughing / coffin
car'd / card
doe / do / dow (= *dough*)
flea / flay
fit / fight (= *did fight*)
jester / gesture
hard / heard / herd
i'le / isle / oil
jerkin / jerking
kill / kiln
least / lest
line / loin
mile / moil (*hard labour*)
nether / neither
own / one
pastor / pasture
pick't her / picture
pour / power
rare / rear
raisins / reasons
share / shear
shoo (*shoe*) / shew (*show*)
stood / stud
tenor / tenure
to / two / toe
war / wear / ware
woo / woe
yea / ye

18.2.7 *Words spelt with ⟨oi⟩*

The study of sound changes is complex, but here is a short explanation of one particular change, in which two sets of words with different vowels in ME and MnE fell together for a time.

From the evidence of the preceding list, *boil*, *oil*, *loin* and *moil* had the same pronunciation as *bile*, *isle*, *line* and *mile*. This can be checked in the poetry of the 17th and early 18th centuries, in which many similar pairs of words consistently rhyme together (see section 18.3.2 on John Dryden). However, this did not mean that their pronunciation at that time was either [baɪl] or [bɔɪl].

⟨*boil*⟩

The verb *boil*, like many other words spelt with the ⟨oi⟩ digraph, came from French and was pronounced [bʊɪl] in ME, though it was usually spelt with ⟨oi⟩. The diphthong was 'unrounded' during the 17th century and changed to [ʌɪ].

We saw evidence in John Hart's *An Orthographie* of the shift of the long vowel [iː] to the diphthong [əɪ], which is almost the same in sound as [ʌɪ], by the 1560s. As a result, words formerly with [iː] and [ʌɪ] fell together, and both were pronounced with the diphthong [əɪ].

After about 1700 the first element of the diphthong shifted further to its present-day pronunciation [aɪ] in words like *bile*. Why, then, do we pronounce *boil* (and similar words) today as [bɔɪl] and not [baɪl]?

The reason is that there was in ME a second set of words spelt with ⟨oi⟩, for example, *choice* and *noise*, with a diphthong pronounced [ɔɪ], not [ʊɪ]. Evidence from the orthoepists suggests that [ʊɪ] words were also pronounced [ɔɪ] by some speakers. Eventually, helped by the spelling, all words spelt with ⟨oi⟩ came to be pronounced [ɔɪ], so that *bile*, by then pronounced [baɪl] ceased to rhyme with *boil*, pronounced [bɔɪl].

18.3 John Dryden

John Dryden (1631–1700), one of the great writers in the English literary tradition, was a poet, dramatist and critic. He was largely responsible for the 'cherished superstition that prepositions must, in spite of the incurable English instinct for putting them late, . . . be kept true to their name & placed before the word they govern' (H. W. Fowler, 1926). Dryden 'went through all his prefaces contriving away the final prepositions that he had been guilty of in his first editions' (ibid.). This is incidental, however, to his recognised eminence as a prose writer.

18.3.1 *Dryden on Chaucer*

Dryden admired Chaucer's poetry, but some aspects of his assessment of Chaucer throw as clear a light on Dryden himself, and the way he and his contemporaries thought about language and writing, as it does on Chaucer. His summary of Chaucer's achievement is often quoted,

> 'Tis sufficient to say according to the Proverb, that here is God's Plenty.

His remarks on Chaucer's language are relevant to our survey of the development of Standard English, and of attitudes to acceptable usage. The earliest English for us is Old English, in texts as far back as the 9th century. Dryden was concerned with the idea of the 'purity' of English, and the notion that it had reached a state of perfection in his day:

> 'From Chaucer the Purity of the English Tongue began . . . Chaucer (lived) in the Dawning of our Language'.

For Dryden, Chaucer's diction 'stands not on an equal Foot with our present English',

> The verse of *Chaucer*, I confess, is not harmonious to us . . . They who liv'd with him, and some time after him, thought it Musical . . . . There is the rude Sweetness of a *Scotch* tune in it, which is natural and pleasing, though not perfect.

and he criticised the editor of an earlier late-16th century printed edition of Chaucer,

> . . . for he would make us believe the Fault is in our Ears, and that there were really Ten Syllables in a Verse where we find but Nine: But this Opinion is not worth confuting; 'tis so gross and obvious an Errour, that Common Sense . . . must convince the Reader, that Equality of Numbers in every Verse which we call *Heroick*, was either not known, or not always practis'd in *Chaucer's* Age. It were an easie Matter to produce some thousands of

> his Verses, which are lame for want of half a Foot, and sometimes a whole one, and which no Pronunciation can make otherwise...
> Chaucer, I confess, is a rough Diamond, and must first be polish'd e're he shines.

Dryden's 'polishing' of Chaucer was done by re-versifying some of *The Canterbury Tales*, making his choice from those *Tales* 'as savour nothing of Immodesty'. In his Preface to the Fables he quotes from Chaucer's *Prologue*, where the narrator 'thus excuses the Ribaldry, which is very gross...'. Dryden then goes on to discuss Chaucer's language,

> You have here a *Specimen* of *Chaucer's* Language, which is so obsolete, that his Sense is scarce to be understood; and you have likewise more than one Example of his unequal Numbers, which were mention'd before. Yet many of his verses consist of Ten Syllables, and the Words not much behind our present *English*.

The following texts consist of the same extract from Chaucer's 'Prologue' to *The Canterbury Tales*, firstly as quoted by Dryden in 1700 from an early printed version as an example of Chaucer's 'obsolete' language and rough versification, and then in a modern edition based on the manuscripts.

Activity 18.7

(i) Study the two versions and comment on the differences between them.
(ii) Read section 13.2.1, which briefly describes the pronunciation of Chaucer's verse.
(iii) Discuss the possible reasons for Dryden's criticism of Chaucer's 'unequal Numbers', that is, his belief that many of Chaucer's lines have fewer than the ten syllables which the verses should have.
(iv) What was 'obsolete' for Dryden in Chaucer's vocabulary and grammar?

Text 145 – Lines from Chaucer's *Prologue*

Dryden's version

But first, I pray you, of your courtesy,
That ye ne arrete it nought my villany,
Though that I plainly speak in this mattere
To tellen you her words, and eke her chere:
Ne though I speak her words properly,
For this ye knowen as well as I,
Who shall tellen a tale after a man
He mote rehearse as nye, as ever He can:
Everich word of it been in his charge,
All speke he, never so rudely, ne large.
Or else he mote tellen his tale untrue,
Or feine things, or find words new:
He may not spare, altho he were his brother,
He mote as well say o words as another.
Christ spake himself full broad in holy Writ,
And well I wote no Villany is it.
Eke *Plato* saith, who so can him rede,
The words mote been Cousin to the dede.

Modern edition from the manuscripts

But first I pray yow of youre curteisye
That ye n'arette it noght my vileynye
Though that I pleynly speke in this mateere
To telle yow hir wordes and hir cheere
Ne thogh I speke hir wordes proprely.
For this ye knowen al so wel as I
Whoso shal telle a tale after a man
He moot reherce as ny as euere he kan
Euerich a word if it be in his charge
Al speke he neuer so rudeliche and large,
Or ellis he moot telle his tale vntrewe
Or feyne thyng or fynde wordes newe.
He may nat spare althogh he were his brother
He moot as wel seye o word as another.
Crist spak hymself ful brode in hooly writ
And wel ye woot no vileynye is it.
Eek Plato seith, whoso that kan hym rede,
The wordes moote be cosyn to the dede.

📖 There is a commentary in the *Text Commentary Book*.

18.3.2 *Evidence of pronunciation from rhymes in Dryden's* Aeneis

When you read poetry from the 16th to the 18th centuries, you will often find pairs of words that should rhyme, but do not do so in present-day pronunciation. It is interesting to examine a few examples at the end of the 17th century, and relate them to what we have learned about pronunciation from the two orthoepists, John Hart in the 16th century (in chapter 15) and Christopher Cooper in the 17th century (in this chapter, section 18.2.2).

The following rhymes from John Dryden's translation of Virgil's Latin *Aeneis*, occur many other times, and are not single examples which might be explained as false or eye rhymes.

Text 146 – couplets from Dryden's *Aeneis*, 1697

⟨ea⟩		
appear	Amidst our course Zacynthian Woods **appear**; And next by rocky Neritos we **steer**:	III 351
	At length, in dead of Night, the Ghost **appears** Of her unhappy Lord: the Spectre **stares**, And with erected Eyes his bloody Bosom **bares**.	I 486
Sea	He calls to raise the Masts, the Sheats **display**; The Chearful Crew with diligence **obey**; They scud before the Wind, and sail in open **Sea**.	V 1084
	Long wandring Ways for you the Pow'rs **decree**: On Land hard Labours, and a length of **Sea**.	II 1058
	Then, from the South arose a gentle **Breeze**, That curl'd the smoothness of the glassy **Seas**:	V 997
Year	When rising Vapours choak the wholsom **Air**, And blasts of noisom Winds corrupt the **Year**.	III 190
	Laocoon, *Neptune's* Priest by Lot that **Year**, With solemn pomp then sacrific'd a **Steer**.	II 267
⟨i⟩		
Wind	His Pow'r to hollow Caverns is **confin'd**, There let him reign, the Jailor of the **Wind**.	I 199
⟨oi⟩		
	For this are various Penances **enjoyn'd**; And some are hung to bleach, upon the **Wind**;	VI 1002
	Did I or Iris give this mad **Advice**, Or made the Fool himself the fatal **Choice**?	X 110
	The passive Gods behold the Greeks **defile** Their Temples, and abandon to the **Spoil** Their own Abodes…	II 471
	But that o'reblown, when Heav'n above 'em **smiles**, Return to Travel, and renew their **Toils**:	X 1144

. . . Resolute to **die**,
And add his Fun'rals to the fate of **Troy**: II 862

⟨**a**⟩

The rest, in Meen, in habit, and in **Face**,
Appear'd a Greek; and such indeed he **was**. III 778

Yet one remain'd, the Messenger of **Fate**;
High on a craggy Cliff Celno **sate**,
And thus her dismall Errand did **relate**. III 21

Then, as her Strength with Years increas'd, **began**
To pierce aloft in Air the soaring **Swan**:
And from the Clouds to fetch the heron and the **Crane**. XI 868

⟨**ar**⟩

O more than Madmen! you your selves shall **bear**
The guilt of Blood and Sacrilegious **War**: VII 821

Loaded with Gold, he sent his Darling, **far**
From Noise and Tumults, and destructive **War**:
Committed to the faithless Tyrant's **Care**. III 73

⟨**oo**⟩

She seem'd a Virgin of the Spartan **Blood**:
With such Array Harpalice **bestrode**
Her Thracian Courser, and outstri'd the rapid **Flood** I 440

His Father Hyrtacus of Noble **Blood**;
His Mother was a Hunt'ress of the **Wood**: IX 223

. . . The Brambles drink his **Blood**;
And his torn Limbs are left, the Vulture's **Food**. VIII 855

Resume your ancient Care; and if the **God**
Your Sire, and you, resolve on Foreign **Blood**: VII 516

⟨**oa**⟩

His knocking Knees are bent beneath the **Load**:
And shiv'ring Cold congeals his vital **Blood**. XII 1308

Maids, Matrons, Widows, mix their common **Moans**:
Orphans their Sires, and Sires lament their **Sons** XI 329

⟨**-y**⟩

Acestes, fir'd with just Disdain, to **see**
The Palm usurp'd without a **Victory**;
Reproch'd Entellus thus . . . V 513

The Pastor pleas'd with his dire **Victory**,
Beholds the satiate Flames in Sheets ascend the **Sky**: X 573

. . . the Coast was **free**
From Foreign or Domestick **Enemy**: III 168

He heav'd it at a Lift: and poiz'd on **high**,
Ran stagg'ring on, against his **Enemy**. XII 1304

The rhyming pairs are recorded on the cassette tape.

appear	[ir]	**Year**	[iːr]	**die**	[aɪ]	**Blood**	[blɒd]	**see**	[siː]
steer	[ir]	**Steer**	[iːr]	**Troy**	[aɪ]	**bestrode**	[bɛstrɒd]	**Victory**	[vɪktəriː]
appears	[erz]	**confin'd**	[aɪnd]	**Face**	[fæs]	**Flood**	[flɒd]	**Victory**	[vɪktərai]
stares	[erz]	**Wind**	[aɪnd]	**was**	[wæs]	**Blood**	[blʊd]	**Sky**	[skaɪ]
bares	[erz]	**enjoyn'd**	[aɪnd]	**Fate**	[feːt]	**Wood**	[wʊd]	**free**	[friː]
display	[eː]	**Wind**	[aɪnd]	**sate**	[seːt]	**Blood**	[blʊd]	**Enemy**	[ɛnəmɪ]
obey	[eː]	**Advice**	[aɪs]	**relate**	[rɛleːt]	**Food**	[fʊd]	**high**	[haɪ]
Sea	[eː]	**Choice**	[aɪs]	**began**	[bɛgæn]	**God**	[gɒd]	**Enemy**	[ɛnəmiː]
decree	[iː]	**defile**	[aɪl]	**Swan**	[swæn]	**Blood**	[blɒd]		
Sea	[iː]	**Spoil**	[aɪl]	**Crane**	[kræn]	**Load**	[lɒd]		
Breeze	[iːz]	**smiles**	[aɪlz]	**bear**	[bɛːr]	**Blood**	[blɒd]		
Seas	[iːz]	**Toils**	[aɪlz]	**War**	[wɛːr]	**Moans**	[moːnz]		
Air	[@iːr]			**far**	[fɛːr]	**Sons**	[sʊnz]		
Year	[@iːr]			**War**	[wɛːr]				
				Care	[kɛːr]				

It seems odd at first that *enemy* could apparently rhyme with either *free*, MnE [friː], and *high*, MnE [haɪ]. But in Dryden's time the vowel of *high* was still in the process of shifting from [iː] to [aɪ], and the vowel of *free* from [eː] to [iː], and at a variable rate in different dialects. Dryden was able to make use of such variant pronunciations. The shifting of these two vowels explains the following word-play in Shakespeare's *The Two Gentlemen of Verona* a century earlier. The dialogue is between Protheus, 'a gentleman of Verona' and Speed, 'a clownish seruant'. The word *Ay* (*yes*) is spelt *I*; *noddy* meant *foolish*.

Text 147 – Shakespeare's *The Two Gentlemen of Verona*

PROTHEUS	But what said she?
SPEED	(*nods, then saies*) I.
PROTHEUS	Nod-I, why that's noddy.
SPEED	You mistooke Sir: I say she did nod; and you aske me if she did nod and I say I.
PROTHEUS	And that set together is noddy.

18.4 North Riding Yorkshire dialect in the 1680s

It was said in an earlier chapter that from the later 15th century, it becomes increasingly rare to find texts which provide evidence of regional forms other than those of the educated London dialect which became established as the standard. Once the grammar and vocabulary of written English were standardised, other dialects were recorded only in texts written for the purpose of presenting dialects as different.

During the 17th century there was a revival of interest in antiquarian studies and of language, two of the many topics discussed by members of the Royal Society. Writing on language included descriptions of the Saxon language of the past, and of contemporary dialects.

One form that this interest in dialect took can be seen in George Meriton's *A Yorkshire Dialogue*, published in York in 1683. Meriton was a lawyer, practising in the North Riding town of Northallerton. The *Dialogue* is a lively representation of a Yorkshire farming family, written in verse couplets, and deliberately full of proverbial sayings. It is therefore only indirect evidence of the authentic spoken North Riding English of the time, but nevertheless gives us plenty of examples of dialectal and traditional vocabulary and grammar.

The spelling of written English had remained virtually unchanged in spite of the efforts of spelling reformers like John Hart in the 16th century, and took no account of the shifts of pronunciation which had taken place since the 14th century. Consequently, the spelling of standard English did not at all accurately indicate the 'polite' accent of the late 17th and early 18th centuries. But when writing in dialect it was (and still is) usual to spell many of the words 'as they were spoken', so that features of dialectal pronunciation were shown as well as the vocabulary and grammar.

In the following short extract, the two young women in the family, Tibb the daughter and Nan the niece, talk about their sweethearts. There are no 'stage directions', so their movements have to be inferred from the dialogue.

Activity 18.8

(i) List some of the probable dialectal pronunciations which the spellings suggest.

(ii) In what ways does the grammar of the dialect differ from the standard English of the late 17th century?

Text 148 – George Meriton's *A Yorkshire Dialogue*, 1683

(*The extract begins at line 155 of the original. The Yorkshire dialectal pronunciation of* <u>*the*</u> is spelt in the *Dialogue* as <u>*'th.*</u>) *F. = Father, M. = Mother, D. = Daughter, N. = Niece.*

A York-shire DIALOGUE, In its pure Natural DIALECT: As it is now commonly Spoken in the North parts of *York-Shire* Being a Miscellaneous discourse, or Hotchpotch of several Country Affaires, begun by a Daughter and her Mother, and continued by the Father, Son, Uncle, Neese, and Land-Lord.

F. What ails our Tibb, that she urles seay ith Newke,
Shee's nut Reet, she leauks an Awd farrand Leauke.
D. Father, Ive gitten cawd, I can scarce tawke,
And my Snurles are seay sayr stopt, I can nut snawke,
N. How duz my Cozen Tibb Naunt I mun nut stay,
I haird sho gat a Cawd the other day,
M. Ey wallaneerin, wilta gang and see,
Shee's aboun 'ith Chawmber, Thou may Clim up 'th Stee.
Shee's on a dovening now gang deftly Nan,
And mack as little din as ee'r Thou can.
N. Your mains flaid, there's an awd saying you knawe
That there's no Carrion will kill a Crawe:
If she be nut as dead as a deaur Naile,
Ile mack her flyer and semper like Flesh Cael,
What Tibb I see, Thou is nut yet quite dead,
Leauke at me woman, and haud up thy head.
D. Ah Nan steeke'th winderboard, and mack it darke,
My Neen are varra sayr, they stoun and warke.
They are seay Gummy and Furr'd up sometime.
I can nut leauke at'th Leet, nor see a stime.
N. Come come, I can mack Thee Leetsome and blythe,
Here will be thy awd Sweet-heart here Belive.
He tell's me seay I say him but last night
O Tibb he is as fine as onny Kneet.
D. Nay Nan Thou dus but jest there's neay sike thing,
He woes another Lasse and gave her a Ring.
N. Away away great feaul tack thou neay Care,
He swears that hee'l love thee for evermare.
And sayes as ever he whopes his Saul to seave,
Hee'l either wed to Thee, or tull his greave . . .

WW

(Modern English)

F. What ails our Tibb, that she crouches* so in the nook,
She's not right, she looks an old fashioned look.
D. Father, I've gotten (a) cold, I can scarce talk,
And my nostrils are so sore stopped (up), I can not inhale,
N. How does my Cousin Tibb aunt I must not stay,
I heard sho got a Cold the other day,
M. Ey alas, wilt thou go and see,
She's above in the Chawmber, Thou may Climb up the ladder.
She's in a doze now go gently Nan,
And make as little din as ever Thou can.
N. You're very worried, there's an old saying you know
That there's no Carrion will kill a Crow:
If she be not as dead as a door Nail,
I'll make her laugh and simper like meat broth,
What Tibb I see, Thou is not yet quite dead,
Look at me woman, and hold up thy head.
D. Ah Nan shut the window-board, and make it dark,
My eyes are very sore, they smart and ache.
They are so Gummy and Furr'd up sometime.
I can not look at the Light, nor see a thing.
N. Come come, I can make Thee Lightsome and blithe,
Here will be thy old Sweet-heart here soon.
He tells me so I saw him but last night
O Tibb he is as fine as any Knight.
D. Nay Nan Thou dost but jest there's no such thing,
He woos another Lass and gave her a Ring.
N. Away away great fool take thou no Care,
He swears that he'll love thee for evermore.
And says as ever he hopes his Soul to save,
He'll either wed to Thee, or till his grave (= *die*).

* *urles* cannot be accurately translated into one standard English word. A contemporary gloss (1684) on the word was, 'To Vrle, is to draw ones self up on a heap'; a later one (1808) was, 'to be pinched with cold'.

A descriptive analysis can be found in the *Text Commentary Book*.

18.5 Loan-words 1650–1699

18.5.1 *French*

The evidence of these loan-words and those adopted in the following centuries suggests that French words taken into English from this time tend to retain both their French spelling and, to some extent, pronunciation. The degree of 'authentic'

French pronunciation by English speakers seems to depend upon the social class of the speaker.

soup	*soupe*	**1653**	aide-de-camp	*aide-de-camp*	**1670**
naïve	*naïve*	**1654**	penchant	*penchant*	**1672**
rapport	*rapporter*	**1662**	beau (n)	*beau*	**1687**
chandelier	*chandelier*	**1663**	commandant	*commandant*	**1687**
jaunty	*gentil*	**1663**	tête-à-tête	*tête-à-tête*	**1697**
champagne	*champagne*	**1664**	ménage	*ménage*	**1698**
envoy	*envoi*	**1664**	salon	*salon*	**1699**
ballet	*ballet*	**1667**			

18.5.2 *Low German*

cruise	*kruisen*	**1651**	snuff (tobacco)	*snuf*	**1863**
slim	*slim*	**1657**	hustle	*husselen*	**1684**
sketch (draw)	*schets*	**1668**	smuggle	*smukkeln*	**1687**

18.5.3 *Latin*

stamen	*stamen*	**1650**	rabies	*rabere*	**1661**
alblum	*album*	**1651**	sinecure	*sine cura*	**1662**
instantaneous	*instantem*	**1651**	tedium	*taedium*	**1662**
larva	*larva*	**1651**	minimum	*minimum*	**1663**
capsule	*capsula*	**1652**	quota	*quota*	**1668**
complex	*compexus*	**1652**	tuber	*tuber*	**1668**
desideratum	*desideratum*	**1652**	serum	*serum*	**1672**
ultimate	*ultimatus*	**1654**	sulcrum	*fulcrum*	**1674**
pallor	*pallor*	**1656**	mica	*mica*	**1684**
erupt	*erumpere*	**1657**	stimulus	*stimulus*	**1684**
exert	*exserere*	**1660**	lens	*lens*	**1693**
pendulum	*pendulum*	**1660**	lumbago	*lumbago*	**1693**
nebula	*nebula*	**1661**	status	*status*	**1693**

18.5.4 *Italian*

regatta	*regatta*	**1652**	pergola	*pergola*	**1675**
gambit	*gambetto*	**1656**	largo	*largo*	**1683**
profile	*profilo*	**1656**	presto	*presto*	**1683**
vista	*vista*	**1657**	sonata	*sonata*	**1694**
dado	*dado*	**1664**	solo	*solo*	**1695**
umbrella	*ombrella*	**1668**	broccoli	*broccoli*	**1699**
vermicelli	*vermicelli*	**1669**			

18.5.5 *Spanish*

siesta	*siesta*	**1655**	matador	*matador*	**1681**
cargo	*cargo*	**1657**	plaza	*plaza*	**1683**
yam	*igname*	**1657**	avocado	*avocado*	**1697**
barbecue	*barbacoa*	**1661**	banana	*banana*	**1697**
vanilla	*vaynilla*	**1662**	tortilla	*tortilla*	**1699**
barracuda	*barracuda*	**1678**			

18.5.6 *Portuguese*

yam	*inhame*	**1657**	port (wine)	*O Porto*	**1691**
cobra	*cobra de capello*	**1668**	banana	*banana*	**1697**
macaw	*macao*	**1668**	teak	*teca*	**1698**

18.5.7 *German*

zinc	*zink*	**1651**
cobalt	*Kobalt*	**1683**

18.5.8 *Urdu and Hindi*

Urdu

bungalow	*bangla*	**1676**
tom-tom	*tam tam* – drum	**1693**
sahib	*sahib* – the original *Oxford English Dictionary* definition is 'A respectful title used by the natives of India in addressing an Englishman or other European (=Sir).'	**1696**

Hindi

cowrie	*kauri* – a sea shell	**1662**
kedgeree	*khichri*	**1662**
mahout	*mahaut* – elephant-driver	**1662**
ghee	*ghi* – cooking oil	**1665**
pundit	*pandit* – a learned man	**1672**
chitty	*chitthi* – a letter or note	**1698**
maharaja	*maharaja* – great king	**1698**

18.5.9 *Arabic*

minaret	*manarat*	**1682**
jinn	*jinn* – evil spirit	**1684**

18.5.10 *Celtic*

galore	Irish *go leor*, Gaelic *gu leor* – plenty	**1675**
ogham	Irish *ogham* – an alphabet of 20 letters used by the ancient British and Irish	**1677**

18.5.11 *Japanese*

saké	*sake,* fermented liquor made from rice	**1687**
soy	*soy*, colloquial form of *sho-yu*, from Chinese *shi* 'salted beans' + *yu* 'oil'; a sauce	**1696**

18.5.12 *Chinese*

ginseng	*jin shin*, the root of the plant; used as a medicine	**1654**
yang	*yang*, in Chinese philosophy, the masculine or positive principle	**1671**
yin	*yin*, in Chinese philosophy, the feminine or negative principle	**1671**
kumquat	*kin ku* 'gold orange', a fruit	**1699**

19. Modern English – the 18th century

A standard language is achieved when writers use prescribed and agreed forms of the vocabulary and grammar, regardless of the dialectal variety of the language which each one may speak. As a result, regional and class dialects, which are themselves no less rule-governed and systematic than an agreed standard, tend to be regarded as inferior. This chapter presents some of the evidence about attitudes towards, and beliefs about the standard language and the dialects in the 18th century.

19.1 Correcting, improving and ascertaining the language

During the 18th century many pamphlets, articles and grammar books were published on the topic of correcting, improving and, if possible, fixing the language in a perfected form. One word which recurred time and time again in referring to the state of the English language was *corruption*. You will find it in the following text, an extract from an article written by Jonathan Swift (1667–1745) in 1710, in the journal *The Tatler*. The complete article took the form of a supposed letter written to *Isaac Bickerstaff*, a pseudonym for Jonathan Swift.

19.1.1 *'The continual Corruption of our English Tongue'*

Activity 19.1

(i) Discuss what the word *corruption* implies as a metaphor of language. Is it a plausible and acceptable concept?
(ii) List the features of contemporary language use that Swift objected to.
(iii) Discuss Swift's argument and his own use of language, for example his irony, and the connotations of words like *Errors*, *Evils*, *Abuses*, *deplorable*, *Depravity*, *Corruption*, *suffer*, *Barbarity*, *Disgrace*, *betrayed*, *Mutilations*, *Coxcomb*.
(iv) Are there any significant differences between Swift's punctuation and present-day conventions?

(The dots in the second Letter (....), quoted within the main letter addressed to 'Isaac Bickerstaff', are part of the punctuation which Swift objected to ('the Breaks at the End of almost every Sentence'). Elsewhere (...) they mark omissions from the original longer text. A few words are explained at the end.)

Text 149 – from *The Tatler*, No. 230, 26 September 1710

The following Letter has laid before me many great and manifest Evils in the World of Letters which I had overlooked; but they open to me a very busie Scene, and it will require no small Care and Application to amend Errors which are become so universal... To Isaac Bickerstaff Esq;

SIR,

There are some Abuses among us of great Consequence, the Reformation of which is properly your Province, tho', as far as I have been conversant in your Papers, you have not yet considered them. These are, the deplorable Ignorance that for some Years hath reigned among our English Writers, the great depravity of our Taste, and the continual Corruption of our Style...

These two Evils, Ignorance and Want of Taste, have produced a Third; I mean, the continual Corruption of our English Tongue, which, without some timely Remedy, will suffer more by the false Refinements of twenty Years past, than it hath been improved in the foregoing Hundred...

But instead of giving you a List of the late Refinements crept into our Language, I here send you the Copy of a Letter I received some Time ago from a most accomplished person in this Way of Writing, upon which I shall make some Remarks. It is in these Terms.

> SIR, I *Cou'dn't* get the Things you sent for all *about Town*.... I *thôt* to *ha'* come down my self, and then *I'd ha' brôut 'um*; but I *han't don't*, and I believe I *can't do't*, that's *Pozz*.... *Tom* begins to *gi'mself Airs* because *he's* going with the *Plenipo's*.... 'Tis said, the *French* King will *bambooz'l* us agen, which *causes many Speculations*. The *Jacks*, and others of that *Kidney*, are very *uppish*, and *alert upon't*, as you may see by their *Phizz's*.... *Will Hazzard* has got the *Hipps*, having lost *to the Tune of* Five hundr'd Pound, *thô* he understands Play very well, *no body better*. He has promis't me upon *Rep*, to leave off Play; but, you know 'tis a Weakness *he's* too apt to *give into*, *thô* he has as much Wit as any Man, *no body more*. He has lain *incog* ever since.... The *Mobb's* very quiet with us now.... I believe you *thot* I *banter'd* you in my Last like a *Country Put*.... I *sha'n't* leave Town this Month, &c.

This Letter is in every Point an admirable Pattern of the present polite Way of Writing; nor is it of less Authority for being an Epistle... The first Thing that strikes your Eye is the Breaks at the End of almost every Sentence; of which I know not the Use, only that it is a Refinement, and very frequently practised. Then you will observe the Abbreviations and Elisions, by which Consonants of most obdurate Sound are joined together, without one softening Vowel to intervene; and all this only to make one Syllable of two, directly contrary to the Example of the Greeks and Romans; altogether of the Gothick Strain, and a natural Tendency towards relapsing into barbarity, which delights in Monosyllables, and uniting of Mute Consonants; as it is observable in all the Northern Languages. And this is still more visible in the next refinement, which consists in pronouncing the first Syllable in a Word that has many, and dismissing the rest; such as *Phizz*, *Hipps*, *Mobb*, *Poz*. *Rep*. and many more; when we are already overloaded with Monosyllables, which are the disgrace of our Language...

The Third Refinement observable in the Letter I send you, consists in the Choice of certain Words invented by some Pretty Fellows; such as *Banter*, *Bamboozle*, *Country Put*, and *Kidney*, as it is there applied; some of which are now struggling for the Vogue, and others are in Possession of it. I have done my utmost for some Years past to stop the Progress of *Mobb* and *Banter*, but have been plainly borne down by Numbers, and betrayed by those who promised to assist me.

In the last Place, you are to take Notice of certain choice Phrases scattered through the Letter; some of them tolerable enough, till they were worn to Rags by servile Imitators. You might easily find them, though they were in a different Print, and therefore I need not disturb them.

These are the false Refinements in our Style which you ought to correct: First, by Argument and fair Means; but if those fail, I think you are to make Use of your Authority as Censor, and by an Annual *Index Expurgatorius* expunge all Words and Phrases that are offensive to good Sense, and condemn those barbarous Mutilations of Vowels and Syllables. In this last Point, the usual pretence is, that they spell as they speak; A Noble Standard for a Language! to depend upon the Caprice of every Coxcomb, who, because Words are the Cloathing of our Thoughts, cuts them out, and shapes them as he pleases, and changes them oftner than his Dress... And upon this Head I should be glad you would bestow some Advice upon several young Readers in our Churches, who coming up from the University, full fraught with Admiration of our Town Politeness, will needs correct the Style of their Prayer Books. In reading the Absolution, they are very careful to say *pardons* and *absolves*; and in the Prayer for the Royal Family, it must be *endue 'um*, *enrich 'um*, *prosper 'um*, and *bring 'um*. Then in their Sermons they use all the modern Terms of Art, *Sham*, *Banter*, *Mob*, *Bubble*, *Bully*, *Cutting*, *Shuffling*, and *Palming*...

I should be glad to see you the Instrument of introducing into our Style that Simplicity which is the best and truest ornament of most Things in Life...

I am, with great Respect,

SIR,

Your, &c.

Some of the contracted or colloquial forms which Swift disliked were:

banter	humorous ridicule (n), to make fun of (vb), *origin unknown, regarded by Swift as slang*
Hipps/hip	hypochondria, depression
incog	incognito, concealed identity
Jacks	lads, chaps
Mobb/mob	*originally shortened from* mobile, *from Latin* mobile vulgus, the movable or excitable crowd, *hence* the rabble
Phizz	physiognomy, face
Plenipos	plenipotentiary, representative
Put	fool, lout, bumpkin (*origin not known*)
Poz	positive, certain
Rep	reputation

The Absolution in *The Book of Common Prayer*, which Swift referred to, contains the words *he pardoneth and absolveth*.

You can see that what Swift disliked was certain new colloquial words and phrases, and fashionable features of pronunciation – all part of spoken usage rather than written. He specifically condemned these as features of *Style*, that is, of deliberate choices of words and structures from the resources of the language. But at the same time he referred in general terms to *the Corruption of our English Tongue*, an evaluative metaphor which implied worsening and decay, as if the style he disliked to hear could affect everyone's use of English, both written and spoken.

This attitude of condemnation, focusing upon relatively trivial aspects of contemporary usage, was taken up time and time again throughout the 18th century, and has continued to the present day. It is important to study it and to assess its effects. One obvious effect is that nonstandard varieties of the language tend to become stigmatized as *substandard*, while Standard English is thought of as the English language, rather than as the prestige dialect of the language.

The language and speech of educated men and women of the south-east, especially in London, Oxford and Cambridge was, as we have already observed, the source of Standard English. This was John Hart's 'best and most perfite English' (section 16.1.1), and George Puttenham's 'vsuall speach of the Court, and that of London and the shires lying about London' (section 16.1.2). The following text from the 1770s illustrates the establishment of this choice:

Activity 19.2

Discuss your response to James Beattie's assertions. Does his argument hold good for the present day?

Text 150 – James Beattie, *Theory of Language*, 1774 (facsimile)

Are, then, all provincial accents equally good? By no means. Of accent, as well as of ſpelling, ſyntax, and idiom, there is a ſtandard in every polite nation. And, in all theſe particulars, the example of approved authors, and the practice of thoſe, who, by their rank, education, and way of life, have had the beſt opportunities to know men and manners, and domeſtick and foreign literature, ought undoubtedly to give the law. Now it is in the metropolis of a kingdom, and in the moſt famous ſchools of learning, where the greateſt reſort may be expected of perſons adorned with all uſeful and elegant accompliſhments. The language, therefore, of the moſt learned and polite perſons in London, and the neighbouring Univerſities of Oxford and Cambridge, ought to be accounted the ſtandard of the Engliſh tongue, eſpecially in accent and pronunciation: ſyntax, ſpelling, and idiom, having been aſcertained by the practice of good authors, and the conſent of former ages.

19.1.2 *Fixing the language* – A Proposal, *1712*

A
PROPOSAL
FOR
Correcting, Improving and Ascertaining
THE
English Tongue;
IN A
LETTER
To the Moſt Honourable
ROBERT
Earl of Oxford *and* Mortimer,
Lord High Treaſurer
OF
GREAT BRITAIN.

LONDON:
Printed for BENJ. TOOKE, at the
Middle-Temple-Gate, Fleetſtreet. 1712.

Swift's concern about the state of the language, as he saw it, was great enough to cause him to publish a serious proposal for establishing some sort of Academy to regulate and maintain the standards of the English language, similar to the Académie Française which had been set up in France in 1634. The arguments used were similar to those of the *Tatler* article of 1710, but Swift introduced also the idea of *ascertaining* the language (*fixing, making it certain*) so that it would not be subject to further change.

Activity 19.3

Comment on the possibility and desirability of 'ascertaining' a language, and on Swift's assertion that a language need not be 'perpetually changing'.

Text 151 – from Jonathan Swift's *A Proposal*, 1712 (facsimile)

My LORD; I do here, in the Name of all the Learned and Polite Perſons of the Nation, complain to Your LORDSHIP, as *Firſt Miniſter*, that our Language is extremely imperfect; that its daily Improvements are by no means in proportion to its daily Corruptions; that the Pretenders to poliſh and refine it, have chiefly multiplied Abuſes and Abſurdities; and, that in many Inſtances, it offends againſt every Part of Grammar.

I ſee no abſolute Neceſſity why any Language ſhould be perpetually changing; for we find many Examples to the contrary.

BUT what I have moſt at Heart is, that ſome Method ſhould be thought on for *aſcertaining* and *fixing* our Language for ever, after ſuch Alterations are made in it as ſhall be thought requiſite. For I am of Opinion, that it is better a Language ſhould not be wholly perfect, than that it ſhould be perpetually changing; and we muſt give over at one Time, or at length infallibly change for the worſe:

BUT where I ſay, that I would have our Language, after it is duly correct, always to laſt; I do not mean that it ſhould never be enlarged: Provided, that no Word which a Society ſhall give a Sanction to, be afterwards antiquated and exploded, they may have liberty to receive whatever new ones they ſhall find occaſion for:

19.2 Dr Johnson's *Dictionary of the English Language*

Dr Samuel Johnson (1709–1784) published *The Plan of a Dictionary of the English Language* in 1747, and completed the dictionary for publication in 1755, by which time he had written the definitions of over 40,000 words, with about 114,000 quotations to illustrate their usage. Knowledge of the etymology of words was limited in the 18th century, but Johnson's dictionary was to remain a standard reference work for over 150 years until the publication of the *Oxford English Dictionary*, completed in 1928.

Among his objectives were the following:

- 'To fix the English language' – although he recognised that this could not be attained, 'language is the work of man, of a being from whom permanence and stability cannot be derived'.
- 'To preserve the purity and ascertain the meaning of our English idiom' (*ascertain* then meaning *to make certain, to prove* (*a thing*) *objectively certain, to fix*).
- To provide a dictionary for popular use.

In the *Plan* he discussed the criteria he proposed to establish in preparing the dictionary:

- 'Foreign words' are to be included, whether 'naturalized and incorporated', like *zenith*, *meridian*, *cynosure*, *equator*, *satellites*, *category*, *cachexy*, *peripneumony*, or still 'alien', like *habeas corpus*, *nisi prius*, *hypostasis*.
- To include 'the peculiar words of every profession' (*peculiar* meaning *belonging to a group of persons, as distinct from others*).
- To include 'the names of species' even though they require no definition – *horse*, *dog*, *cat*, *willow*, *alder*, *dasy*, *rose* because such words still require 'that their accents should be settled, their sounds ascertained, and their etymologies deduced'.
- To settle the orthography, or spelling, of words:

> The chief rule which I propose to follow, is to make no innovation, without a reason sufficient to balance the inconvenience of change; and such reason I do not expect often to find.

- To produce a guide to pronunciation – the accentuation of polysyllables and the pronunciation of monosyllables. He saw danger in variation, when *wound* and *wind*, 'as they are now frequently pronounced', no longer rhymed with *sound* and *mind*.
- To consider the etymology or derivation of words.
- 'Interpreting the words with brevity, fulness and perspicuity.'
- Assigning words to classes – *general*, *poetic*, *obsolete*, *used by individual writers*, *used only in burlesque writing*, *impure and barbarous*.

Both Johnson and Swift disliked *cant*,

> To introduce and multiply cant words is the most ruinous corruption in any language.
>
> (Jonathan Swift, 1755)

> Nor are all words which are not found in the vocabulary, to be lamented as omissions. Of **the laborious and mercantile part of the people**, the diction is in great measure casual and mutable; many of their terms are formed for some temporary or local convenience, and though current at certain times and places, are in others utterly unknown. This **fugitive cant**, which is always in a state of increase or decay, cannot be regarded as any part of the durable materials of a language, and therefore must be suffered to perish with other things unworthy of preservation.
>
> (Samuel Johnson, *Preface to Dictionary*, 1755)

as did other writers on the language (see Text 161). The word *cant* was always used pejoratively, and meant variously,

- *phraseology used for fashion's sake, without being a genuine expression of sentiment*, or
- *an affected stock phrase, repeated as a matter of habit*.

It might also mean *provincial dialect*, *vulgar slang* – whatever the writer found distasteful.

The *Plan* was addressed to his patron, the Earl of Chesterfield, and concluded with a typical Johnsonian rhetorical peroration.

Text 152 – Dr Samuel Johnson's *Plan of a Dictionary*, 1747 (facsimile)

> THIS, my Lord, is my idea of an Engliſh dictionary, a dictionary by which the pronunciation of our language may be fixed, and its attainment facilitated; by which its purity may be preſerved, its uſe aſcertained, and its duration lengthened. And though, perhaps, to correct the language of nations by books of grammar, and amend their manners by diſcourſes of morality, may be taſks equally difficult; yet as it is unavoidable to wiſh, it is natural likewiſe to hope, that your Lordſhip's patronage may not be wholly loſt; that it may contribute to the preſervation of antient, and the improvement of modern writers; that it may promote the reformation of thoſe tranſlators, who for want of underſtanding the characteriſtical difference of tongues, have formed a chaotic dialect of heterogeneous phraſes; and awaken to the care of purer diction, ſome men of genius, whoſe attention to argument makes them negligent of ſtile, or whoſe rapid imagination, like the Peruvian torrents, when it brings down gold, mingles it with ſand.

19.3 The perfection of the language

Dr Johnson again refers to the idea of fixing the language in the Preface of the published *Dictionary* in 1755. He himself, as we have seen, is sceptical of the possibility of success, although he believes in the idea of the perfection and decay of a language:

> Those who have been persuaded to think well of my design, will require that it should fix our language, and put a stop to those alterations which time and chance have hitherto been suffered to make in it without opposition. With this consequence I will confess that I have indulged expectation which neither reason nor experience can justify.
>
> ... tongues, like governments, have a natural tendency to degeneration; we have long preserved our constitution, let us make some struggles for our language.
>
> (from the 'Preface' to Dr Johnson's *Dictionary*, 1755)

Both Swift and Johnson thought that the century from the beginning of Queen Elizabeth's reign in 1558 to the Civil Wars in 1642 was a kind of Golden Age of Improvement in the language, though they did not believe that it had yet reached a 'state of Perfection'. The belief that languages could be improved and brought to a state of perfection was common (though we may not today believe it). Confusion between *language* and *language use* causes the one to be identified with the other, and a period of great writers is called a period of greatness for the language. We have already seen Swift identifying a *style* which he disliked with corruption of the *language*.

19.3.1 The Augustan Age and Classical perfection

Some writers thought that the 'state of perfection' would come in the future, but later 18th-century grammarians placed it in the early and mid 18th-century language of writers like Addison, Steele, Pope and Swift himself. This period is known as the 'Augustan Age' (from the period of the reign of the Roman Emperor Augustus, 27 BC – AD 14, when great writers like Virgil, Horace and Ovid flourished). The language and literature of Classical Rome and Greece were still the foundation of education in the 18th century. Writers copied the forms of Classical literature, like the epic, the ode, and dramatic tragedy, while the Latin and Greek languages were models of perfection in their unchangeable state which writers hoped English could attain. The influence of the sound of Latin and Greek helps to explain Swift's dislike of 'Northern' consonant clusters (see Text 151).

The vernacular Latin language of the 1st century AD had, of course, continued to change, so that after several centuries its many dialects had evolved into French, Italian, Spanish and the other Romance languages. But Classical Latin was fixed and ascertained, because its vocabulary and grammar were derived from the literature of its greatest period. This state seemed to be in complete contrast to contemporary English, and so following Swift, many other writers and grammarians sought to improve the language. Somewhere, in the past or the future, lay the perfected English language.

19.4 'The Genius of the Language'

There are few references to the language of ordinary people by 18th-century writers on language – the grammarians – 'it is beneath a grammarian's attempt' (Anselm Bayly in 1772). But even writers whom they admired were not necessarily taken as models of good English either. Authors' writings were subjected to detailed scrutiny for supposed errors. Grammarians sometimes spoke of 'the Genius of the Language' or 'the Idiom of the Tongue' as a criterion for judgement, the word *genius* meaning sometimes *character* or *spirit*, or simply *grammar*. But this concept in practice meant little more than the intuition of the grammarian, what he thought or felt sounded right, expressed in the Latin phrase *ipse dixit* (*he himself says*). Sometimes this reliance on personal opinion was clearly stated:

> ... *to commute to* I look upon not to be English.
>
> It will be easily discovered that I have paid no regard to authority. I have censured even our best penmen, where they have departed from what I conceive to be the idiom of the tongue, or where I have thought they violate grammar without necessity. To judge by the rule of Ipse dixit is the way to perpetuate error.
>
> (*on the wrong use of prepositions*) ... even by Swift, Temple, Addison, and other writers of the highest reputation; some of them, indeed, with such shameful impropriety as one

> must think must shock every English ear, and almost induce the reader to suppose the writers to be foreigners.
>
> (Robert Baker, *Reflections on the English Language*, 1770)

Notice that Baker condemns *ipse dixit* when applied to 'the best penmen', but not when applied to himself. Often appeals were made to *Reason*, or *Analogy* (a similar form to be found elsewhere in the language):

> In doubtful cases regard ought to be had in our decisions to the analogy of the language.... Of 'Whether he will or *no*' and 'Whether he will or *not*', it is only the latter that is analogical... when you supply the ellipsis, you find it necessary to use the adverb *not*, '*Whether* he will *or* will *not*.'
>
> (George Campbell, *Philosophy of Rhetoric*, 1776)

Grammarians were not always consistent in their arguments, however. They recognised that the evidence for the vocabulary and grammar of a language must be derived from what people actually wrote and spoke, referred to sometimes as Custom:

> Reason permits that we give way to Custom, though contrary to Reason. Analogie is not the Mistress of Language. She prescribes only the Laws of Custom.
>
> (*Art of Speaking*, 1708)

This point of view is argued in greater detail in the following text.

Activity 19.4

Discuss Joseph Priestley's assessment of the relative values of *custom, analogy, the genius of the language*, and *the disapproval of grammarians* in deciding the forms of a standard language.

Text 153 – Joseph Priestley's *Rudiments of English Grammar*, 1769

> It must be allowed, that the custom of speaking is the original, and only just standard of any language. We see, in all grammars, that this is sufficient to establish a rule, even contrary to the strongest analogies of the language with itself. Must not this custom, therefore, be allowed to have some weight, in favour of those forms of speech, to which our best writers and speakers seem evidently prone; forms which are contrary to no analogy of the language with itself, and which have been disapproved by grammarians, only from certain abstract and arbitrary considerations, and when their decisions were not prompted by the genius of the language; which discovers itself in nothing more than in the general propensity of those who use it to certain modes of construction? I think, however, that I have not, in any case, seemed to favour what our grammarians will call an irregularity, but where the genius of the language, and not only single examples, but the general practice of those who write it, and the almost universal custom of all who speak it, have obliged me to do so. I also think I have seemed to favour those irregularities, no more than the degree of the propensity I have first mentioned, when unchecked by a regard to arbitrary rules, in those who use the forms of speech I refer to, will authorize me.

19.5 Bishop Lowth's *Grammar*

One in particular of the many grammar books of the 18th century had a lasting influence on later grammars which were published for use in schools in the late 18th century and throughout the 19th century – Robert Lowth's *A Short Introduction to English Grammar* (1762). Lowth's attitude was prescriptive – that is, he prescribed or laid down what he himself considered to be correct usage.

Text 154 – Robert Lowth's *A Short Introduction to English Grammar*, 1762 (i) (facsimile)

GRAMMAR is the Art of rightly expreſſing our thoughts by Words.

Grammar in general, or Univerſal Grammar, explains the Principles which are common to all languages.

The Grammar of any particular Language, as the Engliſh Grammar, applies thoſe common principles to that particular language, according to the eſtabliſhed uſage and cuſtom of it.

Text 155 – Robert Lowth's *A Short Introduction to English Grammar*, 1762 (ii) (facsimile)

The principal deſign of a Grammar of any Language is to teach us to expreſs ourſelves with propriety in that Language, and to be able to judge of every phraſe and form of conſtruction, whether it be right or not. The plain way of doing this, is to lay down rules, and to illuſtrate them by examples. But beſides ſhewing what is right, the matter may be further explained by pointing out what is wrong.

The words *propriety* and *right* in Text 155 are important, because Lowth was not describing the language in its many varieties, but prescribing what ought to be written in a standard variety of English, and pointing out 'errors' and 'solecisms' with examples from authors like Milton, Dryden and Pope. He described other varieties of usage only in order to condemn them.

The following text is an extract from the Preface, and it typifies this particular attitude to language use. What people actually say and write, even though they may be socially of the highest rank, or eminent authors, is subject to Lowth's prescriptive judgement.

Text 156 – Robert Lowth's *A Short Introduction to English Grammar*, 1762 (iii) (facsimile)

It is now about fifty years ſince Doctor Swift *made a public remonſtrance, addreſſed to the Earl of* Oxford, *then Lord Treaſurer, of the imperfect State of our Language; alledging in particular, "that in many inſtances it "offended againſt every part of "Grammar."* Swift *muſt be allowed to have been a good judge of this matter. He was himſelf very attentive to this part, both in his own writings, and in his remarks upon thoſe of his friends: he is one of our moſt correct, and perhaps our very beſt proſe writer. Indeed the juſtneſs of this complaint, as far as I can find, hath never been queſtioned; and yet no effectual method hath hitherto been taken to redreſs the grievance of which he complains.*

But let us conſider, how, and in what extent, we are to underſtand this charge brought againſt the Engliſh *Language Does it mean, that the* Engliſh *Language as it is ſpoken by the politeſt part of the nation, and as it ſtands in the writings of our moſt approved authors, oftentimes offends againſt every part of Grammar? Thus far, I am afraid, the charge is true.*

Lowth's book was intended for those already well educated. This can be inferred from part of the Preface to his *Grammar*:

> A Grammatical Study of our own Language makes no part of the ordinary method of instruction which we pass thro' in our childhood ... (p. vii)

The use of the first person *we* implies that his readers, like him, will have studied Latin and Greek at school – the *ancient* or *learned* languages. This, however, did not in his opinion provide them with a knowledge of English grammar, even though they lived in polite society and read English literature, activities not followed by most of the population at the time.

Text 157 – Robert Lowth's *A Short Introduction to English Grammar*, 1762 (iv) (facsimile)

Much practice in the polite world, and a general acquaintance with the beſt authors, are good helps, but alone will hardly be ſufficient: we have writers, who have enjoyed theſe advantages in their full extent, and yet cannot be recommended as models of an accurate ſtyle. Much leſs then will what is commonly called Learning ſerve the purpoſe; that is, a critical knowledge of ancient languages, and much reading of ancient authors: *In a word, it was calculated for the uſe of the Learner even of the loweſt claſs. Thoſe, who would enter more deeply into this Subject, will find it fully and accurately handled, with the greateſt acuteneſs of inveſtigation, perſpicuity of explication, and elegance of method, in a Treatiſe intitled* HERMES, *by* JAMES HARRIS *Eſq;* *the moſt beautiful and perfect example of Analyſis that has been exhibited ſince the days of* Ariſtotle.

* *class* as used in this extract does not mean *social class*, but *grade* or *standard of achievement*.

19.6 'The depraved language of the common People'

The standard language recognised by 18th-century grammarians was that variety used by what they called 'the Learned and Polite Persons of the Nation' (Swift) – *polite* in the sense of *polished, refined, elegant, well-bred.* By definition, the language of the common people was inferior. This had far-reaching social consequences, as we shall see later in the chapter. Here is some of the evidence, which also explains why we know much less about the regional, social and spoken varieties of 18th-century English, except what we can infer from novels, plays, letters and other indirect sources – they were not worth the attention of scholars.

Text 158 – On the language of common people

. . . *themselves and Families* (from the *Monthly Review*) . . . a very bad Expression, though very common. It is mere **Shopkeepers cant** and will always be found contemptible in the Ears of persons of any Taste.

(Robert Baker, *Reflections on the English Language*, 1770)

(on *most an end* for *most commonly*) . . . is an expression that would almost disgrace the mouth of **a hackney-coachman**.

(Robert Baker, *Remarks on the English Language*, 1779)

. . . though sometimes it may be difficult, if not impossible to reduce **common speech** to rule, and indeed it is beneath a grammarian's attempt.

(Anselm Bayly, *Plain and Complete Grammar*, 1772)

No absolute monarch hath it more in his power to nobilitate a person of obscure birth, than it is in the power of good use to ennoble words of **low** or **dubious extraction**; such, for instance, as have either arisen, nobody knows how, like *fib*, *banter*, *bigot*, *fop*, *flippant*, among **the rabble**, or like *flimsy*, sprung from the **cant of the manufacturers**.

(George Campbell, *Philosophy of Rhetoric*, 1776)

My Animadversions will extend to such Phrases only as People in decent Life inadvertently adopt. . . . Purity and Politeness of Expression . . . is the only external Distinction which remains between **a gentleman and a valet**; **a lady and a Mantua-maker***.

(Philip Withers, *Aristarchus*, 1788)

* A mantua was a loose gown, so a *Mantua-maker* was a *dress-maker*.

Such comments as these clearly show that the divisions of 18th-century society were marked by language as much as by birth, rank, wealth and education.

19.7 'Propriety & perspicuity of language'

19.7.1 *Formal literary style*

19.7.1.1 *Dr Samuel Johnson*

You will have noticed that the style of Lowth and other grammarians is very formal, its vocabulary and structure unlike that of everyday conversation. Literary prose adopts fashionable choices from the resources of the language at different periods, while ordinary language in speech and writing continues, generally unremarked.

Activity 19.5

Discuss the features of vocabulary and syntax which distinguish this literary style of writing.

Text 159 – Samuel Johnson, from *The Rambler*, No. 38, July 1750

The advantages of mediocrity

...Health and vigour, and a happy constitution of the corporeal frame, are of absolute necessity to the enjoyment of the comforts, and to the performance of the duties of life, and requisite in yet a greater measure to the accomplishment of any thing illustrious or distinguished; yet even these, if we can judge by their apparent consequences, are sometimes not very beneficial to those on whom they are most liberally bestowed. They that frequent the chambers of the sick, will generally find the sharpest pains, and most stubborn maladies among them whom confidence of the force of nature formerly betrayed to negligence and irregularity; and that superfluity of strength, which was at once their boast and their snare, has often, in the latter part of life, no other effect than than it continues them long in impotence and anguish.

Lexical words: **61** – OE 23 = 37.7%; French 32 = 52.5%; Latin 6 = 9.8%.

The words taken from French after the 14th century are: *accomplishment, consequences, impotence, irregularity, beneficial, performance, constitution, distinguished, enjoyment, formerly*, and from Latin, *confidence, requisite, frequent, illustrious, corporeal.*

The words and phrases are often balanced in pairs, in rhetorical parallel, for example,

to the enjoyment of the comforts
and
to the performance of the duties of life

which provide the syntactic formality of this style (compare the informal style of Text 163).

🕮 There is a full analysis in the *Text Commentary Book*.

19.7.1.2 *Edward Harwood and 'elegance of diction'*

A new translation of the *New Testament* was published in 1768.

Text 160 – Edward Harwood's *Liberal Translation of the New Testament* (i) (facsimile)

LIBERAL TRANSLATION

OF THE

NEW TESTAMENT;

BEING

An Attempt to tranſlate the SACRED WRITINGS

WITH THE SAME

Freedom, Spirit, and Elegance,

With which other Engliſh Tranſlations from the Greek Claſſics have lately been executed:

The DESIGN and SCOPE of each Author being ſtrictly and impartially explored, the TRUE SIGNIFICATION and FORCE of the Original critically obſerved, and, as much as poſſible, transfuſed into our Language, and the Whole elucidated and explained upon a new and rational Plan:

With SELECT NOTES, Critical and Explanatory.

BY E. HARWOOD.

The author's intention was

> to cloathe the genuine ideas and doctrines of the Apostles with that propriety and perspicuity, in which they themselves, I apprehend, would have exhibited them had they *now* lived and written in our language.... I *first* carefully perused every chapter to investigate and discover the one true meaning of the Author with all the accuracy and sagacity I could employ.... When I apprehended I had found out the *true* signification of the Original, and the *precise* ideas of the writer at the time he wrote, my *next* study was to adorn them in such language as is *now* written...
>
> Elegance of diction, therefore, hath ever been consulted, but never at the expense of truth and fidelity, which ought ever to be sacred and inviolable in an interpreter of Scripture.
>
> It is pleasing to observe, how much our language, within these very few years, hath been refined and polished, and what infinite improvements it hath lately received.

Harwood attributes *elegance, harmony, copiousness and strength* to the language, and so to his translation, contrasting it with the *Authorized Version* of the Bible published in 1611, which he calls 'the bald and barbarous language of the old vulgar version'.

In present-day linguistic terms, Harwood is really talking about *language use* or *style*, the way in which the resources of *the language* are employed by writers. We would also want to question his principles and beliefs about the separation of *ideas* from the way they are *cloathed in language*. We can best assess his style by comparing one of the most famous passages from St Paul's letters in his version and that in the *bald and barbarous language* of the *Authorized Version* of 1611.

Text 161 – St Paul's *Letter to the Corinthians, chapter 13*

King James Bible, 1611 (modernized spelling)

THOUGH I speak with the tongues of men and of angels, and have not charity, I am become as sounding brass, or a tinkling cymbal.

2 And though I have the gift of prophecy, and understand all mysteries, and all knowledge; and though I have all faith, so that I could remove mountains, and have not charity, I am nothing.

3 And though I bestow all my goods to feed the poor, and though I give my body to be burned, and have not charity, it profiteth me nothing.

4 Charity suffereth long, and is kind; charity envieth not; charity vaunteth not itself, is not puffed up,

5 Doth not behave itself unseemly, seeketh not her own, is not easily provoked, thinketh no evil;

6 Rejoiceth not in iniquity, but rejoiceth in the truth;

7 Beareth all things, believeth all things, hopeth all things, endureth all things.

8 Charity never faileth; but whether there be prophecies, they shall fail; whether there be tongues, they shall cease; whether there be knowledge, it shall vanish away.

9 For we know in part, and we prophecy in part.

10 But when that which is perfect is come, then that which is in part shall be done away.

11 When I was a child, I spake as a child, I understood as a child, I thought as a child: but when I became a man, I put away childish things.

12 For now we see through a glass, darkly; but then face to face: now I know in part; but then shall I know even as also I am known.

13 And now abideth faith, hope, charity, these three; but the greatest of these is charity.

Lexical words 72: OE/ON 50 = 69.5%; OF 20 = 27.8%; French 15th-century 2 = 2.7%.

Two words (2.7%) were adopted in the 15th century – *provoked, vaunteth.* The rest consist largely of core vocabulary from OE and assimilated OF words, which contrasts completely with Edward Harwood's choices in Text 162.

Charity meant *the Christian love of our fellow-men.* The word has developed a more restricted meaning since the 17th century – *benevolence to one's neighbours, especially to the poor, as manifested in action, specifically alms-giving.* Harwood uses *benevolence* in his translation; modern versions use *love.*

Text 162 – Edward Harwood's *Liberal Translation of the New Testament* (ii) (facsimile)

quire the moſt illuſtrious of
theſe ſpiritual gifts—and yet
I can point out to you an en-
dowment, that far tranſcends
all theſe.

CHAP. XIII.

1 COuld I ſpeak all the
languages of men
and of angels, and yet had
an heart deſtitute of benevolence, I am no more than
ſounding braſs or a tinkling
cymbal.
2 And was I endowed with
the ampleſt prophetic powers: could I unravel all the
myſteries of nature: had I
accumulated all the know-
ledge of the ſons of men:
could I exert ſuch ſtupendous
powers as to remove moun-
tains from their baſis, and
transfer them at pleaſure
from place to place—and yet
my heart a ſtranger to benevolence, I am nothing.
3 And ſhould I give away
all I had in the world in cha-
ritable contributions to the
poor: ſhould I even ſurren-
der up my body to the flames
—and yet have an heart de-
void of benevolence, it would
be of no avail to me.
4 Benevolence is unruffled;
is benign: Benevolence che-
riſhes no ambitious deſires:
Benevolence is not oſtenta-
tious; is not inflated with
inſolence.
5 It preſerves a conſiſtent
decorum; is not enſlaved to
ſordid intereſt; is not tranſ-
ported with furious paſſion;
indulges no malevolent deſign.
6 It conceives no delight
from the perpetration of wick-
edneſs; but is firſt to ap-
plaud truth and virtue.
7 It throws a vail of can-
dour over all things: is diſpoſed to believe all things:
views all things in the moſt
favourable light: ſupports
all things with ſerene compo-
ſure.
8 Benevolence ſhall con-
tinue to ſhine with undimi-
niſhed luſtre when all prophetic powers ſhall be no
more, when the ability of
ſpeaking various languages
ſhall be withdrawn, and when
all ſupernatural endowments
ſhall be annihilated.
9 For in this ſtate our
knowledge is defective, our
prophetic powers are limited.
10 But when we arrive in
thoſe happy regions where
perfection dwells, the defective and the limited ſhall be
no more for ever.
11 Juſt as when I was, for
example, in the imperfect
ſtate of childhood; I then
diſcourſed, I underſtood, I
reaſoned in the erroneous
manner children do — but
F 4 when
when I arrived at the matu-
rity and perfection of man-
hood, the defects of my former imperfect ſtate were all
ſwallowed up and forgotten.
12 For in this ſcene of
being our terreſtrial mirrour
exhibits to us but a very dim
and obſcure reflection: but
in an happy futurity we ſhall
ſee face to face—In the pre-
ſent life my knowledge is
partial and limited: in the
future, my knowledge will be
unconfined and clear, like
that divine infallible knowledge, by which I am now
pervaded.
13 In fine, the virtues of
ſuperior eminence are theſe
three, faith, hope, benevolence—but the moſt illuſtrious of theſe is benevolence.

CHAP. XIV.

Lexical words: **140**
14th century & before – OE, ME & ON 36 = 26%; OF 49 = 35%; others 3 = 2%.
15th century & after – French 28 = 20%; Latin 24 = 17%.

Over a quarter of Harwood's lexical vocabulary was adopted in the 16th and 17th centuries from French or Latin. He deliberately used a learned, formal vocabulary, abstract and polysyllabic. The style was justified as *elegant*, *refined*, *polished*, but present-day readers are more likely to find it pompous and so overblown as to read like a parody.

📖 The lexical vocabulary, with derivations, is listed in the *Word Book*.

19.7.1.3 *William Barnes'* A Philological Grammar *(1854)*

This attitude of social and educational superiority to 'bald and barbarous' language was criticised in the mid-19th century by the Dorset poet and grammarian William Barnes (1801–86) in his *A Philological Grammar*, published in 1854:

> In English, purity is in many cases given up for the sake of what is considered to be elegance. Instead of the expression of the common people "I will not be put upon," we are apt to consider it better language to say "I will not be imposed upon", though the word *imposed* is the Latin *impositum*, put upon; from *in*, upon, and *pono*, to put. So that in these and other such cases we use in what we consider the better expression, the very same words as in the worse; or we take, instead of two English words, a Latin compound, which, from the laws upon which languages are constructed, and the limited range of choice which the human mind has in constructing expressions for the same idea, is made of the very simples which we reject.

The technical terminology of academic languagewas also criticised by William Barnes. For example, common terms we use to describe the sounds of language were Englished by him as follows,

	Barnes
speech	breathsound language
writing	type language
vowel	pure breathsound
consonant	clipped breathsound
labials	lip letters
labiodentals	lip-teeth letters
dentals	tongue-teeth letters
alveolars	palate letters
velars	throat letters

19.7.2 *Informal style*

But of course not all writing in the 18th century was in the formal literary style of Harwood and Johnson. Here is a short example taken from a diary.

Text 163 – Thomas Hearne's *Remarks and Collections*, 1715

> MAY 28 (Sat.) This being the Duke of Brunswick, commonly called King George's Birth-Day, some of the Bells were jambled in Oxford, by the care of some of the Whiggish, Fanatical Crew; but as I did not observe the Day in the least my self, so it was little taken notice of (unless by way of ridicule) by other honest People, who are for K. James IIId. who is the undoubted King of these Kingdoms, & 'tis heartily wish'd by them that he may be restored.
>
> This Day I saw one Ward with Dr. Charlett, who, it seems, hath printed several Things. He is a clergy Man. I must inquire about him.

Lexical words: **40** – OE 21 & ON 1 = 22 = 55%; French 16 = 40%; Latin 1 (*Fanatical*) = 2.5%; not known 1 (*Whiggish*) = 2.5%.

🕮 The lexical vocabulary, with derivations, is listed in the *Word Book*.

Most of the words are core vocabulary from OE or OF. The words entering the language after the 14th century are: *Crew*, *several*, *notice*, *undoubted*, *clergy-man*, *ridicule*, *jambled* (=*jangled*), *Fanatical*, *Whiggish*. Syntactically, the first paragraph is a compound-complex sentence, but there is no embedding of clauses, one statement follows another ('right-branching'), so there is no difficulty of understanding. The last two sentences are short and simple.

19.8 Language and social class

Here is a short example of the writing of 'the laborious and mercantile part of the people'. It is an inventory of the goods belonging to a hand-loom weaver, Elkanah Shaw, drawn up in 1773.

Text 164 – Inventory of Elkanah Shaw's property, 1773 (facsimile)

A *tenter* was 'a wooden framework on which cloth is stretched after being milled, so that it may set or dry evenly and without shrinking'. The word survives in the phrase *on tenterhooks*.

November 20 Day 1773 this is Atrue and Perfect
Invetary of the Goods and Chatles of Elknah
Shaw Aprised by us this day And In the year
of our Lord Above writen — £ : s : d
Purse And Aperel — 2 : 2 : 0
One Close praser — 0 : 12 : 0
towo Beds and beding — 2 : 0 : 0
One pare of Lomes — 1 : 5 : 0
two Chists — 0 : 12 : 0
One Clock — 1 : 10 : 0
One Couch Chear — 0 : 11 : 0
One Coberd — 0 : 9 : 0
one table — 0 : 5 : 0
One Chist — 0 : 5 : 0
five Chears and five Stoles — 0 : 5 : 0
One Litle table one Boiler pot — 0 : 4 : 0
One Range and Coulrake and tangs
and Endirns — 0 : 10 : 0
for wone tenter — 1 : 10 : 0
for wool Died and un Died — 30 : 0 : 0
for Six peeces — 18 : 0 : 0
for pots and all huslement — 0 : 10 : 0
60 : 10 : 0

Saml Haigh
[illegible]
Joshua Wrigley junr
Joseph Campinet

The evidence of the quotations in section 19.6 suggests that if the language of the common people was regarded as inferior by the educated upper classes in the 18th century, then their ideas and thoughts would be similarly devalued.

> The best Expressions grow **low and degenrate**, when **profan'd by the populace**, and applied to **mean things**. The use they make of them, infecting them with **a mean and abject Idea**, causes that we cannot use them without **sullying and defiling t**hose things, which are signified by them. But it is no hard matter to discern between **the depraved Language of common People**, and **the noble refin'd expressions of the Gentry**, whose condition and merits have advanced them above the other.
>
> (*Art of Speaking, rendered into English from the French of Messieurs du Port Royal 1676*, 2nd edn, 1708)

Language was regarded as 'the dress of thought' or, to use another simple metaphor, its 'mirror'. It was believed that there was a direct relationship between good language and good thinking. On the one hand was the dominant social class, the Gentry, whose language and way of life are variously described as *polite*, *civilized*, *elegant*, *noble*, *refined*, *tasteful*, and *pure*. On the other hand were 'the laborious and mercantile part of the people', shopkeepers and hackney-coachmen, the rabble, whose language was *vulgar*, *barbarous*, *contemptible*, *low*, *degenerate*, *profane*, *mean*, *abject*, *depraved*.

This view was reinforced by a theory of language which was called 'Universal Grammar'. The following quotations illustrate a belief in the direct connection between language and the mind, or soul, and in the superior value of abstract thought over the senses. They are taken from *Hermes: or a Philosophical Inquiry concerning Language and Universal Grammar*, published in 1751 by James Harris, the author who was commended by Bishop Lowth (see Text 157):

> 'Tis a phrase often apply'd to a man, when speaking, that *he speaks his MIND*; as much as to say, that his Speech or Discourse is *a publishing of some Energie or Motion of his Soul*. The VULGAR merged *in Sense* from their earliest Infancy, and never once dreaming any thing to be worthy of pursuit, but what pampers their Appetite, or fills their Purse, imagine nothing to be *real*, but what may be *tasted*, or *touched*.

For students of language today, the differences between Standard English and regional dialects are seen to be *linguistically* superficial and unimportant. You can convey the same meanings as well in one as the other, although we cannot, in everyday life, ignore the social connotations of regional and nonstandard speech, which are still very powerful in conveying and maintaining attitudes.

In the 18th century, the linguistic differences between refined and common speech were held to match fundamental differences in intellect and morality. The gulf between the two was reinforced by the fact that education was in the 'learned languages' Latin and Greek. The classical Greek language and literature in particular were judged to be the most 'perfect':

> Now the Language of these Greeks was truly like themselves; 'twas conformable to their transcendent and universal Genius.

'Twere to be wished, that those amongst us, who either write or read, with a view to employ their liberal leisure... 'twere to be wished, I say, that the liberal (if they have any relish for letters) would inspect the finished Models of *Grecian Literature*...

(James Harris, *Hermes*, 1751)

As it was believed that the contrasts between the *refined* language of the classically educated class, and the *vulgar* language of the common people, mirrored equal differences in intellectual capabilities and also in virtue or morality, such beliefs had social and political consequences.

The most devastating aspect of 18th century assessments of language was its philosophical justification of this notion of vulgarity.

(Olivia Smith, *The Politics of Language, 1791–1819*, 1984)

These social and political consequences can be demonstrated. The years of the long wars with France (1793–1815) following the French Revolution of 1789 were marked by the political oppression of popular movements for reform. Ideas about language were used to protect the government from criticism. For example, the notion of *vulgarity of language* became an excuse to dismiss a series of petitions to Parliament calling for the reform of the voting system. If the language of the 'labouring classes' was by definition inferior, incapable of expressing coherent thought, and also of dubious moral value, then it was impossible for them to use language properly in order to argue their own case.

Liberty of speech and freedom of discussion in this House form an essential part of the constitution; but it is necessary that persons coming forward as petitioners, should address the House in decent and respectful language.

(*Parliamentary Debates*, xxx.779)

Here are short extracts from three petitions presented to Parliament. The first was presented by 'tradesmen and artificers, unpossessed of freehold land' in Sheffield in 1793, and was rejected; the second, by 'twelve freeholders' from Reading in 1810, was accepted; the third was presented by non-voters from Yorkshire in 1817. At that time, only men who owned freehold land had the vote.

Activity 19.6

(i) Discuss the charge that the language of the first petition was 'indecent and disrespectful', and compare it with another comment made at the time: 'I suspect that the objection to the roughness of the language was not the real cause why this petition was opposed'.

(ii) Discuss the view expressed in Parliament at the time that the language of the second petition, 'though firm as it ought to be, was respectful'.

(iii) The Tory minister George Canning said of the third petition, 'if such language were tolerated, there was an end of the House of Commons, and of the present system of government'. What is objectional in the language?

Text 165 – From a Petition to Parliament, 1793

Your petitioners are lovers of peace, of liberty, and justice. They are in general tradesmen and artificers, unpossessed of freehold land, and consequently have no voice in choosing members to sit in parliament; – but though they may not be freeholders, they are men, and do not think themselves fairly used in being excluded the rights of citizens...

(*Parliamentary Debates*, xxx. 776)

Text 166 – From a Petition to Parliament, 1810

The petitioners cannot conceive it possible that his Majesty's present incapable and arbitrary ministers should be still permitted to carry on the government of the country, after having wasted our resources in fruitless expeditions, and having shewn no vigour but in support of antiquated prejudices, and in attacks upon the liberties of the subject.

(*Parliamentary Debates*, xvi. 955)

Text 167 – From a Petition to Parliament, 1817

The petitioners have a full and immovable conviction, a conviction which they believe to be universal throughout the kingdom, that the House doth not, in any consitutional or rational sense, represent the nation; that, when the people have ceased to be represented, the constitution is subverted; that taxation without representation is slavery...

(*Parliamentary Debates*, xxxv. 81–2)

(Texts 165–7 are quoted in Olivia Smith, op. cit.)

The grammar and spelling of these extracts are perfectly 'correct', but here is an example of a letter of protest against the enclosure of common land, written anonymously by 'the Combin'd of the Parish of Cheshunt' to their local landowner. Nonstandard spelling, punctuation and grammar like this in a petition to Parliament would clearly have provided an excuse for its dismissal.

Text 168 – From a letter to Oliver Cromwell Esquire, of Cheshunt Park, 27 February 1799

Whe right these lines to you who are the Combin'd of the Parish of Cheshunt in the Defence of our Parrish rights which you unlawfully are about to disinherit us of...

Resolutions is maid by the aforesaid Combind that if you intend of inclosing Our Commond fields Lammas Meads Marches &c Whe Resolve before that bloudy and unlawful act is finished to have your hearts bloud if you proceede in the aforesaid bloudy act Whe like horse leaches will cry give, give until whe have split the bloud of every one that wishes to rob the Inosent unborn. It shall not be in your power to say I am safe from the hands of my Enemy for Whe like birds of pray will prively lie in wait to spil the bloud of the aforesaid Charicters whose names and places of abode are as prutrified sores in our Nostrils. Whe declair that thou shall not say I am safe when thou goest to thy bed for beware that thou liftest not thine eyes up in the most mist of flames...

(Quoted in E. P. Thompson, *The Making of the English Working Class*, 1963)

19.9 William Cobbett and the politics of language

William Cobbett (1763–1835) was the son of a farmer from Farnham, Surrey, and self-educated. From 1785 to 1791 he served in a foot regiment in Canada, and left the army after trying, and failing, to bring some officers to trial for embezzlement. He spent the rest of his life in writing, journalism and farming, and became an MP in 1832 after the passing of the Reform Act.

Cobbett began a weekly newspaper, *The Political Register*, in 1802 as a Tory, but soon became converted to the Radical cause of social and Parliamentary reform, and wrote and edited the *Register* until his death in 1835, campaigning against social injustice and government corruption.

We have seen in Section 19.8 how the concept of vulgarity of language was used to deny the value of the meaning and content of petitions to Parliament. Cobbett referred to this in an edition of *The Political Register* which was written in America, where he had gone after the suspension of *habeas corpus* in England.

Text 169 – William Cobbett's *The Political Register*, 29 November 1817

> The present project... is to communicate to all uneducated Reformers, *a knowledge of Grammar*. The people, you know, were accused of presenting petitions *not grammatically correct*. And those petitions were *rejected*, the petitioners being "*ignorant*": though some of them were afterwards *put into prison*, for being "better informed"...
>
> No doubt remains in my mind, that there was more talent discovered, and more political knowledge, by the leaders amongst the Reformers, than have ever been shown, at any period of time, by the Members of the two houses of parliament.
>
> There was only one thing in which any of you were deficient, and that was in the mere art of so arranging the words in your Resolutions and Petitions as to make these compositions what is called *grammatically correct*. Hence, men of a hundredth part of the mind of some of the authors of the Petitions were enabled to cavil at them on this account, and to infer from this incorrectness, that the Petitioners were a set of *poor ignorant creatures,* who knew nothing of what they were talking; a set of the "*Lower Classes*", who ought never to raise their reading above that of children's books, Christmas Carrols, and the like.
>
> For my part, I have always held a mere knowledge of the rules of grammar very cheap. It is a study, which demands hardly any powers of mind. To possess a knowledge of those rules is a pitiful qualification...
>
> Grammar is to literary composition what a linch-pin is to a waggon. It is a poor pitiful thing in itself; it bears no part of the weight; adds not in the least to the celerity; but, still the waggon cannot very well and safely go on without it...
>
> Therefore, trifling, and even contemptible, as this branch of knowledge is *in itself*, it is of vast importance as to the means of giving to the great powers of the mind their proper effect... The grammarian from whom a man of genius learns his rules has little more claim to a share of such a man's renown than has the goose, who yields the pens with which he writes: but, still the pens are *necessary*, and so is the grammar.

Cobbett's writings, like Tom Paine's *The Rights of Man* in 1792 and *The Age of Reason* in 1794, were themselves practical proof that the language of men of humble class origins could be effective in argument, but both Cobbett and Paine wrote in Standard English. Cobbett was well aware of the social connotations of nonstandard language, and wrote an account of how he had taught himself correct grammar. He does not use use the term *standard* himself, and follows the common practice of implying that only this variety of English has *grammar*. He wrote under the name *Peter Porcupine*.

Text 170 – William Cobbett's *The Life and Adventures of Peter Porcupine*, 1796

> One branch of learning, however, I went to the bottom with, and that the most essential branch too, the grammar of my mother tongue. I had experienced the want of a knowledge of grammar during my stay with Mr Holland; but it is very probable that I never should have thought of encountering the study of it, had not accident placed me under a man whose friendship extended beyond his interest. Writing a fair hand procured me the honour of being copyist to Colonel Debeig, the commandant of the garrison...
>
> Being totally ignorant of the rules of grammar, I necessarily made many mistakes in copying, because no one can copy letter by letter, nor even word by word. The colonel saw my deficiency, and strongly recommended study. He enforced his advice with a sort of injunction, and with a promise of reward in case of success.
>
> I procured me a Lowth's grammar, and applied myself to the study of it with unceasing assiduity, and not without some profit; for, though it was a considerable time before I fully comprehended all that I read, still I read and studied with such unremitted attention, that, at last, I could write without falling into any very gross errors. The pains I took cannot be described: I wrote the whole grammar out two or three times; I got it by heart; I repeated it every morning and every evening, and, when on guard, I imposed on myself the task of saying it all over once every time I was posted sentinel. To this exercise of my memory I ascribe the retentiveness of which I have since found it capable, and to the success with which it was attended, I ascribe the perseverance that has led to the acquirement of the little learning of which I am the master.

Cobbett was thus convinced of the need for mastering standard grammar,

> Without understanding this, you can never hope to become fit for anything beyond mere trade or agriculture... Without a knowledge of grammar, it is impossible for you to write correctly; and, it is by mere accident that you speak correctly; and, pray bear in mind, that all well-informed persons judge of a man's mind (until they have other means of judging) by his writing or speaking.
>
> (William Cobbett, *Advice to Young Men*, 1829)

And he followed up his conviction by himself writing a grammar book, in the form of a series of letters addressed to his son.

Text 171 – William Cobbett's *A Grammar of the English Language*, 1817

> ...grammar teaches us *how to make use of words*... to the acquiring of this branch of knowledge, my dear son, there is one motive, which, though it ought, at all times, to be strongly felt, ought, at the present time, to be so felt in an extraordinary degree: I mean that desire which every man, and especially every young man, should entertain to be able to assert with effect the rights and liberties of his country.
>
> (*Introduction*)

> And when we hear a Hampshire plough-boy say, 'Poll Cherrycheek have giv'd I thick handkercher,' we know very well that he *means* to say, 'Poll Cherrycheek has given me this handkerchief:' and yet, we are but too apt to *laugh at him*, and to call him *ignorant*; which is wrong; because he has no pretensions to a knowledge of grammar, and he may be very skilful as a plough-boy.
>
> (*Letter* xvii)

Cobbett is himself conditioned by 18th-century notions of language when he says, 'what he *means* to say...'. Both sentences mean the same, but their differences of expression have social connotations. We would prefer to identify and describe both versions of the sentence as dialectal, each making different choices from the available variants of the grammar of verbs and personal pronouns (*has given/have giv'd*; *me/I*), with the ploughboy using an alternative form *thick* for *this*, described in the *Oxford English Dictionary* as follows:

> *thilk* (archaic and dialectal), from ME *þilke*
> *thick* is in dialect use from Cornwall and Hants to Worcester and Hereford; and also in Pembroke, Glamorgan, and Wexford. In many parts it has also the form *thicky*, *thickee*, or *thicka*. It generally means *that*, but in some parts *this*...

'Cobbett considered grammar, in short, as an integral part of the class structure of England, and the act of learning grammar by one of his readers as an act of class warfare' (Olivia Smith, op. cit.). This conclusion can be inferred from Cobbett's allusions to his own learning the standard grammar from Lowth, such as the following extract from *The Political Register* (shown in Text 172).

There appear to be no significant differences in the grammar of Cobbett's writing that separate today's language from the English of the early 19th century. What we now call Standard English (Cobbett's *knowledge of grammar*) has been established for over 200 years as the only form of the language for writing which obtains universal acceptance.

Text 172 – William Cobbett's *The Political Register*, 6 December 1817 (facsimile)

Vol. 32, No. 35.---Price Two Pence.

COBBETT'S WEEKLY POLITICAL PAMPHLET

1089] LONDON, SATURDAY, DECEMBER 6, 1817. [1090

I have gone into detail as to this anecdote in order to show what power a knowledge of grammar gives to man. During the whole of my military life, I owed even my safety to it; and, it is that, and that alone, which enabled me to pursue and acquire knowledge of a higher order; and, every young man who shall read what I am now writing may be assured, that he can never arrive at fame; that he can never obtain and retain any great degree of influence over the minds of other men, unless he be possessed of this branch of knowledge, which, as I said before, though, *in itself*, contemptible, is the key to all the means of communicating our thoughts to others. It is by the possession of this knowledge, that, sitting here in Long Island, I am able to tell you in England, what I think; and it is the possession of this knowledge by me, that has driven the Boroughmongers to those acts of desperation, which will end in their ruin. It is very true, that *all* men are not born with the same degree of capacity for acquiring knowledge. But, nature has been too fair to give all the capacity to the Aristocracy

This seems to contradict the linguistic statement that 'all living languages are in a constant state of change'. But the grammatical innovations since Cobbett's day are developments of established features, rather than fundamental changes. Once a standard form of writing becomes the norm, then the rate of change in the grammar is slowed down considerably. At the same time, additions and losses to the vocabulary, and modifications in pronunciation, inevitably continue.

19.10 18th-century loan-words

19.10.1 *French*

The pronunciation of most of these loan-words has not been assimilated into English like earlier ME borrowings. They are spoken with varying degrees of approximation to French, but with English stress patterns.

reservoir	*réservoir*	**1705**	morale	*morale*	**1752**
débris	*débris*	**1708**	rouge	*rouge*	**1753**
brunette	*brunette*	**1712**	négligée	*négligée*	**1756**
encore (n)	*encore* (*n*)	**1712**	vis-à-vis	*vis-à-vis*	**1757**
connoisseur	*connoisseur*	**1714**	entrée	*entrée*	**1762**
police	*police*	**1716**	brochure	*brochure*	**1765**
bureau	*bureau*	**1720**	chiffon	*chiffon*	**1765**
chaperon	*chaperon*	**1720**	douche	*douche*	**1766**
ration (n)	*ration* (*n*)	**1720**	boulevard	*boulevard*	**1769**
bouillon	*bouillon*	**1725**	genre	*genre*	**1770**
chute	*chute*	**1725**	passé	*passé*	**1775**
détour	*détour*	**1738**	souvenir	*souvenir*	**1775**
hors d'oeuvre	*hors d'oeuvre*	**1742**	protégé	*protégé*	**1778**
glacier	*glacier*	**1744**	nuance	*nuance*	**1781**
picnic	*pique-nique*	**1748**	ravine	*ravine*	**1781**
etiquette	*etiquette*	**1750**	chignon	*chignon*	**1783**
début	*début*	**1751**	amateur	*amateur*	**1784**
vignette	*vignette*	**1751**	plateau	*plateau*	**1796**
dénouement	*dénouement*	**1752**	crêpe	*crêpe*	**1797**

19.10.2 *Low German*

gin	*genever*	**1714**
mangle	*mangelen*	**1775**

19.10.3 *Latin*

nucleus	*nucleus*	**1704**	maximum	*maximum*	**1740**
inertia	*inertem*	**1713**	insomnia	*insomnis*	**1758**
alibi	*alibi*	**1727**	emanation	*emanere*	**1788**
auditorium	*auditorium*	**1727**	edit	*editus*	**1791**

19.10.4 *Italian*

salvo	*salva*	**1719**
allegro	*allegro*	**1721**
portfolio	*porto folio*	**1722**
cantata	*cantata*	**1724**
forte	*forte*	**1724**
staccato	*staccato*	**1724**
tempo	*tempo*	**1724**
trombone	*trombone*	**1724**
violoncello	*violoncello*	**1724**
oratorio	*oratorio*	**1727**
concerto	*concerto*	**1730**
contralto	*contralto*	**1730**
obbligato	*obbligato*	**1730**
soprano	*soprano*	**1730**
duet	*duetto*	**1740**
malaria	*mal'aria*	**1740**
andante	*andante*	**1742**
aria	*aria*	**1742**
arpeggio	*arpeggiare*	**1742**
libretto	*libretto*	**1742**
loggia	*loggia*	**1742**
influenza	*influenza*	**1743**
adagio	*ad agio*	**1746**
impresario	*impresario*	**1746**
dilettante	*dilettante*	**1748**
lava	*lava*	**1750**
cadenza	*cadenza*	**1753**
pianoforte	*piano e forte*	**1767**
falsetto	*falsetto*	**1774**
diminuendo	*diminuendo*	**1775**
crescendo	*crescendo*	**1776**
prima donna	*prima donna*	**1782**
finale	*finale*	**1783**
maraschino	*marasca*	**1791**
maestro	*maestro*	**1797**
rondo	*rondo*	**1797**
semolina	*semolino*	**1797**
torso	*torso*	**1797**
viola (instrument)	*viola*	**1797**

19.10.5 *Spanish*

flotilla	*flotilla*	**1711**
cigar	*cigarro*	**1735**
adobe	*adobar*	**1748**
lasso	*lazo*	**1768**
albino	*albino*	**1777**
merino	*merino*	**1781**
bolero	*bolero*	**1787**
stevedore	*estivador*	**1788**
picador	*picador*	**1797**

19.10.6 *Portuguese*

verandah	*varanda*	**1711**
palaver	*palavra*	**1735**
commando	*commando*	**1791**

19.10.7 *German*

seltzer	*Nieder-Selters*	**1741**
drill (fabric)	*drell*	**1743**
nickel	*< kupfernickel*	**1755**
pumpernickel	*pumpernickel*	**1756**
quartz	*quartz*	**1756**
feldspar	*feldspat*	**1757**
gneiss	*gneiss*	**1757**
iceberg	*eisberg*	**1774**
noodle	*nudel*	**1779**
waltz	*walzer*	**1781**
meerschaum (pipe)	*meerschaum*	**1799**

19.10.8 *Russian*

knout	*knut* – 'The Knout is a thick hard Thong of Leather of about three Foot and a half long, fasten'd to the end of a handsome Stick about two Foot and a half long, with a Ring or kind of Swivle like a Flail at the end of it, to which the Thong is fasten'd'	**1716**
ukase	*ukase* – A decree or edict, having the force of law, issued by the Russian emperor or government	**1729**
balalaika	*balalaika* – a musical instrument like a guitar	**1738**
parka	*parka* – originally an Aleutian word from Russian for a skin jacket, and recently revived	**1780**

19.10.9 *Urdu and Hindi*

Urdu

sepoy	*sipah* – Anglo-Indian – an Indian soldier under British discipline	**1717**
bangle	*bangri*	**1787**

Hindi

swami	*swami* – master, lord	
	1 a Hindu idol	**1773**
	2 a Hindu religious teacher	**1901**
jungle	*jangal*	**1776**
babu	*babu* – a Hindu title of respect	**1782**
loot	*lut*	**1788**
dinghy	*dengi*	**1794**

19.10.10 *Arabic*

carafe	Fr *carafe* fr Arabic *gharraf*	**1786**
Allah	*allah*	**1702**
tarboosh	*tarbush*	**1702**
hookah	*huqqah* – pipe for smoking	**1763**
ghoul	*ghul* – an evil spirit	**1786**

19.10.11 *Celtic*

banshee	Irish *bean sidhe* – a spirit supposed by the peasantry of Ireland and the Scottish Highlands to wail under the windows of a house where one of the inmates is about to die	**1771**
Sassenach	Gaelic *Sasunnach* – an Englishman	**1771**
claymore	Gaelic *claidheamh mor* – 'great sword'	**1772**
shillelagh	Shillelagh – (the name of a village in Co. Wicklow); an Irish cudgel	**1773**
spalpeen	Irish *spailp'n* – 1 a labourer, 2 a rascal	**1780**
ben	Gaelic *beann*	**1788**
blarney	Irish *Blarney* (cf. *the Blarney stone*) – flattering talk, nonsense	**1796**

19.10.12 *Japanese*

ginkgo	Japanese *ginkgo*, from Chinese *yinhsing*, 'silver apricot'; the maidenhair tree	**1727**
kana	*kana*, Japanese syllabic writing, the chief varieties of which are *hiragana* and *katakana*	**1727**
katakana	*katakana*, from *kata* 'side' + *kana*: one of the two varieties of the Japanese syllabic writing, the characters of which are more angular than the *hiragana*	**1727**
koi	*koi*, a local name in Japan for the common carp	**1727**
Mikado	*mikado*, the title of the Emperor of Japan	**1727**
samurai	*samurai*, a member of the military caste in the former Japanese feudal system	**1727**
Shinto	*shinto*, from Chinese *shin tao* 'way of the gods'; the native religious system of Japan	**1727**
zen	*zen*, 'meditation'; a school of Buddhism that emphasises meditation	**1727**

19.10.13 *Chinese*

ketchup	*kechiap* – a sauce	**1711**
pekoe	*pek-ho* – a superior kind of black tea	**1712**
souchong	*siao-chung* 'small sort'; a variety of tea	**1760**

20. From Old English to Modern English – comparing historical texts

It should be easier for you now to recognise texts from different historical periods of the language, and to describe how they differ from contemporary English. A very short example will illustrate this. It is the first verse from chapter 3 of The Book of Genesis, and illustrates some of the changes in the language from OE to MnE which have been described.

Text 173 – *Genesis*, 3:1

Late 10th century Old English

eac swylce seo næddre wæs geapre þonne ealle þa oðre nytenu þe God geworhte ofer eorþan. and seo næddre cwæþ to þam wife. hwi forbead God eow þæt ge ne æton of ælcon treowe binnan paradisum.

Late 14th century Middle English

But the serpent was feller than alle lyuynge beestis of erthe which the Lord God hadde maad. Which serpent seide to the womman Why comaundide God to ȝou that ȝe schulden not ete of ech tre of paradis.

1611 Early Modern English

Now the serpent was more subtill then any beast of the field, which the Lord God had made, and he said vnto the woman, Yea, hath God said, Ye shall not eat of euery tree of the garden?

1961 Modern English

The serpent was more crafty than any wild creature that the LORD God had made. He said to the woman, 'Is it true that God has forbidden you to eat from any tree in the garden?'

20.1 Commentary on Text 173

The following detailed description of the extracts gives a pattern which can be applied to the comparison of any two or more texts.

Make a series of columns, one for each text, and an extra one to record any reflexes of the older words which have survived into MnE but are not used in later translations. Write down the equivalent words or phrases from each text:

1 OE	*2 ME*	*3 EMnE 1611*	*4 MnE 1961*	*MnE reflex*
eac swylce	but	now	–	such
seo nædre	the serpent	the serpent	the serpent	the adder
wæs	was	was	was	was
geapre	feller	more subtill	more crafty	subtle
þonne	than	then	than	than
ealle	alle	any	any	all
þa oðre	–	any	any	the other
–	lyuinge	–	–	living
nytenu	beestis	beast	wild creature	beast
þe	which	which	that	
God	the Lord God	the Lord God	the LORD God	God
geworhte	hadde maad	had made	had made	wrought
ofer eorþan	of erthe	of the field	wild	over earth
and	–	and	–	and
seo nædre	which serpent	he	he	the adder
cwæþ	seide	said	said	quoth
to þam wife	to the woman	vnto the woman	to the woman	wife
hwi	why	–	–	why
forbead	comaundide	hath . . . said	has forbidden	forbade
eow	ȝou	–	you	you
þæt	that	–	–	that
ge	ȝe	ye	you	(ye)
ne	not	not	–	–
æton	ete	eat	eat	eat
of ælcon treowe	of ech tre	of euery tree	from any tree	of each tree
binnan paradisum	of paradis	of the garden	in the garden	paradise

This table can then be used as data to describe some of the linguistic features of the texts.

20.1.1 Vocabulary

Have any words changed meaning?

- OE *nædre* meant *snake*, *serpent* and is now restricted to one type of snake, the *adder*.
- OE *wif* meant *woman*, but had a more restricted meaning in ME and after.
- OE *geworhte* (*wrought*) is the past tense of *gewyrcan* (*to work*, *make*). Today, *wrought* is used in a specialised sense, and the past tense of *work* is *worked*.

Have any older words been lost from the language?

- OE *eac*, *geapre*, *nytenu* (plural of *nyten* = *animal*), *binnan* are not in the vocabulary of MnE.

- OE *swylce* = MnE *such*, but is used in the phrase *eac swylce* to mean *also, moreover*.
- OE *cwæþ, quoth* is the past tense of *cweþan, to say*. We no longer use *quoth*, an archaic form, but it was used into the 19th century. The present tense *quethe* was in use up to the early 16th century, but is now obsolete.

20.1.2 *Orthography*

Are there any unusual letter forms?

- ⟨þ⟩, ⟨ʒ⟩ and ⟨ð⟩ are not Roman letters.

Can you tell if different spellings of the same word are due to sound changes, or simply different spelling conventions?

- Some spelling conventions must have changed after the OE period, e.g.,

  (i) ⟨qu-⟩ replaced ⟨cw-⟩, as in OE *cwæþ*.
  (ii) ⟨y⟩ and ⟨i⟩ were often interchangeable in ME and EMnE, e.g. *lyuynge, seide, sayd, sotyller, subtill.*
  (iii) *ye* is an abbreviation in EMnE for *the*, the letter ⟨y⟩ standing for the OE letter ⟨þ⟩, MnE ⟨th⟩.
  (iv) ⟨v⟩ in ⟨vnto⟩ – letter ⟨v⟩ was introduced during the ME period, and written for both the consonant [v] and the vowel [u] at the beginning of a word (word-initial), e.g. *verily, vnder*; letter ⟨u⟩ was used in the middle (word-medial) or at the end of a word (word-final), e.g. *lyuynge, vndur* (= *under*), *dust, thou*. They were then variant forms of the same letter, just as today we use upper and lower case variants of the same letters, e.g. ⟨A⟩, ⟨a⟩, ⟨ɑ⟩.

- The spelling is evidence of some sound changes which occurred after the OE period.

  (i) The word *næddre* in OE now has the form *adder*, as well as becoming restricted in meaning. The pronunciation of the phrase *a nadder* is identical to that of *an adder*. The indefinite article *a/an* was not part of OE grammar, so the change of *nadder* to *adder* came later, between the 14th and 16th centuries. The dialectal form *nedder* was still in use at least into the 19th century.
  (ii) The diphthong vowels of *ealle, eorþan, forbead* and *treowe* have smoothed to become single vowels.

It is not possible to recognise all the sound changes from spelling alone, because MnE spelling does not reflect them; e.g. the MnE pronunciation of *was* is [wɒz] but the spelling has not changed since its earlier pronunciation as [wæs].

20.1.3 *Word structure*

Are there changes in word-suffixes (endings)?

- The order of the consonants *re* and *or* of *næddre* and *geworhte* has changed to *er* and *ro*. Other examples are *bird, thresh,* and *run,* which come from OE *brid, þerscan* and *yrnan*. The linguistic term for this reversal of sounds is **metathesis**.
- The pronoun *oðr-e*, however, is not an example of this. It is a shortened form of *oþer-e*, from oðer, and *-e* is a suffix.
- The suffixes on *eall-e, nyten-u, geworht-e, eorþ-an* have been lost.
- The plural *beest-is* has been reduced to *beast-s*.

20.1.4 *Grammar*

Is the OE word-order different from MnE?

- *hwi forbead god eow – why forbade God you*: the **interrogative** in OE was formed by reversing the order of subject and verb, which is no longer grammatical for the simple present and past tenses in MnE except for the simple past or present of *have* or *be*.
- *þæt ge ne æton – that ye ne eat*: the **negative** in OE was formed by placing *ne* before the verb. During the ME period a reinforcing *noght* was added after the verb, which is now the only negative marker, *ne* having been dropped.

20.2 'Your accent gives you away!'

The following texts are historical translations of the same story of Peter's denial from the New Testament, St Matthew's Gospel, chapter 26, vv. 69–75.

Activity 20.1

Make a contrastive study of the language, using some or all of the texts as evidence of some of the principal changes that have taken place since the Old English period in vocabulary, word and sentence structure, spelling and pronunciation.

Text 174 – Late West Saxon Old English *c*. 1050

'þyn spræc þe gesweotolað'
69 Petrus soðlice sæt ute on þam cafertune. þa com to hym an þeowen 7 cwæð. 7 þu
wære myd þam galileiscan hælende. 70 7 he wyðsoc beforan eallum 7 cwæð. nat ic hwæt
þu segst. 71 þa he ut eode of þære dura. þa geseh hyne oðer þynen. 7 sæde þam ðe þar
wæron. 7 þes wæs myd þam nazareniscan hælende. 72 7 he wyðsoc eft myd aðe þæt he
hys nan þyng ne cuðe. 73 þa æfter lytlum fyrste genealæhton þa ðe þær stodon. 7

cwædon to petre. Soðlice þu eart of hym. 7 þyn spræc þe gesweotolað. 74 þa ætsoc he 7
swerede. þæt he næfre þone man ne cuðe. 7 hrædlice þa creow se cocc. 75 ða gemunde
petrus þæs hælendes word þe he cwæð. ærþam þe se cocc crawe. þrywa ðu me wyðscst. 7
he eode ut 7 weop byterlice.

WW 69 Peter truly sat out(side) in the courtyard. then came to him a servant & said. &
thou wast with the galilean saviour. 70 & he denied before all & said. ne-know I
what thou sayest. 71 then he out went of the door. then saw him other servant.&
said to-them that there were. & this (man) was with the nazarean saviour. 72 & he
denied again with oath that he of-him no thing ne-knew. 73 then after little time
approached them that there stood. & said to peter. Truly thou art of him. & thy
speech thee shows. 74 then denied he & swore. that he never the man ne knew. &
immediately then crew the cock. 75 then remembered peter the saviour's words
that he spoke. before that the cock crows thrice thou me deniest. & he went out &
wept bitterly.

Text 175 – 14th-century S Midlands dialect (*The Wycliffite Bible*)

'thi speche makith thee knowun'

69 And Petir sat with outen in the halle; and a damysel cam to hym, and seide, Thou
were with Jhesu of Galilee. 70 And he denyede bifor alle men, and seide, Y woot not
what thou seist. 71 And whanne he ȝede out at the ȝate, another damysel say hym, and
seide to hem that weren there, And this was with Jhesu of Nazareth. 72 And eftsoone
he denyede with an ooth, For I knewe not the man. 73 And a litil aftir, thei that
stooden camen, and seiden to Petir, treuli thou art of hem; for thi speche makith thee
knowun. 74 Thanne he bigan to warie and to swere, that he knewe not the man. And
anoon the cok crewe. 75 And Petir bithouȝte on the word of Jhesu, that he hadde seid,
Bifore the cok crowe, thries thou schalt denye me. And he ȝede out, and wepte bitterli.

Text 176 – Early 16th-century Scots *c.* 1520

(This Scots version was made from Text 175, and is of interest because it makes clear some of the dialectal differences between Scots and Wyclif's Midland dialect.)

'thi speche makis thee knawne'

69 Ande Petir sat without in the hall: and a damycele com to him, and said, Thou was
with Jesu of Galilee. 70 And he denyit before al men, and said, I wate nocht quhat thou
sais. 71 And quhen he yede out at the yet, an vthir damycele saw him, and said to
thame that ware thar, And this was with Jesu of Nazarethe. 72 And eftsone he denyit
with ane athe, For I knew nocht the man. 73 And a litil eftir thai that stude com and
said to Petir, treulie thou art of thame; for thi speche makis thee knawne. 74 Than he
began to warie and to suere that he knew nocht the man. And anon the cok crew.
75 And Petir bethouchte on the word of Jesu, that he had said, Before the cok craw,
thrijse thou sal denye me. And he yede out, and wepit bittirlie.

Text 177 – Early Modern English (*The Rheims Bible*, 1582)

'for euen thy speache doth bevvray thee'

69 But Peter sate vvithout in the court: and there came to him one vvenche, saying:
Thou also vvast vvith IESVS the Galilean. 70 But he denied before them all, saying,
I vvot not vvhat thou sayest. 71 And as he went out of the gate, an other vvenche savv

him, and she saith to them that vvere there, And this felovv also vvas vvith IESVS the
Nazarite. 72 And againe he denied vvith an othe, That I knovv not the man. 73 And
after a litle they came that stoode by, and said to Peter, Surely thou also art of them: for
euen thy speache doth bevvray thee. 74 Then he began to curse and to svveare that he
knevve not the man. And incontinent the cocke crevve. 75 And Peter remembred the
vvord of IESVS vvhich he had said, before the cocke crovv, thou shalt deny me thrise.
And going forth, he vvept bitterly.

Text 178 – Early Modern English (*King James Bible*, 1611)

'for thy speech bewrayeth thee'
69 Now Peter sate without in the palace: and a damosell came vnto him, saying, Thou
also wast with Iesus of Galilee. 70 But hee denied before them all, saying, I know not
what thou saiest. 71 And when he was gone out into the porch, another maide saw
him, and saide vnto them that were there, This fellow was also with Iesus of Nazareth.
72 And againe hee denied with an oath, I doe not know the man. 73 And after a while
came vnto him they that stood by, and saide to Peter, Surely thou also art one of them,
for thy speech bewrayeth thee. 74 Then beganne hee to curse and to sweare, saying,
I know not the man. And immediatly the cocke crew. 75 And Peter remembred the
words of Iesus, which said vnto him, Before the cocke crow, thou shalt denie mee thrice.
And hee went out, and wept bitterly.

Text 179 – 20th-century Scots (*The New Testament in Scots*)

'your Galilee twang outs ye'
69 Meantime, Peter wis sittin furth i the close, whan a servan-queyn cam up an said til
him, 'Ye war wi the man frae Galilee, Jesus, tae, I'm thinkin.' 70 But he denied it afore
them aa: 'I kenna what ye mean,' said he; 71 and wi that he gaed out intil the pend.
Here anither servan-lass saw him an said tae the fowk staundin about, 'This chiel wis wi
yon Nazarean Jesus.' 72 Again Pater wadna tak wi it, but said wi an aith, 'I kenna the
man!'
73 A wee after, the staunders-by gaed up til him an said, 'Ay, but ye war sae wi him,
tae: your Galilee twang outs ye.'
74 At that he fell tae bannin an sweirin at he hed nae kennins o the man ava. An than a
cock crew, 75 an it cam back tae Peter hou Jesus hed said til him, 'Afore the cock
craws, ye will disavou me thrice'; and he gaed out an grat a sair, sair greit.

(*The New Testament in Scots*, trans. William Laughton Lorimer, 1985)

Text 180 – Modern English (*New English Bible*, 1961)

'your accent gives you away!'
69 Meanwhile Peter was sitting outside in the courtyard when a serving-maid accosted
him and said, 'You were there too with Jesus the Galilean.' 70 Peter denied it in face of
them all. 'I do not know what you mean', he said. 71 He then went out to the gateway,
where another girl, seeing him, said to the people there, 'This fellow was with Jesus of
Nazareth.' 72 Once again he denied it, saying with an oath, 'I do not know the man.'
73 Shortly afterwards the bystanders came up and said to Peter, 'Surely you are
another of them; your accent gives you away!' 74 At this he broke into curses and
declared with an oath: 'I do not know the man.' 75 At that moment a cock crew; and
Peter remembered how Jesus had said, 'Before the cock crows you will disown me three
times.' He went outside, and wept bitterly.

Finally, the same Biblical extract in Bislama, a pidgin language based on English, from Vanuatu (formerly the New Hebrides) in the West Pacific. Read it aloud as if it were in phonetic script, because the spelling system is based upon the spoken language, and you should be able to match the sense with the preceding texts. For example, *yad* is pronounced [yɑːd], like English *yard*, *get* is /geːt/, like *gate*, *rusta* like *rooster*, and *save* is a two-syllable word like *savvy*, meaning *know*.

Text 181 – Bislama (*Gud Nyus Bilong Jisas Krais*, 1971)

‘tok bilong yu i tok bilong man Galili ia’
69 Pita i stap sidaon aofsaid long yad bilong haos ia. Nao wan haosgel i kam long em,
i talem long em, i se ‘Yu tu, yu stap wetem man Galili ia, Jisas.’ 70 Be long fes bilong
olgeta evrewan, Pita i haidem samting ia. Em i ansa, i se ‘Mi mi no save samting ia, we
yu yu stap talem.’ 71 Nao em i goaot long get bilong yad ia. Nao wan narafala gel
i lukem em. Nao i talem long ol man we oli stap stanap long ples ia, i se ‘Man ia i wetem
man Naseret ia, Jisas.’ 72 Be Pita i haidem bakegen, i mekem strong tok, nao em
i talem se ‘Mi mi no save man ia.’ 73 Gogo smol taem nomo, ol man ia we oli stap
stanap long ples ia, oli kam long Pita, oli talem long em, oli se, ‘Be i tru ia, yu yu wan
long olgeta. Yu luk, tok bilong yu i tok bilong man Galili ia.’ 74 Nao Pita i mekem tok
we i strong moa, i se ‘Sipos mi mi gyaman, bambae God i givem panis long mi. Mi mi no
save man ia.’ Nao wantaem rusta i singaot. 75 Nao Pita i tingabaot tok ia we Jisas i bin
talem long em, i se ‘Taem rusta i no singaot yet, yu, be bambae yu save haidem tri taem,
se yu no save mi.’ Nao em i go aofsaid, em i kraekrae tumas.

Texts 174–81 are recorded on the cassette tape.

IPA transcription of Text 174 – Late West Saxon Old English *c.* 1050

pɛtrʊs soːθliːtʃə sæt uːtə cn ðaːm kaːvərtuːnə. ðaː coːm toː hɪm ɑːn ðɛːəwən ɑnd kwæθ, ‘ɑnd ðuːwæːrə mɪd ðaːm galɪleːɪʃən hæːləndə’ and heː wɪðsoːk bɛvoːrən æələm ɑnd kwæθ ‘nɑːt ɪtʃ hwæt ðuː sɛɪst’ ðɑː heː uːt eːədə ɔf ðæːrə dʊrə. ðɑː jəzej hɪnə oːðər ðyːnən, ɑnd zæːdə ðaːm ðɛ ðaːr wæːrən, ‘ɑːnd ðɛs wæs mɪd ðaːm nazarenɪʃən hæːlɛnde’ ɑnd heː wɪðsoːk ɛft mɪd ɑːðə θæt heː hɪs nɑːn ðɪŋg nə kuːðə. ðɑː æftər lyːtləm fɪrstə jənɛːəlæːçtən ðɑː ðɛ ðæːr stoːdən, ɑnd kwæːdən toː pɛtrə, ‘soðliːtʃə ðuː æərt ɔf hɪm, ɑnd ðiːn spræːtʃ ðeː jəsweətəlaθ’ ðɑː ætsoːk heː ɑnd swɛrədə ðæt heː næːvrə ðɔnə mɑn nɛ kuːðə, ɑnd hrædliːtʃə ðɑː kreːəw sɛ kɔk. ðɑː jəmʊndə pɛtrʊs ðæs hæːləndəs wɔrd ðɛ heː kwæːθ, ‘æːrðam ðɛ sɛ kɔk krɑːwə, ðryːwa ðuː meː wɪðzækst’ ɑnd heː eːədə uːt ɑnd weːəp bɪtərliːtʃə.

IPA transcription of Text 175 – 14th-century S Midlands dialect

and pɛːtər sæt wɪðuːtən ɪn ðə halə and a daməzəl cɑːm to hɪm and sɛːɪdə, ‘ðuː wɛːrə wɪð ʒeːzʊ ɒv gælɪleː’ and heː dəniədə bɪvoːr al mɛn, and sɛɪdə, ‘iː woːt nɒt hwat ðuː sɛɪst’. and hwanə heː jeːdə uːt æt ðə jɑːtə, ənoːðər daməzəl saɪ hɪm, and sɛːdə to hɛm ðat wɛːrən ðɛːrə, and ðɪs was wɪð ʒeːzʊ ɒv næzærɛθ’. and ɛftsoːnə heː dəniədə wɪð an ɔːθ, ‘fɔr iː kneːwə nɒt ðə man’. and ə lɪtəl æftər, ðɛɪ ðæt stɔːdən cɑːmən, and sɛɪdən to pɛːtər, ‘trɛʊlɪ ðuː art ɒv hɛm, fɔr ðiː speːtʃə maːkəθ ðeː knɔːwən’. ðanə he bɪgan to wɑːriə and to swɛːrə, ðat he kneːwə nɒt ðə man. and anɔːn ðə kɒk kreːwə. and pɛːtər bɪθɔʊxtə ɒn ðə word ɒv ʒeːzʊ, ðæt he hædə sɛɪd, ‘bɪvorə ðe kɒk krɔːwə, θriːəs ðuː ʃælt dɛniə meː. and heː jeːdə uːt, and wɛptə bɪtərli.

IPA transcription of Text 176 – Early 16th-century Scots, *c.* 1520

and peːtər sæt wɪðuːt ɪ ðə hal, and ə damɪsəl cɔːm to hɪm, and saɪd, 'ðuː was wɪθ ʒeːzu ɒv galɪleː' and heː dɛniɪt bɪvɔr al mɛn, and said, 'iː waːt nɒxt xwat ðuː saɪs' and xwɛn heː jeːd uːt at ðə jeːt, ənʊðer damɪsəl saʊ hɪm, and saɪd toː ðam ðat war ðar, 'and ðɪs was wɪθ ʒeːzu ɒv nazərɛθ' and ɛftsoːn heː dɛniɪt wɪθ an ɛːθ, 'fɔr iː knɛʊ nɒxt ðə man' and ə lɪtəl ɛftər ðaɪ ðat stud cɔm and said to peːtər, 'trɛʊli ðuː art ɒv ðam, fɔr ði speːtʃ maks ðeː knaʊn' ðan heː bəgan to wari and to sweːr ðat heː knɛʊ nɒxt ðə man. and anɔn ðə kɒk krɛːʊ. and peːtər bɛθɒʊxt ɒn ðə wɔrd ɒv ʒeːzu, ðat heː had said, 'bɛvɔr ðə kɒk kraʊ, θriːs ðuː sal dɛniː meː' and heː jeːd uːt, and weːpɪt bɪtərliː

IPA transcription of Text 177 – Early Modern English 1582

bʊt peːtər sæt wɪðəʊt ɪn ðə kɔrt ænd ðɛːr kæːm tu hɪm oːn wɛntʃ, sɛiɪŋg 'ðəu alsɔ wæst wɪð dʒɛːzʊs ðə gælɪlɛːən'. bʊt hi dɛnəɪd bɪfɔr ðɛm al, sɛiɪŋg, 'əi wɒt nɒt hwæt ðəu sɛiɪst'. ænd æz hi wɛnt əut ɒv ðə gɛːt, ənʊðər wɛntʃ saʊ hɪm, ænd ʃi sɛɪθ tu ðɛm ðæt wɛr ðɛːr, 'ænd ðɪs fɛlɔʊ alsɔ wæs wɪθ dʒɛːzʊs ðə næzərəit'. ænd əgɛin hi dɛnəɪd wɪð ən ɔːθ, 'ðæt əi knou nɒt ðə mæn'. ænd æftər ə lɪtəl ðɛi kæːm ðæt stuːd bəi, ænd sɛid tu peːtər, 'sjurləi ðəu alsɔ art ɒv ðɛm, fɔr iːvən ðəi speːtʃ dʊθ bəwrɛi ðiː' ðɛn hi bɪgan tu kurs ænd tu swɛːr ðæt hi knɪʊw nɒt ðə mæn. ænd ɪŋkɒntɪnənt ðə kɒk krɪʊw. ænd peːtər rəmɛmbərd ðə wʊrd ɒv dʒɛːzʊs hwɪtʃ hi hæd sɛɪd, 'bɛfɔr ðə kɒk krɔʊ, ðəʊ ʃælt dɛnəi mi θrəis' ænd gɔɪŋg forθ, hi wɛpt bɪtərlɪ.

IPA transcription of Text 178 – Early Modern English 1611

nəʊ peːtər sɛːt wɪðəʊt ɪn ðə pæləs, ənd a dæməzəl kɛːm ʊntu hɪm, seiɪŋg, 'ðəʊ also wæst wɪð dʒeːzʊs ɒv gælɪliː' bʊt hi dənəid bəvɔr ðɛm al, seiɪŋg, 'əi knɔʊ nɒt hwæt ðəu seiɛst'. ænd hwɛn hi wæs gɔn əʊt ɪnto ð pɔrtʃ, ənʊðər meɪd sɔː hɪm, ænd seɪd ʊnto ðɛm ðæt wɛr ðɛr, 'ðɪs fɛlɔː wæs also wɪð dʒeːzʊs əv næzərɛθ' ænd əgɛːɪn hi dɛnəid wɪð ən oːθ, 'əi do nɒt knɔʊ ðə mæn'. ænd æftər ə hwəil kɛːm ʊnto hɪm ðei ðæt stud bəi, ænd sɛɪd to peːtər, 'sjurləi ðəʊ alsɔ art oːn ɒv ðɛm, for ðəi spiːtʃ bɪwrɛːɪɛθ ði'. ðɛn bɪgæn hi to kʊrs ænd to swɛːr, seɪŋg, 'əɪ know nɒt ðə mæn'. ænd ɪmidiətli ðə kɒk krɪuː. ənd peːtər rɛmɛmbərd ðə wʊrdz ɒv dʒezʊs, hwɪtʃ seːɪd ʊnto hɪm, 'bəvɔːr ðə kɒk krɔː, ðəʊ ʃælt dɛnəɪ mi θrəɪs'. ænd hi wɛnt əʊt, ənd wɛpt bɪtərlɪ.

Text 179 – 20th-century Scots

Written Scots text	Standard English spelling
Meantime, Peter wis sittin furth i the close,	Meantime, Peter was sitting forth (*outside*) in the close (*courtyard*)
whan a servan-queyn cam up an said til him,	when a servant-quean (*girl*) came up and said to him,
'Ye war wi the man frae Galilee, Jesus, tae, I'm thinkin.'	'You were with the man from Galilee, Jesus, too, I'm thinking.'
But he denied it afore them aa,	But he denied it before them all
'I kenna what ye mean,' said he	I ken not (*know not*) what you mean,' said he
and wi that he gaed out intil the pend.	and with that he goed (*went*) out into the entry.

Here anither servan-lass saw him an said tae the fowk staundin about, 'This chiel wis wi yon Nazarean Jesus.'	Here another servant-lass saw him and said to the folk standing about, This child (*fellow*) was with yon Nazarean Jesus.'
Again Peter wadna tak wi it, but said wi an aith, 'I kenna the man!' A wee after, the staunders-by gaed up til him an said, 'Ay, but ye war sae wi him, tae,	Again Peter would not take with (*admit* to) it, but said with an oath, 'I ken not the man!' A wee (*little*) after, the standers-by goed (*went*) up to him and said, 'Aye (*yes*), but you were so (*indeed*) with him, too,
your Galilee twang outs ye.'	your Galilee twang (*accent*) outs you (*gives you away*).'
At that he fell tae bannin an sweirin	At that he fell to banning (*cursing*) and swearing
at he hed nae kennins o the man ava.	that he had no kennings (*knowledge*) of the man of all (*at all*) (*cf. Fr du tout*)
An than a cock crew, an it cam back tae Peter hou Jesus hed said til him, 'Afore the cock craws, ye will disavou me thrice.' and he gaed out an grat a sair, sair greit.	And then a cock crew, and it came back to Peter how Jesus had said to him, Before the cock crows, you will disavow me thrice.' and he goed (*went*) out and greeted (*wept*) a sore, sore (*sorrowful*) greet (*weep*)

IPA transcription of Text 179 – 20th-century Scots

miːntɛɪm, piːtə wəz sɪtən fʊrθ ɪ ðə klos, ʌan ə sɛʴvən kwin kam ʌp ən sɛd tɪl ̣ɪm, ji wəʴ wɪ ðə man frɛ galɪli, dʒizəs, teː, am θɪŋkɪn.' bət hi dɪnaɪd ɪt əfor ðəm aː, 'a kɛnə ʌɒt jɪ miːn,' sɛd hiː ənd wɪ ðat hi geːd uːt ɪntɪl ðə pend. hir ənɪðə sɛʴvən-las sɔ hɪm ən sɛd tɛ ðə fok stɔndɪn əbuːt, 'ðɪs tʃiːl wəz wi jɒn næzəriən dʒizəs.' əgen piːtə wadnə tak wi ɪt, bət sɛd wi ən eːθ, 'a kɛnə ðə man'. ə wiː aftə, ðə stɔndɔz baɪ geːd ʌp tɪl ɪm ən sɛd, 'aɪ, bət ji waʴ seː wi əm, teː, jɔʴ galɪli twæŋ uːts ji.' æt ðæt hi fɛl tə bænɪn ən sweːrɪn ət hi hɛd neː kɛnɪnz ə ðə man əva. ən ðan ə kɒk krʉ, ən ɪt kam bak tɛ piːtə hu dʒizəs həd sɛd tɪl ɪm, 'əfor ðə kɒk krɔːz, ji wɪl dɪsəvu mɪ θrɛɪs.' ənd hi geːd uːt ən grat ə sɛr griːt.

IPA transcription of Text 180 – Modern English

miːnwaɪl piːtə wəz sɪtɪŋ aʊtsaɪd ɪn ðə kɔːtjɑːd wɛn ə sɜːviŋ mɛɪd əkɒstɪd hɪm ənd sɛd, juː wɜ ðɛə tu wɪð dʒiːzəs ðə gælɪliən. piːtə dɪnaɪd ɪt ɪn fɛɪs əv ðem ɔːl. aɪ du nɒt̚ nəʊ wɒt̚ ju miːn, hi sɛd. hi ðɛn wɛnt aʊt tə ðə getwɛɪ, wɛəʴ ənʌðə gɜːl, siːɪŋ hɪm, sɛd tə ðə piːpəl ðɛə, ðɪs fɛləʊ wɒz wɪð dʒiːzəs əv næzərɛθ. wʌns əgɛn hi dɪnaɪd ɪt, sɛɪjɪŋ wɪð ən əʊθ, aɪ duː nɒt̚ nəʊ ðə mæn. ʃɔːtli ɑftəwədz ðə baɪstændəz kɛɪm ʌp ənd sɛd tə piːtə, ʃɔːli juː ɑːʴ ənʌðəʴ əv ðɛm; jɔʴ æksənt̚ gɪvz ju əwɛɪ. æt̚ ðɪs hi bɹəʊk ɪntə kɜːsɪz ənd dɪklɛəd wɪð ən əʊθ, aɪ du nɒt̚ nəʊ ðə mæn. æt̚ ðæt̚ məʊmənt ə kɒk kruː, ənd piːtə rɪmɛmbəd haʊ dʒiːzəs hæd sɛd, bɪfɔː ðə kɒk̚ krəʊz ju wɪl dɪsəʊn miː θriː taɪmz. hiː wɛnt aʊtsaɪd ənd wɛpt bɪtəli

Text 181 – Bislama, 1971

Printed text (Bislama is written in a phonemic script):

Bislama	**Standard English**
Pita i stap sidaon aofsaid long yad bilong haos ia.	Peter sat down outside in the yard of the house
Nao wan haosgel i kam long em, i talem long em, i se	And a house-girl came to him, spoke to him and said
'Yu tu, yu stap wetem man Galili ia, Jisas.'	'You too, you were with the Galilean, Jesus.'
Be long fes bilong olgeta evrewan, Pita i haidem samting ia.	But in front of everybody, Peter denied this
Em i ansa, i se	He answered
'Mi mi no save samting ia, we yu yu stap talem.'	'I don't know what you are talking about.'
Nao em i goaot long get bilong yad ia.	And he went out through the gate of the yard.
Nao wan narafala gel i lukem em.	Then another girl saw him.
Nao i talem long ol man we oli stap stanap long ples ia, i se	And she spoke to the people who were standing about in that place.
'Man ia i wetem man Naseret ia, Jisas.'	'This man was with the Nazarean, Jesus.'
Be Pita i haidem bakegen, i mekem strong tok, nao em i talem se 'Mi mi no save man ia.'	But Peter denied it again, vigorously, and said 'I don't know the man.'
Gogo smol taem nomo, ol man ia we oli stap stanap long ples ia,	After a little while, the people who were standing about in that place
oli kam long Pita, oli talem long em, oli se,	came to Peter and said to him,
'Be i tru ia, yu yu wan long olgeta.	'But it's true, you are one of them.
Yu luk, tok bilong yu i tok bilong man Galili ia'	Look! your speech is the speech of a Galilean.'
Nao Pita i mekem tok we i strong moa, i se	And Peter denied it again,
'Sipos mi mi gyaman, bambae God i givem panis long mi.'	'If I'm a liar, God will punish me.'
'Mi mi no save man ia'	'I don't know that man.'
Nao wantaem rusta i singaot.	Then straight away a rooster crowed.
Nao Pita i tingabaot tok ia we Jisas i bin talem long em, i se	And Peter thought about the talk that Jesus had said to him
'Taem rusta i no singaot yet, yu, be bambae yu save haidem tri taem, se yu no save mi'	'Before the cock crows, you will deny (me) three times, say you don't know me.'
Nao em i go aofsaid, em i kraekrae tumas.	And he went outside and cried much.

IPA transcription of Text 181 – Bislama, 1971

pita i stap sɪdaʊn aʊfsaɪd lɒŋ jad bɪlɒŋ haʊs ja.
naʊ wan haʊsgɛl i kam lɒŋ ɛm, i taləm lɒŋ ɛm, i se
ju tu, ju stap wɛtəm man gælɪli ja, dʒizas.
be lɒŋ fes bɪlɒŋ ɒlgɛtə ɛvrɪwan, pita i haɪdəm samtɪŋ ja.
ɛm i ansa, i se
mi mi no save samtɪŋ ja, wɛ ju ju stap taləm.

nau ɛm i goaut lɒŋ get bɪlɒŋ jad ja.
nau wan narəfalə gɛl i lukɪm ɛm.
nau i taləm lɒŋ ɔl man we ɔli stap stanap lɒŋ ples ja, i se
man ja i wɛtəm man nazərɛt ja, dʒizas
be pita i haɪdəm bakəgɛn, i mekəm strɒŋ tɒk, nau ɛm i taləm se
mi mi no save man ja
gogo smɒl taɪm nomɔ, ɔl man ja we ɔli stap stanap lɒŋ ples ja,
ɔli kam lɒŋ pita, ɔli taləm lɒŋ ɛm, ɔli se,
be i tru ja, ju ju wan lɒŋ ɔlgɛta.
ju luk, tɒk bɪlɒŋ ju i tɒk bɪlɒŋ man galɪli ja.
nau pita i mɛkəm tɒk we i strɒŋ moa, i se
sɪpoz mi mi gjaman, baɪmbaɪ gɒd i givəm panɪs lɒŋ mi.
mi mi no save man ja.
nau wantaɪm rusta i sɪŋaut.
nau pita i tɪŋəbaut tɒk ja we dʒizas i bɪn taləm lɒŋ ɛm, i se
taɪm rusta i no sɪŋaut jɛt, ju, bɛ baɪmbaɪ ju save haɪdəm tri taɪm,
se ju no save mi
nau ɛm i go aufsaɪd, ɛm i kraɪkraɪ tumas.

21. Postscript I – to the present day

The object of this book has been to describe how present-day Standard English has developed from its origins in Old English a thousand years ago, and effectively ends in the 18th century, since when there have been only minimal changes in the grammar of the standard language. This is not to deny that there are clear differences between the way that the language has been written and spoken in the 18th, 19th and 20th centuries. But such differences belong rather to *style* or *language use* than to the underlying *language system*. There was in the 18th century a multiplicity of spoken regional and social dialects, largely unrecorded, and this is still so.

In addition, there are today many new 'Englishes' throughout the world as a result of the spread of English as a national and international language. American, Australian, New Zealand, South African, Indian and all other varieties, pidgins and creoles, go without commentary here.

21.1 Some developments in the standard language since the 18th century

21.1.1 *Vocabulary*

There is a constant change in the vocabulary of the language, and it goes without saying that there have been many losses and gains of words since the 18th century. English is a language that has taken in and assimilated words from many foreign languages to add to the core vocabulary of Germanic, French and Latin words, as has been illustrated in the end-of-chapter lists of loan-words.

21.1.2 *Spelling*

The standard orthography was fixed in the 18th century by the agreed practice of printers. Dr Johnson set down accepted spellings in his *Dictionary* of 1755, and had to record some of the arbitrary choices of 'custom':

> ...thus I write, in compliance with a numberless majority, convey and inveigh, deceit and receipt, fancy and phantom.

A few words that you will find in the original versions of 18th-century texts have changed, e.g. *cloathing*, *terrour*, *phantasy*, *publick*, but there are not many. More recently, it has become acceptable to change the ⟨ae⟩ spelling to ⟨e⟩ in a few words of Latin derivation, and to write *medieval* for *mediaeval*, and *archeology* for *archaeology*. Some American spellings have become acceptable in Britain, e.g. *program* as a result of its use in computer programming. With few exceptions, it is true to say that our spelling system was fixed over two hundred years ago, and every attempt to reform it has failed.

21.1.3 *Grammar*

While the underlying rules of the grammar have remained unchanged, their use in speech and writing has continued to develop into forms that distinguish varieties of language use since the 18th century. In present-day English we can observe a greater degree of complexity in both the noun phrase and verb phrase.

Noun phrases

Modifiers of nouns normally precede the head of the NP when they are words (usually adjectives or nouns), e.g. *a* ***red*** *brick*, *the* ***brick*** *wall*, *the* ***red brick*** *wall*, and follow it when they are phrases or clauses, e.g. *the wall* ***between the houses***, ***the wall that was blown down in the gale***. The rule of premodification has been developed so that longer strings of words and phrases now precede the head word in some styles of use. For example, a statement which might be written as,

> There has been a report on the treatment of suspects in police stations in Northern Ireland . . .

can be turned into a NP as,

> A Northern Ireland police station suspect treatment report . . .

in which a series of post-modifying prepositional phrases (PrepPs) – *on the treatment*, *of suspects*, *in police stations*, *in Northern Ireland* – become premodifying NPs within the larger NP. This style is a particular feature of newspaper headlines.

The process of converting clauses with verbs into noun phreases is called **nominalisation**. It is also a prominent marker of academic and formal writing. It enables a writer to omit the agents or actors who actually do things, e.g.

> ***S***   ***P***   ***C***
> There has been no convincing explanation of the attempt . . .

is only the beginning of a longer sentence, and might have been written,

> X has not *convinced* us by *explaining* how Y *attempted* . . .

in which main verbs are used instead of nouns or a modifying participle, and the subjects X and Y would have to be named. This is a trend in style that depends upon the fact that the grammar of English permits nominalisation readily.

Verb phrases

If you compare the possible forms of the verb phrase in contemporary English with any Old English text, you will see that OE verb phrases were generally shorter, and OE grammar lacked the forms of VP that have developed since. In MnE, it is possible to construct VPs like,

she **has been being treated**...
hasn't she **been being treated**?
won't she **have been being treated**?

which use **auxiliary verbs** to combine the grammatical features of **tense** (past or present), **aspect** (perfective or progressive), **voice** (active or passive) and **mood** (declarative or interrogative), to which we can add,

She **seems to manage to be able to keep on being treated**...

in which certain verbs, called **catenatives**, can be strung together in a chain. Such VPs are not common, perhaps, but they are possible, and have developed since the 18th century.

They are examples of the way in which English has become a much more **analytic** language since the OE period, that is, its structures depend upon strings of separate words, and not on the inflections of words. An inflecting language is called **synthetic**.

Another development in the resources of the VP is in the increased use of **phrasal** and **prepositional verbs** like *run across* for *meet*, *put up with* for *tolerate*, *give in* for *surrender*. They are a feature of spoken and informal usage, and though the beginnings of the structure of *verb + particle* can be found in OE, they have increased in numbers considerably in MnE, and new combinations are continually being introduced, often as slang, e.g. *get with it*, later to be assimilated.

21.2 The continuity of prescriptive judgements on language use

We judge others by their speech as much as by other aspects of their behaviour, but some people are much more positive in their reactions. The relationship between social class and language use in the 18th century, which was described in Chapter 19, has been maintained to the present. Here for example is the Dean of Canterbury, Henry Alford D.D., writing in a book called *The Queen's English: Stray Notes on Speaking and Spelling* in 1864.

Text 182 – Dean Henry Alford's *The Queen's English*, 1864 (facsimile)

THE

QUEEN'S ENGLISH:

Stray Notes on Speaking and Spelling.

BY

HENRY ALFORD, D.D.,

DEAN OF CANTERBURY.

LONDON: STRAHAN & Co.
CAMBRIDGE: DEIGHTON, BELL, & CO.
1864.

THE QUEEN'S ENGLISH. 37

51. I pass from spelling to pronunciation. And first and foremost, let me notice that worst of all faults, the leaving out of the aspirate where it ought to be, and putting it in where it ought not to be. This is a vulgarism not confined to this or that province of England, nor especially prevalent in one county or another, but common throughout England to persons of low breeding and inferior education, principally to those among the inhabitants of towns. Nothing so surely stamps a man as below the mark in intelligence, self-respect, and energy, as this unfortunate habit: in intelligence, because, if he were but moderately keen in perception, he would see how it marks him; in self-respect and energy, because if he had these he would long ago have set to work and cured it. Hundreds of stories are current about the absurd consequences of this vulgarism. We remember in *Punch* the barber who, while operating on a gentleman, expressed his opinion, that, after all, the cholera was in the *hair*. "Then," observed the customer, "you ought to be very careful what brushes you use." "Oh, sir," replied the barber, laughing, "I didn't mean the *air* of the *ed*, but the *hair* of the *hatmosphere*." Pronunciation—misuse of the aspirate.

This attitude is that of 18th-century grammarians in their references to 'the depraved language of the common People' (see section 19.6) and of John of Trevisa in the 14th century calling Northern speech 'scharp slyttyng and frotyng and unschape'.

A feature of common usage which is still taught as an error is what is called the 'split infinitive'. Here is Dean Alford:

> A correspondent states as his own usage, and defends, the insertion of an adverb between the sign of the infinitive mood and the verb. He gives as an instance, 'to scientifically illustrate'. But surely this is a practice entirely unknown to English speakers and writers. It seems to me, that we ever regard the to of the infinitive as inseparable from its verb.

The Dean is wrong in his assertion that the practice is 'entirely unknown'. The idea that it is ungrammatical to put an adverb between *to* and the verb was an invention of prescriptive grammarians, but it has been handed on as a **solecism** (violation of the rules of grammar) by one generation of school teachers after another. It has become an easy marker of 'good English', but avoiding it can lead to ambiguity.

The following paragraph appeared in a daily newspaper in August 1989. It shows a journalist trying to avoid the 'split infinitive' at all costs, and failing to make his/her meaning clear.

Correction
Our front page report yesterday on microwave cooking mistakenly stated that in tests of 83 cook-chill and ready-cooked products, Sainsbury's found the instructions on 10 products always failed to ensure the foods were fully heated to 708C. The story should have said the instructions failed always to ensure the foods were fully heated to 708C – that is, they sometimes failed to ensure this.

- The original *always failed to ensure* has one clear meaning, which is not the intended meaning. The adverb *always* modifies the verb *failed*, that is, *the instructions never succeeded in insuring*...
- The correction to *failed always to ensure* is ambiguous, because it is not clear whether *always* modifies *failed* or *ensure*. This ambiguity between *failed always* and *always to ensure* is likely to occur in a compound verb phrase with two verbs (predicators in phase) like *failed to ensure*, because the adverb may either precede or follow the verb it modifies.
- *The instructions failed to always ensure the foods were fully heated* is not ambiguous, and *always* clearly modifies *ensure*. There is no reason why the adverb *always* should not immediately precede *ensure* after the particle *to* that follows *failed*.

21.3 The grammar of spoken English today

The invention of sound recording, and especially of the portable tape recorder, has made it possible for us to study the spoken language in a way that students of language were formerly quite unable to do. It was always known that spoken English differed from written English, but even an experienced shorthand writer would to some extent idealise what was said, and omit features that seemed irrelevant.

Here is a transcription of some recorded informal contemporary spoken English, which uses written symbols to indicate spoken features of the language. The conventions of written punctuation are deliberately not used. The symbols represent intonation and stress patterns, contained in tone-units (units of information into which we divide our speech), each having a tonic syllable marked by stress and a change of pitch.

The speaker is an educated user of Standard English, and the topic is 'linguistic acceptability', but the transcription, even if punctuated with capital letters, full-stops and commas as if it were written, would not be acceptable as written English.

Activity 21.1

(i) Edit the transcription, omitting all non-fluency features which belong to speech only (e.g. hesitations, self-corrections and repetitions), but retaining the identical vocabulary and word order.

(ii) Examine the edited version for evidence of differences between the vocabulary and grammar of informal spoken English and of written English.
(iii) Re-write B's part of the conversation for her, in a style which conforms to the conventions of written Standard English.

For a full analysis, see the Commentary in the *Text Commentary Book*.

Conventions used in the transcription

- The end of a tone-unit (or tone-group) is marked (|).
- The word containing the tonic syllable (or nucleus) is printed in bold type.
- A micro-pause in speech is marked with a stop (.); longer breaks are marked with one or more dashes (–).
- The place where two speakers overlap is marked ([ ]).
-

Text 183 – Contemporary spoken English

The text is part of a longer conversation between two women in their twenties. A is a secretary, B is a university lecturer.

A well what do they **put** | . in a . computing **programme**? | – –
B **well** | you'll hear a lot about it in due **course** | . it's what they call [IL tests / *A* mm] which [stands for / *A* mm] investigating language **acceptability** |
A mm
B and they've done those on groups of **undergraduates** | . we don't know what
A [erm battery things / *B* erm] erm **yes** | . erm sort of . **science** graduates | [*A* erm / **German**] graduates |
B **English** graduates | [and **so** on | / *A* mm | mm |] and **asked** them | – there are various **types** of test they give them | . they give them a **sentence** | and there are four a. there are **three** answers they can give | either it's **acceptable** | it's not **acceptable** |
A mm | – –
B it's **marginal** | . or you **know** | it's somewhere **between** | and then . we **they** | when they mark up the **results** | have a **fourth category** | which is their answer was **incoherent** |
A **yes** |
B if it was heard and they couldn't **hear** it | . if it was written they couldn't **read** it |
A mm |
B that's **one** type | . then there's an **operation** test | they're interested say in . well particularly seeing various **adverbs** | and they write something like I **entirely** | dot dot **dot** | – and the student has to complete the **sentence** | –
A mm | –
B well with **entirely** | they'll nearly all write **agree** with you |
A **yes** | .
B and entirely and agree [go **altogether** | / *A* mm |] mm |

B **collate** or **something** it's called |
A **yeah** |
B [*laughs* – –] and then they in fact try **another** adverb| and then there'll be an absolute **range** of verbs that [**go** with it | / *A* mm |] you know it's quite **interesting** | the way in the **thesis** | they had a sentence with **entirely** | . and **got** people | to er transform it into the **negative** |
B mm |
A this is **very tricky** | . I should have thought there were .
B **yes** | well **quite** | they do that sort of **thing** you see | and then they see what they've **produced** | and then they [sort of / *A* yes |] they score them **up** | in a certain [**way** / *A* yes |] and they'll say have they . erm – –
B have they **done** | what they were **told** to | and if not **why** not | and then there are various reasons why **not** | and they were **scored** | and given a **mark** | and it's quite in[**credible** | / *A* I think that's |] **one** of the most
A **valuable** things | that I've thought was being **done** | in . [in . / ***B*** mm] in the **battery** test | because it **should** relate | quite **directly** | to | the meaning of the **word** | –
B **yes** |

(Adapted from Svartvik and Quirk, *Corpus of English Conversation*.)

21.4 19th- and 20th-century loan-words

21.4.1 *French*

Most of the French words that have been adopted during the last two hundred years have not been assimilated to English pronunciation in the way that earlier borrowings have been. Compare, for example, the pronunciation of *village* (1386) with the various contemporary spoken forms of *garage* (1902) – ['gærɑːdʒ], ['gærɑːʒ], [gə'rɑːdʒ], [gə'rɑːʒ], which retain some aspects of French pronunciation with variant syllable stress, and the assimilated form ['gærɪdʒ], which has followed the pattern of *village* ['vɪlɪdʒ].

The following list is a small sample of 19th- and 20th-century French loan-words. They are in date order.

Activity 21.2

Consider the pronunciation of the words that you are likely to hear among English speakers. How far has assimilation to English patterns of speech taken place?

19th century					
café	*café*	menu	*menu*	foyer	*foyer*
surveillance	*surveillance*	cigarette	*cigarette*	suède	*suède*
liaison	*liaison*	crochet	*crochet*	risqué	*risqué*
de luxe	*de luxe*	fines herbes	*fines herbes*	revue	*revue*
coupon	*coupon*	repertoire	*répertoire*	massage	*massage*
élite	*élite*	matinee	*matiné*	flair	*flair*
laissez-faire	*laissez-faire*	impasse	*impasse*	première (n)	*première*
restaurant	*restaurant*	communiqué	*communiqué*	cliché	*cliché*
coupé	*coupé*	hangar	*hangar*	décor	*décor*
lingerie	*lingerie*	fiancé(e)	*fiancé(e)*	chaffeur	*chauffeur*
chic	*chic*				
20th century					
limousine	*limousine*	fuselage	*fuselage*	collage	*collage*
déjà vu	*déjà vu*	rôtisserie	*rôtisserie*	courgette	*courgette*
haute couture	*haute couture*	camouflage	*camouflage*		

21.4.2 *Italian*

19th century					
bravura	*bravura*	**1813**	vibrato	*vibrato*	**1861**
legato	*legato*	**1815**	mafia	*mafia*	**1875**
alto	*alto*	**1819**	pizzicato	*pizzicato*	**1880**
studio	*studio*	**1819**	tombola	*tombola*	**1880**
replica	*replica*	**1824**	diva	*diva*	**1883**
casino	*casino*	**1831**	spaghetti	*spaghetto*	**1888**
tempera	*tempera*	**1832**			
inferno	*inferno*	**1834**	**20th century**		
intermezzo	*intermezzo*	**1834**	gorgonzola	*gorgonzola*	**1910**
lasagna	*lasagna*	**1846**	ciao	*ciao*	**1929**
salami	*salame*	**1852**	aldente	*al dente*	**1935**
risotto	*risotto*	**1855**	pizza	*pizza*	**1953**
vendetta	*vendetta*	**1855**	scampi	*scampo*	**1953**
piccolo	*piccolo*	**1856**	dolce vita	*dolce vita*	**1961**
magenta	*Magenta*	**1860**	paparazzo	*paparazzo*	**1968**

21.4.3 *Spanish*

19th century					
mustang	*mestengo*	**1808**	canyon	*cañon*	**1837**
ranch	*rancho*	**1808**	cafeteria	*cafeteria*	**1839**
guerilla	*guerrila*	**1819**	bonanza	*bonanza*	**1844**
mescal	*mezcal*	**1828**	tilde	*tilde*	**1864**
patio	*patio*	**1828**	bronco	*bronco*	**1869**
stampede	*estampida*	**1828**	tango	*tango*	**1896**
rodeo	*rodeo*	**1834**			
vamoose	*vamos*	**1834**	**20th century**		
lariat	*la reata*	**1835**	macho	*macho*	**1928**
silo	*silo*	**1835**	machismo	*mach(o) + -ismo*	**1948**

21.4.4 Portuguese

There is little evidence of recent borrowings from Portuguese:

piranha	*piranha*	**1869**
samba	*samba*	**1885**

21.4.5 German

19th century		
schnapps	*schnapps*	**1818**
poodle	*pudel*	**1825**
semester	*semester*	**1927**
alpenstock	*alpenstock*	**1829**
loess	*lösz*	**1833**
yodel	*jodeln*	**1838**
spitz	*spitzhund*	**1842**
umlaut	*umlaut*	**1844**
poltergeist	*poltergeist*	**1848**
zeitgeist	*Zeitgeist*	**1848**
ablaut	*Ablaut*	**1849**
zither	*zither*	**1850**
kindergarten	*Kindergarten*	**1852**
lager (beer)	*lager-bier*	**1853**
schnitzel	*schnitzel*	**1854**
bock	*Eimbockbier, now Einbecker bier, f. Einbeck/Eimbeck, in Hanover*	**1856**
pretzel	*pretzel*	**1856**
edelweiss	*edelweiss*	**1862**
kummel	*kümmel*	**1864**
rucksack	*rucksack*	**1866**
Weltanschauung	*Weltanschauung*	**1868**
kirsch	*kirschwasser*	**1869**
ersatz	*ersatz*	**1875**
leitmotiv	*leitmotiv*	**1876**
delicatessen	*dellikatessen*	**1877**
frankfurter	*Frankfurter wurst*	**1877**
dachshund	*dachshund*	**1881**
hamburger (food)	*Hamburger*	**1889**
seminar	*seminar*	**1889**
hinterland	*hinterland*	**1890**
schwa (=[ə])	*schwa*	**1895**
20th century		
dobermann	*Dobermann pinscher*	**1917**
Gestalt	*Gestalt*	**1922**
Luftwaffe	*Luftwafe*	**1935**
abseil	*abseilen*	**1933**
blitz	*blitzkrieg*	**1940**

21.4.6 Russian

vodka	*vodka*	**1802**
samovar	*samovar*	**1830**
troika	A Russian vehicle drawn by three horses abreast	**1842**
kulak	*kulak*	**1877**
pogrom	*pogrom*, devastation, destruction. An organized massacre in Russia for the destruction or annihilation of any body or class: originally and especially applied to those directed against the Jews	**1882**
borsch	*borshch*	**1884**
borzoi	*borzo*	**1887**
dacha	*dacha*	**1896**

Some loan-words from the Soviet era referring to political issues during the 20th century have acquired a wider reference:

intelligentsia	*intelligentsiya*	**1907**
Bolshevik	*bolshevik*	**1917**
Soviet	*sovét* (council)	**1917**
commissar	*komiss·r*	**1918**
liquidate	in the sense of *to liquidate, wind up*, i.e. *to put an end to, abolish; to stamp out, wipe out; to kill*, after Russian *likvidirovat'*	**1924**
politburo	*politbyuro*, from *politicheskoe*, political + *byuro*, bureau. The highest policy-making committee of the former USSR, or of some other Communist country or party	**1926**
idiogram	*idiogramma* – a diagrammatic or systematised representation of a chromosome complement	**1927**
gopak	*gopak* – a dance	**1929**
agitprop	*agitprop, fr agitsiya* agitation + *propaganda* propaganda	**1934**
socialist realism	*sotsialisticheskia realizm* The official theory of art and literature of the Soviet Communist party	**1934**
babushka	1 grandmother, *fr baba* (peasant) woman 2 a head-scarf	**1938**
apparatchik	*apparatchik* – a member of the apparat	**1941**
troika 2	(*a later, developed meaning from* troika 1 *above*) A group or set of three persons or categories of people associated in power	**1945**
Cominform	the first elements of the Russian forms of *communist* and *information*	**1947**
apparat	*apparat* – the party machine of the Communist party in Russia	**1950**
disinformation	*dezinformatsiya* – the dissemination of deliberately false information	**1955**
sputnik	*sputnik*, literally *travelling companion*; An unmanned artificial earth satellite	**1957**
samizdat	Russian abbreviation of *samoizd·tel'stvo* self-publishing house; The clandestine or illegal copying and distribution of literature	**1967**
kalashnikov	*kalashnikov* – an automatic rifle of Russian manufacture	**1970**
glasnost	*glasnost* – the fact of being public; openness to public scrutiny or discussion	**1972**
refusenik	*refusenik* – partial translation of Russian *otk·znik*, from *otkaz·tí* to refuse. A Jew in the Soviet Union who has been refused permission to emigrate to Israel	**1975**
perestroika	*perestroika* – restructuring – The restructuring or reform of the Soviet economic and political system, first proposed at the 26th Party Congress in 1979 and actively promoted under the leadership of Mikhail Gorbachev from 1985	**1981**
gulag	(*not in Oxford English Dictionary*) the system of forced labour camps for political prisoners in the former Soviet Union	?

21.4.7 *Urdu and Hindi*

Urdu

19th Century		
purdah	*pardah* = *veil, curtain*; the system of the seclusion of Indian women of rank	**1800**
pyjamas	*paejamah*	**1800**

yoga	*yoga* – union	**1820**
tandoor	*tandur* – oven	**1840**
charpoy	*charpai* – light Indian bedstead	**1845**
sitar	*sitar* – musical instrument	**1845**
gymkhana	*gend-khana* – originally Anglo-Indian, 'a place of public resort at a station, where the needful facilities for athletics and games of sorts are provided'	**1861**
khaki	*khak* – '*dusty, dust-coloured*'; a fabric of this colour used in the British army for field-uniforms	**1863**
20th Century		
samosa	*samosa*	**1955**

Hindi

19th century		
pukka	*pakkai* – sure, certain, reliable; cf. *pukka sahib*	**1803**
chapatti	*chapati* – a cake of unleavened bread	**1810**
dacoit	*dakait* – armed rober, pirate	**1810**
gharry	*gari* – a cart or carriage	**1810**
thug	*thag*	
	1 Thug – one of an association of professional robbers and murderers in India, who strangled their victims	**1810**
	2 a ruffian	**1839**
chutney	*chatni*	**1813**
chota	*chota* – small; *chota peg* = a small 'peg' of whisky	**1815**
dhobi	*dhobi* – a washerman	**1816**
popadam	Tamil *pappadam*, contraction from *paruppu adam* 'lentil cake'	**1820**
topi/topee	*topi* – hat cf. Anglo-Indian *sola topi*, worn by Europeans against the sun	**1835**
	sola – an Indian plant; the pith was used in making the topee hats	
lathi	*lathi* – a long heavy stick of bamboo, bound with iron	**1850**
raj	*raj* – sovereignty, rule; *British Raj* = British rule in India before 1947	**1859**
20th century		
biryani	*biryani* – A highly-spiced Indian dish made of meat or vegetables cooked with rice, saffron, and brown lentils	**1932**
tikka	*tikka* – pieces of meat or vegetable marinaded in spices and cooked on a skewer	**1955**

21.4.8 *Arabic*

19th century		
Islam	*islam*	**1818**
wadi	*wadi* – ravine or valley	**1839**
yashmak	*yashmaq* – veil	**1844**
halal	*halal* – lawful food	**1855**
jihad	*jihad* – a religious war	**1869**

21.4.9 *Celtic*

19th century		
mavourneen	Irish *mo mhurnín* – my darling	**1800**
poteen	Irish *poitín* 'little potí', short for *uisge poitín* 'little-pot whiskyí'	**1812**
sporran	Gaelic *sporan*	**1818**
colleen	Irish *cailin* – girl	**1828**
machree	Gaelic *mo chroidhe* – (of) my heart, my dear	**1829**
keen	Irish *caoine* – weeping lamenting	**1830**
menhir	Breton *men hir* – 'long stone'	**1840**
cwm	Welsh *cwm* – valley	**1853**
ceilidh	Irish *céilidhe*, Scots Gaelic *ceilidh*	**1875**
macushla	Irish *mo* my + *cuisle* vein, pulse (of the heart)	**1887**
20th century		
corgi	Welsh *cor-* dwarf + *gi*, from *ci* – dog	**1926**

21.4.10 *Japanese*

19th century		
hiragana	*hiragana*, from *hira* 'plain' + *kana* 'borrowed letter'; the cursive form of Japanese writing, intended for use by women	**1822**
hara-kiri	*hara kiri*, from *hara* 'belly' + *kiri* 'cut' (*seppuku* is said to be a more elegant expression); suicide by disembowelment, as formerly practised by the samurai of Japan, when in circumstances of disgrace, or under sentence of death	**1856**
tycoon	*taikun* 'great lord'; it was originally the title by which the shogun of Japan was described to foreigners	**1857**
Noh	*no*, traditional Japanese masked drama	**1871**
seppuku	*seppuku*, Japanese colloquial pronunciation of *setsu fuku*, from Chinese *qie* 'to cut' + *fu* 'belly' = *hara-kiri*	**1871**
ju-jitsu	*jujutsu*, a Japanese system of wrestling and physical training	**1875**
futon	*futon*, a Japanese bed-quilt	**1876**
sumo	*sumo*, a ritual form of wrestling contest	**1880**
tofu	*tofu*, from Chinese *dÚu* 'beans' + *fu* 'rotten'; a curd made from mashed soya beans	**1880**
netsuke	*netsuke*, a small piece of carved ivory or wood worn by the Japanese on the cord by which articles are suspended from the girdle	**1883**
kimono	*kimono*, a long Japanese robe with sleeves	**1886**
judo	*judo*, from *ju* 'gentleness', + *do*, 'way'; a refined form of ju-jitsu introduced in 1882	**1889**
geisha	*geisha*, a Japanese girl whose profession is to entertain men by dancing and singing	**1891**
banzai	*banzai*, 'ten thousand years'; a shout or cheer used by the Japanese in greeting the emperor or in battle	**1893**
sushi	*sushi*, a Japanese dish of cold boiled rice flavoured with vinegar garnished with fish or cooked egg	**1893**
kamikaze	*kamikaze*, 'divine wind', from *kami* 'god' + *kaze* 'wind'	**1896**
	1 originally used for the divine wind which blew on a night in August 1281, destroying the navy of the invading Mongols	**1945**
	2 Japanese airmen who in the war of 1939–1945 made deliberate suicidal crashes into enemy targets	

bushido	*bushido*, in feudal Japan, the ethical code of the Samurai or military knighthood	**1898**
haiku	*haiku*, form of Japanese verse consisting of 17 syllables	**1899**
kabuki	*kabuki*, from *ka* 'song' + *bu* 'dance' + *ki* 'art, skill'; a traditional form of Japanese drama	**1899**
20th century		
shubunkin	*shu*, 'vermilion' + *bun* 'portion' + *kin* 'gold'; a goldfish	**1917**
dan	*dan*, in Judo, a degree of proficiency	**1941**
bonsai	*bonsai*, a Japanese potted plant or small tree, intentionally dwarfed	**1950**
karate	*karate*, 'empty hand'; a Japanese system of unarmed combat in which hands and feet are used as weapons	**1955**
origami	*origami*, from *ori* 'fold' + *kami* 'paper'; the Japanese art of folding paper into intricate designs	**1956**
yokozuna	*yokozuna*, from *yoko* 'across' + '*zuna*' from *tsuna* 'rope, festoon', originally a sacred straw festoon presented to a champion wrestler; a grand champion sumo wrestler	**1966**
shiatsu	*shiatsu*, 'finger pressure'; a kind of therapy in which pressure is applied with the thumbs and palms to points on the body	**1967**

21.4.11 *Chinese*

19th century		
kow-tow	*ko-tou*, *fr ko* 'knock' + *tou* 'the head'	**1804**
chop-suey	*shap sui*, 'mixed bits'; a Chinese dish	**1888**
20th century		
chow mein	*chow mein 'fried flour'*; fried noodles	**1903**
shih-tzu	*shizigou fr shi* lion + *zi* son + *gou* dog; a small long-coated dog	**1921**
mah jong	*ma-tsiang*, 'sparrows', from *ma*, 'hemp' + *tsiang*, 'small birds'; a game.	**1922**
gung ho	*kung* 'work' + *ho* 'together'; a slogan adopted in the war of 1939–1945 by the United States Marines	**1942**
dim sum	*dim sum*, a savoury Cantonese-style snack	**1948**
wok	*wok*, a bowl-shaped pan used in Chinese cookery	**1952**

22. Postscript II – English spelling today: a summary

22.1 The Roman alphabet and English spelling

An alphabetic system of writing is based on the principle that each of the constituent sounds, or *phonemes*, of the language is represented visually by a sign, a 'graphic shape', in the form of a letter. Individuals pronounce the phonemes differently, but sufficiently similarly for there to be no confusion, just as the individual handwriting or the printed typefaces of a letter can be different, but 'the same letter'. An alphabetic system of writing is therefore *phonemic* in principle and ideally should have one letter for each sound. English uses the **Roman alphabet**, which was originally devised over 2000 years ago for the writing of Latin.

22.2 The contrastive sounds of English

Twenty-six letters for* c. *44 sounds

There are 26 letters in the alphabet. ⟨a e i o u⟩ are the vowel letters, with ⟨y⟩, and they are used in combination to represent 20 vowel sounds. The rest are the consonant letters, some of which are really redundant: ⟨q⟩ in the form ⟨qu⟩ is used for [k] or [kw] so ⟨k⟩ or ⟨kw⟩ could be used, ⟨x⟩ is used for [ks] or [gz] so ⟨ks⟩ or ⟨gz⟩ could be used, and ⟨c⟩ is used for either [s] or [k] and so could be discarded.

The answer to the question 'How many sounds (phonemes) are there in English?' depends on the kind of classification that you use. For example, is a vowel like [aɪ] as in *time*, that glides from one sound to another (a *diphthong*) one phoneme or two? The usual answer is one. The generally accepted classification of the phonemes of Received Pronunciation (RP) gives us 44 – 20 vowels and 24 consonants. As the 26 letters of the Roman alphabet have to represent 44 contrastive sounds, combinations of letters are used, usually in pairs (digraphs), for sounds for which there are no single Roman letters, like ⟨ch⟩, ⟨sh⟩, ⟨th⟩, ⟨ee⟩, ⟨ow⟩, ⟨aw⟩, etc. The system has developed over a long period of time and has never been formally revised or rationalised.

Diacritics

English is the only European language which does not use additional signs as *diacritics*, like ⟨é è ê n ç ü å⟩, though in digraphs like ⟨ch⟩ the letter ⟨h⟩ is being used as a diacritic sign, as is the letter ⟨u⟩ in a word like *dialogue*.

Stress

No spelling convention is normally used to mark the different pronunciations of words that are identical except for stress placement, like the noun *a record* and the verb *to record*, which would be shown in a transcription using the International Phonetic Alphabet (IPA) as ['rɛkɔːd] or [rɪ'kɔːd].

Regional accent

English spelling is neutral to accent. Novelists commonly represent regional accent by mis-spelling, so that a character who says *Wot d'yer think yer doin'?* can be recognised as working-class and vulgar. But this is a convention of fiction. *Wot* and *yer* are examples of *eye-dialect*. The pronunciation of *what* in RP is [wɒt], and *you* in unstressed position is pronounced [jə]. Our spelling system no longer represents current speech in any accent. You can only make accurate reference to sounds in writing by using the symbols of the IPA. Here is a list of the contrastive sounds of English for RP. Other dialectal accents vary in the number of phonemes.

IPA symbol		**RP pronunciation**
Vowels		
Simple vowels		
i	bead	[bid]
ɪ	bid	[bɪd]
ɛ	bed	[bɛd]
æ	bad	[bæd]
ɑ	bard	[bɑd]
ɒ	cod	[kɒd]
ɔ	board	[bɔd]
ʊ	put	[pʊt]
u	shoe	[ʃu]
ʌ	cup	[kʌp]
ɜ	bird	[bɜd]
ə	about, porter	[əbaʊt], [pɔtə]
Diphthongs		
ɛɪ	pay	[pɛɪ]
aɪ	pie	[paɪ]
ɔɪ	boy	[bɔɪ]
əʊ	go	[gəʊ]
aʊ	hound	[haʊnd]
ɪə	beer	[bɪə]
ɛə	bear	[bɛə]
ʊə	cure	[kjʊə]
Consonants		
p	pit	[pɪt]
b	bit	[bɪt]
t	tip	[tɪp]

IPA symbol		**RP pronunciation**
d	did	[dɪd]
k	kick	[kɪk]
g	give	[gɪv]
f	five	[faɪv]
v	vine	[vaɪn]
θ	thumb	[θʌm]
ð	this	[ðɪs]
s	some	[sʌm]
z	zoo	[zu]
ʃ	shoe	[ʃu]
ʒ	measure	[mɛʒə]
h	hot	[hɒt]
tʃ	charge	[tʃɑdʒ]
dʒ	gin	[dʒɪn]
m	mouse	[maʊs]
n	nice	[naɪs]
ŋ	sing	[sɪŋ]
l	leaf	[lif]
r RP = [ɹ] Scots = [ɾ]	run	[ɹʌn] RP [ɾʌn] Scots
j	yacht	[jɒt]
w	wet	[wɛt]
ʔ	The **glottal stop**, which occurs in some people's pronunciation of the medial consonant of words like *butter*, pronounced as *bu'er*, [bʌʔə] or [bʊʔə].	

22.3 The spelling of vowels in English

22.3.1 *Same sound, different spellings*

The following list of words contains selected examples of the range of vowel spellings that has developed in English today. Some groups of words have vowels that are spelt identically, but they are included because they derive from different older spellings that indicate a change from an earlier pronunciation. The original source words are also listed so that you can identify these changes. The variety of spellings illustrates one aspect of the problem of learning the English spelling system.

There are variant pronunciations of the vowels of many words both within RP and between the dialects. For example, *sure* may be pronounced as [ʃɔː] or [ʃʊə], *fire* as [faɪə], [faə] or [fɑː], *either* as [aɪðə] or [iːðə] , *again* as [əgɛn] or [əgɛɪn], *old* as [əʊld] or [ɑʊld], etc.

You can see that few modern English words are still spelt as they were in OE or OF. When you read an OE word remember to give the vowels their 'continental value' in pronunciation, as in Latin. The symbols of the IPA use these Latin values: ⟨a⟩ is [ɑ] or [a] (as in *father*), ⟨æ⟩ is [æ] (*cap*), ⟨e⟩ is [e] or [ɛ] (French é or è), ⟨i⟩ is [i] (*been*), ⟨o⟩ is [o] (French *eau*), ⟨u⟩ is [u] (*moon*), ⟨y⟩ is the vowel [y] (French *mur*).

1	**[iː]**		
⟨ee⟩	geese	ges	OE
	sleep	slæp	OE
	bee	beo	OE
⟨e⟩	be	beon	OE
	evil	yfel	OE
⟨e-e⟩	complete	complet	OF
⟨ea⟩	leaf	leaf	OE
	clean	clæne	OE
	steal	stelan	OE
	mead	meodu	OE
	peace	pes	AF
⟨ie⟩	piece	piece	OF
⟨ei⟩	seize	seizir	OF
⟨ey⟩	key	cæg	OE
⟨i-e⟩	machine	machine	F
⟨eo⟩	people	people	AF
⟨ay⟩	quay	kay	OF
2	**[ɪ]**		
⟨i⟩	sit	sittan	OE
	kin	cynn	OE
⟨y⟩	symbol	symbolum	L
⟨e⟩	pretty	prættig	OE
	England	englaland	OE
	wicked	wicca	OE
	= witch + -ed		
⟨ie⟩	ladies	hlæfdigan	OE
⟨a-e⟩	village	village	OF
⟨ui⟩	build	byldan	OE
	business	bysig	OE
	= busy + ness		
⟨ay⟩	Sunday	sunnandæg	OE
⟨o⟩	women	wifmenn	OE
⟨u⟩	busy	bysig	OE
⟨u-e⟩	minute	minute	OF
3	**[ɛ]**		
⟨e⟩	bed	bedd	OE
	seven	seofon	OE
⟨ea⟩	dead	dead	OE
	sweat	swætan	OE
⟨a⟩	many	mænig	OE
⟨a-e⟩	ate	æt	OE
⟨ai⟩	said	sægde	OE
⟨ay⟩	says	sægpb	OE
⟨u⟩	bury	byrgan	OE
⟨ie⟩	friend	freond	OE
⟨ai⟩	again	ongean	OE
4	**[æ]**		
	narrow	nearwe	OE
	lamb	lamb	OE
⟨ai⟩	plait	pleit	OF

5	**[ɑː]**		
⟨a⟩	bath	bæþ	OE
	ask	ascian	OE
	pass	passer	OF
	father	fæder	OE
⟨ar⟩	part	part	OF
	arm	earm	OE
	far	feor	OE
⟨ear⟩	heart	heorte	OE
⟨er⟩	clerk	clerc	OE
⟨al⟩	calm	calmus	L
⟨au⟩	aunt	aunte	AF
⟨a-e⟩	vase	vase	F
⟨oir⟩	reservoir	réservoir	OF
6	**[ɒ]**		
⟨o⟩	dog	dogga	OE
	holiday	haligdæg	OE
⟨o-e⟩	gone	gan	OE
⟨a⟩	was	wæs	OE
	wash	wascan	OE
⟨ou⟩	cough	kuchen	MDu
⟨ow⟩	knowledge	knaulege	ME
	f. cnawan + -læcan		OE
⟨au⟩	because		ME
	f. bi (OE) +	cause	(OF)
⟨ach⟩	yacht	jaghte	Du
7	**[ɔː]**		
⟨or⟩	cord	corde	OF
	horse	hors	OE
	or	ar	ON
⟨ore⟩	before	beforan	OE
	more	mara	OE
⟨oor⟩	floor	flor	OE
	door	duru	OE
⟨our⟩	four	feower	OE
	court	curt	AF
⟨oa⟩	broad	brad	OE
⟨oar⟩	oar	ar	OE
⟨ou⟩	bought	bohte	OE
⟨aw⟩	saw	seah/sawon	OE
	claw	clawu	OE
	law	lagu	OE
⟨au⟩	cause	cause	OF
⟨ough⟩	bought	bohte	OE
	fought	feaht	OE
	ought	ahte	OE
⟨augh⟩	daughter	dohtor	OE
⟨a⟩	talk	talkien	ME
		f. talu	OE
	hall	heall	OE
	water	wæter	OE
	walk	wealcan	OE
⟨ure⟩	sure	sur	OF

8 **[ʊ]**

⟨u⟩	put	putian	OE
	butcher	bochier	OF
⟨o⟩	wolf	wulf	OE
	woman	wifmann	OE
⟨oo⟩	good	god	OE
	wood	wudu	OE
⟨ou⟩	could	cue	OE

9a **[uː]**

⟨oo⟩	food	foda	OE
	choose	ceosan	OE
	loose	lauss	ON
⟨o⟩	do	don	OE
⟨oe⟩	shoe	scoh	OE
⟨o-e⟩	lose	losian	OE
⟨ou⟩	group	groupe	F
	wound	wundian	OE
⟨ough⟩	through	þurh	OE
⟨ue⟩	blue	bleu	OF
⟨u-e⟩	rude	rude	OF
⟨ew⟩	chew	ceowan	OE

9b **[juː]**

⟨ew⟩	new	niwe	OE
	knew	cneow	OE
	few	feawe	OE
	lewd	læwede	OE
⟨iew⟩	view	viewe	AF
⟨eu⟩	feud	feide	OF
⟨ueue⟩	queue	queue	F
⟨ui⟩	juice	jus	OF
⟨ue⟩	sue	suer	AF
⟨u-e⟩	tune	ton	OF

10 **[ʌ] ~ [ʊ]**

Varies according to dialectal area – RP is [ʌ]

⟨u⟩	sun	sunne	OE
⟨o⟩	son	sunu	OE
	mother	modor	OE
⟨oe⟩	does vb	doþ	OE
⟨ou⟩	young	geong	OE
	country	cuntree	OF
⟨oo⟩	blood	blod	OE
⟨ough⟩	rough	ruh	OE

11 **[ɜː]**

In rhotic areas [r] is pronounced after a vowel, which may then not be [ɜː].

⟨ir⟩	bird	brid/bird	OE
	shirt	scyrte	OE
	her	hire	OE
⟨yr⟩	myrtle	myrtille	OF
⟨er⟩	her	hire	OE
	herd	heord	OE
⟨ear⟩	heard	hyrde	OE
	earth	eorþe	OE
⟨err⟩	err	errer	OF
⟨ur⟩	turn	tyrnan	OE
⟨urr⟩	purr	(*imitative*)	
⟨or⟩	word	word	OE
⟨our⟩	scourge	escorge	OF
⟨olo⟩	colonel	colonello	It

12 **[ə]**

This mid-central 'reduced' vowel is the most frequent in English speech, because it occurs in **unstressed syllables**. These words are only a few of the possible spellings:

col**our**	colour	OF
bor**ough**	burh	OE
doct**or**	doctour	OF
fam**ous**	fameus	OF
fig**ure**	figure	OF
gentle**man** cp gentilz hom		OF
oblige	obliger	OF
particular	particuler	OF
possi**ble**	possible	OF
suppose	supposer	OF
th**e**	se etc	OE

13 **[eɪ]**

⟨a⟩	lady	hlæfdige	OE
⟨a-e⟩	late	læt	OE
	tale	talu	OE
⟨ay⟩	day	dæg	OE
	way	weg	OE
⟨ai⟩	rain	regn	OE
⟨eigh⟩	eight	eahta	OE
⟨ey⟩	they	þeir	ON
⟨ea⟩	great	great	OE
	break	brecan	OE
⟨au⟩	gauge	gauge	AF
⟨ao⟩	gaol	gaole	AF

14a **[aɪ]**

⟨i⟩	child	cild	OE
	climb	climban	OE
⟨i-e⟩	time	tima	OE
	mice	mys	OE
⟨y⟩	cry	cri	OF
⟨ye⟩	dye	deagian	OE
⟨igh⟩	high	heah	OE
	night	niht	OE
⟨eigh⟩	height	hehþu	OE
⟨ie⟩	lie	licgan	OE
⟨ei⟩	either	ægþer	OE
⟨eye⟩	eye	eage	OE

⟨uy⟩	buy	bycgan	OE
⟨ais⟩	aisle	ele	OF
(confused with *island* and OF aile *wing*)			
14b	**[aɪə] ~ [aə] ~ [ɑː]**		
⟨ire⟩	wire	wir	OE
	fire	fyr	OE
⟨oir⟩	choir	quer	OF
		& chorus	L
⟨iar⟩	liar	leogere	OE
⟨ier⟩	briar/brier	brær/brer	OE
15	**[ɔɪ]**		
⟨oi⟩	coin	coin	OF
⟨oy⟩	boy	abuiæ	AF
		= fettered < L boia	
⟨oi-e⟩	noise	noise	OF
	choice	chois	OF
⟨uoy⟩	buoy	boye	MDu
16	**RP [əʊ]**		
Varies a lot in dialectal accents			
⟨o⟩	so	swa	OE
	go	gan	OE
⟨ol⟩	old	eald	OE
	folk	folc	OE
⟨o-e⟩	home	ham	OE
⟨oa⟩	oak	ac	OE
	throat	þrote	OE
⟨oe⟩	toe	ta	OE
⟨ou⟩	soul	sawol	OE
⟨ough⟩	though	þoh	ON
⟨ow⟩	know	cnawan	OE
	grow	growan	OE
	sow	sawan	OE
⟨ew⟩	sew	siwan	OE
⟨au⟩	mauve	mauve	F
⟨oo⟩	brooch	brocher	OF
⟨eau⟩	beau	beau	F

17a	**[aʊ]**		
⟨ou⟩	out	ut	OE
	house	hus	OE
⟨ow⟩	cow	cu	OE
⟨ough⟩	bough	boh	OE
17b	**[aʊə] ~ [aə] ~ [ɑː]**		
⟨our⟩	flour &		
⟨ower⟩	flower	flur	AF
⟨our⟩	our	ure	OE
18	**[ɪə]**		
⟨ea⟩	ear	eare	OE
	dear	deore	OE
	hear	hieran	OE
⟨eer⟩	deer	deor	OE
⟨ere⟩	here	her	OE
⟨ier⟩	fierce	fers	AF
⟨eir⟩	weird	wyrd	OE
⟨ea⟩	idea	idea	L
19	**[ɛə]**		
⟨are⟩	care n	caru	OE
⟨ar-e⟩	scarce	scars	AF
⟨air⟩	air	air	OF
	stair	stæger	OE
⟨ear⟩	bear vb	beran	OE
⟨eir⟩	their	þeirra	ON
⟨ere⟩	there	þær/þer	OE
⟨aer⟩	aerobics	aerobie	F
20a	**[ʊə] ~ [ɔː]**		
⟨u⟩	during	*cf* durant	OF
⟨oor⟩	poor	poure	OF
⟨ure⟩	sure	sur	OF
⟨our⟩	tour	tour	OF
20b	**[jʊə]**		
⟨ure⟩	pure	pur	OF

22.3.2 *Same spelling, different sounds*

The same words from section 22.3.1 are arranged in different sets to show the variety of sounds which each letter may represent:

a
- narrow [æ]
- sat [æ]
- ask [ɑː]
- bath [ɑː]
- father [ɑː]
- pass [ɑː]
- hall [ɔː]
- water [ɔː]
- lady [ɛɪː]
- many [ɛ]
- was [ɒ]
- wash [ɒ]

a–e
- ate [ɛ]
- late [ɛɪ]
- tale [ɛɪ]
- vase [ɒː]
- care [ɛə]
- village [ɪ]

ach
- yacht [ɒ]

ai
- again [ɛ]
- said [ɛ]
- air [ɛə]
- rain [ɛɪ]
- plait [æ]

air
- stair [ɛə]

ais
- aisle [aɪ]

al
- calm [ɑː]
- talk [ɔː]
- walk [ɔː]

ao
- gaol [ɛɪ]

ar
- arm [ɑː]
- far [ɑː]
- part [ɑː]
- particular [əː]
- scarce [ɛə]

au
- aunt [ɑː]
- because [ɒ]
- gauge [ɛɪ]
- mauve [əʊ]

augh
- daughter [ɔː]

aw
- claw [ɔː]
- law [ɔː]
- saw [ɔː]

ay
- day [ɛɪ]
- way [ɛɪ]
- says [ɛ]
- Sunday [ɪ]
- quay [iː]

e
- bed [ɛ]
- seven [ɛ]
- be [iː]
- evil [iː]
- business [ɪ]
- pretty [ɪ]
- wicked [ɪ]
- England [ɪ]
- gentlemen [ə]
- the [ə]

e–e
- complete [iː]

ea
- leaf [iː]
- mead [iː]
- peace [iː]
- steal [iː]
- clean [iː]
- dead [ɛ]
- sweat [ɛ]
- break [ɛɪ]
- great [ɛɪ]
- idea [ɪə]

ear
- bear [ɛə]
- dear [ɪə]
- ear [ɪə]
- earth [ɜː]
- hear [ɪə]
- heard [ɜː]
- heart [ɑː]

ee
- bee [iː]
- geese [iː]
- deer [ɪə]

ei
- either [aɪ]
- seize [iː]
- their [ɛə]

eigh
- eight [ɛɪ]
- height [aɪ]

eir
- weird [ɪə]

eo
- people [iː]

er
- her [ɜː]
- herd [ɜː]
- clerk [ɑː]

ere
- here [ɪə]
- there [ɛə]

err
- err [ɜː]

eu
- feud [juː]

ew
- chew [uː]
- few [juː]
- knew [juː]
- lewd [juː]
- new [juː]
- sew [əʊ]

ey
- key [iː]
- they [ɛɪ]

eye
- eye [aɪ]

i
- kin [ɪ]
- sit [ɪ]
- child [aɪ]
- climb [aɪ]

i–e
- machine [iː]
- mice [aɪ]
- time [aɪ]

ia
- briar [aɪə]
- liar [aɪə]

ie
- friend [ɛ]
- ladies [ɪ]
- lie [aɪ]
- piece [iː]

ier
- fierce [ɪə]

iew
- view [juː]

igh
- high [aɪ]
- night [aɪ]

ir
- bird [ɜː]
- shirt [ɜː]

ire
- fire [aɪə]
- wire [aɪə]

le
- possible [ə]

o
- dog [ɒ]
- holiday [ɒ]
- do [uː]
- lose [uː]
- go [əʊ]
- mother [ʌ]
- son [ʌ]
- wolf [ʊ]
- woman [ʊ]
- old [əʊ]
- so [əʊ]
- women [ɪ]
- oblige [ə]

o–e
- before [ɔː]
- gone [ɒ]
- home [əʊ]

oa
- broad [ɔː]
- oak [əʊ]
- throat [əʊ]

oar
- oar [ɔː]

oe
- does (vb) [ʌ]
- shoe [uː]
- toe [əʊː]

Spelling	Sound
oi	
choice	[ɔɪ]
coin	[ɔɪ]
noise	[ɔɪ]
choir	[aɪə]
oir	
reservoir	[ɑː]
ol	
folk	[əʊ]
olo	
colonel	[ɜː]
oo	
food	[uː]
loose	[uː]
choose	[uː]
blood	[ʌ]
good	[ʊ]
wood	[ʊ]
dbrooch	[əʊ]
oor	[ɔː]
oor	
floor	[ɔː]
poor	[ʊə][ɔː]
or	
cord	[ɔː]
horse	[ɔː]
or	[ɔː]
word	[ɜː]
doctor	[ə]
ore	
more	[ɔː]
ou	
cough	[ɒ]
could	[ʊ]
country	[ʌː]
famous	[ə]
group	[uː]
house	[aʊ]
out	[aʊ]
soul	[əʊ]
young	[ʌ]
ough	
bough	[aʊ]
bought	[ɔː]
fought	[ɔː]
ought	[ɔː]
rough	[ʌ]
though	[əʊ]
through	[uː]
borough	[ə]
our	
court	[ɔː]
four	[ɔː]
flour	[əʊ]
our	[aʊə]
scourge	[ɜː]
tour	[ʊə]
colour	[ə]
ow	
cow	[aʊ]
grow	[əʊ]
know	[əʊ]
sow	[əʊ]
knowledge	[ɒ]
ower	
flower	[aʊə]
oy	
boy	[ɔɪ]
u	
put	[ʊ]
sun	[ʌ]
bury	[ɛ]
business	[ɪ]
busy	[ɪ]
during	[juː]
suppose	[ə]
u–e	
minute (n)	[ɪ]
rude	[uː]
tune	[juː]
ue	
blue	[uː]
sue	[juː]
ueue	
queue	[juː]
ui	
build	[ɪ]
juice	[juː]
ur	
turn	[ɜː]
ure	
sure	[ʊə]
pure	[jʊə]
figure	[ə]
urr	
purr	[ɜː]
uy	
buy	[aɪ]
y	
cry	[aɪ]
symbol	[ɪ]
ye	
dye	[aɪ]
yr	
myrtle	[ɜː]

22.3.3 *Some features of the spelling of vowels*

Some of the reasons for the variety and irregularity of the spelling of English vowels have been discussed in earlier chapters, and are summarized in a survey of the historical development of spelling in chapter 23 following. Test your understanding of the spelling system by discussing possible answers to these questions:

- Why do the same letters represent different sounds? For example, ⟨o⟩ as a single letter in *rot*, [rɒt] as a double letter ⟨oo⟩ in *root*, [ruːt] and in the sequence ⟨ote⟩ in *rote*, [rəʊt]. Similar sequences are *met*, *meet*, *mete* and *cot*, *coot*, *cote*. There are many other pairs of words like *loss/loose*, *bet/beet* in which the double vowel letter is pronounced differently from the single, and *bat/bate*, *win/wine*, *rod/rode*, *cub/cube*, in which the final ⟨e⟩ marks a change in the vowel.
- Why is ⟨ee⟩ always pronounced [iː] as in *bee*, but ⟨ea⟩ varies widely, as in *leaf* [iː], *dead* [ɛ], *heart* [ɑː], *heard* [ɜː], *great* [ɛɪ], *ear* [ɪə], *bear* [ɜə]?
- Why is letter ⟨o⟩ pronounced [ʊ] in *wolf* and [ʌ] or [ʊ] in *son*?
- Why are the vowels of *busy* and *bury* spelt with ⟨u⟩ but pronounced [ɪ] and [ɛ] respectively?

- Why are there eight different pronunciations of the vowel of ⟨-ough⟩?
- Why have many words spelt with ⟨ir⟩, ⟨er⟩ and ⟨ur⟩ lost the pronunciation [ɹ] in RP and other dialectal accents, and are now pronounced [ɜː], whereas other dialects pronounce the ⟨r⟩ and some also differentiate the vowels, e.g. Scots *heard* [hɛɾd], *bird* [bəɾd], etc?

22.4 The spelling of consonants in English

22.4.1 *Grouped by consonant sounds – same sound, different spellings*

1	**[p]**		
⟨p⟩	pill	pille	MDu
	hop (vb)	hoppian	OE
	hoping	hopian	OE
⟨pe⟩	hope (vb)	hopian	OE
⟨pp⟩	hopping	hoppian	OE
	appear	apareir	OF
	hiccough	hiccup ?	
(*assimilated to spelling of cough*)			
	cupboard	cuppe + bord	OE
	receipt	reɪoite	OF
2	**[b]**		
⟨b⟩	rob	rober	OF
	robing	robe	OF
	beauty	beautæ	OF
⟨be⟩	robe	robe	OF
⟨bb⟩	robbing	rober	OF
	rubber	rub + -er	?
	debt	dette	OF
	limb	limr	ON
3	**[t]**		
⟨t⟩	mat	matte	OE
	tell	tellan	OE
	mating	mate	MLG
⟨te⟩	mate	mate	MLG
⟨tt⟩	matting	matte + ing	OE
	attend	atendre	OF
⟨ed⟩	looked	locode	OE
⟨th⟩	Thomas	Thomas	Gk
	castle	castel	AF
4	**[d]**		
⟨d⟩	bid (vb)	biddan	OE
	biding	bidan	OE
	dog	dogga	OE
⟨de⟩	bide	bidan	OE
⟨dd⟩	bidding	biddan + ing	OE
	middle	middel	OE
⟨ed⟩	mugged	mug = -ed	?

5	**[k]**		
⟨k⟩	kind	cynde	OE
⟨c⟩	cake	kaka	ON
	come	cuman	OE
	magic	magique	OF
⟨ck⟩	black	blæc	OE
⟨ch⟩	stomach	stomaque	OF
	choir	quer	OF
		& chorus	L
⟨cc⟩	accord	acord	OF
⟨q⟩	queen	cwen	OE
	conquer	conquerre	OF
6	**[g]**		
⟨g⟩	geese	ges	OE
⟨gg⟩	ragged	roggvaðr	ON
⟨gh⟩	ghost	gast	OE
⟨gu⟩	guard	garder	OF
	gnaw	gnagan	OE
	diaphragm	diaphragma	Gk
7	**[f]**		
⟨f⟩	fit	fitt	OE
	fan	fann	OE
⟨ff⟩	off	of	OE
	suffer	sufrir	AF
⟨gh⟩	enough	genog	OE
	cough	kuchen	MDu
⟨ph⟩	physics	physica	L
8	**[v]**		
⟨v⟩	veal	vel	AF
	vine	vigne	OF
⟨ve⟩	give	giefan	OE
	move	mover	AF
⟨ph⟩	nephew	neveu	OF
⟨f⟩	of	of	OE
9	**[θ]**		
⟨th⟩	thick	þicce	OE
	heath	hæþ	OE

10	**[ð]**		
⟨th⟩	there	þær/þer	OE
	though	þo	ON
	with	wiþ	OE
	whether	hwæþer	OE
11	**[s]**		
⟨s⟩	so	swa	OE
	suit	siute	AF
⟨se⟩	mouse	mus	OE
⟨ss⟩	pass	passer	OF
⟨c⟩	cease	cesser	OF
⟨ce⟩	niece	niece	OF
⟨ps⟩	psalm	sealm	OE
⟨sc⟩	science	science	OF
12	**[z]**		
⟨z⟩	zeal	zelos	Gk
⟨zz⟩	dizzy	dysig	OE
⟨s⟩	bosom	bosm	OE
	cows	cu (cy *pl*)	OE
	was	wæs	OE
⟨se⟩	rose	rose	OE
13	**[ʃ]**		
⟨sh⟩	shoe	scoh	OE
⟨s⟩	sure	sur	OF
⟨ss⟩	mission	mission	F
	assure	aseurer	OF
⟨sch⟩	schedule	cedule	OF
⟨si⟩	mansion	mansion	OF
⟨ti⟩	nation	nation	OF
⟨ci⟩	special	especial	OF
⟨ch⟩	machine	machine	F
14	**[ʒ]**		
⟨ge⟩	beige	beige	F
⟨s⟩	measure	mesure	OF
⟨si⟩	vision	vision	OF
15	**[h]**		
⟨h⟩	hair	hær	OE
	how	hu	OE
	perhaps	per	L
		+ happ + s	ON
⟨wh⟩	who	hwa	OE
	shepherd	sceaphierde	OE
	hour	eure, ore	OF
	vehicle	véhicule	F
	honest	oneste	OF
	hotel	hotel	F
16	**[tʃ]**		
⟨ch⟩	cheese	cese	OE
	rich	rice	OE
⟨tch⟩	watch	wæccan	OE

⟨t⟩	nature	nature	OF
⟨ti⟩	question	question	OF
⟨te⟩	righteous	rihtwis	OE
17	**[dʒ]**		
⟨j⟩	jest	geste	OF
⟨g⟩	gin (drink)	genever	Du
⟨ge⟩	lunge	allonge	F
⟨dge⟩	midge	mycge	OE
⟨gg⟩	suggest	suggerere	L
⟨dj⟩	adjacent	adjacere	L
⟨d⟩	grandeur	grandeur	F
⟨di⟩	soldier	soldier	OF
18	**[m]**		
⟨m⟩	meat	mete	OE
	warm	wearm	OE
⟨mm⟩	summer	sumor	OE
⟨mn⟩	autumn	autompne	OF
⟨lm⟩	salmon	saumon	OF
19	**[n]**		
⟨n⟩	now	nu	OE
	nurse	nurice	OF
⟨nn⟩	dinner	diner	OF
⟨kn⟩	knit	cnyttan	OE
⟨gn⟩	sign	signe	OF
⟨gn⟩	gnaw	gnagan	OE
20	**[ŋ]**		
⟨n⟩	anchor	ancor	OE
	finger	finger	OE
⟨ng⟩	sing	singan	OE
	singer	singan + er	
⟨ngue⟩	tongue	tunge	OE
21	**[l]**		
⟨l⟩	leave	læfan	OE
	blow	blawan	OE
⟨ll⟩	fall	feallan	OE
	silly	sælig	OE
	talk	ME talkien	
		f. talu	OE
	half	healf	OE
22	**[r]**		
⟨r⟩	red	read	OE
	reed	hreod	OE
	dairy	dæge + ery	OE
⟨rr⟩	carry	carier	AF
	mirror	mirour	OF
⟨rh⟩	rhythm	rhythme	F
⟨wr⟩	write	writan	OE
	far	feor	OE
	fir	fyri	ON
	fur	furrer	AF

23	**[j]**		
⟨y⟩	year	gear	OE
	yes	gese	OE
⟨i⟩	spaniel	espaigneul	OF
	muse	muse	OF
	new	niwe	OE
24	**[w]**		
⟨w⟩	weather	weder	OE
	dwindle	dwinan	OE
	wine	win	OE
	witch	wicca	OE
⟨wh⟩	whine	hwinan	OE
	which	hwilc	OE
	wheat	hwæte	OE
	wrist	wrist	OE
	write	writan	OE
	one	an	OE
25	**⟨x⟩ = [ks] = [kʃ]**		
	axe	æx	OE
	luxury	luxurie	OF
26	**⟨x⟩ = [gz]**		
	exact	exactus	L

Words with 'silent' consonant letters			
⟨b⟩	debt	dette	OF
	limb	limr	ON
⟨c⟩	science	science	OF
⟨g⟩	diaphragm	diaphragma	Gk
	sign	signe	OF
	gnaw	gnagan	OE
⟨h⟩	shepherd	sceaphierde	OE
	ghost	gast	OE
	honest	oneste	OF
	hour	ore/eure	OF
	vehicle	væhicule	F
	rhythm	rhythme	F
⟨k⟩	knit	cnyttan	OE
⟨l⟩	half	healf	OE
	salmon	saumon	OF
	talk	ME talkien	
		f talu	OE
⟨n⟩	autumn	autompne	OF
⟨p⟩	cupboard	cuppe + bord	OE
	psalm	sealm	OE
⟨r⟩	far	feor	OE
	fir	fyri	ON
	fur	furrer	AF
⟨t⟩	castle	castel	AF
⟨w⟩	write	writan	OE
	who	hwa	OE
	wrist	wrist	OE
⟨gh⟩	though	þoh	OE

22.4.1 *Some features of the spelling of consonants*

The spelling of consonants is more regular than that of the vowels, but there are a number of apparent anomalies which need to be explained. As before, test your present knowledge now. Chapter 23 will help to explain. A dictionary will also help. This activity looks at only some of the anomalies in the system.

- The pronunciation of consonants spelt with single and double letters does not appear to be different, e.g. *hop*, *hope*, *hopping*, *hoping*. What determines the use of single or double consonant letters, or does it seem to be a random choice?
- Is there a rule for the pronunciation of letter ⟨c⟩ as either [s] or [k]?
- Why and when was OE *cwen* re-spelt *queen*?
- ⟨ough⟩ words vary not only in the pronunciation of the vowel, but in some ⟨gh⟩ is pronounced [f] – *laugh*, *cough*, *trough*. How did this happen?
- Explain why the ⟨h⟩ is not pronounced in words like *hour*, *honest*.
- Why are there 'silent' letters in the spelling of *knight*, *gnaw*, *wrist*, *debt*?

23. Postscript III – the development of present-day English spelling: a summary

23.1 Old English

Old English and the Roman alphabet

The earliest writing which the Angles and Saxons brought over from the Continent in the 5th and 6th centuries used runes (section 3.1.1). Written English began after the establishment of monasteries in the 7th century. Monks wrote and copied Latin manuscripts and therefore adapted the Roman alphabet for the writing of English. By the 10th century a stable spelling system had been established in the West Saxon dialect, which became a standard for written manuscripts throughout the country by the 11th century. This standard was lost in the aftermath of the Norman Conquest (chapters 2–3).

Most of the initial difficulty in deciphering OE writing is caused either by differences in the shape of the letters, most noticeably in ⟨g⟩, ⟨r⟩, and the three shapes for letter ⟨s⟩, and also by the letters that were added to the Roman alphabet to represent sounds that were not used in Latin, ⟨ʒ⟩ *yogh*, ⟨ƿ⟩ *wynn*, ⟨þ⟩ *thorn*, ⟨ð⟩ *eth* and ⟨æ⟩ *ash* (section 3.1.2). Letters ⟨j⟩ ⟨v⟩ and ⟨w⟩ were not in use; ⟨q⟩ and ⟨z⟩ were rare.

23.1.1 *Vowel change from OE to MnE*

Much of the apparent inconsistency in MnE spelling is caused by the fact that changes in the pronunciation of vowels were not matched by appropriate changes in the spelling.

Long and short vowels in OE

Short and long vowels were contrastive in OE (section 3.1.3.1), e.g. *coc* with a short [o] meant *cock*, and with a long [oː] meant *cook*; *ful* with [u] meant *full*, and with [uː] meant *foul*. Sometimes long vowels were written with a double letter, e.g. *cooc* for *cook* or *fuul* for *foul*, but although we now have plenty of words spelt with ⟨ee⟩ and ⟨oo⟩, spellings with ⟨aa⟩, ⟨ii⟩ and ⟨uu⟩ did not survive.

Between the 14th and 17th centuries, in the midlands and south of England, all the long vowels were affected by the Great Vowel Shift (section 15.5). The ME spelling ⟨oo⟩ in *goos* (*goose*) was originally pronounced [oː] but is now [uː].

Why is English home *Scots* hame?

The OE originals of *home* and *hame* were spelt with letter ⟨a⟩ and spoken with the long vowel [ɑː], like, for example, *an* (*one*), *aþ* (*oath*), *ban* (*bone*), *gat* (*goat*), *halig* (*holy*), and *stan* (*stone*). The pronunciation of [ɑː] had shifted enough for writers to spell it with ⟨o⟩, pronounced [ɔː], and still different from [oː], which was also spelt ⟨o⟩. This long low back vowel [ɔː] later shifted to [oː], and finally in present-day RP to the diphthong [əʊ] (section 6.1.4.8).

This 'rounding' of [ɑː] did not happen in the north. Instead, the pronunciation of the vowel in time moved towards the front of the mouth, [ɑː] ⇒ [aː] ⇒ [æː] ⇒ [ɛː] ⇒ [eː]. Evidence for this today is in Scots pronunciation, in contrast to RP:

OE		***MnE RP***		***Scots***	
an	[ɑːn]	one	[wʌn]	ain	[eːn]
aþ	[ɑːθ]	oath	[əʊθ]	aith	[eːθ]
ban	[bɑːn]	bone	[bəʊn]	bane	[beːn]
gat	[gɑːt]	goat	[gəʊt]	gait	[geːt]
halig	[hɑːlɪɣ]	holy	[həʊlɪ]	halie	[heːlɪ]
stan	[stɑːn]	stone	[stəʊn]	stane	[steːn]

What happened to the OE letter

The useful OE letter ⟨**æ**⟩, which distinguished the front vowel [æ] from the back vowel [ɑ] spelt ⟨a⟩, ceased to be used in Middle English writing There were two linked reasons for the loss of the letter. Firstly, it was not used in French spelling, and was one of the casualties of the changes brought about in the aftermath of the Norman Conquest. Secondly, the sound of the long vowel [æː] shifted towards [ɛː], and came to be spelt ⟨e⟩ (section 6.1.4.4).

Examples of OE words with short [æ] which were spelt with ⟨a⟩ in ME are, *æfter*, *æsc*, *cræft*, *græs*, which became *after*, *ash*, *craft*, *grass*. Some OE words with long [æː] which were spelt with ⟨e⟩ in ME are, *dæd*, *þræd*, *hær* which are MnE *deed*, *thread*, *hair*.

What happened to the OE short [y] and long [yː]?

The letter ⟨y⟩ in OE represented a vowel which has since dropped out of most dialectal accents of English – it was like the vowel of the French word *mur* [myr]. It shifted and changed in ME. For example, we find OE *hyll* (*hill*) spelt *hill*, *hell* and *hull*, which is evidence of a different pronunciation in different regions of the country.

This explains the anomaly in present-day spelling described in section 6.1.4.6. We spell *busy* and *bury*, from OE *bysig* and *byrigean*, with letter ⟨u⟩ but pronounce them [bɪzi] and [bɛri], not [bʊzi] and [bʊri]. Spelling and pronunciation each come from different dialectal areas. Usually the spelling of words derived from OE words with ⟨y⟩ corresponds to the particular pronunciation which happens to have come down into Standard English, e.g. *brycg* (*bridge*), *lyft* (*left*), *blyscan* (*blush*).

Long vowels changed similarly, and like all other long vowels, shifted in the Great Vowel Shift later on, e.g., *bryd* (*bride*), *hyf* (*hive*).

The OE verbs *ceosan* (*choose*) and *creopan* (*creep*) were both spelt ⟨eo⟩ for the diphthong [ɛːo]. This diphthong 'smoothed' into a single long vowel, but in *ceosan* it was the end of the 'glide' that lengthened to [oː], and in *creopan* the first part that lengthened to [eː]. So the sequence was *ceosan* ⇒ *chosen* ⇒ *chose* ⇒ *choose* and *creopan* ⇒ *crepen* ⇒ *crepe* ⇒ *creep*. Compare *cleofan* (*cleave*), *seoþan* (*seethe*), *freosan* (*freeze*), *fleotan* (*float*), *sceotan* (*shoot*), etc.

23.1.2 *Consonants from OE to MnE*

Most OE consonants have remained virtually unchanged. By the 11th century however, some consonants were pronounced differently from that suggested by the spelling.

If a spelling system becomes standard and widely used, like the West Saxon system, it does not keep up with changes in pronunciation. So, for example, *scyrte* in late OE was pronounced very much like MnE *shirt* (the same word), though it had begun as something like *skirt*, which has also come down to MnE from the ON word which hadn't changed, and now has a different meaning.

Some OE consonant spellings

Consonant changes that were not reflected in the spelling took place in certain phonetic environments:

Letter	***OE word***		***MnE***	
c = [tʃ]	cese	[tʃeːzə]	cheese	[tʃiːz]
• The original [k] has been 'palatalized' to [tʃ] by the following front vowel				
cg = [dʒ]	mycge	[mydʒə]	midge	[mɪdʒ]
• The ⟨g⟩ had been palatalized in an earlier sound change				
f = [v]	ofer	[ovər]	over	[əʊvə]
s = [z]	dysig	[dyzɪj]	dizzy	[dɪzɪ]
þ = [ð]	hwæþer	[hwæðər]	whether	[wɛðə]
• Voiceless fricatives between vowels became voiced				
g = [j]	gear	[jæər]	year	[jɪə]
• ⟨g⟩ was palatalised before and after [i], and (usually) [æ], [e] and [y]				
g = [ɣ]	fugol	[fuɣəl]	fowl	[faʊl]
• ⟨g⟩ between back vowels became a fricative consonant				
sc	scip	[ʃɪp]	ship	[ʃɪp]
• ⟨sc⟩ before front vowels was palatalized to [ʃ]				

Consonant clusters in OE

Every letter in an OE word was pronounced. There were no 'silent' letters except where two sounds had assimilated, like ⟨sc⟩ [ʃ], and ⟨cg⟩ [dʒ]. For a selection of words whose consonant clusters were later simplified see section 23.3.

The source of a present-day spelling rule

In OE some consonants, as well as vowels, were contrasted by length. Long consonants were written double, for example ⟨tt⟩, ⟨ll⟩, as in the second of these pairs of words,

OE	*MnE*	*OE*	*MnE*
hopian	hope (*vb*)	cwelan	= die
hoppian	hop (*vb*)	cwellan	= kill (*now* quell)

In section 3.1.3.2 we saw that the present tense form of *bledan* (*bleed*) was *blede*, with the long vowel [eː], and that the past tense was *bledde*, also with the long vowel [eː]. We know that long vowels shifted in the Great Vowel Shift, so we have *bleed* with [iː] in MnE, but a short vowel [ɛ] in the past tense *bled*. Therefore the OE long vowel of the past tense must have become short in late OE or early ME. The reason for this must have been that the following long consonant *-dd-* had affected the pronunciation of the vowel, making it short.

After this had taken place, the fact that vowels before double consonants were pronounced short led to a new spelling convention. Double consonants were no longer pronounced long, but in the spelling system a digraph like ⟨tt⟩ came to indicate that the preceding vowel was short, which is the convention we have today.

In OE, a double consonant in writing signified a contrastive sound. In MnE the second consonant is a diacritic, marking the sound of the preceding vowel.

23.2 After 1066 – Middle English

Loss of the standard after the Norman Conquest

After the Norman Conquest, French or Latin were used in official documents, and little written English has survived from 1100 to 1300. The West Saxon standard was lost, and the period of Middle English is known for the wide variety of spellings used in different parts of the country which matched different dialectal pronunciation, vocabulary and grammar.

There is some direct evidence in the continuations of *The Peterborough Chronicle* of language change which the former standard system of West Saxon OE spelling obscured (section 5.3).

A Middle English sound change

A further sound change which took place in the early ME period explains another of the spelling conventions of MnE – the lengthening of short vowels in two-syllable words (section 6.1.4.9). A large set of words became monosyllables in pronunciation with the reduction of the second unstressed syllable, many of them retaining the final letter ⟨e⟩ in spelling.

Because the vowels were now long, they all took part in the later Great Vowel Shift. Their spelling remained the same, however, and is another example of the failure of the spelling system to mark change in pronunciation.

OE		*ME*		*MnE*
cnafa	⇒	knave	⇒	knave
[knava]	⇒	[knaːvə]	⇒	[nɛɪv]
melu	⇒	mele	⇒	meal
[melu]	⇒	[meːlə]	⇒	[miːl]
þrote	⇒	throte	⇒	throat
[þrote]	⇒	[þroːtə]	⇒	[þrəʊt]

Their pronunciation today is one of the pieces of evidence that this lengthening had taken place in early ME. For example, the OE verb *bacan* became ME *baken* and then *bake*. If it had remained with a short vowel, it would have been pronounced like *back* today.

Originally, the final ⟨e⟩ was an inflection and had nothing to do with the sound of the preceding vowel. But in the 16th century, by which time the vowel had become long and had shifted, the final ⟨e⟩ came to be regarded as a diacritic marker of the preceding vowel or diphthong. Richard Mulcaster writes of ⟨e⟩ in 1582 as:

> a letter of maruellous vse in the writing of our tung...whose absence or presence, somtime altereth the vowell.

This explains the 'magic ⟨e⟩', which is said to make the preceding vowel 'sound its name', a simple explanation used by infant teachers when teaching reading.

Lack of standard spelling in Middle English

The notion of a standardized 'correct spelling' was unknown. Here, for example, are some of the different spellings of the words *lady* and *lord* from OE to ME that show changes over time as well as variations in dialect.

MnE	*OE source*	*ME spellings*
lady	hlæfdige (literally loaf-kneader)	hlæfdi hlefdige hlefdi lefdi læfdi lævedi lafdi laidi ledy
lord	hlaford (originally hlafweard, literally loaf-ward, loaf-guardian)	hlafard laford laferde hlouerd laverd leverd lourde lowerd lhord lorde

The influence of the French spelling system in ME

After the Conquest, French-speaking scribes introduced new ways of spelling into English. Many French words were taken into English also, particularly during the 13th and 14th centuries. This accounts for a number of conventions which have remained in the spelling system.

- **Initial ⟨h⟩** – some new French words were spelt with an ⟨h⟩ which was not pronounced.

  honour honest hour

  In some of these the influence of the spelling has re-introduced the [h] in English.

  horrible horror hospital host hostage

  In England *hotel* is pronounced with and without the initial [h].
- **⟨oi⟩** – a new ME diphthong, e.g. *employ*. Most words with the ⟨oi/oy⟩ diphthong are French in origin, e.g. *annoy* (OF *anuier*), *boil* (AF *boiler*), *boy* (AF *abuie*), *choice* (OF *chois*), *joy* (OF *joie*), *moist* (OF *moiste*), *poison* (OF *puison*), etc.
- **⟨c⟩ for [s]**, e.g. *citadel*. The use of ⟨c⟩ for [s] before front vowels [i] and [e] is French, e.g. *centre* (OF *centre*), *city* (OF *cité*), *evidence* (OF *evidence*). This was transferred to some OE words, e.g. *ice* (OE *is*), *mice* (OE *mys*). But *mouse* (OE *mus*) has not been changed, an example of the arbitrary nature of some spelling conventions that have been standardised. Letter ⟨c⟩ pronounced [k] before back vowels [ɑ o u] was not ambiguous, as in *cat*, *coat*, *cut*. Letter ⟨k⟩ also came to be used more, as in *king* (OE *cyning*) and *keen* (OE *cene*).
- **⟨ch⟩ for ⟨c⟩ = [tʃ]**, e.g. *cheese* from OE *cese*. The use of ⟨ch⟩ to distinguish [tʃ] from [k] before front vowels was a useful adoption, e.g. *cheap* (OE *ceap*), *child* (OE *cild*).
- **⟨qu⟩ for ⟨cw⟩ = [kw]**, e.g. *quell* from OE *cwellan*. The digraph ⟨qu⟩ was substituted for the OE ⟨cw⟩ – *queen* (OE *cwen*), *quench* (OE *cwencean*).
- **⟨sh⟩ for ⟨sc⟩ = [ʃ]**, e.g. *shield* from OE *scield*. OE ⟨sc⟩ for [ʃ] was replaced by a variety of letter forms and digraphs in different dialectal areas – ⟨ss⟩, ⟨x⟩, ⟨sch⟩ and ⟨sh⟩. Although ⟨sch⟩ was the most common in ME, as in *schadewe*, *schal*, *schame*, *scharpe* and *sche*, ⟨sh⟩ eventually became standard.
- **⟨ou⟩ for ⟨u⟩ = [uː]**, e.g. *mouse* from OE *mus*. The use of ⟨ou⟩ for the long vowel [uː] spelt ⟨u⟩ in OE was French in origin, e.g. *house* for OE *hus* is simpy a re-spelling, not a change in pronunciation.
- **⟨v⟩** – a new letter, not in OE. A new use for letter ⟨u⟩ and the introduction of an alternative form ⟨v⟩ came from the French. In OE, the voiced consonant [v] did not occur at the beginning of a word, but was a variant of [f] if there were voiced sounds before and after it, as in *hlaford*, [hlavərd], *lufu* [lʊvʊ], so a different letter was not needed. But with the adoption of French words like *vain*, *valley* and *vary*, a letter for the sound was needed. ⟨u⟩ and ⟨v⟩ were alternative 'graphic shapes' for the same letter, e.g.

(i) the consonant [v]

ME	*Source*	*MnE*
ualeie	AF valey	valley
veiage	AF veiage	voyage
ueond	OE feond	fiend
vers	OE fers	verse

(ii) the vowel [u]

ME	*Source*	*MnE*
vnwis	OE unwis	unwise
umble	OF umble	humble
vnglad	OE unglæd	unglad = sad
unclene	OE unclæne	unclean

A convention later developed for using ⟨v⟩ word-initial and ⟨u⟩ word-medial and final.

The influence of Latin spelling – letter ⟨o⟩ for [u]

Because so much copying by scribes was from Latin, the spelling of Latin also had some effects on the spellings of ME.

The short vowel [u] in OE words like *cuman*, *sum*, *munuc*, *sunu*, *wulf* was spelt with letter ⟨o⟩ – *come*, *some*, *monk*, *son*, *wolf*, probably because ⟨u⟩ was an over-used letter. It represented the sound [v] as well as [u], and ⟨uu⟩ was used for [w]. Letter ⟨u⟩ in 'bookhand' writing could also be confused with the 'minim' letters ⟨n⟩ and ⟨m⟩, and letter ⟨o⟩ would have been clearer to read.

The beginnings of a new standard – 15th-century Chancery spelling

The dominance of London as the political and commercial centre of England led to the establishment of the London educated dialect as a standard in writing. In the early 15th century, Henry V encouraged the use of English in official documents rather than French or Latin. So the spelling conventions set up in the Royal Chancery came to be adopted widely as a standard for professional scribes, or 'scriveners'.

Chancery spelling was widely adopted by scriveners as a standard in the 15th century. It made use of some of the conventions of Anglo-Norman spelling which had been first used in the 12th century. They introduced three digraphs for vowels, ⟨ea⟩, ⟨ie⟩ and ⟨eo⟩.The spellings are still part of standard spelling today, although the sounds which they represented are not the same:

⟨**ea**⟩ – during the 15th century scriveners began to use the digraph ⟨ea⟩ for re-spelling words of French origin (see section 15.5.1.4).

⟨**ie**⟩ – '⟨i⟩ before ⟨e⟩ except after ⟨c⟩' – this digraph came from Anglo-Norman also, and was sometimes used for the higher of the two front long vowels [eː],

which later shifted to [iː]. Its use in French loan-words spread to English words like *thief*, from OE *þeof*.

⟨**eo**⟩ – the digraph ⟨eo⟩ was also used for [eː] in French loan-words like *people* (OF *peuple*). So we now have ⟨ea⟩, ⟨ie⟩ and ⟨eo⟩, as well as ⟨ee⟩ and ⟨e-e⟩ as signs for the vowel [eː], now pronounced [iː]. Remember that ⟨ea⟩ is, however, very irregular. You cannot deduce from a word spelt with ⟨ea⟩ what the sound of the vowel is.

The Great Vowel Shift and the effect on spelling

All the following ME words had long vowels. Notice their pronunciation compared with that of the MnE words derived from them. All changed by 'shifting' higher in their place of articulation in the mouth, or becoming new kinds of dipthong. (Some, for example *blood*, have changed further.)

ME		***MnE (RP)***		***ME***		***MnE (RP)***	
knowen	[oː]	*know*	[əʊ]	flod	[oː]	*flood*	[ʌ]
beche	[eː]	*beech*	[iː]	fode	[oː]	*food*	[uː]
biten	[iː]	*bite*	[aɪ]	ground	[uː]	*ground*	[aʊ]
blod	[oː]	*blood*	[ʌ]	ise	[iː]	*ice*	[aɪ]
chesen	[eː]	*choose*	[uː]	leden	[ɛ:]	*lead* (*vb*)	[iː]
crepen	[eː]	*creep*	[iː]	most	[ɔː]	*most*	[əʊ]
cloþ	[ɔː]	*cloth*	[ɒ]	prest	[eː]	*priest*	[iː]
del	[ɛː]	*deal*	[iː]	prude	[yː]	*pride*	[aɪ]
uvel	[yː]	*evil*	[iː]	siþe	[iː]	*scythe*	[aɪ]
doun	[uː]	*down*	[aʊ]	hous	[uː]	*house*	[aʊ]
even	[ɛː]	*even*(*ing*)	[iː]	hwy	[yː]	*why*	[aɪ]

Words spelt with ⟨ough⟩

This is the most often quoted example of the way in which our spelling system has failed to match changes in pronunciation. Here is a list of most of the ⟨-ough⟩ words in present-day English, and the words from which they have derived. Notice that they were spelt in OE with either ⟨g⟩ or ⟨h⟩, which represented a fricative sound [ɣ] no longer in the language, like a strongly articulated and voiced [h]. This sound was later spelt ⟨gh⟩, and in different dialects underwent different changes, as did the vowels.

borough	[bʌrə]	OE burg/burh	*plough*	[plaʊ]	*OE plog/ploh*
bough	[baʊ]	OE bog/boh	*rough*	[rʌf]	*OE ruh*
bought	[bɔt]	OE boht OE broht	*slough*	[slaʊ]	*OE slog/sloh*
brought	[brɔt]	OE brohte	*sought*	[sɔt]	*OE soht*
chough	[tʃʌf]	ME *imitative*	*thorough*	[θʌrə]	*OE þuruh*
cough	[kɒf]	ME coghe	*though*	[ðəʊ]	*ON þoh*
dough	[dəʊ]	OE dag/dah	*thought*	[θɔt]	*OE þoht*
fought	[fɔt]	OE fuht	*through*	[θruː]	*OE þurh*
hiccough	[hɪkʌp]	*imitative origin* – hiccup	*tough*	[tʌf]	*OE toh*
nought	[nɔt]	OE noht	*trough*	[trɒf]	*OE trog/troh*
ought	[ɔt]	OE ahte	*wrought*	[rɔt]	*OE worht*

The following sentence contains words that illustrate every pronunciation:

> A rough-coated dough-faced ploughboy strode coughing and hiccoughing thoughtfully through the streets of the borough.

Later sound changes have left us with a very diversified set because there were regional and social dialectal differences in the pronunciations which developed. There is evidence of *though* and *ought* pronounced with [f] in Smollett's novel *Humphry Clinker* (1771), in which characters say,

> 'but he would never be satisfied, even **thof** she should sweat blood and water in his service...'

> 'But then they **oft** to have some conscience...'

These are both spoken by servants, and so represent the 'vulgar tongue'. Pronunciations varied widely from dialect to dialect and class to class, and the eventual 'standard' choice is arbitrary. Some established pronunciations today in fact came from 'vulgar' as against 'polite' usage.

23.3 Early Modern English

The effects of the printing press

William Caxton set up the first English printing press in 1476. He himself translated many of the books he printed, and wrote prefaces for them, but although the shift of the long vowels (the Great Vowel Shift) was under way, Caxton's spelling did not reflect any changes. It was also inconsistent, and matched the patterns he would have learned as a boy in the early 15th century. His spelling does not follow that of the professional scriveners. Here, for example, are words inconsistently spelt:

al/all	Ilond/ylond
childeren/children	lond/londe
englissh/englysshe	people/peple
ffor/for/fore	scole/Scoolmaysters
fro/from	soune/sowne

Another cause of variability of the spelling in Caxton's printed books was that he employed foreign compositors. They would accept the spelling of the written copy they were setting up, and introduced some foreign conventions, like ⟨gh⟩ for ⟨g⟩, the consonant [g]. One survival of this practice explains the spelling *ghost*, from OE *gast*, ME *gost*.

Caxton's orthography influenced the patterns that in time became standard, but the stable spelling system that was eventually established by printers by the mid-17th century was established more by the many books on spelling and pronunciation that had been published throughout the 16th and early 17th centuries.

New spelling – ⟨oa⟩

One innovation of the mid-16th century was the use of a digraph ⟨oa⟩ to distinguish [ɔː], the lower of two long back vowels, from [oː], spelt ⟨oo⟩ (see section 15.5.1.5). Like all long vowels, these had shifted from their ME sounds. The vowel [ɔː] was in process of shifting to [oː], and [oː] to [uː]. This explains the spelling and pronunciation of, for example, *food* and *goose*, as against *foam* and *load.*

But just as spellings with ⟨ea⟩ are varied in pronunciation now, so are those with ⟨oa⟩ e.g., *broad, board, hoard* [ɔː] and *broach, coach, poach* [əʊ], and with ⟨oo⟩, e.g. *blood* [ʌ], *good* [ʊ], *food* [uː], *brooch* [əʊ]. These are the result of later changes, and variable pronunciation in social and regional dialects. Like the use of ⟨ea⟩ in contrast to ⟨ee⟩, ⟨oa⟩ and ⟨oo⟩ usefully represented contrastive sounds, but later changes have rendered the distinction invalid, leaving us with rather a complicated mess in our spelling system.

Continuing variation in spelling in the 15th and 16th centuries

Inconsistencies and variants in spelling are evident into the 17th century:

- Letters ⟨i⟩ and ⟨y⟩ were generally interchangeable within a word, and ⟨y⟩, ⟨ie⟩ or ⟨ye⟩ at the end.
- The doubling of consonants after short vowels was inconsistent.
- A random final ⟨e⟩ continued to be added to words. This was sometimes done to justify a line of type.

Forms of the word *city* (from OF *cité*) recorded in the *Oxford English Dictionary* illustrate these and other features of former irregularities in spelling:

cyte, cite, scite, cety, cytee, site, citee, cete, cetie, sete, citie, cittie, citte, cytte, syttey, sittey, ciete, cyete, scitie, citty, chitty

The modern practice of printing older texts after Chaucer in modernised spelling has completely obscured the nature of the development of the spelling system. Students of language, however, need to be aware of how our spelling has evolved, so that they can understand its present inconsistencies.

Spelling and printing conventions in William Tyndale's Pentateuch *(1530)*

Here is a facsimile of a page of William Tyndale's 1530 translation of the *Pentateuch*, the *Five Books of Moses* in the Old Testament, in which you can observe the following features in the printing which derived from the handwriting practices of the preceding centuries:

- **⟨þ⟩ and ⟨y⟩** – Letter ⟨þ⟩ had survived into the 15th century in spite of the widespread use of ⟨th⟩. Printers' type founts did not contain this letter, so ⟨y⟩ was used. The words *the* and *that* were often (but not consistently) printed and written as *ye* and *y^t^*, which survived for a long time when ⟨th⟩ was used elsewhere.
- **⟨n⟩ and ⟨m⟩** – Another convention was the use of a tilde ⟨~⟩ or a macron ⟨–⟩ over a vowel to mark a following nasal consonant ⟨n⟩ or ⟨m⟩, as in *takē*,

countenaũce, *rãmes*, *thẽ* for *taken*, *countenaunce*, *rammes* (*rams*), *them*. This seems to have been most frequently used for common words like *and* and *then*, but was not always applied.

- **⟨u⟩ and ⟨v⟩** – ⟨u⟩ and ⟨v⟩ continued as different forms of the same letter (from Latin usage) well into the 17th century, and both were used for either vowel or consonant. The convention was established that the form ⟨v⟩ was used at the beginning of a word, as in *vppon*, *vncleane*, *vayne*, and ⟨u⟩ medially, as in *oure*, *ouer*, *euen*, *foughte*. The distinction between ⟨u⟩ for the vowel and ⟨v⟩ for the consonant, which we use today, dates from the mid-17th century.
- **Long and short ⟨s⟩** – There were two forms of ⟨s⟩, derived from handwriting, of which the long, used initially and medially in a word, has not survived, for example, *ſayde*, *ſent*, *ſhepe* for *sayde*, *sent*, *shepe*.
- **⟨i⟩ and ⟨j⟩** – Until the 17th century letter ⟨i⟩ was used for both the vowel [i] and the consonant [j], as in *iuell*, *iourneys*, *reioysed* for *jewel*, *journeys*, *rejoiced*.

These spelling conventions were purely graphic, and make the language of texts from the 15th to the 17th centuries look stranger than it really is.

Text 184 – William Tyndale's *Pentateuch*, 1530 – facsimile

The fyrst boke of Moses, XXXI. 1–13

¶ The .XXXI. Chapter.

1 ND Iacob herde the wordes of
Labās ſonnes how they ſayde:
Iacob hath takē awaye all that
was oure fathers, and of oure
fathers goodes, hath he gotē all this
2 honoure. And Iacob behelde the countenaũce of Laban, that it was not toward
him as it was in tymes paſt.
3 And the LORde ſayde vnto Iacob:
turne agayne in to the lāde of thy fathers
4 & to thy kynred, & I wilbe with ẏ. Thā
Iacob ſent & called Rahel & Lea to the
5 felde vnto his ſhepe·& ſayde vnto thē: I ſe youre
fathers countenaũce ẏ it is not toward me as in tymes
paſt. Morouer .P.·ẏ God of my father hath bene with
6 me. And ye knowe how that I haue ſerued youre
7 father with all my myghte. And youre father hath
diſceaued me & chaunged my wages .x. tymes: But
8 God ſuffred him not to hurte me. When he ſayde
the ſpotted ſhalbe thy wages, thā all the ſhepe bare
ſpotted. Yf he ſayde the ſtraked ſhalbe thi rewarde,
9 thā bare all the ſhepe ſtraked: thus hath God takē
10 awaye youre fathers catell & geuē thē me. For in
buckynge tyme, I lifted vp myne eyes and ſawe in a
dreame: and beholde, the rammes that bucked the
11 ſhepe were ſtraked, ſpotted and partie. And the
angell of God ſpake vnto me in a dreame ſaynge:
12 Iacob. And I anſwered: here am I. And he ſayde:
lyfte vp thyne eyes ād ſee how all the rāmes that
leape vpon the ſhepe are ſtraked, ſpotted and partie:
13 for I haue ſene all that Laban doth vnto ẏ. I am ẏ
god of Bethell where thou anoynteddeſt the ſtone ād
where thou vowdeſt a vowe vnto me. Now aryſe and

M.C.S. At the cōmaundement of God, Iacob departed frō Laban, & toke hys goodes with hym. Rachel ſtealeth hyr fathers ymages. Laban foloweth Iacob. The couenaunt betwene Laban and Iacob.

'Tinkering with the orthography' in the 16th century

Some oddities of our spelling can be explained by the habit of re-spelling of words in the 16th century in order (sometimes wrongly) to mark their derivation from one of the classical languages, Latin and Greek, although the new spelling did not match the pronunciation. Some of these re-spellings have become standard. Shakespeare satirizes this habit in the character of Holofernes the Pedant, criticising Don Armado in *Loues Labors Lost*:

> He draweth out the thred of his verbositie, finer then the staple of his argument. I abhorre such phanatticall phantasims, such insociable and poynt deuise companions, such rackers of ortagriphie, as to speake dout sine b, when he should say doubt; det, when he shold pronounce debt; d e b t, not d e t: he clepeth a Calfe, Caufe: halfe, haufe: neighbour vocatur nebour; neigh abreuiated ne: this is abhominable, which he would call abbominable, it insinuateth me of insanire: ne intelligis domine, to make frantique lunatique.

The sources of the words mentioned by Holofernes are:

doubt	ME doute fr OF doute fr L dubitare	*half*	OE healf
debt	ME det(te) fr OF dette fr L debitum	*neighbour*	OE neahgebur
calf	OE cælf	*abominable*	ME fr OF fr L abominabilis

More 16th-century re-spellings

Here are some more examples of these 'etymological' changes in spelling:

16th-century re-spelling	*Middle English*	*OE/OF*	*Latin or Greek source*
theatre	teatre	OF teatre	Gk theatron
anthem	antefne	OE antefn	L antiphona
apothecary	apotecarie	OF apotecaire	L apothecarius
comptroller	counterroller	AF contrerollour	L contrarotulare
receipt	receit	AF receite	L recepta
indict	endite	AF enditer	L indictare
victual	vitaile	OF vitaille	L victualia
parliament	parlement	OF parlement	L paraulare + ment
fault	faute	OF faute	L fallita
vault	vaute	OF vaute	L voluta
throne	trone	OF trone	Gk thronos
author	autour	OF autor	L auctor

The next set of words were respelt during the 16th or 17th centuries:

	Derivation	*16th- or 17th-century re-spelling*
amirail	OF a(d)mira(i)l . fr med L a(d)miralis, fr Arabic amir *commander*	**admiral**
amonest	OF amonester fr L admonere	**admonish**
ancre	OE ancor fr L anchora fr Gk agkura	**anchor**
assoil	L absolvere	**absolve**
avauncen	OF avancer fr LL abante *in front* fr L ab *away* + ante *before*	**advance**
avauntage	OF avantage fr avant *in front* fr LL abante: (*see* advance)	**advantage**

	Derivation	***16th- or 17th-century re-spelling***
aventure	OF aventure, aventurer fr L adventurus	**adventure**
avice	OF avis fr L ad *to* + visum	**advice**
caitif	L captivus	**captive**
cedule	OF cedule fr LL schedula	**schedule**
ceptre	OF (s)ceptre fr L sceptrum fr Gk skeptron	**sceptre**
colere	OF colere *bile, anger* fr L cholera fr Gk kholera	**choler**
cors	ME corps, *variant spelling of* cors (corse), fr OF cors f. L corpus	**corpse**
crume	OE cruma	**crumb**
descryve	L describere	**describe**
faucon	OF faucon fr LL falco -onis, perhaps. fr L falx	**falcon**
langage	OF langage ultimately fr L lingua	**language**
nevew	OF neveu fr L nepos	**nephew**
perfit	ME and OF parfit, perfet fr L perfectus	**perfect**
samon	AF sa(u)moun, OF saumon fr L salmo -onis	**salmon**
sent	ME sent fr OF sentir *perceive, smell*, fr L sentire; addition of ⟨c⟩ unexplained	**scent**
sisoures	ME sisoures fr OF cisoires fr LL cisoria, associated with L scindere	**scissors**
sithe	OE siþe	**scythe**
yland	OE igland fr ig *island* + land: first syllable influenced by *isle*, ME ile fr OF ile	**island**

Some of these re-spelt words were in time pronounced differently, according to the letters introduced by analogy with the presumed derivation. In some there was an added consonant:

a[d]miral	a[d]vantage	ca[p]tive	descri[b]e
a[d]monish	a[d]venture	s[ch]edule	fa[l]con
a[b]solve	a[d]vice	cor[p]se	perfe[c]t
a[d]vance			

whereas in others the re-spelling resulted in words with 'silent letters'.

'Silent letters'

ceptre	s[c]eptre	crume	crum[b]	sent	s[c]ent	sithe	s[c]ythe
colere	c[h]oler	samon	sa[l]mon	sisoures	s[c]issors	yland	i[s]land

These words were in addition to others derived from OE whose pronunciation had changed as a result of the loss of spoken consonants. Words in OE beginning with certain pairs of consonants were simplified during the ME and EMnE periods – ⟨cn ~ gn ~ hl ~ hn ~ hr ~ hw ~ wl ~ wr⟩. For some of these, beginning with ⟨kn ~ gn ~ wr⟩, the spelling has remained unchanged. Here is a selection of those words, most of which have come down from OE into MnE:

OE word	***Pronunciation***	***MnE reflex***	***OE word***	***Pronunciation***	***MnE reflex***
cnafa	[knɑvə]	**knave**	hwa	[hwɑː]	**who**
cneo	[kneːə]	**knee**	hwæl	[hwæl]	**whale**
cnif	[kniːf]	**knife**	hwær	[hwæːr]	**where**
cniht	[knɪçt]	**knight**	hwæs	[hwæs]	**whose**
cnyll	[knyll]	**knell**	hwæt	[hwæt]	**what**
gnætt	[gnætt]	**gnat**	hwæte	[hwæːtə]	**wheat**
gnagan	[gnɑɣən]	**gnaw**	hweol	[hweːəl]	**wheel**
hladan	[hlɑdən]	**load**	hwettan	[hwetːən]	**whet**
hlædel	[hlædəl]	**ladle**	hwil	[hwiːl]	**while**
hlæfdige	[hlæːfdijə]	**lady**	hwinan	[hwiːnən]	**whine**
hlaford	[hlɑːvɔrd]	**lord**	hwit	[hwiːt]	**white**
hlaf	[hlɑːf]	**loaf**	hwy	[hwyː]	**why**
hnægan	[hnæɣən]	**neigh**	wlisp	[wlɪsp]	**lisp**
hnutu	[hnutu]	**nut**	wlanc (*proud*)	[wlank]	–
hræfn	[hrævən]	**raven**	wlitan (*to look*)	[wliːtən]	–
hreac	[hrɛːək]	**rick**	wlitig (*beautiful*)	[wlɪtɪj]	–
hring	[hriŋg]	**ring**	wrænna	[wrænːə]	**wren**
hroc	[hroːk]	**rook**	wræþþo	[wræðːə]	**wrath**
hrof	[hroːf]	**roof**	wræstlian	[wræːstliən]	**wrestle**
hrycg	[hrydʒ]	**ridge**	wrist	[wrɪst]	**wrist**

Another sound change not marked in the spelling – loss of post-vocalic ⟨r⟩

Today some English and most American dialects are **rhotic** – that is, the ⟨r⟩ which follows a vowel in words like *hear* and *flour* (post-vocalic ⟨r⟩) is pronounced. All dialects of ME were rhotic. Present-day RP is non-rhotic.

During the 16th and 17th centuries post-vocalic ⟨r⟩ first of all began to affect the pronunciation of its preceding vowel, and then disappeared in some dialects. Spelling was not changed, however. This accounts for the pronunciation in RP and other non-rhotic accents of e.g., *arm* [ɑːm], *person* [pɜːsən], *dirt* [dɜːt], *turf* [tɜːf]. The ⟨r⟩ is no longer pronounced, and the vowels have lengthened or become diphthongs.

23.4 Correct spelling today

The stabilisation of the spelling system was complete by about 1700 in printing, though handwriting remained relatively unstandardised for some time. Samuel Johnson's *Dictionary*, published in 1755, became a standard reference for private use. There have been few changes since the 18th century.

Today most words have one fixed spelling which can be looked up in the dictionaries. The demand for accuracy in spelling is a social and educational fact of life and some questions about the necessity for consistency in spelling are worth debating.

The aim of this chapter has been to show that our present standardised spelling system

- dates back a thousand years or more in its basic patterning,
- reflects the pronunciation of English in the 14th century rather than today – that is, it ignores the Great Vowel Shift,
- also ignores many other subsequent changes in pronunciation that have taken place,
- takes its letter/sound correspondences from several sources, and
- makes arbitrary choices from available variants.

Bibliography

This list is a selection of books which teachers, lecturers and advanced students will find useful for further reading and reference. Separate editions of Old, Middle and Early Modern English texts are not listed.

The history and development of English

Barber, Charles, *The English Language: A Historical Introduction* (Cambridge: Cambridge University Press, 1993).

Baugh, A. C. and Cable, T., *A History of the English Language*, 4th edn (London: Routledge & Kegan Paul, 1993).

Blake, N. F., *A History of the English Language* (London: Macmillan, 1996).

Crystal, David (ed.), *Cambridge Encyclopedia of the English Language* (Cambridge: Cambridge University Press, 1995).

Hogg, Richard M. (general editor), *Cambridge History of the English Language* (Cambridge: Cambridge University Press):
- vol. 1: Hogg, Richard M. (ed.), *The Beginnings to 1066* (1992).
- vol. 2: Blake, Norman (ed.), *1066–1476* (1992).
- vol. 5: Burchfield, Robert, *English in Britain & Overseas: Origin & Development* (1994).

Leith, Dick, *A Social History of English* (London: Routledge & Kegan Paul, 1983).

Partridge, A. C., *A Companion to Old & Middle English Studies* (London: Deutsch, 1982).

Pyles, T. and Algeo, J., *The Origins & Development of the English Language*, 3rd edn (New York: Harcourt Brace Jovanovich, 1982).

Scragg, D. G., *A History of English Spelling* (Manchester: Manchester University Press, 1974).

Strang, Barbara, *A History of English* (London: Methuen, 1970).

Old English

Bradley, S. A. J., *Anglo-Saxon Poetry* (translation) (London: Dent, 1982).

Davis, N., *Sweet's Anglo-Saxon Primer*, 9th edn (Oxford: Oxford University Press, 1953).

Mitchell, B., *An Invitation to Old English & Anglo-Saxon England* (Oxford: Blackwell, 1995).
Mitchell, B. and Robinson, F. C., *A Guide to Old English*, 5th edn (Oxford: Blackwell, 1986).
Quirk, R. and Wrenn, C. L., *An Old English Grammar* (London: Methuen, 1957).
Quirk, R., Adams, V. and Davy, D., *Old English Literature: A Practical Introduction* (London: Edward Arnold, 1975).
Swanton, Michael, *Anglo-Saxon Prose* (translation) (London: Dent, 1975).
Swanton, Michael, *The Anglo-Saxon Chronicle* (translation) (London: Dent, 1996).
Sweet, H., *The Student's Dictionary of Anglo-Saxon, 1896* (Oxford: Oxford University Press, reprint, 1978).

Middle English

Burnley, D., *A Guide to Chaucer's Language* (London: Macmillan, 1983).
Bennett, J. A. W. and Smithers, G. V., *Early Middle English Verse & Prose*, 2nd edn (anthology) (Oxford: Oxford University Press, 1968).
Sisam, K., *Fourteenth Century Verse & Prose* (Oxford: Oxford University Press, 1921).

Early Modern English

Barber, Charles, *Early Modern English* (London: Deutsch, 1976).
Blake, N. F., *The Language of Shakespeare* (London: Macmillan, 1985).

Modern English

Barber, Charles, *Linguistic Change in Present-Day English* (London: Oliver & Boyd, 1964).
Foster, B., *The Changing English Language* (London: Macmillan, 1968).
Potter, S., *Changing English* (London: Deutsch, 1969).
Quirk, R., Greenbaum, S., Leech, G. and Svartvik, J., *A Comprehensive Grammar of the English Language* (London: Longman, 1985).

Index